ILLINOIS HISTORY

ILLINOIS HISTORY

An Annotated Bibliography

ELLEN M. WHITNEY, *Compiler*
JANICE A. PETTERCHAK, *Editor*
SANDRA M. STARK, *Associate Editor*

Prepared under the auspices of the Illinois
State Historical Library and the Illinois State
Historical Society

Bibliographies of the States of the United States, Number 4
Carol Bondhus Fitzgerald, Series Editor

GREENWOOD PRESS
Westport, Connecticut • London

Library of Congress Cataloging-in-Publication Data

Whitney, Ellen M.
    Illinois history : an annotated bibliography / Ellen M. Whitney,
compiler ; Janice A. Petterchak, editor, Sandra M. Stark, associate
editor.
        p.   cm.—(Bibliographies of the states of the United States,
ISSN 1060–5711 ; no. 4)
    "Prepared under the auspices of the Illinois State Historical
Library and the Illinois State Historical Society."
    Includes bibliographical references and index.
    ISBN 0–313–28235–8
    1. Illinois—History—Bibliography.   I. Petterchak, Janice A.
II. Stark, Sandra M.   III. Illinois State Historical Library.
IV. Title.   V. Series.
Z1277.W47   1995
[F541]
016.9773—dc20   94–42122

British Library Cataloguing in Publication Data is available.

Library of Congress Catalog Card Number: 94–42122
ISBN: 0–313–28235–8
ISSN: 1060–5711

First published in 1995

Greenwood Press, 88 Post Road West, Westport, CT 06881
An imprint of Greenwood Publishing Group, Inc.

Printed in the United States of America

The paper used in this book complies with the
Permanent Paper Standard issued by the National
Information Standards Organization (Z39.48–1984).

10 9 8 7 6 5 4 3 2 1

CONTENTS

SERIES FOREWORD

The name of each state and territory conjures a distinct image: the legacy of its own ethnic, geographic and economic heritage. These disparate states have been united to produce a country that is "not merely a nation but a teeming nation of nations" (Walt Whitman, "Preface," *Leaves of Grass*, 1855).

The richness of local history and its relevance to national history becomes more apparent as many states and academic institutions reevaluate the importance of cultural diversity. Yet if the nation has been late in recognizing aspects of its regional history, its people have not. While the indigenous population may have left little written documentation, their presence and influence have been studied by other means, and they are included in this series. Since the beginnings of European settlement, the inhabitants of the states and territories have left vast quantities of records, observations, and studies. Succeeding scholars have produced books, articles, dissertations, technical reports, government documents, oral histories, and other special resources which chronicle and interpret local history. Much of this vast body of material has not been indexed or published and distributed largely for regional appreciation.

The book-length bibliographies in this series systematically review the many components of local, state, and regional history within the chronological framework of the states' histories. Scholars specializing in state and territorial history present annotated citations to the standard sources, and more importantly, to materials perhaps unknown outside its immediate area.

The bibliographers identify and describe available primary materials, and narrative and interpretative writing on topics in local history. Whether used as an interdisciplinary guide to all the states, or as a guide to one state, the series offers the opportunity for a fuller understanding of the national heritage, even as it reveals topics in need of further research.

Carol Bondhus Fitzgerald

PREFACE

This volume in the Greenwood Press series Bibliographies of the States of the United States is co-sponsored by the Illinois State Historical Library and Illinois State Historical Society, both of which publish and distribute works related to the history of Illinois. We therefore relied heavily on those publications in guiding our work and forming the core of this volume.

Throughout the compilation process, we were also guided by a vision of the user of the bibliography as one or more of the following: the history scholar beginning research in a field new to him or her; the graduate student working on a thesis; a high school or college student writing a term paper; the librarian searching for the answer to a patron's reference question.

Our goal, therefore, was to include the major historical publications related to Illinois. Anyone wishing to pursue a subject further is advised to consult the footnotes and bibliographies of the scholarly works named herein. Important regional or national histories are listed only if Illinois people, events, or source materials figure prominently. We remind the user that this is a *selected* list of sources: for nearly every entry related to a subject, scores of others are not given.

In the volumes of this series, most entries are presented within a chronological framework. Many articles and books, however, do not fit neatly within such a structure. Indeed, the chronological structure for one state's history rarely coincides with that of another state. But insofar as possible, entries are presented chronologically. A source containing information related to two or more chronological periods--as outlined in the Table of Contents--is listed either with general histories or under a subject heading.

As a rule, entries are annotated only when their titles do not adequately describe their content. The compiler made no attempt to list all editions of a work, although reprint information is sometimes given.

Several kinds of items related to Illinois have been excluded: 1) county and town histories and atlases--unless they are of unquestioned general interest and illustrate broader political and social issues, 2) fiction, 3) poetry, 4) juvenile literature, 5) textbooks, 6) Civil War regimental histories, 7) most theses and dissertations, 8) territorial and state session laws and revised statutes, 9) genealogical studies of individual families, 10) routine government documents, 11) tourist guides and promotional materials, 12) routine news coverage in newspapers and magazines, 13) technical, scientific, and economic treatises, 14) city directories, and 15) foreign-language publications. Literary criticism is also excluded, but biographies of poets and novelists do appear, as do historical accounts of literary publications and literary movements. Other limitations and exclusions are noted in the introductory paragraphs to the various sections.

Members of the Illinois State Historical Library staff were most helpful in the preparation of this work. We thank, in particular, Cheryl Schnirring, manuscript curator; Sadie Shontz, who assisted with the compilation; Kathryn Harris, head of reference and technical services; Jill Blessman, head of acquisitions, who also helped proofread the typescript; Gloria Gibbons and Jane Ehrenhart of the cataloging staff; and Thomas Schwartz, state historian. James A. Edstrom of the Illinois Newspaper Project (a National Endowment for the Humanities program for cataloging all known Illinois newspapers) compiled the section on representative newspapers. Preparation of camera-ready copy for the publisher was the work of Sandra Stark.

This project received substantial financial support through the Illinois State Historical Library division of the Illinois Historic Preservation Agency and from the following generous donors to the Illinois State Historical Society:

American National Bank Foundation
Ameritech
William Blair & Company Foundation
Elizabeth F. Cheney Foundation
Gaylord Donnelley
R. R. Donnelley & Sons Company
International Business Machines, Springfield office
James H. Oughton, Jr.
Walgreens

We are also grateful to Professor John Hallwas of Western Illinois University (chairman of the Historical Library Committee of the Illinois State Historical Society) for his invaluable assistance in reading the manuscript and offering suggestions for its improvement.

Ellen M. Whitney, Compiler
Janice A. Petterchak, Editor

CHRONOLOGY

10,000 BC- 8000 BC	Paleo Indians roam the area, briefly occupying small camps in coniferous forests and subsisting on large game and wild plants.
8000 BC- 500 BC	Archaic period Indians inhabit deciduous forests in small groups, hunt deer and small game, weave baskets, and grind seeds with stones.
500 BC- AD 900	Woodland culture Indians develop maize agriculture, build villages and burial mounds, invent the bow and arrow for hunting, and begin making pottery.
900- 1500	Indians of the Mississippian culture improve agricultural methods, build temple mounds and large fortified villages. Most of the settlements are abandoned prior to the historic period.
1673	French explorers Jacques Marquette (1637-1675) and Louis Jolliet (1645-1700) descend the Mississippi to the Arkansas River and return to Wisconsin via the Illinois River--the first Europeans to reach the Illinois country.
1675	Marquette founds a mission at the Great Village of the Illinois, near present Utica.
1680	French traders René Robert Cavelier, Sieur de La Salle (1643-1687) and Henry de Tonty (1650-1704) build Fort Crèvecoeur on the Illinois River, near present Peoria.
	Iroquois Indians destroy the Great Village of the Illinois.
1682	La Salle and Tonty build Fort St. Louis across the Illinois River from the Great Village of the Illinois site.

1696	Jesuit priest Pierre François Pinet (1660-1704?) establishes the Guardian Angel mission at present Chicago.
1699	Priests of the Quebec Seminary of Foreign Missions found the Holy Family mission at Cahokia, the first permanent settlement in the Illinois country.
1703	Jesuit priest Gabriel Marest (1662-1714) moves the Immaculate Conception mission from present St. Louis to Kaskaskia.
1717	Illinois becomes part of the French colony of Louisiana.
1718	John Law (1671-1729) is granted a French charter for colonizing the Mississippi Valley; his "Mississippi Bubble" scheme bursts in 1720.
1720	Fort de Chartres in Randolph County becomes the seat of military and civilian government in Illinois.
1730	In a major battle, hostile Fox Indians are massacred in east-central Illinois by French troops and Indian allies.
1763	French and Indian (Seven Years') War ends; Illinois country is ceded to Britain by the Treaty of Paris.
1769	According to legend, northern tribes besiege and starve Illinois Indians tribes at Fort St. Louis, now known as Starved Rock.
1778	George Rogers Clark (1752-1818) defeats the British at Kaskaskia, securing the Illinois country for Virginia.
1779	Jean Baptiste Point du Sable (1745?-1818) establishes a trading post at present Chicago.
1783	Treaty of Paris extends the United States boundary to include the Illinois country.
1784	Virginia relinquishes its claim to Illinois.
1787	Northwest Ordinance places Illinois in the Northwest Territory.
1788	Arthur St. Clair (1734-1818) becomes the first governor of the Northwest Territory.

1800   Congress creates the Indiana Territory, which includes Illinois.

1803   Kaskaskia Indians cede nearly all of their Illinois lands to the United States.

United States Army establishes Fort Dearborn at present Chicago.

1804   William Clark (1770-1838) and his troops depart from Camp Dubois, Madison County, to join Meriwether Lewis (1774-1809) for westward explorations.

1809   Congress organizes the Illinois Territory, with Kaskaskia the capital, Ninian Edwards (1775-1833) the governor.

1811   The first coal mine in Illinois is opened in Jackson County.

New Madrid, Missouri, earthquake, the largest in United States history, damages southern Illinois (recurs in 1812).

1812   Potawatomi Indians massacre fifty-two troops and civilians in destroying Fort Dearborn.

1813   Land offices are opened at Kaskaskia and Shawneetown.

1814   The first newspaper in the state, the *Illinois Herald*, is published at Kaskaskia.

1816   Fort Armstrong is built at Rock Island, and Fort Dearborn is rebuilt at Chicago.

The first bank in Illinois, at Shawneetown, is chartered by the territorial legislature.

1817   Morris Birkbeck (1764-1825) and George Flower (1780-1862) establish an English settlement at Albion.

War of 1812 veterans begin receiving 160-acre land warrants in the Illinois Military Tract, a region between the Illinois and Mississippi rivers.

1818	Illinois becomes the twenty-first state, with Kaskaskia the capital and Shadrach Bond (1773-1832) the first governor. Population of the state is 34,620.
1819	Kickapoo Indians move west of the Mississippi, relinquishing most claims to central Illinois lands.
1820	Vandalia becomes the state capital.
1821	General Assembly charters a state bank at Vandalia, with branches at Shawneetown, Edwardsville, and Brownsville.
1823	Galena becomes a center for lead mining.
1824	Voters defeat a constitutional convention call to permit slavery in the state.
1825	Gurdon S. Hubbard (1802-1886) establishes the Vincennes Trace from southern Illinois to Lake Michigan.
	General Assembly enacts the first public school law and levies a school tax.
	Marquis de Lafayette (1757-1834) visits Kaskaskia and Shawneetown on a tour of the United States.
1827	John Mason Peck (1789-1858) founds Rock Spring Seminary, the first college in the state.
1829	Chippewa, Ottawa, and Potawatomi cede lands in northern Illinois by treaty at Prairie du Chien.
1830	The first state prison is built at Alton.
	Abraham Lincoln (1809-1865) moves to Illinois from Indiana.
	James Hall (1793-1858) launches *Illinois Monthly Magazine*, the first literary periodical published west of Ohio.
1832	Black Hawk War ends with Sauk and Fox Indians leaving the Illinois lands they had ceded in 1804.

1833   Treaty of Chicago provides for United States acquisition and settlement of the last remaining Indian lands in Illinois.

1835   General Assembly grants a charter for the Jacksonville Female Academy, the first institution in the state for women's education.

1836   Illinois and Michigan Canal construction is begun between Lake Michigan and the Illinois Valley; completed in 1848.

Galena and Chicago Union Railroad is chartered; completed twelve years later.

1837   Chicago receives a city charter; William Ogden (1805-1877) becomes the first mayor.

At Alton a pro-slavery mob murders abolitionist editor Elijah P. Lovejoy (b. 1802).

John Deere (1804-1886) of Grand Detour designs a self-scouring steel plow.

1838   Northern Cross Railroad construction is begun between Meredosia and Springfield; the line is completed in 1842.

1839   Cherokee Indians pass through southern Illinois on the "Trail of Tears" to Oklahoma.

Springfield becomes the state capital.

National Road is completed from Cumberland, Maryland, to Vandalia.

Joseph Smith (1805-1844) chooses Nauvoo as headquarters for the Mormon church.

1841   Chicagoan John S. Wright (1815-1874) begins publishing *Prairie Farmer* magazine.

1842   British author Charles Dickens (1812-1870) visits southern Illinois, described in his *American Notes* (1842).

1844   Anti-Mormons assassinate Mormon leaders Joseph and Hyrum (b. 1800) Smith at Carthage.

1846   Mormons leave Nauvoo for the Great Salt Lake Basin in Utah.

Donner party leaves Springfield by wagon train for California; forty-two perish in Sierra Mountains snowstorms.

Erik Jansson (1808-1850) and Jonas Olson (1802?-1898) establish a Swedish religious colony at Bishop Hill.

1847   Joseph Medill (1823-1899) founds the *Chicago Tribune.*

Jacksonville educator Jonathan Baldwin Turner (1805-1899) introduces Osage orange hedges as farm fencing.

Inventor Cyrus Hall McCormick (1809-1884) opens a plant in Chicago for manufacturing wheat reapers.

1848   Chicago Board of Trade is organized; it is now the largest and oldest commodity futures exchange in the world.

1849   Ètienne Cabet (1788-1856) establishes a French Icarian communal settlement at Nauvoo.

1850   Population of the state is 851,470.

Illinois Central Railroad receives the first federal land grant for rail construction.

1853   The first state fair is held in Springfield.

General Assembly enacts legislation to prevent free blacks from settling in the state.

1855   General Assembly adopts a free public school system.

1856   Illinois Central Railroad is completed between Chicago, Galena, and Cairo.

The first railroad bridge across the Mississippi River is completed between Rock Island and Davenport, Iowa.

Rand McNally is established in Chicago; by 1880 it is the world's largest mapmaking company.

Chicago Historical Society is founded, with William H. Brown (1796-1867) the first president.

1858   Republican Abraham Lincoln and Democrat Stephen A. Douglas (1813-1861) hold seven debates in the United States Senate contest; Douglas wins the election.

1860   Lincoln is elected President of the United States, defeating three other candidates.

Luxury steamer *Lady Elgin* sinks in Lake Michigan; nearly three hundred perish.

1861   Civil War begins; Cairo becomes a troop and supply center for the Union Army.

1862   Union League of America is founded in Pekin for the promotion of patriotism and Union loyalty.

1864   Lincoln is reelected President.

1865   General Assembly repeals measures against black settlement (Black Laws); is the first state legislature to ratify the Thirteenth Amendment abolishing slavery.

Lincoln is assassinated in Washington, D.C.; buried in Springfield.

Chicago Union Stock Yards opens; by 1900 employs more than one third of packing industry laborers in the nation.

1866   Grand Army of the Republic is established in Decatur; the first GAR convention is held in Springfield.

1867   General Assembly establishes the Illinois Industrial University at Champaign-Urbana, renamed the University of Illinois in 1885.

George M. Pullman (1831-1897) founds the Pullman Palace Car Company in Chicago, manufacturing railroad sleeping cars.

Illinois Normal University geologist John Wesley Powell (1834-1902) begins surveys of the Rocky Mountain region; becomes director of the United States Geological Survey in 1880.

1868　　　　　Ulysses S. Grant (1822-1885), Civil War general from Galena, is elected President of the United States.

Marshall Field & Co. department store opens in downtown Chicago; at his death, Field (1834-1906) is the city's wealthiest citizen.

1871　　　　　Chicago Fire destroys eighteen thousand downtown buildings, with losses estimated at $200 million.

1872　　　　　Chicagoan John Jones (1816-1879) becomes a Cook County commissioner, the first African-American to hold elective office in Illinois.

Chicago merchant Aaron Montgomery Ward (1844-1913) establishes the first large-scale mail order business.

General Assembly grants communities taxing authority to establish and maintain public libraries.

1873　　　　　Frances Willard (1839-1898) founds the Woman's Christian Temperance Union in Evanston.

Joseph F. Glidden (1813-1906) of DeKalb develops barbed wire fencing, patented in 1874.

1876　　　　　United States Supreme Court establishes in *Munn v. Illinois* the principle that business of a public nature is subject to state regulation.

1877　　　　　General Assembly establishes the Illinois National Guard.

1878　　　　　Bell Telephone Company of Illinois begins service in Chicago.

1880   Leslie E. Keeley (1832-1900) and John R. Oughton (1858-1925) establish the Keeley Institute in Dwight for treatment of alcoholism; by 1900 franchised sanitoriums are operating in many states.

1883   General Assembly enacts the first compulsory school attendance legislation.

              William LeBaron Jenney (1832-1907) designs the ten-story Home Insurance Building in Chicago, generally known as the world's first skyscraper.

1886   Haymarket Square bombing and riot in Chicago during a labor rally cause several deaths; eight anarchists are convicted, four are hanged, and one dies in prison.

1888   Chicago attorney Melville W. Fuller (1833-1910) is named Chief Justice of the United States Supreme Court.

1889   Jane Addams (1860-1935) and Ellen Gates Starr (1859-1940) open Hull House, one of the nation's first settlement houses, for foreign-born residents of Chicago.

              Evangelist Dwight L. Moody (1837-1899) founds the Chicago Bible Institute for training missionaries to foreign lands.

              Illinois State Historical Library is established by the state legislature; in 1899, a membership-support organization, the Illinois State Historical Society, is founded.

              John Mitchell (1870-1919) of Spring Valley becomes president of the United Mine Workers of America (to 1908).

1890   University of Chicago is incorporated, with William Rainey Harper (1856-1906) the first president.

1891   Chicago Symphony Orchestra is established, with Christian Theodore Thomas (1835-1905) the first conductor.

              African-American surgeon Daniel Hale Williams (1858-1931) organizes Provident Hospital in Chicago, the first black hospital in the United States; performs the first open-heart surgery in 1893.

1892	Chicago attorney Myra Bradwell (1831-1894) becomes the first woman admitted to practice before the United States Supreme Court.
	Canal construction to reverse the Chicago River flow is begun; completed in 1900.
	Illinois and Mississippi (Hennepin) Canal construction is begun between the Illinois and the Rock rivers; completed in 1907.
	Adlai Stevenson I (1835-1914) of Bloomington is elected Vice President of the United States on the ticket with Grover Cleveland.
1893	World's Columbian Exposition is held in Chicago, commemorating the 400th anniversary of European exploratory voyages to the western hemisphere.
	General Assembly establishes regulations for child labor and factory inspections.
	Governor John Peter Altgeld (1847-1902) pardons three imprisoned Haymarket anarchists.
1894	Pullman factory strike in Chicago becomes a national railway strike; federal troops are called to quell mob violence.
	Chicago attorney Clarence Darrow (1857-1938) unsuccessfully defends socialist leader Eugene V. Debs (1855-1926) on charges relating to the Pullman strike.
1896	Salem native William Jennings Bryan (1860-1925) wins the first of three presidential nominations; is defeated each time.
1898	United Mine Workers win labor disputes at Pana and Virden, after eleven miners and guards are killed.
1899	General Assembly creates the first juvenile court system in the nation.
1900	Population of the state is 4,821,550.

Chicago Sanitary & Ship Canal opens between Chicago and Lockport.

Frank Lloyd Wright (1869-1959) establishes a studio in Oak Park for designing "prairie style" architecture.

Chicago newspaperman Theodore Dreiser (1871-1945) launches his literary career with *Sister Carrie*, the first major novel set in Chicago.

1903   Fire destroys the Iroquois Theater in Chicago; nearly six hundred perish.

Joseph G. Cannon (1836-1926), Danville, elected to the United States House of Representatives in 1872, begins the first of four successive terms as Speaker of the House (to 1911).

1905   Paul P. Harris (1869-1947) and other Chicago businessmen organize the Rotary Club.

Eugene Debs, Mary Harris "Mother" Jones (1843?-1930), and others found the Industrial Workers of the World union in Chicago.

1906   Chicago White Sox defeat crosstown rival Chicago Cubs in the baseball World Series.

1908   Springfield race riot leads to formation of the National Association for the Advancement of Colored People (NAACP) in 1909.

1909   Coal mine fire at Cherry, resulting in 259 deaths, is one of the worst mine disasters in history.

Architect Daniel Burnham (1846-1912) designs the "Chicago Plan" for development of the lakefront and business district.

1910   William D. Boyce (1858-1929), Chicago and Ottawa businessman, founds the Boy Scouts of America.

Winchester native and Northwestern University Dental School dean Greene V. Black (1836-1915) receives the first International Miller Prize in dental science.

1911   Chicago sculptor Lorado Taft (1860-1936) completes his most famous work, "The Indian" (later called "Black Hawk"), a massive statue overlooking Rock River in Ogle County.

1912   Harriet Monroe (1860-1936) launches *Poetry: A Magazine of Verse* in Chicago; includes writings of Springfield poet Vachel Lindsay (1879-1931).

1913   General Assembly grants women the right to vote for presidential electors and provides state aid for county road construction.

1915   Poet and novelist Edgar Lee Masters (1869-1950) publishes *Spoon River Anthology*, a volume on small-town Illinois.

Excursion steamer *Eastland* capsizes in the Chicago River; 812 perish.

1917   With support from Governor Frank O. Lowden (1861-1943) General Assembly adopts a modern civil administrative code for state government.

In May and July Illinois National Guard troops are sent to East St. Louis to quell race riots.

Chicago White Sox defeat the New York Giants in the World Series.

1918   Voters approve a $60 million bond issue for paving state roads.

Influenza epidemic causes thirty-two thousand deaths in the state.

Robert Paul Prager (b. 1886), a German-born socialist suspected of disloyalty to the United States, is lynched by a pro-war mob in Collinsville.

1919   Chicago White Sox players (the "Black Sox") are accused of gambling on the World Series, which they lost to the Cincinnati Red Legs.

              Chicago race riots leave thirty-eight dead and more than five hundred injured; a thousand residents are left homeless.

1920   John L. Lewis (1880-1969) of Springfield is elected president of the United Mine Workers of America (to 1960).

              Governor Lennington Small (1862-1936) pardons twenty members of the Communist Labor party convicted under the Illinois Sedition Act.

1921   George Halas's (1895-1983) football team, the Staleys, moves from Decatur to Chicago, and wins the national championship; in 1922 the Staleys become the Chicago Bears.

1922   Decatur manufacturer A. E. Staley (1867-1940) opens the first commercial soybean-processing plant.

              In the "Herrin Massacre," three union miners and twenty strikebreakers are killed in mob violence at a strip mine in Williamson County.

1924   At the University of Illinois' new Memorial Stadium, Harold "Red" Grange (1904-1991), the "Galloping Ghost," scores four touchdowns in twelve minutes against the University of Michigan.

1925   Charles Gates Dawes (1865-1951) of Evanston becomes Vice President with President Calvin Coolidge (1872-1933); receives the Nobel Peace Prize for the "Dawes Plan" to restore the German economy after World War I.

              The worst tornado in United States history devastates parts of Illinois, Missouri, and Indiana; 695 deaths.

              Chicago Cardinals win the professional football championship; repeat in 1947.

1926   Aviator Charles Lindbergh (1902-1974) begins daily mail delivery flights between Chicago and St. Louis.

1929   Gunmen of Alphonse Capone (1899-1947) murder seven rival
               Chicago mobsters in the "St. Valentine's Day Massacre."

1930   Utilities founded by Chicagoan Samuel Insull (1859-1938), and
               valued at more than $2 billion, produce one tenth of the nation's
               electric power.

1931   Jane Addams wins the Nobel Peace Prize.

1932   Disgruntled United Mine Workers organize the Progressive
               Miners of America at Gillespie and Benld, eventually enlisting
               twenty thousand members.

               The number of unemployed Chicago workers during the Great
               Depression reaches 750,000.

               Chicago Bears win the professional football championship;
               repeat in 1933, 1940, 1941, 1943, 1946, 1963, and 1986.

1933   Century of Progress International Exposition commemorates the
               centennial of the incorporation of Chicago (held again in 1934).

               Chicago mayor Anton J. Cermak (b. 1873) dies in Miami,
               Florida, in an assassination attempt on President-elect Franklin
               Roosevelt (1882-1945).

               Chicago Tribune sports editor Arch Ward (1896-1955)
               organizes the first baseball All-Star Game, played at Comiskey
               Park and won by the American League.

               Illinois and Michigan Canal is closed to river traffic.

1934   Chicago Black Hawks win the National Hockey League
               championship (Stanley Cup); repeat in 1938 and 1961.

1937   General Assembly creates an unemployment compensation
               system.

               On Memorial Day, Chicago police fire on strikers at Republic
               Steel, resulting in ten deaths.

1939   Chicago author Richard Wright (1908-1960) publishes *Native Son*, set in Chicago and the first major novel about the black experience in America.

1940   Chicago theater-chain owner John Balaban (1894-1957) establishes WBKB, the first television station in Illinois.

1942   University of Chicago scientists, led by Nobel Prize winner (1938) Enrico Fermi (1901-1954), achieve the first self-sustaining nuclear reaction.

1945   Chicago Cubs win the National League pennant, lose the World Series to the Detroit Tigers.

            American Airlines inaugurates direct air service from Chicago to London.

1949   Orchard Place Airport in Chicago is renamed O'Hare Field, Chicago International Airport in honor of Lieutenant Commander Edward H. O'Hare (1914-1943), Congressional Medal of Honor recipient killed in World War II.

1950   Population of the state is 8,712,176.

            Gwendolyn Brooks (b. 1917) becomes the first African-American woman to win a Pulitzer Prize; is named Illinois poet laureate in 1968.

1951   Illinois and Mississippi Canal is closed to river traffic.

1952   Governor Adlai Stevenson (1900-1965) is the Democratic nominee for president; defeated by Republican Dwight Eisenhower (1890-1969).

1953   State Auditor Orville Hodge (1904-1986) is convicted of $1.5 million theft of state funds.

1954   In Des Plaines, Raymond A. Kroc (1902-1984) opens the first in a chain of McDonald's fast-food restaurants.

1955   Richard J. Daley (1902-1976) is elected to the first of six terms as Chicago mayor.

1957   The nation's first nuclear power generating station is activated
                    at Argonne National Laboratory in DuPage County.

1958   The first section of Illinois toll roads is opened from O'Hare
                    International Airport to the Wisconsin border.

                    Fire at Our Lady of Angels elementary school in Chicago
                    claims the lives of ninety-two children and three nuns.

1959   Everett M. Dirksen (1896-1969) is elected Republican leader of
                    the United States Senate.

                    Chicago White Sox win their first American League
                    championship since the 1919 Black Sox scandal but lose the
                    World Series to the Los Angeles Dodgers.

                    Chicago native Lorraine Hansberry (1930-1965) wins the New
                    York Drama Critics Circle Award for *A Raisin in the Sun*, the
                    first play by an African-American woman to be presented on
                    Broadway.

1962   General Assembly names Pulitzer Prize-winner Carl Sandburg
                    (1878-1967) the first poet laureate of Illinois.

                    Governor Otto Kerner (1908-1976) leads businessmen on the
                    first Illinois trade mission to Europe.

1964   General Assembly approves an at-large election of 177
                    representatives after the 1963 veto of a reapportionment bill.

1966   Illinois for the first time leads the nation in exports of
                    agricultural and manufactured products.

1968   Civil disorder erupts during the Democratic National
                    Convention in Chicago; police report 650 arrests.

1970   After the death of Secretary of State Paul Powell (b. 1902),
                    $800,000 is found in shoeboxes in his Springfield hotel room.

                    Voters adopt a new Constitution, the first in one hundred years.

"Chicago Seven" defendants are convicted on charges relating to violence at the 1968 Democratic National Convention; the decision is overturned in 1972.

1971   Chicago political and civil rights leader Jesse Jackson (b. 1941) founds Operation PUSH -- People United to Save (later Serve) Humanity.

Chicago Union Stock Yards closes.

Abraham Lincoln Home in Springfield is designated the first national historic site in Illinois

1972   Two Illinois Central commuter trains collide in Chicago; forty-five passengers are killed and more than two hundred are injured.

1973   Otto Kerner is convicted on charges involving the sale of racetrack stock while governor.

1974   The world's tallest building, Sears Tower in downtown Chicago, is completed.

1974   General Assembly approves a state lottery.

1976   James R. Thompson (b. 1936) is elected to the first of four gubernatorial terms (to 1991), the longest-serving governor in Illinois history.

Chicago author Saul Bellow (b. 1915) wins the Nobel Prize in Literature.

1979   Jane Byrne (b. 1934) becomes the first female mayor of Chicago.

American Airlines crash at O'Hare International Airport kills 275, the worst air disaster in United States history.

Centralia native Roland Burris (b. 1937) becomes Comptroller, the first African-American to hold a statewide elective office in Illinois.

1980   Ronald Reagan, born (1911) in Tampico, is elected United States President; John B. Anderson (b. 1922) of Rockford is defeated as an Independent candidate.

1981   Morton Grove ordinance bans the possession of handguns, the most restrictive gun control measure in the nation.

            Peoria native John B. "Jack" Brickhouse (b. 1916) retires after broadcasting more than five thousand Chicago Cubs and White Sox games; receives the National Baseball Hall of Fame Ford C. Frick Award in 1983.

1982   General Assembly fails to ratify the proposed equal rights amendment to the United States Constitution.

1983   Harold Washington (1922-1987) is elected the first African-American mayor of Chicago.

1984   Seventeen Chicago attorneys, police officers, and judges are indicted in Operation Greylord on charges of improperly influencing court cases; convictions include the first for a sitting state court judge in Illinois.

1988   Diamond-Star Motors, an automobile manufacturing venture between Mitsubishi Motors of Japan and the Chrysler Corporation, opens in Bloomington.

1989   Clarence Page (b. 1947) of the *Chicago Tribune* is the first African-American columnist to win a Pulitzer Prize.

1990   Population of the state is 11,430,602.

1991   Chicago Bulls win the first of three consecutive National Basketball Association championships.

1992   Carol Moseley-Braun (b. 1947) of Chicago becomes the first African-American woman elected to the United States Senate.

1993   The worst floods in the state's history ravage western and southern Illinois.

COUNTY SEATS
STATE OF ILLINOIS

PREPARED BY THE
DEPARTMENT OF TRANSPORTATION
OFFICE OF PLANNING AND PROGRAMMING

IN COOPERATION WITH THE
U. S. DEPARTMENT OF TRANSPORTATION
FEDERAL HIGHWAY ADMINISTRATION

I. CHRONOLOGICAL PERIODS

A. PREHISTORY

Technical archaeological reports are excluded from this section, although many series publications that do include such reports are listed. A few broad archaeological reports on the Cahokia Mounds group are given in the Historic Sites section.

1. Bagg, Rufus M. "Notes on the Distribution of the Mastodon in Illinois," in *Studies from the Geological Department.* University Studies, vol. 3, no. 2 (January 1909). Urbana, Ill.: University Press.

2. Bareis, Charles J. *Preservation Archaeology: Interstate 270, Madison, St. Clair, and Monroe Counties, Illinois.* Springfield: Illinois Department of Transportation, 1978.

3. Belting, Natalia Maree. "The Piasa--It Isn't a Bird." *Journal of the Illinois State Historical Society* 66 (1973): 302-5. The author identifies the petroglyph above Alton as a water monster, a symbol of evil among the Algonquian and Siouan Indians.

4. Bennett, Gwen Patrice. *A Bibliography of Illinois Archaeology.* Illinois State Museum Scientific Papers, vol. 21. Springfield: Illinois State Museum (in cooperation with the Illinois Archaeological Survey), 1984. A project of the Lands Unsuitable for Mining Program, this volume was designed to be used as a guide in designating such areas by the state Department of Mines and Minerals, after consultation with specified state environmental and scientific agencies. Entries are arranged alphabetically by principal author, with a cross-index by county.

5.   Bennett, John W. *Archaeological Explorations in Jo Daviess County, Illinois: The Work of William Baker Nickerson (1895-1901) and the University of Chicago (1926-32).* Chicago: University of Chicago Press, 1945. Nickerson worked under direction of the Peabody Museum, Harvard University. After his death, his field notes were donated to the University of Chicago.

6.   *Bulletin of the Archaeological Society of Illinois.* Vol. 1, no. 1 (1938). Succeeded by *Quarterly Bulletin of the Illinois State Archaeological Society,* vol. 2, no. 1 (September 1939)--to date.

7.   Cole, Fay-Cooper, and others. *Kincaid: A Prehistoric Illinois Metropolis.* Chicago: University of Chicago Press, 1951. Designed for the layman and nonspecialist, this volume discusses four cultural groups that successively occupied villages along the Ohio River and on the border between Pope and Massac counties in Illinois. Appendixes add details for the archaeology specialist.

8.   _____, and Deuel, Thorne. *Rediscovering Illinois: Archaeological Explorations in and around Fulton County.* Chicago: University of Chicago Press, 1937. A technical study, but very readable.

9.   Deuel, Thorne. "Illinois Records of 1000 A.D." *Journal of the Illinois State Historical Society* 41 (1948): 219-30. The archaeology of Hopewellian sites in Illinois. Reprinted as Illinois State Museum Reports of Investigations, no. 2. Springfield, 1948.

10.   Emerson, Thomas E. *Mississippian Stone Images in Illinois.* Illinois Archaeological Survey Circular, no. 6. Urbana, 1982.

11.   Hyde, George E. *Indians of the Woodlands: From Prehistoric Times to 1725.* Norman: University of Oklahoma Press, 1962. Does not reflect changes in archaeological chronologies resulting from radiocarbon dating introduced in 1950.

12.   Illinois Archaeological Survey. *Bulletin.* Nos. 1-10 (1959-75). Published irregularly. Became *Illinois Archaeology: Journal of the Archaeological Survey* in 1989.

13.   _____. *Circular.* No. 1 (October 1976)--to date. Published irregularly.

14.   _____. *Monograph.* 1969--to date.

15. _____. *Special Publication.* No. 1 (1973)--to date. Issued irregularly.

16. Illinois State Archaeological Society. *Journal . . .* vols. 1 (May 1942)--10 (April 1950); n.s. vols. 1 (July 1950)--3 (January 1954); succeeded by *Central States Archaeological Journal,* vols. 1 (July 1954)--to date. The latter *Journal* is the combined publication of the Illinois society with eleven other similar archaeological groups.

17. Illinois State Museum. Reports of Investigations. No. 1 (1948)--to date. Generally technical descriptions of excavations at both prehistoric and historic sites. Many Reports also contain information about the geology and environment of the sites. No. 45 was issued in 1990. Reports of general interest are listed separately herein in the appropriate category.

18. Jefferies, Richard W. *The Archaeology of Carrier Mills: 10,000 Years in the Saline Valley of Illinois.* Carbondale: Southern Illinois University Press, 1987. The story of human life at three sites, from excavations funded by the Peabody Coal Company and now destroyed by mines. A scholarly study accessible to the general reader, the publication also includes an account of Lakeview (a nineteenth-century settlement of black freedmen) part of which lay within the Carrier Mills Archaeological District.

19. Kampsville Archeological Center. *Kampsville Seminars in Archeology.* Vol. 1 (1982)--to date.

20. _____. *Research Series.* Vol. 1 (1985)--to date. A series of investigations for the Illinois Department of Transportation conducted under the auspices of the Illinois Archaeological Survey, in cooperation with other state and federal agencies.

21. _____. *Technical Reports.* Vol. 1 (1985)--to date.

22. McGregor, John C. *The Pool and Irving Villages: A Study of Hopewell Occupation in the Illinois River Valley.* Urbana: University of Illinois Press, 1958. A documentation of man's early existence in the Illinois River Valley. A valuable pioneering study, but some data have been superseded.

23. Markman, Charles W. *Chicago before History: The Prehistoric Archaeology of a Modern Metropolitan Area.* Studies in Illinois Archaeology, no. 7. Springfield: Illinois Historic Preservation Agency, 1991.

24. Merwin, Bruce W. "An Aboriginal Village Site in Union County." *Journal of the Illinois State Historical Society* 28, no. 1 (April 1935): 78-91. Study of Indian earthworks in the Mississippi bottom, near Anna.

25. Morse, Dan F., and Morse, Phyllis A. *Archaeology of the Central Mississippi Valley.* New World Archaeological Record series. New York: Academic Press, 1983. Includes the Cahokia Mounds site.

26. Peithmann, Irvin M. *Echoes of the Red Man: Archaeological and Cultural Survey of Indians of Southern Illinois.* New York: Exposition Press, 1955.

27. Quimby, George Irving. *Indian Life in the Upper Great Lakes, 11,000 B.C. to A.D. 1800.* Contribution of the Chicago Natural History Museum. Chicago: University of Chicago Press, 1960. How the geological history of the Great Lakes area affected the environment and the inhabitants.

28. Robbins, Peggy. "The Koster Dig." *American History Illustrated* 9 (February 1975): 29-34.

29. Silverberg, Robert. *Mound Builders of Ancient America: The Archaeology of a Myth.* Greenwich, Conn.: New York Graphic Society, 1968.

30. Struever, Stuart, and Holton, Felicia Antonelli. *Koster: Americans in Search of Their Prehistoric Past.* Garden City, N.Y.: Anchor Press, Doubleday, 1979. A story of the discovery and excavation of the Koster site in the lower Illinois River Valley. Written for the general reader.

31. Temple, Wayne C. "The Piasa Bird: Fact or Fiction." *Journal of the Illinois State Historical Society* 49 (1956): 308-27. Early French travelers reported a drawing of a mythical creature on the Mississippi River bluffs. Around these descriptions many legends were later elaborated. The author summarizes most of the published material about the drawing. Reprinted as Illinois State Museum Reports of Investigations, no. 5 (Springfield, 1956).

32. Terrell, John Upton. *American Indian Almanac.* New York: World, 1971. Brief accounts of prehistoric peoples, divided into ten geographical regions.

33. Woods, William I., ed. *Prehistoric Agriculture: Observations from the Midwest.* Studies in Illinois Archaeology, no. 8. Springfield: Illinois Historic Preservation Agency, 1992.

B. FRENCH PERIOD, 1673-1763

1. Bibliographies and General Works

34. Balesi, Charles J. *The Time of the French in the Heart of North America, 1673-1818.* Chicago: Alliance Francaise, 1992.

35. Beckwith, Hiram W., ed. *Collections of the Illinois State Historical Library, Volume I.* Springfield, 1903. Contains translations of the official account of Father Jacques Marquette's discoveries in the Mississippi Valley, various papers of the Sieur de La Salle, the so-called memoir of Henri de Tonty, the 1758 report by Charles Philippe Aubry, from Fort de Chartres, recounting the expedition he led to Fort Duquesne, as well as documents relating to George Rogers Clark's Illinois campaigns of 1778-79 and 1780.

36. Beers, Henry Putney. *The French & British in the Old Northwest: A Bibliographical Guide to Archive and Manuscript Sources.* Detroit: Wayne State University Press, 1964.

37. _____. *French and Spanish Records of Louisiana: A Bibliographical Guide to Archive and Manuscript Sources.* Baton Rouge and London: Louisiana State University Press, 1989. A well-written administrative history and a description of major sources, presented in a narrative bibliography. There is a separate 50-page bibliography related to French and Spanish records, as well as a good index with many Illinois references. The person beginning research in this period would be well advised to consult this invaluable source.

38. _____. *The French in North America: A Bibliographical Guide to French Archives, Reproductions, and Research Missions.* Baton Rouge: Louisiana State University Press, 1957. On the French records acquired by the Illinois Historical Survey, see pages 159-65.

39. Caldwell, Norman Ward. *The French in the Mississippi Valley, 1740-1750.* Illinois Studies in the Social Sciences, vol. 26, no. 3. Urbana: University of Illinois Press, 1941. An account of the administration and economy of the colonies.

40. Caruso, John A. *The Mississippi Valley Frontier: The Age of French Exploration and Settlement.* Indianapolis: Bobbs-Merrill, 1966. A cursory and often inaccurate survey.

41. Giraud, Marcel. *A History of French Louisiana.* 5 vols. to date. Two volumes have been issued in translation by Louisiana State University Press. *Volume One: The Reign of Louis XIV, 1698-1715,* translated by Joseph C. Lambert and revised and corrected by the author (1974) and *Volume Five: The Company of the Indies, 1723-1731,* translated by Brian Pearce (1991).

42. Kellogg, Louise Phelps. *The French Régime in Wisconsin and the Northwest.* Madison: State Historical Society of Wisconsin, 1925.

43. McDermott, John Francis, ed. *The French in the Mississippi Valley.* Urbana: University of Illinois Press, 1965. Fourteen significant papers from a 1964 conference commemorating the bicentennial of the founding of St. Louis. Among them are Joseph P. Donnelly's "Pierre Gibault and the Critical Period of the Illinois Country, 1768-78"; "Colonial Fortifications and Military Architecture in the Mississippi Valley," by Samuel Wilson, Jr.; and three articles on research resources: "The Seminary of Quebec--Resources for the History of the French in the Mississippi Valley," by Noël Baillargeon; "Resources in Detroit for the History of the French in the Mississippi Valley," by James M. Babcock; and "Manuscript Sources in Louisiana for the History of the French in the Mississippi Valley," by Winston De Ville.

44. Mumford, Helen W. *The French Governors of Illinois, 1718-1765.* Evanston, Ill.: National Society of the Colonial Dames of America in the State of Illinois, 1963.

45. Osman, Eaton G. *The Last of a Great Indian Tribe: A Chapter of Colonial History.* Chicago: A. Flanagan, 1923. Originally published under the title "Starved Rock." A history of Starved Rock during the French regime.

46. Pease, Theodore Calvin, ed. *Anglo-French Boundary Disputes in the West, 1749-1763.* Collections of the Illinois State Historical Library, vol. 27. Springfield, 1936. A 171-page introduction provides the diplomatic and historical background necessary to a full understanding of documents related to the boundary controversies of the era of the Seven Years' War. Items are presented in French, with English translations.

47. _____, and Werner, Raymond C., eds. *The French Foundations, 1680-1693.* Collections of the Illinois State Historical Library, vol. 23. Springfield, 1934. Documents presented in the original French, with English translations. Among the items are La Salle's 9 November 1680 report on the Illinois country (which the editors say Margry garbled) and the Degannes memoir (pages 302-96), actually written by Pierre de Liette, Henri de Tonty's nephew. The latter document, the editors say, is "the best of the early accounts of the Illinois country and its Indians."

48. _____, and Jenison, Ernestine, eds. *Illinois on the Eve of the Seven Years' War, 1747-1755.* Collections of the Illinois State Historical Library, vol. 29. Springfield, 1940. Documents selected for this volume represent, the editors say, "the writings of the people who labored to maintain the cause of France in the West"--more particularly in the Illinois country. Items are presented in the original French, with English translations.

49. Thwaites, Reuben Gold, comp. and ed. *The French Regime in Wisconsin.* Collections of the State Historical Society of Wisconsin, vols. 16-18. Madison, 1902-8. A vast collection of documents containing many references to the Illinois country and the Illinois Indians. The volumes are indexed separately.

2. Explorers and Missionaries and Their Discoveries

50. Charlevoix, Pierre François Xavier de. *Journal of a Voyage to North America.* With notes, introduction, and index by Louise Phelps Kellogg. 2 vols. Chicago: Caxton Club, 1923. Reprint of the original London edition, 1761. The index has many Illinois-related entries, especially for the Illinois tribe. See John Lee Allaman's "Western Illinois in Charlevoix's History and Journal." *Western Illinois Regional Studies* 7, no. 1 (Spring 1984): 5-15.

51. Cox, Isaac Joslin, ed. *The Journeys of René Robert Cavelier, Sieur de La Salle . . .* New York: Barnes, 1905. Contains the narratives of Hennepin, Tonty, and other men of their period.

52. Cross, Marion E., trans. and ed. *Father Louis Hennepin's Description of Louisiana.* Minneapolis: University of Minnesota Press, 1938. A new translation of the first printed account of the Illinois country.

53. Delanglez, Jean. "The Cartography of the Mississippi." *Mid-America* 31 (1949): 29-52.

54. _____. "The Discovery of the Mississippi: Primary Sources." *Mid-America* 16 n.s. (1945): 219-31.

55. _____. "The Discovery of the Mississippi: Secondary Sources." *Mid-America* 17 n.s. (1946): 3-22.

56. _____. "The Jolliet Lost Map of the Mississippi." *Mid-America* 17 n.s. (1946): 67-144.

57. _____. "La Salle, 1669-1673." *Mid-America* 8 n.s. (1937): 197-216, 237-53.

58. _____. *Life and Voyages of Louis Jolliet, 1645-1700.* Institute of Jesuit History Publications, vol. 6. Chicago, 1948. Biographical information about Jolliet, along with a critical examination of the source material on which knowledge of his explorations is based.

59. _____. "Marquette's Autograph Map of the Mississippi River." *Mid-America* 16 n.s. (1945): 30-53.

60. _____. "The 'Recit des voyages et des decouvertes du Pere Jacques Marquette.' " *Mid-America* 17 n.s. (1946): 173-94, 211-58.

61. _____. "The 1674 Account of the Discovery of the Mississippi." *Mid-America* 15 n.s. (1944): 301-24. The author proves that the "Account" was the work of Claude Dablon, Jesuit Superior at Quebec.

62. _____. "The Voyages of Tonti in North America, 1678-1704." *Mid-America* 15 n.s. (1944): 255-300. A fully documented calendar of Tonty's twenty-six years in North America, with maps.

63. Donnelly, Joseph P. *Jacques Marquette, S. J., 1637-1675.* Chicago: Loyola University Press, 1968.

64. Gaither, Frances. *The Fatal River: The Life and Death of La Salle.* New York: Holt, 1931.

65. Garraghan, Gilbert Joseph. *Marquette.* New York: American Press, 1937.

66. _____. "Some Hitherto Unpublished Marquettiana." *Mid-America* 7 n.s. (1936): 15-26.

67. _____. *Some Newly Discovered Marquette and La Salle Letters.* Archivum Historicum Societatis Jesu, vol. 4. Rome: Soc. Tip. A. Macioce E Pisani-Isola Liri, 1935.

68. Hamilton, Raphael N. *Marquette's Explorations: The Narratives Reexamined.* Madison: University of Wisconsin Press, 1970. A scholarly study of the accounts of Marquette's voyage with Jolliet in 1673 and the establishment of the mission at the great village of the Kaskaskia near Starved Rock. An indispensable tool for historians of the French period.

69. Hennepin, Louis. *A New Discovery of a Vast Country in America by Father Louis Hennepin; Reprinted from the Second London Issue of 1698.* 2 vols. Edited by Reuben Gold Thwaites. Chicago: McClurg, 1903. Many entries relate to Illinois and the Illinois tribe.

70. Joutel, Henri. *Joutel's Journal of La Salle's Last Voyage, 1684-7.* Edited by Henry Reed Stiles, with a bibliography of the discovery of the Mississippi by Appleton P. C. Griffin. Albany, N. Y.: J. McDonough, 1906.

71. Kellogg, Louise Phelps, ed. *Early Narratives of the Northwest, 1634-1699.* New York: Scribner's, 1917. Contains the narratives of Marquette and Tonty.

72. Knight, Robert, and Zeuch, Lucius H. *The Location of the Chicago Portage Route of the Seventeenth Century . . .* Chicago Historical Society's Collection, vol. 12. Chicago, 1928.

73. La Salle, René Robert, Cavelier de. *Relation of the Discoveries and Voyages of Cavelier de La Salle from 1679 to 1681: The Official Narrative.* Translated by Melville B. Anderson. Notes by Pierre Margry. Chicago: Caxton Club, 1901.

74. "La Salle on the Mississippi." *American Heritage,* April 1957, pp. 4-19, 71-91. Sixteen of 28 paintings, by George Catlin, in the series "La Salle on the Mississippi," are reproduced, along with text from Francis Parkman's *La Salle and the Discovery of the Great West* that illuminates the paintings. Two paintings are of the great Illinois village on the Illinois River.

75. Margry, Pierre, ed. *Découvertes et établissements des français dans l'ouest et dans le sud de l'Amérique Septenrionale (1614-1754).* 6 vols. Paris: Maisonneuve, 1879-88. See the criticism by Jean Delanglez of this collection of French documents (*Mid-America* 8 n.s. [1937]: 197-216 and 237-53).

76. Meehan, Thomas A. *Man with the Iron Hand and Heart: Story of Henri de Tony* [Tonty], *Catholic Explorer and Adventurer.* Huntington, Ind.: Our Sunday Visitor Press, 1943.

77. Munro, William Bennett. *Crusaders of New France: A Chronicle of the Fleur-de-lis in the Wilderness.* The Chronicles of America Series, vol. 4. New

Haven, Conn.: Yale University Press, 1918. Chapter 6 deals with La Salle's explorations.

78. Murphy, Edmund R. *Henry de Tonty: Fur Trader of the Mississippi.* Baltimore: Johns Hopkins Press, 1941.

79. O'Dea, Arthur J., and Garraghan, Gilbert Joseph. "Marquette's Titles to Fame." *Mid-America* 9 n.s. (1938): 30-36.

80. Parkman, Francis. *La Salle and the Discovery of the Great West.* Pt. 3 of France and England in North America: A Series of Historical Narratives. 11th ed., rev., Boston: Little, Brown, 1879.

81. Quaife, Milo Milton, ed. *The Western Country in the 17th Century: The Memoirs of Lamothe Cadillac and Pierre Liette.* Lakeside Classics, no. 45. Chicago: R. R. Donnelley, 1947. Reprint, Secaucus, N.J.: Citadel Press, 1962.

82. Shea, John Gilmary, ed. *Discovery and Exploration of the Mississippi Valley, with the Original Narratives of Marquette, Allouez, Membré, Hennepin, and Anastase Douay.* New York: Redfield, 1852. Reprint, Albany: Joseph McDonough, 1903.

83. _____, ed. *Early Voyages up and down the Mississippi, by Cavelier, St. Cosme, Le Sueur, Gravier, and Guignas.* Albany: Joel Munsell, 1861.

84. Steck, Francis Borgia. *Marquette Legends.* Edited by August Reyling. New York: Pageant Press, 1960. A summation of essays published earlier, some printed privately, the most important of which demonstrated that Father Jacques Marquette was not the author of the famous journal ascribed to him and first published in 1681. Later scholars have overwhelmingly agreed with Steck's conclusions.

85. _____. "What Became of Jolliet's Journal?" *The Americas* 5 (1948): 172-99.

86. Thwaites, Reuben Gold. *Father Marquette.* New York: Appleton, 1902.

87. _____, ed. *The Jesuit Relations and Allied Documents: Travels and Explorations of the Jesuit Missionaries in New France, 1610-1791 . . .* 73 vols. Cleveland: Burrows Brothers, 1896-1901. Volumes 72 and 73 are the index. Under the entries "Indians" as well as under specific tribal names are many pages of references. There are also many references under "Illinois (country)" and

"Illinois (state)." See also Donnelly, Joseph P. *Thwaites' Jesuit Relations: Errata and Addenda.* Chicago: Loyola University Press, 1967.

88. Tonty, Henri de. *Relation of Henri de Tonty Concerning the Explorations of La Salle from 1678 to 1683.* Translated by Melville B. Anderson. Chicago: Caxton Club, 1898.

89. Weddle, Robert S., ed.; Morkovsky, Mary Christine, and Galloway, Patricia, assoc. eds. *La Salle, the Mississippi, and the Gulf: Three Primary Documents.* Translated by Ann Linda Bell and Robert S. Weddle. College Station: Texas A & M Press, 1987. One of the three superbly edited and translated documents is the "Minet Relation," unknown to scholars until 1981. Minet based the document on oral reports to him from two members of La Salle's 1682 expedition to the Illinois country and the Mississippi Valley.

3. Settlements, Missions, Trading Posts, and Forts

90. Belting, Natalia Maree. "The French Villages of the Illinois Country." *Canadian Historical Review* 24 (1943): 14-23. Brief histories of Kaskaskia, Fort de Chartres, Prairie du Rocher, St. Philippe, and Cahokia, in Illinois, and Ste. Genevieve, in Missouri.

91. _____. "Kaskaskia, 'The Versailles of the West.' " *Indiana Magazine of History* 41 (1945): 1-18. Business and social history of the first settlers.

92. _____. *Kaskaskia under the French Regime.* Illinois Studies in the Social Sciences, vol. 29, no. 3. Urbana: University of Illinois Press, 1948.

93. Briggs, Winstanley. "Le Pays des Illinois." *William and Mary Quarterly* 3d ser. 47 (1990): 30-56. Compares French villages in the Illinois country with New England villages. A brief but comprehensive study of all aspects of village life and governance, with valuable annotations.

94. Brown, Margaret Kimball. "The Kaskaskia Manuscripts." *Illinois Libraries* 62 (1980): 312-24. A detailed history of various official French records that were cataloged, calendared, indexed, and microfilmed under direction of the author.

95. _____. "Uncovering the Mystery of the Three Forts de Chartres." *Illinois Magazine* 16, no. 9 (November 1977): 23-29.

96. _____, and Dean, Lawrie Cena, eds. *The Village of Chartres in Colonial Illinois, 1720-1765.* New Orleans: Polyanthos Press, 1977. More than one thousand pages in facsimile reproduction of typed copies of documents from the parishes of Fort de Chartres, St. Philippe, and Prairie du Rocher. The documents consist of baptismal, marriage, and death records; real estate records and other notarial records (1718-19); and court records. Church records are presented both in French and English translation; the others, in translation only. The volume has a name index and is a valuable research resource.

97. Faris, John T. *The Romance of Forgotten Towns.* New York: Harper, 1924. Contains chapters on Kaskaskia, Cahokia, and Fort de Chartres. Chapter 11, about Kaskaskia, was reprinted separately by the Public Library of Fort Wayne and Allen County, Indiana, in 1955.

98. Fortier, Edward Joseph. "The Establishment of the Tamarois Mission." *Transactions of the Illinois State Historical Society, 1908,* pp. 233-39.

99. Garraghan, Gilbert Joseph. "Chicago under the French Regime." *Transactions of the Illinois State Historical Society, 1930,* pp. 184-99.

100. _____. "Earliest Settlements of the Illinois Country." *Catholic Historical Review* 15, n.s. 9, January 1930, pp. 351-62. A summary of recent (1929) research about the first settlements at Cahokia, Kaskaskia, and Chicago, Illinois, and Vincennes, Indiana.

101. _____. "New Light on Old Cahokia." *Illinois Catholic Historical Review* 11 (1928-29): 99-146.

102. Gums, Bonnie L. *Archaeology at French Colonial Cahokia.* Illinois Historic Preservation Agency Studies in Illinois Archaeology, no. 3. Springfield, 1988.

103. Jelks, Edward B.; Ekberg, Carl J.; and Martin, Terrance J. *Excavations at the Laurens Site, Probable Location of Fort de Chartres I.* Illinois Historic Preservation Agency Studies in Illinois Archaeology, no. 5. Springfield, 1989. The original fort, built about 1720 (at the Laurens Site), is approximately one kilometer southeast of Fort de Chartres State Historic Site.

104. Lagron, Arthur. "Fort Crèvecoeur." *Journal of the Illinois State Historical Society* 5 (1912-13): 451-57.

105. McCarthy, William P. "The Chevalier Macarty Mactigue." *Journal of the Illinois State Historical Society* 61 (1968): 41-57. Macarty, as commandant of the Illinois country in the 1750s, supervised construction of a new Fort de Chartres and mustered the command of troops and Native Americans sent to Fort Niagara in 1759.

106. McDermott, John Francis, ed. *Frenchmen and French Ways in the Mississippi Valley.* Urbana: University of Illinois Press, 1969. Among the papers herein, presented at a 1967 conference, are "New Light on Fort Massac," by John B. Fortier, and "François Saucier, Engineer of Fort de Chartres, Illinois," by Walter J. Saucier and Kathrine Wagner Seineke--which supersedes the outdated writings on Saucier by John Francis Snyder.

107. _____, ed. *Old Cahokia: A Narrative and Documents Illustrating the First Century of Its History.* St. Louis: St. Louis Historical Documents Foundation, 1949. Some of the documents carry the story of Cahokia and its manners and customs to the 1820s.

108. _____. "The Poverty of the Illinois French." *Journal of the Illinois State Historical Society* 27 (1934-35): 195-201. The French settlements, once prosperous, suffered in the British and territorial periods from floods, weather that destroyed crops, decline of the Indian trade, and unscrupulous administrators who plundered the villages.

109. Meehan, Thomas A. "Jean Baptiste Point du Sable, the First Chicagoan." *Journal of the Illinois State Historical Society* 56 (1963): 439-53.

110. Mulkey, Floyd. "Fort St. Louis at Peoria." *Journal of the Illinois State Historical Society* 37 (1944): 301-16. Fort St. Louis at the lower end of Lake Peoria succeeded the first fort by that name, located on Starved Rock. The second fort was finally abandoned in 1720.

111. Palm, Mary Borgias, Sister. *The Jesuit Missions of the Illinois Country, 1673-1763.* Cleveland: Sisters of Notre Dame, 1933.

112. Rowland, Dunbar, and Sanders, A. G., eds. *Mississippi Provincial Archives, French Dominion.* 3 vols. Jackson: Press of the Mississippi Department of Archives and History, 1927-32. Many references to the settlements and Indians of the Illinois country.

113. Snyder, John Francis. *Captain John Baptiste Saucier at Fort Chartres in the Illinois, 1751-1763.* Peoria, Ill.: Smith & Schaefer, 190₁. Saucier, an officer in the French Army at Fort de Chartres, was an ancestor of the author's. Snyder's information about the fort is outdated. Reprinted from *Transactions of the Illinois State Historical Society, 1919*, pp. 215-63.

114. Waller, Elbert. "Forts of the American Bottom." *Transactions of the Illinois State Historical Society, 1928*, pp. 203-12.

115. Walthall, John A., ed. *French Colonial Archaeology: The Illinois Country and the Western Great Lakes.* Urbana: University of Illinois Press, 1991.

116. _____, and Benchley, Elizabeth. *The River L'Abbe Mission: A French Colonial Church for the Cahokia Illini on Monks Mound.* Illinois Historic Preservation Agency Studies in Illinois Archaeology, no. 2. Springfield, 1987.

4. Miscellany

117. Brown, Margaret Kimball. "Allons, Cowboys." *Journal of the Illinois State Historical Society* 76 (1983): 273-82. An account of the roundup of cattle and horses in the Illinois country for the combined French and Indian campaign against the Chickasaw on the lower Mississippi in 1739-40.

118. Caldwell, Norman Ward. "Charles Juchereau de St. Denys, a French Pioneer in the Mississippi Valley." *Mississippi Valley Historical Review* 28 (1941-42): 563-80.

119. Delisle, Legardeur. "A Search for Copper on the Illinois River: The Journals of Legardeur Delisle, 1722." Edited by Stanley Faye. *Journal of the Illinois State Historical Society* 38 (1945): 38-57. Delisle was a military officer who accompanied François Philippe Renault to Illinois.

120. Douglas, Walter B. "The Sieurs de St. Ange." *Transactions of the Illinois State Historical Society, 1909*, pp. 135-46.

121. Ekberg, Carl J. "Black Slavery in Illinois, 1720-1765." *Western Illinois Regional Studies* 12, no. 1 (Spring 1989): 5-19.

122. _____, with Pregaldin, Anton J. "Marie Rouensa-Oucateona and the Foundations of French Illinois." *Illinois Historical Journal* 84 (1991): 146-60. The daughter of a Kaskaskia chief, Marie Rouensa married two Frenchmen and became a prosperous resident of the village of Kaskaskia.

123. Fortier, John B., and Chaput, Donald. "A Historical Reexamination of Juchereau's Illinois Tannery." *Journal of the Illinois State Historical Society* 62 (1969): 385-406. Charles Juchereau de St. Denys operated a tannery and established a short-lived colony on the Ohio in late 1702.

124. McDermott, John Francis. *A Glossary of Mississippi Valley French.* Washington University Studies, n.s., Language and Literature, no. 12. St. Louis, 1941.

125. Pearson, Emmet F. "First Hospital in the Illinois Country." *Journal of the Illinois State Historical Society* 70 (1977): 299-301. Describes the house used as a hospital for Fort de Chartres after 1739 and discusses the early surgeons there and elsewhere in the Illinois country.

126. Seineke, Kathrine Wagner. "Three Canadiennes and the Men They Married: An Intimate Look at Some Eighteenth Century French Colonials of the Mississippi Valley." *French Canadian and Acadian Genealogical Review* 2 (1969): 71-119. Traces the lives and family histories of three Canadiennes who lived in, or visited, the Illinois country. A concise history of the French occupancy, giving many of the major sources for that history.

127. Thompson, Charles Manfred. "Monetary System of Nouvelle France." *Journal of the Illinois State Historical Society* 4 (1911-12): 145-56.

128. Walthall, John A., and Emerson, Thomas E., eds. *The Calumet & the Fleur-de-lys: Archaeology of Indian and French Contact in the Midcontinent.* Washington: Smithsonian Institution Press, 1992.

C. BRITISH PERIOD, 1763-1783

1. Bibliographies and General Works

129. Alvord, Clarence Walworth, and Carter, Clarence Edwin, eds. *The Critical Period, 1763-1765.* Collections of the Illinois State Historical Library, vol. 10. Springfield, 1915.

130. Alvord, Clarence Walworth. *The Mississippi Valley in British Politics: A Study of Trade, Land Speculation, and Experiments in Imperialism Culminating in the American Revolution.* 2 vols. Cleveland: Arthur H. Clark, 1917.

131. _____, and Carter, Clarence Edwin, eds. *The New Régime, 1765-1767.* Collections of the Illinois State Historical Library, vol. 11. Springfield, 1916.

132. _____, and Carter, Clarence Edwin, eds. *Trade and Politics, 1767-1769.* Collections of the Illinois State Historical Library, vol. 16. Springfield, 1921.

133. Alvord, Clarence Walworth. "Virginia and the West: An Interpretation." *Mississippi Valley Historical Review* 3 (1916-17): 19-38.

134. Carter, Clarence Edwin. *Great Britain and the Illinois Country, 1763-1774.* Washington: American Historical Association, 1910. Reprints, Port Washington, N.Y.: Kennikat Press, 1970, and Freeport, N.Y.: Books for Libraries Press, 1971. Winner of the 1908 Justin Winsor prize in American history.

135. Gephart, Ronald M., comp. *Revolutionary America, 1763-1789: A Bibliography.* Washington: Library of Congress, 1984. A 2-volume bibliography, with 14,810 entries, that includes items published through 1972. Published material only is included; but under the heading "Research Aids," 315 guides to manuscript collections are listed. Illinois-related items can be located through the topical-chronological table of contents.

136. Kellogg, Louise Phelps. *The British Régime in Wisconsin and the Northwest.* Madison: State Historical Society of Wisconsin, 1935. History through the War of 1812.

137. Kinnaird, Lawrence, ed. *Spain in the Mississippi Valley, 1765-1794: Translations of Materials from the Spanish Archives in the Bancroft Library.* Vols. 2 and 3 of *Annual Report of the American Historical Association for the year 1945.* Washington: Government Printing Office, 1946, 1949.

138. Pittman, Philip. *The Present State of the European Settlements on the Mississippi, with a Geographical Description of the River.* London: Printed for J. Nourse, 1770. Facsimile reprint, with an introduction and notes by John Francis McDermott, Memphis: Memphis State University Press, 1977. In preparing his introduction and footnotes, McDermott consulted, among other manuscript sources for the British period, the papers of General Thomas Gage and Sir Jeffrey Amherst in the William L. Clements Library at the University of Michigan and the Frederick Haldimand Papers at the British Museum, London. Pittman's account includes descriptions of Kaskaskia, Prairie du Rocher, Fort de Chartres, Cahokia, and St. Philippe, as well as general accounts of the Illinois country and its residents, both Native American and European.

2. The American Revolution

139. "The Army Led by Col. George Rogers Clark in His Conquest of the Illinois, 1778-9." *Transactions of the Illinois State Historical Society, 1903,* pp. 166-78. With notes by Dr. John Francis Snyder. The rosters printed here contain notations about land grants due these men or already given to them for their service.

140. Baldwin, Carl R. *Captains of the Wilderness: The American Revolution on the Western Frontier.* Belleville, Ill.: Tiger Rose Publishing, 1986. Lives of some of the people who played a role in the Revolution in Illinois.

141. Barnhart, John D. "A New Evaluation of Henry Hamilton and George Rogers Clark." *Mississippi Valley Historical Review* 37 (1950-51): 643-52.

142. Bodley, Temple. "George Rogers Clark's Relief Claims." *Journal of the Illinois State Historical Society* 29 (1936-37): 103-20. Attempts to gain reimbursement from Virginia for obligations Clark had incurred during the Revolutionary War.

143. Butterfield, Consul Willshire. *History of George Rogers Clark's Conquest of the Illinois and Wabash Towns, 1778 and 1779.* 1904; reprint, Boston: Gregg Press, 1972.

144. Carter, Clarence Edwin. "Documents Relating to the Occupation of the Illinois Country by the British." *Transactions of the Illinois State Historical Society, 1907,* pp. 201-21. Although France ceded the Illinois country in 1763, the British were unable to reach Illinois until 1765, the year these documents were dated.

145. Chaput, Donald. "Treason or Loyalty: Frontier French in the American Revolution." *Journal of the Illinois State Historical Society* 71 (1978): 242-51. The author concludes that, by and large, the thousands of French in the Ohio Valley, Great Lakes, and Mississippi River areas favored the British. He discusses in particular several who did not do so or whose loyalties shifted.

146. Clark, George Rogers. *The Conquest of the Illinois.* Lakeside Classics, no. 18, edited by Milo Milton Quaife. Chicago: R. R. Donnelley, 1920. Clark's memoir, written in 1798 and 1799, is here transcribed into "clear and grammatical English." A literal transcription appears in James Alton James, ed. *The George Rogers Clark Papers.*

147. Cook, Minnie G. "Virginia Currency in the Illinois Country." *Transactions of the Illinois State Historical Society, 1912*, pp. 122-41. George Rogers Clark paid many of the bills for his troops with debased currency issued by the state of Virginia.

148. Cummings, J. E. "The Burning of Sauk-e-nuk: The Westernmost Battle of the Revolution." *Journal of the Illinois State Historical Society* 20 (1927-28): 49-62.

149. Drumm, Stella M. "The British-Indian Attack on Pain Court (St. Louis)." *Journal of the Illinois State Historical Society* 23 (1930-31): 642-51. The settlements in Illinois were also threatened, and after the British were repulsed on 26 May 1780, Colonel John Montgomery led an expedition after the retreating forces. Based in large part on the Voorhis Collection of Clark Manuscripts in the Missouri Historical Society, St. Louis.

150. *The French, the Indians, and George Rogers Clark in the Illinois Country: Proceedings of an Indiana American Revolution Bicentennial Symposium . . .* Indianapolis: Indiana Historical Society, 1977.

151. Graebner, Norman A. "The Illinois Country and the Treaty of Paris of 1783." *Illinois Historical Journal* 78 (1985): 2-16. The American treaty commissioners were successful in sustaining American claims to the Illinois country against claims made by the French and Spanish as well as the British.

152. Harding, Margery Heberling, comp. *George Rogers Clark and His Men: Military Records, 1778-1784.* Frankfort: Kentucky Historical Society, 1981. More than two hundred military rolls, principally pay rolls, from the Illinois Papers in the Virginia State Library, Archives Division, are transcribed and indexed.

153. Harrison, Lowell H. *George Rogers Clark and the War in the West.* Lexington: University Press of Kentucky, 1976. A brief but balanced account designed for a popular audience.

154. Hauberg, John H. "Hard Times in Illinois in 1780." *Journal of the Illinois State Historical Society* 44 (1951): 231-40.

155. Havighurst, Walter. "A Sword for George Rogers Clark." *American Heritage*, October 1962, pp. 56-64. An exciting succinct account of Clark's capture of Vincennes, for which the state of Virginia belatedly presented him with a pension and a sword.

156. Horsman, Reginald. "Great Britain and the Illinois Country in the Era of the American Revolution." *Journal of the Illinois State Historical Society* 69 (1976): 100-109.

157. Hulbert, Archer Butler. *Historic Highways of America.* 16 vols. Cleveland: Arthur H. Clark, 1902-5. In volume 8 (*Military Roads of the Mississippi Basin: The Conquest of the Old Northwest*) Hulbert traces George Rogers Clark's route across Illinois, pages 15-71 and 221-30.

158. James, James Alton. "An Appraisal of the Contributions of George Rogers Clark to the History of the West." *Mississippi Valley Historical Review* 17 (1930-31): 98-115.

159. _____, ed. *George Rogers Clark Papers, 1771-1781; George Rogers Clark Papers, 1781-1784.* Collections of the Illinois State Historical Library, vols. 8 and 19. Springfield, 1912 and 1926. In addition to Clark's own papers, the collection includes documents relating to his campaigns in the Northwest and the creation of the Illinois country as a county of Virginia.

160. _____. "Illinois and the Revolution in the West, 1779-1780." *Transactions of the Illinois State Historical Society, 1910*, pp. 63-71. Useful summary of military activities, the establishment of government, Native American affairs, and problems of funding and supply.

161. _____. "Oliver Pollock, Financier of the Revolution in the West." *Mississippi Valley Historical Review* 16 (1929-30): 67-80.

162. _____. "Oliver Pollock and the Winning of the Illinois Country." *Transactions of the Illinois State Historical Society, 1934*, pp. 33-59. Pollock was a merchant in Spanish Louisiana, whose firm was one of the principal outlets for goods produced in the Illinois country. During the American Revolution he honored George Rogers Clark's bills of credit for supplies needed in the Illinois country.

163. _____. "The Significance of the Attack on St. Louis, 1780." *Proceedings of the Mississippi Valley Historical Association* 2 (1908-9): 199-217.

164. _____. "The Significance of the Sesquicentennial Celebration of the American Revolution West of the Allegheny Mountains." *Journal of the Illinois State Historical Society* 19 (1926-27): 13-35.

165. _____. "Some Problems of the Northwest in 1779." In *Essays in American History Dedicated to Frederick Jackson Turner.* Edited by Guy Stanton Ford. New York: Holt, 1910, pp. 57-83.

166. _____. "Spanish Influence in the West during the American Revolution." *Mississippi Valley Historical Review* 4 (1917-18): 193-208.

167. Kellogg, Louise Phelps. "Indian Diplomacy during the Revolution in the West." *Transactions of the Illinois State Historical Society, 1929*, pp. 47-57.

168. Lambert, Joseph I. "Clark's Conquest of the Northwest." *Indiana Magazine of History* 36 (1940): 337-50.

169. McDermott, John Francis. "The Myth of the 'Imbecile Governor': Captain Fernando de Leyba and the Defense of St. Louis in 1780." *The Spanish in the Mississippi Valley, 1762-1804*, edited by John Francis McDermott. Urbana: University of Illinois Press, 1974, pp. 314-405.

170. Meese, William A. "Rock River in the Revolution." *Transactions of the Illinois State Historical Society, 1909*, pp. 97-103. On an expedition against Native Americans who had attacked St. Louis in May 1780, John Montgomery's troops proceeded to Peoria and then burned the Sauk village on Rock River.

171. Nasatir, A. P. "The Anglo-Spanish Frontier in the Illinois Country during the American Revolution, 1779-1783." *Journal of the Illinois State Historical Society* 21 (1928-29): 291-358.

172. Pease, Theodore Calvin, and Pease, Marguerite Jenison. *George Rogers Clark and the Revolution in Illinois, 1763-1787: A Sesquicentennial Memorial.* Springfield: Illinois State Historical Library and Society, 1929. A brief history of British control of the Illinois country, including accounts of Clark's capture of Kaskaskia on 4 July 1778, events of the Revolution, 1778-81, and of area activities until 1790, when Illinois was organized as St. Clair County under the Ordinance of 1787.

173. Pease, Theodore Calvin, "1780: The Revolution at Crisis in the West." *Journal of the Illinois State Historical Society* 23 (1930-31): 664-81.

174. Quaife, Milo Milton, ed. *The Capture of Old Vincennes: The Original Narratives of George Rogers Clark and of His Opponent Gov. Henry Hamilton.* Indianapolis: Bobbs-Merrill, 1927.

175. Randall, James Garfield. "George Rogers Clark's Service of Supply." *Mississippi Valley Historical Review* 8 (1921-22): 250-63.

176. Rickey, Don Jr. "The British-Indian Attack on St. Louis, May 26, 1780." *Missouri Historical Review* 55 (1960-61): 35-45. The British recruited Indians in Illinois to join their ranks; the Americans across the river at Kaskaskia and Cahokia came to the aid of the Spanish and then, with the Spanish, launched an attack on the Sauk village on Rock River.

177. Schuyler, Robert Livingston. *The Transition in Illinois from British to American Government.* New York: Columbia University Press, 1909.

178. Seineke, Kathrine Wagner. *The George Rogers Clark Adventure in the Illinois and Selected Documents of the American Revolution at the Frontier Posts.* Introduction by Robert Mize Sutton. New Orleans: Polyanthos, 1981. Book 1 of this volume is an account of Clark's campaign in the Illinois country. Book 2 has reproductions, or a calendar listing, of more than four hundred documents (from American, British, Canadian, French, and Spanish archives) that constitute a documentary history of the Old Northwest, 1757-84.

179. Sheehan, Bernard W. " 'The Famous Hair Buyer General': Henry Hamilton, George Rogers Clark, and the American Indian." *Indiana Magazine of History* 79 (March 1983): 1-28.

180. Skaggs, David Curtis, ed. *The Old Northwest in the American Revolution: An Anthology.* Madison: State Historical Society of Wisconsin, 1977. Many of the twenty-one contributions, by outstanding scholars, are related to Illinois. There is a bibliography but no index.

181. Sosin, Jack M. *The Revolutionary Frontier, 1763-1783.* Histories of the American Frontier series. New York: Holt, 1967. Reprint, Albuquerque: University of New Mexico Press, 1974.

182. Stevens, Paul L. " 'To Invade the Frontiers of Kentucky'? The Indian Diplomacy of Philippe de Rocheblave, Britain's Acting Commandant at Kaskaskia, 1776-1778." *Filson Club History Quarterly* 64 (1990): 205-46.

183. Sutton, Robert Mize. "George Rogers Clark and the Campaign in the West: The Five Major Documents." *Indiana Magazine of History* 76 (December 1980): 334-45.

184. Thompson, David G. "Thomas Bentley and the American Revolution in Illinois." *Illinois Historical Journal* 83 (1990): 2-12.

185. Thwaites, Reuben Gold. *How George Rogers Clark Won the Northwest and Other Essays in Western History.* Chicago: McClurg, 1903. Chapter 3 includes a history of the Black Hawk War.

186. Waller, George M. *The American Revolution in the West.* Chicago: Nelson-Hall, 1976.

187. _____. "George Rogers Clark and the American Revolution in the West." *Indiana Magazine of History* 72 (1976): 1-20.

188. Woolard, F. M. "Route of Colonel George Rogers Clark and His Army from Kaskaskia to Vincennes." *Transactions of the Illinois State Historical Society, 1907,* pp. 48-63.

3. Miscellany

189. Alvord, Clarence Walworth, and Carter, Clarence Edwin, eds. *Earnest Invitation to the Inhabitants of Illinois by an Inhabitant of Kaskaskia.* Club of Colonial Reprints of Providence, R.I., 1908. Originally published in Philadelphia by Du Simitiere in 1772. The Alvord and Carter edition was a facsimile reprint in French. An English version, translated and edited by Lydia Marie Brauer, was published in the *Transactions of the Illinois State Historical Society, 1908,* pages 261-68. The community pleads with the British to establish a government in the Illinois country.

190. Boyd, C. E. "The County of Illinois." *American Historical Review* 4 (1898-99): 623-35. In October 1778 Virginia annexed Illinois as a county and made provisions for its government, which was more or less in place until 1790.

191. Evans, Emory G. "The Colonial View of the West." *Journal of the Illinois State Historical Society* 69 (1976): 84-90. Comments on the economic value of the western territories by both British and colonial American writers.

192. Foster, Olive S., and Hempstead, Mary C. *The Revolutionary War Period, 1763-1787, in Publications of the Illinois State Historical Library and Society.* Springfield: Illinois Bicentennial Commission, 1973.

193. Gage, Thomas. *The Correspondence of General Thomas Gage with the Secretaries of State, and with the War Office and the Treasury, 1763-1775.* 2 vols. Compiled and edited by Clarence Edwin Carter. New Haven, Conn.: Yale University Press, 1931, 1933. The original letters of General Gage are in the William L. Clements Library at the University of Michigan.

194. Gordon, Harry. "Extract from Journal of Captain Harry Gordon." *Missouri Historical Society Collections* 3, no. 4 (1911): 437-43. Excellent descriptions of the French and Indian villages in the Kaskaskia-Fort de Chartres area in 1766.

195. Hanna, Charles A. *The Wilderness Trail, or the Ventures and Adventures of the Pennsylvania Traders on the Allegheny Path, with Some New Annals of the Old West, and the Records of Some Strong Men and Some Bad Ones.* 2 vols. New York: Putnam, 1911. Contains extensive quotations from primary sources, with frequent references to settlements and Native Americans in the Illinois country. Good index.

196. *The Illinois-Wabash Land Company Manuscript.* Introduction by Clarence Walworth Alvord. Chicago: C. H. McCormick, 1915. A facsimile photograph of a "manuscript book, being a contract with Indians for land in the Illinois." That and other documents related to the land contract and copied into the manuscript book are dated 1772-79.

197. Marks, Anna Edith. "William Murray, Trader and Land Speculator in the Illinois Country." *Transactions of the Illinois State Historical Society, 1919*, pp. 183-212.

198. Murray, Myles N., and Zoda, Robert V. *William Murray, Esq.: Land Agent in the Illinois Territory before the Revolutionary War.* Brooklyn, N.Y.: Theo. Gaus, Ltd., 1987. A portrayal of the founder of the Illinois-Wabash Land Company as a Revolutionary hero.

199. Oaks, Robert F., ed. "George Morgan's 'Memorandums': A Journey to the Illinois Country, 1770." *Journal of the Illinois State Historical Society* 69 (1976): 185-200. Morgan's day-by-day account of his trip from Fort Pitt down the Ohio and up the Mississippi with supplies for trading in the Illinois country. The memoranda also include copies of letters and reports of his difficulties with British officers at Fort de Chartres. The original documents are in the Baynton, Wharton, and Morgan Papers, Pennsylvania State Archives, Harrisburg.

200. Peckham, Howard. *Pontiac and the Indian Uprising.* Princeton, N.J.: Princeton University Press, 1947. Leader of a great Indian confederacy, Pontiac was murdered near Cahokia in 1769.

201. Savelle, Max. *George Morgan, Colony Builder.* New York: Columbia University Press, 1932. During the British régime Morgan came to trade in the Illinois country as a partner in the Philadelphia firm of Baynton, Wharton, and Morgan.

202. Scott, Rose Moss. "Preliminary Treaty Signed at a Point Which Is Now Palermo, Edgar County, Illinois, in 1765, Giving the Eastern Mississippi Valley to Anglo-Saxon Civilization." *Transactions of the Illinois State Historical Society, 1922,* pp. 123-26. Principal signers were George Croghan, representing British authority, and Pontiac, representing the Indians of Illinois.

203. Sosin, Jack M. "The French Settlements in British Policy for the North American Interior, 1760-1774." *Canadian Historical Review* 39 (1958): 185-208.

204. Storm, Colton. "The Notorious Colonel Wilkins." *Journal of the Illinois State Historical Society* 40 (1947): 7-22. As commandant of the Illinois country, 1768-71, John Wilkins's administration was notorious except for his handling of Indian affairs. The writer speculates that the "indefensible" behavior of Wilkins in Illinois may have been due to a head injury suffered in the French and Indian War.

205. Sutton, Robert Mize. "George Morgan, Early Illinois Businessman: A Case of Premature Enterprise." *Journal of the Illinois State Historical Society* 69 (1976): 173-84. George Morgan, as representative of the Philadelphia firm in which he was a partner, began to trade at Kaskaskia in 1766 and remained there until 1771 when unsettled conditions and difficulties with the British military establishment led to his departure.

206. Thomas, Charles M. "Successful and Unsuccessful Merchants in the Illinois Country." *Journal of the Illinois State Historical Society* 30 (1937-38): 429-40. Compares British firms, especially Baynton, Wharton, and Morgan, with French and Spanish traders.

207. Thwaites, Reuben Gold, comp. and ed. *The British Regime in Wisconsin.* Collections of the State Historical Society of Wisconsin, vol. 18. Madison, 1908, pp. 223-468. Many references to Illinois and the Illinois Indian tribe.

D. AMERICAN TERRITORIAL PERIOD, 1783-1818

1. Description and Travel

208. Collot, Victor. "A Journey in North America." *Transactions of the Illinois State Historical Society, 1908*, pp. 269-310. Extracts from the 1826 English edition of Collot's account of travel in the West in 1796. Includes good descriptions of Fort Massac, of roads from that place to Kaskaskia, and of the navigation of the Ohio and the Mississippi rivers to the mouth of the Missouri River.

209. Evans, Salome Paddock. "The Diary of Salome Paddock Evans." Edited by Louisa I. Enos. *Journal of the Illinois State Historical Society* 13 (1920-21): 370-77. Descriptions of a wagon trip from Vermont to St. Louis in 1815 and 1816.

210. Fearon, Henry Bradshaw. *Sketches of America: A Narrative of a Journey of Five Thousand Miles through the Eastern and Western States of America; Contained in Eight Reports Addressed to the Thirty-nine English Families by Whom the Author Was Deputed, in June 1817, to Ascertain Whether Any and What Part of the United States Would Be Suitable for Their Residence. With Remarks on Mr. Birkbeck's "Notes" and "Letters."* London: Printed for Longman, Hurst, Reese, Orme, & Brown, 1818. On Illinois, pages 255-66, 336-40, 450-51.

211. Flower, George. *The Errors of Emigrants: Pointing out Many Popular Errors Hitherto Unnoticed; with a Sketch of the Extent and Resources of the New States of the North American Union, and a Description of the Progress and Present Aspect of the English Settlement in Illinois, Founded by Morris Birkbeck and George Flower, in the Year 1817.* London: Cleave, 1841. Reprint, Mid-American Frontier series, New York: Arno, 1975.

212. Hunter, George. *The Western Journals of Dr. George Hunter, 1796-1805.* Edited by John Francis McDermott. Transactions of the American Philosophical Society, n.s., vol. 53, pt. 4. Philadelphia, July 1963. Includes the journal of a 1796 trip from Philadelphia to the Illinois country. Hunter crossed Illinois from Vincennes, Indiana, to Kaskaskia and St. Louis and returned to Vincennes, both ways by land.

213. Keating, William H. *Narrative of an Expedition to the Source of St. Peter's River . . . under the Command of Stephen H. Long, Major U.S.T.E.* 2 vols. Philadelphia: H. C. Carey and I. Lea, 1824.

214. Long, Stephen H. *Voyage in a Six-Oared Skiff to the Falls of Saint Anthony in 1817.* Collections of the Historical Society of Minnesota, 1860. Reprint (2d ed.), Collections of the Minnesota Historical Society 2 (1889): 9-88. On the return trip down the Mississippi, Long visited and described Rock Island, Fort Armstrong, the Sauk village on Rock River, and Fort Edwards.

215. McDermott, John Francis, ed. "Audubon's 'Journey up the Mississippi.' " *Journal of the Illinois State Historical Society* 35 (1942): 148-73. An account of John James Audubon's 1810 journey, written much later and published in 1829. Audubon discusses life in the Osage and Shawnee villages on the Ohio River and on the Mississippi below Cape Girardeau, Missouri.

216. McKnight, Robert. "To Illinois in 1811." *Journal of the Illinois State Historical Society* 36 (1943): 208-10, 408. Journal of travels from Ohio to Kentucky and Vincennes, Indiana, thence across Illinois to St. Louis and St. Charles, Missouri.

217. Pike, Zebulon. *An Account of Expeditions to the Sources of the Mississippi.* Philadelphia: C. & A. Conrad, 1810.

218. Schermerhorn, John F., and Mills, Samuel J. *A Correct View of That Part of the United States Which Lies West of the Allegheny Mountains, with Regard to Religion and Morals.* Hartford, Conn.: Peter B. Gleason, 1814. An 1813 description of Illinois Territory is on pages 31-32.

219. Schultz, Christian Jr. *Travels on an Inland Voyage through the States of New York, Pennsylvania, Virginia, Ohio, Kentucky and Tennessee, and through the Territories of Indiana, Louisiana, Mississippi, and New-Orleans, Performed in the Years 1807 and 1808, Including a Tour of Nearly Six Thousand Miles.* 2 vols. in 1. New York: Printed by Isaac Riley, 1810. The author visited Prairie du Rocher and Fort de Chartres.

220. Storm, Colton. "Lieutenant John Armstrong's Map of the Illinois River, 1790." *Journal of the Illinois State Historical Society* 37 (1944): 48-55. Reproduction of the map and transcription of place names on the map, with present-day equivalents. The original is in the Josiah Harmar Papers, William L. Clements Library, University of Michigan.

221. Volney, C. F. *View of the Climate and Soil of the United States of America, to Which Are Annexed Some Accounts of Florida, the French Colony on the Scioto, Certain Canadian Colonies, and the Savages or Natives.* London: J. Johnson, 1804. Describes the road from Vincennes, Indiana, to Kaskaskia.

2. Military Affairs

222. Barnhart, John D., ed. "A New Letter about the Massacre at Fort Dearborn." *Indiana Magazine of History* 41 (1945): 187-99. The 17 December 1812 letter by Walter K. Jordan, printed and compared with other contemporary accounts.

223. Caldwell, Norman Ward. "Cantonment Wilkinson." *Mid-America* 31 (1949): 3-28. History of the short-lived post near the site of the Grand Chain, a six-mile-long chain of rocks on the Ohio River in Pulaski County.

224. _____. "Civilian Personnel at the Frontier Military Post, 1790-1814." *Mid-America* 38 (1956): 101-19.

225. _____. "The Enlisted Soldier at the Frontier Post, 1790-1814." *Mid-America* 37 (1955): 195-204.

226. _____. "The Frontier Army Officer, 1794-1814." *Mid-America* 37 (1955): 101-28. Many examples from United States Army posts in what is now Illinois.

227. Callaway, James. "James Callaway in the War of 1812: Letters, Diary, and Rosters." Edited by Edgar B. Wesley. *Missouri Historical Society Collections* 5 (1927-28): 38-81. In his introduction, the editor discusses several military actions in which Illinois men took part. Callaway, from Missouri, also discusses Illinois men and the battle at Credit Island. The article includes a drawing of Fort Johnson, made by Callaway. The Callaway Collection is in the Missouri Historical Society, St. Louis.

228. "Daughters of 1812 Honor Memory of Thomas Higgins, Famous Indian Fighter." *Journal of the Illinois State Historical Society* 17 (1924-25): 740-45. Contains an account of an Indian attack on Hill's Fort (Bond County), 21 August 1814.

229. East, Ernest Edward. "Lincoln and the Peoria French Claims." *Journal of the Illinois State Historical Society* 42 (1949): 41-56. History of claims for property destroyed by soldiers in the War of 1812 to final court settlement in 1867.

230. Forsyth, Thomas. "Letter-Book of Thomas Forsyth, 1814-1818." Edited by Reuben Gold Thwaites. *Collections of the State Historical Society of*

Wisconsin 11 (1888): 316-55. Most of the letters deal with Indian relations during and after the War of 1812.

231.   Fredriksen, John C., comp.   *Free Trade and Sailors' Rights: A Bibliography of the War of 1812.* Westport, Conn.: Greenwood, 1985. The compiler lists ninety-nine citations under "Illinois Territory."

232. Hamilton, Holman, ed. "Zachary Taylor in Illinois." *Journal of the Illinois State Historical Society* 34 (1941): 84-91. An autobiographical sketch written in 1816, from the Taylor Papers in the Library of Congress. Taylor includes copies of orders that illuminate his service in the War of 1812 on the Illinois, Indiana, and Missouri frontiers.

233. Hammes, Raymond H., comp. and ed. "Illinois Militiamen--August 1, 1790." *Illinois Libraries* 59 (1977): 308-19. Militiamen in service on that date were each awarded land grants of one hundred acres by act of Congress.

234. Helderman, Leonard C. "The Northwest Expedition of George Rogers Clark, 1786-1787." *Mississippi Valley Historical Review* 25 (1938-39): 317-34. In June 1786 a small Kentucky force engaged the Indians near Shawneetown in one of the episodes that preceded Clark's expedition against Indians of the Upper Wabash.

235. Holden, Robert J. "Governor Ninian Edwards and the War of 1812: The Military Role of a Territorial Governor." *Selected Papers in Illinois History, 1980.* Springfield: Illinois State Historical Society, 1982. Pp. 1-8.

236.   Hutson, Austin.   "Killed by Indians." *Journal of the Illinois State Historical Society* 5 (1912-13): 96-103. A highly embellished account of an Indian attack in Crawford County in 1812 that resulted in the deaths of six members of the Isaac Hutson, Sr. family.

237. Jackson, Donald. "Old Fort Madison--1808-1813." *Palimpsest* 47 (1966): 1-64. The fort, located in Iowa, on the Mississippi, was important in the history of relations with the Sauk and Fox.

238. Johnson, Charles Beneulyn. "On and about the National Road in the Early Fifties." *Transactions of the Illinois State Historical Society, 1922,* pp. 59-65. Most of the article deals with Indian attacks in Bond County during the War of 1812.

239. Kinzie, Juliette Augusta Magill. *Mrs. John H. Kinzie. Narrative of the Massacre at Chicago, Aug. 15, 1812, and of Some Preceding Events.* Chicago: Ellis & Fergus, 1844. With some changes this account of the Fort Dearborn massacre was reprinted as chapters 18 and 19 of the author's *Wau-Bun.* It was also reprinted as number 30 in Fergus' Historical Series.

240. Kirkland, Joseph. "Chicago Massacre in 1812." *Magazine of American History* 28 (1892): 111-22. Mrs. Nathan Heald's account of the Fort Dearborn massacre.

241. "Letters of the War of 1812." *Journal of the Illinois State Historical Society* 46 (1953): 332-33. Forty-eight letters of Colonel Henry S. Dodge, presented to the Illinois State Historical Library.

242. Lippincott, Thomas. "The Wood River Massacre." *Journal of the Illinois State Historical Society* 4 (1911-12): 504-9. Reprinted from the *Sangamo Journal* (Springfield), 2 April 1841. An 1832 narrative about the War of 1812 episode.

243. McVicker, George G. "A Chapter in the Warfare against the Indians in Illinois during the Year 1812: Copy of a Letter Found in 'Genius of Liberty,' Published at Uniontown, Pa., January 14, 1813." *Journal of the Illinois State Historical Society* 24 (1931-32): 342-43. In a letter dated 7 November 1812, McVicker recounts information received from Governor Ninian Edwards about his march with a command of volunteers to the head of Peoria Lake, where they attacked a force of Kickapoo and Miami Indians and destroyed several villages.

244. Meese, William A. "Credit Island, 1814-1914: Historical Address Delivered on the Island at the Celebration of the One-Hundredth Anniversary of the Battle." *Journal of the Illinois State Historical Society* 7, no. 4 (January 1915): 349-73. At Credit Island, on the Mississippi River, a group of Sauk and Fox Indians, under the command of British troops, held their position and control of the Upper Mississippi.

245. Musham, H. A. "Where Did the Battle of Chicago Take Place?" *Journal of the Illinois State Historical Society* 36 (1943): 21-40. Location of the famous, though minor, War of 1812 action, 15 August 1812, known as the Fort Dearborn massacre.

246. Quaife, Milo Milton. "A Forgotten Hero of Rock Island." *Journal of the Illinois State Historical Society* 23 (1930-31): 652-63. The hero was British Sergeant James Keating, who with a single three-pound gun was primarily responsible for the British recapture of the fort at Prairie du Chien, Wisconsin, in 1814 and later, with more guns, for the British-Indian repulse of Zachary Taylor's United States force at Credit Island.

247. _____, ed. "The Fort Dearborn Massacre." *Mississippi Valley Historical Review* 1 (1914): 561-73. Quaife presents several contemporary documents that challenge massacre narratives by the Kinzie family.

248. Richmond, Volney P. "The Wood River Massacre." *Transactions of the Illinois State Historical Society, 1901*, pp. 93-95. The massacre occurred in Madison County in 1814 during the war with Britain.

249. "A Speck of Indian Warfare on the Frontier of Illinois in 1811." *Journal of the Illinois State Historical Society* 5 (1912-13): 119-20. The murder of A. M. Price in Madison County was the first Indian attack in Illinois in the War of 1812.

250. "Stephen H. Long's Plan for New Fort at Peoria." *Journal of the Illinois State Historical Society* 47 (1954): 417-21. Fort Clark was erected at Peoria during the War of 1812 by United States troops from St. Louis and volunteers from Illinois and Missouri. Long's plans and map, dated 1816, were for a proposed permanent post nearby. The original documents are in the National Archives, Washington.

251. Stevens, Frank Everett. "Illinois in the War of 1812-1814." *Transactions of the Illinois State Historical Society, 1904*, pp. 62-197. Contains considerable primary source material.

252. Sword, Wiley. *President Washington's Indian War: The Struggle for the Old Northwest, 1790-1795.* Norman: University of Oklahoma Press, 1985.

253. Williams, Mentor L., ed. "John Kinzie's Narrative of the Fort Dearborn Massacre." *Journal of the Illinois State Historical Society* 46 (1953): 343-62. Kinzie's reminiscence, located by the editor, was recorded in 1820 by Captain David Bates Douglas, a member of the expedition led by Lewis Cass and Henry R. Schoolcraft. This narrative corrects many errors in other better-known accounts, with which the editor compares Kinzie's.

254. Woolard, F. M. "Reminiscences of a Tragedy in Pioneer Life." *Journal of the Illinois State Historical Society* 2, no. 3 (October 1909): 42-48. The murder by Indians of a young man in western Edwards County during the War of 1812, and his father's retribution.

3. Politics and Government

George Rogers Clark captured Kaskaskia in 1776, and the Illinois country, technically, was thereafter administered by the state of Virginia. Great Britain ceded its western lands to the United States in 1783, and the new territorial government was authorized by the Ordinance of 1787 but was not established until 1790.

255. Allinson, May. "The Government of Illinois, 1790-1799." *Transactions of the Illinois State Historical Society, 1907*, pp. 277-92.

256. Alvord, Clarence Walworth, ed. *Cahokia Records, 1778-90.* Collections of the Illinois State Historical Library, vol. 2. Springfield, 1907. Original documents, mainly court records, provide an excellent description of life in Cahokia. The introduction to this volume, retitled "The County of Illinois," was separately reprinted in 1907.

257. _____. "The Finding of the Kaskaskia Records." *Transactions of the Illinois State Historical Society, 1906*, pp. 27-31. Reported by E. G. Mason to have been destroyed, early Kaskaskia records were located by Alvord in 1905 in the Randolph County Courthouse at Chester. Many of these documents are printed in *Cahokia Records* and *Kaskaskia Records*, both edited by Alvord, q.v.

258. _____. *Illinois in the Eighteenth Century: A Report on the Documents in Belleville, Illinois, Illustrating the Early History of the State.* Bulletin of the Illinois State Historical Library, vol. 1, no. 1 (Springfield, 1905). The records at Belleville comprise those that were removed to Cahokia when Randolph County was separated from St. Clair in 1795 (the remaining records of the Illinois country were left at Kaskaskia before being removed to Chester). The most important of the Cahokia records were published in a volume of that name, edited by Alvord, q.v.

259. _____, ed. *Kaskaskia Records, 1778-90.* Collections of the Illinois State Historical Library, vol. 5. Springfield, 1910. Original documents concerned with the political center of the Illinois country in the years of near-anarchy before the establishment of government under the Northwest Ordinance.

260. Barnhart, John D. "The Southern Influence in the Formation of Illinois." *Journal of the Illinois State Historical Society* 32 (1939): 358-78. The author concludes that the southern backgrounds of a majority of members of the 1818 constitutional convention resulted in "slight changes towards greater democracy" and nationalism while protecting "existing slavery and indentured servitude."

261. Billington, Ray A. "The Historians of the Northwest Ordinance." *Journal of the Illinois State Historical Society* 40 (1947): 397-413.

262. Bloom, Jo Tice. "The Congressional Delegates from the Northwest Territory, 1799-1803." *Old Northwest* 3 (1977): 3-21.

263. _____. "Peaceful Politics: The Delegates from Illinois Territory, 1809-1818." *Old Northwest* 6 (1980): 203-15.

264. Brant, Irving. "Madison and the Empire of Free Men." *Journal of the Illinois State Historical Society* 48 (1955): 402-23. James Madison was president when Illinois became a separate territory in 1809 and in innumerable important ways contributed to establishing democratic principles in the new territory.

265. Burgess, Charles E. "John Rice Jones, Citizen of Many Territories." *Journal of the Illinois State Historical Society* 61 (1968): 58-82.

266. Carter, Clarence Edwin, comp. and ed. *The Territory Northwest of the River Ohio, 1787-1803*. The Territorial Papers of the United States, vol. 2. Washington: Government Printing Office, 1934. Volume 3 in the series completes the papers of the Northwest Territory.

267. _____. *The Territory of Illinois, 1809-1814*. The Territorial Papers of the United States, vol. 16. Washington: Government Printing Office, 1948.

268. _____. *The Territory of Illinois, 1814-1818*. The Territorial Papers of the United States, vol. 17. Washington: Government Printing Office, 1950.

269. _____. *The Territory of Indiana, 1800-1810*. The Territorial Papers of the United States, vol. 7. Washington: Government Printing Office, 1939.

270. _____. *The Territory of Indiana, 1810-1816*. The Territorial Papers of the United States, vol. 8. Washington: Government Printing Office, 1939.

271. Horsman, Reginald. "American Indian Policy in the Old Northwest, 1783-1815." *William and Mary Quarterly*, 3d ser. 18 (1961): 35-53.

272. _____. *The Frontier in the Formative Years, 1783-1815*. New York: Holt, 1970. Has excellent analyses of the governments of Indiana and Illinois territories. The index has other entries for Illinois.

273. _____.   "Thomas Jefferson and the Ordinance of 1784."   *Illinois Historical Journal* 79 (1986): 99-112.

274. "The Illinois Constitutional Convention of 1818." Introduction by Richard V. Carpenter. *Journal of the Illinois State Historical Society* 6 (1913-14): 327-424. The introduction contains biographical sketches of convention members. The journal of convention proceedings, then the only known copy in existence, is reprinted.

275. James, Edmund J., ed. *The Territorial Records of Illinois.* Publications of the Illinois State Historical Library, no. 3 (for bibliographic reference, this publication is considered *Transactions of the Illinois State Historical Society, 1901*). Includes the Executive Register, 1809-18; Journal of the Executive Council, 1812; and Journal of the House of Representatives, 1812.

276. Pease, Theodore Calvin, ed. *The Laws of the Northwest Territory, 1788-1800.* Collections of the Illinois State Historical Library, vol. 17. Springfield, 1925. Illinois was part of the Northwest Territory until 1800, when Indiana Territory was created.

277. Philbrick, Francis S., ed. *Laws of Illinois Territory, 1809-1818.* Collections of the Illinois State Historical Library, vol. 25. Springfield, 1950. In a 477-page introduction, the editor discusses laws of the first and second stages of territorial government, the legal basis of territorial government, the Northwest Ordinance of 1787, and administrative problems that arose under that plan.

278. _____.   *The Laws of Indiana Territory, 1801-1809.* Collections of the Illinois State Historical Library, vol. 21. Springfield, 1930. In a 225-page introduction, the editor discusses both the legal antecedents and administration of the laws. Appendixes list the territorial and county officers, 1800-1809, as well as prominent attorneys, and provide annotated biographical sketches.

279. _____.   *Pope's Digest, 1815.* 2 vols. Collections of the Illinois State Historical Library, vols. 28 and 30. Springfield, 1938 and 1940. Reprint of the first digest and revised edition of Illinois laws, prepared by Nathaniel Pope and published in two volumes by Matthew Duncan. Philbrick examined all extant records, down to 1830, in the thirteen counties of the state that constituted Illinois Territory. In the introduction to the first volume, he discusses the evolution of later state codes and revised statutes, and presents biographical information about the state's early attorneys.

280. Quaife, Milo Milton. "The Significance of the Ordinance of 1787." *Journal of the Illinois State Historical Society* 30 (1937-38): 415-28.

281. Shriner, Phillip R. "America's Other Bicentennial." *Old Northwest* 9 (1983): 219-35. Historiography of the Northwest Ordinance of 1787.

282. Suppiger, Joseph E. "Amity to Enmity: Ninian Edwards and Jesse B. Thomas." *Journal of the Illinois State Historical Society* 67 (1974): 201-11. Edwards, as governor of Illinois Territory, and Thomas, as one of the three federal judges in the territory, soon after their appointments were engaged in a power struggle over territorial administration and policy.

283. Sutton, Robert Mize. "The Northwest Ordinance: A Bicentennial Souvenir." *Illinois Historical Journal* 81 (1988): 13-24. Historiography and historical background of the Ordinance of 1787.

284. Taylor, Robert M. Jr., ed. *The Northwest Ordinance, 1787: A Bicentennial Handbook.* Indianapolis: Indiana Historical Society, 1987.

285. Thornbrough, Gayle, and Riker, Dorothy, eds. *Journals of the General Assembly of Indiana Territory, 1805-1815.* Indiana Historical Collections, vol. 32. Indianapolis, 1950. Illinois was part of Indiana Territory until 1809.

286. Williams, Frederick D. *The Northwest Ordinance: Essays on Its Formulation, Provisions, and Legacy.* East Lansing: Michigan State University Press, 1988.

4. Miscellany

287. Biggs, William. "Narrative of the Capture of William Biggs by the Kickapoo Indians in 1788." *Transactions of the Illinois State Historical Society, 1902,* pp. 202-15. Biggs was captured in Monroe County, Illinois, and held for three weeks in Indiana before he ransomed himself with the help of a French trader. This account was written thirty-eight years after the event. A letter of 1789 in which he also described the kidnapping is in the *Journal of the Illinois State Historical Society* 6 (1913-14): 129-33.

288. Davis, James E. "New Aspects of Men and New Forms of Society: The Old Northwest, 1790-1820." *Journal of the Illinois State Historical Society* 69 (1976): 164-72. An account of frontiersmen and their attitudes that illustrates both intellectual life and social customs.

289. Gunn, John H. "Witchcraft in Illinois." *Magazine of American History* 14 (1885): 458-63. In the 1790s two slaves were executed for witchcraft after conviction by a local court.

290. Hammes, Raymond H., comp. and ed. "Squatters in Territorial Illinois: The First Americans to Settle Outside the American Bottom after the Revolutionary War." *Illinois Libraries* 59 (1977): 319-82.

291. "The High Cost of Entertainment" [Statement of charges for supplies issued by John Rice Jones to a delegation of Sauk and Fox Indians at Kaskaskia, 24 May 1794--6 July 1794]. *Journal of the Illinois State Historical Society* 35 (1942): 296. Original document in the Illinois State Historical Library.

292. Lindley, Robert. "The Cannon-Stark Indian Massacre and Captivity." Edited by Milo Custer. *Journal of the Illinois State Historical Society* 11 (1918-19): 586-91. See also ibid., 17. The murders took place in Wabash County in 1815.

293. Lux, Leonard. *The Vincennes Donation Lands.* Indiana Historical Society Publications, vol. 15, no. 4. Indianapolis, 1949. In 1788 the Confederation Congress authorized grants of four hundred acres of land to each head of family who had settled at Vincennes before 1783. Later grants were authorized for militiamen and for those who had held land in the Vincennes Common. Many of the grants were in Illinois.

294. McCluggage, Robert W. "The Pioneer Squatter." *Illinois Historical Journal* 82 (1989): 47-54. Graphic descriptions of the first pioneers and their way of life. After the War of 1812, changing land policies made it possible for squatters to become landowners.

295. McDermott, John Francis. "The Library of Barthelemi Tardiveau." *Journal of the Illinois State Historical Society* 29 (1936-37): 89-91. Tardiveau came to the Illinois country in 1787.

296. McMurtrie, Douglas C. *Negotiations for the Illinois Salt Springs, 1802-1803.* Chicago: Privately printed, 1938. Reprinted from the *Bulletin of the Chicago Historical Society* 2 (1937): 86-91. By agreement of 17 September 1802, representatives of six Native American tribes ceded to the United States a four-mile-square area that included the salt lick on the Saline River.

297. Oglesby, Richard E. "Pierre Menard, Reluctant Mountain Man." *Missouri Historical Society Bulletin* 24 (1967-68): 3-19. As a partner in the St. Louis

Missouri Fur Company, Menard left his home at Kaskaskia to be part of the company's first fur-trading expedition in 1808-9.

298. Peck, John Mason. *"Father Clark," or, the Pioneer Preacher: Sketches and Incidents of Rev. John Clark.* New York: Sheldon, Lamport & Blakeman, 1855. Excellent account of life in the early American settlements.

299. _____. "An Historical Sketch of the Early American Settlements in Illinois, from 1780 to 1800, Read before the Illinois State Lyceum, at Its Anniversary, August 16, 1832." *Western Monthly Magazine* 1 (1833): 73-83.

300. Penick, James Jr. *The New Madrid Earthquakes of 1811-1812.* Columbia: University of Missouri Press, 1976.

301. "Petition for Slavery in Kaskaskia and Cahokia." *Journal of the Illinois State Historical Society* 47 (1954): 94-96. In a petition to Congress, 28 December 1802, residents of Indiana Territory seek removal of the Northwest Ordinance slavery ban; they also ask for various land grants and a reserve of timber near the salt springs. The petition as published for circulation is in the Illinois State Historical Library.

302. Posey, John Thornton. "A Federalist on the Frontier: General Thomas Posey." *Illinois Historical Journal* 83 (1990): 247-57. A Revolutionary War officer from Virginia, Posey ended his career as territorial governor of Indiana and then as United States Indian agent at Shawneetown.

303. _____. *General Thomas Posey: Son of the American Revolution.* East Lansing: Michigan State University Press, 1992.

304. Reynolds, John. *The Pioneer History of Illinois, Containing the Discovery in 1673, and the History of the Country to the Year 1818, When the State Government Was Organized.* Chicago: Fergus Printing, 1887. Reprint, Ann Arbor, Mich.: University Microfilms, 1968. More than three fourths of this volume is devoted to Illinois as an American territory. There are biographies of early settlers, many of them known to Reynolds, who was governor of Illinois, 1830-34. Especially interesting are the author's accounts of social life and customs on the Illinois frontier, to which Reynolds moved from Tennessee with his father's family in 1800.

305. Smelser, Marshall. "Material Customs in the Territory of Illinois." *Journal of the Illinois State Historical Society* 29 (1936-37): 5-41. Deals with day-to-day life, 1800-1818.

306. Zochert, Donald. "Illinois Water Mills, 1790-1818." *Journal of the Illinois State Historical Society* 65 (1972): 173-201. The author identified forty-two millers of this period and provided fully annotated sketches of each man and his mill.

E. STATEHOOD AND THE EXPANSIONIST ERA, 1818-1854

1. General Works

307. Billington, Ray A. "The Frontier in Illinois History." *Journal of the Illinois State Historical Society* 43 (1950): 28-45. Overview of the Illinois economy through the 1830s.

308. Buck, Solon Justus. *Illinois in 1818.* Springfield: Illinois Centennial Commission, 1917. Introductory volume to The Centennial History of Illinois series. 2d ed., rev., with an introduction by Allan Nevins, Urbana: University of Illinois Press, 1967.

309. Ford, Thomas. *A History of Illinois, from Its Commencement as a State in 1818 to 1847, Containing a Full Account of the Black Hawk War, the Rise, Progress and Fall of Mormonism, the Alton and Lovejoy Riots, and Other . . . Events.* Published posthumously; edited by James Shields. Chicago: S. C. Griggs, and New York: Ivison and Phinney, 1854. Issued in 2 vols. as Lakeside Classics, nos. 43-44, edited by Milo M. Quaife. Chicago: R. R. Donnelley, 1945-46; facsimile reprint, Ann Arbor, Mich.: University Microfilms, 1968. As governor, 1842-46, Ford was not a disinterested reporter of the events he describes, but his work is nonetheless valuable. For the contemporary furor his history caused, see the documents published in Alvord, no. 774.

310. Pease, Theodore Calvin. *The Frontier State, 1818-1848.* The Centennial History of Illinois, vol. 2. Springfield: Illinois Centennial Commission, 1918. Reprint, The Sesquicentennial History of Illinois, vol. 2, with an introduction by Robert W. Johannsen, Urbana: University of Illinois Press, 1987.

311. Sutton, Robert Mize. "Illinois' Year of Decision, 1837." *Journal of the Illinois State Historical Society* 58 (1965): 34-53. How three 1837 developments--the state's internal improvements program, the invention of the steel plow, and the lynching of abolitionist Elijah Lovejoy--helped to shape the state's history.

2. Agriculture and the Land

312. Ankli, Robert E. "Agricultural Growth in Antebellum Illinois." *Journal of the Illinois State Historical Society* 63 (1970): 387-98.

313. Baxter, David J. "William Cullen Bryant, Illinois Landowner." *Western Illinois Regional Studies* 1 (1978): 1-14.

314. Gara, Larry. "Yankee Land Agent in Illinois." *Journal of the Illinois State Historical Society* 44 (1951): 120-41. Land speculation by the Boston and Western Land Company, 1835-43.

315. Gates, Paul Wallace. "Disposal of the Public Domain in Illinois, 1848-1856." *Journal of Economic and Business History* 3 (1931): 216-40. The author discusses government land policies, land speculation, location of military warrants, and grants to railroads.

316. _____. *Landlords and Tenants on the Prairie Frontier: Studies in American Land Policy.* Ithaca, N.Y.: Cornell University Press, 1973. A collection of nine articles that deal especially with Indiana and Illinois.

317. Henlein, Paul C. *Cattle Kingdom in the Ohio Valley, 1783-1860.* Lexington: University of Kentucky Press, 1959. One of the five cattle-feeding regions considered is the Sangamon River Valley in the 1830s.

318. McCullough, John. "Farming in Illinois in 1837." *Journal of the Illinois State Historical Society* 27 (1934-35): 235-37. In a letter of 30 August 1837, McCullough writes from Macoupin County of farm life, wages, and prices.

319. Park, Siyoung. "Land Speculation in Western Illinois: Pike County, 1821-1835." *Journal of the Illinois State Historical Society* 77 (1984): 115-28. The author discusses large-scale speculators in the Illinois Military Tract, which was included in the bounds of Pike County in 1821.

320. _____. "Perception of Land Quality and the Settlement of Northern Pike County, 1821-1836." *Western Illinois Regional Studies* 3 (1980): 5-21. A detailed study of public land sales shows that land was desired for its investment value rather than for its eventual use.

321. Power, Richard Lyle. *Planting Corn Belt Culture: The Impress of the Upland Southerner and Yankee in the Old Northwest.* Indiana Historical Society Publications, vol. 17. Indianapolis, 1953. Farming methods as well as social aspects of frontier and pioneer life. Many of the sources and examples are from Illinois.

322. Rezab, Gordana. "Land Speculation in Fulton County, 1817-1832." *Western Illinois Regional Studies* 3 (1980): 22-35.

323. Schmidt, Hubert G. "Farming in Illinois a Century Ago as Illustrated in Bond County." *Journal of the Illinois State Historical Society* 31 (1938): 138-59.

324. Walker, Juliet E. K. "Legal Processes and Judicial Challenges: Black Land Ownership in Western Illinois." *Western Illinois Regional Studies* 6, no. 2 (Fall 1983): 23-48. The focus of the article is land ownership by Frank McWhorter, but the content is broader--dealing with the history of land ownership by blacks in both Illinois and the nation.

325. Walters, William D. Jr., and Mansberger, Floyd R. "Initial Field Location in Illinois." *Agricultural History* 57 (1983): 289-96. Maps of the original land surveys in northern Illinois show that the first fields were cultivated on land that was entirely prairie (except near Galena and Lake Michigan, where "prairies were almost entirely absent") but within a few miles of woodland.

326. Young, James Harvey, ed. "Land Hunting in 1836." *Journal of the Illinois State Historical Society* 45 (1952): 241-51. Isaac Miller Wetmore describes his 1836 trip to Knox County and his search for land in north-central Illinois. Vivid descriptions of crops and terrain.

3. Business

327. Abbott, Carl. *Boosters and Businessmen: Popular Economic Thought and Urban Growth in the Antebellum Middle West.* Contributions in American Studies, no. 53. Westport, Conn.: Greenwood, 1981. Chicago and Galena are two of the four cities analyzed.

328. Beard, William D. " 'I have labored hard to find the law': Abraham Lincoln for the Alton and Sangamon Railroad." *Illinois Historical Journal* 85 (1992): 209-20.

329. Brandt, Frank Erwin. "Russel Farnham, Astorian." *Transactions of the Illinois State Historical Society, 1930*, pp. 210-34. This sketch of the redoubtable employee of the American Fur Company is valuable especially for reports of the fur trade of the firm Farnham and Davenport in the late 1820s and early 1830s.

330. Everhart, Duane K. "The Leasing of Mineral Lands in Illinois and Wisconsin." *Journal of the Illinois State Historical Society* 60 (1967): 117-36.

331. Frueh, Erne Rene. "Retail Merchandising in Chicago, 1833-1848." *Journal of the Illinois State Historical Society* 32 (1939): 149-72.

332. Haeger, John Denis. "Eastern Money and the Urban Frontier: Chicago, 1833-1842." *Journal of the Illinois State Historical Society* 64 (1971): 267-84.

333. _____. *The Investment Frontier: New York Businessmen and the Economic Development of the Old Northwest.* Albany: State University of New York Press, 1981. Haeger's thesis is that eastern speculators did not unduly exploit the frontier but contributed substantially to its growth and development in the period 1830-45.

334. Holt, Glen E. "The Birth of Chicago: An Examination of Economic Parentage." *Journal of the Illinois State Historical Society* 76 (1983): 82-94. The author argues that Chicago's founding and early growth owed more to federal and state policies (i.e., the establishment of Fort Dearborn, the Illinois and Michigan Canal, and the improvement of Chicago's harbor) than to local entrepreneurs.

335. "Lincoln's Carriage Maker." *Journal of the Illinois State Historical Society* 50 (1957): 412-16. Extracts from the business records of Obed Lewis of Springfield show representative prices and details of purchases and repairs for the Lincoln vehicles, 1852-59.

336. McLear, Patrick E. "The Galena and Chicago Union Railroad: A Symbol of Chicago's Economic Maturity." *Journal of the Illinois State Historical Society* 73 (1980): 17-26. Economic development of northern Illinois traced through the history of this railroad, the first section of which was opened in 1848.

337. _____. "Land Speculators and Urban and Regional Development: Chicago in the 1830's." *Old Northwest* 6 (Summer 1980): 137-51.

338. _____. "Speculation, Promotion, and the Panic of 1837 in Chicago." *Journal of the Illinois State Historical Society* 62 (1969): 135-46.

339. _____. "William Butler Ogden: A Chicago Promoter in the Speculative Era and the Panic of 1837." *Journal of the Illinois State Historical Society* 70 (1977): 283-91.

340. Smith, Alice E. *George Smith's Money.* Madison: State Historical Society of Wisconsin, 1966. Illinois and Wisconsin banking history in the years following the Panic of 1837.

341. Tilton, Clint Clay. "John W. Vance and the Vermilion Salines." *Transactions of the Illinois State Historical Society, 1931,* pp. 156-67.

342. Walker, Juliet E. K. "Occupational Distribution of Frontier Towns in Pike County: An 1850 Census Survey." *Western Illinois Regional Studies* 5 (1982): 146-71.

343. Walters, William D. Jr. "Early Western Illinois Town Advertisements: A Geographical Inquiry." *Western Illinois Regional Studies* 8, no. 1 (Spring 1985): 5-15.

344. _____. "The Fanciful Geography of 1836." *Old Northwest* 9 (1983-84): 331-43. The author reconstructs the "geographical pattern of townsite speculation" in central Illinois, 1835-37.

345. White, Elizabeth Pearson. "Captain Benjamin Godfrey and the Alton and Sangamon Railroad." *Journal of the Illinois State Historical Society* 67 (1974): 466-86. The railroad was chartered in 1847, and the first trip from Alton to Springfield was completed 9 September 1852.

346. Wilkey, Harry L. "Infant Industries in Illinois: As Illustrated in Quincy, 1836-1856." *Journal of the Illinois State Historical Society* 32 (1939): 474-97.

4. Description and Travel

347. Ampère, Jean-Jacques. "A Frenchman in America: Two Chapters from Ampère's Promenade en Amèrique, 1851." Translated by Mildred H. Crew. *Journal of the Illinois State Historical Society* 38 (1945): 207-26.

348. Armytage, W. H. G. "James Stuart's Journey up the River Mississippi in 1830." *Mid-America* 31 (1949): 92-100.

349. Atkinson, Eleanor. "The Winter of the Deep Snow." *Transactions of the Illinois State Historical Society, 1909*, pp. 47-62. The deep snow began in January 1831.

350. Bigelow, Ellen. "Letters Written by a Peoria Woman in 1835: By Boat, Wagon, Horse and Foot to Peoria in the Days of Pioneers." *Journal of the Illinois State Historical Society* 21 (1928-29): 335-53.

351. Bingham, Henry Vest. "The Road West in 1818: The Diary of Henry Vest Bingham." Edited by Marie George Windell. *Missouri Historical Review* 40 (1945-46): 21-54, 174-204. Describes routes across Illinois as well as the Kaskaskia and Delaware Indians he met in the state.

352. Blane, William N. *An Excursion through the United States and Canada during the Years 1822-23.* London: Printed for Baldwin, Cradock & Joy, 1824.

353. Bottorff, Rachael Ann. "Log Cabin Hospitality on the Illinois Frontier." *Western Illinois Regional Studies* 9, no. 2 (Fall 1986): 36-46.

354. Bryant, William Cullen. *Letters of a Traveller, or, Notes on Things Seen in Europe and America.* New York: Putnam, 1850.

355. Buckingham, James Silk. *The Eastern and Western States of America.* 3 vols. London: Fisher, Son & Co., 1842.

356. Buckingham, Joseph H. "Illinois as Lincoln Knew It: A Boston Reporter's Record of a Trip in 1847." Edited by Harry E. Pratt. *Transactions of the Illinois State Historical Society, 1937*, pp. 109-87. Buckingham was a delegate to the Chicago Harbor and River Convention. He was accompanied by Abraham Lincoln during part of a trip from Chicago to St. Louis, up the Mississippi to Galena, and overland back to Chicago.

357. Caird, James. *Prairie Farming in America, with Notes by the Way on Canada and the United States.* London: Longman, Brown, Green, Longmans & Roberts, 1859.

358. Candler, John. *A Friendly Mission: John Candler's Letters from America, 1853-1854.* Indianapolis: Indiana Historical Society, 1951. In their travels John Candler and two other English Quakers went from Terre Haute, Indiana, to Springfield, Illinois, by stage and thence to Chicago by rail.

359. Caton, John Dean. "John Dean Caton's Reminiscences of Chicago in 1833 and 1834." Edited by Harry E. Pratt. *Journal of the Illinois State Historical Society* 28, no. 1 (April 1935): 5-25.

360. Clark, John A. *Gleanings by the Way.* Philadelphia: W. J. and J. K. Simon, and New York: R. Carter, 1842. Clark visited the "great Western Valley" in 1837.

361. Curran, Isaac B. "The 'Pleisures' of Western Traveling." *Journal of the Illinois State Historical Society* 46 (1953): 305-8. Detailed account, 29 June 1840, of Curran's trip from New York to Springfield, Illinois. Original in the Illinois State Historical Library.

362. Dickson, William. "Travel on the Western Illinois Frontier: The Memoir of William Dickson." Edited by William Roba. *Western Illinois Regional Studies* 9, no. 2 (Fall 1986): 60-69. Dickson traveled in northwestern Illinois in 1834 and 1836. A typescript copy of the memoir is in the Rock Island County Historical Society library.

363. Dobell, William. "Original Letters--A Description of the Illinois Country." *Journal of the Illinois State Historical Society* 15 (1922-23): 524-30. In a letter of 6 January 1842, dated at Albion, Dobell describes agriculture and daily activities of the settlers.

364. *Emigrant's Hand-book: The State of Illinois, with Notices of the Valley of the Mississippi; Descriptive of That Fertile Region of the Republic . . . with Suggestions to Emigrants, and Letters from a Rambler in the West.* Reprinted from the American ed., London: G. B. Dyer, 1842. Abridged from *Illinois in 1837.* Philadelphia: Mitchell, 1837.

365. Ernst, Ferdinand. "Travels in Illinois in 1819." *Transactions of the Illinois State Historical Society, 1903*, pp. 150-65. Ernst explored most of southern and central Illinois.

366. Featherstonhaugh, G. W. *Excursion through the Slave States, from Washington on the Potomac to the Frontier of Mexico; with Sketches of Popular Manners and Geological Notices.* 2 vols. London: J. Murray, 1844. In volume 1, pages 250-53, the author describes the country between Vincennnes, Indiana, and St. Louis, Missouri.

367. Fenstermaker, J. Van. "A Description of Sangamon County, Illinois, in 1830." *Agricultural History* 39 (1965): 136-40. The Rev. John G. Berger of the

First Presbyterian Church in Springfield wrote this description for a Pennsylvania newspaper.

368. Flagg, Edmund. *The Far West, or, a Tour Beyond the Mountains: Embracing Outlines of Western Life and Scenery; Sketches of the Prairies, Rivers, Ancient Mounds, Early Settlements of the French, etc.* 2 vols. New York: Harper, 1838.

369. Foreman, Grant. "English Settlers in Illinois." *Journal of the Illinois State Historical Society* 34 (1941): 303-43. Descriptions of life and opportunities in Illinois, 1830-50, by English settlers throughout the state, from letters published in English newspapers.

370. Fuller, Margaret. *Summer on the Lakes in 1843.* 1844. Reprint, with an introduction by Susan Belasco Smith, Urbana: University of Illinois Press, 1991. From Chicago, Fuller traveled across northern Illinois and to central Illinois.

371. Gould, M. J. "Wanderings in the West in 1839." Edited by Earl W. Hayter. *Journal of the Illinois State Historical Society* 33 (1940): 389-411. Before moving to Illinois, Gould made a horseback trip through the central and northern parts of the state and recorded his observations.

372. Gustorf, Frederick Julius. *The Uncorrupted Heart: Journal and Letters of Frederick Julius Gustorf, 1800-1845.* Edited by Fred Gustorf. Columbia: University of Missouri Press, 1969. Portions of the journal that relate to 1835 and 1836 travels in Illinois were published in the *Journal of the Illinois State Historical Society* 55 (1962): 136-56 and 255-70.

373. Hallwas, John E. "Childe Harold in the Mississippi Valley: Edmund Flagg's *The Far West.*" *Old Northwest* 3 (1977): 379-88.

374. _____, ed. "Quincy and Meredosia in 1842: Charles Carter Langdon's Travel Letters." *Western Illinois Regional Studies* 2 (1979): 127-37.

375. Havighurst, Walter. "The Way to Future City." *Journal of the Illinois State Historical Society* 69 (1976): 224-37. Based on travel accounts and early narratives, this article describes a number of frontier communities in Illinois, including one on the Ohio called Future City.

376. Hoffman, Charles Fenno. *A Winter in the West.* 2 vols. New York: Harper, 1835. 2d ed. (2 vols. in 1), London: Bentley, 1835.

377. Hone, Philip. "The Western Trip of Philip Hone." Edited by Paul McClelland Angle. *Journal of the Illinois State Historical Society* 38 (1945): 277-94. Hone describes an 1847 trip from Cairo up the Mississippi and the Illinois rivers to Peru and thence by stagecoach to Chicago, where he attended the Harbor and River Convention.

378. Hulbert, Eri Baker. "A Merchant of Early Chicago: Four Letters of Eri Baker Hulbert." Edited by Elizabeth Wyant. *Journal of the Illinois State Historical Society* 28, no. 2 (July 1935): 100-109. Letters of 1836 and 1837 provide excellent descriptions of Chicago and the surrounding countryside as well as life in the community, especially merchandising, churches, land speculation, and health.

379. James, Edwin, comp. *Account of an Expedition from Pittsburgh to the Rocky Mountains, Performed in the Years 1819, 1820, by Order of the Hon. J. C. Calhoun, Secretary of War, under the Command of Maj. S. H. Long, of the U. S. Top. Engineers; Compiled from the Notes of Major Long, Mr. T. Say, and Other Gentlemen of the Party.* 3 vols. London: Longman, Hurst, Rees, Orme, & Brown, 1823. Reprinted in Reuben Gold Thwaites, ed. *Early Western Travels, 1748-1846 . . .* , vols. 14-17. Descriptions of Illinois are in volume 14, pages 92-102, 120-21.

380. Jones, A. D. *Illinois and the West, with a Township Map, Containing the Latest Surveys and Improvements.* Boston: Weeks, Jordan, and Philadelphia: W. Marshall, 1838.

381. Jones, Dallas L. "Chicago in 1833: Impressions of Three Britishers." *Journal of the Illinois State Historical Society* 47 (1954): 167-75. Two writers, Charles J. Latrobe and Patrick Shirreff, and immigrant Charles Cleaver describe Chicago.

382. _____. "Illinois in the 1830's: Impressions of British Travelers and Immigrants." *Journal of the Illinois State Historical Society* 47 (1954): 252-63.

383. Kearny, Stephen Watts. "Journal of Stephen Watts Kearny." Edited by Valentine Mott Porter. *Missouri Historical Society Collections* 3 (1908): 8-29, 99-131. Kearny's 1820 travel accounts include descriptions of Sauk and Fox villages on the Mississippi.

384. Larwill, Joseph. "Journal of a Trip to Illinois, 1823." Manuscript, Illinois State Historical Library. Extract printed in the *Journal of the Illinois State*

Historical Society 34 (1941): 136. Describes Shawneetown and mines in the area.

385. Latrobe, Charles Joseph. *The Rambler in North America, 1832-1833.* 2 vols. New York: Harper, 1835. Describes the Potawatomi gathered at Chicago in 1833 for treaty negotiations.

386. Levinge, Richard G. A. *Echoes from the Backwoods or Sketches of Transatlantic Life.* 2 vols. London: J. & D. A. Darling, 1849. Chapter 18 is titled "Prairies of Illinois."

387. Logan, James. *Notes of a Journey through Canada, the United States of America, and the West Indes.* Edinburgh: Fraser, 1838. The author traveled by stage and steamer from Chicago to St. Louis.

388. Loomis, Chester A. *A Journey on Horseback through the Great West in 1825* . . . Bath, N.Y.: Plaindealer Press, [182?]. Loomis visited Kaskaskia and Vandalia.

389. McDermott, John Francis. *Seth Eastman's Mississippi: A Lost Portfolio Recovered.* Urbana: University of Illinois Press, 1973. The history and description of seventy-five miniature watercolors painted 1846-48 (black and white reproductions).

390. McIlvaine, Mabel, comp. *Reminiscences of Chicago during the Forties and Fifties.* Lakeside Classics, no. 11. Chicago: R. R. Donnelley, 1913. Selections from writings of William Bross, Charles Cleaver, and Joseph Jefferson, and an account of Chicago's first railroad systems.

391. _____. *Reminiscences of Early Chicago.* Lakeside Classics, no. 10. Chicago: R. R. Donnelley, 1912. Includes selections from Charles Fenno Hoffman, Harriet Martineau, John Wentworth, John Dean Caton, and Jonathan Young Scammon.

392. Manford, Erasmus. *Twenty-five Years in the West.* Chicago: E. Manford, 1867. Rev. ed., 1875. An 1844 trip across flood-swollen streams and roads in eastern Illinois.

393. Martineau, Harriet. *Society in America.* 3 vols. London: Saunders & Otley, 1837. Excellent descriptions of the prairies near Chicago and of early Illinois roads and hotels.

394. Mason, Richard Lee. *Narrative of Richard Lee Mason in the Pioneer West, 1819.* Heartman's Historical Series, no. 6. New York: Printed for C. F. Heartman, 1915. The author describes Kaskaskia and some of its prominent residents, as well as the nearby village of Kaskaskia Indians.

395. Morrison, Anna R. "Diary of Anna R. Morrison, Wife of Isaac L. Morrison." *Journal of the Illinois State Historical Society* 7, no. 1 (April 1914): 34-50. An 1840 stage trip from St. Louis to Springfield and social life in Springfield and Jacksonville.

396. Oliver, William. *Eight Months in Illinois, with Information to Emigrants.* Newcastle-upon-Tyne: William Andrew Mitchell, 1843. Reprint, Chicago: W. M. Hill, 1924; facsimile reprint, Ann Arbor, Mich.: University Microfilms, 1968 (Illinois Sesquicentennial ed.). A native of England, the author traveled in Illinois in 1841.

397. Paddock, Gaius. "Is the Sangamon River Navigable?" *Journal of the Illinois State Historical Society* 13 (1920-21): 48-50. The author was present when Abraham Lincoln demonstrated the model of a steamboat he had designed for navigating the Sangamon.

398. Paulding, James Kirke. "A Tour of Illinois in 1842." Edited by Mentor L. Williams. *Journal of the Illinois State Historical Society* 42 (1949): 292-312. Published originally in *Graham's Magazine* 34 (1849): 16-25.

399. Peyton, John Lewis. *Over the Alleghanies and across the Prairies: Personal Recollections of the Far West, One and Twenty Years Ago.* London: Simpkin, Marshall & Co., 1869. Includes a description of the Illinois capital (Springfield) in 1848.

400. Quaife, Milo Milton, ed. *Pictures of Illinois One Hundred Years Ago.* Lakeside Classics, no. 16. Chicago: R. R. Donnelley, 1918. Contains Morris Birkbeck's observations of Illinois in 1817, William N. Blane's account of a tour of southern Illinois in 1822, and Henry R. Schoolcraft's narrative of a journey up the Illinois River in 1821, as well as a copy of the Chicago Treaty of 1821. Schoolcraft's account was taken from his *Travels in the Central Portions of the Mississippi Valley . . . ,* published in 1825.

401. Schoolcraft, Henry R. *Narrative Journal of Travels through the Northwestern Regions of the United States . . . in the Year 1820 .* Albany, N.Y.: E. & E. Hosford, 1821. Reprint, edited by Mentor L. Williams, East Lansing: Michigan State College Press, 1953. Includes descriptions of Chicago and the surrounding countryside as well as the Fox Indian village at Dubuque, Iowa, which he visited 7 August 1820. Index in the reprint is inadequate.

402. _____. *Narrative of an Expedition through the Upper Mississippi to Itasca Lake, the Actual Source of River* . . . New York: Harper, 1834. A preliminary expedition started in 1831, but the principal trip took place in 1832. Appendixes include two lengthy papers by Schoolcraft on the Chippewa language as well as a report on the lead mine country of northwestern Illinois and southern Wisconsin.

403. _____. *Summary Narrative of an Exploratory Expedition to the Sources of the Mississippi River in 1820, Resumed and Completed by the Discovery of Its Origin in Itasca Lake in 1832* . . . Philadelphia: Lippincott, Grambo, 1855. Contains Schoolcraft's journal of his 1820 trip and other reports.

404. _____. *Travels in the Central Portions of the Mississippi Valley, Comprising Observations on Its Mineral Geography, Internal Resources, and Aboriginal Population.* New York: Collins & Hannay, 1825. Describes Illinois geography and settlements, pages 162-63, 186-226, 294-336; the last fourth of the book deals with negotiations at Chicago for an 1821 treaty with the Ottawa, Chippewa, and Potawatomi; Schoolcraft served as a treaty commissioner.

405. Scott, James L. *Journal of a Missionary Tour through Pennsylvania, Ohio, Indiana, Illinois, Iowa, Wiskonsin and Michigan* . . . Providence, R.I.: The author, 1843.

406. Snyder, John Francis. "Charles Dickens in Illinois." *Journal of the Illinois State Historical Society* 3, no. 3 (October 1910): 7-22.

407. Stevens, Frank Everett. *James Watson Webb's Trip across Illinois in 1822.* Sycamore, Ill.: Sycamore Tribune Print, 1924.

408. Stewart, Robert. "Rev. R. Stewart's Journal--Extracts." [6 February--6 April 1852], from the *Presbytery Reporter* (Alton, 1 May 1852), reprinted in the *Journal of the Illinois State Historical Society* 41 (1948): 449-52. Descriptions of travel through southern Illinois.

409. Stone, Alvan. "Extracts from the Memoir of Alvan Stone." *Journal of the Illinois State Historical Society* 3, no. 4 (January 1911): 85-97. Extracts from the young Baptist minister's diary and letters, 1830-33, provide excellent descriptions of Illinois.

410. Stuart, James. *Three Years in North America.* 2 vols. From the 2d London ed., New York: J. & J. Harper, 1833. Stuart traveled up the Mississippi and across Illinois in 1830 (pages 191-250). He describes the English settlement in Edwards County.

411. Thompson, Scerial. "The Cherokee Cross Egypt." *Journal of the Illinois State Historical Society* 44 (1951): 289-304. Route of the migrating Cherokee in 1837 and 1838-39 across southern Illinois on the old road from Golconda to Cape Girardeau, Missouri.

412. Thurston, John Gates. *A Journal of a Trip to Illinois in 1836.* Mount Pleasant, Mich.: John Cumming, 1971.

413. Verhaegen, Pierre. "From St. Louis to Springfield in 1836." *Journal of the Illinois State Historical Society* 26 (1933-34): 308-9. A letter describing a stagecoach trip, the prairies, and a night at a stagestop.

414. Wild, J. C. *The Valley of the Mississippi, Illustrated in a Series of Views, Painted and Lithographed by J. C. Wild, Accompanied with Historical Descriptions.* Edited by Lewis Foulk Thomas. St. Louis: Published, in 9 numbers, by the artist; printed by Chambers & Knapp, 1841. Reprint, St. Louis: Hawthorne Publishing, 1981. Includes views and descriptions of several Illinois towns and sites.

5. Health and Medicine

415. Coleman, Charles H., ed. "Coles County in the 1840's." *Journal of the Illinois State Historical Society* 45 (1952): 168-72. Extracts from the letters of Dr. Hiram Rutherford, now in the Illinois State Historical Library.

416. Hood, Humphrey. "Selected Letters of Humphrey Hood, Litchfield Physician: Part I, 1852-1856." Edited by Elizabeth Gegenheimer. *Journal of the Illinois State Historical Society* 72 (1979): 193-212.

417. Koehler, G. "Lottery Authorized in 1819 by the State of Illinois to Raise Funds for Improving the Public Health by Draining the Ponds in the American Bottoms." *Transactions of the Illinois State Historical Society, 1928,* pp. 195-202.

418. Levine, Norman D., ed. *Malaria in the Interior Valley of North America.* Urbana: University of Illinois Press, 1964. Reprint of a substantial portion of a book with the same title by Dr. Daniel Drake; interesting for its comments on all aspects of frontier life.

419. Rezneck, Samuel. "Diary of a New York Doctor in Illinois, 1830-1831." *Journal of the Illinois State Historical Society* 54 (1961): 25-50. Asa Fitch was a 21-year-old physician when he arrived in Greenville. He discusses not only his medical practice but also details of day-to-day life.

420. Rutherford, Hiram. *On the Illinois Frontier: Dr. Hiram Rutherford, 1840-1848*. Edited by Willene and George Hendrick. Southern Illinois University Medical Humanities Series. Carbondale: Southern Illinois University Press, 1981. Early letters by Dr. Rutherford and newspaper accounts written when he was elderly.

421. Young, James Harvey. "Patent Medicines: The Early Post-Frontier Phase." *Journal of the Illinois State Historical Society* 46 (1953): 254-64. The author examined Illinois newspapers of 1820-40 to assess the impact of patent medicines.

6. Immigration and Settlement

a. Colony Settlements

(1) At Bishop Hill

422. Anderson, Theodore J. *100 Years: A History of Bishop Hill, Illinois; Also Biographical Sketches of Many Early Swedish Pioneers in Illinois*. Chicago: T. G. Anderson, 1947. The first Swedish settlement in Illinois, now a state historic site.

423. Barton, H. Arnold. "The Eric-Janssonists and the Shifting Contours of Community." *Western Illinois Regional Studies* 12, no. 2 (Fall 1989): 16-35.

424. "Bibliography of English Language Publications on Bishop Hill." *Western Illinois Regional Studies* 12, no. 2 (Fall 1989): 105-8.

425. Dawson, Elise Schebler. "The Folk Genre Paintings of Olof Krans as Historical Documents." *Western Illinois Regional Studies* 12, no. 2 (Fall 1989): 82-104. Krans's paintings illustrate the agricultural work of the Bishop Hill colony.

426. "An Early Description of Bishop Hill." *Journal of the Illinois State Historical Society* 47 (1954): 424-25. Report on the colony in 1847.

427. Elmen, Paul. *Wheat Flour Messiah: Eric Jansson of Bishop Hill.* Carbondale: Southern Illinois University Press, for the Swedish Pioneer Historical Society, 1976. Biography of the Swedish religious dissident who led followers to Bishop Hill.

428. Erdahl, Sivert. "Eric Janson and the Bishop Hill Colony." *Journal of the Illinois State Historical Society* 18 (1925-26): 503-74.

429. Isaksson, Olov, and Hallgren, Sören. *Bishop Hill: Svensk Koloni Pa Prairien/Bishop Hill, Illinois: A Utopia on the Prairie.* Stockholm: LT Publishing House, and Chicago: Swedish Pioneer Historical Society, 1969. Parallel texts in Swedish and English.

430. Jacobson, Margaret E. "The Painted Record of a Community Experiment-- Olaf Krans and His Pictures of the Bishop Hill Colony." *Journal of the Illinois State Historical Society* 34 (1941): 164-76.

431. Lagerberg, Matt. "The Bishop Hill Colonists in the Gold Rush." *Journal of the Illinois State Historical Society* 48 (1955): 466-69. The journal and letters of Rev. Jonas W. Olson quoted here also provide information about the latter years of the colony at Bishop Hill.

432. Mikkelsen, Michael. *The Bishop Hill Colony: A Religious Communistic Settlement in Henry County, Illinois.* 1892. American Utopian Adventure reprint series. Philadelphia: Porcupine Press, 1972. Includes Sivert Erdahl's article on Bishop Hill and its founder (Erik Jansson), which appeared in the October 1925 *Journal of the Illinois State Historical Society.*

433. Nelson, Charles H. "Toward a More Accurate Approximation of the Class Composition of the Erik Janssonists." *Swedish Pioneer Historical Quarterly* 26 (1975): 3-15.

434. Nelson, Ronald E. "Bishop Hill: Swedish Development of the Western Illinois Frontier." *Western Illinois Regional Studies* 1 (1978): 109-20.

435. _____. "The Bishop Hill Colony: What They Found." *Western Illinois Regional Studies* 12, no. 2 (Fall 1989): 36-45. The physical environment of Henry County and five "Yankee Colony" settlements in the area; some of the latter were primarily land speculation schemes.

436. _____. "The Building of Bishop Hill." *Western Illinois Regional Studies* 12, no. 2 (Fall 1989): 46-60.

437. Norton, John E.   " 'And Utopia became Bishop Hill.' "   *Historic Preservation*, vol. 25, no. 4 (October-December 1972), pp. 4-7, 9-12.   Includes Sparks, Esther. "Olof Krans, Prairie Painter," p. 9.

438. _____, ed.   " 'For It Flows with Milk and Honey': Two Immigrant Letters about Bishop Hill." *Swedish Pioneer Historical Quarterly* 24 (1973): 163-79. The letters, dated 1847, were written by Anders Andersson and Anders Larsson.

439. Pratt, Harry Edward, ed.   "The Murder of Eric Janson, Leader of Bishop Hill Colony." *Journal of the Illinois State Historical Society* 45 (1952): 55-69. Six documents, all dated 1850, from the Governor Augustus C. French Papers in the Illinois State Historical Library, are reproduced.

440. Setterdahl, Lilly, ed.   "Emigrant Letters by Bishop Hill Colonists from Nora Parish." *Western Illinois Regional Studies* 1 (1978): 121-75.

441. _____, and Wilson, J. Hiram.   "Hotel Accommodations in the Bishop Hill Colony." *Swedish Pioneer Historical Quarterly* 29 (1978): 180-97.   Includes descriptions of the Bjorklund Hotel and other structures in the colony.

442. Swank, George.   *Bishop Hill, Showcase of Swedish History: A Pictorial History and Guide.* Galva?, Ill.: Bishop Hill Heritage Association, 1965.

443. _____.   *Painter Krans: OK of Bishop Hill Colony.* Galva, Ill.: Galvaland Press, 1976.

444. Wagner, Jon.   "Living in Community: Daily Life in the Bishop Hill Colony." *Western Illinois Regional Studies* 12, no. 2 (Fall 1989): 61-81.

445. Wheeler, Wayne.   "Eric Janssonism: Community and Freedom in Nineteenth-Century Sweden and America." *Western Illinois Regional Studies* 12, no. 2 (Fall 1989): 7-15.

(2) Of English

446. Birkbeck, Morris.   *Letters from Illinois.* Philadelphia: M. Carey & Son, 1818.   There were many reprints issued that year, both in Dublin and London.

One, by Taylor and Hessey of London, was reprinted by University Microfilms, Ann Arbor, Mich., 1968.

447. _____. *Notes on a Journey in America, from the Coast of Virginia to the Territory of Illinois, with Proposals for the Establishment of a Colony of English.* Philadelphia: Caleb Richardson, 1817. A reprint of an 1818 3d ed. (New York: Augustus M. Kelley, 1971) has the added title line *To Which Is Added Letters from Illinois.* In 1968, University Microfilms, Ann Arbor, Mich., reprinted a fourth edition, issued originally in London by James Ridgway.

448. Boewe, Charles. *Prairie Albion: An English Settlement in Pioneer Illinois.* Carbondale: Southern Illinois University Press, 1962. Extracts from letters, diaries, and other primary documents are woven into a coherent narrative.

449. Cobbett, William. *A Year's Residence in the United States of America* . . . 3 pts. 2d ed., London: Sherwood, Neely, and Jones, 1819. Part 3 contains Thomas Hulme's journal (1818) of a visit to the English settlement in Illinois; Cobbett's letter of 18 December 1818, responding to Morris Birkbeck's accounts of Illinois and plea for settlers; and Cobbett's letter of 9 January 1819, criticizing Henry Fearon.

450. Colyer, Walter. "The Fordhams and La Serres of the English Settlement in Edwards County." *Transactions of the Illinois State Historical Society, 1911,* pp. 43-54.

451. Dukes, Edgar L., ed. "George Flower of Albion Seeks a Loan." *Journal of the Illinois State Historical Society* 49 (1956): 221-27. In an 1842 letter to a British attorney, Flower asks to borrow money because of financial difficulties owing to the failure of the state's two banks.

452. Faux, William. *Memorable Days in America: Being a Journal of a Tour to the United States, Principally Undertaken to Ascertain, by Positive Evidence, the Condition and Probable Prospects of British Emigrants; Including Accounts of Mr. Birkbeck's Settlement in the Illinois.* London: W. Simpkin and R. Marshall, 1823. Reprinted in Reuben Gold Thwaites, ed. *Early Western Travels,* vols. 11 and 12, and by AMS Press, New York, 1969.

453. Flower, George. *History of the English Settlement in Edwards County, Illinois, Founded in 1817 and 1819, by Morris Birkbeck and George Flower.* Preface and annotations by E. B. Washburne. Chicago Historical Society's Collection, vol. 1. Chicago: Fergus Printing, 1882. Reprint, Ann Arbor, Mich.: University Microfilms, 1968.

454. Flower, Richard. *Letters from Lexington and the Illinois, Containing a Brief Account of the English Settlement in the Latter Territory, and a Refutation of the Misrepresentations of Mr. Cobbett.* London: J. Ridgway, 1819. Reprinted in Reuben Gold Thwaites, ed. *Early Western Travels*, vol. 10.

455. _____. *Letters from the Illinois, 1820, 1821; Containing an Account of the English Settlement at Albion and Its Vicinity, and a Refutation of Various Misrepresentations, Those More Particularly of Mr. Cobbett.* London: J. Ridgway, 1822. Reprinted in Reuben Gold Thwaites, ed. *Early Western Travels*, vol. 10.

456. Fordham, Elias Pym. *Personal Narrative of Travels in Virginia, Maryland, Pennsylvania, Ohio, Indiana, Kentucky, and of a Residence in the Illinois Territory, 1817-1818.* Edited by Frederic Austin Ogg. Cleveland: Arthur H. Clark, 1906.

457. Hall, William. "From England to Illinois in 1821: The Journal of William Hall." Edited by Jay Monaghan. *Journal of the Illinois State Historical Society* 39 (1946): 21-67 and 208-53. The journal begins with an account of the voyage of the Hall family from London and continues for several years after arrival at the English Settlement in Edwards County.

458. Hendrickson, Walter B. "An Owenite Society in Illinois." *Indiana Magazine of History* 45 (1949): 175-82. The Illinois community was the short-lived Wanborough Society in Edwards County. A contemporary copy of the agreement of organization, in the Illinois State Historical Library, is published.

459. Hulme, Thomas. *A Journal Made during a Tour in the Western Countries of America, September 30, 1818--August 7, 1819 . . .* Reprinted from William Cobbett's *A Year's Residence in the United States of America* in Reuben Gold Thwaites, ed. *Early Western Travels*, vol. 10.

460. Ironside, R. G., ed. *Frontier Settlement.* University of Alberta Studies in Geography Monograph 1. Alberta: University of Alberta, 1974. The chapter by Brian P. Birch, "Initial Perception of Prairie--An English Settlement in Illinois," discusses the role of aesthetics in Morris Birkbeck's selection of land in Illinois.

461. Macdonald, Donald. *The Diaries of Donald Macdonald, 1824-1826.* With an introduction by Caroline Dale Snedeker. Indiana Historical Society Publications, vol. 14, no. 2. Indianapolis, 1942. The diarist describes the English settlement in Edwards County and other nearby communities in southeastern Illinois.

462. Miller, Keith L. "Planning, Proper Hygiene, and a Doctor: The Good Health of the English Settlement." *Journal of the Illinois State Historical Society* 71 (1978): 22-29.

463. Rodman, Jane. "The English Settlement in Southern Illinois, 1815-1825." *Indiana Magazine of History* 43 (1947): 329-62.

464. _____. "The English Settlement in Southern Illinois as Viewed by English Travelers, 1815-1825." *Indiana Magazine of History* 44 (1948): 37-68.

465. Salter, Mary Ann. "Bankrupts and Scoundrels: Some Minor Figures in the English Settlement." *Transactions of the Illinois State Historical Society: Selected Papers from the Seventh Annual History Symposium and the Eighth Annual Illinois History Symposium* [1986 and 1987]. Springfield, 1989. Pp. 11-19.

466. _____. "George Flower Comes to the Illinois Country: A New Look at Motivations." *Journal of the Illinois State Historical Society* 69 (1976): 213-23. Based on a collection of letters recently given to the Illinois State Historical Library.

467. _____. "Morris Birkbeck's Empire on the Prairies: Speculation, Philanthropy, or Mania?" *Selected Papers in Illinois History, 1981.* Springfield: Illinois State Historical Society, 1982. Pp. 1-6.

468. _____. "Quarreling in the English Settlement: The Flowers in Court." *Journal of the Illinois State Historical Society* 75 (1982): 101-14.

469. Shoemaker, L. E. "A Biography of Morris Birkbeck." *Journal of the Illinois State Historical Society* 23 (1930-31): 339-43.

470. Smith, Charles Wesley. "A Contribution toward a Bibliography of Morris Birkbeck and the English Settlement in Edwards Co., Ill., Founded by Morris Birkbeck and George Flower, 1817-18." *Transactions of the Illinois State Historical Society, 1905*, pp. 167-77.

471. Sparks, Edwin Erle, ed. *The English Settlement in the Illinois: Reprints of Three Rare Tracts on the Illinois Country, with Map and a View of a British Colony House at Albion.* London: Museum Book Store and Cedar Rapids, Iowa: Torch Press, 1907. The three tracts are an 1819 pamphlet by Morris Birkbeck (issued in response to a publication by William Cobbett) and two by Richard

Flower: *Letters from Lexington and the Illinois* (1819) and *Letters from the Illinois, 1820, 1821* (1822).

472. Thomson, Gladys Scott. *A Pioneer Family: The Birkbecks in Illinois, 1818-1827.* London: Jonathan Cape, 1953. Letters from Morris Birkbeck and his children to relatives in London add substantially to the history of the English Settlement in Illinois.

473. Walker, Janet R., and Burkhardt, Richard W. *Eliza Julia Flower: Letters of an English Gentlewoman; Life on the Illinois-Indiana Frontier, 1817-1861.* Muncie, Ind.: Ball State University, 1991. Eliza was the wife of George Flower.

474. Welby, Adlard. *Visit to North America and the English Settlements in Illinois, with a Winter Residence at Philadelphia . . .* London: J. Drury, 1821. Reprinted in Reuben Gold Thwaites, ed. *Early Western Travels*, vol. 12, pp. 248-59.

475. Williams, Daniel E. "English Gentlemen and American Backwoodsmen: A Confrontation in Edwards County, Illinois, 1816-1820." *Selected Papers in Illinois History, 1980.* Springfield: Illinois State Historical Society, 1982. Pp. 9-16.

476. Wood, Thomas J. " 'Blood in the Moon': The War for the Seat of Edwards County, 1821-1824." *Illinois Historical Journal* 85 (1992): 143-60. The contest went to Albion in the English Settlement, much to the chagrin of American-born settlers, among whom anti-British sentiment was strong.

477. Woods, John. *Two Years' Residence in the Settlement on the English Prairie, in the Illinois Country, United States, with an Account of Its Animal and Vegetable Production, Agriculture, &c., a Description of the Principal Towns, Villages, &c. &c., with the Habits and Customs of the Back-Woodsmen.* 1822. Reprint, edited by Paul McClelland Angle, Lakeside Classics, no. 66. Chicago: R. R. Donnelley, 1968. Also reprinted in Reuben Gold Thwaites, ed. *Early Western Travels*, vol. 10, pp. 179-357.

(3) Of Mormons

478. Allaman, John Lee. "Joseph Smith's Visits to Henderson County." *Western Illinois Regional Studies* 8, no. 1 (Spring 1985): 46-55.

479. Allen, James B. *Trials of Discipleship: The Story of William Clayton, a Mormon.* Urbana: University of Illinois Press, 1987. Clayton was a secretary to Joseph Smith, Jr., and Allen's account of the Nauvoo years is based on Clayton's journals.

480. Arrington, Joseph Earl. "Destruction of the Mormon Temple at Nauvoo." *Journal of the Illinois State Historical Society* 40 (1947): 414-25. Dedicated in April 1846, the temple was destroyed by fire on 9 October 1848.

481. _____. "Panorama Paintings in the 1840s of the Mormon Temple in Nauvoo." *Brigham Young University Studies* 22 (Winter 1982): 193-211.

482. Arrington, Leonard J., and Bitton, Davis. *The Mormon Experience: A History of the Latter-day Saints.* New York: Knopf, 1979. Brief but good accounts of the Mormons at Nauvoo.

483. Beardsley, Harry M. "The Mormons in Illinois." *Transactions of the Illinois State Historical Society, 1933,* pp. 45-54. A critical analysis of Mormonism and Joseph Smith, Jr.

484. Bennett, Richard E. " 'A Samaritan had passed by': George Miller, Mormon Bishop, Trailblazer, and Brigham Young Antagonist." *Illinois Historical Journal* 82 (1989): 2-16.

485. Berry, Orville F. "The Mormon Settlement in Illinois." *Transactions of the Illinois State Historical Society, 1906,* pp. 88-102.

486. Best, Christy. *Guide to Sources for Studies of Mormon Women, in the Church Archives, The Church of Jesus Christ of Latter-day Saints.* Salt Lake City: Historical Department, Church of Jesus Christ of Latter-day Saints, 1976. Several of these manuscript collections concern life at Nauvoo.

487. Bishop, M. Guy; Lacey, Vincent A.; and Wixon, Richard. "Death at Mormon Nauvoo, 1843-1845." *Western Illinois Regional Studies* 9, no. 2 (Fall 1986): 70-83. A detailed mortality study.

488. Bishop, M. Guy. "Sex Roles, Marriage, and Childrearing at Mormon Nauvoo." *Western Illinois Regional Studies* 11, no. 2 (Fall 1988): 30-45.

489. Bitton, Davis. *Guide to Mormon Diaries & Autobiographies.* Provo, Utah: Brigham Young University Press, 1977. The index has many entries under the subject heading "Nauvoo."

490. Bringhurst, Newell G. "Fawn M. Brodie, 'Mormondom's Lost Generation,' and *No Man Knows My History.*" *Journal of Mormon History* 16 (1990): 11-23. The author considers the writings of many other Mormons and non-Mormons of Brodie's generation.

491. Brodie, Fawn. *No Man Knows My History: The Life of Joseph Smith.* New York: Knopf, 1946. A scholarly study called by one reviewer the "first objective" biography of Smith. For the Mormon point of view, see Bringhurst, above.

492. Buckingham, Clyde E. "Mormonism in Illinois." *Journal of the Illinois State Historical Society* 32 (1939): 173-92. See also the letter from S. A. Burgess, historian of the Reorganized Church of Jesus Christ of Latter Day Saints, written in response to this article and published in the *Journal* 33 (1940): 116-24.

493. Cannon, Donald Q. "Reverend George Moore Comments on Nauvoo, the Mormons, and Joseph Smith." *Western Illinois Regional Studies* 5 (1982): 5-16. Moore was a Unitarian minister at Quincy, who visited Nauvoo several times in the years 1840-45.

494. Cook, Lyndon W. "William Law, Nauvoo Dissenter." *Brigham Young University Studies* 22 (Winter 1982): 47-72.

495. Davis, Inez Smith. *The Story of the Church: A History of the Church of Jesus Christ of Latter Day Saints, and of Its Legal Successor, the Reorganized Church of Jesus Christ of Latter Day Saints.* Independence, Mo.: Herald Publishing House, 1938.

496. Enders, Donald L. "A Dam for Nauvoo: An Attempt to Industrialize the City." *Brigham Young University Studies* 18 (Winter 1978): 151-78.

497. Esplin, Ronald K. "Life in Nauvoo, June 1844: Vilate Kimball's Martyrdom Letters." *Brigham Young University Studies* 19 (Winter 1979): 231-40.

498. _____. "The Significance of Nauvoo for Latter-day Saints." *Journal of Mormon History* 16 (1990): 71-86. Descriptions of Mormon Nauvoo and its conservation and restoration, as well as of Joseph Smith's teachings propounded there.

499. Fish, Joseph. *The Life and Times of Joseph Fish, Mormon Pioneer.* Edited by John H. Krenkel. Danville, Ill.: Interstate, 1970. Fish's diary contains accounts of his early life at Nauvoo.

500. Flake, Chad J., ed. *A Mormon Bibliography, 1830-1930: Books, Pamphlets, Periodicals, and Broadsides Relating to the First Century of Mormonism.* Salt Lake City: University of Utah Press, 1978. A ten-year supplement, compiled by Flake and Larry W. Draper, was published in 1989. Items are arranged by author and indexed by year of publication; the supplement includes a title index.

501. Flanders, Robert B. *Nauvoo: Kingdom on the Mississippi.* Urbana: University of Illinois Press, 1965. Illinois Books ed., 1975. An excellent history of Mormonism for the years 1839-46.

502. Gardner, Hamilton. "The Nauvoo Legion, 1840-1845: A Unique Military Organization." *Journal of the Illinois State Historical Society* 54 (1961): 181-97.

503. Gayler, George R. "Governor Ford and the Death of Joseph and Hyrum Smith." *Journal of the Illinois State Historical Society* 50 (1957): 391-411. A study of Governor Thomas Ford's failure in 1844 to calm the unrest in Hancock County and prevent the murders of the Mormon leaders Joseph and Hyrum Smith.

504. _____. "The Mormons and Politics in Illinois, 1839-1844." *Journal of the Illinois State Historical Society* 49 (1956): 48-66.

505. Givens, George W. *In Old Nauvoo: Everyday Life in the City of Joseph.* Salt Lake City: Deseret Book, 1990. A comprehensive social history of the town in the years 1839-46, with such chapters as Food and Drink, Sickness and Death, Courtship and Marriage, Children and Childhood, Women and Mothers, as well as those more commonplace on farming, recreation, the church, etc. Well written and carefully annotated.

506. Godfrey, Kenneth W. "Joseph Smith and the Masons." *Journal of the Illinois State Historical Society* 64 (1971): 79-90.

507. Gregg, Thomas. *History of Hancock County, Illinois, together with an Outline History of the State and a Digest of State Laws.* Chicago: Chas. C. Chapman, 1880. Gregg's chapter "The Mormon Period," pages 242-378, is the most important non-Mormon source for Illinois Mormon history, except for the *Warsaw Signal* and, perhaps, Thomas Ford's history of Illinois.

508. Hallwas, John E., and Launius, Roger D., eds. *Cultures in Conflict: A Documentary History of the Mormon War in Illinois.* Logan: Utah State University Press, forthcoming.

509. Hallwas, John E. "Mormon Nauvoo from a Non-Mormon Perspective." *Journal of Mormon History* 16 (1990): 53-69. Winner of the John Whitmer Historical Association for the finest article of the year in Mormon studies--the first non-Mormon scholar to win the award. Excellent bibliography.

510. Hampshire, Annette P. "Thomas Sharp and Anti-Mormon Sentiment in Illinois." *Journal of the Illinois State Historical Society* 72 (1979): 82-100. Sharp was editor of the anti-Mormon newspaper *Warsaw Signal*, 1842-45.

511. _____. "The Triumph of Mobocracy in Hancock County, 1844-1846." *Western Illinois Regional Studies* 5 (1982): 17-37. A good account of the civil unrest and the breakdown of civil authority that led to the Mormon War.

512. Hill, Marvin S. *Quest for Refuge: The Mormon Flight from American Pluralism.* Salt Lake City: Signature Books, 1989.

513. Howard, Richard P. "The Nauvoo Heritage of the Reorganized Church." *Journal of Mormon History* 16 (1990): 41-52.

514. Kimball, James L. Jr. "The Nauvoo Charter: A Reinterpretation." *Journal of the Illinois State Historical Society* 64 (1971): 66-78.

515. Kimball, Stanley B. "The Mormons in Illinois, 1838-1846." *Journal of the Illinois State Historical Society* 74 (1971): 4-21. An introduction to an issue of the *Journal* devoted to the Mormons that constitutes a general history of the Mormons in that period.

516. _____, comp. *Sources of Mormon History in Illinois, 1839-48: An Annotated Catalog of the Microfilm Collection at Southern Illinois University.* Southern Illinois University at Edwardsville, Lovejoy Library Bibliographic Contributions, no. 1. Carbondale, 1964. 2d ed., rev. and enl., 1966. The microfilm collection at Southern Illinois University at Edwardsville consists of photocopies of most of the available sources.

517. Klaus, J. Hansen. *Quest for Empire: The Political Kingdom of God and the Council of Fifty in Mormon History.* East Lansing: Michigan State University Press, 1967. Reprint, Lincoln: University of Nebraska Press, 1974.

Joseph Smith's efforts towards developing a political kingdom of God at Nauvoo, with himself at its head.

518. Laub, George. "George Laub's Nauvoo Journal." Edited by Eugene England. *Brigham Young University Studies* 18 (Winter 1978): 151-78.

519. Launius, Roger D. "American Home Missionary Society Ministers and Mormon Nauvoo: Selected Letters." *Western Illinois Regional Studies* 8, no. 1 (Spring 1985): 16-45. The letters are from the American Home Missionary Society Collection at the Amistead Research Center, New Orleans.

520. _____, and McKiernan, F. Mark. *Joseph Smith Jr.'s Red Brick Store.* Western Illinois Monograph Series, no. 5. Macomb: Western Illinois University, 1985. Smith's store served as an unofficial community center at Nauvoo. The monograph includes 1842 daybook entries from the store.

521. Launius, Roger D. *Joseph Smith III: Pragmatic Prophet.* Urbana: University of Illinois Press, 1988. This biography presents a sound account of the controversy that followed the death of Joseph Smith and the succession of Brigham Young as leader of the Mormons; Joseph Smith III later organized dissident groups into the Reorganized Church of Jesus Christ of Latter Day Saints.

522. _____. "Joseph Smith III and the Mormon Succession Crisis, 1844-1846." *Western Illinois Regional Studies* 6, no. 1 (Spring 1983): 5-22.

523. _____, and Hallwas, John E., eds. *Kingdom on the Mississippi Revisited: Nauvoo in Mormon History.* Urbana: University of Illinois Press, forthcoming. A collection of fourteen articles.

524. Leonard, Glen M. "Recent Writing on Mormon Nauvoo." *Western Illinois Regional Studies* 11, no. 2 (Fall 1988): 69-93. Lists publications from 1978 until this article appeared.

525. _____. "Remembering Nauvoo: Historiographical Considerations." *Journal of Mormon History* 16 (1990): 25-39.

526. Linn, William Alexander. *The Story of the Mormons from the Date of Their Origin to the Year 1901.* New York: Macmillan, 1902. For a history of the Mormons in Illinois, see pages 219-356.

527. McGavin, E. Cecil. *The Nauvoo Temple.* Salt Lake City: Deseret Book, 1962. Primarily a tract written by a Mormon for Mormons planning to restore the temple.

528. McKiernan, F. Mark. *The Voice of One Crying in the Wilderness: Sidney Rigdon, Religious Reformer, 1793-1876.* Lawrence, Kans.: Coronado Press, 1971. Rigdon was an important leader in the early days of the Mormons in Illinois.

529. Marsh, Eudocia Baldwin. "Mormons in Hancock County: A Reminiscence." Edited by Douglas L. Wilson and Rodney O. Davis. *Journal of the Illinois State Historical Society* 64 (1971): 22-65.

530. Miller, Daniel E., and Miller, Delia S. *Nauvoo: The City of the Saints.* Salt Lake City: Peregrine Smith, 1974.

531. Newell, Linda King, and Avery, Valeen Tippets. *Mormon Enigma: Emma Hale Smith.* Garden City, N.Y.: Doubleday, 1984. A scholarly, clear-sighted study of the wife of the Mormon prophet Joseph Smith and the mother of Joseph Smith III, first president of the Reorganized Church of Jesus Christ of Latter Day Saints.

532. Oaks, Dallin H., and Hill, Marvin S. *Carthage Conspiracy: The Trial of the Accused Assassins of Joseph Smith.* Urbana: University of Illinois Press, 1975.

533. Poll, Richard D. "Nauvoo and the New Mormon History: A Bibliographical Survey." *Journal of Mormon History* 5 (1978): 105-23. Covers items published in the 1960s and 1970s until the date of this article.

534. "Recollections of the Nauvoo Temple." An unsigned description from the *Illinois Journal*, 9 December 1853, is reprinted in the *Journal of the Illinois State Historical Society* 38 (1945): 481-85.

535. Sloan, James. "Mormon Nauvoo in 1842." *Journal of the Illinois State Historical Society* 46 (1953): 313-15. A letter of 27 March 1842 from Nauvoo (original in the Illinois State Historical Library) provides a description of the city.

536. Smith, Andrew F. "Dr. John Cook Bennett's Tomato Campaign." *Old Northwest* 16 (1992): 61-75. A short-term member of the Mormon community at Nauvoo, Bennett advocated cultivation of the tomato there, as he had done elsewhere since the early 1830s.

537. Smith, Joseph Jr. "A New Mormon Letter." *Journal of the Illinois State Historical Society* 40 (1947): 85-86. A letter of 4 May 1841 from Smith to Oliver Granger, acquired by the Illinois State Historical Library, deals primarily with church financial matters, although he adds that three hundred immigrants had arrived at Nauvoo in less than a week.

538. _____. *The Papers of Joseph Smith: Volume 1, Autobiographical and Historical Writings.* Edited by Dean C. Jessee. Salt Lake City: Deseret Book Co., 1989.

539. Sorensen, Parry D. "Nauvoo Times and Seasons." *Journal of the Illinois State Historical Society* 55 (1962): 117-35. The Mormon paper was published from November 1839 through 15 February 1846.

540. Stout, Hosea. *On the Mormon Frontier: The Diary of Hosea Stout, 1844-1861.* Edited by Juanita Brooks. 2 vols. Salt Lake City: University of Utah Press and Utah State Historical Society, 1964. The diary of this influential leader, superbly edited, begins at Nauvoo. The first 117 pages are concerned with life there until 9 February 1846, when Stout was on the west bank of the Mississippi en route to the West.

541. Tanner, Terence A. "The Mormon Press in Nauvoo, 1839-1846." *Western Illinois Regional Studies* 11, no. 2 (Fall 1988): 5-29.

542. Taylor, Samuel W. *The Kingdom or Nothing: The Life of John Taylor, Militant Mormon.* New York: Macmillan, 1976. Chapter 6 deals with Taylor and "The Rise and Fall of Nauvoo."

543. Walgren, Kent L. "James Adams: Early Springfield Mormon and Freemason." *Journal of the Illinois State Historical Society* 75 (1982): 121-36. Adams was an associate of Mormon founder Joseph Smith Jr.

544. Winn, Kenneth H. *Exiles in a Land of Liberty: Mormons in America, 1830-1846.* Chapel Hill: University of North Carolina Press, 1989. A reinterpretation of Mormonism that sees the religion as a protest against the disorder in America that threatened republicanism. The last third of the book is a succinct reappraisal of the Mormons in Illinois.

(4) Of Icarians

545. Barnes, Sherman B. "An Icarian in Nauvoo." *Journal of the Illinois State Historical Society* 34 (1941): 233-44. Two letters of the Nauvoo Icarian Pierre Roux, published in France in 1839, led the author to conclude that a principal reason for the failure of the community was the fierce individualism of the residents.

546. Bush, Robert D. "Communism, Community, and Charisma: The Crisis in Icaria at Nauvoo." *Old Northwest* 3 (1977): 409-28.

547. Chicoineau, Jacques C. "Étienne Cabet and the Icarians." *Western Illinois Regional Studies* 2 (1979): 5-19.

548.   Miller, Mrs. I. G.   "The Icarian Community of Nauvoo, Illinois." *Transactions of the Illinois State Historical Society, 1906*, pp. 103-7.

549.   Prudhommeaux, Jules Jean.   *Icarie et son Fondateur Étienne Cabet: Contribution à l'étude du Socialisme Expérimental.* 1907. American Utopian Adventure reprint series. Philadelphia: Porcupine Press, 1972. An excellent treatise.

550. Shaw, Albert. *Icaria: A Chapter in the History of Communism.* American Utopian Adventure reprint series.   Philadelphia: Porcupine Press, 1972. Originally published in 1884, this study is outdated.

551. Snider, Felicie Cottet. "A Short Sketch of the Life of Jules Leon Cottet, a Former Member of the Icarian Community." *Journal of the Illinois State Historical Society* 7, no. 3 (October 1914): 200-217.

552. Sutton, Robert P., ed. "An Icarian Embarkation: Le Havre to Nauvoo, 1854." Translated by Lloyd and William Gundy. *Western Illinois Regional Studies* 9, no. 1 (Spring 1986): 19-33. The diarist is unknown, but the original was printed in a pamphlet by Étienne Cabet.

553. _____. Les Icariens: *The Utopian Dream in Europe and America.* Urbana: University of Illinois Press, 1994.

554. _____, and Smithson, Rulon N., eds. " 'Mon cher Emile': The Cabet-Baxter Letters, 1854-1855." *Western Illinois Regional Studies* 2 (1979): 20-37. The letters, from Étienne Cabet at Nauvoo to Emile Baxter, are on deposit at Newberry Library, Chicago.

555. Sutton, Robert P. "Utopian Fraternity: Ideal and Reality in Icarian Recreation." *Western Illinois Regional Studies* 6, no. 1 (Spring 1983): 23-37.

556. Vallet, Émile. *Communism: History of the Experiment at Nauvoo of the Icarian Settlement.* Edited by H. Roger Grant. Reprint, Illinois State Historical Society Pamphlet Series, no. 6. Springfield, 1971. A good study of a secular utopian society of the 1850s.

(5) Others

557. Coggeshall, John M. " 'God Bless the Dutch!' The Emergence of a German-American Ethnic Group in St. Clair County, Illinois, 1833-1858." *Selected Papers in Illinois History, 1982.* Springfield: Illinois State Historical Society, 1984. Pp. 20-30.

558. Dawson, George E. "The Integral Phalanx." *Transactions of the Illinois State Historical Society, 1907*, pp. 85-97. The Phalanx was a short-lived communitarian society (based on the principles of Charles Fourier), established in Sangamon County in 1845.

559. Grant, H. Roger. "Utopias That Failed: The Antebellum Years." *Western Illinois Regional Studies* 2 (1979): 38-51. In addition to Bishop Hill and the Icarian community at Nauvoo, the author mentions five other short-lived Fourier-based communities in Illinois.

560. Hirsch, Helmut. "Theodor Erasmus Hilgard, Ambassador of American-ism." *Journal of the Illinois State Historical Society* 37 (1944): 164-72. One of the German immigrant gentlemen-farmers known as "Latin peasants" for their educational attainments, Hilgard championed most things American in articles and books and letters to his homeland. In the United States, Hilgard lived near Belleville in St. Clair County.

561. Hubbard, Anson M. "A Colony Settlement: Geneseo, Illinois, 1836-1837." *Journal of the Illinois State Historical Society* 29 (1936-37): 403-31. Original Geneseo settlers were Congregationalists from New York.

562. Klett, Ada M. "Belleville Germans Look at America, 1833-1845." *Journal of the Illinois State Historical Society* 40 (1947): 23-37. Extracts from letters in the Engelmann-Kircher Family Letters and Papers, in the Illinois State Historical Library, describe pioneer life in the Belleville area.

563. "Letters from New Switzerland, 1831-1832." *Journal of the Illinois State Historical Society* 49 (1956): 431-44. Joseph Suppiger and Salomon (or Soloman) Koepfli write letters back to Switzerland from Highland that constitute comprehensive accounts of all aspects of pioneer settlement and immigration to Illinois.

564. Newbauer, Ella C. "The Swiss Settlement of Madison County, Illinois." *Transactions of the Illinois State Historical Society, 1906*, pp. 232-37. Highland was the principal Swiss settlement, but there were several others in the county.

565. Poage, George Rawlings. "The Coming of the Portuguese." *Journal of the Illinois State Historical Society* 18 (1925-26): 101-35. The story of Protestant Portuguese from Madeira who settled in central Illinois in 1849.

566. Qualey, Carlton C. "The Fox River Norwegian Settlement." *Journal of the Illinois State Historical Society* 27 (1934-35): 133-77. History of the first Norwegian settlement (1834) in the Midwest.

567. Stroble, Paul E. Jr. "Ferdinand Ernst and the German Colony at Vandalia." *Illinois Historical Journal* 80 (1987): 101-10. Ernst visited Vandalia in 1819 and moved there with a group of immigrants the following year.

568. Suppiger, Joseph; Koepfli, Salomon; and Koepfli, Kaspar. *Journey to New Switzerland: Travel Account of the Koepfli and Suppiger Family to St. Louis on the Mississippi and the Founding of New Switzerland in the State of Illinois.* Translated by Raymond J. Spahn. Edited by John C. Abbott. Carbondale: Southern Illinois University Press, 1987. An account by the German-speaking Swiss who settled in 1831 at what became Highland.

569. Trautmann, Frederic, ed. and trans. "Eight Weeks on a St. Clair County Farm in 1851: Letters by a Young German." *Journal of the Illinois State Historical Society* 75 (1982): 162-78. The letter writer was Carl Köhler, who visited the farm of Friedrich Karl Hecker, near a community of refugees from the 1830 German revolution. Hecker himself fled Germany after the 1848 uprising.

570. Villard, Oswald Garrison. "The 'Latin Peasants' of Belleville, Illinois." *Journal of the Illinois State Historical Society* 35 (1942): 7-20. The so-called "Latin peasants" were well-educated German immigrants who settled in St. Clair County in the 1830s and 1840s.

b. Settlers and Settlements in General

571. Alderfer, William K. "The Artist Gustav Pfau." *Journal of the Illinois State Historical Society* 60 (1967): 383-90. Pfau's drawings illustrate frontier life along the Mississippi in the early 1840s.

572. Angle, Paul McClelland, ed. *Pioneers: Narratives of Noah Harris Letts and Thomas Allen Banning, 1825-1865.* Lakeside Classics, no. 70. Chicago: R. R. Donnelley, 1972. The Letts family moved to La Salle County in 1830 and the Banning family to McDonough County in 1836. Banning's narrative has little about the family's life in Illinois since they moved to Kansas when he was still a boy. These narratives, Angle says, are among the few that tell the stories of unsuccessful pioneers.

573. Ballance, Charles. "The Journal of Charles Ballance of Peoria." Edited by Ernest E. East. *Journal of the Illinois State Historical Society* 30 (1937-38): 70-84. Entries, 1831-43, provide good accounts of travel through Illinois as well as of the real estate business in Peoria.

574. Beach, Richard H. "A Letter from Illinois Written in 1836." *Journal of the Illinois State Historical Society*, vol. 3, no. 3 (October 1910), pp. 91-98. A valuable letter describing all aspects of life in the state.

575. Bergendoff, Conrad. "The Beginnings of Swedish Immigration into Illinois a Century Ago." *Journal of the Illinois State Historical Society* 41 (1948): 16-27.

576. Bohman, George V. "A Poet's Mother: Sarah Snell Bryant in Illinois." *Journal of the Illinois State Historical Society* 33 (1940): 166-89. Based on family letters, this article is an excellent account of the social life and customs on the frontier and of life in Princeton, where the Bryants settled in 1835.

577. Bray, Robert, and Bushnell, Paul. "From New England to the Old Northwest: The American Odyssey of the Jeremiah Greenman Family." *Journal of the Illinois State Historical Society* 69 (1976): 201-12. The authors trace the family's hegira from Rhode Island to Illinois, 1775-1830.

578. Bridges, Roger Dean. "Dark Faces on the Antebellum West Central Illinois Landscape." *Western Illinois Regional Studies* 6, no. 2 (Fall 1983): 67-80. Racism and anti-black sentiment in the fourteen counties west of the Illinois River in pre-Civil War Illinois, with some discussion of the successful free blacks in the area.

579. Buckingham, Clyde E. "Early Settlers of the Rock River Valley." *Journal of the Illinois State Historical Society* 35 (1942): 236-59. Contains many descriptions of the area by early travelers.

580. Burlend, Rebecca. *A True Picture of Emigration.* Lakeside Classics, no. 34, edited by Milo Milton Quaife. Chicago: R. R. Donnelley, 1936. The story of a family that emigrated from England to Pike County in 1831.

581. Campbell, Archibald. "Letters from a Cass County Farmer." Edited by A. Cameron Grant. *Journal of the Illinois State Historical Society* 64 (1971): 327-36. The letters are dated 1851-56.

582. Clarke, Charles James Fox. "Sketch of Charles James Fox Clarke with Letters to His Mother." Edited by Charles R. Clarke. *Journal of the Illinois State Historical Society* 22 (1929-30): 559-81. The letters (1834-43) describe life in central Illinois.

583. Curran, Nathaniel B. "Anna Durkee Tauzin Young, 1753-1839: Connecticut Lady, Illinois Pioneer." *Journal of the Illinois State Historical Society* 77 (1984): 94-100. The story of a remarkable grandmother who came to Madison County with her grandchildren in 1817.

584. Davis, James E. "Settlers in Frontier Illinois: Primary Evidence, Persistent Problems, and the Historian's Craft." *Selected Papers in Illinois History, 1981.* Springfield: Illinois State Historical Society, 1982. Pp. 7-14. An examination of primary accounts of those who settled in Illinois in the years 1820-50 or who visited the state in that period.

585. East, Ernest Edward. "The Inhabitants of Chicago, 1825-1831." *Journal of the Illinois State Historical Society* 37 (1944): 131-63. A list of the inhabitants with biographical information from official records of Peoria County (of which Cook County was then a part), as well as from other sources.

586. Ellsworth, Oliver. "Ninety-Eight Years Ago in Bloomington." *Journal of the Illinois State Historical Society* 28, no. 3 (October 1935): 204-13. In a letter of 19 October 1837, Ellsworth describes Bloomington and farm life and prices.

587. Eslinger, Ellen T. "Cultural Heritages of Naperville, Illinois: The Pennsylvania Germans." *Transactions of the Illinois State Historical Society: Selected Papers from the Fifth and Sixth Illinois History Symposiums of the Illinois State Historical Society* [1984 and 1985]. Springfield, 1988. Pp. 119-28.

588. Faragher, John Mack. *Sugar Creek: Life on the Illinois Prairie.* New Haven: Yale University Press, 1986. A well-written scholarly account of community and family life in Sangamon County before the Civil War. Local history of state and national importance.

589. Farnham, Eliza. *Life in Prairie Land.* New York: Harper, 1846. Reprint, with an introduction by John E. Hallwas, Urbana: University of Illinois Press, 1988. Farnham moved to Tazewell County in the 1830s. She provides a distinctively female perception of frontier settlement and reflects concern for the natural world as well.

590. Hallwas, John E. "John Regan's 'Emigrant's Guide': A Neglected Literary Achievement." *Illinois Historical Journal* 77 (1984): 269-94. Regan immigrated to central Illinois from Scotland in 1842. A schoolmaster and newspaper editor, Regan published the *Emigrant's Guide* in 1852.

591. Hamilton, Henry Edward. *Incidents and Events in the Life of Gurdon Saltonstall Hubbard, Collected from Personal Narratives and Other Sources, and Arranged by His Nephew.* Chicago: Rand McNally, 1888. Reissued, with an introduction by Caroline M. McIlvaine, as *The Autobiography of Gurdon Saltonstall Hubbard . . .* Lakeside Classics, no. 9. Chicago: R. R. Donnelley, 1911. Hubbard's own account, which ends at 1830, is primarily about his life as a trader with the Indians of northeastern Illinois.

592. Harper, Charles A. "An Appraisement of the Property of the Rev. James McGeoch, 1833." *Journal of the Illinois State Historical Society* 24 (1931-32): 141-60. Detailed listing of household items, clothes, and books in the large library of the McLean County minister.

593. Hays, Lorena L. *To the Land of Gold and Wickedness: The 1848-59 Diary of Lorena L. Hays.* Edited by Jeanne Hamilton Watson. St. Louis: Patrice Press, 1988. From 1839 to 1853 Hays lived in Pike County. The first third of her diary, together with the editor's introduction, provides a substantial social history of the place and times. The second and third parts of the volume concern her trip to California and her years there.

594. Henry, John. "The Memoirs of John Henry: A Pioneer of Morgan County." Edited by C. H. Rammelkamp. *Journal of the Illinois State Historical Society* 18 (1925-26): 39-75. Henry served in both the Black Hawk War and the Civil War, and as a state legislator and congressman. He was personally involved with most of the major political figures and social issues of his day, and his memoir is thus quite remarkable. It includes sketches of Governor Joseph Duncan and the cattleman Jacob Strawn.

595. Iles, Elijah. *Sketches of Early Life and Times in Kentucky, Missouri, and Illinois.* Springfield, Ill.: Springfield Printing, 1883.

596. Johnson, T. Walter. "Charles Reynolds Matheny, Pioneer Settler of Illinois (1786-1839)." *Journal of the Illinois State Historical Society* 33 (1940): 438-68. Prominent in local and state government, Matheny lived in several Illinois communities before settling in Springfield in 1821.

597. Jordan, Philip D. "The Life and Works of James Gardiner Edwards." *Journal of the Illinois State Historical Society* 23 (1930-31): 462-502. Edwards founded the first Jacksonville newspaper in 1830; he later lived in Iowa.

598. Kinzie, Juliette Augusta Magill. *Wau-Bun, The Early Day in the North West.* London: Sampson, Low, Son & Co.; New York: Derby & Jackson; Chicago: D. B. Cooke & Co.; Cincinnati: H. W. Derby & Co., 1856. Reprints, Lakeside Classics, no. 30, Chicago: R. R. Donnelley, 1932; and Urbana: University of Illinois Press, 1992, with an introduction by Nina Baym. Delightful and reliable reminiscences of life at Chicago, with recollections of the many Indians who visited the Chicago and Fort Winnebago subagencies, as well as narratives of the Fort Dearborn massacre and several trips on the Illinois and Wisconsin frontier.

599. Lawrence, Barbara, and Branz, Nedra, eds. *The Flagg Correspondence: Selected Letters, 1816-1854.* Carbondale: Southern Illinois University Press, 1986. Two hundred letters among members of the family of Gershom Flagg, who left Vermont in 1816 and settled in Madison County, Illinois, in 1818. The letters, together with the footnotes, offer a comprehensive account of life in early Illinois. The original letters are in the Illinois Historical Survey, University of Illinois at Urbana-Champaign and Southern Illinois University at Edwardsville. Twenty-four early letters (edited by Solon J. Buck) are reprinted from the *Transactions of the Illinois State Historical Society, 1910*, pp. 139-83.

600. Lebron, Jeanne. "Colonel James W. Stephenson, Galena Pioneer." *Journal of the Illinois State Historical Society* 35 (1942): 347-67. Personal letters filed with Stephenson's estate papers not only provide biographical information but also illustrate the social and political life of a prominent politician-officeholder of northwestern Illinois in the 1830s.

601. "Letters from Ogle and Carroll Counties, 1838-1857." *Transactions of the Illinois State Historical Society, 1907*, pp. 247-61. All but two of the letters fall within the 1830s and 1840s. Excellent descriptions of day-to-day life, land sales, cost of living, etc. James H. and Sarah A. Smith were the principal correspondents.

602. McLear, Patrick E. " '. . . And Still They Came'--Chicago from 1832-36." *Journal of the West* 7 (1968): 397-404.

603. McPheeters, Addison. "The Reminiscences of Addison McPheeters." *Journal of the Illinois State Historical Society* 67 (1974): 212-26. McPheeters was a pioneer settler in Kentucky, Missouri, and Illinois. He discusses agriculture, manners and customs, business ventures, and service in the Black Hawk War.

604. Mills, Abel. "Autobiography of Abel Mills." *Journal of the Illinois State Historical Society* 19 (1926-27): 94-239. Valuable for its account of farm life and activities of the Society of Friends (Quakers) in north-central Illinois.

605. Patton, James Welch, ed. "Letters from North Carolina Emigrants in the Old Northwest, 1830-1834." *Mississippi Valley Historical Review* 47 (1960-61): 263-77. Principally letters from the Cress and Ludewick families in Montgomery County.

606. Phelps, Caroline. "Caroline Phelps' Diary." *Journal of the Illinois State Historical Society* 23 (1930-31): 209-39. A courageous young woman, wife of an Indian trader from Lewistown, Illinois, recounts harrowing adventures as she traveled to join her husband at his trading posts in Iowa.

607. Regan, John. *The Emigrant's Guide to the Western States of America; or, Backwoods and Prairies.* Rev. ed. Edinburgh: Oliver and Boyd, 1852. The author emigrated from Scotland to Illinois in 1842, and the book offers practical information for the emigrant--costs of building a house, prices of food and clothing, prices received by the farmer for agricultural products, etc.

608. Reid, Harvey. *Biographical Sketch of Enoch Long, an Illinois Pioneer.* Chicago Historical Society's Collection, vol. 2. Chicago: Fergus Printing, 1884. Long was a businessman in Alton and a lead miner at Galena.

609. Riley, Glenda. "The 'Female Frontier' in Illinois." *Mid-America* 67 (1985): 69-82. From the "abundant" sources the author has located, she constructs reliable portrayals of the lives of Illinois frontierswomen.

610. Ross, Harvey Lee. *The Early Pioneers and Pioneer Events of the State of Illinois.* Chicago: Eastman Brothers, 1899. Reprint, Astoria, Ill.: Stevens Publishing, 1970.

611. Rutledge, James McGrady. "The Memoirs of James McGrady Rutledge, 1814-1899." Introduction and notes by Fern Nance Pond. *Journal of the Illinois State Historical Society* 29 (1936-37): 76-88, 432-33. The memoirs deal with Abraham Lincoln and life at New Salem.

612. Sackett, Mary. "Mary Sackett's Journal, 1841-1842." Photoduplicated. Kirkwood, Mo.: W. M. Underwood, 1986. Excellent accounts of the Sackett family's journey by way of the Great Lakes to Laona, Winnebago County, and of their life in Illinois.

613. Snyder, John Francis. *Adam W. Snyder and His Period in Illinois History, 1817-1842.* Virginia, Ill.: E. Needham, 1906.

614. _____. "The Old French Towns of Illinois in 1839: A Reminiscence." *Journal of the Illinois State Historical Society* 36 (1943): 345-67. Snyder discusses many of the Illinois political leaders who lived in the area, as well as the towns themselves.

615. Soady, Fred W. Jr. " 'In These Waste Places': Pekin, Illinois, 1824-1849." *Journal of the Illinois State Historical Society* 57 (1964): 156-71. The development of a town--socially, governmentally, and economically--in its first twenty-five years.

616. Spencer, John W. *Reminiscences of Pioneer Life in the Mississippi Valley.* Davenport, Iowa: Griggs, Watson & Day, 1872. Reprinted in Milo Milton Quaife, ed. *The Early Day of Rock Island and Davenport . . .* Lakeside Classics, no. 40. Chicago: R. R. Donnelley, 1942. The Quaife edition also includes J. M. D. Burrows' *Fifty Years in Iowa* (1888). Spencer's tale deals primarily with pioneer life, Indian affairs, and the Black Hawk War; Burrows' narrative is concerned with frontier businesses.

617. Stroble, Paul E. Jr. *High on Okaw's Western Bank: Vandalia, Illinois, 1819-39.* Urbana: University of Illinois Press, 1992. During the years considered, Vandalia was capital of the state. Stroble sets the town's history in a broad framework of social, economic, and political developments.

618. Tillson, Christiana Holmes. *Reminiscences of Early Life in Illinois by Our Mother.* Amherst, Mass.: Privately printed, 1873. Reprinted as *A Woman's Story* *of Pioneer Illinois.* Lakeside Classics, no. 17, edited by Milo Milton Quaife. Chicago: R. R. Donnelley, 1919. Mrs. Tillson immigrated to Illinois in 1822.

619. Tingley, Donald Fred. "Illinois Days of Daniel Parker, Texas Colonizer." *Journal of the Illinois State Historical Society* 51 (1958): 388-402. The frontier minister Daniel Parker settled near the Wabash River in Illinois in 1816 and within a few years became a prominent antislavery state senator. The author discusses the religious and political views held by Parker.

620. Tonsor, Stephen J., ed. " 'I Am My Own Boss': A German Immigrant Writes from Illinois." *Journal of the Illinois State Historical Society* 54 (1961): 392-404. Three letters from Adolf von Aman of White County, dated 1828 and 1831.

621. Tunnell, Calvin. "Prowling Monsters of the Greene County Desert." *Journal of the Illinois State Historical Society* 55 (1962): 81-87. In a letter to his granddaughter, Tunnell describes life on the frontier in 1819.

622. Washburne, Elihu B. "Letter of E. B. Washburne to John Dixon." *Journal of the Illinois State Historical Society* 6 (1913-14): 214-31. The letter, dated 15 December 1874, consists of reminiscences of pioneer life and early settlers in northwestern Illinois.

623. Wright, Erastus. "He Had His 'Dish Right Side Up.' " *Journal of the Illinois State Historical Society* 47 (1954): 91-94. In letters of 1826 and 1827, Springfield merchant Erastus Wright describes such varied subjects as a hanging, land sales, his new home, and a threatened Indian war. Original manuscript owned by Lincoln College, Lincoln, Illinois.

7. Intellectual Life and Education

624. Baker, Clara Martin. "Books in a Pioneer Household." *Journal of the Illinois State Historical Society* 32 (1939): 261-87.

625. Bone, Robert E. "Rock Creek Lyceum." *Journal of the Illinois State Historical Society* 19 (1926-27): 63-76.

626. Bone, Robert Gehlmann. "Education in Illinois before 1857." *Journal of the Illinois State Historical Society* 50 (1957): 119-40. Both public-school education and the development of early teachers' colleges (first called Normal Universities).

627. Burtschi, Mary. *James Hall of Lincoln's Frontier World.* Vandalia, Ill.: The Little Brick House, 1977.

628. Chase, Philander. "Selected Letters from the Bishop Chase Correspondence." Edited by David R. Pichaske. *Western Illinois Regional Studies* 5 (1982): 105-35. Several of the letters concern Chase's fund-raising and planning for Jubilee College. The letters printed are from the Cullom-Davis Library at Bradley University; other Chase letters are in the Kenyon College Archives.

629. Congdon, Harriet Rice. "The Early History of Monticello Seminary." *Transactions of the Illinois State Historical Society, 1924*, pp. 58-63. Traces the history of the seminary from its founding in 1838 to 1857.

630. Eversole, Mildred, ed. "Canton College: An Early Attempt at Higher Education in Illinois." *Journal of the Illinois State Historical Society* 34 (1941): 334-43. A brief history of the short-lived college, with letters of 1836, by Joel Wright, a trustee, and of 1838, by N. W. Dewey, a professor. The original letters are in the Illinois State Historical Library.

631. Flanagan, John T. "The Destruction of an Early Illinois Library." *Journal of the Illinois State Historical Society* 49 (1956): 387-93. The library of John Mason Peck, which the author calls probably "the most important" in the state at the time, was destroyed by fire in 1852. Peck describes many of its contents in a letter to John Russell of 12 November 1852, which is reproduced.

632. _____. *James Hall, Literary Pioneer of the Ohio Valley.* Minneapolis: University of Minnesota Press, 1941. A good survey of Hall's literary significance.

633. _____. "James Hall, Pioneer Vandalia Editor and Publicist." *Journal of the Illinois State Historical Society* 48 (1955): 119-36.

634. _____. "James Hall and the Antiquarian and Historical Society of Illinois." *Journal of the Illinois State Historical Society* 34 (1941): 439-52. The society survived only a short time after its founding in 1827.

635. Hall, James. "The Autobiography of James Hall, Western Literary Pioneer." Edited by David Donald. *Ohio State Archaeological and Historical Quarterly* 56 (1947): 295-304. Hall discusses his literary and legal work in Illinois.

636. Hallwas, John E. "Illinois Poetry: The Lincoln Era." *Selected Papers in Illinois History, 1981.* Springfield: Illinois State Historical Society, 1982. Pp. 15-23.

637. _____, ed. *The Poems of H.: The Lost Poet of Lincoln's Springfield.* Peoria, Ill.: Ellis Press, 1982. A good literary detective story as well as a collection of poems from the man who had seventy poems published in a Springfield newspaper, 1831-46.

638. Hildner, Ernest G. "Colleges and College Life in Illinois One Hundred Years Ago." *Transactions of the Illinois State Historical Society, 1942*, pp. 19-31.

639. *Illinois Monthly Magazine.* 2 vols. (October 1830--September 1832). All knowledge was within the purview of this literary magazine, edited by James Hall. It contained articles on Illinois environment and geology, Illinois towns, Indian relations, foreign affairs, and medicine, as well as poetry and fiction.

640. Jamison, Isabel. "Literature and Literary People of Early Illinois." *Transactions of the Illinois State Historical Society, 1908*, pp. 123-39.

641. Johannsen, Robert W. "History on the Illinois Frontier: Early Efforts to Preserve the State's Past." *Journal of the Illinois State Historical Society* 68 (1975): 121-42. The first (short-lived) state historical society was founded in 1827 at Vandalia. There, on the frontier, it was one of several programs and organizations that reflected the lively intellectual life of the community.

642. Kaufman, Polly Welts. *Women Teachers on the Frontier.* New Haven: Yale University Press, 1984. Includes letters from two women who taught in Illinois in the 1850s. A chart gives biographical information about 224 women teachers sent west by the National Popular Education Board; many of them taught in Illinois. Based on formidable research.

643. Kindig, Everett W. " 'I Am in Purgatory Now': Journalist Hooper Warren Survives the Illinois Frontier." *Illinois Historical Journal* 79 (1986): 185-96. The hand-to-mouth life of a frontier editor and the precarious existence of several early newspapers.

644. McClelland, Clarence Paul. "The Education of Females in Early Illinois." *Journal of the Illinois State Historical Society* 36 (1943): 378-407. Establishment of seminaries and colleges for women.

645. McDermott, John Francis. "The Library of John Hay of Cahokia and Belleville." Missouri Historical Society's *Glimpses of the Past* 9 (1952-53): 183-86. The appraisal of Hay's estate, dated 9 December 1842 in St. Clair County, listed more than 250 volumes in his library.

646. Monaghan, Jay. "Literary Opportunities in Pioneer Times." *Journal of the Illinois State Historical Society* 33 (1940): 412-37. Literature available during the first half of the nineteenth century.

647. Moore, Ensley. "A Notable Illinois Family." *Transactions of the Illinois State Historical Society, 1907*, pp. 315-23. Members of the Goudy family were printers and publishers in Jacksonville.

648. Nortrup, Jack. "College Letters of Samuel Willard." *Journal of the Illinois State Historical Society* 66 (1973): 444-54. Letters from Illinois College in the 1830s and 1840s. The originals are in the Illinois State Historical Library.

649. _____. "The Troubles of an Itinerant Teacher in the Early Nineteenth Century." *Journal of the Illinois State Historical Society* 71 (1978): 279-87. Based on the Samuel Willard Papers in the Illinois State Historical Library, this article recounts the teaching experiences and day-to-day life of teacher Frances Langdon Willard, who moved to Illinois in 1835 and in 1836 opened the first of several private schools she was to establish.

650. Peck, John Mason. "Letters by John Mason Peck." Edited by John T. Flanagan. *Journal of the Illinois State Historical Society* 47 (1954): 264-99. The letters, addressed to John Russell, are now in the Russell Papers in the Illinois State Historical Library. The letters concern Russell's and Peck's mutual interests in writing and publishing, education, and religion.

651. Pichaske, David R. "Jubilee College: Bishop Chase's School of Prophets." *Old Northwest* 2 (1976): 281-97. In 1835 Philander Chase started planning for the college, which was in operation 1840-62. It is now a state historic site.

652. Pratt, Harry Edward. "Peter Cartwright and the Cause of Education." *Journal of the Illinois State Historical Society* 28, no. 4 (January 1936): 271-78. Work of the pioneer minister on behalf of schools.

653. _____. "The Springfield Mechanics Union, 1839-1848." *Journal of the Illinois State Historical Society* 34 (1941): 130-34. The union was typical of organizations formed in this era for the self-improvement of members and the education of their children. It offered literary and political lectures, provided charitable assistance to its members, and established a private school.

654. Randall, Randolph C. *James Hall, Spokesman of the New West.* Columbus: Ohio State University Press, 1964. Detailed, scholarly biography.

655. Schwartz, Thomas F. "The Springfield Lyceums and Lincoln's 1838 Speech." *Illinois Historical Journal* 83 (1990): 45-49. Primarily a history of the lyceum movement and the two lyceums in Sangamon County.

656. Shultz, Esther. "James Hall in Shawneetown." *Journal of the Illinois State Historical Society* 22 (1929-30): 388-400; "James Hall in Vandalia," ibid. 23 (1930): 92-112.

657. Starke, Aubrey. "Books in the Wilderness." *Journal of the Illinois State Historical Society* 28, no. 4 (January 1936): 258-70.

658. Stevens, Frank Everett. "Hooper Warren." *Journal of the Illinois State Historical Society* 4 (1911-12): 271-87. Warren was a strong abolitionist who edited several newspapers in early statehood days.

659. Still, Bayrd. "Evidences of the 'Higher Life' on the Frontier: As Illustrated in the History of Cultural Matters in Chicago, 1830 to 1850." *Journal of the Illinois State Historical Society* 28, no. 2 (July 1935): 81-99. Libraries, theatre, music, public lectures, public schools, newspapers, etc.

660. Taylor, Richard S. "Western Colleges as 'Securities of Intelligence & Virtue': The Towne-Eddy Report of 1846." *Old Northwest* 7 (1981): 41-65. Joseph Towne and Ansel Eddy went to Illinois for the Western College Society to report on the colleges it helped support--including Illinois College and a previously unsuccessful applicant for financial assistance, Knox College.

661. Travous, R. Louise. "Pioneer Illinois Library." *Journal of the Illinois State Historical Society* 42 (1949): 446-53. Catalog of the 216 books in the Edwardsville library in 1819 and a history of the library to 1825.

8. Internal Improvements

662. Boritt (Borit), Gabor S. "Lincoln and Taxation during His Illinois Legislative Years." *Journal of the Illinois State Historical Society* 61 (1968):

365-73. Lincoln became an advocate of increased taxation to support the state's internal improvements program.

663. Bronson, Howard G. "Early Illinois Railroads: The Place of the Illinois Central Railroad in Illinois History Prior to the Civil War." *Transactions of the Illinois State Historical Society, 1908*, pp. 171-83.

664. Conzen, Michael P., and Carr, Kay J., eds. *The Illinois & Michigan Canal National Heritage Corridor: A Guide to Its History and Sources.* DeKalb: Northern Illinois University Press, 1988. A detailed, annotated bibliography related to all aspects of the corridor, in addition to four analytical essays, one by each of the editors and by G. Gray Fitzsimons and Gerald W. Adelmann, Jr.

665. Davis, John. "A Diary of the Illinois-Michigan Canal Investigation, 1843-1844." Edited by Guy A. Lee. *Transactions of the Illinois State Historical Society, 1941*, pp. 38-72.

666. Davis, John Chandler Bancroft. *Report upon the Condition, and Sources of Business of the Illinois Central Railroad, Made at the Request of the Board of Directors, by J. C. Bancroft Davis, January 26th, 1855.* New York: G. S. Roe, Printer, 1855.

667. Elazar, Daniel J. "Gubernatorial Power and the Illinois and Michigan Canal: A Study of Political Development in the Nineteenth Century." *Journal of the Illinois State Historical Society* 58 (1965): 396-423.

668. Fergus, Robert, comp. *Chicago River-and-Harbor Convention: An Account of Its Origin and Proceedings . . . together with Statistics concerning Chicago . . .* Fergus' Historical Series, no. 18. Chicago, 1882. The convention was held in July 1847.

669. Gates, Paul Wallace. "The Struggle for the Charter of the Illinois Central Railroad." *Transactions of the Illinois State Historical Society, 1933*, pp. 55-66.

670. Hardin, Thomas L. "The National Road in Illinois." *Journal of the Illinois State Historical Society* 60 (1967): 5-22. Between 1830 and 1840 the road was under construction from the Indiana line to Vandalia, where it ended.

671. Howard, Robert P. "The Great Canal Scrip Fraud: The Downfall of Governor Joel A. Matteson." *Selected Papers in Illinois History, 1980.* Springfield: Illinois State Historical Society, 1982. Pp. 25-30.

672. Illinois and Michigan Canal. *Documents Relating to the Negotiation Which Has Been Carried on with the Foreign Creditors of Illinois, for the Purpose of Raising Funds to Complete This Work* . . . Boston: Samuel N. Dickinson, Printer, 1844.

673. "The Importance of Steamboats." *Journal of the Illinois State Historical Society* 47 (1954): 426-28. A report from the *Galena Gazette* of 9 December 1837 describes commerce along the Galena levee throughout that year, and a report from the 28 April 1848 *Ottawa Gazette* describes traffic on the newly opened Illinois and Michigan Canal.

674. Kane, Lucile M.; Holmquist, June D.; and Gilman, Carolyn, eds. *The Northern Expeditions of Stephen H. Long: The Journals of 1817 and 1823 and Related Documents.* St. Paul: Minnesota Historical Society Press, 1978. Long crossed Illinois on his 1823 expedition, mapped the Chicago Portage, and recommended construction of a canal between the Illinois River and Lake Michigan.

675. Krenkel, John H. *Illinois Internal Improvements, 1818-1848.* Cedar Rapids, Iowa: Torch Press, 1958.

676. _____. "Internal Improvements in Illinois Politics, 1837-1842." *Mid-America* 31 (April 1949): 67-91.

677. Lamb, John Michael. "The Politics of Transportation: The History of a Political Conflict and Its Links to Railroad Development and the Illinois and Michigan Canal." *Selected Papers in Illinois History, 1980.* Springfield: Illinois State Historical Society, 1982. Pp. 17-24.

678. _____. *William Gooding: Chief Engineer, I. and M. Canal.* Lockport: Illinois Canal Society, 1982.

679. Lightner, David L. "Construction Labor on the Illinois Central Railroad." *Journal of the Illinois State Historical Society* 66 (1973): 285-301.

680. McCampbell, Coleman. "H. L. Kinney and Daniel Webster in Illinois in the 1830's." *Journal of the Illinois State Historical Society* 47 (1954): 35-44. Kinney was an entrepreneur, land speculator, and contractor for a portion of the Illinois and Michigan Canal. He entertained Daniel Webster when the latter visited his lands in Illinois.

681. McConnel, George M. "Recollections of the Northern Cross Railroad." *Transactions of the Illinois State Historical Society, 1908*, pp. 145-52.

682. Nettels, Curtis. "The Mississippi Valley and the Constitution, 1815-29." *Mississippi Valley Historical Review* 11 (1924-25): 332-57. Constitutional arguments and congressional actions in relation to internal improvements in the new frontier states.

683. Putnam, James William. *The Illinois and Michigan Canal: A Study in Economic History.* Illinois Centennial Publication. Chicago: University of Chicago Press, 1918.

684. Stratton, H. J. "The Northern Cross Railroad." *Journal of the Illinois State Historical Society* 28, no. 2 (July 1935): 5-52. Includes a good brief discussion of the other railroads authorized by the state's internal improvements act as well as the history of the Northern Cross.

685. Teaford, Jon C. "The State and Industrial Development: Public Power Development in the Old Northwest." *Old Northwest* 1 (March 1975): 11-34. Efforts of state leaders in Ohio, Indiana, and Illinois to further economic development through the creation and administration of new water power sources in the early nineteenth century. The author continues the story of canals through the early years of the twentieth century.

686. Weik, Jesse W. "An Unpublished Chapter in the Early History of Chicago." *Journal of the Illinois State Historical Society* 7, no. 4 (January 1915): 329-48. Weik recorded the reminiscences of James M. Bucklin, chief engineer for the Illinois and Michigan Canal.

687. Williams, Mentor L. "The Background of the Chicago Harbor and River Convention, 1847." *Mid-America* 19 n.s. (1948): 219-32.

688. _____. "The Chicago River and Harbor Convention, 1847." *Mississippi Valley Historical Review* 35 (1948-49): 607-26. The author also discusses the impetus the convention gave to the development of railroads.

9. Law and Lawlessness

689. Allaman, John Lee. "Greenbush Vigilantes: An Organizational Document." *Western Illinois Regional Studies* 10, no. 1 (Spring 1987): 32-41. The

"Greenbush Mutual Protecting Company" was organized in Warren County in 1850.

690. Ander, Oscar Fritiof. "Law and Lawlessness in Rock Island Prior to 1850." *Journal of the Illinois State Historical Society* 52 (1959): 526-43.

691. Bonney, Edward. *The Banditti of the Prairies: A Tale of the Mississippi Valley; An Authentic Narrative of Thrilling Adventures in the Early Settlement of the Western Country.* Chicago: D. B. Cooke, 1856. Probably the work of a ghostwriter, this volume tells how Bonney, a detective, tracked down the murderers of George Davenport, killed in 1845 at Rock Island. The author also discusses conflicts between the Mormons and their neighbors at Nauvoo.

692. Davis, Rodney O. "Judge Ford and the Regulators, 1841-1842." *Selected Papers in Illinois History, 1981.* Springfield: Illinois State Historical Society, 1982. Pp. 25-36.

693. Jones, Robert Huhn. "Three Days of Violence: The Regulators of the Rock River Valley." *Journal of the Illinois State Historical Society* 59 (1966): 131-42. In 1841 the "Regulators" were formed to fight the Driscoll gang of outlaws terrorizing northern Illinois.

694. Rose, James A. "The Regulators and Flatheads in Southern Illinois." *Transactions of the Illinois State Historical Society, 1906*, pp. 108-21. The Regulators were a vigilante group, formed in response to the inability of civil authorities to control crime; the criminals became known as the Flatheads.

695. Snively, W. D. Jr., and Furbee, Louanna. *Satan's Ferryman: A True Tale of the Old Frontier.* New York: Ungar, 1968. A scholarly study of James Ford and William Potts and the crimes they were accused of perpetrating on the Ford's Ferry Road along the Ohio River.

10. Manners and Customs

696. Bloom, Arthur W. "Tavern Theatre in Early Chicago." *Journal of the Illinois State Historical Society* 74 (1981): 217-29.

697. Briggs, Harold E., and Briggs, Ernestine B. "The Early Theatre in Chicago." *Journal of the Illinois State Historical Society* 39 (1946): 165-78.

698. _____. "The Early Theatre in the Upper Mississippi Valley." *Mid-America* 31 (1949): 131-62. Contains information on theatre in Galena in the 1830s.

699. Briggs, Harold E. "Entertainment and Amusement in Cairo, 1848-1858." *Journal of the Illinois State Historical Society* 47 (1954): 231-51.

700. Brown, Caroline Owsley. "Springfield Society before the Civil War." *Journal of the Illinois State Historical Society* 15 (1922-23): 477-500. Contains many anecdotes about prominent state political figures.

701. Clinton, Katherine B. "Pioneer Women in Chicago, 1833-1837." *Journal of the West* 12 (1973): 317-24.

702. Cole, Arthur Charles. "Illinois Women of the Middle Period." *Journal of the Illinois State Historical Society* 13 (1920-21): 312-23. Discussion of women's suffrage, temperance, and philanthropic and professional activities in the 1840s and 1850s.

703. "Correspondence from the First State Fair." *Journal of the Illinois State Historical Society* 43 (1950): 62-67. Reports from the *New York Tribune* of 1853.

704. Dale, Edward Everett. "The Food of the Frontier." *Journal of the Illinois State Historical Society* 40 (1947): 38-61.

705. Doolittle, Clara Matteson. "An Illinois First Family: The Reminiscences of Clara Matteson Doolittle." Edited by James T. Hickey. *Journal of the Illinois State Historical Society* 69 (1976): 3-16. Charming reminiscences by a daughter of Governor Joel Matteson's. She recalls life in the old house used by the governor, then in the present Executive Mansion, which was built during her father's term, and finally in the family's own palatial home across the street from the Executive Mansion. She also describes her brother's death of typhoid fever in an army camp during the Civil War.

706. Duncan, Elizabeth Caldwell Smith. "Diary of Mrs. Joseph Duncan . . ." Edited by Elizabeth Duncan Putnam. *Journal of the Illinois State Historical Society* 21 (1928-29): 1-92. Entries for 1841-48 describe the day-to-day life of a well-connected woman in Jacksonville. The original diary is in the Davenport (Iowa) Public Museum.

707. Flanagan, John T. "Hunting in Early Illinois." *Journal of the Illinois State Historical Society* 72 (1979): 2-12.

708. Ghent, Jocelyn Maynard. "The Golden Dream and the Press: Illinois and the California Gold Rush of '49." *Journal of the West* 17 (April 1978): 17-27.

709. Hickey, James T. "The Lincoln's Globe Tavern: A Study in Tracing the History of a Nineteenth-Century Building." *Journal of the Illinois State Historical Society* 56 (1963): 629-53. The author discusses the Lincolns' life at Globe Tavern, as well as the social life of Springfield that centered on the tavern in the years 1835-54.

710. Jamison, Isabel. "The First Official Thanksgiving in Illinois." *Journal of the Illinois State Historical Society* 11 (1918-19): 370-78. The year was 1842.

711. Kane, Charles P. "Wedding of the First White Couple in the Territory Which Became the County of Sangamon." *Transactions of the Illinois State Historical Society, 1906*, pp. 57-64. Philo Beers and Martha Stillman were married in 1820.

712. Lee County Columbian Club, comp. *Recollections of the Pioneers of Lee County.* Dixon, Ill.: Inez A. Kennedy, 1893.

713. O'Ryan, Mary Ann. "A Tale of Two Women: Life in the Old Northwest, 1830-1835." *Transactions of the Illinois State Historical Society: Selected Papers from the Seventh Annual History Symposium and the Eighth Annual History Symposium* [1986 and 1987]. Springfield, 1989. Pp. 27-34. Social life and customs in Chicago. The two women were Eliza Chappell and Juliette Kinzie.

714. Parrish, Braxton. "Pioneer Preacher's Autobiography." *Journal of the Illinois State Historical Society* 49 (1956): 424-31. Reminiscences of pioneer life in Franklin County by a man who was both a Methodist minister and long-term state legislator.

715. Pond, Fern Nance, ed. "New Salem Community Activities: Documentary." *Journal of the Illinois State Historical Society* 48 (1955): 82-101. The editor presents minutes and other records of a literary society and a prohibition society of the early 1830s.

716. *Quincy Whig*, 9 July 1845.   An extract describing a Fourth of July celebration is reprinted in the *Journal of the Illinois State Historical Society* 34 (1941): 256.

717. Rezab, Gordana, ed. "The Memoir of William T. Brooking, McDonough County Pioneer: Part 1." *Western Illinois Regional Studies* 4 (1981): 5-24. The family came to Macomb in 1834.

718. _____. "The Memoir of William T. Brooking, McDonough County Pioneer. Part 2." *Western Illinois Regional Studies* 4 (1981): 136-51. Covers the years 1844-54, and his militia service in the so-called Mormon War.

719. Riley, Glenda. "The 'Female Frontier' in Early Illinois." *Mid-America* 67 (1985): 69-89. Life on the frontier based on letters and books written by frontier women.

720. Swingley, Upton. "Gold Rush Fever Hits Mount Morris." *Journal of the Illinois State Historical Society* 42 (1949): 457-62. Includes reminiscences of growing up in Ogle County, 1839-50, as well as of going to California in 1850.

721. Wilmeth, Don B. "The MacKenzie-Jefferson Theatrical Company in Galena, 1838-1839." *Journal of the Illinois State Historical Society* 60 (1967): 23-36.

11. Military Affairs

722. Allaman, John Lee. "Uniforms and Equipment of the Black Hawk War and the Mormon War." *Western Illinois Regional Studies* 13, no. 1 (Spring 1990): 5-18.

723. Anderson, Robert. "Robert Anderson to E. B. Washburne." *Journal of the Illinois State Historical Society* 10 (1917-18): 422-28. In this letter of 10 May 1870 Anderson recalls his experiences in the Black Hawk War.

724. Armstrong, Perry A. *The Sauks and the Black Hawk War, with Biographical Sketches, etc.* Springfield, Ill.: H. W. Rokker, 1887. Colorful, but undocumented, narrative. Despite the title there are biographical sketches of only four Native Americans and nine white men prominent in the Black Hawk War.

725. Barbour, James. *Letter from the Secretary of War Transmitting the Information Required by a Resolution of the House of Representatives . . . in*

Relation to the Hostile Disposition of Indian Tribes on the Northwestern Frontier. 21 May 1828. U.S. Congress. House. 20th Cong., 1 sess. H. Doc. 277 (serial 175). Washington, 1828. Enclosures report on the so-called Winnebago War of 1827 and the likelihood of further difficulties in 1828.

726. Beckwith, Hiram W., ed. *The Winnebago Scare.* Fergus' Historical Series, no. 10. Chicago, 1877. The narrative of Hezekiah Cunningham, as edited by Beckwith.

727. Bishop, W. W., comp. *A Journal of the Twelve Months Campaign of Gen. Shields' Brigade, in Mexico, in the Years 1846-7. Compiled from Notes of Lieutenants J. J. Adams & H. C. Dunbar.* St. Louis: Cathcart, Prescott,1847. Bishop was a captain in the 3d Regiment of Illinois Volunteers.

728. "A Black Hawk War Payroll." *Journal of the Illinois State Historical Society* 47 (1954): 411-13. Description of procedures for paying volunteer soldiers, and specific amounts paid to Captain Elijah Iles's company, which included Abraham Lincoln (one of three companies in which Lincoln served in the war).

729. Burton, C. M., comp. and ed. "The Black Hawk War: Papers of Gen. John R. Williams." *Collections and Researches Made by the Michigan Pioneer and Historical Society* 21 (1902): 313-471. The papers are related to the movements of Michigan Territory volunteers during the war.

730. Canaday, Dayton W. "Voice of the Volunteer of 1847." *Journal of the Illinois State Historical Society* 44 (1951): 199-209. Story of the *Picket Guard*, a camp newspaper published in Saltillo, Mexico, in 1847. Six of the paper's seven issues are in the Illinois State Historical Library.

731. Cooke, Philip St. George. *Scenes and Adventures in the Army, or Romance of Military Life.* Philadelphia: Lindsay & Blakiston, 1857. In chapters 22-27, Cooke, an officer in the 6th United States Infantry, outlines his movements in the Black Hawk War.

732. "Earliest Known Lincoln--Black Hawk War Discharge." *Journal of the Illinois State Historical Society* 52 (1959): 544-46. Discussion of the discharge written and signed by Captain Lincoln 24 July 1832. From the collections of the Illinois State Historical Library.

733. Eby, Cecil. *"That Disgraceful Affair," the Black Hawk War.* New York: Norton, 1973. An exciting, dramatic account of the frontier conflict. The author goes too far in debunking frontier heroes, depends too heavily on nineteenth-century writers, and has little ethnographical background.

734. Ehinger, Augustus Frederic. "Diary of the Travels of Augustus Ehinger." Edited by Charles F. Ward. Typescript. Roswell, N.M., 1978? The diarist was a member of Company H, 2d Regiment, Illinois Volunteers.

735. Engelmann, Adolph. "The Second Illinois in the Mexican War: Mexican War Letters of Adolph Engelmann, 1846-1847." Translated and edited by Otto B. Engelmann. *Journal of the Illinois State Historical Society* 26 (1933-34): 357-452.

736. Everett, Edward. "A Narrative of Military Experience in Several Capacities." *Transactions of the Illinois State Historical Society, 1905*, pp. 179-236. The author was a member of a Quincy rifle company that was called to active duty during the so-called Mormon War. The author also describes his service in the Mexican War and the Civil War.

737. Flint, Timothy. *Indian Wars of the West; Containing Biographical Sketches of Those Pioneers Who Headed the Western Settlers in Repelling the Attacks of the Savages, together with a View of the Character, Manners, Monuments, and Antiquities of the Western Indians.* Cincinnati: E. H. Flint, 1833. Chapter 14, on the Black Hawk War, is a typical contemporary diatribe against the Sauk and Fox Indians.

738. Hagan, William T. "The Dodge-Henry Controversy." *Journal of the Illinois State Historical Society* 50 (1957): 377-84. The controversy--between supporters of Henry Dodge of Michigan Territory and James D. Henry of Illinois--about the predominant leader in bringing the 1832 Black Hawk War to a conclusion is resolved in favor of Dodge.

739. _____. "General Henry Atkinson and the Militia." *Military Affairs* 23 (1959): 194-97. In this brief history of the Black Hawk War, Hagan concludes that Atkinson was too cautious and conservative in commanding the militia.

740. Hall, Thomas B. *Medicine on the Santa Fe Trail.* Dayton, Ohio: Morningside Bookshop, 1971. Medical history of the 1st Regiment, Illinois Infantry, en route to Santa Fe in the Mexican War.

741. Hauberg, John H. "The Black Hawk War, 1831-1832." *Transactions of the Illinois State Historical Society, 1932*, pp. 91-134.

742. Henderson, Alfred J. "A Morgan County Volunteer in the Mexican War." *Journal of the Illinois State Historical Society* 41 (1948): 383-401. Based on the letters of John B. Duncan, an attorney in Jacksonville.

743. Hendrickson, Walter B., ed. "The Happy Soldier: The Mexican War Letters of John Nevin King." *Journal of the Illinois State Historical Society* 46 (1953): 13-27, 151-70. King served first in a Sangamon County company of volunteers and later in the quartermaster's department. The letters printed here, and many others, are now in the King Family Papers in the Illinois State Historical Library.

744. Hilyard, James Powell. "Sixty Years in the West." Typescript, 1980, by Mrs. Dale A. Hilyard, in the Illinois State Historical Library. Hilyard served with the 4th Regiment, Illinois Infantry, in the Mexican War. The reminiscences also contain graphic accounts of pioneer life.

745. Illinois. Adjutant General's Office. *Records of the Service of Illinois Soldiers in the Black Hawk War, 1831-32, and in the Mexican War, 1846-8 . . . with an Appendix Giving a Record of the Services of the Illinois Militia, Rangers, and Riflemen, in Protecting the Frontier from the Ravages of the Indians from 1810 to 1813.* Springfield: H. W. Rokker, 1882. More complete rosters of Black Hawk War troops are in no. 772.

746. Jackson, Donald, and Peterson, William J. "The Black Hawk War." *Palimpsest* 43 (1962): 65-112.

747. Jamison, Isabel. "Independent Military Companies of Sangamon County in the 30's." *Journal of the Illinois State Historical Society*, vol. 3, no. 4 (January 1911): 22-48.

748. Lambert, Joseph I. "The Black Hawk War." *Journal of the Illinois State Historical Society* 32 (1939): 442-73. An account by a United States Cavalry officer.

749. McCall, George A. *Letters from the Frontiers, Written during a Period of Thirty Years' Service in the Army of the United States.* Philadelphia: Lippincott, 1868. Includes documents and reminiscences about the 1831 campaign against Black Hawk.

750. Matson, Nehemiah. *Memories of Shaubena with Incidents Relating to the Early Settlement of the West.* Chicago: D. B. Cooke, 1878. Accounts of the life of the Potawatomi leader and the Black Hawk War. A fuller account, with a slightly different title--*Memories of Shaubena, with Incidents Relating to Indian Wars and the Early Settlement*--was published in Chicago by R. Grainger in 1882. Still valuable for frontier attitudes and obscure information, although dated, unannotated, and often inaccurate.

751. Myers, Lee. "Illinois Volunteers in New Mexico, 1847-1848." *New Mexico Historical Review* 47 (1972): 5-32.

752. Newlands, R. W. "The Black Hawk War: An Account of the Discovery of the Graves of the Men Who Fell in the 'Battle of Stillman's Run,' on May 14, 1832." *Transactions of the Illinois State Historical Society, 1901*, pp. 117-20. The site was excavated in 1899, and the General Assembly authorized a monument at the site in 1901.

753. Nichols, Roger L. *Black Hawk and the Warrior's Path*. American Biographical History Series. Arlington Heights, Ill.: Harlan Davidson, 1992. Not annotated but has excellent critical bibliography.

754. _____. "The Black Hawk War in Retrospect." *Wisconsin Magazine of History* 65 (1981-82): 238-46.

755. Powell, William. "William Powell's Recollections, in an Interview with Lyman C. Draper." *Proceedings of the State Historical Society of Wisconsin . . . 1912* . Madison, 1913. Pp. 146-79. Includes Powell's recollections with a company of Menominee called into United States service in the Black Hawk War.

756. Prince, Ezra M. "The Fourth Illinois Infantry in the War with Mexico." *Transactions of the Illinois State Historical Society, 1906*, pp. 172-87.

757. Quaife, Milo Milton. "The Northwestern Career of Jefferson Davis." *Transactions of the Illinois State Historical Society, 1923*. pp. 58-69. Not dependable; for example, Quaife is incorrect in his assertion that Davis was with his regiment of regulars during the 1832 campaign against Black Hawk.

758. Roland, Charles P. *Albert Sidney Johnston, Soldier of Three Republics*. Austin: University of Texas Press, 1964. Chapter 3 deals with the Black Hawk War.

759. Rooney, Elizabeth B. "The Story of the Black Hawk War." *Wisconsin Magazine of History* 40 (1957): 274-83.

760. "Saltillo." *Journal of the Illinois State Historical Society* 42 (1949): 467-68. Extracts from a soldiers' newspaper, the *Picket Guard*, describe camp life in Saltillo, Mexico.

761. Scanlan, P. L. "The Military Record of Jefferson Davis in Wisconsin." *Wisconsin Magazine of History* 24 (1940-41): 174-82. The author accounts for Davis's whereabouts during the 1831 and 1832 campaigns against Black Hawk.

762. Scott, Winfield. *Memoirs of Lieut.-General Scott, LL.D.* 2 vols. New York: Sheldon, 1864. Chapter 18 is Scott's account of his service in the Black Hawk War.

763. Smith, Henry. *The Expedition against the Sauk and Fox Indians, 1832.* New York, 1914. Reprinted from the *Military and Naval Magazine of the United States*, August 1833. Smith was a regular army captain in General Henry Atkinson's command and a participant in the march against Black Hawk.

764. Stark, William F. *Along the Black Hawk Trail.* Sheboygan, Wis.: Zimmermann Press, 1984. The author followed Black Hawk's trail during the Black Hawk War and has produced both a history of the war and an illustrated guide for others to follow. There are photographs of signs, monuments, markers, artifacts, and landscapes connected with the war.

765. Stevens, Frank Everett. *The Black Hawk War.* Chicago: F. E. Stevens, 1903. Marred by obvious bias against the Indians, though based on the many contemporary documents he amassed (some reprinted).

766. _____. "A Forgotten Hero: James Dougherty Henry." *Transactions of the Illinois State Historical Society, 1934*, pp. 77-120. Henry was considered a hero by his contemporaries for his service in the Black Hawk War.

767. Tennery, Thomas D. *The Mexican War Diary of Thomas D. Tennery.* Edited by D. E. Livingston-Little. Norman: University of Oklahoma Press, 1970. Tennery served in the 4th Illinois Infantry.

768. Thayer, Crawford Beecher, comp. and ed. *Hunting a Shadow: The Search for Black Hawk.* An Eye-Witness Account of the Black Hawk War of 1832. Published privately, 1981. A chronological account with extracts from a single original document reprinted under many dates. This volume includes the dates 1 July--24 July 1832. In the Eyewitness series, the author also published *The Battle of Wisconsin Heights*, 1983, and *Massacre at Bad Axe*, 1984.

769. Thomas, William. "The Winnebago 'War' of 1827." *Transactions of the Illinois State Historical Society, 1907*, pp. 265-69. Thomas was quartermaster sergeant of the regiment ordered to Galena to protect the frontier from expected Winnebago hostilities that never materialized. The regiment marched to southern Wisconsin without seeing any Indians.

770. Thwaites, Reuben Gold. "The Story of the Black Hawk War." *Collections of the State Historical Society of Wisconsin* 12 (1892): 216-65.

771. Wakefield, John Allen. *History of the War between the United States and Sac and Fox Indians and Other Disaffected Tribes of Indians in the Years Eighteen Hundred and Twenty-seven, Thirty-one, and Thirty-two.* Jacksonville, Ill.: C. Goudy, 1834. Reprint, edited by Frank Everett Stevens, Chicago: Caxton Club, 1908. The 1827 episode was the Winnebago War.

772. Whitney, Ellen M., comp. and ed. *The Black Hawk War, 1831-32.* Vol. 1: *Illinois Volunteers*; introduction by Anthony F. C. Wallace. Vol. 2 (in 3 pts.): *Letters and Papers.* Collections of the Illinois State Historical Library, vols. 35-38. Springfield, 1970-78. The introduction, "Prelude to Disaster," also separately published, provides an ethnohistorical background to the Black Hawk War with the Sauk and Fox Indians. Accompanying the letters and papers in volume 2 are biographical sketches of the letter-writers and people mentioned in the letters.

773. Young, Otis E. "The United States Mounted Ranger Battalion, 1832-1833." *Mississippi Valley Historical Review* 41 (1954-55): 453-70. Predecessor of the 1st Dragoons (later the 1st Cavalry), the battalion included two companies raised in Illinois--Captain Jesse B. Browne's at Danville and Captain Matthew Duncan's at Vandalia. Several of the companies patrolled northern Illinois and southern Wisconsin in late 1832 and 1833 to guard against hostilities with the Winnebago.

12. Politics and Government

a. In General

774. Alvord, Clarence Walworth., ed. *Governor Edward Coles.* Collections of the Illinois State Historical Library, vol. 15. Springfield, 1920. Contains the *Sketch of Edward Coles*, by Elihu B. Washburne, originally published by the Chicago Historical Society in 1882, and a collection of original documents by and about Coles. A calendar of papers, 1797-1858, lists the documents in both the Washburne *Sketch* and the appendixes.

775. Angle, Paul McClelland, ed. "The Early Settlers: A Realistic Picture." *Journal of the Illinois State Historical Society* 37 (1944): 266-69. A letter from attorney Benjamin Willis, 26 December 1834 (in the Illinois State Historical Library), offers succinct descriptions of the state's political leaders as well as of the town of Quincy.

776. _____. "The Peoria Truce." *Journal of the Illinois State Historical Society* 21 (1928-29): 500-505. Angle debunks the two-part tale that Abraham Lincoln and Stephen A. Douglas agreed not to make further political speeches after 16 October 1854 and that Douglas broke the truce.

777. Branz, Nedra, and Lawrence, Barbara. "A Prairie Farmer and Loco Focos, Speculators, Nullifiers &c. &c." *Old Northwest* 9 (1983-84): 345-66. Letters (1828-51) between Gershom Flagg of Illinois and a variety of correspondents illustrate the depth of political knowledge of one Illinois farmer. Flagg was also an informative commentator on social life and customs of the frontier. The original letters are in the Lovejoy Library, Southern Illinois University at Edwardsville.

778. Bray, Robert. "The Cartwright-Lincoln Acquaintance." *Old Northwest* 13 (1987): 111-30. The early acquaintance of Peter Cartwright and Abraham Lincoln stemmed from their campaigns for the legislature in 1832. Lincoln later successfully defended Cartwright's grandson on a murder charge.

779. Caton, John Dean. *Early Bench and Bar of Illinois.* Chicago: Chicago Legal News, 1893. A reminiscence of courts, cases, and lawyers, rather than a presentation of biographies.

780. Cole, Arthur Charles, ed. *The Constitutional Debates of 1847.* Collections of the Illinois State Historical Library, vol. 14. Springfield, 1919. An appendix has biographical sketches of convention members.

781. Danbom, David B. "The Young America Movement." *Journal of the Illinois State Historical Society* 67 (1974): 294-306. A coalition of young Democrats, primarily active 1849-53, who were strong supporters of Stephen A. Douglas.

782. Davidson, Martha McNiell. "Southern Illinois and Neighboring States at the Whig Convention of 1840." *Transactions of the Illinois State Historical Society, 1914*, pp. 150-59. The convention met at Springfield in June.

783. Davis, Rodney O. "Lobbying and the Third House in the Early Illinois General Assembly." *Old Northwest* 14 (1988-89): 267-84. Lobbyists of the era 1821-55, often members of the state's judiciary, constituted the so-called "Third House."

784. _____. " 'The People in Miniature': The Illinois General Assembly, 1818-1848." *Illinois Historical Journal* 81 (1988): 95-108. An analytical study of the legislature's increasing power and the consequent public dissatisfaction that led to the constitutional convention of 1847.

785. East, Ernest Edward. "The 'Peoria Truce': Did Douglas Ask for Quarter?" *Journal of the Illinois State Historical Society* 29 (1936-37): 70-75. An examination of contemporary newspapers shows that there was no truce between Lincoln and Douglas not to give speeches after 16 October 1854.

786. Fehrenbacher, Don E. "The Post Office in Illinois Politics of the 1850's." *Journal of the Illinois State Historical Society* 46 (1953): 60-70.

787. Greene, Evarts Boutell, and Alvord, Clarence Walworth, eds. *The Governors' Letter-Books, 1818-1834.* Collections of the Illinois State Historical Library, vol. 4. Springfield, 1909.

788. Greene, Evarts Boutell, and Thompson, Charles Manfred, eds. *Governors' Letter-Books, 1840-1853.* Collections of the Illinois State Historical Library, vol. 7. Springfield, 1911.

789. Harris, Gibson. "Three Letters from a Lincoln Law Student." Edited by Roger D. Bridges. *Journal of the Illinois State Historical Society* 66 (1973): 79-87. Harris discusses politics and the Lincoln-Herndon law office, where he read law in 1846. Photocopies of the letters are in the Illinois State Historical Library.

790. Herriott, F. I. "Senator Stephen A. Douglas and the Germans in 1854." *Transactions of the Illinois State Historical Society, 1912*, pp. 142-58.

791. Jamison, Isabel. "The Young Men's Convention and Old Soldiers' Meeting at Springfield, June 3-4, 1840." *Transactions of the Illinois State Historical Society, 1914*, pp. 160-71. The meetings mentioned in the title were preliminary to the statewide Whig convention at Springfield in June, of which a detailed account is given.

792. Kelly, Edith Packard. "Northern Illinois in the Great Whig Convention of 1840." *Transactions of the Illinois State Historical Society, 1914*, pp. 137-49.

793. King, Ameda Ruth. "The Last Years of the Whig Party in Illinois, 1847 to 1856." *Transactions of the Illinois State Historical Society, 1925*, pp. 108-54.

794. Leichtle, Kurt E. "The Rise of Jacksonian Politics in Illinois." *Illinois Historical Journal* 82 (1989): 93-107. The author shows how political leaders of the period 1822-31 were unable to adapt to the new national party system.

795. "Letters to Gustav Koerner, 1837-1863." *Transactions of the Illinois State Historical Society, 1907*, pp. 222-46. Letters from many of the state's political leaders.

796. Maidenbaum, Aryeh. "Sounds of Silence: An Aspect of Lincoln's Whig Years." *Illinois Historical Journal* 82 (1989): 167-76. Lincoln's positions on Mormon and abolitionist issues.

797. Pease, Theodore Calvin, ed. *Illinois Election Returns, 1818-1848.* Collections of the Illinois State Historical Library, vol. 18. Springfield, 1923. Returns are given for all state and national officers from Illinois.

798. Pratt, Harry Edward. "A Beginner on the Old Eighth Judicial Circuit." *Journal of the Illinois State Historical Society* 44 (1951): 241-48. Sketch of beginning attorney Leonard Swett and letters about his practice, 1849-54, in the Illinois State Historical Library.

799. Shankman, Arnold. "Partisan Conflicts, 1839-1841, and the Illinois Constitution." *Journal of the Illinois State Historical Society* 63 (1970): 336-67.

800. Sweet, William W. "Peter Cartwright in Illinois History." *Transactions of the Illinois State Historical Society, 1921*, pp. 116-23.

801. Thompson, Charles Manfred. "Elections and Election Machinery in Illinois, 1818-1848." *Journal of the Illinois State Historical Society* 7, no. 4 (January 1915): 379-88.

802. _____. "Genesis of the Whig Party in Illinois." *Transactions of the Illinois State Historical Society, 1912*, pp. 86-92.

803. _____. *The Illinois Whigs before 1846.* University of Illinois Studies in the Social Sciences, vol. 4, no. 1. Urbana, 1915.

804. Tingley, Donald Fred. "The Jefferson Davis--William H. Bissell Duel." *Mid-America* 38 (1956): 146-55. At the time of the threatened duel in 1850, Bissell was an Illinois representative in Congress and Davis was a senator from Mississippi. The affair was smoothed over before the duel arrangements were finalized.

805. "Turn About Is Fair Play." *Journal of the Illinois State Historical Society* 47 (1954): 191-92. A discussion of the agreement in the 1840s among three Whigs--Abraham Lincoln, John J. Hardin, and Edward D. Baker--not to campaign against each other for the Whig nomination for Congress, thereby giving each a turn.

806. Wilson, Terry. "The Business of a Midwestern Trial Court: Knox County, Illinois, 1841-1850." *Illinois Historical Journal* 84 (1991): 249-67.

807. Wilson, William. "Politics, 1840." *Journal of the Illinois State Historical Society* 33 (1940): 127-28. Letter of 4 June 1840 describing a mammoth Springfield rally for William Henry Harrison. Original in the Illinois State Historical Library.

b. Racism and the Antislavery Movement

808. Beecher, Edward. *Narrative of Riots at Alton, in Connection with the Death of Rev. Elijah P. Lovejoy. Alton, Ill. . . .* Alton, Ill.: G. Holton, 1838. Reprints, New York: Dutton, 1965, and New York: Haskell House, 1970. Merton Dillon calls this "probably the most eloquent defense of freedom of inquiry ever written in this country."

809. Berfield, Karen. "Three Antislavery Leaders of Bureau County." *Western Illinois Regional Studies* 3 (1980): 46-65. The three subjects are John Howard Bryant, Julian Bryant, and Owen Lovejoy.

810. Birkbeck, Morris. *An Appeal to the People of Illinois on the Question of a Convention.* Shawneetown, Ill.: C. Jones, 1823. Birkbeck opposed a constitutional convention, whose proponents hoped to legalize slavery in Illinois.

811. Bowen, A. L. "Antislavery Convention Held in Alton, Illinois, October 26-28, 1837." *Journal of the Illinois State Historical Society* 20 (1927-28): 329-56.

812. Bridges, Roger Dean, ed. "John Mason Peck on Illinois Slavery." *Journal of the Illinois State Historical Society* 75 (1982): 179-217. Articles by Peck called "Slavery in Illinois" appeared originally in 1847 and 1848; three articles titled "The Colored Population of Illinois" appeared in 1853. All are reprinted here.

813. Dillon, Merton Lynn. "Abolitionism Comes to Illinois." *Journal of the Illinois State Historical Society* 53 (1960): 389-403. Abolition sentiment in southern and central Illinois steadily gained momentum in the years 1831-55.

814. _____. "The Antislavery Movement in Illinois, 1824-1835." *Journal of the Illinois State Historical Society* 47 (1954): 149-66.

815. _____. *Elijah P. Lovejoy, Abolitionist Editor.* Urbana: University of Illinois Press, 1961. Lovejoy's death at the hands of an Alton mob in 1837 was a major influence in galvanizing abolitionists throughout the nation. Dillon presents analytical bibliographies for both the antislavery movement and Lovejoy.

816. _____. "John Mason Peck: A Study of Historical Rationalization." *Journal of the Illinois State Historical Society* 50 (1957): 385-90. Although the prominent clergyman-educator had opposed the abolitionists of the 1830s in Illinois, his later claims to have supported them have never been corroborated.

817. _____. "Sources of Early Antislavery Thought in Illinois." *Journal of the Illinois State Historical Society* 50 (1957): 36-50.

818. Dugan, Frank H. "An Illinois Martyrdom." *Transactions of the Illinois State Historical Society, 1938*, pp. 111-57. Account of the murder of abolitionist editor Elijah P. Lovejoy.

819. Gill, John G. "Elijah Lovejoy's Pledge of Silence." *Bulletin of the Missouri Historical Society* 14 (1957-58): 167-77.

820. _____. *Tide without Turning: Elijah P. Lovejoy and Freedom of the Press.* Boston: Starr King Press, 1958.

821. Jones, James Pickett. "The Illinois Negro Law of 1853: Racism in a Free State." *Illinois Quarterly* 40, no. 2 (Winter 1977): 5-22.

822. Jones, Stanley L. "John Wentworth and Anti-Slavery in Chicago to 1856." *Mid-America* 36 (1954): 147-60.

823. Kilby, Clyde S. "Three Antislavery Prisoners." *Journal of the Illinois State Historical Society* 52 (1959): 419-30. The later stories of three Illinois abolitionists who had been imprisoned in Missouri in the 1840s for their antislavery activities.

824. Kuhns, Frederick Irving. *The American Home Missionary Society in Relation to the Antislavery Controversy in the Old Northwest.* Billings, Mont.: The author, 1959.

825. Landon, Fred. "Benjamin Lundy in Illinois." *Journal of the Illinois State Historical Society* 33 (1940): 57-67. After Elijah Lovejoy's death, Lundy came to Illinois, where he published the abolitionist newspaper *Genius of Liberty.*

826. Lawrence, George A. "Benjamin Lundy, Pioneer of Freedom." *Journal of the Illinois State Historical Society* 6 (1913-14): 175-205.

827. Lincoln, William S. *Alton Trials . . . for a Riot Committed in Alton, on the Night of the 7th of November, 1837, in Unlawfully and Forcibly Entering the Warehouse of Godfrey, Gilman & Co., and Breaking up and Destroying a Printing Press; Written out from Notes Taken at the Time of Trial.* New York: John F. Trow, 1838.

828. Lovejoy, Joseph C., and Lovejoy, Owen. *Memoir of the Rev. Elijah P. Lovejoy, Who Was Murdered in Defence of the Liberty of the Press, at Alton, Illinois, Nov. 7, 1837.* New York: John S. Taylor, 1838. The authors were brothers of Elijah Lovejoy, and the first two thirds of the *Memoir* consists primarily of family letters. The remainder of the book is devoted to a tribute to Lovejoy and reports of antislavery activities and the trial of the rioters whose actions led to Lovejoy's death.

829. McCoy, Drew R. *The Last of the Fathers: James Madison and the Republican Legacy.* Cambridge: Cambridge University Press, 1989. On pages 311-28 the author discusses slavery as it related to Madison's young friend Edward Coles, who moved to Illinois in order to free his slaves and who often discussed the issue with Madison.

830. Muelder, Hermann R. *Fighters for Freedom: A History of Anti-Slavery Activities of Men and Women Associated with Knox College.* New York: Columbia University Press, 1959.

831. _____. "Galesburg, Hot-bed of Abolitionism." *Journal of the Illinois State Historical Society* 35 (1942): 216-35. History of antislavery activities, 1836-48.

832. Rammelkamp, Charles Henry. "Illinois College and the Antislavery Movement." *Transactions of the Illinois State Historical Society, 1908*, pp. 192-203.

833. Richardson, Eudora Ramsay. "The Virginian Who Made Illinois a Free State." *Journal of the Illinois State Historical Society* 45 (1952): 5-22. The Virginian was Edward Coles, who served as governor of Illinois, 1822-26.

834. Silbey, Joel H. "The Slavery-Extension Controversy and Illinois Congressmen, 1846-50." *Journal of the Illinois State Historical Society* 58 (1965): 378-95.

835. Simon, Paul. *Lovejoy: Martyr to Freedom.* St. Louis: Concordia Publishing House, 1964.

836. Spencer, Donald S. "Edward Coles: Virginia Gentleman in Frontier Politics." *Journal of the Illinois State Historical Society* 61 (1968): 150-63.

837. Stevens, Wayne Edson. "The Shaw-Hansen Election Contest: An Episode of the Slavery Contest." *Journal of the Illinois State Historical Society* 7, no. 4 (January 1915): 389-401. The contested election for state representative between Nicholas Hansen and John Shaw was decided by the legislature in favor of Shaw in order to gain the two-thirds vote necessary to call for a referendum in 1824 for a constitutional convention, which was expected to be proslavery. The convention was voted down.

838. Sutton, Robert Mize. "Edward Coles and the Constitutional Crisis in Illinois, 1822-1824." *Illinois Historical Journal* 82 (1989): 33-46. A sketch of the cultivated Virginian who moved to Illinois, freed his slaves, and continued to work against the legalization of slavery in his new home. In 1824 he was instrumental in defeating a proposal for a new constitutional convention, which had been advocated by proslavery forces.

839. Tanner, Henry. *The Martyrdom of Lovejoy: An Account of the Life, Trials, and Perils of Rev. Elijah P. Lovejoy, Who Was Killed by a Pro-Slavery Mob, at Alton, Ill., on the Night of November 7, 1837.* Chicago: Fergus Printing, 1881.

840. Tregillis, Helen Cox, comp. *River Roads to Freedom: Fugitive Slave Notices and Sheriff Notices Found in Illinois Sources.* Bowie, Md.: Heritage Books, 1988. The notices are dated 1819-35.

841. Washburne, Elihu B. *Sketch of Edward Coles, Second Governor of Illinois, and of the Slavery Struggle of 1823-4.* Prepared for the Chicago Historical Society. Chicago: McClurg, 1882.

842. Wolf, Hazel Catherine. *On Freedom's Altar: The Martyr Complex in the Abolition Movement.* Madison: University of Wisconsin Press, 1952. One chapter, "The First Martyr," is devoted to Elijah Lovejoy.

13. Religion

843. Bray, Robert. "Beating the Devil: Life and Art in Peter Cartwright's *Autobiography.*" *Illinois Historical Journal* 78 (1985): 179-94.

844. Bridges, Roger Dean. "Founding the Illinois Baptist Convention, 1830-1834." *American Baptist Quarterly* 3 (September 1984): 235-46.

845. Cartwright, Peter. *Autobiography of Peter Cartwright, the Backwoods Preacher.* Edited by W. P. Strickland. Cincinnati: Hitchcock & Walden and New York: Phillips & Hunt, 1856. Reprint, with an introduction, bibliography, and index by Charles L. Wallis, Nashville, Tenn.: Abingdon Press, 1956.

846. Cleary, Thomas. "The Organization of the Catholic Church in Central Illinois." *Mid-America* 6 n.s. (1935): 105-24.

847. Crissey, Elwell. *Horse Preacher: A Methodist Circuit Rider Travels the Prodigious Tallgrass Prairies of Illinois during the 1830's.* Tigard, Oreg.: Blue Water Publishing, 1989.

848. Crook, Richard J. *Jesse Walker, Pioneer Preacher.* Plainfield, Ill.: Enterprise Printing, 1976. The first presiding elder of the Illinois District of the Methodist church, Walker established missions to the Indians of the Illinois River country.

849. Davis, Charles G. "The Reverend John Brich: His Life and Tragic Death." *Journal of the Illinois State Historical Society* 38 (1945): 227-37. Brich was a pioneer Presbyterian minister in Illinois, who froze to death while traveling in Henry County.

850. Dietrichson, Johannes. *A Pioneer Churchman.* Edited by E. Clifford Nelson. New York: Twayne, 1973. Dietrichson was a pastor of the Norwegian Lutheran church, who traveled and worked among his countrymen in Illinois and Wisconsin in the 1840s. His travel narrative and a journal of work in Wisconsin are presented here.

851. Elbert, E. Duane. "The American Roots of German Lutheranism in Illinois." *Illinois Historical Journal* 78 (1985): 97-112. The neglected story of German Lutherans in frontier Illinois.

852. Fogde, Myron J. "Primitivism and Paternalism: Early Denominational Approaches in Western Illinois." *Western Illinois Regional Studies* 3 (1980): 105-40.

853. Garraghan, Gilbert Joseph. *The Jesuits of the Middle United States.* 3 vols. New York: America Press, 1938. On the Illinois missions, see volume 1, pages 243-54.

854. Heinl, Frank J. "Congregationalism in Jacksonville and Early Illinois." *Journal of the Illinois State Historical Society* 27 (1934-35): 441-62.

855. Hobart, Chauncey. *Peter Cartwright, a Life Sketch: New Facts about the Old Hero.* Red Wing, Minn.: Red Wing Printing, 1889. A short personal sketch by a contemporary and fellow minister.

856. _____. *Recollections of My Life: Fifty Years of Itinerancy in the Northwest.* Red Wing, Minn.: Red Wing Printing, 1885.

857. Mazzuchelli, Samuel. *The Memoirs of Father Samuel Mazzuchelli, O.P.* Chicago: Priory Press, 1967. Reprinted from a 1915 translation of the 1844 edition. In book 2, chapters 4 and 17, are accounts of the church at Galena; in chapter 43 the author discusses the Mormons.

858. Milburn, William Henry. *Ten Years of Preacher-Life: Chapters from an Autobiography.* London: Sampson Low, Son & Co., and New York: Derby & Jackson, 1859. Contains accounts of frontier and pioneer life. An extract (from pages 147-50) describing an 1846 boat, stagecoach, and wagon trip in Illinois was published in the *Journal of the Illinois State Historical Society* 35 (1942): 184-86.

859. Pennewell, Almer M. *A Voice in the Wilderness: Jesse Walker, "the Daniel Boone of Methodism."* Niles, Ill.: The author, n.d. Reprint, Nashville, Tenn.: Parthenon Press, 1958.

860. Willis, John Randolph. *God's Frontiersmen: The Yale Band in Illinois.* Washington, D.C.: University Press of America, 1979. Biographies of fifteen members of the band, formed at Yale University, who served as Congregational ministers, college founders, antislavery leaders, and agents of the American Home Missionary Society in Illinois and elsewhere in the Midwest in the early nineteenth century.

F. CIVIL WAR ERA, 1855-1870

By and large, the kind of regimental histories that appeared in vast numbers soon after the war are not included in this bibliography. Reminiscences, diaries, and letters that are listed herein under Military Actions and Soldier Life do include histories of some regiments. General campaign histories of book length and biographies of Union generals whose commands included Illinois soldiers are, for the most part, not listed, unless the generals themselves were from Illinois.

1. Bibliographies and Indexes

861. Burton, William L. *Descriptive Bibliography of Civil War Manuscripts in Illinois.* Published for the Civil War Centennial Commission of Illinois by Northwestern University Press, 1966. The compiler describes the Civil War manuscripts found in twenty-two Illinois libraries or archives. The entries are arranged alphabetically by the name of the originator of the manuscript or collection. There is also a good index to the manuscript descriptions.

862. Cole, Garold L. *Civil War Eyewitnesses: An Annotated Bibliography of Books and Articles, 1955-1986.* Columbia: University of South Carolina Press, 1988. Contains almost fourteen hundred entries, with excellent appraisals, and an index that lists regiments (by state), battles, and campaigns, as well as authors and editors. More than fifty Illinois units are listed in the index.

863. Dornbusch, C. E., comp. *Regimental Publications and Personal Narratives of the Civil War. Volume I, Northern States; Part I, Illinois.* New York: New York Public Library, 1961. This checklist is an updated revision of one issued in 1913 by the War Department Library.

864. Hallwas, John E. "Civil War Accounts as Literature: Illinois Letters, Diaries, and Personal Narratives." *Western Illinois Regional Studies* 13, no. 1 (Spring 1990): 46-60. The author discusses, and gives examples from, many of the documents that have literary merit.

865. Munden, Kenneth W., and Beers, Henry Putney. *Guide to Federal Archives Relating to the Civil War.* National Archives Publication, no. 63-1. Washington: National Archives and Records Service, General Services Administration, 1962. A good index locates Illinois records in the Archives.

866. Murdock, Eugene C. *The Civil War in the North: A Selective Annotated Bibliography.* New York: Garland, 1987. A valuable listing of 5,599 titles--both books and periodicals. The index includes many Illinois entries; there is a separate category for Illinois military units (Items 1460-1521).

867. Nevins, Allan; Robertson, James I. Jr.; and Wiley, Bell I., eds. *Civil War Books: A Critical Bibliography.* 2 vols. Baton Rouge: Louisiana State University Press, for the U.S. Civil War Centennial Commission, 1967, 1969. Divided into fifteen subject areas (each assigned to a different specialist), these volumes contain approximately 5,100 entries (books or pamphlets), each with a critical annotation. A cumulative index in volume 2 includes titles, authors, and subjects; there are many index entries for Illinois and Lincoln. The 5,100 entries are believed by the editors to be the best-known and most likely to be studied of the estimated 60,000 volumes and pamphlets on the subject.

868. Newman, Ralph Geoffrey, and Long, E. B. "A Basic Civil War Library: A Bibliographical Essay." *Journal of the Illinois State Historical Society* 56 (1963): 391-411.

869. Tubbs, William B. "Bibliography of Illinois Civil War Regimental Sources in the Illinois State Historical Library." Publication forthcoming, 1994.

2. General Works

870. *Civil War History.* Vol. 1 (1955)--to date. Published quarterly by the University of Iowa, 1955-67, and by Kent State University, 1968 to the present.

871. Cole, Arthur Charles. *The Era of the Civil War, 1848-1870.* The Centennial History of Illinois, vol. 3. Springfield: Illinois Centennial Commission, 1919. Reprint, The Sesquicentennial History of Illinois, vol. 3, with an introduction by John Y. Simon, Urbana: University of Illinois Press, 1987.

872. Fiske, John. *The Mississippi Valley in the Civil War.* Boston: Houghton Mifflin, 1900. This narrative by a popular historian recounts the campaigns in which Illinois troops were engaged.

873. Hicken, Victor. *Illinois in the Civil War.* Urbana: University of Illinois Press, 1966. 2d ed., rev., 1991. The story of Illinois men and units in battle. The revised edition has an expanded bibliography brought up to date, with many previously unlisted manuscript sources and regimental histories.

874. Hood, Humphrey. "Selected Letters of Humphrey Hood, Litchfield Physician: Part II, 1862-1867." Edited by Elizabeth Gegenheimer. *Journal of the Illinois State Historical Society* 72 (1979): 242-56. Hood discusses recruitment, politics and government, battles and campaigns, civilian life--indeed, every aspect of the era.

875. Illinois. Civil War Centennial Commission. *Illinois Military Units in the Civil War.* Springfield, 1962.

876. *Illinois Civil War Sketches.* Springfield: Civil War Centennial Commission, 1963 ff. A series of ten pamphlets: 1) *The Preachers' Regiment,* by Elizabeth Rissler; 2) *Illinois Catholics in the Civil War,* by Helene H. Levene; 3) *Illinois Jews in the Civil War,* by Bernard Wax; 4) *The Schoolmasters' Regiment,* by Elizabeth Rissler; 5) *The Copperheads in Illinois,* by Donald F. Tingley; 6) *Colonel Grant of the Illinois Volunteers,* by John Y. Simon; 7) *Illinois Railroads in the Civil War,* by Robert Mize Sutton; 8) *Illinois Negroes in the Civil War,* by Arvarh E. Strickland; 9) *Illinois Camps, Posts, and Prisons,* by Victor Hicken; and 10) *The Constitutional Convention of 1862,* by Mark A. Plummer.

877. Monteiro, George, ed. "John Hay and the Union Generals." *Journal of the Illinois State Historical Society* 69 (1976): 46-66. Monteiro has identified Hay as the author of six unsigned reviews of seven Civil War histories that appeared in 1881 and 1882. The reviews are printed along with the evidence for attributing each to Hay.

3. Description and Travel

878. Brooks, Noah. " 'The Empire City of the West': A View of Chicago in 1864." Edited by P. J. Staudenraus. *Journal of the Illinois State Historical Society* 56 (1963): 340-49. Descriptions by the journalist Noah Brooks.

879. Carson, Caroline McKinley. "I Remember." *Journal of the Illinois State Historical Society* 66 (1973): 341-48. This reminiscence of a trip by covered wagon across the prairies of Illinois in 1869 described travel as primitive as that a half-century earlier.

880. Clark, Jerusha Whitmarsh. "Childhood Reminiscences of Princeton." *Journal of the Illinois State Historical Society* 49 (1956): 95-110. Mrs. Clark recalls how her family lived in the 1850s.

881. Coatsworth, Stella S. *The Loyal People of the North-west: A Record of Prominent Persons, Places and Events, during Eight Years of Unparalleled American History.* Chicago: Church, Goodman & Donnelley, 1869. Coatsworth describes the war atmosphere in Chicago and her visit to Belmont, Missouri, and Cairo, Illinois, in late 1861. At the latter place she attended a New Year's Eve party.

882. Cook, Frederick Francis. *Bygone Days in Chicago: Recollections of the 'Garden City' of the Sixties.* Chicago: McClurg, 1910.

883. Dicey, Edward. *Six Months in the Federal States.* 2 vols. London: Macmillan, 1863. Dicey describes the Illinois prairies in the 1860s.

884. Johnson, Charles Beneulyn. *Illinois in the Fifties, or, a Decade of Development, 1851-1860.* Champaign: Flanigan-Pearson, 1918. Approximately thirty pages are devoted to politics.

885. Keiser, Thomas. "The Prince of Wales in the United States: A Harbinger of English Opinion of the Civil War." *Illinois Historical Journal* 83 (1990): 235-46. This account of the Illinois portion of the Prince's 1860 journey deals primarily with his bird-hunting near Dwight.

886. McIlvaine, Mabel, comp. *Reminiscences of Chicago during the Civil War.* Lakeside Classics, no. 12. Chicago: R. R. Donnelley, 1914. Reprint, New York: Citadel Press, 1967.

887. Rose, George. *The Great Country; or, Impressions of America.* London: Tinsley Brothers, 1868. The author visited the United States shortly after the Civil War. His narrative includes descriptions of Chicago and Mississippi River travel.

888. Woods, N. A. *The Prince of Wales in Canada and the United States.* London: Bradbury & Evans, 1861. Woods describes 1860 political rallies in

Chicago for Lincoln and Douglas as well as the prairies near Dwight, where the Prince went shooting, and a train trip from there to St. Louis. The Prince was Albert Edward, later Edward VII, the first member of the British royal family to visit the West.

4. Dissent and Civil Unrest

889. Anderson, William M. "The Fulton County War at Home and in the Field." *Illinois Historical Journal* 85 (1992): 23-36. Civil War dissent in microcosm, with discussions of the draft and mobilization problems, military discipline, county newspapers, and the Emancipation Proclamation.

890. Cole, Arthur E. "Lincoln and the American Tradition of Civil Liberty." *Transactions of the Illinois State Historical Society, 1926*, pp. 102-11. Focuses on threats to civil liberties in Illinois and the reactions of Illinois newspapers to threats elsewhere.

891. Coleman, Charles H., and Spence, Paul H. "The Charleston Riot, March 28, 1864." *Journal of the Illinois State Historical Society* 33 (1940): 7-56. Episodes of violence between Union supporters and Peace Democrats, or Copperheads, were frequent before the riot, which primarily involved Union soldiers on leave and Copperheads gathered in town for Coles County Circuit Court.

892. Ellis, Mrs. L. E. "The *Chicago Times* during the Civil War." *Transactions of the Illinois State Historical Society, 1932*, pp. 135-81.

893. Gridley, J. N. "A Case under an Illinois Black Law." *Journal of the Illinois State Historical Society* 4 (1911-12): 401-25. The Cass County case was instituted in 1862 against a young African-American who had (illegally under an 1853 law) come to Illinois with a returning Civil War soldier. The lad was found guilty but fled the county when threatened by a mob as he was awaiting appeal.

894. _____. "The Husted or Jacksonville Raid." *Journal of the Illinois State Historical Society* 5 (1912-13): 207-11. Farmers from Cass County (reportedly members of Knights of the Golden Circle and opponents of the draft and Civil War) flocked to Jacksonville in support of John Husted, one of their number, who faced a court hearing in 1863 on charges of attempted murder. The case was dismissed, and there was no disorder in the town. Also called the Dog Fennel War.

895. Hofer, J. M. "Development of the Peace Movement in Illinois during the Civil War." *Journal of the Illinois State Historical Society* 24 (1931-32): 110-28.

896. Klement, Frank L. "Copperhead Secret Societies in Illinois during the Civil War." *Journal of the Illinois State Historical Society* 48 (1955): 152-80.

897. _____. *Copperheads in the Middle West.* Chicago: University of Chicago Press, 1960.

898. _____. *Dark Lanterns: Secret Political Societies, Conspiracies, and Treason Trials in the Civil War.* Baton Rouge: Louisiana State University Press, 1984. An important revisionist study of secret societies in the Midwest, which holds that most members of such societies were loyal citizens.

899. Monaghan, Jay. "Morgan County's Dog Fennel War: An Account of the Cass County Invasion of Jacksonville in 1863." *Journal of the Illinois State Historical Society* 39 (1946): 447-58. A group of several hundred farmers arrived in Jacksonville on 14 September and caused panic in the town until it was learned that they were there in connection with a court case, not to protest the war or the draft.

900. Morrow, Ralph E. "Methodists and 'Butternuts' in the Old Northwest." *Journal of the Illinois State Historical Society* 49 (1956): 34-47. Schisms in the Methodist church caused by the Civil War.

901. Reed, Scott Owen. "Military Arrests of Lawyers in Illinois during the Civil War." *Western Illinois Regional Studies* 6, no. 2 (Fall 1983): 5-22.

902. Tenney, Craig D. "To Suppress or Not to Suppress: Abraham Lincoln and the Chicago *Times*." *Civil War History* 27 (1981): 248-59. Lincoln's response to an 1863 order by Major General Ambrose E. Burnside suppressing the Chicago *Times* for disloyalty to the Union.

903. Tingley, Donald Fred. "The Clingman Raid." *Journal of the Illinois State Historical Society* 56 (1963): 350-63. Activities of a gang of desperadoes in Montgomery, Fayette, and Bond counties in 1864.

5. Education

904. Beyer, Richard Lawrence. "The Southern Illinois College." *Journal of the Illinois State Historical Society* 27 (1934-35): 330-40. The college flourished briefly in Carbondale.

905. Carr, Kay J. "Community Dynamics and Educational Decisions: Establishing Public Schools in Belleville and Galesburg." *Illinois Historical Journal* 84 (1991): 25-38. Effect of social structure and demographics on the organization of public schools under the 1855 state act for free school systems.

906. Hetherington, Norriss S. "Financing Education and Science in Nineteenth-Century America: The Case of Cleveland Abbe, the Chicago Astronomical Society and the First University of Chicago." *Journal of the Illinois State Historical Society* 68 (1975): 319-23. The young astronomer Cleveland Abbe declined an appointment as assistant director of the University of Chicago observatory because he would have had to raise funds for his own salary.

907. Kedro, M. James, ed. "Letters Home: An Illinois Coed in the 1850's." *Journal of the Illinois State Historical Society* 70 (1977): 196-200. Melinda Hall (later Mrs. Ezra M. Aylesworth) writes from Berean College in Jacksonville. The letters are dated 1855 and 1856.

908. Manierre, George. "Reminiscences of Lake Forest Academy and Its Students from the Opening of the Academy in the Fall of 1859 to the Year 1863, Inclusive." *Journal of the Illinois State Historical Society* 10 (1917-18): 394-407.

909. Smith, Grace Partridge. "Wayland Female Institute (Alton, 1853-1856)." *Journal of the Illinois State Historical Society* 38 (1945): 58-70.

910. Urban, William. "Monmouth College in the Civil War." *Journal of the Illinois State Historical Society* 71 (1978): 13-21. The author discusses the students at Monmouth who enlisted in Civil War units and also offers substantial historical accounts of the college and the town of Monmouth.

6. Military Actions and Soldier Life

911. Adams, David Wallace. "Illinois Soldiers and the Emancipation Proclamation." *Journal of the Illinois State Historical Society* 67 (1974): 407-21. The vote of soldiers on the proposed Illinois Constitution of 1862 and their letters home illustrate their support of the Republican party and the Emancipation Proclamation.

912. Affeld, Charles E. "Pvt. Charles E. Affeld Describes the Mechanicsburg Expeditions." Edited by Edwin C. Bearss. *Journal of the Illinois State*

Historical Society 56 (1963): 233-56. Affeld was a cannoneer in Battery B, 1st Illinois Light Artillery.

913. _____. "Pvt. Charles E. Affeld Reports Action West of the Mississippi." Edited by Edwin C. Bearss. *Journal of the Illinois State Historical Society* 60 (1967): 267-96. Diary of the Vicksburg campaign.

914. Allen, Winthrop S. G. "Civil War Letters of Winthrop S. G. Allen." Edited by Harry E. Pratt. *Journal of the Illinois State Historical Society* 24 (1931-32): 553-77. Letters, 1862-63, from Camp Butler, Illinois, and camps in Virginia, Pennsylvania, and Maryland. Allen served with the 12th Illinois Cavalry.

915. Anderson, William M. "Colonel Lawler and the Lawless Eighteenth Illinois Infantry." *Selected Papers in Illinois History, 1982.* Springfield: Illinois State Historical Society, 1984. Pp. 31-41. Lawler's ineffectual efforts to bring discipline to the unit.

916. Andrus, Onley. *The Civil War Letters of Sergeant Onley Andrus.* Edited by Fred Albert Shannon. Illinois Studies in the Social Sciences, vol. 28, no. 4. Urbana, 1947. Andrus was a member of the 95th Illinois Infantry.

917. Bear, Henry C. *The Civil War Letters of Henry C. Bear, A Soldier in the 116th Illinois Volunteer Infantry.* Edited by Wayne C. Temple. Harrogate, Tenn.: Lincoln Memorial University, 1961. Letters written in diary form to his wife, but designed to be read by other family members, cover the five months of Bear's active duty in late 1862 and 1863.

918. Brown, D. Alexander. *Grierson's Raid.* Urbana: University of Illinois Press, 1954. The 1863 raid across Mississippi to Baton Rouge, Louisiana, designed to divert attention from Grant's move on Vicksburg and to destroy supply lines, was led by Benjamin Grierson of Jacksonville.

919. Burdette, Robert Jones. *The Drums of the 47th.* Indianapolis: Bobbs-Merrill, 1914. One of the best memoirs of Illinois veterans. An extract was reprinted in no. 3866.

920. Camm, William. "Diary of Colonel William Camm, 1861 to 1865." Edited by Fritz Haskell. *Journal of the Illinois State Historical Society* 18 (1925-26): 793-969. Camm was an officer of the 14th Illinois Infantry.

921. Campbell, Robert W. "Brief History of the 17th Regiment, Illinois Volunteer Infantry--1861-1864." *Transactions of the Illinois State Historical Society, 1914*, pp. 184-90.

922. Capron, Thaddeus H. "War Diary of Thaddeus H. Capron, 1861-1865." *Journal of the Illinois State Historical Society* 12 (1919-20): 330-406. The so-called diary actually consists of extracts from the letters of Capron, who served with the 55th Illinois Infantry, 1861-65.

923. Chambers, Joel R. *War Fever Cured: The Civil War Diary of Private Joel R. Chambers, 1864-1865*. Edited by Cheryl H. Beneke and Carol D. Summer; Phillip C. Neal, assistant editor. Memphis, Tenn.: Citizens Education, Counsel, Inc., 1980. The diarist enlisted in January 1864 and participated in battles at Resaca, Kenesaw Mountain, Atlanta, Jonesboro, and Nashville.

924. Clausius, Gerhard P. "The Little Soldier of the 95th: Albert D. J. Cashier." *Journal of the Illinois State Historical Society* 51 (1958): 380-87. The little soldier was an Irish immigrant woman who maintained her imposture until 1911.

925. Connelly, Henry C. "Recollections of the War between the States." *Journal of the Illinois State Historical Society* 5 (1912-13): 458-74, 6 (1913-14): 72-111. Connelly served with the 14th Illinois Cavalry.

926. Connolly, James Austin. *Three Years in the Army of the Cumberland*. Edited by Paul McClelland Angle. Bloomington: Indiana University Press, 1959. Reprinted from the *Transactions of the Illinois State Historical Society, 1928*, pp. 215-438, with minor editorial changes. Connolly served with the 123d Illinois Infantry and later as a division inspector with the 14th Army Corps.

927. "Contributions to State History: William H. H. Ibbetson, Co. D, 122d Reg. Ill." *Transactions of the Illinois State Historical Society, 1930*, pp. 235-73. Contains Ibbetson's diary, 8 October 1862--8 August 1864, and a muster roll of the company. The company served in Tennessee, Mississippi, Alabama, and Kentucky. Excellent descriptions of soldier life.

928. Crippin, Edward W. "The Diary of Edward W. Crippin, Private 27th Illinois Volunteers, War of the Rebellion, August 7, 1861, to September 19, 1863." Edited by Robert J. Kerner. *Transactions of the Illinois State Historical Society, 1909*, pp. 220-82.

929. Culver, J. F. *"Your Affectionate Husband, J. F. Culver": Letters Written during the Civil War*. Edited by Leslie W. Dunlap; notes by Edwin C. Bearss.

Iowa City: Friends of the University of Iowa Libraries, 1978. Culver was in the 129th Illinois Infantry.

930. Davis, Rodney O. "Private Albert Cashier As Regarded by His/Her Comrades." *Illinois Historical Journal* 82 (1989): 108-12. Recently discovered correspondence reveals that men of the 95th Illinois thought highly of the comrade they had not known was a woman.

931. DeRosier, Arthur H. Jr., ed. and comp. *Through the South with a Union Soldier.* Johnson City: East Tennessee State University, 1969. Letters, 1862-65, written by A. A. and C. L. Dunham, privates in the 129th Illinois Infantry.

932. Dickinson, John N. "The Civil War Years of John Alexander Logan." *Journal of the Illinois State Historical Society* 56 (1963): 212-32. Traces Logan's exemplary military career from the Battle of Belmont in 1861 through the Battle of Ezra Church in July 1864.

933. Drake, George. *The Mail Goes Through; or, The Civil War Letters of George Drake (1846-1918): Over Eighty Letters Written from August 9, 1862 to May 29, 1865, by an 85th Illinois Vol.* Compiled and edited by Julia A. Drake. San Angelo, Tex.: Anchor Publishing, 1964.

934. East, Ernest Edward. "Lincoln's Russian General." *Journal of the Illinois State Historical Society* 52 (1959): 106-22. Sketch of the Civil War and postwar careers of John Basil Turchin, onetime Russian military officer later employed in the Illinois Central engineering department in Illinois, who rose from colonel of the 19th Illinois Infantry to commander of several different brigades in the 14th Army Corps.

935. Eisenschiml, Otto. "The 55th Illinois at Shiloh." *Journal of the Illinois State Historical Society* 56 (1963): 193-211.

936. Fischer, LeRoy H. "Cairo's Civil War Angel, Mary Jane Safford." *Journal of the Illinois State Historical Society* 54 (1961): 229-45. Safford was "probably the first woman in the West to carry on military hospital relief." She later became a physician and surgeon.

937. Forbes, S. A. "Grierson's Cavalry Raid." *Transactions of the Illinois State Historical Society, 1907,* pp. 99-130. Benjamin H. Grierson was colonel of the 6th Illinois Cavalry and commanded that unit and the 7th in the successful April 1863 raid from Tennessee to Baton Rouge, Louisiana, sent out to destroy railroads and telegraph lines to the rear of Vicksburg. Forbes was a member of the 7th.

938. French, A. S. "Civil War Letters." *Journal of the Illinois State Historical Society* 15 (1922-23): 531-34. Two letters of 1863 written from the Vicksburg area.

939. Gertz, Elmer. "Three Galena Generals." *Journal of the Illinois State Historical Society* 50 (1957): 24-35. The Civil War careers of three men from Galena: John A. Rawlins, Ely S. Parker, and Augustus L. Chetlain.

940. Grant, U. S. *Personal Memoirs of U. S. Grant.* 2 vols. New York: Charles L. Webster, 1885-86. Grant describes his life at Galena, pages 210-28, and the outbreak of the rebellion and his service with the Illinois troops, beginning on page 229. His reports of the Civil War continue through volume one and all of volume two.

941. Greenbie, Marjorie Barstow. *Lincoln's Daughters of Mercy.* Athens, Ohio: Lawhead Press, 1944. Among the women who did the work of the United States Sanitary Commission were three from Illinois: Mary Livermore of Chicago, Mary Ann Bickerdyke of Galesburg, and Mary Safford of Cairo. These women, and their counterparts in other states, worked with soldiers in the field, operating kitchens, laundries, and hospitals.

942. Hess, Earl J. "The Obscurity of August Mersy: A German-American in the Civil War." *Illinois Historical Journal* 79 (1986): 127-38. A onetime German military officer, Mersy remained obscure, despite his service as lieutenant colonel and colonel of the 9th Illinois Infantry, which saw action throughout the war with the Army of the Tennessee.

943. Holaday, Clayton A. "Joseph Kirkland's Company K." *Journal of the Illinois State Historical Society* 49 (1956): 295-307. Illinois writer and publisher Joseph Kirkland based his novel on the company in which he served--Company C, 12th Illinois Infantry.

944. Hopkins, Vivian C., ed. "Soldiers of the 92nd Illinois: Letters of William H. Brown and His Fiancée, Emma Jane Frazey." *Bulletin of the New York Public Library* 73 (1969): 114-39.

945. Huch, Ronald K. "Fort Pillow Massacre: The Aftermath of Paducah." *Journal of the Illinois State Historical Society* 66 (1973): 62-70. Colonel S. G. Hicks of the 40th Illinois Infantry was commander at Paducah when his men (including 120 from the 122d Illinois) refused to surrender to Nathan Bedford Forrest's superior force. Also in Hicks's command were 274 African-American troops in the 1st Kentucky Heavy Artillery. The author proposes that Forrest's later massacre of African-American recruits at Fort Pillow was made in revenge.

946. Irvine, Dallas, comp. *Military Operations of the Civil War: A Guide-Index to the Official Records of the Union and Confederate Armies.* National Archives Publication, no. 68-11. 5 vols. Washington, 1968-80. The *Official Records* series is indexed herein by theaters of operations. Illinois men, for instance, took part in the Battle of Shiloh in Mississippi in the main western theater of operations. *Official Records* reports on that battle, then, are indexed under "Mississippi" in volume 4 (for the main western theater).

947. Jenkins, W. H. "The Thirty-Ninth Illinois Volunteers, Yates Phalanx." *Transactions of the Illinois State Historical Society, 1914,* pp. 130-36.

948. Jones, James Pickett. *"Black Jack": John A. Logan and Southern Illinois in the Civil War.* Tallahassee: Florida State University, 1967.

949. Kaiser, Leo M., ed. "Letters from the Front." *Journal of the Illinois State Historical Society* 56 (1963): 150-63. Excerpts from the letters of eleven Civil War soldiers. The original letters are in the Chicago Historical Society.

950. Kincaid, William I. "Camp Butler." *Journal of the Illinois State Historical Society* 14 (1921-22): 382-85. The author recalls his two years there, first as patient and then as steward at the Civil War hospital.

951. Kircher, Henry A. *A German in the Yankee Fatherland: The Civil War Letters of Henry A. Kircher.* Edited by Earl J. Hess. Kent, Ohio: Kent State University Press, 1983. Kircher's original letters are in the Illinois State Historical Library. He served briefly in the 9th Illinois Infantry before transferring to the 12th Missouri Infantry, most of whose members were German-speaking.

952. "Letters Written by Dr. James R. Zearing to His Wife, Lucinda Helmer Zearing, during the Civil War, 1861-1865." *Transactions of the Illinois State Historical Society, 1921,* pp. 150-202. Vivid descriptions of battlefield casualties and treatment of the sick and wounded, as well as of the southern towns he passed through or was stationed in.

953. Litvin, Martin, ed. *Voices of the Prairie Land.* 2 vols. Galesburg, Ill.: Mother Bickerdyke Historical Collection, 1972. Manuscript material, with narrative by the editor, from a variety of people, among them James L. Burkhalter, commander of Company F, 86th Illinois Infantry, in the Civil War.

954. Lowe, Donald V. "Army Memoirs of Lucius W. Barber." *Journal of the Illinois State Historical Society* 56 (1963): 298-315. A summary of the 1894 book *Army Memoirs of Lucius W. Barber*, long out of print. Barber's diary records his service of four and one-half years in the 15th Illinois Infantry.

955. Lutz, Earle. "The *Stars and Stripes* of Illinois Boys in Blue." *Journal of the Illinois State Historical Society* 46 (1953): 132-41. History of newspapers published in the field by Illinois troops, with a bibliography.

956. Maul, David T. "Five Butternut Yankees." *Journal of the Illinois State Historical Society* 56 (1963): 177-92. The five butternut Yankees were former Confederate prisoners who served with the 23d Illinois Infantry (the Irish Brigade).

957. Miers, Earl Schenck, ed. *Grant's Civil War, Selected and Edited from His Personal Memoirs.* New York: Collier Books, 1962.

958. Morris, W. S.; Hartwell, L. D.; and Kuykendall, J. B. *History: 31st Regiment, Illinois Volunteers, Organized by John A. Logan.* 1902. Reprint, with a foreword by John Y. Simon, Herrin, Ill.: Crossfire Press, 1991.

959. Mosman, Chesley A. *The Rough Side of War: The Civil War Journal of Chesley A. Mosman, 1st Lieutenant, Company D, 59th Illinois Volunteer Infantry Regiment.* Edited by Arnold Gates. Garden City, N.Y.: Basin Publishing, 1987.

960. Murray, Donald M., and Rodney, Robert M. "Colonel Julian E. Bryant, Champion of the Negro Soldier." *Journal of the Illinois State Historical Society* 56 (1963): 257-81. Julian Bryant, nephew of William Cullen Bryant, was a teacher of drawing at Illinois State Normal University when he volunteered for service. His drawings that appear here illustrate soldier life. In 1863 he became an officer of African-American troops raised in the South.

961. Newsome, Edmund. *Experience in the War of the Great Rebellion.* Reprint of 2d ed., Murphysboro, Ill.: Jackson County Historical Society, 1984. Newsome served in the 81st Illinois Infantry, and his volume includes both a regimental history and his diary of events through the Vicksburg campaign, the Red River expedition, and battles at Nashville and Mobile.

962. Orendorff, Henry. *We Are Sherman's Men: The Civil War Letters of Henry Orendorff.* Edited by William M. Anderson. Western Illinois Monograph Series, no. 6. Macomb: Western Illinois University, 1986. Orendorff wrote of the soldier's everyday life through the Vicksburg and Atlanta campaigns, the March to the Sea, and the campaign in the Carolinas.

963. Orme, William Ward. "Civil War Letters of Brigadier General William Ward Orme, 1862-1866." Edited by Harry E. Pratt. *Journal of the Illinois State Historical Society* 23 (1930): 246-315. These letters, and many other Orme papers, are now in the Illinois State Historical Library.

964. Parks, George E. "One Story of the 109th Illinois Volunteer Infantry Regiment." *Journal of the Illinois State Historical Society* 56 (1963): 282-97. Officers of the regiment (all from Union County, except for those of Company K) were "disgracefully" discharged for incompetence and for having failed to march to support troops under attack at Holly Springs, Mississippi, in December 1862. The author argues their case.

965. Partridge, Charles A. "The Ninety-Sixth Illinois at Chickamauga." *Transactions of the Illinois State Historical Society, 1910,* pp. 72-80.

966. Pitkin, William A. "Michael K. Lawler's Ordeal with the Eighteenth Illinois." *Journal of the Illinois State Historical Society* 58 (1965): 357-77. In late 1861 Lawler was courtmartialed for irregularities in his regiment, but his conviction was reversed.

967. Schwartz, Ezekiel Koehler. *Civil War Diary of Ezekiel Koehler Schwartz, March 1863 to June 1865, and History of E. K. Schwartz Family.* Shelbyville, Ill.: Shelby County Historical & Genealogical Society, 1989. Schwartz served, 1862-65, in the 115th Illinois Infantry.

968. Simon, John Y. "Daniel Harmon Brush and the Eighteenth Illinois Infantry." *Selected Papers in Illinois History, 1982.* Springfield: Illinois State Historical Society, 1984. Pp. 42-50.

969. _____. "From Galena to Appomattox: Grant and Washburne." *Journal of the Illinois State Historical Society* 58 (1965): 165-89. How Congressman Elihu Washburne, Grant's friend in Galena, used political influence to help shape Grant's military career.

970. Smith, Benjamin T. *Private Smith's Journal: Recollections of the Late War.* Edited by Clyde C. Walton. Lakeside Classics, no. 61. Chicago: R. R. Donnelley, 1963. Smith was in the 51st Illinois Infantry.

971. Smith, Harold F. "Mulligan and the Irish Brigade." *Journal of the Illinois State Historical Society* 56 (1963): 164-76. The unit, headed by James A. Mulligan, was an over-strength independent regiment (the 23d) that was in service throughout the Civil War.

972. Sterling, Bob [Robert W.]. "Discouragement, Weariness, and War Politics: Desertions from Illinois Regiments during the Civil War." *Illinois Historical Journal* 82 (1989): 239-62. The author discusses problems of recruiting, the draft, and military discipline, as well as such political issues as the Emancipation Proclamation.

973. Stillwell, Leander. "In the Ranks at Shiloh." *Journal of the Illinois State Historical Society* 15 (1922-23): 460-76. Stillwell's account of the battle, in which he took part, was written in 1890.

974. _____. *The Story of a Common Soldier of Army Life in the Civil War, 1861-1865.* Erie, Kans.: Press of the Erie Record, 1917. Reprint, Time-Life Books, 1983. One of the best memoirs from Illinois.

975. Strong, Robert Hale. *A Yankee Private's Civil War.* Edited by Ashley Halsey. Chicago: Regnery, 1961.

976. Tebbetts, William H. "The Story of an Ordinary Man." Edited by Paul McClelland Angle. *Journal of the Illinois State Historical Society* 33 (1940): 212-32. Tebbetts's letters, 1853-62, deal with his work as a teacher and farmer, and his subsequent service in the 45th Illinois Infantry. He was killed at Shiloh, 6 April 1862. The letters are in the Illinois State Historical Library.

977. Thompson, Mitchel Andrew. *Dear Eliza . . . The Letters of Mitchel Andrew Thompson, May, 1862--August 1864.* Edited by Mary Bess Henderson, Evelyn Janet Young, and Anna Irene Nadelhoffer. Ames, Iowa: Carter Press, 1976. Thompson served in the 83d Illinois Infantry, raised at Monmouth in 1862.

978. Turchin, John B. *Chickamauga.* Chicago: Fergus Printing, 1888.

979. Turchin, Nadine. " 'A Monotony Full of Sadness': The Diary of Nadine Turchin, May, 1863-April 1864." Edited by Mary Ellen McElligott. *Journal of* *the Illinois State Historical Society* 70 (1977): 27-89. The wife of Illinois General John Basil Turchin accompanied him through campaigns in Missouri, Kentucky, Tennessee, and Alabama, and recorded events of the campaigns. The only one extant of her several diaries is printed.

980. Waters, Joseph G. "Letters from the 84th Regiment." Reprinted from the *Macomb Journal* in Hallwas, *Illinois Literature*, no. 3866. In addition to vividly portraying soldier life, Waters describes the Battle of Stone's River.

981. White, Patrick H. "Civil War Diary of Patrick H. White." *Journal of the Illinois State Historical Society* 15 (1922-23): 640-63. White served with a Chicago battery from 1861 until he was captured in 1864. He discusses several campaigns in the West.

982. Wilcox, Charles E. "With Grant at Vicksburg--From the Civil War Diary of Captain Charles E. Wilcox." Edited by Edgar L. Erickson. *Journal of the Illinois State Historical Society* 30 (1937-38): 441-503. Wilcox served in the 33d Illinois Infantry.

983. Wilder, Jeremy H. "The Thirty-seventh Illinois at Prairie Grove." *Arkansas Historical Quarterly* (1990): 3-19.

984. Wilkin, Jacob W. "Personal Reminiscences of General U. S. Grant." *Transactions of the Illinois State Historical Society, 1907*, pp. 131-40. Wilkin was in the 130th Illinois Infantry, and this account is more a narrative of the Vicksburg campaign than a reminiscence about Grant.

985. Willis, Charles W. *Army Life of an Illinois Soldier*. Washington, D.C.: Globe Printing, 1906.

7. Mobilization, Organization, and Supply

986. Ayers, James T. *The Civil War Diary of James T. Ayers, Civil War Recruiter*. Edited, with introduction, by John Hope Franklin. Occasional Publications of the Illinois State Historical Society, no. 50. Springfield, 1947.

987. Baumann, Ken. *Arming the Suckers, 1861-1865: A Compilation of Illinois Civil War Weapons*. Dayton, Ohio: Morningside House, 1989. Compiled from required quarterly reports prepared by company and battery ordnance officers and other primary sources.

988. Burton, William L. "Ethnic Regiments in the Civil War: The Illinois Experience." *Selected Papers in Illinois History, 1980.* Springfield: Illinois State Historical Society, 1982. Pp. 31-39.

989. _____. *Melting Pot Soldiers: The Union's Ethnic Regiments.* Ames: Iowa State University Press, 1988. Includes discussions of ethnic units from Illinois.

990. Dayton, Aretas. "The Raising of Union Forces in Illinois during the Civil War." *Journal of the Illinois State Historical Society* 34 (1941): 401-38.

991. "Draft Exemption Certificate, Civil War." *Journal of the Illinois State Historical Society* 37 (1944): 365. The original of the 3 November 1864 certificate, reproduced here, is in the Illinois State Historical Library.

992. Franklin, John Hope. "James T. Ayers, Civil War Recruiter." *Journal of the Illinois State Historical Society* 40 (1947): 267-97.

993. "Grant Takes Command at Cairo." *Journal of the Illinois State Historical Society* 38 (1945): 242-44. A letter of 28 September 1886 from Richard J. Oglesby (in the Oglesby Papers in the Illinois State Historical Library).

994. Hanchett, William. "An Illinois Physician and the Civil War Draft, 1864-1865: Letters of Dr. Joshua Nichols Speed." *Journal of the Illinois State Historical Society* 59 (1966): 143-60. Dr. Speed served in the headquarters of the provost marshal for the 9th congressional district at Mt. Sterling. He examined draftees to determine their fitness for military service.

995. Hicken, Victor. "The Record of Illinois' Negro Soldiers in the Civil War." *Journal of the Illinois State Historical Society* 56 (1963): 529-51. The author discusses both those who enrolled from Illinois and those added to Illinois units in the South.

996. Illinois. Adjutant General's Office. *Report of the Adjutant General of the State of Illinois . . . 1861-1866 . . .* 8 vols. Springfield: Baker, Bailhache, 1867. Revised editions issued in 1886 and in 1900-1902. The latter edition has a 9th volume that includes Black Hawk, Mexican, and Spanish-American war records.

997. Lash, Jeffrey N. "A Politician Turned General: Stephen A. Hurlbut and Military Patronage in Illinois, 1861-62." *Selected Papers in Illinois History, 1981.* Springfield: Illinois State Historical Society, 1982. Pp. 37-49.

998. Laudermilk, John I. "Recruiting Gunboat Sailors in Civil War Chicago." *Transactions of the Illinois State Historical Society: Selected Papers from the Seventh Annual History Symposium and the Eighth Annual History Symposium* [1986 and 1987]. Springfield, 1989. Pp. 41-49. Sailors were recruited for the Western Flotilla.

999. Merrill, James M. "Cairo, Illinois: Strategic Civil War River Port." *Journal of the Illinois State Historical Society* 76 (1983): 242-56. Development of the United States Navy's Western Flotilla (later called the Mississippi Squadron), which was based at Cairo. Union gunboats, some of which were converted steamboats, participated in attacks on various Confederate strongholds on the Cumberland and Mississippi rivers.

1000. Moore, Ensley. "Grant's First March." *Transactions of the Illinois State Historical Society, 1910*, pp. 55-62. As colonel of the 21st Illinois Infantry, Ulysses S. Grant drilled the unit, then marched overland from Springfield to the Illinois River, where orders were received to go to Palmyra, Missouri.

1001. Pearson, Emmet F. "The Historic Hospitals of Cairo." *Journal of the Illinois State Historical Society* 77 (1984): 21-32. Military hospitals were established in camps and on a steamboat during the Civil War. Sisters of the Holy Cross at Notre Dame in South Bend, Indiana, who staffed and administered the military hospitals, later established an infirmary at Cairo that cared for marine patients. The author also discusses the medical history of the community up to 1919.

1002. Peterson, William S. "A History of Camp Butler, 1861-1866." *Illinois Historical Journal* 82 (1989): 74-92. A comprehensive, scholarly study. Camp Butler was both a training ground for Union soldiers and a prisoner-of-war camp for Confederate soldiers.

1003. Phillips, Christopher. "Peoria's Reaction to the Outbreak of the Civil War." *Western Illinois Regional Studies* 9, no. 1 (Spring 1986): 34-47.

1004. Pitkin, William A. "When Cairo Was Saved for the Union." *Journal of the Illinois State Historical Society* 51 (1958): 284-305. A history of Cairo from the time in 1861 when Illinois troops were concentrated there to protect the strategic juncture of the Ohio and Mississippi rivers until early 1862, when the town was a staging point for Grant's Tennessee campaign.

1005. Sheppley, Helen Edith. "Camp Butler in the Civil War Days." *Journal of the Illinois State Historical Society* 25 (1932-33): 285-317.

1006. Sterling, Robert E. "Civil War Draft Resistance in Illinois." *Journal of the Illinois State Historical Society* 64 (1971): 244-66.

1007. United States Adjutant-General's Office. *Official Army Register of the Volunteer Force of the United States Army for the Years 1861, '62, '63, '64, '65.* 8 vols. Washington, 1865-67. Indiana, Illinois, pt. 6.

8. Politics and Government

a. In General

1008. Baringer, William Eldon. "Campaign Technique in Illinois, 1860." *Transactions of the Illinois State Historical Society, 1932,* pp. 203-81.

1009. Costigan, David. "James Washington Singleton and the Politics of Principle." *Transactions of the Illinois State Historical Society: Selected Papers from the Seventh Annual History Symposium and the Eighth Annual History Symposium* [1986 and 1987]. Springfield, 1989. Pp. 35-40. Biographical sketch of a Civil War pacifist who later became a member of Congress.

1010. Crissey, Elwell. *Lincoln's Lost Speech, the Pivot of His Career.* New York: Hawthorn Books, 1967. The speech, given at the Bloomington, Illinois, anti-Nebraska convention in 1856, is still lost, but the author gives brief sketches of the seventy men who attended and an account of the convention itself. See Howard, no. 1028, for a comprehensive report on the many factions that were to become the Republican party.

1011. Cross, Jasper W. "The Civil War Comes to 'Egypt.' " *Journal of the Illinois State Historical Society* 44 (1951): 160-69. Despite the southern background and the Democratic sentiments of many southern Illinois residents, the region strongly supported the Union cause.

1012. Cunningham, J. O. "The Bloomington Convention of 1856 and Those Who Participated in It." *Transactions of the Illinois State Historical Society, 1905,* pp. 101-10. Passage of the Kansas-Nebraska Act galvanized opponents of slavery to join forces in opposing Stephen A. Douglas.

1013. Dante, Harris L. "Western Attitudes and Reconstruction Politics in Illinois." *Journal of the Illinois State Historical Society* 49 (1956): 149-62.

1014. *Debates and Proceedings of the Constitutional Convention of the State of Illinois, Convened at the City of Springfield, Tuesday, Dec. 13, 1869.* 2 vols. Springfield: E. L. Merritt & Brother for the Illinois Constitutional Convention, 1870.

1015. Dick, David B. "Resurgence of the Chicago Democracy, April-November, 1861." *Journal of the Illinois State Historical Society* 56 (1963): 139-49.

1016. Dickerson, O. M. *The Illinois Constitutional Convention of 1862.* University Studies, vol. 1, no. 9 (March 1905). Urbana, Ill.: University Press.

1017. East, Ernest Edward, ed. "The Campaign of 1860 in Peoria." *Journal of the Illinois State Historical Society* 37 (1944): 362-63. In a letter of 29 August 1860, Richard Jacques describes party rallies (original letter in the Peoria Public Library).

1018. Fehrenbacher, Don E. "The Judd-Wentworth Feud." *Journal of the Illinois State Historical Society* 45 (1952): 197-211. How the feud between two Chicago Republicans affected Lincoln's political operations in the late 1850s.

1019. Formisano, Ronald P., and Shade, William G. "The Concept of Agrarian Radicalism." *Mid-America* 52 (1970): 3-30. A detailed study of the fourteen most prominent Democratic delegates to the 1862 Illinois constitutional convention, showing that their positions then and later were not those held by agrarian radicals, as exemplified by Greenbackers and Grangers.

1020. Gienapp, William E., ed. "The 1856 Election: An Unpublished Lincoln Letter." *Journal of the Illinois State Historical Society* 70 (1977): 18-21. In a letter of 27 June 1856, Lincoln discusses Illinois politics and politicians. The original letter is in the Illinois State Historical Library.

1021. _____. "Nativism and the Creation of a Republican Majority in the North before the Civil War." *Journal of American History* 72 (1985-86): 529-59.

1022. Hamilton, Holman. *Prologue to Conflict: The Crisis and Compromise of 1850.* Lexington: University of Kentucky Press, 1964. Especially valuable for its treatment of Stephen A. Douglas as a statesman and for its detailed analysis of congressional action.

1023. Herriott, F. I. "The Conference in the Deutsches Haus, Chicago, May 14-15, 1860: A Study of Some of the Preliminaries of the National Republican

Convention of 1860." *Transactions of the Illinois State Historical Society, 1928,* pp. 101-91. The role played by German-Americans "in the rise of the Republican party to place and power between 1840 and 1860." The article contains brief biographical sketches of the German-Americans who attended the conference.

1024. _____. "Memories of the Chicago Convention of 1860." *Annals of Iowa* 3d ser. 12 (1915-21): 446-66. The Republican convention at which Lincoln was nominated for the presidency.

1025. Hicken, Victor. "John A. McClernand and the House Speakership Struggle of 1859." *Journal of the Illinois State Historical Society* 53 (1960): 163-78. The Illinois Democratic congressman lost the speakership but assumed, incorrectly, that he and his allies had saved the Democratic party for Douglas.

1026. Hickey, James T. "Oglesby's Fence Rail Dealings and the 1860 Decatur Convention." *Journal of the Illinois State Historical Society* 54 (1961): 5-24.

1027. Hossack, John. *Speech of John Hossack, Convicted of a Violation of the Fugitive Slave Law, before Judge Drummond, of the United States District Court, Chicago, Ill.* New York: American Anti-Slavery Society, 1860. Reprinted (facsimile) as no. 11 in *Anti-Slavery Tracts,* ser. 2, nos. 1-14, 1860, Westport, Conn.: Negro Universities Press, 1970. Reprinted also in *Journal of the Illinois State Historical Society* 41 (1948): 67-74; and see "John Hossack's Fate," ibid., pp. 284-85.

1028. Howard, Victor B. "The Illinois Republican Party; Part I: A Party Organizer for the Republicans in 1854." *Journal of the Illinois State Historical Society* 64 (1971): 125-60. ". . . Part II: The Party Becomes Conservative, 1855-1856." Ibid., pp. 285-311.

1029. Jones, James Pickett. "John A. Logan, Freshman in Congress, 1859-1861." *Journal of the Illinois State Historical Society* 56 (1963): 36-60.

1030. _____. "Radical Reinforcement: John A. Logan Returns to Congress." *Journal of the Illinois State Historical Society* 68 (1975): 324-36. Logan's service as a Radical Republican in Congress in 1867-68.

1031. Jones, Stanley L. "Agrarian Radicalism in Illinois' Constitutional Convention of 1862." *Journal of the Illinois State Historical Society* 48 (1955): 271-82. The agrarian radicals sought to elect anti-bank delegates to the convention as well as to use the convention to regulate railroads and corporations and protect homesteads from forced sale. In spite of economic discontent in the state, the new constitution was voted down by the people. Reprinted in Scheiber, no. 4086.

1032. Kimball, E. L. "Richard Yates: His Record as Civil War Governor of Illinois." *Journal of the Illinois State Historical Society* 23 (1930-31): 1-83.

1033. Klement, Frank L. "Middle Western Copperheadism and the Genesis of the Granger Movement." *Mississippi Valley Historical Review* 38 (1951-52): 679-94. Reprinted in Scheiber, no. 4086.

1034. Meerse, David E. "Origins of the Buchanan-Douglas Feud Reconsidered." *Journal of the Illinois State Historical Society* 67 (1974): 154-74. The author discusses Senator Douglas's recommendations and President Buchanan's political appointments of Illinoisans and shows that the patronage situation did not result in a Douglas-Buchanan "feud" in 1857 but played "an insignificant role" in their later disagreement over the application of popular sovereignty in Kansas.

1035. Monaghan, Jay. "Did Abraham Lincoln Receive the Illinois German Vote?" *Journal of the Illinois State Historical Society* 35 (1942): 133-39. An analysis of census and voting figures, particularly in St. Clair County, shows that in 1860 the German vote was indeed an important factor in Lincoln's election.

1036. Nortrup, Jack. "Richard Yates: A Personal Glimpse of the Illinois Soldiers' Friend." *Journal of the Illinois State Historical Society* 56 (1963): 121-38. Governor Yates helped furnish supplies and medical workers for Illinois troops.

1037. _____. "A Western Whig in Washington." *Journal of the Illinois State Historical Society* 64 (1971): 419-41. The author discusses national issues that concerned Richard Yates as a congressman from Illinois, 1851-55.

1038. _____. "Yates, the Prorogued Legislature, and the Constitutional Convention." *Journal of the Illinois State Historical Society* 62 (1969): 5-34.

1039. Ochs, Robert D. "An Illinois State Agent in Washington: The Activities of Harry Dewitt Cook, 1865-1871." *Journal of the Illinois State Historical Society* 31 (1938): 449-81. Cook's principal duties were to expedite the processing of Civil War back pay claims, bounties, and pensions to veterans. Based on his letter books in the Illinois State Historical Library.

1040. Oder, Broeck N. "Andrew Johnson and the 1866 Illinois Election." *Journal of the Illinois State Historical Society* 73 (1980): 189-200. Johnson's campaigning in seventeen Illinois counties led to Republican gains in fourteen of those counties and, indeed, increased all voter participation.

1041. Olden, Peter H. "Anton C. Hesing: The Rise of a Chicago Boss." *Journal of the Illinois State Historical Society* 35 (1942): 260-87. Hesing, a German-American, dominated Chicago Republican politics in the post-Civil War years.

1042. Palmer, George Thomas, ed. "A Collection of Letters from Lyman Trumbull to John M. Palmer, 1854-1858." *Journal of the Illinois State Historical Society* 16 (1923-24): 20-41. These letters are now in the John M. Palmer Collection (II) in the Illinois State Historical Library. Three of the letters concern the 1858 campaign.

1043. "Political Rally at Galena in 1864." *Journal of the Illinois State Historical Society* 45 (1952): 76-79. A description of Richard J. Oglesby's oratory.

1044. Pratt, Harry Edward. "The Repudiation of Lincoln's War Policy in 1862: Stuart-Swett Congressional Campaign." *Journal of the Illinois State Historical Society* 24 (1931-32): 129-40. John Todd Stuart, the Democrat, won the 8th District seat from Republican Leonard Swett, even though the district had been re-formed in 1860 to favor the Republicans.

1045. "A Prelude to the Birth of the Republican Party." *Journal of the Illinois State Historical Society* 46 (1953): 311-13. A letter of 3 April 1856, from Elihu B. Washburne to Richard Yates, regarding plans for the May anti-Nebraska convention at Bloomington.

1046. Prince, Ezra M., ed. "Meeting of May 29, 1900, Commemorative of the Convention of May 29, 1856, That Organized the Republican Party in the State of Illinois." *Transactions of the McLean County Historical Society, Bloomington, Illinois* 3 (1900). A collection of nineteen speeches and articles about the 1856 convention, including many contemporary newspaper reports.

1047. Robinson, Michael C. "After Lincoln: The Transformation of the Illinois Republican Party, 1865-1872." *Selected Papers in Illinois History, 1982.* Springfield: Illinois State Historical Society, 1984. Pp. 51-56.

1048. Rozett, John M. "Racism and Republican Emergence in Illinois, 1848-1860: A Re-evaluation of Republican Negrophobia." *Civil War History* 22 (June 1976): 101-15.

1049. Sanger, Donald Bridgman. "The Chicago Times and the Civil War." *Mississippi Valley Historical Review* 17 (1930-31): 557-80. The *Times* was fiercely anti-Lincoln and pro-slavery.

1050. Senning, John P. "The Know-Nothing Movement in Illinois, 1854-1856." *Journal of the Illinois State Historical Society* 7, no. 1 (April 1914): 7-33.

1051. Smith, William Hawley. "Old-Time Campaigning and the Story of a Lincoln Campaign Song." *Journal of the Illinois State Historical Society* 13 (1920-21): 23-32. The author describes an 1860 Springfield rally for Lincoln.

1052. Spencer, Ivor D., ed. "Chicago Helps to Reelect Lincoln." *Journal of the Illinois State Historical Society* 63 (1970): 167-79. Extracts from the 1866 volumes *Huit Mois en Amérique (Eight Months in America)* by Ernest Duvergier de Hauranne.

1053. Stoler, Mildred C. "The Democratic Element in the New Republican Party in Illinois, 1856-1860." *Transactions of the Illinois State Historical Society, 1942*, pp. 32-71.

1054. Zornow, William Frank. "McClellan and Seymour in the Chicago Convention of 1864." *Journal of the Illinois State Historical Society* 43 (1950): 282-95.

b.   Lincoln-Douglas Debates and the Campaign of 1858

1055. Angle, Paul McClelland, ed. *Created Equal? The Complete Lincoln-Douglas Debates of 1858.* Collections of the Illinois State Historical Library, vol. 33. Chicago: University of Chicago Press, 1958. In addition to the texts of the debates, this volume includes three preliminary speeches by Lincoln, two by Douglas, newspaper accounts of other speeches made between the debates, and an introduction by Angle. An earlier collection of the debates, edited by Edwin Erle Sparks, is volume 3 of the Collections series.

1056. Coleman, Charles H. *The Lincoln-Douglas Debate at Charleston, Illinois, September 18, 1858.* Eastern Illinois University Bulletin 220 (1 October 1957). Events that led to the debates, a summary of the debates, and sketches of

Charleston friends of Lincoln's.   In addition to an annotated text of the Charleston debate, Coleman gives voting statistics for Coles County and a political chronology, 1854-58.

1057. Collins, Bruce.   "The Lincoln-Douglas Contest of 1858 and Illinois' Electorate." *Journal of American Studies* 20 (1986): 391-420. Although the debates dealt with "the grandest of national issues," the author concludes that in the counties, people were preoccupied with many other issues that influenced their votes.

1058. Davis, William. "A Newcomer Observes the Climax of the 1858 Lincoln-Douglas Campaign." Edited by Mark Plummer and Michael Maher. *Illinois Historical Journal* 81 (1988): 181-90.

1059. Fischer, LeRoy H. "Lincoln's 1858 Visit to Pittsfield, Illinois." *Journal of the Illinois State Historical Society* 61 (1968): 350-64.

1060.   Heckman, Richard Allen.   *Lincoln vs Douglas: The Great Debates Campaign.* Washington, D.C.: Public Affairs Press, 1967.

1061. _____. "Out-of-State Influences and the Lincoln-Douglas Campaign of 1858." *Journal of the Illinois State Historical Society* 59 (1966): 30-47.

1062. Herriott, F. I. "Iowa and the First Nomination of Abraham Lincoln." *Annals of Iowa* 3d ser. 8 (1907-9): 444-66. The Lincoln-Douglas debates as reported in Iowa. Two prominent men from that state who attended a debate immediately wrote of Lincoln as the "next President."

1063. Holzer, Harold, comp. and ed. *The Lincoln-Douglas Debates: The First Complete, Unexpurgated Text.* New York: Harper Collins, 1993.

1064.   Johannsen, Robert W.   "The Lincoln-Douglas Campaign of 1858: Background and Perspective." *Journal of the Illinois State Historical Society* 73 (1980): 242-62.

1065. King, Willard L., and Nevins, Allan. "The Constitution and Declaration of Independence as Issues in the Lincoln-Douglas Debates." *Journal of the Illinois State Historical Society* 52 (1959): 7-32.

1066. Krug, Mark M. "Lyman Trumbull and the Real Issues in the Lincoln-Douglas Debates." *Journal of the Illinois State Historical Society* 57 (1964): 380-96.

1067. Lightner, David L. "Abraham Lincoln and the Ideal of Equality." *Journal of the Illinois State Historical Society* 75 (1982): 289-308.

1068. Lincoln, Abraham. *Abraham Lincoln's "House Divided" Address, Delivered in Springfield, before the Illinois State Republican Convention, June 16, 1858.* Introduction by Clyde C. Walton. Illinois State Historical Society Pamphlet Series, no. 1. Springfield, 1958.

1069. McMurtry, R. Gerald. "The Different Editions of the 'Debates of Lincoln and Douglas.' " *Journal of the Illinois State Historical Society* 27 (1934-35): 133-77.

1070. Magdol, Edward. "Owen Lovejoy's Role in the Campaign of 1858." *Journal of the Illinois State Historical Society* 51 (1958): 403-16. The abolitionist congressman Owen Lovejoy became a strong supporter of Lincoln's.

1071. Monaghan, Jay. "When Were the *Debates* First Published?" *Journal of the Illinois State Historical Society* 42 (1949): 344-47. Evidence that the published Lincoln-Douglas *Debates* were a part of the campaign literature for Lincoln's nomination for president.

1072. Muelder, Hermann R. "The Moral Lights Around Us." *Journal of the Illinois State Historical Society* 52 (1959): 248-62. Moral issues of the Lincoln-Douglas debates, adapted from the author's *Fighters for Freedom*.

1073. Pratt, Harry Edward. "The Great Debates." *Illinois Blue Book, 1953-1954.* Pp. 2-30. Reprint, rev., Illinois State Historical Library, 1955, 1956.

1074. Satz, Ronald N. "The African Slave Trade and Lincoln's Campaign of 1858." *Journal of the Illinois State Historical Society* 65 (1972): 269-79.

1075. Schapsmeier, Edward L., and Schapsmeier, Frederick H. "Lincoln and Douglas: Their Versions of the West." *Journal of the West* 7 (1968): 542-52.

1076. Sigelschiffer, Saul. *The American Conscience: The Drama of the Lincoln-Douglas Debates.* New York: Houghton Mifflin, 1973.

1077. Simon, John Y. "Union County in 1858 and the Lincoln-Douglas Debate." *Journal of the Illinois State Historical Society* 62 (1969): 267-92.

1078. Zarefsky, David. *Lincoln, Douglas, and Slavery: In the Crucible of Public Debate.* Chicago: University of Chicago Press, 1990. An examination of the debates as rhetorical texts.

9. Prisoners and Prisons

1079. Chandler, Josephine Craven. "An Episode of the Civil War: A Romance of Coincidence." *Journal of the Illinois State Historical Society* 17 (1924-25): 352-68. The war careers of two Springfield men, Edward R. Roberts and Edward P. Strickland, who served together for a time, met again in a Confederate prison, escaped separately, and met still again in Springfield, each believing the other to have been recaptured.

1080. Eisendrath, Joseph L. Jr. "Chicago's Camp Douglas, 1861-1865." *Journal of the Illinois State Historical Society* 53 (1960): 37-63. Camp Douglas was both a mobilization center for Union troops and a prison for captured Confederates. Most of the article is devoted to the camp as a prison.

1081. Gilbert, William H. "Transient Prisoner: The Reminiscences of William H. Gilbert." Edited by Alvin R. Sunseri. *Journal of the Illinois State Historical Society* 74 (1981): 41-50. Gilbert writes of his seventeen months in six Confederate prisons.

1082. Hall, George P. "Fourteen Months in Rebel Prisons." Printed in the *Macomb Journal,* 1879-80, and reprinted for the first time in Hallwas, *Illinois Literature,* no. 3866.

1083. Moore, Hugh. "A Reminiscence of Confederate Prison Life." Edited by Clifford H. Haka. *Journal of the Illinois State Historical Society* 65 (1972): 451-61. Moore, from Salem, was serving in the 111th Illinois Infantry when he was captured.

1084. Quinn, Camilla A. Corlas. "Forgotten Soldiers: The Confederate Prisoners at Camp Butler, 1862-1863." *Illinois Historical Journal* 81 (1988): 35-44.

1085. Rogan, Lafayette. "A Confederate Prisoner at Rock Island: The Diary of Lafayette Rogan." Edited by John H. Hauberg. *Journal of the Illinois State Historical Society* 34 (1941): 26-49.

1086. Tusken, Roger, ed. " 'In the Bastile of the Rebels.' " *Journal of the Illinois State Historical Society* 56 (1963): 316-39. Excerpts from the diary of George R. Lodge, 53d Illinois Infantry, who was held in Confederate prisons from July 1863 until March 1865.

10. Miscellany

1087. Ander, Oscar Fritiof, and Nordstrom, Oscar L., comps. and eds. *The American Origin of the Augustana Synod from Contemporary Lutheran Periodicals, 1851-1860: A Collection of Source Material.* Augustana Historical Society Publications, vol. 9. Rock Island, Ill.: Augustana Historical Society, 1942. This volume includes documents that illustrate (1) the establishment of educational institutions by Swedish Lutherans and (2) conflicts between foreign-born and native Americans.

1088. Bailey, J. W. *Knox College, by Whom Founded and Endowed; Also a Review of a Pamphlet Entitled "Rights of Congregationalists in Knox College."* Chicago: Press & Tribune Book & Job Printing Office, 1860.

1089. Baker, Nina Brown. *Cyclone in Calico.* Boston: Little, Brown, 1952. An account of the Civil War nursing career of Mary Ann Bickerdyke.

1090. Beyer, Richard Lawrence. "Baseball in Cairo: A Footnote to Illinois History." *Journal of the Illinois State Historical Society* 33 (1940): 234-37. Account of an 1867 game between Cairo and Paducah teams.

1091. Cain, Louis P. "William Dean's Theory of Urban Growth: Chicago's Commerce and Industry, 1854-1871." *Journal of Economic History* 45 (June 1985): 241-49.

1092. Carter, C. C. "Illinois' First Showman." *Journal of the Illinois State Historical Society* 34 (1941): 371-75. Cyrus Carter started a traveling magic show with music.

1093. Clark, Dwight F. "The Wreck of the *Lady Elgin*." *Journal of the Illinois State Historical Society* 39 (1946): 407-18. The *Lady Elgin* was struck amidship by another Great Lakes steamer and sank offshore near Evanston on 7 September 1860. Almost three hundred people lost their lives; the casualty count was never exact.

1094. Congregational General Association of Illinois, Committee on Knox College. *Rights of Congregationalists in Knox College, Being the Report of a Committee of Investigation of the General Association of Illinois.* Chicago: Church, Goodman & Cushing, 1859.

1095. Curran, Nathaniel B. "General Isaac B. Curran: Gregarious Jeweler." *Journal of the Illinois State Historical Society* 71 (1978): 273-78. This account of Isaac Curran's life illustrates social life and customs of a prosperous and politically prominent Springfield family.

1096. Davis, Margaret Burton. *The Woman Who Battled for the Boys in Blue: Mother Bickerdyke, Her Life and Labors for the Relief of Our Soldiers . . .* San Francisco: Printed and sold by A. T. Dewey, 1886.

1097. Epstein, Dena J. *Music Publishing in Chicago before 1871: The Firm of Root and Cady, 1858-1871.* Detroit Studies in Music Bibliography, no. 14. Detroit: Information Coordinators, 1969.

1098. Fortney, John F. M. "The Wreck of the *James Watson*: A Civil War Disaster." *Journal of the Illinois State Historical Society* 37 (1944): 213-28. In a letter of 4 March 1865, Fortney describes the steamer wreck on the Mississippi; twenty soldiers lost their lives. The original letter is in the Illinois State Historical Library.

1099. Freedman, Stephen. "The Baseball Fad in Chicago, 1865-1870: An Exploration of the Role of Sport in the Nineteenth-Century City." *Journal of Sport History* 5 (Summer 1978): 42-64.

1100. Gates, Paul Wallace. "The Land Policy of the Illinois Central Railroad, 1851-1870." *Journal of Economic and Business History* 3 (1931): 554-73.

1101. _____. "Large-Scale Farming in Illinois, 1850 to 1870." *Agricultural History* 6 (1932): 14-25.

1102. _____. "The Promotion of Agriculture by the Illinois Central Railroad, 1855-1870." *Agricultural History* 5 (1931): 57-76.

1103. Gertz, Elmer. "Charles A. Dana and the *Chicago Republican*." *Journal of the Illinois State Historical Society* 45 (1952): 124-35. Dana established the *Republican* in 1865 but served as editor only a year.

1104. Hamilton, E. Bentley. "The Union League: Its Origin and Achievements in the Civil War." *Transactions of the Illinois State Historical Society, 1921*, pp. 110-15. The Union League was a Civil War secret society organized to support the Union and to counteract the pernicious influence of the Knights of the Golden Circle.

1105. Hansen, Harry. "How to Give away an Opera House." *Journal of the Illinois State Historical Society* 39 (1946): 419-24. An 1867 money-making scheme to sell the Crosby Opera House in Chicago by lottery.

1106. Holt, Marilyn Irvin. "Placing Out in Illinois: Emigration for the Poor, 1855-1863." *Transactions of the Illinois State Historical Society: Selected Papers from the Fifth and Sixth Illinois History Symposiums of the Illinois State Historical Society* [1984 and 1985]. Springfield, 1988. Pp. 35-47. The New York Children's Aid Society gathered up indigent adults and orphans and shipped them by railroad to Illinois (and other states), where local clergymen found lodging and employment for them.

1107. Hudson, Anna Ridgely. "A Girl of the Sixties: Excerpts from the Journal of Anna Ridgely." Edited by Octavia Roberts Corneau. *Journal of the Illinois State Historical Society* 22 (1929-30): 401-46. The editor calls the journal a "simple chronicle of social life" in Springfield through the Civil War years.

1108. *Illinois State Register* (Springfield), 2 July 1866. Extract of a story describing a baseball game between Jacksonville and Springfield teams is reprinted in the *Journal of the Illinois State Historical Society* 34 (1941): 256-57.

1109. Karamanski, Theodore J. *Rally 'Round the Flag: Chicago and the Civil War*. Chicago: Nelson-Hall, 1993.

1110. Keefe, Thomas M. "Catholic Issues in the Chicago Tribune before the Civil War." *Mid-America* 57 (1975): 227-45. Anti-Catholic and anti-Irish policies prevailed, 1853-61.

1111. Kramp, Larry. "Willie Lincoln, Civil War Correspondent." *Journal of the Illinois State Historical Society* 49 (1956): 67-70. Lincoln's ten-year-old son reports the death of Colonel Elmer Ellsworth in a letter to a friend. The letter is in the Illinois State Historical Library.

1112. Mabbott, Thomas O., and Jordan, Philip D. "The Prairie Chicken: Notes on Lincoln and Mrs. Kirkland." *Journal of the Illinois State Historical Society* 25 (1932-33): 154-66. The *Prairie Chicken*, published at Tilton by Joseph

Kirkland, was one of several periodicals issued during the Civil War in support of the United States Sanitary Commission. Extracts, printed here, include articles by Kirkland's mother and Kirkland's own reminiscences about Abraham Lincoln.

1113. McMurtry, R. Gerald. "Lincoln Patriotics." *Journal of the Illinois State Historical Society* 52 (1959): 123-29. Patriotics were envelopes bearing illustrations commemorating or condemning the Civil War and Lincoln.

1114. Noe, Kenneth W. " 'The Conservative': A Civil War Soldier's Musical Condemnation of Civil War Copperheads." *Journal of the Illinois State Historical Society* 84 (1991): 268-72. Aden E. Cherington of Illinois wrote the song in protest to William Lodge's newspaper, the *Piatt County Conservative*, which Cherington believed to be inadequately supportive of abolitionist policy.

1115. Norberg, Carl A. "First European Ship Direct to Chicago." *Inland Seas* 42 (1986): 74-77. The sailing ship was the schooner *Sleipner*, which arrived in 1862, carrying freight as well as Norwegian immigrants.

1116. Olsson, Nils William. "Naturalizations of Swedes in Rock Island County, IL, 1855-1864." *Swedish-American Genealogist* 2 (March 1982): 18-27.

1117. Packard, Elizabeth Parsons Ware. *Great Disclosure of Spiritual Wickedness in High Places; with an Appeal to the Government to Protect the Inalienable Rights of Married Women . . .* Boston: The author, 1865. An account of the trial, 11-19 January 1864, at Kankakee, brought by application of Mrs. Packard "under the *Habeas Corpus Act*, to be discharged from imprisonment by her husband in their own house." Mrs. Packard later wrote several books about her incarceration and her activities on behalf of mental patients.

1118. Phifer, Louisa Jane. "Letters from an Illinois Farm, 1864-1865." Edited by Carol Benson Pye. *Journal of the Illinois State Historical Society* 66 (1973): 387-403.

1119. "The Prairie Chicken: A Rarity." *Journal of the Illinois State Historical Society* 47 (1954): 84-88. Joseph Kirkland published the literary periodical for a year, 1864-65.

1120. Quinn, Camilla A. Corlas. *Lincoln's Springfield in the Civil War.* Western Illinois Monograph Series, no. 8. Macomb: Western Illinois University, 1991. Compelling narrative of social life and customs in the war years.

1121. _____. "Soldiers on Our Streets: The Effects of a Civil War Military Camp on the Springfield Community." *Illinois Historical Journal* 86 (1993): 245-56. Shortly after Camp Butler was established northeast of Springfield, residents of the town went on frequent excursions there to watch drills and listen to bands. But as the number of troops increased and the war progressed, soldiers from the camp brought disorder and fear to the streets of Springfield.

1122. Raines, Edgar F. Jr. "The American Missionary Association in Southern Illinois, 1856-1862: A Case Study in the Abolition Movement." *Journal of the Illinois State Historical Society* 65 (1972): 246-68.

1123. Rammelkamp, Charles Henry. "The Reverberations of the Slavery Conflict in a Pioneer College." *Mississippi Valley Historical Review* 14 (1927-28): 447-61. Effects of the slavery issue on Illinois College in the 1850s and 1860s.

1124. Renner, Richard Wilson. "Ye Kort Martial: A Tale of Chicago Politics, Theatre, Journalism, and Militia." *Journal of the Illinois State Historical Society* 66 (1973): 376-86. A misunderstanding among the officers assigned to review militia units in an 1858 parade led to a court-martial that was lampooned by the press and by a theatrical production.

1125. Robinson, Luther E. "Ephraim Elmer Ellsworth, First Martyr of the Civil War." *Transactions of the Illinois State Historical Society, 1923*, pp. 111-32. The colorful young Zouave officer was shot by a civilian in Alexandria, Virginia. The article contains several letters from Ellsworth.

1126. Sapinsley, Barbara. *The Private War of Mrs. Packard.* New York: Paragon House, 1991. A modern account of Elizabeth Packard's revolutionary actions to protect her own (and thus women's) civil rights and to reform the state's policies for the mentally ill.

1127. Schmidt, Hubert G. "Jediah F. Alexander, Civil War Editor." *Journal of the Illinois State Historical Society* 40 (1947): 135-53. Alexander edited the *Greenville Journal* in Bond County.

1128. "The Story of the Runaway Balloon." *Journal of the Illinois State Historical Society* 15 (1922-23): 501-6. The episode took place at the Illinois State Fair, held in 1858 at Centralia.

1129. Sutton, Robert Mize. *The Illinois Central in Peace and War, 1858-1868.* Urbana: University of Illinois, 1948. Reprint, The Railroads series, New York: Arno, 1981.

1130. Talbot, William L. "The Warsaw Boat Yard." *Western Illinois Regional Studies* 7, no. 2 (Fall 1984): 5-17.

1131. Temple, Wayne C. "The Pike's Peak Gold Rush." *Journal of the Illinois State Historical Society* 44 (1951): 147-59. Illinoisans who went to Colorado, 1858-60, and the effect of the Gold Rush on business and transportation in Illinois.

1132. _____. "Tinsmith to the Late Mr. Lincoln: Samuel S. Elder." *Journal of the Illinois State Historical Society* 71 (1978): 176-84. This sketch is illustrative of both business activities and social life and customs of the era.

1133. Urban, William. "The Temperance Movement in Monmouth, 1857-1859." *Western Illinois Regional Studies* 13, no. 2 (Fall 1990): 32-45.

1134. Vest, Eugene B. "When Dio Lewis Came to Dixon." *Journal of the Illinois State Historical Society* 40 (1947): 298-312. A physician of homeopathy and hydropathy, Lewis was a champion of physical-culture education and temperance. This account of his stay in Dixon in 1858 illustrates manners and customs.

1135. Voegeli, V. Jacque. *Free but Not Equal: The Midwest and the Negro during the Civil War.* Chicago: University of Chicago Press, 1967.

1136. Young, John Edward. "An Illinois Farmer during the Civil War: Extracts from the Journal of John Edward Young, 1859-66." *Journal of the Illinois State Historical Society* 26 (1933-34): 70-135. The complete original journal is in the Illinois State Historical Library.

G. LATE NINETEENTH CENTURY, 1871-1899

1. General Works

1137. Bogart, Ernest L., and Thompson, Charles Manfred. *The Industrial State, 1870-1893.* The Centennial History of Illinois, vol. 4. Springfield: Illinois Centennial Commission, 1920. Reliable but dull and dated.

1138. Ginger, Ray. *Altgeld's America: The Lincoln Ideal Versus Changing Realities.* New York: Funk & Wagnalls, 1958. A search for sources of the reform spirit that began to rise in industrial Chicago and Illinois in the late nineteenth century.

1139. Keiser, John H. *Building for the Centuries: Illinois, 1865 to 1898.* The Sesquicentennial History of Illinois, vol. 4. Urbana: Published for the Illinois Sesquicentennial Commission and the Illinois State Historical Society by the University of Illinois Press, 1977. This excellent volume--well-written, detailed, and scholarly--replaces volume 4 (by Bogart and Thompson) in the original Centennial History of Illinois series. Full bibliography and appendixes with population and manufacturing statistics.

2. Agriculture and Farmers' Organizations

1140. Britt, Albert. *An America That Was: What Life Was Like on an Illinois Farm Seventy Years Ago.* Barre, Mass.: Barre Publishers, 1964.

1141. Buck, Solon Justus. *The Agrarian Crusade: A Chronicle of the Farmer in Politics.* The Chronicles of America Series, vol. 45. New Haven: Yale University Press, 1920.

1142. _____. "Agricultural Organization in Illinois, 1870-1880." *Journal of the Illinois State Historical Society* 3, no. 1 (April 1910): 10-23.

1143. _____. *The Granger Movement: A Study in Agricultural Organization and Its Political, Economic, and Social Manifestations, 1870-1880.* Harvard Historical Studies, vol. 19. Cambridge, Mass., 1913. Reprint, Lincoln: University of Nebraska Press, 1963. Illinois railroad law is discussed on pages 123-58 of the 1913 edition. Other Illinois agricultural and Grange issues are discussed throughout the book.

1144. Ferris, William G. "The Disgrace of Ira Munn." *Journal of the Illinois State Historical Society* 68 (1975): 202-12. This account involves the storage of grain from the Midwest, state regulation of grain elevators, and an attempt by grain dealers and speculators to corner the wheat market. Chicago Board of Trade member Ira Munn was convicted of violating the state's 1871 warehouse act; his name became famous from the United States Supreme Court decision (*Munn* v. *Illinois*) that validated the Illinois law.

1145. Iftner, George H. "Memorial to James L. Reid, Pioneer Corn Breeder." *Journal of the Illinois State Historical Society* 48 (1955): 427-30. On a farm in

Tazewell County, Reid developed Reid's Yellow Dent Corn, which was the source of many present hybrids.

1146. Marsh, Charles W. *Recollections, 1837-1910.* Chicago: Farm Implement News, 1910. One of the inventors of the Marsh harvester discusses Illinois farming and industry.

1147. Paine, A. E. *The Granger Movement in Illinois.* University Studies, vol. 1, no. 8 (September 1904). Urbana, Ill.: University Press.

1148. Scott, Roy V. *The Agrarian Movement in Illinois, 1880-1896.* Illinois Studies in the Social Sciences, vol. 52. Urbana: University of Illinois Press, 1962.

1149. _____. "Grangerism in Champaign County, Illinois, 1873-1877." *Mid-America* 43 (1961): 139-63.

1150. _____. "John Patterson Stelle, Agrarian Crusader from Southern Illinois." *Journal of the Illinois State Historical Society* 55 (1962): 229-49.

1151. _____. "Milton George and the Farmers' Alliance Movement." *Mississippi Valley Historical Review* 45 (1958-59): 90-109.

1152. Zerbe, Richard O. Jr. "The Origin and Effect of Grain Trade Regulations in the Late Nineteenth Century." *Agricultural History* 56 (1982): 172-93; comments by Jonathan Lurie, 211-14.

3. Business, Labor, and Industry

1153. Altgeld, John Peter. *Reasons for Pardoning Fielden, Neebe & Schwab, the Haymarket Anarchists.* 1893. Reprint, Chicago: Charles H. Kerr, 1986.

1154. Avrich, Paul. *The Haymarket Tragedy.* Princeton, N.J.: Princeton University Press, 1984. A narrative history based on impressive research.

1155. Boston, Ray. "General Matthew Mark Trumbull, Respectable Radical." *Journal of the Illinois State Historical Society* 66 (1973): 159-76. The British-born Chicago attorney and champion of labor is probably best known for his efforts to free the Haymarket anarchists.

1156. Boyle, O. D. *History of Railroad Strikes: A History of the Railroad Revolt of 1877; the American Railroad Union Strike on the Great Northern in 1894 and Its Participation in the Pullman Car Strikes of the Same Year.* Washington, D.C.: Brotherhood Publishing, 1935.

1157. Busch, Francis X. "The Haymarket Riot and the Trial of the Anarchists." *Journal of the Illinois State Historical Society* 48 (1955): 247-70.

1158. Calmer, Alan. *Labor Agitator: The Story of Albert R. Parsons.* New York: International Publishers, 1937. Parsons was one of the anarchists hanged for the Haymarket affair.

1159. Carr, Clark E. *History of Bringing the Atchison, Topeka & Santa Fe Railway to Galesburg.* Galesburg: Wagoner Printing, 1913.

1160. Carwardine, William Horace. *The Pullman Strike.* Chicago: Charles H. Kerr, 1894. Reprint, for the Illinois Labor History Society, 1971. The author, a Methodist minister in Pullman, wrote this book before the strike ended; it is a valuable contribution to the history of the strike, the strikers, and the community.

1161. Cary, Lorin Lee. "Adolph Germer and the 1890's Depression." *Journal of the Illinois State Historical Society* 68 (1975): 337-43. Young Adolph Germer's experiences as a coal miner led to his becoming a United Mine Workers official and a member of the Socialist party.

1162. Chapin, John R. "The Infamous Pullman Strike as Revealed by the Robert Todd Lincoln Collection." *Journal of the Illinois State Historical Society* 74 (1981): 179-98. The collection is in the Illinois State Historical Library.

1163. Charrney, Theodore Sherwin. "The Potatoe Ships." *Transactions of the Illinois State Historical Society: Selected Papers from the Seventh Annual History Symposium and the Eighth Annual History Symposium* [1986 and 1987]. Springfield, 1989. Pp. 69-73. Producers in Michigan shipped their potatoes to Chicago, and ship captains sold them directly from the ships.

1164. Cleveland, Grover. *The Government in the Chicago Strike of 1894.* Princeton, N.J.: Princeton University Press, 1913.

1165. Cobb, Stephen G. *Reverend William Carwardine and the Pullman Strike of 1894: The Christian Gospel and Social Justice.* Lewiston, N.Y.: Edwin Mellen Press, 1992.

1166. Crawford, T. C. "Pullman Company and Its Striking Workmen." *Harper's Weekly* 38 (1894): 677, 684-89.

1167. David, Henry. *The History of the Haymarket Affair: A Study in the American Social-Revolutionary and Labor Movements.* New York: Farrar, 1936. 2d ed., New York: Russell & Russell, 1958.

1168. Destler, Chester McArthur. "The Opposition of American Businessmen to Social Control during the 'Gilded Age.' " *Mississippi Valley Historical Review* 39 (1952-53): 641-72. Contains many examples from Illinois.

1169. East, Ernest Edward. "The Distillers' and Cattle Feeders' Trust, 1887-1895." *Journal of the Illinois State Historical Society* 45 (1952): 101-23.

1170. *First Infantry, Illinois National Guard, Second Annual Military Ball, Wednesday, October 9, 1895.* Chicago: Rogers & Wells, 1895. Contains accounts of the regiment's actions in the 1886 stockyards riots and in the Pullman Strike.

1171. Foner, Philip S., ed. *The Autobiographies of the Haymarket Martyrs.* New York: Humanities Press, 1969. These autobiographies were first printed in the *Knights of Labor*, published in Chicago.

1172. Garrett, Romeo B. "The Role of the Duryea Brothers in the Development of the Gasoline Automobile." *Journal of the Illinois State Historical Society* 68 (1975): 174-80. The Duryea brothers, of Wyoming, Illinois, manufactured their automobiles in Springfield, Massachusetts, and Peoria Heights, Illinois, 1893-98.

1173. Gernon, Blaine Brooks. "Hinckley's Railroad Empire." *Journal of the Illinois State Historical Society* 47 (1954): 361-72. Francis Edward Hinckley developed several short lines in Illinois.

1174. Gottlieb, Amy Zahl. "British Coal Miners: A Demographic Study of Braidwood and Streator, Illinois." *Journal of the Illinois State Historical Society* 72 (1979): 179-92.

1175. Griffin, Donald W. "Community Functions in the Late Nineteenth Century: A Photographic Essay." *Western Illinois Regional Studies* 13, no. 2 (Fall 1990): 78-94. The photographs portray businesses as well as social life and customs.

1176. Gutman, Herbert G. "The Braidwood Lockout of 1874." *Journal of the Illinois State Historical Society* 53 (1960): 5-28. The three coal companies at Braidwood locked out the miners when they refused to accept lower wages. The companies capitulated after fourteen weeks.

1177. _____. "The Workers' Search for Power: Labor in the Gilded Age" in Morgan, H. Wayne, ed. *The Gilded Age: A Reappraisal.* Syracuse, N.Y.: Syracuse University Press, 1963. Reprinted in Scheiber, no. 4086.

1178. Harahan, Joseph P., ed. " 'Police Force' in the Arsenal Shops: A Document on the 1899 Machinists' Strike at Rock Island Arsenal." *Journal of the Illinois State Historical Society* 74 (1981): 119-29.

1179. Hicken, Victor. "The Virden and Pana Mine Wars of 1898." *Journal of the Illinois State Historical Society* 52 (1959): 263-78.

1180. Hirsch, Eric L. *Urban Revolt: Ethnic Politics in the Nineteenth-Century Chicago Labor Movement.* Berkeley: University of California Press, 1990.

1181. Husband, Joseph. *The Story of the Pullman Car.* Chicago: McClurg, 1917.

1182. "Illinois' First Electric Street Railway." *Journal of the Illinois State Historical Society* 46 (1953): 328. The trolley line started operations in Ottawa in 1889.

1183. Jebsen, Harry Jr. "The Role of Blue Island in the Pullman Strike of 1894." *Journal of the Illinois State Historical Society* 67 (1974): 275-93.

1184. Keiser, John H. "Black Strikebreakers and Racism in Illinois, 1865-1900." *Journal of the Illinois State Historical Society* 65 (1972): 313-26. African-Americans were brought from the South to replace striking coal miners.

1185. Lindsey, Almont. "Paternalism and the Pullman Strike." *American Historical Review* 44 (1938-39): 272-89.

1186. _____. *The Pullman Strike: The Story of a Unique Experiment and of a Great Labor Upheaval.* Chicago: University of Chicago Press, 1942. Reprint, Phoenix Books, 1964. A scholarly account of the 11 May 1894 strike. The "unique experiment" was the company town of Pullman, now a part of Chicago.

1187. McMurry, Donald LeCrone. *The Great Burlington Strike of 1888: A Case History in Labor Relations.* Cambridge, Mass.: Harvard University Press, 1956. General offices and the eastern terminal of the Burlington were in Chicago.

1188. Manning, Thomas G., ed. *The Chicago Strike of 1894: Industrial Labor in the Nineteenth Century.* New York: Holt, 1960. Reprint, 1966.

1189. Nelson, Bruce C. *Beyond the Martyrs: A Social History of Chicago's Anarchists, 1870-1900.* New Brunswick, N.J.: Rutgers University Press, 1988.

1190. Parsons, Lucy Eldine. *Life of Albert R. Parsons, with Brief History of the Labor Movement in America.* Chicago: The author, 1889.

1191. Plummer, Mark A. "Governor Richard J. Oglesby and the Haymarket Anarchists." *Selected Papers in Illinois History,* 1981. Springfield: Illinois State Historical Society, 1982. Pp. 50-59.

1192. Remington, F. "Chicago under the Law." *Harper's Weekly* 38 (1894): 703-5.

1193. _____. "Chicago under the Mob." *Harper's Weekly* 38 (1894): 680-81.

1194. _____. "Withdrawal of the U.S. troops." *Harper's Weekly* 38 (1894): 748-49.

1195. Roediger, Dave, and Rosemont, Franklin, eds. *Haymarket Scrapbook.* Chicago: Charles H. Kerr, 1986.   A collection of illustrations and written materials related to the riot.

1196. Sampson, Robert D. " 'Honest men and law-abiding citizens': The 1894 Railroad Strike in Decatur." *Illinois Historical Journal* 85 (1992): 74-88.

1197. Seng, R. A., and Gilmour, J. V. *Brink's, the Money Movers: The Story of a Century of Service.* Chicago: Lakeside Press, R. R. Donnelley, 1959.

1198. Sereiko, George Eugene. "Chicago and Its Book Trade, 1871-1893." Ph.D. dissertation, Case Western Reserve University, 1973. Ann Arbor, Mich.: University Microfilms. History of both bookselling and publishing.

1199. Sigmund, Elwin W. "Railroad Strikers in Court: Unreported Contempt Cases in 1877." *Journal of the Illinois State Historical Society* 49 (1956): 190-209.

1200. *Souvenir, Governor's Guard, Co. C, Fifth Infantry, Illinois National Guard, Springfield, Illinois.* Springfield, Ill.: Illinois State Register, n.d. History of the National Guard unit that was called to active duty to preserve order during the coal mine strike at Pana and the Pullman Strike, both in the 1890s.

1201. Stead, William Thomas. *Chicago To-day: The Labour War in America.* Mass Violence in America series. Reprint of the 1894 ed., New York: Arno Press, 1969.

1202. Stein, Leon, comp. *The Pullman Strike.* New York: Arno Press, 1969. Reprints of four works about the 1894 strike.

1203. Suhrbur, Thomas J. "The Economic Transformation of Carpentry in Late Nineteenth-Century Chicago." *Illinois Historical Journal* 81 (1988): 109-24. The account closes with the acceptance of unions by carpenters.

1204. Tarr, Joel Arthur. "The Chicago Anti-Department Store Crusade of 1897: A Case Study in Urban Commercial Development." *Journal of the Illinois State Historical Society* 64 (1971): 161-72.

1205. _____. "J. R. Walsh of Chicago: A Case Study in Banking and Politics, 1881-1905." Reprinted from *Business History Review*, vol. 40, in Walsh, James, comp. *The Irish: America's Political Class.* The Irish-Americans series. New York: Arno, 1976.

1206. Turner, Henry Lathrop, ed. *Souvenir Album and Sketch Book, First Infantry, I. N. G. of Chicago.* Chicago: Knight & Leonard, 1890? This unit was called to duty in the 1874 lockout of Braidwood miners, the 1877 railroad strikes, and the 1886 stockyards strike. The *Album* contains biographical sketches and photographs of many regimental officers, as well as company rosters.

1207. U. S. Strike Commission, 1894. *Report on the Chicago Strike of June-July 1894, by the United States Strike Commission . . . with Appendices Containing Testimony, Proceedings, and Recommendations.* U. S. Congress. Senate. 53d Cong., 3 sess. Exec. Doc., vol. 2, no. 7. Washington, 1895.

1208. Wilson, Howard A. "William Dean Howells's Unpublished Letters about the Haymarket Affair." *Journal of the Illinois State Historical Society* 56 (1963): 5-19. Letters in this article are from Knox College, Galesburg.

1209. Wish, Harvey. "Governor Altgeld Pardons the Anarchists." *Journal of the Illinois State Historical Society* 31 (1938): 424-48.

1210. _____. "The Pullman Strike: A Study in Industrial Warfare." *Journal of the Illinois State Historical Society* 32 (1939): 288-312.

1211. Writers' Program, Illinois. *Annals of Labor and Industry in Illinois . . .* 3 vols. (January, February, March 1890; April, May, June 1890; and July, August, September 1890). Chicago, 1939, 1940, 1941. Extracts from newspapers and periodicals.

4. Manners and Customs

1212. Anderson, Russell H. "The First Automobile Race in America." *Journal of the Illinois State Historical Society* 47 (1954): 343-59. The 1895 Thanksgiving Day race took place in Chicago.

1213. Clinton, Katherine B. "An Illinois Family of the 1870's." *Journal of the Illinois State Historical Society* 66 (1973): 198-204. The life and times of a family in northwestern Illinois, as revealed in family letters.

1214. Crane, Frances Noel. "Creal Springs, Village with a Past." *Journal of the Illinois State Historical Society* 37 (1944): 173-77. Description of life at a typical Illinois spa, to which visitors came to drink the mineral waters and take the baths. The village also had a flourishing college and conservatory of music.

1215. Dowell, Cheryl Wexell. "Dear Diary, 1886-1890: Clara Lindbeck Writes from Bishop Hill." *Illinois Historical Journal* 82 (1989): 231-38. This article, based on Lindbeck's diary, presents an unusually full account of daily life in a small town.

1216. "First-Hand Report of an 1877 Wedding." *Journal of the Illinois State Historical Society* 47 (1954): 421-23. An elaborate wedding and the following week-long celebration in Springfield are described in a letter from one of the guests.

1217. Garvey, Timothy J. "The Artist Is Out: Recreations of the 'Little Room' and 'Eagle's Nest.' " *Transactions of the Illinois State Historical Society: Selected Papers from the Fifth and Sixth Illinois History Symposiums of the Illinois State Historical Society* [1984 and 1985]. Springfield, 1988. Pp. 59-67.

1218. Grierson, Alice Kirk. *The Colonel's Lady on the Western Frontier: The Correspondence of Alice Kirk Grierson.* Edited by Shirley A. Leckie. Women in the West series. Lincoln: University of Nebraska Press, 1989. Many of the Grierson family letters (1866-88) were written from Jacksonville. The Illinois State Historical Library has a large collection of Benjamin H. Grierson papers, from which many of the letters were drawn.

1219. Harrington, Estelle Messenger. *Ida Amelia: A True Story Connected with the Messenger Family of Illinois (St. Clair County).* St. Louis: The author, 1940.

1220. Hendrickson, Walter B. "Commencement Week in 1876." *Journal of the Illinois State Historical Society* 43 (1950): 13-27. The town of Jacksonville, with its colleges and other public institutions, had many commencement festivities.

1221. Holst, David L. "Charles G. Radbourne: The Greatest Pitcher of the Nineteenth Century." *Illinois Historical Journal* 81 (1988): 255-68. The Illinois minor league pitcher who rose to fame with the Buffalo Bisons and the Providence Grays of the National League.

1222. Masters, Edgar Lee. *The Sangamon.* The Rivers of America. New York: Farrar, 1942. Life in central Illinois in the 1880s. A University of Illinois Press edition (1988) has a helpful introduction by Charles E. Burgess.

1223. Mayne, Isabella Maud Rittenhouse. *Maud.* Edited by Richard Lee Strout. New York: Macmillan, 1939. Extracts from the diary of Maud Rittenhouse (later Mayne), who discusses social life in Cairo, 1881-95.

1224. Ralph, Julian. "Chicago's Gentle Side." *Harper's New Monthly Magazine* 87 (June-November 1893): 286-98. Chicago's women as leaders of social and cultural life as well as of reform movements.

1225. Riley, Glenda. "From Ireland to Illinois: The Life of Helen Ross Hall." *Illinois Historical Journal* 81 (1988): 163-80. Based on Mrs. Hall's memoir in the McLean County Historical Society, this is the story of an Irish immigrant family that settled in Bloomington in 1868.

1226. Shiffler, Harold C. "The Chicago Church-Theater Controversy of 1881-1882." *Journal of the Illinois State Historical Society* 53 (1960): 361-75. Protestant clergymen protested the entertainment at Chicago's four major theatres.

1227. Trutter, John Thomas, and Trutter, Edith English. *The Governor Takes a Bride: The Celebrated Marriage of Cora English and John R. Tanner,*

Governor of Illinois (1897-1901). Carbondale: Southern Illinois University Press, for the Illinois State Historical Society, 1977. The wedding took place in December 1896, and the Tanners shortly thereafter moved into the newly renovated Executive Mansion, which the authors describe.

1228. Van Bolt, Roger H. " 'Cap' Anson's First Professional Baseball Contract." *Journal of the Illinois State Historical Society* 45 (1952): 262-68. Biographical sketch of the player for the Rockford "Forest City Baseball Club"; accompanying the sketch is the text of Anson's 1871 contract, which is in the Illinois State Historical Library.

1229. Writers' Project of the Works Project Administration in the State of Illinois, comp. "Camp Lincoln." *Journal of the Illinois State Historical Society* 34 (1941): 271-302. Camp Lincoln, Springfield, is still operated by the National Guard, but the writers concentrate on the period when the camp played an important role in the social life of the area.

5. Medicine and Science

1230. Arnold, Lois Barber. *Four Lives in Science: Women's Education in the Nineteenth Century.* New York: Schocken Books, 1984. One of the four subjects is Louisa C. Allen Gregory, who established the School of Domestic Science and Art at the University of Illinois. The curriculum included training in science.

1231. Cooke, M. Francis, Sister. *Doors That Never Close: A Centennial History of St. John's Hospital.* Springfield, Ill.: Sangamon County Historical Society, 1975.

1232. Davenport, F. Garvin. "John Henry Rauch and Public Health in Illinois, 1877-1891." *Journal of the Illinois State Historical Society* 50 (1957): 277-93. Rauch was a progressive physician who headed the State Board of Health.

1233. _____. *Rise of the Dental Profession in Illinois, 1870-1900.* Monmouth: Kellogg Printing Company, 1975.

1234. _____. "The Sanitation Revolution in Illinois, 1870-1900." *Journal of the Illinois State Historical Society* 66 (1973): 306-26. The movement for acceptance of such public health measures as sewage disposal, inside plumbing, control of waste products from factories and packinghouses, sanitary milk and food supplies, and pure water.

1235. Morgan, H. Wayne. " 'No, Thank You. I've Been to Dwight': Reflections on the Keeley Cure for Alcoholism." *Illinois Historical Journal* 82 (1989): 147-66. History of the early days of the Keeley treatment and its founder, Dr. Leslie Keeley.

6. Politics and Government

1236. Barnes, James A. "Illinois and the Gold-Silver Controversy, 1890-1896." *Transactions of the Illinois State Historical Society, 1931*, pp. 35-59.

1237. Cantrall, Daniel. "The Illinois State Board of Public Charities and the County Poorhouses, 1870-1900: Institutional Ideals vs. County Realities." *Transactions of the Illinois State Historical Society: Selected Papers from the Fifth and Sixth Illinois History Symposiums of the Illinois State Historical Society* [1984 and 1985]. Springfield, 1988. Pp. 49-57.

1238. Davis, Allen F. "Jane Addams vs. the Ward Boss." *Journal of the Illinois State Historical Society* 53 (1960): 247-65. Addams learned "the realities of ward politics" in her several efforts to unseat 19th Ward Alderman John Powers in the late 1890s.

1239. Destler, Chester McArthur. "Consummation of a Labor-Populist Alliance in Illinois, 1894." *Mississippi Valley Historical Review* 27 (1940-41): 589-602.

1240. Di Nunzio, Mario R. "Lyman Trumbull, the States' Rights Issue, and the Liberal Republican Revolt." *Journal of the Illinois State Historical Society* 66 (1973): 364-75.

1241. Jensen, Richard J. "The Religious and Occupational Roots of Party Identification: Illinois and Indiana in the 1870's." *Civil War History* 16 (1970): 325-43.

1242. Newcombe, Alfred W. "Alson J. Streeter, an Agrarian Liberal." *Journal of the Illinois State Historical Society* 38 (1945): 414-45 and 39 (1946): 68-95. Robert Cowdrey of the United Labor party and Alson J. Streeter of the Union Labor party, both of Illinois, were two of the eight candidates for president of the United States in 1888.

1243. Pitkin, William A. "Shelby M. Cullom, Presidential Prospect." *Journal of the Illinois State Historical Society* 49 (1956): 375-86. Cullom sought the Republican nomination in 1888 and 1892.

1244. Pixton, John E. Jr. "Charles G. Dawes and the McKinley Campaign." *Journal of the Illinois State Historical Society* 48 (1955): 283-306. Dawes led the Illinois campaign for McKinley's nomination and election to the presidency in 1896.

1245. Roberts, Sidney I. "The Municipal Voters' League and Chicago's Boodlers." *Journal of the Illinois State Historical Society* 53 (1960): 117-48. The league was founded in 1896 to fight city corruption.

1246. Scharnau, Ralph William. "Thomas J. Morgan and the United Labor Party of Chicago." *Journal of the Illinois State Historical Society* 66 (1973): 41-61. The short-lived party that Morgan led was an attempt to unite conservative and radical labor groups with "pure and simple" trade unionists to act against the anti-labor legislation that followed the 1886 strike at McCormick Harvester Works and the Haymarket riot.

1247. Schlup, Leonard. "The Congressional Career of the First Adlai E. Stevenson." *Illinois Quarterly* 38, no. 2 (Winter 1975): 5-19. Stevenson was elected to Congress in 1874 and 1878; defeated in '76, '80, and '82.

1248. Searles, William C. "Governor Cullom and the Pekin Whiskey Ring Scandal." *Journal of the Illinois State Historical Society* 51 (1958): 28-41. Cullom was the 1876 Republican gubernatorial candidate when he was rumored to have been involved with two United States Treasury Department officials who absconded with more than $100,000. No charges were ever filed against Cullom, and he won the governorship and then a seat in the United States Senate.

1249. Tompkins, C. David. "John Peter Altgeld as a Candidate for Mayor of Chicago in 1899." *Journal of the Illinois State Historical Society* 56 (1963): 654-76.

1250. Wish, Harvey. "John Peter Altgeld and the Background of the Campaign of 1896." *Mississippi Valley Historical Review* 24 (1937-38): 503-18.

1251. _____. "John Peter Altgeld and the Election of 1896." *Journal of the Illinois State Historical Society* 30 (1937-38): 353-84.

7. Social Problems

1252. Allaman, John Lee. "The Crime, Trial, and Execution of William W. Lee of East Burlington, Illinois." *Western Illinois Regional Studies* 6 (1983): 49-68.

In 1876 Lee was executed at the Henderson County jail for the gruesome murder of a prostitute in his employ.

1253. Black, Paul V. "Employee Alcoholism on the Burlington Railroad, 1876-1902." *Journal of the West* 17 (October 1978): 5-11.

1254. Cha-Jua, Sundiata Keita. " 'Join hands and hearts with law and order': The 1893 Lynching of Samuel J. Bush and the Response of Decatur's African American Community." *Illinois Historical Journal* 83 (1990): 187-200.

1255. Downey, Dennis B. "William Stead and Chicago: A Victorian Jeremiah in the Windy City." *Mid-America* 68 (1986): 153-66. The muckraking British journalist and social reformer William Stead exposed the political corruption and moral turpitude of Chicago in his book *If Christ Came to Chicago.*

1256. Gara, Larry. "A Glorious Time: The 1874 Abolitionist Reunion in Chicago." *Journal of the Illinois State Historical Society* 65 (1972): 280-92. According to the author, the reunion "did not reverse the national mood of reconciliation that culminated in the removal of federal troops from the South and the virtual abandonment of the rights of southern black people."

1257. Hall, Andy. "The Ku Klux Klan in Southern Illinois in 1875." *Journal of the Illinois State Historical Society* 46 (1953): 363-72.

1258. Kirkland, Joseph. "Among the Poor of Chicago." *Scribner's Magazine* 12 (1892): 2-27.

1259. Lederer, Francis L. II. "Nora Marks, Investigative Reporter." *Journal of the Illinois State Historical Society* 68 (1975): 306-18, and "Nora Marks--Reinvestigated." Ibid. 73 (1980): 61-64. As a "special writer" for the *Chicago Tribune*, Eleanor Stackhouse (later Atkinson) investigated social life and social problems as well as government agencies. Nora Marks was her pen name.

1260. Raines, Edgar F. Jr. "The Ku Klux Klan in Illinois, 1867-1875." *Illinois Historical Journal* 78 (1985): 17-44. Activities of the Klan in southern Illinois and government efforts to suppress its racist and criminal operations.

1261. Roberts, Clarence N. "The Crusade against Secret Societies and the National Christian Association." *Journal of the Illinois State Historical Society* 64 (1971): 382-400. The crusade was led in the late nineteenth century by Jonathan Blanchard, president of Wheaton College.

1262. Schwarz, Richard W. "Dr. John Harvey Kellogg as a Social Gospel Practitioner." *Journal of the Illinois State Historical Society* 57 (1964): 5-22. Kellogg operated a medical mission and a medical college on Chicago's South Side.

1263. Smith, Beverly A. "Murder in a Rural Setting: Logan County Homicides, 1865-1900." *Western Illinois Regional Studies* 13, no. 1 (Spring 1990): 61-79.

1264. _____. "The Murder of Zura Burns, 1883: A Case Study of a Homicide in Lincoln." *Illinois Historical Journal* 84 (1991): 218-34.

1265. _____. "People v. Weyrich (1877): A Nineteenth-Century Murder Case." *Old Northwest* 14 (1988): 107-29. In 1877 Peter Weyrich was poisoned by his wife, Anna, but she was acquitted. The author examines the court system and the "image and reality" of the female murderer.

1266. Smith, Jonathan. "The Redeemed of 1874: The Women's Temperance Crusade in Bloomington, Illinois." *Transactions of the Illinois State Historical Society: Selected Papers from the Seventh Annual History Symposium and the Eighth Annual History Symposium* [1986 and 1987]. Springfield, 1989. Pp. 51-58.

1267. Stead, William Thomas. *If Christ Came to Chicago: A Plea for the Union of All Who Love in the Service of All Who Suffer.* Chicago: Laird & Lee, 1894.

8. Spanish-American War

1268. Bolton, H. W., ed. *History of the Second Regiment, Illinois Volunteer Infantry, from Organization to Muster-out.* Chicago: R. R. Donnelley, 1899.

1269. Bunzey, Rufus S. *History of Companies I and E, Sixth Regt., Illinois Volunteer Infantry from Whiteside County; Containing a Detailed Account of Their Experiences While Serving as Volunteers in the Porto Rican Campaign during the Spanish-American War of 1898. Also a Record of the Two Companies as State Troops from the Date of Organization to April 30th, 1901.* Morrison, Ill., 1901.

1270. Gatewood, Willard B. Jr. "An Experiment in Color: The Eighth Illinois Volunteers, 1898-1899." *Journal of the Illinois State Historical Society* 65 (1972): 293-312.

1271. _____. *"Smoked Yankees" and the Struggle for Empire: Letters from Negro Soldiers, 1898-1902.* Urbana: University of Illinois Press, 1971. Includes letters from members of the 8th Illinois Volunteers.

1272. Goode, W. T. *The "Eighth Illinois," by Corporal W. T. Goode, Company F, Eighth Illinois Volunteer Regiment, United States Volunteers.* Chicago: Blakely Printing, 1899.

1273. *Historical Sketch of the Oakland Rifles and Co. C. 4th Infantry, I.N.G. Presented Nov. 21, 1889.* Chicago: Foster, Roe & Crone, 1889?

1274. Illinois. Adjutant-General's Office. *Adjutant-General's Report Containing the Complete Muster-out Rolls of the Illinois Volunteers Who Served in the Spanish-American War, 1898 and 1899.* 5 vols. Springfield: Phillips Brothers, 1902-4.

1275. Lacey, Edwin M. "The Cuban Diary of Edwin M. Lacey." Edited by Donald F. Tingley. *Journal of the Illinois State Historical Society* 56 (1963): 20-35. Lacey served in the 4th Illinois Volunteer Infantry Regiment and the 2d U.S. Volunteer Signal Corps, 1898-99.

1276. Pease, William H. "Samuel Fallows, Expansionist." *Journal of the Illinois State Historical Society* 46 (1953): 265-76. Educator, minister, Civil War veteran, and social crusader, Fallows held patriotic and social views that led to his advocacy of territorial acquisition and economic imperialism.

1277. Skinner, John R. *History of the Fourth Illinois Volunteers in Their Relation to the Spanish-American War for the Liberation of Cuba and Other Island Possessions of Spain.* Logansport, Ind.: Wilson, Humphreys, 1899.

1278. Wade, Louise Carroll. "Hell Hath No Fury like a General Scorned: Nelson A. Miles, the Pullman Strike, and the Beef Scandal of 1898." *Illinois Historical Journal* 79 (1986): 162-84. Wade relates General Miles's Pullman Strike experiences to his charges four years later that Chicago meatpackers supplied his troops with tainted meat. A court of inquiry exonerated the suppliers.

9. World's Columbian Exposition

1279. Anderson, Norman D. *Ferris Wheels: An Illustrated History.* Bowling Green, Ohio: Bowling Green State University Popular Press, 1992. The huge vertical wheel built by George Washington Gale Ferris became the symbol for the World's Columbian Exposition.

1280. Badger, Reid. *The Great American Fair: The World's Columbian Exposition & American Culture.* Chicago: Nelson-Hall, 1979.

1281. Bancroft, Hubert Howe. *The Book of the Fair: An Historical and Descriptive Presentation of the World's Science, Art, and Industry, as Viewed from the Columbian Exposition at Chicago in 1893 . . .* 2 vols. Chicago and San Francisco: Bancroft, 1893. Also issued by Bancroft in 1893 was a fin-de-siècle edition of ten volumes, accompanied by ten portfolios of colored plates.

1282. Bolotin, Norman, and Laing, Christine. *The World's Columbian Exposition.* Washington: Preservation Press, National Trust for Historic Preservation, 1992.

1283. Bunner, H. C. "The Making of the White City." *Scribner's Magazine* 12 (1892): 398-418.

1284. Burg, David F. *Chicago's White City of 1893.* Lexington: University Press of Kentucky, 1976. A critique of the architects and architecture of the exposition.

1285. Burnham, Daniel. *The Final Official Report of the Director of the World's Columbian Exposition.* 2 vols. Introduction by Joan E. Draper; preface by Thomas Hines. New York: Garland, 1989. Photographic reproduction of the original typewritten manuscript pages as they were mounted with photographs in bound volumes. The original photographs and drawings are of great interest to students of architecture but as reprinted in gray are greatly compromised.

1286. Cassell, Frank A. "Welcoming the World: Illinois' Role in the World's Columbian Exposition." *Illinois Historical Journal* 79 (1986): 230-44.

1287. Downey, Dennis B. "The Congress on Labor at the 1893 World's Columbian Exposition." *Journal of the Illinois State Historical Society* 76 (1983): 131-38.

1288. _____. "Tradition and Acceptance: American Catholics and the Columbian Exposition." *Mid-America* 63 (1981): 79-92.

1289. Dybwad, G. L., and Bliss, Joy V. *Annotated Bibliography: World's Columbian Exposition, Chicago 1893.* Albuquerque, N.M.: The Book Stops

Here, 1992. The volume contains 2,467 numbered items. Entries from any one periodical are listed together under the periodical name--with the result that the authors say they examined more than 2,700 items. Good index.

1290. Gilbert, James. *Perfect Cities: Chicago's Utopias of 1893*. Chicago: University of Chicago Press, 1991. The utopias are the World's Columbian Exposition; the planned company town of Pullman; and the utopias envisioned by a) Dwight Moody's religious crusade and b) books about the city and plans for its further development.

1291. Johnson, Rossiter, ed. *A History of the World's Columbian Exposition Held in Chicago in 1893*. 4 vols. New York: Appleton, 1897-98.

1292. Lederer, Francis L. II. "Competition for the World's Columbian Exposition: The Chicago Campaign." *Journal of the Illinois State Historical Society* 65 (1972): 382-95.

1293. McCarthy, Michael P. "Should We Drink the Water? Typhoid Fever Worries at the Columbian Exposition." *Illinois Historical Journal* 86 (1993): 2-14.

1294. Millet, F. D. "The Decoration of the Exposition." *Scribner's Magazine* 12 (1892): 692-709.

1295. Neufeld, Maurice. "The White City: The Beginnings of a Planned Civilization in America." *Journal of the Illinois State Historical Society* 27 (1934-35): 71-93. A social and cultural evaluation of the World's Columbian Exposition.

1296. Ralph, Julian. "Chicago: The Main Exhibit." *Harper's New Monthly Magazine* 84 (December 1891--May 1892): 425-36. The city itself as the main exhibit of the World's Columbian Exposition.

1297. Sandweiss, Eric. "Around the World in a Day: International Participation in the World's Columbian Exposition." *Illinois Historical Journal* 84 (1991): 2-14.

1298. Wilson, Robert E. "The Infanta at the Fair." *Journal of the Illinois State Historical Society* 59 (1966): 252-71. An account of Spain's official representative, the Infanta Eulalia, at the World's Columbian Exposition.

10. Miscellany

1299. Abramoske, Donald J. "The Founding of the *Chicago Daily News.*" *Journal of the Illinois State Historical Society* 59 (1966): 341-53. The *News* was founded by Melville E. Stone in December 1875. The author discusses other newspapers of that period as well.

1300. "The Angel Gabriel's Ledger." *Journal of the Illinois State Historical Society* 32 (1939): 390-94. An iron bridge over the Rock River at Dixon collapsed in 1873; several people on the bridge were rescued.

1301. Angle, Paul McClelland, ed. *The Great Chicago Fire, October 8-9, 1871, Described by Eight Men and Women Who Experienced Its Horrors and Testified to the Courage of Its Inhabitants.* Picture selection by Mary Frances Rhymer. Chicago: Chicago Historical Society, 1971. A new and enlarged edition of a 1946 publication.

1302. Berrell, George Barton. "George Barton Berrell's Piscatorial Summer of 1878." Edited by Harriet Bell Carlander and Kenneth D. Carlander. *Bulletin of the Missouri Historical Society* 7 (1950-51): 413-39. Fishing in Illinois near the Mississippi River in Madison and St. Clair counties.

1303. Burford, Cary Clive. *The Chatsworth Wreck: A Saga of Excursion Train Travel in the American Midwest in the 1880s.* Fairbury, Ill.: Blade Publishing, 1949.

1304. Charney, Wayne Michael, and Stamper, John W. "Nathan Clifford Ricker and the Beginning of Architectural Education in Illinois." *Illinois Historical Journal* 79 (1986): 257-66. Ricker, the first architecture student at the University of Illinois, was later a faculty member there.

1305. DeCotton, L. "A Frenchman's Visit to Chicago in 1886." Translated by Georges J. Joyaux. *Journal of the Illinois State Historical Society* 47 (1954): 45-56.

1306. Ellis, Thomas Harding. "A Description of the Chicago Fire of 1871." Edited by Robert H. Woody. *Mississippi Valley Historical Review* 33 (1946-47): 607-16. The editor provides a good brief bibliography of the fire.

1307. Fine, Howard D. "The Koreshan Unity: The Chicago Years of a Utopian Community." *Journal of the Illinois State Historical Society* 68 (1975): 213-27.

The Koreshan Unity was a communistic millennial community that flourished in Chicago, 1886-1903, before moving to Florida.

1308. Frizzell, Robert W. "German Freethinkers in Bloomington: Sampling a Forgotten Culture." *Transactions of the Illinois State Historical Society: Selected Papers from the Fifth and the Sixth Illinois History Symposiums of the Illinois State Historical Society* [1984 and 1985]. Springfield, 1988. Pp. 15-23. Prominent members of the late nineteenth-century German immigrant community who rejected traditional religion.

1309. Garvey, Timothy J. "Conferring Status: Lorado Taft's Portraits of an Artistic Community." *Illinois Historical Journal* 78 (1985): 162-78. In the late 1890s Taft sculpted busts of eight of his literary and artistic friends in an effort to place them on par with leaders in other fields in Chicago.

1310. Hendrickson, Walter B. "Jacksonville Artists of the 1870's." *Journal of the Illinois State Historical Society* 70 (1977): 258-75.

1311. Hutchison, William R. "Disapproval of Chicago: The Symbolic Trial of David Swing." *Journal of American History* 59 (1971-72): 30-47. A Presbyterian minister, Swing was an adherent of a liberal theology, which led to his 1874 trial for heresy by the Chicago Presbytery. He was acquitted.

1312. Kirkham, E. Bruce. "Harriet Beecher Stowe's Western Tour." *Old Northwest* 1 (March 1975): 35-49. On her 1873 tour Mrs. Stowe visited and presented "readings" in Springfield, Bloomington, and Chicago.

1313. Kogan, Herman, and Cromie, Robert. *The Great Fire: Chicago, 1871.* New York: Putnam, 1971.

1314. McIlvaine, Mabel, comp. *Reminiscences of Chicago during the Great Fire.* Lakeside Classics, no. 13. Chicago: R. R. Donnelley, 1915.

1315. Miller, Ross. *American Apocalypse: The Great Fire and the Myth of Chicago.* Chicago: University of Chicago Press, 1990. The author shows how the city "consciously exploited its own tragedy as an archetype of the modern struggle against adversity," becoming "America's most dynamic city between 1871 and 1894."

1316. Musham, H. A. "The Great Chicago Fire, October 8-10, 1871." *Transactions of the Illinois State Historical Society, 1940,* pp. 69-189.

1317. Oblinger, Carl D. *Religious Mimesis: Social Bases for the Holiness Schism in Late Nineteenth-Century Methodism: The Illinois Case, 1869-1885.* Evanston, Ill.: Institute for the Study of American Religion, 1973.

1318. Panagopoulos, E. P. "Chicago and the War between Greece and Turkey in 1897." *Journal of the Illinois State Historical Society* 49 (1956): 394-404. The city supplied both funds and troops to the Greeks. The Greek- and Armenian-Americans were particularly active, though support was widespread.

1319. Pauly, John J. "The Great Chicago Fire as a National Event." *American Quarterly* 36 (Winter 1984): 668-83.

1320. Peterson, William S. "Kipling's First Visit to Chicago." *Journal of the Illinois State Historical Society* 63 (1970): 290-301. The visit occurred in 1889.

1321. Robertson, Darrel M. *The Chicago Revival, 1876: Society and Revivalism in a Nineteenth-Century City.* Metuchen, N.J.: Scarecrow Press, 1989. An account of the revival led by Dwight L. Moody.

1322. Schlereth, Wendy Clauson. *The Chap-Book: A Journal of American Intellectual Life in the 1890's.* Ann Arbor, Mich.: UMI Research Press, 1982. A history of the short-lived magazine, published first at Harvard and then in Chicago.

1323. Schuyler, Montgomery. "Glimpses of Western Architecture: Chicago." *Harper's New Monthly Magazine* 83 (June-November 1891): 395-406, 559-70.

1324. Scofield, Charles Josiah. "Reminiscences of a Centenarian." *Journal of the Illinois State Historical Society* 47 (1954): 88-91. Description of the writer's legal education and law practice.

1325. Sennett, Richard. *Families against the City: Middle Class Homes of Industrial Chicago, 1872-1890.* Cambridge, Mass.: Harvard University Press, 1970. A study of the changing Chicago neighborhood of Union Park.

1326. Smith, Nina B. " 'This Bleak Situation': The Founding of Fort Sheridan, Illinois." *Illinois Historical Journal* 80 (1987): 13-22. The fort was established north of Chicago in response to the Haymarket riot of May 1886.

1327. Spector, Robert M. "Woman Against the Law: Myra Bradwell's Struggle for Admission to the Illinois Bar." *Journal of the Illinois State Historical Society* 68 (1975): 228-42.

1328. Stamm, Martin. " 'The Great Wave of Fire' at Chicago: The Reminiscences of Martin Stamm." Edited by Kathy Ranalletta. *Journal of the Illinois State Historical Society* 70 (1977): 149-60. An Evangelical minister recalls the fire of October 1871.

1329. Stoutemyer, Helen Louise Plaster. *The Train That Never Arrived: A Saga of the Niagara Excursion Train That Wrecked between Chatsworth and Piper City, August 10, 1887*. Fairbury, Ill.: Cornbelt Press, 1980. The train on the Toledo, Peoria and Western rail line was headed for Niagara Falls.

1330. Swing, David. "Memory of the Chicago Fire." *Scribner's Magazine* 11 (1892): 691-96.

1331. Thoreson, Trygve. "Mark Twain's Chicago." *Journal of the Illinois State Historical Society* 73 (1980): 277-90.

1332. Turnbaugh, Roy C. Jr. "Ethnicity, Civic Pride, and Commitment: The Evolution of the Chicago Militia." *Journal of the Illinois State Historical Society* 72 (1979): 111-22. Good background for state militia law and militia history. By Act of 1877 the Illinois Militia became the Illinois National Guard, and the militia gradually changed from a social organization to one used for civil control--its first test being the 1877 railroad strike.

1333. "When Chicago Burned." *American Heritage* 14 (August 1963): 54-61.

1334. Wright, Carroll D. *The Italians in Chicago: A Social and Economic Study*. Ninth Special Report of the Commissioner of Labor. Washington: Government Printing Office, 1897. Reprint, New York: Arno, 1970. The American Immigration Collection, Ser. II. A detailed statistical study (begun in 1896) of 1,348 families, embracing 6,773 persons, of whom 4,493 were born in Italy. The interviewers sought comprehensive details about personal and business life: birthplace, kind of employment, number of hours worked, wages, number of children, illnesses during the year, literacy, school attendance, etc.

H. EARLY TWENTIETH CENTURY, 1900-1928

1. General Works

1335. Bogart, Ernest L., and Mathews, John M. *The Modern Commonwealth, 1893-1918*. The Centennial History of Illinois, vol. 5. Springfield: Illinois

Centennial Commission, 1920.   Superseded by Donald F. Tingley's *The Structuring of a State* (1980) in the Sesquicentennial History of Illinois series.

1336. Tingley, Donald Fred. *The Structuring of a State: The History of Illinois, 1899 to 1928.* The Sesquicentennial History of Illinois, vol. 5. Urbana: Published for the Illinois Sesquicentennial Commission and the Illinois State Historical Society by the University of Illinois Press, 1980. This volume replaces volume 5 in the original Centennial History of Illinois series. An authoritative, fascinating portrayal of Illinois history. Carefully annotated, with full bibliography.

2. Civil Unrest and Crime

1337. Angle, Paul McClelland. *Bloody Williamson: A Chapter in American Lawlessness.* New York: Knopf, 1952. Reprint, with an introduction by John Y. Simon, Urbana: University of Illinois Press, 1992. Primarily concerned with union activities among coal miners, the massacre of twenty miners at Herrin in 1922, and the investigations that followed; with added discussions of the Ku Klux Klan, the Birger and Shelton criminal gangs of the same era, and family feuds of the 1860s that gave the county its "bloody" appellation.

1338. Asher, Robert, ed. "Documents of the Race Riot at East St. Louis." *Journal of the Illinois State Historical Society* 65 (1972): 327-36. Documents about the 1917 riot, from the Sherman Papers in the Illinois State Historical Library.

1339. Barrett, James R. "Unity and Fragmentation: Class, Race, and Ethnicity on Chicago's South Side, 1900-1922." *Journal of Social History* 18 (Fall 1984): 37-55.

1340. DeChenne, David. "Recipe for Violence: War Attitudes, the Black Hundred Riot, and Superpatriotism in an Illinois Coalfield, 1917-1918." *Illinois Historical Journal* 85 (1992): 221-38. Mob violence in the coal-mining towns of southwestern Illinois against those deemed to be pro-German.

1341. DeNeal, Gary. *A Knight of Another Sort: Prohibition Days and Charlie Birger.* Danville, Ill.: Interstate, 1981.

1342. Haller, Mark H. "Urban Crime and Criminal Justice: The Chicago Case." *Journal of American History* 57 (1970): 619-35. The author examines the "interrelations of crime, criminal justice, and reform" in the years 1900-1930.

He concludes that the criminal underworld had a "secure place within the social structure of Chicago."

1343. Hickey, Donald R. "The Prager Affair: A Study in Wartime Hysteria." *Journal of the Illinois State Historical Society* 62 (1969): 117-34. The lynching of a German-born socialist, Robert Paul Prager, at Collinsville in 1918.

1344. Kobler, John. *Capone: The Life and World of Al Capone.* New York: Putnam, 1971. Written for the general public but based on primary sources.

1345. Krohe, James Jr. *Summer of Rage: The Springfield Race Riot of 1908.* Sangamon County Historical Society Bicentennial Studies in Sangamon History. Springfield, 1973.

1346. Landesco, John. *Organized Crime in Chicago: Part III of the Illinois Crime Survey, 1929.* With a new introduction by Mark H. Haller. Chicago: University of Chicago Press, 1968.

1347. Norvell, Stanley B., and Tuttle, William M. Jr. "Views of a Negro during 'The Red Summer' of 1919." *Journal of Negro History* 51 (1966): 209-18. The "views" were expressed in a letter from Norvell, an African-American veteran of World War I, to Victor B. Lawson, editor of the *Chicago Daily News.*

1348. Pearson, Ralph L. "Charles S. Johnson and the Chicago Commission on Race Relations." *Illinois Historical Journal* 81 (1988): 211-20. The commission was appointed by Governor Frank O. Lowden to study race relations in Chicago, especially the causes of the 1919 riot in that city; the commission named Johnson associate executive secretary.

1349. Rudwick, Elliott M. *Race Riot at East St. Louis, July 2, 1917.* Carbondale: Southern Illinois University Press, 1964. Reprint, Blacks in the New World series, Urbana: University of Illinois Press, 1982. A well-documented analysis of the events of the riot and its origin, as well as of the trials that followed.

1350. Sandburg, Carl. *The Chicago Race Riots, July, 1919.* With preface by Ralph McGill and introductory note by Walter Lippman. New York: Harcourt, Brace, 1969.

1351. Schmuhl, Robert. "History, Fantasy, Memory: Ben Hecht and a Chicago Hanging." *Illinois Historical Journal* 83 (1990): 146-58. The victim was Grover Cleveland Redding, a Chicago black man convicted of killing a man during the violence that erupted during a parade and demonstration on Chicago's South Side.

1352. Schoenberg, Robert J. *Mr. Capone*. New York: William Morrow, 1992. Mr. Capone was the notorious gangster Al Capone.

1353. Senechal, Roberta. *The Sociogenesis of a Race Riot: Springfield, Illinois, in 1908*. Blacks in the New World series, Urbana: University of Illinois Press, 1990.

1354. Small, Curtis G. *Mean Old Jail*. Harrisburg, Ill.: Register Publishing Co., 1970. The author's father was sheriff of Saline County; the family lived at the jail, 1922-26. Small recalls such infamous figures as Charley Birger.

1355. Stroud, Jessie Ruth. "Ma of the Fierce Jones Gang--or, Teaching Country School in the Gangster Region." *Journal of the Illinois State Historical Society* 62 (1969): 65-71. Stroud's reminiscence of teaching in southern Illinois and her encounters with some southern Illinois gangsters.

1356. Tuttle, William M. Jr. "Contested Neighborhoods and Racial Violence: Prelude to the Chicago Riot of 1919." *Journal of Negro History* 55 (1970): 266-88.

1357. _____. *Race Riot: Chicago in the Red Summer of 1919*. New York: Atheneum, 1970. A sensitive and scholarly study.

3. Education

1358. Bartow, Beverly. "Isabel Bevier at the University of Illinois and the Home Economics Movement." *Journal of the Illinois State Historical Society* 72 (1979): 21-38.

1359. Bonser, Frederick Gordon. *A Statistical Study of Illinois High Schools*. University Studies, vol. 1, no. 3 (May 1902). Urbana: University Press. A survey of curriculum and textbooks in 1900.

1360. Candeloro, Dominic. "The Chicago School Board Crisis of 1907." *Journal of the Illinois State Historical Society* 68 (1975): 396-406.

1361. Dorris, Jonathan Truman. *An Illini-Bluegrass School Master: Seventy-five Years in the Classroom*. Richmond: Eastern Progress Press, Eastern Kentucky

State College, 1964. Dorris was a teacher or superintendent of schools in several Illinois schools in the early twentieth century.

1362. Hicken, Victor. "The Golden Years: Western Illinois University, 1905-1914." *Journal of the Illinois State Historical Society* 65 (1972): 419-33.

1363. James, Edmund J. *Sixteen Years at the University of Illinois: A Statistical Study of the Administration of President Edmund J. James.* Urbana: University of Illinois Press, 1920. A much broader report than the subtitle indicates.

1364. Rodnitzky, Jerome Leon. "David Kinley: A Paternal President in the Roaring Twenties." *Journal of the Illinois State Historical Society* 66 (1973): 5-19. Kinley was president of the University of Illinois.

1365. _____. "Farm and Gown: The University of Illinois and the Farmer, 1904-1918." *Journal of the Illinois State Historical Society* 72 (1979): 13-20.

1366. _____. "President James and His Campaigns for University of Illinois Funds." *Journal of the Illinois State Historical Society* 63 (1970): 69-90. James was president of the university, 1904-19.

1367. Smith, Joan K. "Progressive School Administration: Ella Flagg Young and the Chicago Schools, 1905-1915." *Journal of the Illinois State Historical Society* 73 (1980): 27-44.

4. Immigration and Ethnic Groups

1368. Bator, Joseph. "The Immigrants' Protective League in the Aftermath of the Restriction of Immigration, 1921-1929." *Transactions of the Illinois State Historical Society: Selected Papers from the Seventh Annual History Symposium and the Eighth Annual History Symposium* [1986 and 1987]. Springfield, 1989. Pp. 75-80.

1369. Bicha, Karel D. "The Survival of the Village in Urban America: A Note on Czech Immigrants in Chicago to 1914." *International Migration Review* 5 (1971): 72-74.

1370. Buroker, Robert L. "From Voluntary Association to Welfare State: The Illinois Immigrants' Protective League, 1908-1926." *Journal of American History* 58 (1971-72): 643-60.

1371. Cassens, David E. "The Bulgarian Colony of Southwestern Illinois, 1900-1920." *Illinois Historical Journal* 84 (1991): 15-24.

1372. Grossman, James R. "Blowing the Trumpet: The *Chicago Defender* and Black Migration during World War I." *Illinois Historical Journal* 78 (1985): 82-96.

1373. _____. *Land of Hope: Chicago, Black Southerners, and the Great Migration.* Chicago: University of Chicago Press, 1989. The author discusses the migration of African-Americans to Chicago in 1916-18.

1374. Leonard, Henry B. "The Immigrants' Protective League of Chicago, 1908-1921." *Journal of the Illinois State Historical Society* 66 (1973): 271-84.

1375. Oberg, Elmer B. "The Farm Life of a Swedish Immigrant in Illinois, circa 1900-1925." *Swedish-American Historical Quarterly* 36 (July 1985): 168-85.

1376. Reisler, Mark. "The Mexican Immigrant in the Chicago Area during the 1920's." *Journal of the Illinois State Historical Society* 66 (1973): 144-58.

1377. Rubenstein, Asa. "Midwestern Jewish Commitment and Practical American Idealism: The Early History of the Sinai Temple, Champaign, Illinois." *Journal of the Illinois State Historical Society* 75 (1982): 82-100.

1378. Trotter, Joe William, ed. *The Great Migration in Historical Perspective: New Dimensions of Race, Class, and Gender.* Blacks in the Diaspora series. Bloomington: Indiana University Press, 1991. In addition to two historiographical essays by the editor, this collection includes James R. Grossman's "The White Man's Union: The Great Migration and the Resonance of Race and Class in Chicago, 1916-1922."

5. Literature and the Arts

1379. Abegglen, Homer N. "The Chicago Little Theatre, 1912-1917." *Old Northwest* 3 (1977): 153-72.

1380. Dukore, Bernard F. "Maurice Browne and the Chicago Little Theatre." *Theatre Survey* 3 (1962): 59 ff.

1381. Fetherling, Dale, and Fetherling, Doug. *Carl Sandburg at the Movies: A Poet in the Silent Era, 1920-1927.* Metuchen, N.J.: Scarecrow Press, 1985. This collection of Sandburg's movie reviews provides an interesting look at life and entertainment in the 1920s.

1382. Gazell, James Albert. "The High Noon of Chicago's Bohemias." *Journal of the Illinois State Historical Society* 65 (1972): 54-68. Discussion of the Fifty-seventh Street colony of artists and writers and the north side colony called Towertown.

1383. Hansen, Harry. *Midwest Portraits: A Book of Memories and Friendships.* New York: Harcourt, Brace, 1923. Essays on midwestern writers, including several who were Illinois natives or who had substantial careers in the state; among them, Carl Sandburg, Floyd Dell, Robert Herrick, Ben Hecht, Max Bodenheim, Edgar Lee Masters, Lew Sarett, Wallace Smith, and Harriet Monroe.

1384. Joost, Nicholas. *Years of Transition: The Dial, 1912-1920.* Barre, Mass.: Barre Publishers, 1967. The third periodical by the name *Dial* was edited in Chicago, 1880-1918.

1385. Kahler, Bruce R. "Joseph Twyman and the Arts-and-Crafts Movement in Chicago." *Selected Papers in Illinois History, 1981.* Springfield: Illinois State Historical Society, 1982. Pp. 60-69. Twyman's work as an apostle of the arts-and-crafts movement was best known through the interior decoration of houses and buildings.

1386. Kramer, Dale. *Chicago Renaissance: The Literary Life in the Midwest, 1900-1930.* New York: Appleton, 1966. Chapters on Floyd Dell, Carl Sandburg, Edgar Lee Masters, Vachel Lindsay, Harriet Monroe, and Margaret Anderson, among others.

1387. Massa, Ann. " 'The Columbian Ode' and *Poetry: A Magazine of Verse*: Harriet Monroe's Entrepreneurial Triumphs." *Journal of American Studies* 20 (1986): 51-69.

1388. Rich, J. D., and Seligman, K. L. "New Theatre of Chicago, 1906-1907." *Educational Theatre Journal* 26 (March 1974): 53-68.

1389. Tanselle, G. Thomas. "Vachel Lindsay Writes to Floyd Dell." *Journal of the Illinois State Historical Society* 57 (1964): 366-79. Article is based on letters, 1909-12, in the Floyd Dell Papers in the Newberry Library.

1390. Tingley, Donald Fred. "Ellen Van Volkenburg, Maurice Browne, and the Chicago Little Theatre." *Illinois Historical Journal* 80 (1987): 130-46.

1391. _____. "The 'Robin's Egg Renaissance': Chicago and the Arts, 1910-1920." *Journal of the Illinois State Historical Society* 63 (1970): 35-54.

1392. Williams, Ellen. *Harriet Monroe and the Poetry Renaissance: The First Ten Years of Poetry, 1912-22.* Urbana: University of Illinois Press, 1977.

6. Military Affairs

Many counties published honor rolls of World War I veterans--some with biographical information; similar rolls appear in county histories. Such county rolls are not included in the sources below. Illinois men were absorbed into scores of United States Army units. Some Illinois National Guard units, however, did maintain their identity though given new United States Army designations. Only the latter category is represented in the listings that follow.

1393. Albert, Warren G. *Battery "A" in France, 1917-1918.* Danville, Ill.: Interstate, 1919? The battery was originally from Danville.

1394. Allen, Waldo M., comp. *331st Field Artillery, United States Army, 1917-1919.* Chicago?, 1919. The unit's officers, from Illinois, trained at Fort Sheridan; and the men, from Illinois and Wisconsin, trained at Camp Grant.

1395. *Battery B, 123rd Field Artillery.* N.p., n.d. The two companies in the battery, previously part of the 6th Illinois Infantry, were from Aledo and Sterling.

1396. *Being the Story of a Light Field Artillery Battery from Illinois during the World War.* Chicago: Gunthorp-Warren Printing, 1930. Battery C of the 149th Field Artillery.

1397. *Black Hawk, Company "F," 311th Ammunition Train, 86th Division.* Rockford, Ill.: Rockford Printing, 1919?

1398. Blech, Gustavus M. *Personal Memoirs of the World War.* Chicago, 1924. Reprinted from the *American Journal of Clinical Medicine.* A Chicago physician, Blech served as a medical officer in the war.

1399. Bowen, Joseph T. "The War Work of the Women of Illinois." *Transactions of the Illinois State Historical Society, 1919,* pp. 93-100.

1400. Braddan, William S. *Under Fire with the 370th Infantry (8th I.N.G.) A.E.F.: "Lest You Forget"; Memoirs of the World War.* Chicago: n.d. Braddan was chaplain of the unit, whose members were "composed largely of men from the Berean Baptist Church," an African-American church in Chicago.

1401. Coltrin, C. W. "History of the 123rd Field Artillery Home Folks' Association." Chicago, 1920? Typescript in Illinois State Historical Library. The association was a non-military relief and support organization. The unit was composed of Illinois men.

1402. Currey, Joseph Seymour. *Illinois Activities in the World War, Covering the Period from 1914 to 1920.* 3 vols. Chicago: Thos. B. Poole, 1921.

1403. Dickson, Frank E. "Military Achievements of Illinois in the World War." *Blue Book of Illinois, 1919-1920.* Springfield, 1919. Pp. 82-96. Dickson was Illinois adjutant general, and his report precedes ten others (pages 97-128), all of which deal with Illinois during the war.

1404. Dumont, Henry, ed. *The History of Company F, 2nd Infantry I.R.M.* La Grange, Ill., 1929. This unit of reserve militia from the Chicago area was one of four regiments organized to replace units that had been nationalized. Their only active duty was service during the 1919 Chicago race riot.

1405. Elbert, E. Duane. "Smile, and Work, and Serve: The Legacy of an Illinois Officer in World War I." *Illinois Historical Journal* 79 (1986): 33-58. Letters of Andrew Dunn of Charleston, written from England and France. He was killed in action.

1406. *Fighting Men of Illinois: An Illustrated Historical Biography Compiled from Private and Public Authentic Records.* Chicago: Publishers Subscription, 1918. Photographs and brief sketches of World War I soldiers.

1407. Gilmore, William E. "History of Headquarters Company, One Hundred and Forty-Ninth Field Artillery, from June 30, 1917, to May 10, 1919." *Journal of the Illinois State Historical Society* 17 (1924-25): 21-143.

1408. Goedeken, Edward A. "A Banker at War: The World War I Experiences of Charles Gates Dawes." *Illinois Historical Journal* 78 (1985): 195-206. Dawes was purchasing agent for the American Expeditionary Forces.

1409. Harrison, Carter H. *With the American Red Cross in France, 1918-1919.* Chicago: R. F. Seymour, 1947.

1410. Hines, Henry J., in collaboration with Sidney Birdsall. *Hardtack and Bullets.* Elgin, Ill.: Lowrie & Black, 1919. Reminiscences of service with Company E, 129th Regiment, Illinois National Guard.

1411. *The History and Achievements of the Fort Sheridan Officers' Training Camps.* Chicago: Fort Sheridan Association, 1920.

1412. Hokanson, Nels M. "The Foreign Language Division of the Chicago Liberty Loan Campaign." *Journal of the Illinois State Historical Society* 67 (1974): 429-39. The author recalls his service directing the sale of war bonds to non-English-speaking people during World War I.

1413. Huidekoper, Frederic Louis. *The History of the 33rd Division, A.E.F.* Illinois in the World War, vols. 1-4. Springfield: Illinois State Historical Library, 1921. The fourth volume is a portfolio of maps.

1414. Husband, Lori, comp. *Chicago World War I Draftees, Districts 3, 4, 5 and 70.* Park Forest, Ill.: The compiler, 1990. Names, with some street addresses, from the four Chicago draft board districts. The list was compiled from the July and August 1918 issues of the *Chicago Defender.*

1415. Illinois. Adjutant-General's Office. *Roster of the Illinois National Guard and Illinois Naval Militia as Organized When Called by the President for World War Service, 1917.* Springfield, 1929.

1416. _____. *Roster of the Illinois National Guard on the Mexican Border, 1916-1917.* Springfield, 1928.

1417. Illinois. State Council of Defense. *Final Report of the State Council of Defense of Illinois, 1917-1918-1919* . . . Springfield: State of Illinois, 1919.

1418. Illinois. State Council of Defense, Women's Committee. *Final Report* . . . *April 1917--July 1919.* Chicago: Hildman Printing, 1919.

1419. *Illinois in the World War: An Illustrated History of the Thirty-third Division* . . . 2 vols. Chicago: States Publications Society, 1921.

1420. Jahelka, Joseph. "The Role of Chicago Czechs in the Struggle for Czechoslovak Independence." *Journal of the Illinois State Historical Society* 31 (1938): 381-410.

1421. Jenison, Marguerite Edith, ed. *War Documents and Addresses.* Illinois in the World War, vol. 6. Springfield: Illinois State Historical Library, 1923.

1422. _____. *The War-Time Organization of Illinois.* Illinois in the World War, vol. 5. Springfield: Illinois State Historical Library, 1923.

1423. Judy, Will. *A Soldier's Diary: A Day-to-Day Record in the World War.* Chicago: Judy Publishing, 1930. Judy was an army field clerk with the 33d Division.

1424. Leach, William James. *Poems and War Letters.* Peoria, Ill.: Manual Arts Press, 1922. The Methodist minister from central Illinois served in World War I in France with the YMCA.

1425. Little, John G. *The Official History of the Eighty-Sixth Division.* Chicago: States Publications Society, 1921. The division, composed of men from northern Illinois, Wisconsin, and Minnesota, trained at Camp Grant, near Rockford.

1426. MacArthur, Charles G. *A Bug's-Eye View of the War.* Privately printed for Battery F, 149th Field Artillery, 1919. Most members of the battery were from Illinois.

1427. McCann, Irving Goff. *With the National Guard on the Border: Our National Military Problem.* St. Louis: C. V. Mosby, 1917. McCann was chaplain of the 1st Infantry, Illinois National Guard. A history of the unit (1874-1917) is in an appendix.

1428. McCormick, Robert R. *With the Russian Army: Being the Experiences of a National Guardsman.* New York: Macmillan, 1915. McCormick's father was United States ambassador to Russia.

1429. McGrath, John F., comp. *War Diary of the 354th Infantry; Missouri, Kansas, Nebraska, Colorado, Minnesota, Wisconsin, Arizona, Illinois; 89th Division.* Trier, Germany: J. Lintz, 1920? McGrath was regimental historian.

1430. MacLeish, Kenneth. *Kenneth: A Collection of Letters Written by Lieut. Kenneth MacLeish, U.S.N.R.F.C., Dating from His Enlistment and during His Services in the Aviation Corps of the United States Navy.* Edited and arranged by his mother. Chicago: Privately printed, 1919.

1431. Patton, John H. "Narrative of an Officer . . . of [the] 8th Illinois." In Sweeney, W. Allison. *History of the American Negro in the Great World War* . . . Chicago: Cuneo-Henneberry, 1919, pp. 164-79.

1432. Sanborn, Joseph B.; Malstrom, George V.; and others. *The 131st U.S. Infantry (First Infantry, Illinois National Guard) in the World War* . . . Chicago, 1919.

1433. Searcy, Earl B. *Looking Back.* Springfield, Ill.: Journal Press, 1921. Searcy served with the 78th Division of the American Expeditionary Forces in France.

1434. *The Sentinel; Sixth Corps Area, Fort Sheridan, Illinois, Camp McCoy, Wisconsin.* Vol. 3 (1928). Chicago: Military Training Camps Association of the United States, 1928. Yearbook for the Citizens' Military Training Camps at the two posts.

1435. Shearer, Benjamin F. "An Experiment in Military and Civilian Education: The Students' Army Training Corps at the University of Illinois." *Journal of the Illinois State Historical Society* 72 (1979): 213-24. The program was conducted by the War Department in 1918.

1436. Sheets, William. "From Oblong, Crawford County, Illinois, to Jefferson Barracks, to the Rio Grande, on to the Rhine, and Return." Typescript in Illinois State Historical Library. The document consists of letters written by Sheets, who served in Company C, of the 2d Engineers, 2d Division, of the American Expeditionary Forces.

1437. States Publications Society. *Illinois in the World War: An Illustrated Record Prepared with the Cooperation and under the Direction of the Leaders in the State's Military and Civilian Organizations.* Chicago, 1920.

1438. Thornton, Earle C., comp. *Record of Events and Roster of the 129th U.S. Infantry (Formerly 3rd Ill. N.G.), 65th Brigade, 33rd Division* . . . N.p., 1919? Contains chronologies and extracts from diaries as well as unit rosters.

1439. Turner, Thomas F. *Diary of the Q.M.C. Band during Its Organization and Development in France.* Compiled and edited by Harry E. Stinson. Atlanta, Ill.: Crihfield Bros. Press, 1920. The publisher, Robert Crihfield, was a member of the band; there were several other Illinois members.

1440. *War Diary of Ambulance Co. 129, 108th Sanitary Train, 33rd Division.* Chicago, 1919. Most company members were from Chicago.

7. Politics, Government, and Social Problems

1441. Bagby, Wesley M. "The 'Smoke Filled Room' and the Nomination of Warren G. Harding." *Journal of American History* 41 (1954-55): 657-74. One of the key players in the 1920 Republican convention, and also a candidate for the nomination, was Illinois Governor Frank O. Lowden.

1442. Baker, John D. "The Character of the Congressional Revolution of 1910." *Journal of American History* 60 (1973-74): 679-91. Democrats and insurgent Republicans joined forces to limit the power of House Speaker Joseph G. Cannon of Illinois.

1443. Barrett, James R. "Life in 'The Jungle': An Immigrant Working-Class Community on Chicago's South Side in Fiction and in Fact, 1900-1910." *Transactions of the Illinois State Historical Society: Selected Papers from the Fifth and Sixth Illinois History Symposiums of the Illinois State Historical Society* [1984 and 1985]. Springfield, 1988. Pp. 97-106.

1444. Buenker, John D. "Dynamics of Chicago Ethnic Politics, 1900-1930." *Journal of the Illinois State Historical Society* 67 (1974): 175-99.

1445. _____. "Edward F. Dunne: The Urban New Stock Democrat as Progressive." *Mid-America* 50 (1968): 3-21.

1446. _____. "Illinois and the Four Progressive-Era Amendments to the United States Constitution." *Illinois Historical Journal* 80 (1987): 210-27.

1447. _____. "The Illinois Legislature and Prohibition, 1907-1919." *Journal of the Illinois State Historical Society* 62 (1969): 363-84.

1448. _____. "Illinois Socialists and Progressive Reform." *Journal of the Illinois State Historical Society* 63 (1970): 368-86.

1449. _____. "The New-Stock Politicians of 1912." *Journal of the Illinois State Historical Society* 62 (1969): 35-52. The rise of members of ethnic and religious minorities to significant roles in the Democratic party.

1450. _____.   *Urban Liberalism and Progressive Reform.*   New York: Scribner's, 1973.

1451. Davis, John McCan.   *The Breaking of the Deadlock; Being an Accurate and Authentic Account of the Contest of 1903-4 for the Republican Nomination for Governor of Illinois . . .* Springfield, Ill., 1904.

1452. Elazar, Daniel J., ed.   "Working Conditions in Chicago in the Early 20th Century: Testimony before the Illinois Senatorial Vice Committee, 1913."   *American Jewish Archives* 21 (1969): 149-71.

1453. Flanagan, Maureen A.   *Charter Reform in Chicago.*   Carbondale: Southern Illinois University Press, 1987.   A detailed history of the voters' rejection of a new city charter in 1907.

1454. _____.   "The Ethnic Entry into Chicago Politics: The United Societies for Local Self-Government."   *Journal of the Illinois State Historical Society* 75 (1982): 2-14.   In 1906 Chicago's ethnic groups joined together to protect "personal liberties" and oppose restrictions on the sale of liquor.   To that end they led the movement to reject the new home-rule charter for the city that had been adopted by the 1907 charter convention.

1455. Gottlieb, Amy Zahl.   "The Illinois Workmen's Compensation Act, 1911: The Role of the British Immigrant Coal Miner."   *Selected Papers in Illinois History, 1980.*   Springfield: Illinois State Historical Society, 1982. Pp. 63-68.

1456. Havig, Alan R.   "The Raymond Robins Case for Progressive Republicanism."   *Journal of the Illinois State Historical Society* 64 (1971): 401-18.   In 1916, after Theodore Roosevelt declined the nomination of the Progressive party, the social reformer Raymond Robins supported the candidacy of Republican Charles Evans Hughes, who, he believed, offered a "more hopeful base for progressive reform."

1457. Heidebrecht, Paul H.   "Clifford Barnes and the Decline of Protestant Power."   *Transactions of the Illinois State Historical Society: Selected Papers from the Fifth and Sixth Illinois History Symposiums of the Illinois State Historical Society* [1984 and 1985].   Springfield, 1988. Pp. 1-13.   Onetime minister, Illinois College president, and social activist, Barnes founded the Chicago Sunday Evening Club.

1458. *Illinois: First Administrative Report of the Director of Departments under the Civil Administrative Code, Together with the Adjutant General's Report.* July 1, 1917, to June 30, 1918. Springfield, 1918.

1459. Kirkland, Wallace. *The Many Faces of Hull House: The Photographs of Wallace Kirkland.* Edited by Mary Ann Johnson. Urbana: University of Illinois Press, 1989.

1460. Lindstrom, Andrew F. "Lawrence Stringer, A Wilson Democrat." *Journal of the Illinois State Historical Society* 66 (1973): 20-40.

1461. Luthy, Godfrey G. "Lowden Refused the Vice-Presidential Nomination." *Journal of the Illinois State Historical Society* 45 (1952): 73-75. Luthy was a delegate to the Republican convention in 1924, when Frank O. Lowden refused the nomination.

1462. McCarthy, Michael P. "Prelude to Armageddon: Charles E. Merriam and the Chicago Mayoral Election of 1911." *Journal of the Illinois State Historical Society* 67 (1974): 505-18.

1463. Petterchak, Janice A. "Conflict of Ideals: Samuel Gompers v. 'Uncle Joe' Cannon." *Journal of the Illinois State Historical Society* 74 (1981): 31-40. Unsuccessful efforts of AFL leader Gompers to defeat Illinois Congressman (and Speaker of the House) Joseph Cannon in 1906 and 1908. Based on the Cannon Papers in the Illinois State Historical Library.

1464. Piott, Steven L. *The Anti-Monopoly Persuasion: Popular Resistance to the Rise of Big Business in the Midwest.* Contributions in Economics and Economic History, no. 60. Westport, Conn.: Greenwood, 1985. The author bases his argument on Illinois and Missouri case studies.

1465. Reed, Christopher Robert. "Organized Racial Reform in Chicago during the Progressive Era: The Chicago NAACP, 1910-1920." *Michigan Historical Review* 14 (Spring 1988): 75-99.

1466. Roberts, Daniel A. "A Chicago Political Diary, 1928-1929." Edited by Daniel J. Roberts. *Journal of the Illinois State Historical Society* 71 (1978): 30-56. A Republican attorney, Roberts was a member of the board that administered parks in the western part of the city.

1467.   Schlup, Leonard.   "The Last Hurrah: Adlai E. Stevenson and the Presidential Election of 1912." *Illinois Quarterly* 43, no. 4 (Summer 1981): 30-40.

1468.   _____.   "Lewis Green Stevenson and the 1928 Vice-Presidential Question." *Illinois Quarterly* 40, no. 3 (Spring 1978): 49-61.

1469.   Schmidt, John R.   *"The Mayor Who Cleaned Up Chicago": A Political Biography of William E. Dever.*   DeKalb: Northern Illinois University Press, 1989.

1470.   Schottenhamel, George.   "How Big Bill Thompson Won Control of Chicago." *Journal of the Illinois State Historical Society* 45 (1952): 30-49. Republican election politics, 1905-31.

1471.   Skokkebaek, Mette.   "Concerns of Organized Labor, 1902-18: The Belleville Trades and Labor Assembly, Illinois." *American Studies in Scandinavia* 13, no. 2 (1981): 81-92.

1472.   Sparling, Samuel E.   "Chicago's Voters' League." *Outlook* 71 (1902): 495-98.

1473.   Stevens, Errol Wayne.   "The Socialist Party of America in Municipal Politics: Canton, Illinois, 1911-1920." *Journal of the Illinois State Historical Society* 72 (1979): 257-72.   Coal-mining and manufacturing companies gave labor unions and the Socialist party a foothold in central Illinois.

1474.   Stone, Ralph A.   "Two Illinois Senators among the Irreconcilables." *Mississippi Valley Historical Review* 50 (1963-64): 443-65.   The Illinois "irreconcilables" who opposed the Treaty of Versailles and the League of Nations were Medill McCormick and Lawrence Y. Sherman.

1475.   Stovall, Mary E.   "The *Chicago Defender* in the Progressive Era." *Illinois Historical Journal* 83 (1990): 159-72.   Editor Robert Abbott "championed only those Progressive goals that contributed to equality and justice for blacks."

1476.   Tarr, Joel Arthur.   "President Theodore Roosevelt and Illinois Politics, 1901-1904." *Journal of the Illinois State Historical Society* 58 (1965): 245-64.

1477.   Thurner, Arthur W.   "The Mayor, the Governor, and the People's Council." *Journal of the Illinois State Historical Society* 66 (1973): 125-43.

Illinois politics, free speech, and a peace movement in the era of Chicago Mayor William Hale Thompson and Governor Frank Lowden.

1478. Travis, Anthony R. "The Origin of Mothers' Pensions in Illinois." *Journal of the Illinois State Historical Society* 68 (1975): 421-28.

1479. Tucker, Cynthia Grant. *A Woman's Ministry: Mary Collson's Search for Reform as a Unitarian Minister, a Hull House Social Worker, and a Christian Science Practitioner.* Philadelphia: Temple University Press, 1984.

1480. Waller, Robert A. "Norman L. Jones versus Len Small in the Illinois Gubernatorial Campaign of 1924." *Journal of the Illinois State Historical Society* 72 (1979): 162-78. National politics complicated the already complex election.

1481. Wheeler, Adade Mitchell. "Conflict in the Illinois Woman Suffrage Movement of 1913." *Journal of the Illinois State Historical Society* 76 (1983): 95-114.

1482. Williams, Donald Edward. "Dawes and the 1924 Republican Vice-Presidential Nomination." *Mid-America* 44 (1962): 3-18.

1483. Wooddy, Carroll Hill. *The Case of Frank L. Smith: A Study in Representative Government.* Chicago: University of Chicago Press, 1931. A detailed account of the political background and the United States Senate proceedings that excluded Smith from membership in that body in 1928.

8. Miscellany

1484. Barbour, Frances M.; Neely, Julia Jonah; and Trovillian, Mae. "The Light That Failed: The Decline of a Unique Educational Venture." *Journal of the Illinois State Historical Society* 64 (1971): 442-44. Account of an unsuccessful attempt in 1926-27 at establishing John Wesley College in a remote section of southern Illinois.

1485. Bennett, Dianne, and Graebner, William. "Safety First: Slogan and Symbol of the Industrial Safety Movement." *Journal of the Illinois State Historical Society* 68 (1975): 243-56.

1486. Bial, Raymond, and Schlipf, Frederick A., eds. *Upon a Quiet Landscape: The Photographs of Frank Sadorus.* Urbana, Ill.: Champaign County Historical

Archives at the Urbana Free Library, 1983. Sixty-six remarkable photographs from a collection of 350 glass negatives, 1908-12, illustrate life on the Illinois prairie.

1487. Borough, Reuben W. "The Chicago I Remember, 1907." *Journal of the Illinois State Historical Society* 59 (1966): 117-30. Borough recalls his work as a reporter for the *Chicago Daily Socialist*. He was deeply involved in the Socialist party and social reform activities in the city.

1488. Buenker, John D. "The New Era Business Philosophy of the 1920s." *Illinois Quarterly* 38, no. 3 (Spring 1976): 20-49.

1489. Cook, Philip L. "Zion City, Illinois--The Kingdom of Heaven and Race." *Illinois Quarterly* 38, no. 2 (Winter 1975): 50-61. History of John Alexander Dowie's utopian community from 1901 to 1906. Dowie was a champion of civil rights for African-Americans, about two hundred of whom lived in Zion.

1490. Evans, James F. "The Sheetwriter: Rural Confidence Man in Illinois." *Journal of the Illinois State Historical Society* 67 (1974): 548-54. Sheetwriters were magazine salesmen, with shady schemes galore, who approached farmers at fairs, sales, and carnivals.

1491. Felknor, Peter S. *The Tri-State Tornado: The Story of America's Greatest Tornado Disaster.* Ames: Iowa State University Press, 1992. The 1925 storm hit Missouri, Illinois, and Indiana. The volume includes eyewitness reports of fourteen survivors.

1492. Fuller, Lillian Beck. "Public Health Nursing in Chicago in the 1920's: The Reminiscences of Lillian Beck Fuller, R.N." Edited by Joellen Beck W. Hawkins. *Journal of the Illinois State Historical Society* 76 (1983): 195-204. The writer's reminiscences provide a lively illustration of medical and social conditions of the era.

1493. Grant, H. Roger. *Spirit Fruit: A Gentle Utopia.* DeKalb: Northern Illinois University Press, 1988. The Spirit Fruit utopian group lived in Chicago and Ingleside 1904-14. The author also writes of other utopian experiments in the area.

1494. _____. "The Spirit Fruit Society: A Perfectionist Utopia in the Old Northwest, 1899-1915." *Old Northwest* 9 (Spring 1983): 23-36.

1495. Halberg, Carl V. " 'For God, Country, and Home': The Ku Klux Klan in Pekin, 1923-1925." *Journal of the Illinois State Historical Society* 77 (1984): 82-93. An unusual story of the Klan's operation of a local newspaper and the manipulation of its own image.

1496. Illinois Centennial Commission. *The Centennial of the State of Illinois: Report of the Centennial Commission.* Springfield, 1920.

1497. McCarthy, Michael P. "Chicago Businessmen and the Burnham Plan." *Journal of the Illinois State Historical Society* 63 (1970): 228-56. Daniel Burnham's comprehensive plan for Chicago was financed by two businessmen's organizations. Major features of the plan are outlined.

1498. Moline, Norman T. *Mobility and the Small Town, 1900-1930: Transportation Change in Oregon, Illinois.* University of Chicago Department of Geography, Research Paper no. 132. Chicago, 1971. Concentrates on improved roads and highways and the changes they fostered in the community.

1499. Murphy, James L. *The Reluctant Radicals: Jacob L. Beilhart and the Spirit Fruit Society.* Lanham, Md.: University Press of America, 1989.

1500. O'Rourke, Alice A. "Cooperative Marketing in McLean County." *Journal of the Illinois State Historical Society* 64 (1971): 173-91.

1501. Person, Carl E. *The Lizard's Trail: A Story from the Illinois Central and Harriman Lines Strike of 1911 to 1915 Inclusive.* Chicago: Lake Publishing, 1918. Edward H. Harriman had been a powerful director of the Illinois Central and many other rail lines. He died in 1909.

1502. Petterchak, Janice A. "The Guy Mathis Collection." *Journal of the Illinois State Historical Society* 71 (1978): 288-98. The collection in the Illinois State Historical Library, described and illustrated in this article, consists of seventeen hundred glass negatives and prints made in the years 1900-1905 by Springfield photographer Guy Mathis.

1503. Semrad, Alberita Napier Richards. "Wing Dams and Riprap." *Journal of the Illinois State Historical Society* 71 (1978): 264-71. Reminiscences of summer life in the early 1900s on Mississippi River steamboats in the United States Corps of Engineers construction fleet, with excellent descriptions of the engineers' work.

1504. Stegh, Leslie J. "Putting America in the Driver's Seat: The Deere-Clark Motor Car Company." *Illinois Historical Journal* 81 (1988): 242-54. The story of the short-lived company that produced about one hundred automobiles in 1906-7 in East Moline.

1505. Stone, Ralph A. "Illinois Miners and the Birth of the Cooperative League U.S.A." *Selected Papers in Illinois History, 1981.* Springfield: Illinois State Historical Society, 1982. Pp. 70-85. In 1918 the cooperative stores of Illinois miners were the most successful in the nation.

1506. Stout, Steve. "Tragedy in November: The Cherry Mine Disaster." *Journal of the Illinois State Historical Society* 72 (1979): 57-69. History of the 1909 fire at the St. Paul Coal Company in Cherry that resulted in the deaths of 259 miners.

1507. Tap, Bruce. "Suppression of Dissent: Academic Freedom at the University of Illinois." *Illinois Historical Journal* 85 (1992): 2-22.

1508. Taylor, Richard S. "New Thought in the Twenties: The Case of Springfield, Illinois." *Historian* 49 (1987): 329-47. Springfield's proponents of the New Thought religious movement both exemplified and deviated from its stated principles.

1509. Vining, James W. "Slater Burgesser and His Famous Spring." *Western Illinois Regional Studies* 5 (1982): 184-94. William Slater Burgesser owned the famed Ripley Mineral Springs, whose water was bottled under the name "New Life Mineral Water Company."

1510. Wacker, Grant. "Marching to Zion: Religion in a Modern Utopian Community." *Church History* 54 (1985): 496-511. The role of religious motivation in the history of Zion, Illinois.

1511. Walters, Karen A. "McLean County and the Influenza Epidemic of 1918-1919." *Journal of the Illinois State Historical Society* 74 (1981): 130-33.

1512. Warne, Colston Estey. *The Consumers' Co-operative Movement in Illinois.* Chicago: University of Chicago Press, 1926.

1513. Wilson, Harold S. *McClure's Magazine and the Muckrakers.* Princeton, N.J.: Princeton University Press, 1970. S. S. McClure, founder of the magazine, was a graduate of Knox College in Illinois; the author shows how the college was always an influence on the magazine.

1514. Wrone, David R. "Illinois Pulls out of the Mud." *Journal of the Illinois State Historical Society* 58 (1965): 54-76. A study of the "good roads movement" that led to state financing of paved roads in the 1920s.

I. DEPRESSION, THE NEW DEAL, AND WORLD WAR II, 1929-1949

1. Depression and the New Deal

1515. Annunziata, Frank. "Donald R. Richberg and American Liberalism: An Illinois Progressive's Critique of the New Deal and Welfare State." *Journal of the Illinois State Historical Society* 67 (1974): 531-47.

1516. Beito, David T. *Taxpayers in Revolt: Tax Resistance during the Great Depression.* Chapel Hill: University of North Carolina Press, 1989. Three chapters deal with the Chicago tax strike of 1930-33.

1517. Biles, Roger. "Henry Horner and the New Deal in Illinois." *Mid-America* 74 (1992): 37-57.

1518. Brace, Beverly Waltmire. *The Humboldt Years, 1930-1939.* Chicago: Adams Press, 1977. A study by the daughter of William Baily Waltmire of his work as pastor of the Humboldt Park Methodist Church. The volume illustrates the devastating impact of the Depression on a working-class Chicago neighborhood.

1519. Brown, Malcolm, and Webb, John N. *Seven Stranded Coal Towns: A Study of an American Depressed Area.* Federal Works Agency, Work Projects Administration, Division of Research, Research Monograph 23. Washington: Government Printing Office, 1941. Effects of the declining coal industry on the towns of Bush, Johnston City, Carrier Mills, Herrin, West Frankfort, Zeigler, and Eldorado in Franklin, Williamson, and Saline counties.

1520. Brune, Lester H. " 'Union Holiday--Closed Till Further Notice': The 1936 General Strike at Pekin, Illinois." *Journal of the Illinois State Historical Society* 75 (1982): 29-38.

1521. Eaklor, Vicki L. "The Illinois Symphony Orchestra, 1936-1942: Microcosm of a Cultural New Deal." *Selected Papers in Illinois History, 1980.* Springfield: Illinois State Historical Society, 1982. Pp. 69-77. The symphony, an organization of professional musicians located in Chicago, was sponsored by the Federal Music Project of the Works Progress Administration.

1522. Esbitt, Milton. "Bank Portfolios and Bank Failures during the Great Depression: Chicago." *Journal of Economic History* 46 (1986): 455-62.

1523. Glick, Frank G. *The Illinois Emergency Relief Commission.* Chicago: University of Chicago Press, 1940.

1524. Gordon, Rita Werner. "The Change of the Political Alignment of Chicago's Negroes during the New Deal." *Journal of American History* 56 (1969-70): 584-603. The change was the shift to the Democratic party.

1525. Gosnell, Harold F. *Machine Politics: Chicago Model.* Chicago: University of Chicago Press, 1937. Reprint, 1968. An excellent study of Chicago politics, 1928-36.

1526. Hastings, Robert J. *A Nickel's Worth of Skim Milk: A Boy's View of the Great Depression.* 2d ed., Shawnee Books. Carbondale: Southern Illinois University Press, 1986. The author grew up in the southern Illinois town of Marion.

1527. _____. *A Penny's Worth of Minced Ham: Another Look at the Great Depression.* 2d ed., Shawnee Books. Carbondale: Southern Illinois University Press, 1986.

1528. Illinois Emergency Relief Commission (later Illinois Public Aid Commission). *Monthly Bulletin,* 1933-41.

1529. Jones, Gene D. L. "The Chicago Catholic Charities, the Great Depression, and Public Monies." *Illinois Historical Journal* 83 (1990): 13-30.

1530. _____. "The Origin of the Alliance between the New Deal and the Chicago Machine." *Journal of the Illinois State Historical Society* 67 (1974): 253-74. The author discusses the downstate-metropolitan conflict in Illinois politics that led to the preeminence of the Chicago machine, despite Governor Henry Horner's reelection in 1936.

1531. Kiefer, E. Kay, and Fellows, Paul E. *Hobnail Boots and Khaki Suits: A Brief Look at the Great Depression and the Civilian Conservation Corps as Seen through the Eyes of Those Who Were There.* Chicago: Adams Press, 1983. Includes reminiscences of several men who served at Illinois camps.

1532. Kohn, Walter S. G. "Illinois' Convention Ratifies the Twenty-first Amendment." *Journal of the Illinois State Historical Society* 56 (1963): 692-712.

Congress provided that the 21st Amendment, which nullified the 18th (or Prohibition) Amendment, should be ratified by state conventions. The Illinois convention ratified the amendment 10 July 1933.

1533. Littlewood, Thomas B. "FDR, the New Deal, and Illinois." *Selected Papers in Illinois History, 1982.* Springfield: Illinois State Historical Society, 1984. Pp. 1-10.

1534. Mavigliano, George J., and Lawson, Richard A. *The Federal Art Project in Illinois, 1935-1943.* Carbondale: Southern Illinois University Press, 1990. In addition to a scholarly history of the project, lengthy appendixes list all of the project artists and administrators in Illinois, murals completed, public sculptures, job classifications and salaries, and other craft and art projects in the state.

1535. Meyers, W. Cameron. "Henry Horner and Richard Finnegan: Footnote to a Friendship." *Journal of the Illinois State Historical Society* 55 (1962): 341-69. Finnegan was editor of the *Chicago Daily Times* and advised Horner throughout his successful gubernatorial campaign in 1932 and his subsequent administration.

1536. Miller, Kristie. "Ruth Hanna McCormick and the Senatorial Election of 1930." *Illinois Historical Journal* 81 (1988): 191-210. McCormick was the Republican party candidate for the United States Senate.

1537. Park, Marlene, and Markowitz, Gerald E. *Democratic Vistas: Post Offices and Public Art in the New Deal.* Philadelphia: Temple University Press, 1984. Study of murals and sculpture commissioned by the Treasury Department's Section on Fine Arts. Illinois was one of the major beneficiaries; an appendix lists all commissions by state and city.

1538. Reed, Christopher Robert. "Black Chicago Political Realignment during the Depression and New Deal." *Illinois Historical Journal* 78 (1985): 242-56. The realignment was from the Republican to the Democratic party.

1539. Strickland, Arvarh E. "The New Deal Comes to Illinois." *Journal of the Illinois State Historical Society* 63 (1970): 55-68.

1540. Terkel, Louis (Studs). *Hard Times: An Oral History of the Great Depression.* New York: Pantheon, 1970. Includes many interviews with Chicagoans.

1541. Van Sickle, Frederick Mercer. "A Special Place: Lake Forest and the Great Depression, 1929-1940." *Illinois Historical Journal* 79 (1986): 113-26.

1542. Weiss, Stuart. "Kent Keller, the Liberal Bloc, and the New Deal." *Journal of the Illinois State Historical Society* 68 (1975): 143-58.

2. Labor

1543. Adelman, William J. *The Memorial Day Massacre of 1937.* Chicago: Illinois Labor History Society, 1973? Ten union strikers were killed by police at Chicago's Republic Steel plant in 1937.

1544. Booth, Stephane Elise. "A Coal-Mining Activist in the Fields of Southern Illinois, 1932-1938." *Selected Papers in Illinois History, 1981.* Springfield: Illinois State Historical Society, 1982. Pp. 86-94. The activist was Gerry Allard, who edited a newspaper published by the Progressive Mine Workers of America.

1545. Bork, William. *Massacre at Republic Steel.* Chicago: Illinois Labor History Society, 1975.

1546. Cary, Lorin Lee. "The Reorganized United Mine Workers of America, 1930-1931." *Journal of the Illinois State Historical Society* 66 (1973): 245-70.

1547. Newell, Barbara Warne. *Chicago and the Labor Movement: Metropolitan Unionism in the 1930's.* Urbana: University of Illinois Press, 1961.

1548. Oblinger, Carl D. *Divided Kingdom: Work, Community, and the Mining Wars in the Central Illinois Coal Fields during the Great Depression.* Springfield: Illinois State Historical Society, 1991. Based on thirty-seven taped interviews (1985-86) with miners and their families.

1549. Young, Dallas M. "Origin of the Progressive Mine Workers of America." *Journal of the Illinois State Historical Society* 40 (1947): 313-30. Conflicts among labor unions in the coal mines of Illinois.

3. World War II

In addition to the books and articles listed below, another source of information about World War II is the many camp and war-plant newspapers, which can be found in libraries throughout the state.

1550. Armstrong, Paul G. "Historical Report on the Organization and Operation of the Selective Service System in Illinois." Mimeographed, 1947? In Illinois State Historical Library. Armstrong was state director of the system, 1940-47. The report was compiled for the United States Director of Selective Service.

1551. Army and Navy Publishing Company of Louisiana, Baton Rouge. *George Field, Army Air Forces Advanced Flying School (TE); Army Air Forces Southeast Training Center* [at Maxwell Field, Alabama]. Baton Rouge, La., 1943. George Field was located near Lawrenceville, Illinois.

1552. Barker, Robert A. *Philippine Diary: A Journal of Life as a Japanese Prisoner of War*. Chicago: The Robert A. Barker Foundation, 1990. Barker, a native of Springfield, made entries in the diary from 24 May 1942 through 5 June 1944. He was being transported to Japan when his ship was sunk.

1553. Barringer, Floyd S. *Wartime Odyssey: Letters Written by a Son to His Father, July 1941--July 1944*. Springfield, Ill.: The author, 1987. Both men were physicians, and the younger wrote especially of his service at a military hospital in England.

1554. _____. *Wartime Odyssey: A Sequel, July 1944--April 1946*. Springfield, Ill.: The author, 1989.

1555. Bawden, Harry E., ed. *The Achievement of Rock Island Arsenal, World War II*. Davenport, Iowa: Bawden Brothers, 1948.

1556. Bordner, Marjorie Rich. *From Cornfields to Marching Feet: Camp Ellis, Illinois*. Dallas, Tex.: Curtis Media Corporation, 1993. Memoirs of 174 people who worked or served at the camp, as well as original documents, photographs, and out-of-print histories and reports.

1557. Burton, Robert O. *The Story of Camp Ellis*. Macomb, Ill.: Macomb Daily Journal, 1945. Reprinted in Bordner, above. The World War II military installation was built on the site of Bernadotte and nearby farms in Fulton County in 1942-43.

1558. Cole, Wayne C. "The America First Committee." *Journal of the Illinois State Historical Society* 44 (1951): 305-22. National headquarters of the committee was in Chicago, and General Robert E. Wood was national chairman.

1559. Erikson, Stanley, and Roach, Elinor. "The War Records Program of the Illinois War Council." *Journal of the Illinois State Historical Society* 37 (1944):

117-30. The Council's Division of War Records and Research, created in 1942, evolved a program to preserve the records necessary for compiling a "comprehensive history of Illinois at war."

1560. Freeman, L. Willard. "Mayo General Hospital." *Journal of the Illinois State Historical Society* 44 (1951): 26-31. The United States Army hospital was located at Galesburg, 1943-46.

1561. Hanna, John Perry II. *Diary of an Illinois Farmer . . . 1941-1947.* N.p., ca. 1980. The diary entries under the above title first appeared as a column in the *Chicago Daily News.* Excellent accounts of farm life as well as of homefront reactions to war news.

1562. Havighurst, Robert J., and Morgan, H. Gerthon. *The Social History of a War-Boom Community.* New York: Longmans, Green, 1951. A case study of the wartime transformation of a town of 1,235 to one of 6,600, with employment of 10,000 in 1944 at the Chicago Bridge and Iron Company shipyards at Seneca.

1563. *Historical Lineage, Illinois National Guard, Illinois Naval Militia.* Springfield: Illinois Military and Naval Department, 1 July 1953. Traces units back to their creation, many to the late nineteenth century.

1564. Hope, Pamela M. *The Homesick Angel.* Taylorville, Ill.: Bill and Pam Hope, 1989. The Homesick Angel was a World War II B-24, in the 11th Bombardment Group, 98th Squadron. The gripping account of its service in the South Pacific is based on members' reminiscences and Bill Hope's diary.

1565. "Illinois, Great in Peace, Hurls All Her Resources into Mighty War Program." *Blue Book of the State of Illinois, 1941-1942.* Pp. 504-47.

1566. *The Illinois War Council, 1941-1945, Organization, Procedure, and Recommendations: Final Report of the Executive Director.* Springfield: State of Illinois, 1945.

1567. Independent Engineering Company, O'Fallon, Illinois. *Source Book of Historical Material Concerning the Portable Oxygen Generators Manufactured by Independent Engineering Company, O'Fallon, Illinois, 1939-1945.* O'Fallon, 1945.

1568. Jannotta, A. Vernon. "LCI (L) Flotilla 24: Composition, War History, Officer Roster, 3rd Grand Reunion." Cincinnati: LCI (L) Flotilla 24, 1955. Chicagoan Jannotta was commander of the flotilla.

1569. Kleber, Victor. *Selective Service in Illinois, 1940-1947: A Complete History of the Operation of the Selective Service System in Illinois from Its Inception on September 16, 1940, to Its Termination on March 31, 1947.* Springfield, 1948.

1570. Marsh, Robert. "The Illinois Hemp Project at Polo in World War II." *Journal of the Illinois State Historical Society* 60 (1967): 391-410. German prisoners-of-war from Camp Grant helped harvest the hemp, which was then processed at a plant in Polo.

1571. Morgan, Ivan. "The 1942 Mid-Term Elections in Illinois." *Journal of the Illinois State Historical Society* 76 (1983): 115-30. Impact of the war and national politics on elections in Illinois.

1572. *The 106th Cavalry Group in Europe, 1944-1945.* Augsburg, Germany: J. P. Himmer, 1945. World War II actions described by the men involved. The unit contained many men from Illinois.

1573. Pabel, Reinhold. *Enemies Are Human.* Philadelphia: Winston, 1955. Pabel was a German prisoner-of-war at Camp Ellis in Illinois when he escaped and built a new life as an American.

1574. Richter, Anton H., trans. and ed. "A German P.O.W. at Camp Grant: The Reminiscences of Heinz Richter." *Journal of the Illinois State Historical Society* 76 (1983): 61-70.

1575. *Sakowicz Jug: The Serviceman's Newspaper; Published as a Means of Communication for Men and Women of Our Neighborhood and the Vicinity Who Are in the Service of Their Country.* No. 1 (October 1942)--no. 44 (May 1946). Published and edited every two months by Sigmund S. Sakowicz in Chicago. The file of papers was bound with the title as given. Each issue had news from servicemen as well as neighborhood news.

1576. Schacht, John N. *Three Faces of Midwestern Isolationism: Gerald P. Nye, Robert E. Wood, John L. Lewis.* Iowa City, Iowa: Center for the Study of the Recent History of the United States, 1981.

1577. Schneider, James Colvill. *Should America Go to War? The Debate over Foreign Policy in Chicago, 1939-1941.* Chapel Hill: University of North Carolina Press, 1989.

1578. Schneider, James G. *The Navy V-12 Program: Leadership for a Lifetime.* Boston: Houghton Mifflin, 1987. Among the 131 colleges that participated in the program, four were in Illinois: Illinois Institute of Technology, Illinois State Normal University, Northwestern University, and the University of Illinois at Urbana-Champaign.

1579. Schrock, Vernon L. *The Meanderings of a Marine.* Peoria, Ill.: Courier Printing, 1947. Reminiscences of an Illinois man who served in the South Pacific.

1580. "353rd Fighter Group's 1983 Reunion Memoir." Springfield, Ill.: Oral History Office, Sangamon State University, 1984. Personal narratives, recorded and transcribed by Horace Waggoner.

1581. United States Adjutant-General's Office. *World War II Honor List of Dead and Missing: State of Illinois.* Washington: War Department, 1946.

1582. United States Army Air Force. *Scott Field . . . United States Army Air Corps. A Pictorial and Historical Review of Scott Field, Illinois.* St. Louis: Everett Schneider, 1942.

1583. United States Navy Department, Office of Public Information. *State Summary of War Casualties [Illinois].* Washington: U.S. Navy, 1946.

1584. Watters, Mary. *Illinois in the Second World War.* 2 vols. Springfield: Illinois State Historical Library, 1951-52. The volumes are subtitled *Operation Homefront* and *The Production Front.*

1585. Wilbur, Fred E. *Bud: A Young Man in a War.* Edina, Minn.: Burgess Publishing, 1991. Letters, 1941-45, from Wilbur, of Downers Grove, who served in the Marine Corps in the South Pacific.

1586. Woodstrup, Thomas E. *A Flip on a Jackstay.* Sycamore, Ill.: The author, 1992. A collection of letters between Woodstrup and his mother written during World War II when he was in the United States Navy.

4. Miscellany

1587. Beyer, Richard Lawrence. "Hell and High Water: The Flood of 1937 in Southern Illinois." *Journal of the Illinois State Historical Society* 31 (1938): 5-

21. Eight counties were "either completely or partly inundated" in "one of the major catastrophes in the history of this state."

1588. Biles, Roger. *Big City Boss in Depression and War: Mayor Edward J. Kelly of Chicago.* DeKalb: Northern Illinois University Press, 1984. Kelly was mayor from 1933 to 1947.

1589. Burbank, Lyman B. "Chicago Public Schools and the Depression Years of 1928-1937." *Journal of the Illinois State Historical Society* 64 (1971): 365-81.

1590. Collier, James Lincoln. *Benny Goodman and the Swing Era.* New York: Oxford University Press, 1989. Goodman was born in Chicago.

1591. Dorn, Jacob H. " 'Religion and Reform in the City': The Re-Thinking Chicago Movement of the 1930s." *Church History* 55 (1986): 323-37. The organized efforts of leading Chicago clergymen to inform the city's residents about the need for social and political reform.

1592. Edwards, Jerome E. *The Foreign Policy of Col. McCormick's Tribune, 1929-1941.* Reno: University of Nevada Press, 1971.

1593. Freeman, Lucy. *"Before I Kill More . . ."* New York: Crown, 1955. Life of William Heirens, who kidnapped and murdered six-year-old Suzanne Degnan in Chicago in 1946.

1594. Hiller, Ernest Theodore. *Houseboat and River-Bottoms People.* Illinois Studies in the Social Sciences, vol. 24, no. 1. Urbana: University of Illinois, 1939. The author studied river-front residents (683 households) in six Illinois counties, four on the Ohio, one on the Mississippi, and one (Alexander) on both rivers. He reports land use and occupancy, kinds of employment, unemployment and welfare statistics, housing, family structure, literacy level, and the effects of environment.

1595. Homel, Michael W. "Lilydale School Campaign of 1936: Direct Action in the Verbal Protest Era." *Journal of Negro History* 59 (1974): 228-41. Development (1912-20) of Lilydale, a nearly all-black community on the far South Side of Chicago. The 1936 campaign was a protest against the area's substandard temporary schools.

1596. Hufft, Jane Wolf, and Loftis, Anne Nevins, eds. "Excerpts from the Letters of Lewis Omer to Allan Nevins, 1930-1953." *Illinois Historical Journal*

81 (1988): 25-34. A college professor (Nevins) and a farm owner (Omer) discuss politics, farming, and books.

1597. McCollum, Dannel Angus. "Origins of the 'Champaign System': Prelude to the McCollum Case, 1945-1948." *Journal of the Illinois State Historical Society* 75 (1982): 137-47. The "Champaign System" was a program of weekly religious classes instituted in 1940 in the public school system at Champaign. The program was challenged in the courts by Vashti McCollum and eventually declared unconstitutional. The author discusses events that preceded initiation of the court case.

1598. Meier, August, and Rudwick, Elliott M. "Negro Protest at the Chicago World's Fair, 1933-34." *Journal of the Illinois State Historical Society* 59 (1966): 161-71. The protesters sought legal redress against discrimination in public accommodations.

1599. Purdue, Earl. *Horse Creek and the Great Depression.* Kell, Ill.: The author, 1983. Farm life in southern Illinois from the Great Depression to 1975.

1600. Reed, Christopher Robert. "A Reinterpretation of Black Strategies for Change at the Chicago World's Fair, 1933-1934." *Illinois Historical Journal* 81 (1988): 2-12. Chicago's African-American citizens used the fair as an opportunity to campaign for civil and economic rights.

1601. Reid, Robert L., and Viskochil, Larry A., eds. *Chicago and Downstate: Illinois as Seen by the Farm Security Administration Photographers, 1936-1943.* Visions of Illinois series. Urbana: University of Illinois Press and the Chicago Historical Society, 1989. Photographs arranged both topically and chronologically in eleven chapters, with an introduction that establishes the historical, social, and economic framework.

1602. Russell, Herbert K., comp. *A Southern Illinois Album: Farm Security Administration Photographs, 1936-1943.* With a foreword by F. Jack Hurley. Carbondale: Southern Illinois University Press, 1990.

1603. Sadler, Charles. " 'Political Dynamite': The Chicago Polonia and President Roosevelt in 1944." *Journal of the Illinois State Historical Society* 71 (1978): 119-32.

1604. Trobaugh, Lee Margaret. *All They Had Was a Song: The Story of the Egyptian Choral Club, 1934-1946.* West Frankfort, Ill.: The author, 1986. A story of the club and its founder, Frank Trobaugh, who not only presented many concerts but also founded a community concert association and the Egyptian Music Festival.

1605. Trolander, Judith Ann. *Settlement Houses and the Great Depression.* Detroit: Wayne State University Press, 1975.

1606. Ubriaco, Robert D. Jr. "The Yalta Conference and Its Impact on the Chicago Congressional Elections of 1946." *Illinois Historical Journal* 86 (1993): 225-44. Polish-Americans in Chicago, disillusioned by the Yalta decision to leave a Communist puppet government in place in Poland, began to abandon the Democratic party. As a result, three incumbent Democratic congressmen lost their seats in the 1946 elections.

1607. Weaver, Leon H. *School Consolidation and State Aid in Illinois.* Illinois Studies in the Social Sciences, vol. 27, no. 4. Urbana: University of Illinois, 1944.

J. 1950 TO THE PRESENT

1. Education

1608. Beadle, Muriel. *Where Has All the Ivy Gone? A Memoir of University Life.* Garden City, N.Y.: Doubleday, 1972. Reminiscences by the wife of George Beadle, who became president of the University of Chicago in 1960.

1609. Butler, David L. *Retrospect at a Tenth Anniversary: Southern Illinois University at Edwardsville.* Carbondale: Southern Illinois University Press, 1976.

1610. Collins, Marva, and Tamarkin, Civia. *Marva Collins' Way.* Los Angeles: J. P. Tarcher, 1982. Collins discusses the successful teaching techniques used at her Westside Preparatory School in Chicago.

1611. O'Connell, Mary. *School Reform Chicago Style: How Citizens Organized to Change Public Policy.* Chicago: Center for Neighborhood Technology, 1991.

1612. Peterson, Paul E. *School Politics Chicago Style.* Chicago: University of Chicago Press, 1976.

1613. Rosen, George. *Decision-Making Chicago Style: The Genesis of a University of Illinois Campus.* Urbana: University of Illinois Press, 1980. Public decisions involved in the development of the Chicago Circle campus and the impact of those decisions on a Chicago neighborhood.

1614. Sherman, Richard G. "Constitutionalism and the Illinois Community College System: A Case of Dissenting Taxpayers, 1966-68." *Illinois Historical Journal* 83 (1990): 85-96.

2. Politics and Government

1615. Anton, Thomas J. *The Politics of State Expenditure in Illinois*. Urbana: University of Illinois Press, 1966. A study of the state appropriations procedure, through consideration of the 1961 and 1963 biennial budgets. Procedures have since been changed, but the author's account of political influences on the budgeting process is still of interest.

1616. Bernard, Richard M. *Snowbelt Cities: Metropolitan Politics in the Northeast and Midwest since World War II*. Bloomington: Indiana University Press, 1990. Chicago is one of the cities studied.

1617. Bisnow, Mark. *Diary of a Dark Horse: The 1980 Anderson Presidential Campaign*. Carbondale: Southern Illinois University Press, 1983. The campaign of Illinois Congressman John B. Anderson is discussed by one of his advisors.

1618. Burman, Ian D. *Lobbying at the Illinois Constitutional Convention*. Studies in Illinois Constitution Making. Urbana: University of Illinois Press, for the Institute of Government and Public Affairs, 1973.

1619. Byrne, Jane. *My Chicago*. New York: Norton, 1992. A condensed history of Chicago and an autobiography of the city's first woman mayor.

1620. Cohn, Rubin G. *To Judge with Justice: History and Politics of Illinois Judicial Reform*. Studies in Illinois Constitution Making. Urbana: University of Illinois Press, for the Institute of Government and Public Affairs, 1973. This study of the constitutional basis of the judicial system deals primarily with the judicial amendment of 1962 and the constitution of 1970.

1621. Day, J. Edward. *My Appointed Round: 929 Days as Postmaster General*. New York: Holt, 1965.

1622. Elzy, Martin I. "Illinois Viewed from the Johnson White House." *Journal of the Illinois State Historical Society* 74 (1981): 3-16. Substantive and political issues as they affected Illinois in the 1960s.

1623. Farber, David. *Chicago '68.* Chicago: University of Chicago Press, 1988. An account of the conflict between the "radicals" and city authorities at the national Democratic convention in Chicago.

1624. Felsenthal, Carol. *The Sweetheart of the Silent Majority: The Biography of Phyllis Schlafly.* Garden City, N.Y.: Doubleday, 1981.

1625. Fisher, Glenn W. *Taxes and Politics: A Study of Illinois Public Finances.* Urbana: University of Illinois Press, 1969. Outdated, but useful for the 1960-65 period.

1626. FitzGerald, Kathleen. *Brass, Jane Byrne, and the Pursuit of Power.* Chicago: Contemporary Books, 1981.

1627. Forde, Kevin M. *The Government of Cook County: A Study in Governmental Obsolescence.* Loyola University Center for Research in Urban Government, publication no. 13. Chicago, 1967.

1628. Gertz, Elmer, and Pisciotte, Joseph P. *Charter for a New Age: An Inside View of the Sixth Illinois Constitutional Convention.* Studies in Illinois Constitution Making. Urbana: University of Illinois Press, for the Institute of Government and Public Affairs, 1980.

1629. Gertz, Elmer. *For the First Hours of Tomorrow: The New Illinois Bill of Rights.* Studies in Illinois Constitution Making. Urbana: University of Illinois Press, for the Institute of Government and Public Affairs, 1972. History of the committee that drafted the rights bill of the 1970 constitution.

1630. Gove, Samuel Kimball, and Masotti, Louis H., eds. *After Daley: Chicago Politics in Transition.* Urbana: University of Illinois Press, 1982. A collection of essays.

1631. Gove, Samuel Kimball. *Reapportionment and the Cities: The Impact of Reapportionment on Urban Legislation in Illinois.* Loyola University Center for Research in Urban Government, publication no. 12. Chicago, 1967.

1632. _____, and Kitsos, Thomas B. *Revision Success: The Sixth Illinois Constitutional Convention.* State Constitutional Convention Studies, no. 8. New York: National Municipal League, 1974.

1633. Granger, Bill, and Granger, Lori. *Fighting Jane: Mayor Jane Byrne and the Chicago Machine.* New York: Dial Press, 1980.

1634. Green, Paul M., and Holli, Melvin G., eds. *Restoration, 1989: Chicago Elects a New Daley.* Chicago: Lyceum Books, 1991.

1635. Illinois. Commission to Study State Government. *Organization and Functioning of the State Government: Report . . . Submitted to the 67th Illinois General Assembly.* Springfield, 1950. The commission, headed by Walter V. Schaefer, was the Illinois version of the national Hoover Commission.

1636. *Illinois Issues.* Published monthly eleven times a year (the August-September issue is a double number) by Sangamon State University, Springfield; cosponsored by the University of Illinois. 1975--to date. Devoted to public policy and governmental issues, with book reviews and news of appointments and court decisions.

1637. Judd, Dennis R., and Mendolson, Robert E. *The Politics of Urban Planning: The East St. Louis Experience.* Urbana: University of Illinois Press, 1973. Failure of plans for urban redevelopment under the Model Cities programs in the 1960s was due, the authors argue, to the ideology of planners who either did not consider the needs of the community or failed to understand the political processes by which the plans may have been effected.

1638. Kallina, Edmund F. Jr. *Courthouse over White House: Chicago and the Presidential Election of 1960.* Gainesville: University Presses of Florida, 1988.

1639. Kenney, David. *Making a Modern Constitution: The Illinois Experience.* Murphysboro, Ill.: Jackson County Historical Society, 1991. Based on the 1969-70 convention journal and record as well as contemporary newspapers and the author's own diaries.

1640. Kleppner, Paul; Dahlberg, Richard E.; Tobias, Ruth Anne; Himmelberger, Kevin M.; and Vaupel, Richard P. *Political Atlas of Illinois.* DeKalb: Northern Illinois University Press, 1988. An atlas of Illinois counties and the 59 senate and 118 house districts of the Illinois General Assembly (1982-86) with election returns and statistical profiles of each district and county drawn from the census (i.e., education, income, types of employment, ethnic populations).

1641. Lockwood, Brocton, with Harlan H. Mendenhall. *Operation Greylord: Brocton Lockwood's Story*. Carbondale: Southern Illinois University Press, 1989. A southern Illinois judge assigned to Chicago, Lockwood wore a tape recorder in a sting operation that exposed extensive corruption among Chicago judges and attorneys.

1642. Mailer, Norman. *Miami and the Siege of Chicago: An Informal History of the Republican and Democratic Conventions of 1968*. New York: World Publishing, 1968.

1643. Mattick, Hans W., and Sweet, Ronald P. *Illinois Jails: Challenge and Opportunity for the 1970's*. Illinois Law Enforcement Commission Publication no. 8-70. Chicago, 1970. Based on The Illinois Jails Survey of 1967-68 by the Center for Studies in Criminal Justice at the University of Chicago Law School.

1644. Monypenny, Phillip. *The Impact of Federal Grants in Illinois*. Urbana: University of Illinois Institute of Government and Public Affairs, 1958.

1645. Nowlan, James D., ed. *Inside State Government: A Primer for Illinois Managers*. Urbana: University of Illinois Institute of Government and Public Affairs, 1982. Rev. ed., Chicago: Neltnor House, 1991.

1646. _____. *A New Game Plan for Illinois*. Chicago: Neltnor House, 1989. A thoughtful and provocative study, with a good bibliography.

1647. O'Reilly, Kenneth. "Adlai E. Stevenson, McCarthyism, and the FBI." *Illinois Historical Journal* 81 (1988): 45-60.

1648. Schapsmeier, Edward L., and Schapsmeier, Frederick H. "Paul H. Douglas: From Pacifist to Soldier-Statesman." *Journal of the Illinois State Historical Society* 67 (1974): 307-23.

1649. _____. "Scott W. Lucas of Havana: His Rise and Fall as Majority Leader in the United States Senate." *Journal of the Illinois State Historical Society* 70 (1977): 302-20.

1650. Simon, Jeanne. *Codename Scarlett: Life on the Campaign Trail*. New York: Continuum, 1989. Account of the 1988 presidential campaign by the wife of candidate Paul Simon.

1651. Simon, Paul. *Winners and Losers, the 1988 Race for the Presidency: One Candidate's Perspective*. New York: Continuum, 1989.

1652. Stein, David Lewis. *Living the Revolution: The Yippies in Chicago.* Indianapolis: Bobbs-Merrill, 1969. Conflict at the 1968 Democratic convention.

1653. Steiner, Gilbert Y., and Gove, Samuel Kimball. *Legislative Politics in Illinois.* Urbana: University of Illinois Press, 1960. A valuable study of behind-the-scenes forces that determine legislative policy.

1654. Suttles, Gerald D. *The Man-Made City: The Land-Use Confidence Game in Chicago.* Chicago: University of Chicago Press, 1990. The chaotic nature of so-called city planning in Chicago, 1976-87.

1655. Thiem, George. *The Hodge Scandal: A Pattern of American Political Corruption.* New York: St. Martin's Press, 1963. In 1956 *Chicago Daily News* reporter Thiem first exposed thefts by State Auditor Orville E. Hodge, who became the first elected state official sentenced to prison.

1656. Tuohy, James, and Warden, Rob. *Greylord: Justice, Chicago Style.* New York: Putnam, 1989. An inside investigation of the Chicago court system that led to the indictment and conviction of several judges, attorneys, and other court officers.

1657. Van der Slik, Jack; Pernacciaro, Samuel J.; and Kenney, David. "Patterns of Partisanship in a Nonpartisan Representational Setting: The Illinois Constitutional Convention." *American Journal of Political Science* 18 (February 1974): 95-116.

1658. Woodard, David E. "Reflections on Otto Kerner as a Civil Rights Leader." *Transactions of the Illinois State Historical Society: Selected Papers from the Seventh Annual History Symposium and the Eighth Annual History Symposium* [1986 and 1987]. Springfield, 1989. Pp. 81-90.

3. Social Problems

1659. Altman, Jack, and Ziporyn, Marvin. *Born to Raise Hell: The Untold Story of Richard Speck.* New York: Grove Press, 1967. Speck killed eight nurses in Chicago in 1966. This book is the story of the preliminaries to his trial and the trial itself.

1660. Bailey, Robert Jr. *Radicals in Urban Politics: The Alinsky Approach.* Chicago: University of Chicago Press, 1974. A study of community organization in the Chicago Austin neighborhood.

1661. Cahill, Tim. *Buried Dreams: Inside the Mind of a Serial Killer; Based on the Investigative Reporting of Russ Ewing.* New York: Bantam Books, 1986. The convicted killer is John Wayne Gacy.

1662. Colander, Pat. *Thin Air: The Life and Mysterious Disappearance of Helen Brach.* Chicago: Contemporary Books, 1982. The body of the Brach candy heiress still has not been found.

1663. Dawley, David. *A Nation of Lords: The Autobiography of the Vice Lords.* Garden City, N.Y.: Anchor Press, Doubleday, 1973. Study of a Chicago street gang.

1664. Fish, John Hall. *Black Power/White Control: The Struggle for the Woodlawn Organization in Chicago.* Princeton, N.J.: Princeton University Press, 1973. A community development study.

1665. Garrow, David J., ed. *Chicago 1966: Open Housing Marches, Summit Negotiations, and Operation Breadbasket.* Brooklyn, N.Y.: Carlson, 1989. Activities of the Chicago Freedom Movement.

1666. Keiser, R. Lincoln. *The Vice Lords, Warriors of the Streets.* Case Studies in Cultural Anthropology. New York: Holt, 1969.

1667. Kennedy, Patrick D. "Reactions against the Vietnam War and Military-Related Targets on Campus: The University of Illinois as a Case Study, 1965-1972." *Illinois Historical Journal* 84 (1991): 101-18.

1668. Knoepfle, Peg. *After Alinsky: Community Organizing in Illinois.* Springfield: *Illinois Issues*, Sangamon State University, 1990.

1669. Kotlowitz, Alex. *There Are No Children Here: The Story of Two Boys Growing Up in the Other America.* New York: Doubleday, 1991. Life in the Henry Horner Homes, a Chicago public housing project.

1670. Linedecker, Clifford L. *The Man Who Killed Boys.* New York: St. Martin's Press, 1980. A study of John Wayne Gacy.

1671. McClory, Robert. *The Man Who Beat Clout City.* Chicago: Swallow Press, 1977. The subject is Renault Robinson, a Chicago policeman who organized the Afro-American Patrolmen's League and ultimately went to the federal courts to end discrimination in the police department.

1672. Monroe, Sylvester, and Goldman, Peter, with Vern E. Smith, Terry E. Johnson, Monroe Anderson, and Jacques Chenet. *Brothers: Black and Poor--A True Story of Courage and Survival.* A Newsweek Book. New York: William Morrow, 1988. The stories of twelve black men who grew up together in the housing projects of Chicago's South Side.

1673. O'Brien, Darcy. *Murder in Little Egypt.* New York: New American Library, Penguin Books, 1990. Story of the once-respected physician Dr. John Dale Cavaness, who was convicted of murdering one son and suspected of murdering another.

1674. Pierson, Robert L. *Riots Chicago Style.* Great Neck, N.Y.: Todd & Honeywell, 1984. A Chicago police officer reports on the 1968 riots at the Democratic convention and those following the assassination of Martin Luther King.

1675. Protess, David L., and Warden, Rob. *Gone in the Night: The Dowaliby Family's Encounter with Murder and the Law.* New York: Delacorte, 1993. David Dowaliby was tried for the abduction and murder of his young stepdaughter, Jaclyn, in 1988. He was found guilty, but the verdict was reversed by the Illinois Appellate Court. The murder is still unsolved.

1676. Sale, Richard T. *The Blackstone Rangers: A Reporter's Account of Time Spent with the Street Gang on Chicago's South Side.* New York: Random House, 1972.

1677. Squires, Gregory D.; Bennett, Larry; McCourt, Kathleen; and Nyden, Philip. *Chicago: Race, Class, and the Response to Urban Decline.* Comparative American Cities series. Philadelphia: Temple University Press, 1987.

1678. Stout, Steve. *The Starved Rock Murders.* Utica, Ill.: Utica House, 1982. A well-researched and well-written account of the 1960 murders of three women at Starved Rock State Park.

1679. Sullivan, Terry, with Peter T. Maiken. *Killer Clown.* New York: Grosset & Dunlap, 1983. John Wayne Gacy, the serial killer, performed as a clown for young children.

1680. Suttles, Gerald D. *The Social Order of the Slum: Ethnicity and Territory in the Inner City.* Studies of Urban Society. Chicago: University of Chicago Press, 1968. A sociological study of the slum area of Chicago's Near West Side in the 1960s.

1681. Thrasher, Frederic Milton. *The Gang: A Study of 1,313 Gangs in Chicago.* Abridged, with a new introduction by James F. Short, Jr. Chicago: University of Chicago Press, 1963.

1682. Vogel, Steve. *Reasonable Doubt: A True Story of Lust and Murder in the American Heartland.* Chicago: Contemporary Books, 1989. An account of the 1983 murders of the David Hendricks family and of Hendricks's trial and conviction. (Hendricks won a second trial, at which he was found not guilty.)

1683. Weber, Don W., and Bosworth, Charles Jr. *Precious Victims.* New York: Penguin, 1991. A true crime story (by the prosecuting attorney and a *St. Louis Post-Dispatch* reporter, respectively) of the trial and conviction of Paula Sims for the suffocation death of one of her two murdered daughters.

4. Miscellany

1684. Allen, James Sloan. *The Romance of Commerce and Culture: Capitalism, Modernism, and the Chicago-Aspen Crusade for Cultural Reform.* Chicago: University of Chicago Press, 1983. The author discusses the relation between Walter Paepcke (Chicago industrialist and a founder of the Aspen Institute) and a group of University of Chicago luminaries whose ideas greatly influenced the 1950s.

1685. Bennett, Larry. *Fragments of Cities: The New American Downtowns and Neighborhoods.* Columbus: Ohio State University Press, 1990. Chicago is treated extensively.

1686. Dahm, Charles, in collaboration with Robert Ghelardi. *Power and Authority in the Catholic Church: Cardinal Cody in Chicago.* Notre Dame, Ind.: University of Notre Dame Press, 1981. An unbalanced anti-Cody treatise.

1687. Derber, Milton, comp. *Labor in Illinois: The Affluent Years, 1945-1980.* Urbana: University of Illinois Press, 1989. Collection of essays by the compiler and graduate students in the Institute of Labor and Industrial Relations at the University of Illinois.

1688. Elazar, Daniel J., et al. *Cities of the Prairie Revisited: The Closing of the Metropolitan Frontier.* Cities of the Prairie series. Lincoln: University of Nebraska Press, 1986. Continues the study of ten metropolitan areas (eight in Illinois) from 1961 to 1976. An earlier volume, published in 1970 (New York: Basic Books) covered the years 1946-61.

1689. Forbes, John. *The Springfield Mitre: A History of the Politics and Consequences of an Episcopal Election in Illinois, 1962-1967.* Pelham, N.Y.: American Church Publications, 1971. The election took place in the Springfield diocese of the Episcopal church.

1690. Fortner, Robert S., and Hoag, Richard L. "The Concern over Nuclear Power: An Illinois Context." *Illinois Quarterly* 42, no. 2 (Winter 1979): 5-14. An analysis of public attitudes towards the nuclear power plants in Grundy County.

1691. Gertz, Elmer. *Gertz v. Robert Welch, Inc.: The Story of a Landmark Libel Case.* Carbondale: Southern Illinois University Press, 1992. Case of civil rights attorney Gertz against Robert Welch, head of the John Birch Society.

1692. Goudy, Frank W. "Foreign Ownership of Farmland in Western Illinois." *Western Illinois Regional Studies* 5 (1982): 65-83.

1693. Greising, David, and Morris, Laurie. *Brokers, Bagmen, and Moles: Fraud and Corruption in the Chicago Futures Market.* New York: John Wiley, 1991. This account of the federal investigation of the futures market and the indictment in 1989 of forty-five Chicago traders and a trader's clerk also traces the history of the Chicago Board of Trade and the Chicago Mercantile Exchange.

1694. Hair, C. Edwin. *Our Christmas Disaster.* Mt. Vernon, Ill.: L. S. Wood Printing, 1952. The disaster was the 21 December 1951 explosion at New Orient Mine 2 at West Frankfort.

1695. Heinz, John P., and Laumann, Edward O. *Chicago Lawyers: The Social Structure of the Bar.* New York: Russell Sage Foundation and American Bar Foundation, 1982. An analysis of the profession, not of individual lawyers.

1696. Katz, Donald R. *The Big Store: Inside the Crisis and Revolution at Sears.* New York: Viking, 1987.

1697. Krohe, James Jr. *Breadbasket or Dust Bowl? The Future of Illinois Farmland.* Springfield: *Illinois Issues,* Sangamon State University, 1982. Sponsored by the Joyce Foundation, the Illinois Department of Agriculture, and *Illinois Issues* of Sangamon State University.

1698. Littlewood, Thomas B. *Coals of Fire: The* Alton Telegraph *Libel Case.* Carbondale: Southern Illinois University Press, 1988. After losing a 1980 libel suit, the *Telegraph* was sold to a large newspaper chain. This volume is an account of not only the suit but also a flawed legal system and the demise of independent publishers.

1699. McCrohan, Donna. *The Second City: A Backstage History of Comedy's Hottest Troupe.* New York: Perigee Books, 1987.

1700. Mann, John. "MVR at Fifteen." *Western Illinois Regional Studies* 8, no. 2 (Fall 1985): 66-73. A history of the literary magazine *Mississippi Valley Review*, published since 1970 by the Department of English at Western Illinois University.

1701. Morgan, Hugh. "The West Frankfort Mine Disaster." *Selected Papers in Illinois History, 1981.* Springfield: Illinois State Historical Society, 1982. Pp. 95-107.

1702. Moyer, Reed. *Competition in the Midwestern Coal Industry.* Harvard Economic Studies, vol. 122. Cambridge, Mass.: Harvard University Press, 1964. An important scholarly study that analyzes coal mining in Illinois, Indiana, and western Kentucky in the 1960s.

1703. Polovchak, Walter, with Kevin Klose. *Freedom's Child: A Courageous Teenager's Story of Fleeing His Parents--and the Soviet Union--to Live in America.* New York: Random House, 1988.

1704. Powers, Ron. *Far from Home: Life and Loss in Two American Towns.* New York: Random House, 1991. A study of two imperiled towns: Cairo, Illinois, and Kent, Connecticut--Cairo from strained race relations and the flight of industry, and Kent from overdevelopment.

1705. Pruter, Robert. *Chicago Soul.* Music in American Life series. Urbana: University of Illinois Press, 1991. A history of soul music, its performers, and concomitant businesses, in Chicago, from the 1960s to the 1980s.

1706. Raizman, David. "The Contribution of Regional Arts: A Conversation with George M. Irwin of Quincy." *Western Illinois Regional Studies* 10, no. 2 (Fall 1987): 49-63.

1707. Robertson, Mary Lou. "Traditional & Acculturative Medical Practices among the Ethnic Lao: A Study in Rockford & Elgin, Illinois." *Southeast Asia Review* 9 (1984): 1-97.

1708. Sweet, Jeffrey, ed. *Something Wonderful Right Away: An Oral History of the Second City and the Compass Players.* New York: Avon, 1978.

1709. Swenson, Russell G., and Miner, Pamela Olson. "The Character of New Small Farms in Western Illinois." *Western Illinois Regional Studies* 10, no. 1 (Spring 1987): 83-93.

1710. Terkel, Louis (Studs). *Division Street: America.* New York: Pantheon, 1967. Interviews with Chicagoans from all walks of life constitute a documentary of American attitudes.

1711. Walker, Daniel. *Rights in Conflict: Chicago's 7 Brutal Days.* New York: Grosset & Dunlap, 1968. A report (submitted to the National Commission on the Causes and Prevention of Violence) on the violence that occurred during the Democratic convention in Chicago in 1968. The report, under the title *Rights in Conflict: Convention Week in Chicago, August 25-29, 1968*, was published by Dutton in 1968, with an introduction by Max Frankel.

II. SUBJECTS

Books and articles related to the subjects listed below appear in the chronological sections if the content concerns only one chronological period. Titles in the following sections contain information on two or more chronological periods. All of the Native American titles are presented here, however, regardless of chronology.

A. DESCRIPTION AND TRAVEL

1. Bibliographies

1712. Buck, Solon Justus. *Travel and Description, 1765-1865; Together with a List of County Histories, Atlases, and Biographical Collections and a List of Territorial and State Laws.* Collections of the Illinois State Historical Library, vol. 9. Springfield, 1914. Reprints, Burt Franklin: Research & Source Work Series 827; New York: Lenox Hill Pub. & Dist., 1971. A comprehensive annotated listing of volumes of travel and description. Full bibliographic information is given for all known editions, as well as the location of the volumes. Especially valuable are Buck's introductions to the three bibliographical sections: travel and description; county histories, atlases, and biographical collections; and territorial and state laws.

1713. Hubach, Robert R., comp. "They Saw the Early Midwest: A Bibliography of Travel Narratives, 1673-1850." *Journal of the Illinois State Historical Society* 47 (1954): 385-97. The narratives listed are those that appeared in early and little-known historical publications of Illinois, Indiana, Michigan, Ohio, and Wisconsin.

1714. _____, comp. "They Saw the Early Midwest: A Bibliography of Travel Narratives, 1722-1850." *Journal of the Illinois State Historical Society* 46 (1953): 283-89. A listing of narratives printed in major historical magazines.

1715. _____, comp. "Unpublished Travel Narratives of the Early Midwest, 1720-1850: A Preliminary Bibliography." *Mississippi Valley Historical Review* 42 (1955-56): 525-48.

2. General Accounts

1716. Bonnell, Clarence. *The Illinois Ozarks*. Harrisburg, Ill.: Register Publishing, 1946. Descriptions of sites in southern Illinois by an amateur geologist and naturalist. A few brief historic accounts.

1717. Hubach, Robert R. "Illinois, Host to Well-Known Nineteenth Century Authors." *Journal of the Illinois State Historical Society* 38 (1945): 446-67. Discussion of the visits of such writers as William Cullen Bryant, Charles Dickens, Oscar Wilde, Walt Whitman, Ralph Waldo Emerson, and many others. Footnotes constitute a bibliography of travel narratives.

1718. Hurt, James. *Writing Illinois: The Prairie, Lincoln, and Chicago*. Urbana: University of Illinois Press, 1992. The prairie, Lincoln, and Chicago, as interpreted by various writers.

1719. Jones, A. D. *Illinois and the West, with a Township Map Containing the Latest Surveys and Improvements*. Boston: Weeks, Jordan, 1838.

3. Travel Narratives

1720. Angle, Paul McClelland, comp. and ed., assisted by Mary Lynn McCree. *Prairie State: Impressions of Illinois, 1673-1967*. Chicago: University of Chicago Press, 1968. Angle states that his emphasis is on "the descriptive rather than the narrative."

1721. Beadle, J. H. *Western Wilds and the Men Who Redeem Them: An Authentic Narrative, Embracing an Account of Seven Years Travel and Adventure in the Far West, Wild Life in Arizona, Perils of the Plains, Life in the Cañon and*

Death on the Desert . . . Adventures among the Red and White Savages of the West . . . the Mountain Meadow Massacre, the Custer Defeat, Life and Death of Brigham Young, etc. Cincinnati: Jones Brothers Publishing, 1879. The author describes and gives brief histories of the Mormon and Icarian settlements at Nauvoo.

1722. Pierce, Bessie Louise, ed. *As Others See Chicago: Impressions of Visitors, 1673-1933.* Chicago: University of Chicago Press, 1933.

1723. Thwaites, Reuben Gold, ed. *Early Western Travels, 1748-1846: A Series of Annotated Reprints of Some of the Best and Rarest Contemporary Volumes of Travel Descriptive of the Aborigines and Social and Economic Conditions in the Middle and Far West, during the Period of Early American Settlement.* 32 vols. Cleveland: Arthur H. Clark, 1904-7. The last two volumes are an analytical index. In volume 31, pages 13-18, is a list of the reprints published in the series.

1724. Walton, Clyde C. "As They Saw Illinois, 1765-1828." *Illinois Blue Book, 1957-1958.* Pp. 11-33. Reprint, Springfield: Illinois State Historical Library, 1959. A collection of excerpts from vivid travel accounts.

B. ECONOMIC HISTORY

1. Agriculture and the Land

a. Bibliographies

1725. Bardolph, Richard. *Agricultural Literature and the Early Illinois Farmer.* Illinois Studies in the Social Sciences, vol. 29, nos. 1 and 2. Urbana: University of Illinois Press, 1948. The author considers books, newspapers, and periodicals for the farmer in the years 1760-1870.

1726. Bercaw, Louise O.; Hannay, A. M.; and Colvin, Esther M., comps. *Bibliography of Land Settlement with Particular Reference to Small Holdings and Subsistence Homesteads.* United States Department of Agriculture Miscellaneous Publication no. 172. Washington: Government Printing Office, 1934. Entries are descriptive; the Illinois section (items 858-66) mainly concerns Great Depression-era projects; the index shows other entries under Illinois and Chicago.

1727. Bowers, Douglas, comp. *A List of References for the History of Agriculture in the United States, 1790-1840.* Davis: Agricultural History Center, University of California at Davis, 1969. Illinois, pp. 22-25.

1728. Edwards, Everett E., comp. *A Bibliography of the History of Agriculture in the United States.* United States Department of Agriculture Miscellaneous Publication no. 84. Washington: Government Printing Office, 1930. In addition to general references, arranged by subject, there are sections for each state. For Illinois (pages 115-17) there are 36 entries.

b. In General

1729. Aldrich, S. R. *Illinois Field Crops and Soils.* University of Illinois Agricultural Extension Service, Circular 901. January 1965.

1730. Ankli, Robert E. "Horses vs. Tractors on the Corn Belt." *Agricultural History* 54 (1980): 134-48. Based on Illinois and Iowa records.

1731. Bardolph, Richard. "Illinois Agriculture in Transition, 1820-1870." *Journal of the Illinois State Historical Society* 41 (1948): 244-64, 415-37.

1732. Bigolin, Stephen J. *The Barbed Wire Saga.* Gurler Chronicle, no. 9. DeKalb, Ill.: Gurler Heritage Association, 1983. Two DeKalb County men, Jacob Haish and Joseph Farwell Glidden, made substantial improvements in barbed wire, and both manufactured and marketed their wire, though Glidden's design was the one that survived.

1733. Bogue, Allan G. "Farming in the Prairie Peninsula, 1830-1890." *Journal of Economic History* 23 (1963): 3-29. Reprinted in Scheiber, no. 4086. The author defines the prairie peninsula as the triangle "flaring westward from the upper valley of the Wabash" that includes "most of central and northern Illinois and almost all of Iowa."

1734. _____. *From Prairie to Corn Belt: Farming on the Illinois and Iowa Prairies in the Nineteenth Century.* Chicago: University of Chicago Press, 1963.

1735. Bogue, Margaret Beattie. *Patterns from the Sod: Land Use and Tenure in the Grand Prairie, 1850-1900.* Collections of the Illinois State Historical Library, vol. 34. Springfield, 1959.

1736. _____. "The Swamp Land Act and Wet Land Utilization in Illinois, 1850-1890." *Agricultural History* 25 (1951): 169-80.

1737. Caraway, Charles. *Foothold on a Hillside: Memories of a Southern Illinoisan.* Shawnee Series. Carbondale: Southern Illinois University Press, 1986. Farm life from the 1890s to the 1960s.

1738. Carlson, Theodore L. *The Illinois Military Tract: A Study of Land Occupation, Utilization, and Tenure.* Illinois Studies in the Social Sciences, vol. 32, no. 2. Urbana: University of Illinois Press, 1951. The Military Tract was that extensive area between the Illinois and Mississippi rivers set aside as bounty land for soldiers in the War of 1812. The author traces the economic development of the region from its early settlement in 1818 to 1900.

1739. *Circular.* University of Illinois at Urbana-Champaign. Cooperative Extension Service. No. 1 (1897?)--to date. Issued irregularly by various agencies at the university, currently by the Cooperative Extension Service.

1740. Clark, John G. *The Grain Trade in the Old Northwest.* Urbana: University of Illinois Press, 1966. Distribution of agricultural products from territorial days to 1860--first by water and then by railroad.

1741. Coon, Reuben L., ed. *History of the Illinois State Agricultural Society, Containing Summary of the Growth of the Illinois State Fair from 1853 to 1941.* Springfield, Ill.: Williamson Press, 1941? The first history of the state fair, this booklet was based on careful research.

1742. Crabb, Richard. *The Hybrid-Corn Makers: Prophets of Plenty.* New Brunswick, N.J.: Rutgers University Press, 1947. 2d ed., Wheaton, Ill.: West Chicago Publishing, 1992, with a special 84-page introductory section reporting developments in corn-hybridization, 1942-92.

1743. Curran, William Reid. "Indian Corn: Genesis of Reid's Yellow Dent." *Journal of the Illinois State Historical Society* 11 (1918-19): 576-85. Yellow Dent was developed by James L. Reid.

1744. Davenport, Eugene. "On the Agricultural Development of Illinois since the Civil War." *Transactions of the Illinois State Historical Society, 1919,* pp. 101-6.

1745. Dillon, Jessie M. "Normal and the Norman Horse Industry: Percherons of Today." *Journal of the Illinois State Historical Society* 29 (1936-37): 364-

402. Members of the Dillon family came to Illinois in the 1820s and brought with them several draft horses. In mid-century they acquired their first Norman horse (or Percheron).

1746. Esposito, Margaret. *Places of Pride: The Work and Photography of Clara R. Brian.* Photographs edited by Tona Schenck. Bloomington, Ill.: McLean County Historical Society, 1989. Brian was the first McLean County Home Bureau adviser (1918-45). This collection of one hundred of her photographs, together with the biographical sketch by Esposito, constitutes a "slice-of-life" history of farm life in the first half of the twentieth century.

1747. Evans, James F. *Prairie Farmer and WLS: The Burridge D. Butler Years.* Urbana: University of Illinois Press, 1969. Butler assumed control of the *Prairie Farmer* in 1909.

1748. Farlow, Lawrence. *The Farmers Elevator Movement in Illinois.* N.p.: Farmers Grain Dealers Association of Illinois, 1928.

1749. Fitzgerald, Deborah. *The Business of Breeding: Hybrid Corn in Illinois, 1890-1940.* Ithaca, N.Y.: Cornell University Press, 1990.

1750. Gates, Paul Wallace. "Cattle Kings in the Prairies." *Mississippi Valley Historical Review* 35 (1948-49): 379-412. Cattle feeders and breeders in Illinois from the 1830s to the 1940s.

1751. _____. "Frontier Landlords and Pioneer Tenants." *Journal of the Illinois State Historical Society* 38 (1945): 143-206. Reprint, Ithaca, N.Y.: Cornell University Press, 1945. Discussion of large landholdings in Illinois to the end of the nineteenth century.

1752. Gregory, Owen. "The Chicago Board of Trade's Archives." *Agricultural History* 56 (1982): 326-27. The papers are located at the University of Illinois at Chicago Circle.

1753. Hammes, Raymond H. "Land Transactions in Illinois Prior to the Sale of Public Domain." *Journal of the Illinois State Historical Society* 77 (1984): 101-14. The first sale of public lands in Illinois was recorded at the Kaskaskia Land Office in 1814. The author discusses land alienation prior to that time.

1754. Harris, Benjamin Franklin. "Autobiography of Benjamin Franklin Harris." Edited by Mrs. Mary Vose Harris. *Transactions of the Illinois State Historical Society, 1923*, pp. 72-110. Harris, who lived in Illinois from 1835 until his death in 1905, had one of the largest stock farms in the state, located in Champaign County. The so-called autobiography is a third-person narrative with extracts from the original autobiography and from Harris's day books. Known locally as a "cattle king," Harris also raised horses, hogs, and sheep.

1755. Hayter, Earl W. "Barbed Wire Fencing--A Prairie Invention: Its Rise and Influence in the Western States." *Agricultural History* 13 (1939): 180-207. Barbed wire was perfected and manufactured in Illinois.

1756. Hedlund, Earl C. *The Transportation Economics of the Soybean Processing Industry.* Illinois Studies in the Social Sciences, vol. 33, no. 1. Urbana, 1952.

1757. Heinl, Frank J. "Pioneer Nurserymen in Illinois." *American Nurserymen* 15 July 1950, p. 25.

1758. Henry, Patricia. "Illinois State Fair: Then and Now." *Illinois Magazine* 23, no. 4 (July-August 1984), supplement, pp. 1A-8A.

1759. Herget, James E. "Taming the Environment: The Drainage District in Illinois." *Journal of the Illinois State Historical Society* 71 (1978): 107-18. After the federal government turned over swamp lands to the states by statute of 1850, the state transferred title to the counties. Illinois passed a general ditch law in 1865; the author traces the history of drainage districts to 1972.

1760. Illinois State Horticultural Society. *Transactions . . .* Vols. 1--11 (1856-66); n.s. vols. 1--84 (1867-1950?). Continued as *Transactions of the Illinois State Horticultural Society and the Illinois Fruit Council,* vols. 85--114 (1951-80), and as *Transactions of the Illinois State Horticultural Society for the Year . . . ,* vols. 115 (1981)--to date.

1761. Jacobs, Leonard J. "Kings of the Hill: Illini Huskers, 1924-1941." *Journal of the Illinois State Historical Society* 76 (1983): 205-12. A description of the sport of corn-husking and accounts of some of the Illinois farmers who were champion huskers.

1762. Kellar, Herbert A. "The Reaper as a Factor in the Development of the Agriculture of Illinois, 1834-1865." *Transactions of the Illinois State Historical Society, 1927,* pp. 105-14.

1763. Kruckman, Laurence, and Whiteman, Darrell L. "Barns, Buildings, and Windmills: A Key to Change on the Illinois Prairie." *Journal of the Illinois State Historical Society* 68 (1975): 257-66. Covers the period 1850-1974.

1764. Lacey, John J. *Farm Bureau in Illinois.* Bloomington, Ill.: Illinois Agricultural Association, 1965. This official history of the Illinois Agricultural Association is an important contribution to state agricultural history.

1765. Love, Martin M. "William H. Ashley, Land Speculator." *Western Historical Quarterly* 6 (April 1975): 241-43. Traces Ashley's purchase of military bounty land warrants in Fulton County.

1766. McCallum, Henry D., and McCallum, Frances T. *The Wire That Fenced the West.* Norman: University of Oklahoma Press, 1965. The Illinoisans who perfected and manufactured barbed wire are discussed at length.

1767. McClelland, Clarence Paul. "Jacob Strawn and John T. Alexander, Central Illinois Stockmen." *Journal of the Illinois State Historical Society* 34 (1941): 177-208.

1768. Olsen, Nils A. *Journal of a Tamed Bureaucrat: Nils A. Olsen and the BAE, 1925-1935.* Edited by Richard Lowitt. Ames: Iowa State University Press, 1980. Onetime farmer from Kankakee, Olsen headed the Bureau of Agricultural Economics, 1928-35. His journal reflects his positions on critical farm policies and is a valuable contribution to agricultural history.

1769. *Prairie Farmer Centennial Number.* 11 January 1941. The issue presents a history of Illinois agriculture.

1770. Price, H. Wayne. "The Double-Crib Log Barns of Calhoun County." *Journal of the Illinois State Historical Society* 73 (1980): 140-60.

1771. Rikoon, J. Sanford. *Threshing in the Midwest, 1820-1940.* Midwestern History and Culture series. Bloomington: Indiana University Press, 1988.

1772. Rogin, Leo. *The Introduction of Farm Machinery in Its Relation to the Productivity of Labor in the Agriculture of the United States during the Nineteenth Century.* University of California Publications in Economics, vol. 9. Berkeley, 1931. Reprint, Johnson Reprint, 1966.

1773. Rohrbough, Malcolm J. *The Land Office Business: The Settlement and Administration of American Public Lands, 1789-1837.* 1968. Rev. ed., Belmont,

Calif.: Wadsworth Publishing, 1990. The index to this valuable source has many Illinois and Illinois-related entries.

1774. Salamon, Sonya. *Prairie Patrimony: Family, Farming, and Community in the Midwest.* Studies in Rural Culture. Chapel Hill: University of North Carolina Press, 1992.

1775. Saloutos, Theodore, and Hicks, John D. *Agricultural Discontent in the Middle West, 1900-1939.* Madison: University of Wisconsin Press, 1951.

1776. Schob, David E. *Hired Hands and Plowboys: Farm Labor in the Midwest, 1815-60.* Urbana: University of Illinois Press, 1975.

1777. _____. "Sodbusting on the Upper Midwestern Frontier, 1820-1860." *Agricultural History* 47 (1973): 47-56.

1778. Severson, Harold. *Architects of Rural Progress: A Dynamic Story of the Electric Cooperatives as Service Organizations in Illinois.* Springfield: Association of Illinois Electric Cooperatives, 1966?

1779. Smith, Malcolm L. *Working with People, Bugs and Apples: An Old Fashioned Family, L. M. and Grace Smith, Parents of Ten.* Washington, D.C.: Malcolm L. Smith, 1979. Based on extensive family papers, this volume not only provides an account of the fieldwork of a state entomologist but also offers a detailed account of family life on an orchard in southern Illinois from the turn of the century to 1966.

1780. Socolofsky, Homer E. *Landlord William Scully.* Lawrence: The Regents Press of Kansas, 1979. Scully became the owner of vast landholdings throughout the United States, especially in Illinois. His life is a fascinating study of progressive land management.

1781. _____. "William Scully: His Early Years in Illinois, 1850-1865." *Journal of the West* 4 (1965): 41-55.

1782. Stewart, Charles Leslie. *Land Tenure in the United States with Special Reference to Illinois.* University of Illinois Studies in the Social Sciences, vol. 5, no. 3. Urbana, 1916. Covers the years 1850-1910.

1783. Swenson, Russell G. "Wind Engines in Western Illinois." *Western Illinois Regional Studies* 7, no. 1 (Spring 1984): 61-79.

1784. *Transactions of the Illinois State Agricultural Society.* Vols. 1-8 (1853-70), published under this title. Later volumes were titled *Transactions of the Department of Agriculture of the State of Illinois with Reports from County Agricultural Societies . . .* With volume 56 (1918) the series was discontinued.

1785. Ulen, Thomas S. "The Regulation of Grain Warehousing and Its Economic Effects: The Competitive Position of Chicago in the 1870s and 1880s." *Agricultural History* 56 (1982): 194-214. Traces the history of grain transportation and warehousing from the 1830s to the period of concentration in the late nineteenth century; with comments by Jonathan Lurie.

1786. University of Illinois (Urbana-Champaign). Agricultural Experiment Station. *Bulletin.* Vol. 1 (May 1888)--to date. A few separate titles from the *Bulletin* are listed in this bibliography.

1787. University of Illinois (Urbana-Champaign). College of Agriculture. *Special Publication.* No. 1 (1960)--to date.

1788. University of Illinois (Urbana-Champaign). Department of Agricultural Economics, Agricultural Experiment Station. *AERR* (Agricultural Economics Research Report). No. 1? No. 2 (1954)--no. 205 (1988).

1789. Whitaker, James W. *Feedlot Empire: Beef Cattle Feeding in Illinois and Iowa, 1840-1900.* Ames: Iowa State University Press, 1975. An important work in an often-neglected aspect of agricultural history.

1790. Wills, Walter J. *Farm Cooperatives in Illinois.* Southern Illinois University School of Agriculture Publication no. 4. Carbondale, 1958?

1791. Woodman, Harold D. "Chicago Businessmen and the 'Granger' Laws." *Agricultural History* 36 (1962): 16-24. Chicago businessmen, especially the grain traders, joined farmers in the 1860s and 1870s in their push for state regulation of railroads and warehouse monopolies.

2. Business, Labor, and Industry

1792. Achilles, Rolf. *Made in Illinois: A Story of Illinois Manufacturing.* Chicago: Illinois Manufacturers' Association, 1993. Issued in honor of the Manufacturers' Association centennial, this volume provides brief histories of more than six hundred companies producing goods that were invented, developed, or manufactured for the first time in Illinois.

1793. Andrews, Wayne. *Battle for Chicago.* New York: Harcourt, 1946. Chicago's wealthiest businessmen and their influence from the post-Civil War years to the 1940s.

1794. Appleton, John B. *The Iron and Steel Industry of the Calumet District: A Study in Economic Geography.* University of Illinois Studies in the Social Sciences, vol. 13, no. 2. Urbana, 1927. The district lies partially in metropolitan Chicago and partially in Indiana.

1795. Babcock, Milton. "Fire Marks in Illinois." *Journal of the Illinois State Historical Society* 42 (1949): 348-51. Fire marks were small metal house plates issued by insurance companies.

1796. Banton, O. T., ed. *80 Years of Banking, 1860-1940.* Decatur, Ill.: Privately printed, 1940. A history of Decatur's Millikin National Bank and its founder, businessman/philanthropist James Millikin.

1797. Barrett, James R. *Work and Community in the Jungle: Chicago's Packinghouse Workers, 1874-1922.* The Working Class in American History series. Urbana: University of Illinois Press, 1987. A broad scholarly study that considers urbanization, immigration, racial problems, and the effects of World War I on labor and the economy.

1798. Beckner, Earl R. *A History of Labor Legislation in Illinois.* Social Science Studies, Directed by the Local Community Research Committee of the University of Chicago, no. 13. Chicago: University of Chicago Press, 1929.

1799. Bisno, Abraham. *Abraham Bisno, Union Pioneer: An Autobiographical Account of Bisno's Early Life and the Beginnings of Unionism in the Women's Garment Industry.* Foreword by Joel Seidman. Madison: University of Wisconsin Press, 1967. Bisno's first organizing work was done in Chicago, where he also served as a state factory inspector.

1800. Broehl, Wayne G. Jr. *John Deere's Company: A History of Deere & Company and Its Times.* Garden City, N.Y.: Doubleday, 1984. A comprehensive scholarly study that is a model of its kind; includes studies of the men who have managed the company from its inception to the present. In addition to farm implements, the company produces industrial and construction equipment.

1801. Cartlidge, Oscar. *Fifty Years of Coal Mining.* Oregon City, Oreg.: Oregon City Enterprise, 1933. An account of the author's experiences in Illinois as a miner, mine manager, engineer, and state inspector.

1802. Casson, Herbert N. *The Romance of the Reaper.* New York: Doubleday, 1908. A popular account.

1803. Caterpillar Tractor Co. *Fifty Years on Tracks.* Peoria, Ill., 1954. Caterpillar was formed in 1925 with the merger of the C. L. Best Tractor Company and the Holt Manufacturing Company.

1804. Clemen, R. A. *The American Livestock and Meat Industry.* New York: Ronald Press, 1923. Abridged reprint, New York: Johnson Reprint, 1966.

1805. Cohen, Lizabeth. *Making a New Deal: Industrial Workers in Chicago, 1919-1939.* New York: Cambridge University Press, 1990.

1806. Coleberd, Robert E. Jr. "John Williams, A Merchant Banker in Springfield, Illinois." *Agricultural History* 42 (1968): 259-65. Williams's business career spanned four decades, 1824-64. Based in part on the Black and Williams Papers in the Illinois State Historical Library.

1807. Coleman, McAlister. *Men and Coal.* New York: Farrar, 1943. Not limited to Illinois, this volume nevertheless discusses the state's extensive involvement in the development of miners' unionism.

1808. Cornell, James Jr. *The People Get the Credit: The First One Hundred Years of the Spiegel Story, 1865-1965.* Chicago? 1964.

1809. *Crain's Illinois Business.* Vol. 1, no. 1 (Winter 1982)--to date.

1810. Currey, Joseph Seymour. *Manufacturing and Wholesale Industries of Chicago.* 3 vols. Chicago: Thomas B. Poole, 1918. An economic history of Chicago with sketches of both companies and their leaders. Index in volume 3.

1811. Darby, Edwin. *It All Adds Up: The Growth of Victor Comptometer Corporation.* Chicago: The corporation, 1968.

1812. Darling, Sharon. *Chicago Furniture: Art, Craft, and Industry, 1833-1983.* Chicago Historical Society, in association with Norton, New York, 1984.

1813. Dowrie, George William. *The Development of Banking in Illinois, 1817-1863.* University of Illinois Studies in the Social Sciences, vol. 2, no. 4. Urbana, 1913.

1814. Eavenson, Howard N. *The First Century and a Quarter of American Coal Industry.* Pittsburgh: Privately printed, and Baltimore: Waverly Press, 1942. Valuable statistical data and a good general history put the state's coal-mining past in perspective.

1815. Ebert, Albert E. "Early History of the Drug Trade of Chicago." *Transactions of the Illinois State Historical Society, 1903*, pp. 234-74 and *Transactions . . . 1905* , pp. 237-60.

1816. Eilert, John W. "Illinois Business Incorporations, 1816-1869." *Business History Review* 37 (1963): 169-81.

1817. Emmet, Boris, and Jeuck, John E. *Catalogues and Counters: A History of Sears, Roebuck and Company.* Chicago: University of Chicago Press, 1950.

1818. Ericsson, Henry, with Lewis E. Myers. *Sixty Years a Builder: The Autobiography of Henry Ericsson.* Chicago: A. Kroch & Son, 1942. In recounting his work as a builder and contractor, this Swedish immigrant to Chicago also relates the history of many technical building developments.

1819. Fargo, Charlyn. "Sweet on Illinois." *State Journal-Register*, 3 March 1994, Heartland sec., pp. 4A-7A. Histories of four Illinois candy-makers: three in Chicago--Frango Chocolates of Marshall Field & Company, Fannie May, and Tootsie Roll--and Leaf Industries, formerly the Heath Candy Company of Robinson.

1820. Ferris, William G. *The Grain Traders: The Story of the Chicago Board of Trade.* East Lansing: Michigan State University Press, 1988.

1821. Fine, Lisa M. *The Souls of the Skyscraper: Female Clerical Workers in Chicago, 1870-1930.* Women in the Political Economy series. Philadelphia: Temple University Press, 1990.

1822. Forrestal, Dan J. *The Kernel and the Bean: The 75-Year Story of the Staley Company.* New York: Simon & Schuster, 1982. This manufacturer of products from corn and soybeans is located in Decatur.

1823. Freedman, Stephen. "Organizing the Workers in a Steel Company Town: The Union Movement in Joliet, 1870-1920." *Illinois Historical Journal* 79 (1986): 2-18.

1824. Garner, John S. "Leclaire, Illinois: A Model Company Town, 1890-1934." *Journal of the Society of Architectural Historians* 30 (1971): 219-27. The town was established in Madison County by N. O. Nelson, founder of the N. O. Nelson Manufacturing Company, which made plumbing equipment and was a pioneer in profit-sharing and cooperative ownership for the employees. The town eventually became part of Edwardsville.

1825. Gazel, Neil R. *Beatrice: From Buildup through Breakup.* Urbana: University of Illinois Press, for the University of Illinois Bureau of Economic and Business Research, 1990. This history of the Beatrice Food Company exemplifies food industry and trade in the United States.

1826. Glenn, John M. "The Industrial Development of Illinois." *Transactions of the Illinois State Historical Society, 1921,* pp. 55-72. Contains brief sketches of industrial pioneers, many now little known, and lists the products of principal manufacturing towns.

1827. Grimstead, Wayde. *50 Years of Inland Steel, 1893-1943.* Chicago: Inland Steel, 1943.

1828. Haeger, John Denis. "The American Fur Company and the Chicago of 1812-1835." *Journal of the Illinois State Historical Society* 61 (1968): 117-39.

1829. Hallwas, John E., ed. *The Legacy of the Mines: Memoirs of Coal Mining in Fulton County, Illinois.* Canton: Spoon River College, 1993. Forty-two memoirs--about shaft mining, strip mining, mining towns, and mining families.

1830. Heinl, Frank J. *1839-1939: Centennial, J. Capps & Sons, Ltd.* Jacksonville, Ill.: Jacksonville Journal-Courier, 1939. History of the clothing-manufacturing firm.

1831. Helle, Sheldon Lyle. *Logging on the Mississippi River in the Twentieth Century.* Savanna, Ill.: The author, 1982?

1832. _____. *Ninety-Eight Years of Helle Sawmill History, 1882-1980: Forty Years of Sawmill History in Savanna, Illinois, 1940-1980.* Savanna, Ill.: The author, 1980?

1833. Herndon, Booton. *Satisfaction Guaranteed: An Unconventional Report to Today's Consumers.* New York: McGraw Hill, 1972. A history of Montgomery Ward, with emphasis on recent officers and development.

1834. Hicken, Victor. "Mine Union Radicalism in Macoupin and Montgomery Counties." *Western Illinois Regional Studies* 3 (1980): 173-91. A survey of coal miners and their unions from the late nineteenth century through the 1930s.

1835. Hill, Howard Copeland. "The Development of Chicago as a Center of the Meat Packing Industry." *Mississippi Valley Historical Review* 10 (1923-24): 253-73.

1836. Hoge, Cecil C. *The First Hundred Years Are the Hardest: What We Can Learn from the Century of Competition between Sears and Wards.* Berkeley, Calif.: Ten Speed Press, 1988.

1837. Huston, Francis M. *Financing an Empire: History of Banking in Illinois.* 4 vols. Chicago: S. J. Clark Publishing, 1926.

1838. *Illinois Business Review.* A monthly publication (bimonthly since December 1981) of the University of Illinois Bureau of Economic and Business Research, January 1944--to date.

1839. Jackson, Carlton. *The Dreadful Month.* Bowling Green, Ohio: Bowling Green State University Popular Press, 1982. December seems to be the "dreadful month" for coal mine accidents. The author discusses three Illinois disasters, two of which took place in December--Moweaqua, 24 December 1932, and West Frankfort, 31 December 1951--and the 25 March 1947 explosion at Centralia. The Moweaqua and West Frankfort disasters led to improved state and federal safety procedures.

1840. James, F. Cyril. *The Growth of Chicago Banks.* Vol. 1, *The Formative Years, 1816-1896.* Vol. 2, *The Modern Age, 1897-1938.* New York: Harper, 1938.

1841. Kalisch, Philip A. "Death Down Below: Coal Mine Disasters in Three Illinois Counties." *Journal of the Illinois State Historical Society* 65 (1972): 5-21. The history of twenty-four mine disasters, 1904-51, in Franklin, Saline, and Williamson counties in southern Illinois.

1842. Kantowicz, Edward R. *True Value: John Cotter--70 Years of Hardware.* Chicago: Regnery, 1986. History of the successful firm that was started in Illinois.

1843. Kogan, Herman. *Lending Is Our Business: The Story of Household Finance Corporation.* Chicago: Household Finance Corporation, 1965.

1844. Latham, Frank B. *1872-1972, A Century of Serving Consumers: The Story of Montgomery Ward.* Chicago, 1972.

1845. Lurie, Jonathan. *The Chicago Board of Trade, 1859-1905: The Dynamics of Self-Regulation.* Urbana: University of Illinois Press, 1979.

1846. _____. "The Chicago Board of Trade, the Merchants' Exchange of St. Louis, and the Great Bucket Shop War, 1882-1905." *Bulletin of the Missouri Historical Society* 29 (1972-73): 243-59.

1847. Lyons, Norbert. *The McCormick Reaper Legend: The True Story of a Great Invention.* Foreword by Robert Hall McCormick III. New York: Exposition Press, 1955. The case for Robert Hall McCormick, not his son Cyrus, as inventor of the reaper.

1848. McLear, Patrick E. "John Stephen Wright and Urban and Regional Promotion in the Nineteenth Century." *Journal of the Illinois State Historical Society* 68 (1975): 407-20. Wright's career as a businessman and land speculator in Chicago was far less successful than that as publisher of promotional materials about Chicago and the Midwest, especially the *Prairie Farmer*.

1849. Macmillan, Don, and Jones, Russell. *John Deere: Tractors and Equipment; Volume One, 1837-1959; Volume Two, 1960-1990.* St. Joseph, Mich.: American Society of Agricultural Engineers, 1988, 1991.

1850. Marckhoff, Fred R. "Currency and Banking in Illinois before 1865." *Journal of the Illinois State Historical Society* 52 (1959): 365-418.

1851. Meyerowitz, Joanne J. *Women Adrift: Independent Wage Earners in Chicago, 1880-1930.* Chicago: University of Chicago Press, 1988. The author discusses the kinds of jobs held by women, as well as their private lives and place in society.

1852. Miller, Keith L. "Petroleum and Profits in the Prairie State, 1889-1980: Straws in the Cider Barrel." *Illinois Historical Journal* 77 (1984): 162-76. The economic impact of three oil booms in the state.

1853. _____. "Plucking the Apple without Rooting up the Tree: Environmental Concern in the Production of Prairie State Petroleum." *Illinois Historical Journal* 84 (1991): 161-72.

1854. Murphy, Lucy Eldersveld. "Businesswomen and Separate Spheres in the Midwest, 1850-1880." *Illinois Historical Journal* 80 (1987): 155-76. Based on an Illinois directory of 1864-65 and the United States censuses of 1870 and 1880, and buttressed by newspaper accounts and little-known reminiscences, the author makes a substantial contribution to women's and business history.

1855. Myers, Jacob M. "History of the Gallatin County Salines." *Journal of the Illinois State Historical Society* 14 (1921-22): 337-50.

1856. Newcomen Society of the United States. *Index to Publications (1933-1984)* . . . Compiled by Gretchen R. Randle, Paula Field, and Nancy Arnold. Exton, Pa.: The society, 1986. This publication has three indexes: number, author, and subject. Total number of publications (in pamphlet form) is 1,234; "Supplement . . . 1985 to Present" (photoduplicated) brings the total number to 1,403. The society operates the Thomas Newcomen Library and Museum in Steam Technology and Industrial History at Exton. Its publications are histories of businesses presented by their owners or chief executive officers. Many are from Illinois.

1857. Noble, Sean. "The Wicks Organ Company." *State Journal-Register* (Springfield, Ill.), 7 September 1990. Heartland sec., pp. 10A-13A. Brief history of the Highland company.

1858. Nourse, Hugh O. *The Electronics Industry and Economic Growth in Illinois.* Springfield: Illinois Department of Business and Economic Development, 1967.

1859. O'Brien, Francis J. *The Fabulous Franklin Story: The History of the Franklin Life Insurance Company.* Chicago: Rand McNally, 1972.

1860. Orear, Leslie, and Diamond, Stephen H. *Out of the Jungle: The Packinghouse Workers Fight for Justice and Equality.* Chicago: Hyde Park Press, 1968. A pictorial history of the United Packinghouse, Food, and Allied Workers, AFL-CIO.

1861. Pacyga, Dominic A. *Polish Immigrants and Industrial Chicago: Workers on the South Side, 1880-1922.* Urban Life and Urban Landscape Series. Columbus: Ohio State University Press, 1991. Polish-American immigrants lived in the South Side neighborhoods of Packingtown and Steel City and worked primarily in meatpacking and steel production.

1862. Paul, John R., and Parmalee, Paul W. *Soft Drink Bottling: A History with Special Reference to Illinois.* Springfield: Illinois State Museum, 1973. This volume contains a descriptive list of Illinois bottling companies in the years 1860-1930, as well as information about their plants and products. There are also historical sketches of some Illinois companies, passim.

1863. Payne, Walter A., general ed. *Benjamin Holt: The Story of the Caterpillar Tractor.* Stockton, Calif.: University of the Pacific, 1982. Holt was the inventor of the Caterpillar tractor.

1864. Pegram, Thomas R. "The Illinois Manufacturers' Association: A Case Study of Interest Group Politics in the Progressive Era." *Transactions of the Illinois State Historical Society: Selected Papers from the Fifth and Sixth Illinois History Symposiums of the Illinois State Historical Society* [1984 and 1985]. Springfield, 1988. Pp. 83-96. The IMA was founded in 1893 to challenge the 1893 Sweatshop Act in court.

1865. Platt, Harold L. *The Electric City: The Growth of the Chicago Area, 1880-1930.* Chicago: University of Chicago Press, 1991. Traces the history of Chicago utilities, emphasizing Commonwealth Edison and its president, Samuel Insull, and shows how the development and regulation of power affected politics, suburban growth, industrial development, as well as personal life.

1866. Polos, N. C. "Marshall Field, the 'Merchant Prince,' and Robert E. Wood, the 'Soldier Merchant.' " *Journal of the West* 25 (January 1986): 28-38.

1867. *Quarterly Review of Economics and Business.* Published by the Bureau of Economic and Business Research, University of Illinois at Urbana-Champaign. Vols. 1-31 (February 1961--Winter 1991). Continued as *Quarterly Review of Economics and Finance: Journal of the Midwest Economics Association.* Vol. 32 (Spring 1992)--to date.

1868. Rodgers, Daniel T. *The Work Ethic in Industrial America, 1850-1920.* Chicago: University of Chicago Press, 1974. The author explains that this is "a study not of work but of ideas about work." As such, it provides a sound basis for the study of both labor and industry.

1869. *Sangamo: A History of Fifty Years.* Chicago: Privately printed, 1949. Contains "Forty Years of Sangamo," by R. C. Lanphier and "Sangamo in Peace and War," by B. P. Thomas. Histories of the Sangamo Electric Company of Springfield. A supplement, titled *Part Three: Sangamo, 1949-1959*, by John H.

Schacht, was published by Sangamo in 1960? The company manufactured electric meters, and during World War II produced many special military devices.

1870. Schafer, Joseph. *The Wisconsin Lead Region.* Publications of the State Historical Society of Wisconsin. Wisconsin Domesday Book, General Studies, vol. 3. Madison, 1932. Galena and Jo Daviess County, Illinois, were part of the lead region.

1871. Schneirov, Richard, and Suhrbur, Thomas J. *Union Brotherhood, Union Town: The History of the Carpenters' Union of Chicago, 1863-1987.* Carbondale: Southern Illinois University Press, 1988.

1872. Scott, George Tressler. "Seven Brothers in Dry Goods in Illinois." *Journal of the Illinois State Historical Society* 49 (1956): 227-32. An account of the merchandising ventures in northern Illinois of the Scott brothers, several of whom were later associated with Carson, Pirie, Scott & Company.

1873. Scott, Harold W. *The Sugar Creek Saga: Chronicles of a Petroleum Geologist.* Urbana: University of Illinois Foundation and the Department of Geology, University of Illinois, 1986. Scott illustrates the changes in oil consumption by the example of the Sugar Creek community in Iroquois County.

1874. Severson, Robert F. Jr.; Niss, James F.; and Winkelman, Richard D. "Mortgage Borrowing As a Frontier Developed: A Study of Mortgages in Champaign County, Illinois, 1836-1895." *Journal of Economic History* 26 (1966): 147-68. The loans were rural, urban, and industrial in nature, and the lenders were private persons as well as government agencies and financial institutions.

1875. Sharer, Amy A. "Life on Zinc Street: Functional Corporate Benevolence at Matthiessen and Hegeler Zinc, 1881-1903." *Transactions of the Illinois State Historical Society: Selected Papers from the Seventh Annual History Symposium and the Eighth Annual History Symposium* [1986 and 1987]. Springfield, 1989. Pp. 59-68. History of a zinc-producing and coal-mining company that offered laborers unusual company benefits.

1876. Smalley, Orange A., and Sturdivant, Frederick D. *The Credit Merchants: A History of Spiegel, Inc.* Carbondale: Southern Illinois University Press, 1973. The company was founded in 1865; this centennial history is based on original business records.

1877. Smith, George Washington. "The Salines of Southern Illinois." *Transactions of the Illinois State Historical Society, 1904*, pp. 245-58. Salt-making in Gallatin County. The salt springs in the county were worked from prehistoric times to the late nineteenth century.

1878. Solomon, Ezra, and Bilbija, Zarko G. *Metropolitan Chicago: An Economic Analysis.* Glencoe, Ill.: Free Press, 1960.

1879. Staley, Eugene. *History of the Illinois State Federation of Labor.* Social Science Studies, no. 15 [i.e. 16]. Chicago: University of Chicago Press, 1930.

1880. Starke, Aubrey. "The Indigenous Iron Industry of Illinois." *Journal of the Illinois State Historical Society* 27 (1934-35): 432-40. Iron ore was extracted and smelted in Hardin County from about 1837 to 1883.

1881. Stevens, Wayne Edson. *The Northwest Fur Trade.* University of Illinois Studies in the Social Sciences, vol. 14, no. 3. Urbana, 1928.

1882. Stroud, Gene S., and Donahue, Gilbert E., comps. *Labor History in the United States: A General Bibliography.* Institute of Labor and Industrial Relations, University of Illinois, Bibliographic Contributions, no. 6. Urbana, 1961. A good index sets out entries related to Illinois and, in particular, to Chicago.

1883. Taylor, Charles H., ed. *History of the Board of Trade of the City of Chicago.* 3 vols. Chicago: Robert O. Law, 1917. Volume 3 contains biographies of sixty-three members of the Board of Trade.

1884. Thomas, R. G. "Bank Failures in Chicago before 1925." *Journal of the Illinois State Historical Society* 28, no. 3 (October 1935): 188-203.

1885. Thompson, Fred, comp. *The I.W.W.: Its First Fifty Years (1905-1955).* Chicago: Industrial Workers of the World, 1955. New information is provided only for the years 1930-55.

1886. Tuttle, William M. Jr. "Labor Conflict and Racial Violence: The Black Worker in Chicago, 1894-1919." *Labor History* 10 (1969): 408-32.

1887. Twyman, Robert W. *History of Marshall Field & Co., 1852-1906.* Philadelphia: University of Pennsylvania Press, 1954.

1888. Wade, Louise Carroll. *Chicago's Pride: The Stockyards, Packingtown, and Environs in the Nineteenth Century.* Urbana: University of Illinois Press, 1987. In addition to presenting business and labor history from the early 1830s to 1893, the author analyzes the political and social history of Lake Township, in which the stockyards and packinghouses were located.

1889. Walsh, Margaret. *The Rise of the Midwestern Meat Packing Industry.* Lexington: University of Kentucky Press, 1982. Covers the years 1840-90.

1890. Weems, Robert E. Jr. "The Chicago Metropolitan Mutual Assurance Company: A Profile of a Black-Owned Enterprise." *Illinois Historical Journal* 86 (1993): 15-26. One of Chicago's oldest continuing black firms, the insurance company was founded in 1925.

1891. Weil, Gordon L. *Sears, Roebuck, U.S.A.: The Great American Catalog Store and How It Grew.* New York: Stein & Day, 1977.

1892. Wendell, C. H. *150 Years of International Harvester.* Crestline Series. Osceola, Wis.: Motorbooks International, 1993. The history begins with the 1831 reaper developed by Cyrus Hall McCormick; the volume includes illustrations and descriptions of farm implements produced since that time--by other companies as well as those that eventually became part of the McCormick empire.

1893. _____. *150 Years of J. I. Case.* Edited and designed by George H. Dammann. Sarasota, Fla.: Crestline Publishing, 1991. J. I. Case merged with International Harvester in 1985; the company's new name is Case-IH. The book contains histories of many Illinois farm-implement manufacturers that Case absorbed. Lavishly illustrated.

1894. Wendt, Lloyd, and Kogan, Herman. *Give the Lady What She Wants: The Story of Marshall Field & Company.* Chicago: Rand McNally, 1952. As much women's and social history as that of a business. Covers the first hundred years of the store, 1852-1952.

1895. White, Allison Carll. "Monuments to Their Skill: Urbana-Champaign Carpenters, Contractors, and Builders, 1850-1900." *Illinois Historical Journal* 85 (1992): 37-46. Still standing are several houses that illustrate the work of the skilled craftsmen in the twin cities.

1896. Willett, Howard L. *Willett and the March of Time: The History of a Company and a Family.* Privately printed, 1959. Three generations of Willetts in the Chicago transportation business, from horse-drawn vehicles to modern trucks.

1897. Zunz, Oliver. *Making America Corporate, 1870-1920.* Chicago: University of Chicago Press, 1990. The social impact of changes and growth in business as revealed through the study of several businesses, including McCormick Harvester and the Chicago, Burlington & Quincy Railroad.

3. Transportation

a. Railroads

The citations that follow are, for the most part, general histories of railroad lines in Illinois that operated for more than a decade or two. In the nineteenth century scores of new lines were proposed, and some even opened for business. Research libraries and railroad buffs therefore have extensive collections of railroad ephemera--schedules, prospectuses, charters, incorporation papers, court cases, bylaws, reports to stockholders, rosters of employees, etc.--not included in this volume.

1898. Ackerman, William K. *Early Illinois Railroads: A Paper Read before the Chicago Historical Society, Tuesday Evening, February 20, 1883 . . . Notes by Hon. John Wentworth. Also, an Appendix with the Breese-Douglas Correspondence on the Inception and Origin of the Illinois-Central Railroad and the Origin of Names of Stations on the Illinois-Central Railroad.* Fergus' Historical Series, no. 23. Chicago, 1884.

1899. _____. *Historical Sketch of the Illinois-Central Railroad, together with a Brief Biographical Record of Its Incorporators and Some of Its Early Officers.* Chicago: Fergus Printing, 1890. Ackerman was president of the railroad, but his history is not always accurate.

1900. Agnew, Dwight L. "Beginning of the Rock Island Lines." *Journal of the Illinois State Historical Society* 46 (1953): 407-24.

1901. Bach, Ira J., and Wolfson, Susan. *A Guide to Chicago's Train Stations, Present and Past.* Athens: Ohio University Press, 1986.

1902. Boylan, Josephine. "The Illinois Railroad and Its Successors." *Journal of the Illinois State Historical Society* 30 (1937-38): 180-92. A private railroad built in 1837 from the Mississippi (in present East St. Louis) southeast to coal mines on the bluffs. After several changes of ownership, the line was absorbed by the Southern Railway system in 1900.

1903. *A Brief History of the Chicago and North Western Line.* Chicago: Chicago and North Western Railway Co., 1942.

1904. Brownson, Howard Gray. *History of the Illinois Central Railroad to 1870.* University of Illinois Studies in the Social Sciences, vol. 4, nos. 3 and 4. Urbana, 1915.

1905. Burford, Cary Clive. "The Twilight of the Local Passenger Train in Illinois." *Journal of the Illinois State Historical Society* 51 (1958): 161-80.

1906. Calkins, Earnest Elmo. "Genesis of a Railroad." *Transactions of the Illinois State Historical Society, 1935,* pp. 39-72. History of the Peoria and Oquawka Railroad, chartered by the General Assembly in 1849; that line and the Northern Cross line eventually merged and became the Chicago, Burlington, & Quincy, along with other lesser-known lines absorbed by mid-century.

1907. Campbell, George V. *Days of the North Shore Line.* Delavan, Wis.: National Bus Trader, 1985.

1908. Casey, Robert J., and Douglas, W. A. S. *Pioneer Railroad: The Story of the Chicago and North Western System.* New York: Whittlesey House, 1948.

1909. *The Chicago, Rock Island & Pacific Railway and Representative Employees . . .* Chicago: Biographical Publishing, 1900. Primarily biographical.

1910. Corbin, Bernard, and Kerka, William. *Steam Locomotives of the Burlington Route.* Red Oak?, Iowa, 1960.

1911. Corliss, Carlton J. *Main Line of Mid-America: The Story of the Illinois Central.* New York: Creative Age Press, 1950.

1912. _____. *Trails to Rails: A Story of Transportation Progress in Illinois.* Chicago: Illinois Central System, 1934.

1913. "Country Correspondence." *Journal of the Illinois State Historical Society* 42 (1949): 468-70. A letter published in the *Alton Weekly Courier* in 1853 from a Decatur correspondent describes construction and labor troubles on the Illinois Central Railroad.

1914. Davis, James Leslie. *The Elevated System and the Growth of Northern Chicago*. Northwestern University Studies in Geography, no. 10. Evanston, Ill.: Northwestern University, 1965.

1915. Douglas, George H. *Rail City: Chicago, USA*. San Diego: Howell-North Books, 1981.

1916. Edson, William D. "The Illinois Terminal: Corporate Structure and Steam Power." *Railroad History* 145 (Autumn 1981): 106-9.

1917. French, Chauncey Del. *Railroadman*. New York: Macmillan, 1938. Biography of Henry Clay French of Illinois, a railroad employee who rose from messenger to switchman-yardmaster.

1918. Gates, Paul Wallace. *The Illinois Central Railroad and Its Colonization Work*. Harvard Economic Studies, vol. 42. Cambridge, Mass.: Harvard University Press, 1934. Reprint, New York: Johnson Reprint, 1968. Covers the early settlement of Illinois as well as the Illinois Central's promotion of settlement to 1900, by which time the railroad had made between 40,000 and 45,000 individual land sales in disposing of its approximate two and one-half million-acre land grants.

1919. Gordon, Joseph Hinckley. *Illinois Railway Legislation and Commission Control since 1870*. University Studies, vol. 1, no. 6 (March 1904). Urbana: University Press.

1920. Grant, H. Roger. "The Combination Railroad Station in the Old Northwest." *Old Northwest* 4 (June 1978): 95-118.

1921. _____. *The Corn Belt Route: A History of the Chicago Great Western Railroad Company*. DeKalb: Northern Illinois University Press, 1984.

1922. _____. "The Illinois Small-Town Depot." *Selected Papers in Illinois History, 1980*. Springfield: Illinois State Historical Society, 1982. Pp. 53-62.

1923. Gustafson, Carl P. *The Dairy Route: A History of the Elgin & Belvidere Electric Company*. Crystal Lake, Ill.: Gustafson Publications, 1967.

1924. Hayes, William Edward. *Iron Road to Empire: The History of 100 Years of the Progress and Achievements of the Rock Island Lines*. New York: Simmons-Boardman, 1953. Hayes was an assistant to the president of the Rock

Island lines, and this volume is therefore written from the management viewpoint.

1925. Hilton, George W., and Due, John Fitzgerald. *The Electric Interurban Railways of America.* Stanford, Calif.: Stanford University Press, 1960. Illinois lines constitute an important part of this history.

1926. Holbrook, Stewart H. *The Story of American Railroads.* New York: Crown, 1947.

1927. *Interurban to Milwaukee.* Central Electric Railfans' Association Bulletin 106. Chicago, 1962. History of the Chicago, North Shore and Milwaukee Railroad to 1926.

1928. Johnson, James David, comp. *Aurora 'n' Elgin: Being a Compendium of Word and Picture Recalling the Everyday Operations of the Chicago, Aurora and Elgin Railroad.* Wheaton, Ill.: Traction Orange, 1965.

1929. _____, comp.; photographs by Thomas Hollister and paintings by Robert T. Pernau. *A Century of Chicago's Streetcars, 1858-1958: A Pictorial History of the World's Largest Street Railway.* Wheaton, Ill.: Traction Orange, 1964.

1930. _____, comp. *The Lincoln Land Traction.* Wheaton, Ill.: Traction Orange, 1965. Story of the Illinois Traction Co. System, the electric railway of central Illinois that was in operation until 1956.

1931. Keister, Philip L. *Cars of the Rockford and Interurban Railway.* Bulletin/Electric Railway Historical Society, no. 21. Chicago, 1956?

1932. _____. *The Lee County Central Electric Railway.* Bulletin/Electric Railway Historical Society, no. 48. Chicago, 1967.

1933. _____. *The Rockford and Interurban Railway.* Bulletin/Electric Railway Historical Society, no. 22. Chicago, 1956.

1934. Kester, Elmer E. "Illinois Terminal--1949." *Trolley Sparks.* Central Electric Railfans' Association Bulletin 82 (January 1949): 3-13. This account of the Illinois Terminal begins with its incorporation in 1895.

1935. Knudsen, Charles T. *Chicago and North Western Railway Steam Power, 1848-1956, Classes A-Z.* Chicago: Knudsen Publications, 1965.

1936. Lemly, James Hutton. *The Gulf, Mobile and Ohio.* Homewood, Ill.: Richard D. Irwin, 1953.

1937. Licht, Walter. *Working for the Railroad: The Organization of Work in the Nineteenth Century.* Princeton, N.J.: Princeton University Press, 1983. Covers the years 1830-77.

1938. Lind, Alan R. *Chicago Surface Lines: An Illustrated History.* Park Forest, Ill.: Transport History Press, 1974. 3d ed., 1979. Electric streetcars and trains, 1858 to today. According to the author, many of the streetcars were reincarnated as CTA rapid transit cars.

1939. _____. *Limiteds along the Lakefront: The Illinois Central in Chicago.* Park Forest, Ill.: Transport History Press, 1986. The Illinois Central electrified its suburban trains in 1926. This history deals with all of the company's trains from 1852 on and its Chicago offices and stations as well.

1940. Maiken, Peter T. *Night Trains: The Pullman System in the Golden Years of American Rail Travel.* Chicago: Lakme Press, 1989.

1941. Marre, Louis A. *Rock Island Diesel Locomotives, 1930-1980.* Cincinnati: Railfax Inc., 1982.

1942. Matejka, Michael G., and Koos, Greg. *Bloomington's C & A Shops: Our Lives Remembered.* Urbana: University of Illinois Press, 1988. Oral history interviews with twenty-four former employees of the Chicago and Alton Railroad shops at Bloomington, with an historical sketch by Mark Wyman of Illinois State University.

1943. Middleton, William D. *North Shore: America's Fastest Interurban.* San Marino, Calif.: Golden West Books, 1964.

1944. _____. *South Shore, the Last Interurban.* San Marino, Calif.: Golden West Books, 1970.

1945. Morgan, David Page. *Fast Mail, the First 75 Years: A History of the Burlington Railroad's Mail Service between Chicago and Council Bluffs-Omaha, 1884-1959.* Chicago: Chicago, Burlington & Quincy Railroad Company, 1959.

1946. Mureen, E. W. *A History of the Fulton County Narrow Gauge Railway, the Spoon River "Peavine."* Railway & Locomotive Historical Society Bulletin, no. 61A. Boston: Baker Library, Harvard Business School, 1943.

1947. Olmsted, Robert P., and McMillan, Joe. *The 5:10 to Suburbia: Chicago's Suburban Railroads, 1960-1975.* Janesville, Wis.: Sultze Print, 1975. On some suburban routes the trains used were the same diesels used on the regular lines, whereas other lines were still mainly electric.

1948. Olmsted, Robert P. *Interurbans to the Loop; North Shore Line, South Shore Line.* Janesville, Wis., 1969.

1949. _____. *Rock Island Recollections.* Woodridge, Ill.: McMillan Publications, 1982. Accounts of famous locomotives and trains. Lavishly illustrated, like all of Olmsted's books.

1950. _____. *Six Units to Sycamore: Chicago Great Western in Illinois.* Woodridge, Ill.: McMillan, 1967. Reprint, 1982.

1951. _____. *Trail of the Zephyrs: The Burlington Route in Northern Illinois.* [n.p., 1970]

1952. Overton, Richard C. *Burlington Route: A History of the Burlington Lines.* New York: Knopf, 1965.

1953. _____. *Burlington West: A Colonization History of the Burlington Railroad.* Cambridge, Mass.: Harvard University Press, 1942. Most of the book concerns disposal of federal land grants. Because the Burlington was started in Illinois, this volume covers the railroad's early history and contains much incidental information about other lines in the state.

1954. Pearson, Henry Greenleaf. *An American Railroad Builder, John Murray Forbes.* Boston: Houghton Mifflin, 1911. President of Michigan Central Railroad (1846-55) and Chicago, Burlington, & Quincy Railroad (1857-98).

1955. Prescott, D. C. *Early Day Railroading from Chicago: A Narration with Some Observations.* Chicago: David B. Clarkson, 1910. An anecdotal history that concentrates especially on the Chicago and North Western Railway.

1956. Raia, William A. *Spirit of the South Shore.* River Forest, Ill.: Heimburger House Publishing, 1984. A history in photographs, with informative legends.

1957. Robertson, William E. *The Woodstock and Sycamore Traction Company.* Delavan, Wis.: National Bus Trader, 1985.

1958. Schrader, Fred L. "History [of] Chicago, Peoria & St. Louis Railroad Company." Mimeographed, 1952, in Illinois State Historical Library.

1959. Stover, John F. *History of the Baltimore and Ohio Railroad.* West Lafayette, Ind.: Purdue University Press, 1987.

1960. _____. *History of the Illinois Central Railroad.* Railroads of America. New York: Macmillan, 1975.

1961. Stringham, Paul H. *Illinois Terminal: The Electric Years.* Glendale, Calif.: Interurban Press, 1989. Illinois Terminal was part of the Illinois Traction System, made up of many companies financed by the same syndicate.

1962. _____. *76 Years of Peoria Street Cars.* Electric Railway Historical Society, Bulletin 46. Chicago, 1965.

1963. Stromquist, Shelton. *A Generation of Boomers: The Pattern of Railroad Labor Conflict in Nineteenth-Century America.* The Working Class in American History. Urbana: University of Illinois Press, 1987.

1964. "Travel Handicaps and Hospitality." *Journal of the Illinois State Historical Society* 46 (1953): 196. An account of the difficulties involved in transferring from the Burlington to the Rock Island Railroad in 1863.

1965. Wallin, Richard R.; Stringham, Paul H.; and Szwajkart, John. *Chicago & Illinois Midland.* San Marino, Calif.: Golden West Books, 1979.

1966. White, John H. Jr. "Chicago Locomotive Builders." *Railway Bulletin,* no. 22 (April 1970): 52-60.

1967. _____. *The Pioneer, Chicago's First Locomotive.* Chicago: Chicago Historical Society, 1976.

1968. Whitney, Richard. *Old Maud: The Story of the Palatine, Lake Zurich & Wauconda Railroad.* Polo, Ill.: Transportation Trails, 1992.

1969. Yates, JoAnne. *Control through Communication: The Rise of System in American Management.* Baltimore: Johns Hopkins University Press, 1989. The author illustrates her study of internal communication in corporations with three firms as case studies; one is the Illinois Central.

1970. Yungmeyer, D. W. "An Excursion into the Early History of the Chicago and Alton Railroad." *Journal of the Illinois State Historical Society* 38 (1945): 7-37.

b. Trails, Highways, and Bridges

1971. Agnew, Dwight L. "Jefferson Davis and the Rock Island Bridge." *Iowa Journal of History* 47 (1949): 3-14. As secretary of war, Davis attempted to thwart the progress of the bridge-builders, in favor of a southern route to the Pacific; but he was overruled in federal court and the railroad bridge opened in 1856--the first bridge across the Mississippi. The Railroad Bridge Company had been granted a charter by the state of Illinois.

1972. Baber, Adin. "Early Trails of Eastern Illinois." *Journal of the Illinois State Historical Society* 25 (1932-33): 49-62.

1973. Birk, Russell Charles. "Shortest Route to the Galena Lead Mines: The Lewistown Road." *Journal of the Illinois State Historical Society* 66 (1973): 187-97.

1974. Boylan, Josephine. "Illinois Highways, 1700-1848: Roads, Rivers, Ferries, Canals." *Journal of the Illinois State Historical Society* 26 (1933-34): 5-59. No annotations, but information is based primarily on county records and state session laws. Includes a list of public roads laid out between 1818 and 1848.

1975. Burchard, Edward L. "Early Trails and Tides of Travel in the Lead Mine and Black Hawk Country." *Journal of the Illinois State Historical Society* 17 (1924-25): 565-603.

1976. "Century-Old Covered Bridge." *Journal of the Illinois State Historical Society* 47 (1954): 107-8. A brief history of the bridge spanning Little Mary's Creek near Bremen.

1977. Cunningham, J. O. "The Danville and Fort Clark Road." *Journal of the Illinois State Historical Society* 4 (1911-12): 212-17. Portions of the road followed Kickapoo trails.

1978. Dorsey, Florence. *The Story of James B. Eads: Road to the Sea and the Mississippi River.* New York: Rinehart, 1947. Account of the construction of the bridge across the Mississippi at East St. Louis.

1979. Eaton, Thelma. *The Covered Bridges of Illinois.* Ann Arbor, Mich.: Edwards Brothers, 1968. Valuable source book, with descriptions and histories of all the state's known covered bridges, some of which are on the National Register of Historic Places.

1980. Enos, Zimri. "The Old Indian Trail, Sangamon County, Illinois." *Journal of the Illinois State Historical Society* 4 (1911-12): 218-26. The trail passed through a Kickapoo village.

1981. Hauberg, John H. "Indian Trails Centering at Black Hawk's Village." *Transactions of the Illinois State Historical Society, 1921*, pp. 87-109. Many different Sauk and Fox trails in northwestern Illinois are located.

1982. Hulbert, Archer Butler. *The Old National Road.* Columbus, Ohio: F. J. Heer, 1901. Now U.S. 40, the Old National Road was completed in Illinois from the Indiana line to Vandalia.

1983. "Illinois' Covered Bridges." *Journal of the Illinois State Historical Society* 43 (1950): 149-50.

1984. Jordan, Philip D. *The National Road.* Indianapolis: Bobbs-Merrill, 1948.

1985. Quaife, Milo Milton. *Chicago's Highways, Old and New, from Indian Trail to Motor Road.* Chicago: D. F. Keller, 1923. Facsimile reprint, Ann Arbor, Mich.: University Microfilms, 1968. A delightful scholarly story of transportation in northern Illinois.

1986. Rennick, Percival Graham. "The Peoria and Galena Trail and Coach Road and the Peoria Neighborhood." *Journal of the Illinois State Historical Society* 27 (1934-35): 351-431.

1987. Schneider, Norris F. *The National Road: Main Street of America.* Columbus: Ohio Historical Society, 1975. This famous road reached Vandalia, Illinois, in 1839; it eventually became part of U.S. 40.

1988. Scott, Quinta, and Kelly, Susan Croce. *Route 66: The Highway and Its People.* Norman: University of Oklahoma Press, 1988.

1989. Sculle, Keith A. "Jacob Allaman, Covered-Bridge Builder." *Journal of the Illinois State Historical Society* 76 (1983): 139-49. Account of the life of Allaman and the bridges he built in Henderson County.

1990. _____. "Lessons from the Landscape: The Stone Arch Bridges of Monroe County, Illinois." *Illinois Historical Journal* 83 (1990): 113-26.

1991. Shaw, Fayette B. "Transportation in the Development of Joliet and Will County." *Journal of the Illinois State Historical Society* 30 (1937-38): 85-134. A study far broader than its title implies, affecting other parts of the state and including discussions of Indian trails, highways, the Illinois and Michigan Canal, railroads, and numerous other businesses.

1992. Spooner, H. L. "The Other End of the Great Sauk Trail." *Journal of the Illinois State Historical Society* 29 (1936-37): 121-34. The trail led from the Mississippi to Fort Malden at Amherstburg, Ontario.

1993. Steward, John F. "The Sac and Fox Trail." *Journal of the Illinois State Historical Society* 4 (1911-12): 157-64.

1994. Swanson, Leslie C. *Covered Bridges in Illinois, Iowa and Wisconsin.* Moline, Ill.: Swanson Publishing, 1960.

1995. "Vermilion County Covered Bridge Burned." *Journal of the Illinois State Historical Society* 49 (1956): 248-49. This short article lists the eleven bridges surviving in Illinois in 1956.

1996. Wallis, Michael. *Route 66: The Mother Road.* New York: St. Martin's Press, 1990.

1997. Wingert, Edward E. "Rock River and Its Crossings." *Journal of the Illinois State Historical Society* 20 (1927-28): 282-302. Both highway and railroad crossings are discussed.

c. Water Transportation

1998. Ashton, Bessie L. *The Geonomic Aspects of the Illinois Waterway.* University of Illinois Studies in the Social Sciences, vol. 14, no. 2. Urbana: 1927.

1999. Baldwin, Leland D. *The Keelboat Age on Western Waters.* Pittsburgh: University of Pittsburgh Press, 1941.

2000. Barr, Vernon F. "The Illinois Waterway." *Western Illinois Regional Studies* 7, no. 2 (Fall 1984): 77-86.

2001. Blust, Frank A. "The U.S. Lake Survey, 1841-1974." *Inland Seas* 32 (1976): 91-104. The federal agency known as the Lake Survey made navigation charts for the Great Lakes.

2002. Braun, Mark S. *Chicago's North Shore Shipwrecks.* Polo, Ill.: Transportation Trails, 1992.

2003. Burton, William L. "The Life and Death of Bloody Island: A Ferry Tale." *Western Illinois Regional Studies* 11, no. 1 (Spring 1988): 5-22. Engineering works in the Mississippi at St. Louis and operations of ferries there, 1795-1850.

2004. Cuthbertson, George A. *Freshwater.* Toronto: Macmillan Co. of Canada, 1931. Great Lakes ships and shipping.

2005. Dowling, Edward J. "Red Stacks in the Sunset." *Journal of the Illinois State Historical Society* 40 (1947): 176-99. History of the Goodrich steamship line, 1852-1933.

2006. Draine, Edwin H., and Meyer, Donald G. *Port of Chicago: Unification Study.* Chicago, 1970.

2007. Feltner, Charles E., and Feltner, Jeri Baron. *Great Lakes Maritime History: Bibliography and Sources of Information.* Dearborn, Mich.: Seajoy Publications, 1982.

2008. Flower, Elliott. "Chicago's Great River-Harbor." *Century* 63 (1901-2): 483-92.

2009. Gould, E. W. *Fifty Years on the Mississippi, or Gould's History of River Navigation* . . . St. Louis: Nixon-Jones Printing, 1889. Gould also describes steamboats and traffic on the Illinois River, pages 521-25.

2010. Graff, Maurice O. "The Lake Michigan Water Diversion Controversy: A Summary Statement." *Journal of the Illinois State Historical Society* 34 (1941): 453-71. Water was first diverted from Lake Michigan to dilute Chicago sewage emptying into the Chicago Drainage Canal and later diverted to insure adequate flowage for a deep Lakes-to-the-Gulf waterway, now known as the Illinois Waterway.

2011. Griffin, Donald W. "The Hennepin Canal as Community." *Western Illinois Regional Studies* 10, no. 1 (Spring 1987): 42-51.

2012. _____. "Recollections of the Hennepin Canal." *Western Illinois Regional Studies* 4 (1981): 50-76. Officially the Illinois and Mississippi Canal, this waterway, opened in 1907, linked the Illinois and Mississippi rivers. Commercial operations ceased in 1951.

2013. Havighurst, Walter. *The Long Ships Passing.* New York: Macmillan, 1926. An account of Great Lakes shipping.

2014. Hoagland, H. E. *Wage Bargaining on the Vessels of the Great Lakes.* University of Illinois Studies in the Social Sciences, vol. 6, no. 3. Urbana, 1917.

2015. Lamb, John Michael. "Canal Boats on the Illinois and Michigan Canal." *Journal of the Illinois State Historical Society* 71 (1978): 211-24. History of commercial traffic on the canal from 1848 to 1912.

2016. _____. "I. & M. Canal Locks." Photoduplicated. Lockport: Illinois Canal Society, 1981. History of the locks to 1981.

2017. Larson, Gustav E. "More Notes on Rock River Navigation." *Journal of the Illinois State Historical Society* 34 (1941): 245-49.

2018. _____. "Notes on Rock River Navigation." *Journal of the Illinois State Historical Society* 33 (1940): 341-58. The author's story ends in the late 1860s when railroads supplanted the river as a means of transportation.

2019. Lee, Henry W. "The Calumet Portage." *Transactions of the Illinois State Historical Society, 1912,* pp. 24-48. The author examined the writings of French missionaries and other early travelers to locate the portage and other geographical features, as well as Native American villages.

2020. *Mississippi and Ohio Rivers: Southern and Western Inland Steam Vessels on the Ohio.* Edited by Elizabeth Stanton Anderson; drawings by Samuel Ward Stanton. Upper Montclair, N.J.: H. Kneeland Whiting, 1975. This small book includes reproductions of thirty-nine pen and ink sketches of turn-of-the-century steamboats, with short histories of the vessels.

2021. Newton, Gerald A.; McFarland, John A.; and Griffin, Donald W. "The Hennepin Canal: New Life for an Old Waterway." *Western Illinois Regional Studies* 7, no. 2 (Fall 1984): 34-46.

2022. Petersen, William J. "Floating Namesakes of the Sucker State: Some Upper Mississippi Steamboats." *Transactions of the Illinois State Historical*

Society, 1939, pp. 6-26. Includes descriptions of steamboats named for several Illinois towns as well as for the state itself.

2023. _____. *Steamboating on the Upper Mississippi.* Iowa City: State Historical Society of Iowa, 1937. Reprint, 1968.

2024. Russell, Joseph A., et al. *The St. Lawrence Seaway: Its Impact, by 1965, upon Industry of Metropolitan Chicago and Illinois Waterway-Associated Areas.* 2 vols. Chicago: Association of Commerce and Industry, 1959-60.

2025. Swanson, Leslie C. *Canals of Mid-America.* Moline, Ill.: The author, 1964.

2026. Swift, James V. "Only Lock on the Wabash River." *Journal of the Illinois State Historical Society* 46 (1953): 194-95. A dam and lock were at the Grand Rapids at Mount Carmel.

2027. Toole, Robert C. "Competition and Consolidation: The Galena Packet Co., 1847-63." *Journal of the Illinois State Historical Society* 57 (1964): 229-48.

2028. Tweet, Roald D. *A History of the Rock Island District, Corps of Engineers.* Rock Island, Ill.: U. S. Army Engineer District, Rock Island, 1975. Engineering projects on the Mississippi are the focus of this work; one chapter concerns the Illinois and Mississippi Canal (also called the Hennepin Canal).

2029. _____. "Taming the Rapids of the Upper Mississippi." *Western Illinois Regional Studies* 7, no. 2 (Fall 1984): 47-76. Geology of, and engineering improvements at, the Des Moines River rapids and the Rock Island rapids of the Mississippi.

2030. Wallace, Agnes. "The Wiggins Ferry Monopoly." *Missouri Historical Review* 42 (1947-48): 1-19. The ferry operated between East St. Louis and St. Louis, 1797-1902.

2031. Waller, Robert A. "The Illinois Waterway from Conception to Completion, 1908-1933." *Journal of the Illinois State Historical Society* 65 (1972): 125-41.

2032. *Waterways Journal.* Vol. 1 (April 1887)--to date. Issued weekly. Devoted to the marine profession, yachting, and commercial interests of all inland waterways.

2033. Way, Frederick Jr. *Way's Packet Directory, 1848-1983: Passenger Steamboats of the Mississippi River System Since the Advent of Photography in Mid-Continent America.* Athens: Ohio University Press, 1983. Descriptions of almost six thousand steamboats, with information about owners and places of operation. Photographic section features thirty-two plates.

2034. Willoughby, William R. *The St. Lawrence Waterway: A Study in Politics and Diplomacy.* Madison: University of Wisconsin Press, 1961.

d. In General

2035. Baier, Royce, and Walters, William D. Jr. *Brick Streets in Illinois: A Brief History and Guide to Their Preservation and Maintenance.* Illinois Preservation Series, no. 12. Springfield: Illinois Historic Preservation Agency, Division of Preservation Services, 1991.

2036. Barrett, Paul. "Public Policy and Private Choice: Mass Transit and the Automobile in Chicago between the Wars." *Business History Review* 49 (1975): 473-97.

2037. Elliott, Eugene C. "The First Airship." *Journal of the Illinois State Historical Society* 24 (1931-32): 105-9. The first attempt to fly a heavier-than-air plane was made by Hugh Newell in Vermilion County in 1841. The plane was too heavy to fly.

2038. Hallion, Richard. "A Source Guide to the History of Aeronautics and Astronautics." *American Studies International* 20 (Spring 1982): 3-50.

2039. Lee, Judson Fiske. "Transportation: A Factor in the Development of Northern Illinois Previous to 1860." *Journal of the Illinois State Historical Society* 10 (1917-18): 17-85. Study of how lake transportation affected the development of Chicago, as well as a history of plank roads, railroads, and river travel.

2040. Scamehorn, Howard Lee. *Balloons to Jets: A Century of Aeronautics in Illinois, 1855-1955.* Occasional Publications of the Illinois State Historical Society, no. 52. Chicago: Regnery, 1957.

2041. _____. "Thomas Scott Baldwin, the Columbus of the Air." *Journal of the Illinois State Historical Society* 49 (1956): 163-89. Baldwin was a prominent balloonist and parachutist from Quincy. He also developed an early dirigible and a biplane.

2042.   Steiger, William A.   "Lindbergh Flies Air Mail from Springfield." *Journal of the Illinois State Historical Society* 47 (1954): 133-48.   The flights between Chicago and St. Louis were inaugurated in 1926.

C. EDUCATION

1. General Works

2043.   Babcock, Kendric C.   "The Expansion of Higher Education in Illinois." *Transactions of the Illinois State Historical Society, 1925*, pp. 41-53.

2044.   Brown, Donald R.   "Jonathan Baldwin Turner and the Land-Grant Idea." *Journal of the Illinois State Historical Society* 55 (1962): 370-84.   Turner was the originator and promoter of the proposal to use land grants for developing at least one college in each state for agricultural and industrial training. Turner's campaign culminated in the Morrill Act of 1862.

2045.   Cook, John Williston.   *Educational History of Illinois: Growth and Progress in Educational Affairs of the State from the Earliest Day to the Present, with Portraits and Biographies.*   Chicago: Henry O. Shepard, 1912.

2046.   Diner, Steven J.   *A City and Its Universities: Public Policy in Chicago, 1892-1919.*   Chapel Hill: University of North Carolina Press, 1980.   The influence of the University of Chicago and Northwestern University on reform movements in the city of Chicago.

2047.   Henthorne, Mary Evangela, Sister.   "Foundations of Catholic Secondary Education in Illinois." *Mid-America* 6 n.s. (1935): 145-71.

2048.   Illinois Board of Higher Education.   *A Provisional Master Plan.* Springfield: Illinois Board of Higher Education, 1964.

2049.   James, Edmund J.   *The Origin of the Land Grant Act of 1862 (The So-Called Morrill Act) and Some Account of Its Author, Jonathan B. Turner.* University Studies, vol. 4, no. 1. Urbana: University of Illinois, 1910.   By the Morrill Act, states were granted public land for the endowment of agricultural and mechanical-arts colleges.

2050. Kucera, Daniel W. *Church-State Relationships in Education in Illinois.* Washington, D.C.: Catholic University Press, 1955. A scholarly study encompassing the relationships from 1673 to 1953.

2051. Moore, Margaret King. "The Ladies' Association for Educating Females, 1833-37." *Journal of the Illinois State Historical Society* 31 (1938): 166-87. A private society in Jacksonville (later affiliated with the General Federation of Women's Clubs in America) that raised funds to pay tuition for prospective teachers. Contributions were sought nationwide.

2052. Nowlan, James D. *The Politics of Higher Education: Lawmakers and the Academy in Illinois.* Urbana: University of Illinois Press, 1976.

2053. Pillsbury, W. L. "Early Education in Illinois." *Sixteenth Biennial Report of the Superintendent of Public Instruction of the State of Illinois.* Springfield, 1886. Pp. civ-cciii.

2054. Sanders, James W. *The Education of an Urban Minority: Catholics in Chicago, 1833-1865.* New York: Oxford University Press, 1977.

2055. Smith, Timothy L. "Uncommon Schools: Christian Colleges and Social Idealism in Midwestern America, 1820-1950," in *Indiana Historical Society Lectures, 1976-1977.* Indianapolis, 1978.

2. Primary and Secondary Schools and Teachers

2056. Belting, Paul E. "The Development of the Free Public High School in Illinois to 1860." *Journal of the Illinois State Historical Society* 11 (1918-19): 269-369, 467-566.

2057. Bronson, Flora Adelaide Holcomb. " 'Mother by the Tens': Flora Adelaide Holcomb Bronson's Account of Her Life as an Illinois Schoolteacher, Poet, and Farm Wife, 1851-1927." Edited by Justin Leiber, James Pickering, and Flora Bronson White. *Journal of the Illinois State Historical Society* 76 (1983): 283-307. The latter half of the reminiscence deals with the author's schooldays at the teachers' college at Normal (now Illinois State University) and her teaching days in the state in the 1870s and 1880s and her later family life.

2058. Cleary, Minnie Wait. "History of the Illinois School for the Deaf." *Journal of the Illinois State Historical Society* 35 (1942): 368-89. The school, located in Jacksonville, opened in January 1846.

2059. Daniel, Philip T. K. "History of Discrimination against Black Students in Chicago Secondary Schools." *History of Education Quarterly* 20 (Summer 1980): 147-62.

2060. Gutowski, Thomas W. "Student Initiative and the Origins of the High School Extracurriculum: Chicago, 1880-1915." *History of Education Quarterly* 28 (Spring 1988): 49-72.

2061. Hendrickson, Walter B. *From Shelter to Self-Reliance: A History of the Illinois Braille and Sight Saving School.* Jacksonville: Illinois Braille and Sight Saving School, 1972. A complete history of the institution that was a pioneer in the development of teaching techniques for the visually handicapped.

2062. _____. "The Three Lives of Frank H. Hall." *Journal of the Illinois State Historical Society* 49 (1956): 271-93. Hall was a teacher, school administrator, and agriculturist, as well as the inventor of a Braille-writer and a stereotypemaker for printing books in Braille. For many years he headed the Illinois Braille and Sight Saving School. See also the addendum, "Frank H. Hall and Progressive Education," ibid. 50 (1957): 89-91.

2063. Herget, James E. "Democracy Revisited: The Law and School Districts in Illinois." *Journal of the Illinois State Historical Society* 72 (1979): 123-38. Public education history from 1647 to 1955.

2064. Herrick, Mary J. *The Chicago Schools: A Social and Political History.* Beverly Hills, Calif.: Sage Publications, 1971. An inclusive history from 1833 to the date of publication.

2065. Hogan, David John. *Class and Reform: School and Society in Chicago, 1880-1930.* Philadelphia: University of Pennsylvania Press, 1985.

2066. Johnson, Charles Beneulyn. "The Subscription School and the Seminary in Pioneer Days." *Transactions of the Illinois State Historical Society, 1925,* pp. 54-59.

2067. McCaul, Robert L. *The Black Struggle for Public Schooling in Nineteenth-Century Illinois.* Carbondale: Southern Illinois University Press, 1987.

2068. Meier, August, and Rudwick, Elliott M. "Early Boycotts of Segregated Schools: The Alton, Illinois Case, 1897-1908." *Journal of Negro Education* 36 (1967): 394-402.

2069. Murphy, Marjorie. "Taxation and Social Conflict: Teacher Unionism and Public School Finance in Chicago, 1898-1934." *Journal of the Illinois State Historical Society* 74 (1981): 242-60.

2070. Paul, Norma A. *Study and Memos: Religious Orders and Their Schools in Illinois, 1834-1939.* N.p., 1970? The author gives brief histories of the orders, names the elementary and secondary schools of each order, then gives annual enrollment figures and sources of information.

2071. Peterson, Charles E. Jr. "The *Common School Advocate*: Molder of the Public Mind." *Journal of the Illinois State Historical Society* 57 (1964): 261-69. Published only in 1837, the *Advocate* was the first Illinois periodical devoted to educational matters.

2072. Pulliam, John. "Changing Attitudes toward Free Public Schools in Illinois, 1825-1860." *History of Education Quarterly* 7 (1967): 191-208.

2073. Walker, W. G. "The Development of the Free Public High School in Illinois during the Nineteenth Century." *History of Education Quarterly* 4 (1964): 264-79.

2074. Wrigley, Julia. *Class Politics and Public Schools: Chicago, 1900-1950.* New Brunswick, N.J.: Rutgers University Press, 1982.

3. Colleges and Universities

Recruiting brochures, commencement invitations and programs, catalogs and bulletins, yearbooks, publications for alumni, and student newspapers are not included unless they contain extensive histories of their colleges.

a. Illinois College

2075. Caine, L. Vernon. *To Heights Beyond: The Story of Illinois College, 1955-1973.* Carbondale: Southern Illinois University Press, for Illinois College, 1986.

2076. *Centennial Celebration of the Founding of Illinois College, October Twelfth, Thirteenth, Fourteenth, and Fifteenth, Nineteen Hundred and Twenty-nine.* Chicago: Lakeside Press, 1930?

2077. Frank, Charles E. *Pioneer's Progress: Illinois College, 1829-1979.* Carbondale: Southern Illinois University Press, for Illinois College, 1979. Part 1 is an abridgment of Rammelkamp's 1928 history.

2078. Gibson, Harold E. *Sigma Pi Society of Illinois College, 1843-1971: A History of a Literary Society.* Jacksonville, Ill.: Sigma Pi Society, 1972.

2079. Rammelkamp, Charles Henry. "Fundamentalism and Modernism in a Pioneer College." *Journal of the Illinois State Historical Society* 21 (1928-29): 395-408. The successful struggle of Illinois College President J. M. Sturtevant to maintain intellectual freedom against those who sought to impose narrow denominational control of the institution.

2080. _____. *Illinois College: A Centennial History, 1829-1929.* New Haven: Yale University Press, for Illinois College, 1928.

2081. Yeager, Iver Franklin. *Church and College on the Illinois Frontier: The Beginnings of Illinois College and the United Church of Christ in Central Illinois, 1829 to 1867.* Jacksonville: Illinois College, 1980.

2082. _____, ed. *Sesquicentennial Papers: Illinois College.* Carbondale: Southern Illinois University Press, for Illinois College, 1982.

b. Illinois State University

2083. Champagne, Roger J. *A Place of Education: Illinois State University, 1967-1977.* Normal: Illinois State University Foundation, 1978.

2084. _____. *The Thirteenth Decade: Illinois State University, 1977-1987.* Normal: Illinois State University, 1989.

2085. Cook, John Williston, and McHugh, James V. *A History of the Illinois State Normal University, Normal, Illinois.* Bloomington, Ill.: Pantagraph Printing, 1882.

2086. Harper, Charles A. *Development of the Teachers College in the United States, with Special Reference to the Illinois State Normal University.* Bloomington, Ill.: McKnight & McKnight, 1935.

2087. Marshall, Helen E. "Charles E. Hovey, Educator and Soldier." *Journal of the Illinois State Historical Society* 50 (1957): 243-76. The career of the prominent Illinois schoolman who became the first president of Illinois State University in 1857 and later served as a Union brigadier general.

2088. _____. *The Eleventh Decade, Illinois State University, 1957-1967.* Normal: Illinois State University, 1967.

2089. _____. *Grandest of Enterprises: Illinois State Normal University, 1857-1957.* Normal: Illinois State Normal University, 1956.

2090. _____. "The Town and the Gown." *Journal of the Illinois State Historical Society* 50 (1957): 141-67. A history of Illinois State Normal University and its relationships with the town of Normal.

2091. Sands, Theodore, and Parker, Rose E. "Special Education, Then and Now." *Journal of the Illinois State Historical Society* 50 (1957): 190-203. Development of the special education program at Illinois State Normal University.

2092. Welch, Eleanor Weir. "A Library Grows Up." *Journal of the Illinois State Historical Society* 50 (1957): 176-89. Development of the library at Illinois State University, 1857-1957.

c. Knox College

2093. Gettleman, Marvin E. "John H. Finley's Illinois Education." *Journal of the Illinois State Historical Society* 62 (1969): 147-69. The *New York Times* editor attended Illinois public schools and Knox College.

2094. Muelder, Hermann R. *Missionaries and Muckrakers: The First Hundred Years of Knox College.* Urbana: University of Illinois Press, 1984.

2095. Sherwin, Proctor Fenn, ed. *Record of the Centenary of Knox College and Galesburg.* Galesburg, Ill.: The college, 1938.

2096. Webster, Martha Farnham. *Seventy-Five Significant Years: The Story of Knox College, 1837-1912* Galesburg, Ill.: Wagoner Printing, 1912.

d. McKendree College

2097. Chamberlin, M. H. "Historical Sketch of McKendree College." *Transactions of the Illinois State Historical Society, 1904*, pp. 328-64.

2098. Eaton, William. " 'Scholarship, Virtue, and Religion': Robert Allyn and McKendree College, 1863-1874." *Illinois Historical Journal* 78 (1985): 129-42.

2099. Farthing, Paul, and Farthing, Chester, eds. *Philo History: Chronicles and Biographies of the Philosophian Literary Society of McKendree College.* Lebanon, Ill.: Published for the Society, 1911.

2100. *Souvenir Catalogue of the Platonian Literary Society of McKendree College, Lebanon, Ill. . . .* St. Louis: Nixon-Jones Printing, 1901.

2101. Walton, William Clarence. *Centennial, McKendree College, with St. Clair County History.* Lebanon, Ill.: McKendree College, 1928.

2102. Weil, Oscar E. "The Movement to Establish Lebanon Seminary, 1833-1835." *Journal of the Illinois State Historical Society* 59 (1966): 384-406. Lebanon Seminary, which opened in 1828, later became McKendree College.

e. MacMurray College

2103. Harker, Joseph R. "Progress in the Illinois Conference, 1824-1924." *Journal of the Illinois State Historical Society* 18 (1925-26): 159-74. The president of MacMurray College, 1893-1925, Harker discusses the founding by the Methodist church of McKendree College, DePauw University, MacMurray, Illinois Wesleyan, and several other seminaries and academies.

2104. Hendrickson, Walter B. *Forward in the Second Century of MacMurray College: A History of 125 Years.* Jacksonville, Ill.: MacMurray College, 1972. A brief but knowledgeable and sympathetic history that illustrates the problems and successes of the midwestern liberal arts college.

2105. McClelland, Clarence Paul. "The Morning-Star of Memory." *Journal of the Illinois State Historical Society* 40 (1947): 253-66. Thumbnail history of MacMurray College, presented by its president on the occasion of its centennial celebration.

2106. Watters, Mary. *The First Hundred Years of MacMurray College.* Springfield, Ill.: Williamson Publishing, 1947.

f. Monmouth College

2107. Beth, Loren P. "Monmouth Literary Societies." *Journal of the Illinois State Historical Society* 43 (1950): 120-36. History of the four societies at Monmouth College, the last of which disbanded in 1933.

2108. Crow, Mary B. "The Sorority Movement at Monmouth College." *Western Illinois Regional Studies* 4 (1981): 37-49.

2109. Davenport, F. Garvin. *Monmouth College: The First Hundred Years, 1853-1953.* Cedar Rapids, Iowa: Torch Press, 1953.

2110. _____. "The Pioneers of Monmouth College." *Journal of the Illinois State Historical Society* 46 (1953): 45-59.

2111. Urban, William, with Mary B. Crow, Charles Speel, and Samuel Thompson. *A History of Monmouth College through Its Fifth Quarter-Century.* Monmouth, Ill.: Monmouth College, 1979.

g. Northwestern University

2112. Clark, Dwight F. "A Forgotten Evanston Institution: The Northwestern Female College." *Journal of the Illinois State Historical Society* 35 (1942): 115-32. History of a school that later became a part of Northwestern University.

2113. Dillon, Mary Earhart. "Frances Willard as an Illinois Teacher." *Transactions of the Illinois State Historical Society, 1939*, pp. 27-37. The climax of her teaching career was the presidency of the Evanston College for Ladies, later absorbed by Northwestern University.

2114. Rein, Lynn Miller. *Northwestern University School of Speech: A History.* Evanston, Ill.: Northwestern University, 1981.

2115. Scott, Franklin D., ed. *A Pictorial History of Northwestern University, 1851-1951.* Evanston, Ill.: Northwestern University Press, 1951.

2116. Sedlak, Michael W., and Williamson, Harold F. *The Evolution of Management Education: A History of the Northwestern University J. L. Kellogg Graduate School of Management, 1908-1983.* Urbana: University of Illinois Press, 1983. More a commemorative than an analytical study.

2117. Ward, Estelle Frances. *The Story of Northwestern University*. New York: Dodd, Mead, 1924.

2118. Wilde, Arthur Herbert, ed. *Northwestern University: A History, 1855-1905*. 4 vols. New York: University Publishing Society, 1905.

2119. Williamson, Harold F., and Wild, Payson S. *Northwestern University: A History, 1850-1975*. Evanston, Ill.: Northwestern University, 1976.

h.   Southern Illinois University

2120. Everson, David H., and Miller, Roy E. *SIU Student Attitudes toward University Authority: A Profile*. Carbondale: Public Affairs Research Bureau, Southern Illinois University, 1970.

2121. Lentz, Eli G. *Seventy-five Years in Retrospect, From Normal School to Teachers College to University: Southern Illinois University, 1874-1949*. Carbondale: Southern Illinois University, 1955.

2122. Mitchell, Betty. *Delyte Morris of SIU*. Carbondale: Southern Illinois University Press, 1988. Biography of the president who transformed Southern Illinois University from a small teacher-training institution to a university of some 35,000 students.

2123. Neckers, James W. *The Building of a Department: Chemistry at Southern Illinois University, 1927-1967*. Carbondale: Southern Illinois University, 1979. A nuts-and-bolts account of how a university operates and evolves, by the man who was primarily responsible for developing a nationally recognized chemistry department there.

2124. Plochmann, George Kimball. *The Ordeal of Southern Illinois University*. Carbondale: Southern Illinois University Press, 1959. History of the school, 1943-55, during its transformation from a small teachers' college to a large university.

2125. *Quarter Centennial Anniversary Souvenir of the Southern Illinois State Normal University*. Carbondale: Carbondale Free Press, for the Alumni Association, 1899.

i. University of Chicago

2126. Block, Jean F. *The Uses of Gothic: Planning and Building the Campus of the University of Chicago, 1892-1932.* Chicago: University of Chicago Library, 1983.

2127. Bulmer, Martin. *The Chicago School of Sociology: Institutionalization, Diversity, and the Rise of Sociological Research.* Chicago: University of Chicago Press, 1984. A valuable resource for the history of sociology.

2128. Ellsworth, Frank L. *Law on the Midway: The Founding of the University of Chicago Law School.* Chicago: Law School of the University of Chicago, 1977.

2129. Fisher, Daniel Jerome. *The Seventy Years of the Department of Geology, University of Chicago, 1892-1961.* Chicago: University of Chicago, 1963.

2130. Goodspeed, Thomas Wakefield. *The Story of the University of Chicago, 1890-1925.* Chicago: University of Chicago Press, 1925. Also incorporates a brief account of the first University of Chicago (1856-86).

2131. McNeill, William Hardy. *Hutchins' University: A Memoir of the University of Chicago, 1929-1950.* Chicago: University of Chicago Press, 1991.

2132. Murphy, William Michael, and Bruckner, D. J. R., eds. *The Idea of the University of Chicago: Selections from the Papers of the First Eight Chief Executives of the University of Chicago from 1891 to 1975.* Chicago: University of Chicago Press, 1976.

2133. Persons, Stow. *Ethnic Studies at Chicago, 1905-45.* Urbana: University of Illinois Press, 1987. A study of the "Chicago school" of social scientists at the University of Chicago, with a bibliography.

2134. Richardson, John Jr. *The Spirit of Inquiry: The Graduate Library School at Chicago, 1925-51.* Chicago: American Library Association, 1982.

2135. Rucker, Darnell. *The Chicago Pragmatists.* Minneapolis: University of Minnesota Press, 1969. The community of scholars at the University of Chicago from the late nineteenth century to about 1930.

2136. Shils, Edward, ed. *Remembering the University of Chicago, Teachers, Scientists, and Scholars.* Chicago: University of Chicago Press, 1991.

"Intellectual biographies" of almost fifty teachers in the years 1920-70, based on recollections of their colleagues and students.

2137. Storr, Richard J. *Harper's University: The Beginnings; A History of the University of Chicago*. Chicago: University of Chicago Press, 1966.

2138. Streeter, Robert E., ed. *One in Spirit: A Retrospective of the University of Chicago on the Occasion of Its Centennial*. 2d ed. Chicago: University of Chicago, 1991. The university was incorporated in 1890 and classes began in 1892.

2139. Vincent, George E. "The University of Chicago." *Outlook* 71 (1902): 839-51.

2140. Ward, F. Champion, ed. *The Idea and Practice of General Education: An Account of the College of the University of Chicago, by Present and Former Members of the Faculty*. Chicago: University of Chicago Press, 1950. Reprint, 1992.

      j. University of Illinois

2141. Burford, Cary Clive, *We're Loyal to You, Illinois*. Danville, Ill.: Interstate, 1952. A history of the University of Illinois bands and conductor Albert Austin Harding.

2142. Dilliard, Irving. "When Woodrow Wilson Was Invited to Head the University of Illinois." *Journal of the Illinois State Historical Society* 60 (1967): 357-82. Wilson was offered the post in 1892.

2143. Ebert, Roger, comp. *An Illini Century: One Hundred Years of Campus Life*. Urbana: University of Illinois Press, 1967.

2144. Grotzinger, Laurel. "The University of Illinois Library School, 1893-1942." *Journal of Library History* 2 (1967): 129-41.

2145. Hardin, Thomas L. "The University of Illinois and the Community-Junior College Movement, 1901-1965." *Illinois Historical Journal* 79 (1986): 82-98.

2146. Hatch, Richard A., comp. *Some Founding Papers of the University of Illinois*. Urbana: University of Illinois Press, 1967. Sponsored by the committee on the centennial of the university.

2147. Hildner, Ernest G. "Higher Education in Transition, 1850-1870." *Journal of the Illinois State Historical Society* 56 (1963): 61-73. The opening of the University of Illinois in 1868 marked the transition of higher education from classical colleges centered on Greek, Latin, and mathematics to state-supported schools emphasizing practical and applied arts and sciences.

2148. *Illini Years, 1868-1950: A Picture History of the University of Illinois.* Urbana: University of Illinois Press, 1950. Based on the research of Carl Stephens, university historian.

2149. Johnson, Henry C. Jr., and Johanningmeier, Erwin V. *Teachers for the Prairie: The University of Illinois and the Schools, 1863-1945.* Urbana: University of Illinois Press, 1972. More a history of the University of Illinois College of Education than of the university's relations with public schools.

2150. Johnson, Ronald M. "Schoolman among Scholars: Andrew S. Draper at the University of Illinois, 1894-1904." *Illinois Historical Journal* 78 (1985): 257-72. A study of the University of Illinois president noted for his administrative skills and service to public school education.

2151. Moores, Richard Gordon. *Fields of Rich Toil: The Development of the University of Illinois College of Agriculture.* Urbana: University of Illinois Press, 1970.

2152. Nevins, Allan. *Illinois.* American College and University Series. New York: Oxford University Press, 1917. A history of the University of Illinois.

2153. Solberg, Winton U. *The University of Illinois, 1867-1894: An Intellectual and Cultural History.* Urbana: University of Illinois Press, 1968.

2154. _____. "The University of Illinois Struggles for Public Recognition, 1867-1894." *Journal of the Illinois State Historical Society* 59 (1966): 5-29.

2155. Turner, Fred H. "Misconceptions Concerning the Early History of the University of Illinois." *Transactions of the Illinois State Historical Society, 1932,* pp. 63-90.

2156. Weller, Allen Stuart. *100 Years of Campus Architecture at the University of Illinois.* Urbana: University of Illinois Press, for the Committee on the Centennial of the University, 1968.

k. Wheaton College

2157. Bechtel, Paul M. *Wheaton College: A Heritage Remembered, 1860-1984.* Wheaton, Ill.: Harold Shaw Publishers, 1984.

2158. Taylor, Richard S. "Religion and Higher Education in Gilded Age America: The Case of Wheaton College." *American Studies*, Spring 1981, pp. 57-70. History of the college and its religious ties, 1860-82.

2159. Willard, Warren Wyeth. *Fire on the Prairie: The Story of Wheaton College.* Wheaton, Ill.: Van Kampen Press, 1950.

l. Others

2160. Adams, Harold K. *History of Eureka College.* Eureka, Ill.: Board of Trustees of Eureka College, 1982.

2161. Aksler, Samuel. "Asher Library." *Jewish Book Annual* 31 (1973-74): 58-61. The library is at Spertus College of Judaica in Chicago.

2162. Altenhofen, Aurelia, Sister. *Rosary College: Transition and Progress, 1949-1974.* Privately printed, 1977. Established by the Dominican Sisters as Santa Clara College in 1901, the school changed its name to Rosary College and moved from Wisconsin to River Forest, Illinois, in 1922.

2163. Baepler, Walter August. *A Century of Blessing, 1846-1946: Concordia Theological Seminary, Springfield, Illinois.* N.p., 1946? This seminary of the Missouri Synod of the Lutheran church closed in 1976.

2164. *Barat College: Celebrating 75 Years in Lake Forest; Special Anniversary Report, Fall, 1979.* [Lake Forest, Ill.: The college, 1979]

2165. Berchtold, Theodore A. *To Teach, to Heal, to Serve! The Story of the Chicago College of Osteopathic Medicine: The First 75 Years (1900-1975).* Chicago: The college, 1975.

2166. Bergendoff, Conrad. *Augustana--A Profession of Faith: A History of Augustana College, 1860-1935.* Rock Island, Ill.: Augustana College Library, 1969.

2167. _____. "A Century-Old Monument: Augustana College's Main." *Swedish-American Historical Quarterly* 35 (July 1984): 267-81.

2168. Bledig, Alice R. "The Origin and Development of the Nursing Program at Southeastern Illinois College, 1955-1985." Ph.D. dissertation, Southern Illinois University, 1985.

2169. *Bradley Polytechnic Institute: The First Decade, 1897-1907.* Peoria, Ill.: Bradley University, 1908.

2170. Brinkman, Gabriel. "Quincy College." In *New Catholic Encyclopedia.* New York: McGraw Hill, 1967.

2171. Button, Henry Warren. "James Park Slade, Nineteenth-Century Schoolman." *Journal of the Illinois State Historical Society* 54 (1961): 374-91. Slade was a teacher, principal, and county superintendent of schools in St. Clair County before becoming state superintendent in 1879. He later headed Almira College in Greenville.

2172. Camp, Norman Harvey. *The Moody Bible Institute of Chicago: A Brief Historical Sketch.* Chicago: Moody Bible Institute, 1915.

2173. Carlson, Leland H. *A History of North Park College, Commemorating the Fiftieth Anniversary, 1891-1941.* Chicago, 1941.

2174. *Celebrating 25 Years of Class.* This history of Lake Land College, Mattoon, was an insert in the *Summer Class Schedule 1992.*

2175. Chase, Virginius H. "Jubilee College and Its Founder." *Journal of the Illinois State Historical Society* 40 (1947): 154-67. The founder was Philander Chase, Episcopal bishop of Illinois.

2176. Coleman, Charles H. *Eastern Illinois State College: Fifty Years of Public Service.* Eastern Illinois State College Bulletin, no. 189. Charleston, 1950. Eastern was authorized by the state legislature in 1895.

2177. _____. "The Normal School Comes to Charleston." *Journal of the Illinois State Historical Society* 41 (1948): 117-35.

2178. Concordia College. *Changeless Change: Concordia College, 125 Years, 1864-1989.* River Forest, Ill.: The college, 1989?

2179. Crankshaw, Ned. "Changing Images at Shimer College: From Rural Home to Collegiate Quadrangle." *Illinois Historical Journal* 86 (1993): 159-80.

2180. DeBlois, Austen Kennedy. *The Pioneer School: A History of Shurtleff College, the Oldest Educational Institution in the West.* Chicago: Fleming H. Revell, 1900.

2181. Dickinson, Elmira J., ed. *A History of Eureka College with Biographical Sketches and Reminiscences.* St. Louis: Christian Publishing, 1894.

2182. Donnay, Donald E. "The Development of Olney Central College, an Eastern Illinois Community College, 1956-1984." Ph.D. dissertation, Southern Illinois University at Carbondale, 1991.

2183. Douthit, Jasper Lewis, ed. *Shelby Seminary Memorial, 1854-1869.* Shelbyville, Ill.: Printed at the office of Our Best Words, 1886.

2184. Dukes, Edgar L. "The Southern Collegiate Institute, 1891-1916." *Journal of the Illinois State Historical Society* 38 (1945): 295-318. The college was in Albion.

2185. Elgin Community College. *Catalog, 1993-1994.* Elgin, Ill.: The college, 1993. Contains an "Historical Summary" of the school's development, in chronological form, from 10 January 1949 to the present.

2186. *Elmhurst College Magazine.* Vol. 4, no. 3 (1971). This issue, titled "Elmhurst College, 1871-1971," is devoted to a history of the school.

2187. Evjen, Harry. "Illinois State University, 1852-1868." *Journal of the Illinois State Historical Society* 31 (1938): 54-71. History of a private Lutheran college at Springfield.

2188. Falbe, Lawrence, and Andersen, Wendy, eds. *Contexts: A Celebration of the Augustana College Library.* Augustana College Library New Series, no. 1. Rock Island, Ill.: East Hall Press, 1991.

2189. Ferguson, W. F. *Causes of Failure and Success in Founding Western Colleges: An Inaugural Address Delivered before the Board of Trustees of McDonough College, Illinois, March 31, 1852.* Cincinnati: John D. Thorpe, for McDonough College, 1852. The college was in Macomb.

2190. Flood, Robert G., and Jenkins, Jerry B. *Teaching the Word, Reaching the World: Moody Bible Institute, the First 100 Years.* Chicago: Moody Press, 1985.

2191. *Founder's Day, September 14, 1986: Black Hawk College, 40th Anniversary, Forty Years of Growth and Excellence.* This program contains an historical chronology of the college, located near Moline.

2192. Frederick, Duke. *Early Times at Northeastern: A Memoir.* Chicago: Northeastern Illinois University, 1978.

2193. Freitag, Alfred J. *College with a Cause: A History of Concordia Teachers College.* River Forest, Ill.: Concordia Teachers College, 1964.

2194. *General Register of Lake Forest College, 1857-1914.* Lake Forest, Ill., 1914.

2195. Gleicher, David. "The Origins and Early Years of Chicago's Hebrew Theological College." *Tradition: A Journal of Orthodox Jewish Thought* 27, no. 2 (Winter 1993): 56-68.

2196. Gray, Francis Jerome. "Quincy College--Eleven Years without a Home." *Quincy College Alumni Bulletin,* Spring 1971, pp. 14-18.

2197. Greene, William W. *Semi-Centennial History of the Alpha Zeta Society of Shurtleff College, together with Complete Rosters of Active and Honorary Members.* Alton, Ill.: Melling & Gaskins, 1898.

2198. Grote, Caroline. *Housing and Living Conditions of Women Students in the Western Illinois State Teachers College at Macomb--School Years 1926-1927, 1927-1928, and 1928-1929.* Teachers College, Columbia University, Contributions to Education, no. 507. New York, 1932.

2199. Habig, Marion Alphonse. "Educational Institutions" in *Heralds of the King: The Franciscans of the St. Louis-Chicago Sacred Heart Province, 1858-1958.* Chicago: Franciscan Herald Press, 1958. Includes information about Quincy College.

2200. Hamlin, Griffith A. *Monticello: The Biography of a College.* Fulton, Mo.: Published by William Woods College for the Monticello College Foundation, 1976.

2201. Hayter, Earl W. *Education in Transition: The History of Northern Illinois University, 1899-1974*. DeKalb: Northern Illinois University Press, 1974.

2202. Heck, Arch O. *The Hedding Roll*. Columbus, Ohio, 1973. Photocopy from typescript. A roll since 1867 of students, faculty, and members of the boards of trustees of the college at Abingdon, Illinois. The second part of the book consists of biographical sketches.

2203. Hicken, Victor. *The Purple and the Gold: The Story of Western Illinois University*. Macomb: Western Illinois University Foundation, 1970.

2204. *History of Westfield College, Founded at Westfield, Illinois, February 15, 1865* . . . Dayton, Ohio: United Brethren Publishing House, 1876.

2205. Idisi, C. Onokata. "Shawnee College: An Analysis of the Organization and Establishment of a Post-secondary Institution." Ph.D. dissertation, Southern Illinois University, 1979. The college is located at Ullin.

2206. *Illinois Central College: Celebrating 25 Years of Learning for Living*. Appendix to the North Central Self Study Report, Spring 1992. A brief history and detailed description of the East Peoria institution.

2207. Illinois Institute of Technology. *Converging Visions: The Making of a University*. Chicago: IIT, 1990? Brief history, with chronology.

2208. *John A. Logan College: 25th Anniversary, Sharing the Past, Shaping the Future--History, 1967-1992*. This history of the college at Carterville is the program for the 25th anniversary celebration, 13 September 1992.

2209. Johnson, Daniel T. "Financing the Western Colleges, 1844-1862." *Journal of the Illinois State Historical Society* 65 (1972): 43-53. The Western College Society was formed in the East as a means of raising money for Presbyterian and Congregational colleges in the West.

2210. Jordahl, Donald C. "John Brown White and Early Women's Education: A History of Almira College." *Journal of the Illinois State Historical Society* 72 (1979): 101-10. Almira College at Greenville was chartered in 1857; it later became coeducational, and in 1892 the name was changed to Greenville College.

2211. *Kaskaskia College Catalog, 1993-1995: A Vital Sign for Your Future*. Centralia, Ill., 1993. Contains a brief history.

2212. Kearney, Edmund W., with the assistance of Thomas A. DePasquale. *Chicago State College, 1869-1969: A Centennial Retrospective.* Chicago, 1969. Now Chicago State University.

2213. Lelon, Thomas Charles. "The Emergence of Roosevelt College of Chicago: A Search for an Ideal." Ph.D. dissertation, University of Chicago, 1973.

2214. Lentz, Harold H. *The Miracle of Carthage: History of Carthage College, 1847-1974.* Lima, Ohio: C.S.S. Publishing, 1975.

2215. Leonard, Edwin S. Jr. *As the Sowing: The First Fifty Years of the Principia.* St. Louis: The Principia, 1980. History of the college at Elsah.

2216. Lester, Marilyn A. *History of the National College of Education Libraries, 1920-1978.* Evanston, Ill.: The college, 1987.

2217. Lindley, Lester G. *To Fulfill This Mission: A History of Kendall College, 1934-1984.* Photoduplicated, 1984? Formerly Evanston Collegiate Institute, Kendall became a four-year college in 1976.

2218. Lindstrom, Andrew F., and Carruthers, Olive. *Lincoln, the Namesake College: A Centennial History, 1865-1965.* Lincoln, Ill., 1965.

2219. Macauley, Irene. *The Heritage of Illinois Institute of Technology.* Chicago: Illinois Institute of Technology, 1978.

2220. McCarty, Eva, Sister. *The Sinsinawa Dominicans: Outline of Twentieth Century Development, 1901-1949.* Dubuque, Iowa: Hoermann Press, 1952. Early history of Rosary College, founded by members of the Dominican order.

2221. McClure, James Gore King. *The Story of the Life and Work of the Presbyterian Theological Seminary, Chicago, Founded by Cyrus H. McCormick* . . . Chicago: Lakeside Press, R. R. Donnelley, 1929.

2222. McConagha, Glenn L. *Blackburn College, 1837-1987: An Anecdotal and Analytical History of the Private College.* Carlinville, Ill.: Blackburn College, 1988.

2223. McGiffert, Arthur Cushman Jr. *No Ivory Tower: The Story of the Chicago Theological Seminary.* Chicago: Chicago Theological Seminary, 1965.

2224. *McHenry County College: Catalog & Planning Guide, 1993-1994.* Crystal Lake, Ill.: The college, 1993. Contains a brief history of the college.

2225. Melvin, George R. "Northeastern Illinois University: The History of a Comprehensive State University." Ph.D. dissertation, University of Chicago, 1979.

2226. Mertz, James J. *Madonna Della Strada Chapel, Loyola University.* Chicago: Loyola University Press, 1975.

2227. Messenger, Janet Graveline. *The Story of the National College of Education, 1886-1986.* Evanston, Ill.: The college, 1985.

2228. Miller, L. W. "Higher Education in Dixon." *Journal of the Illinois State Historical Society* 39 (1946): 259-62. Concerns the Dixon Collegiate Institute, opened in 1855, and the Northern Illinois Normal School and Business College, opened in 1881.

2229. Miller, Mary. *A Chance for All: A Historical Diary of the Early Years of Danville Junior College.* Danville, Ill.: The college, 1980. Now Danville Area Community College.

2230. Mills, Albert Taylor. *My Forty Years at Millikin.* Decatur, Ill., 1948? Mills taught history and political science from 1903, when the college opened, to 1943.

2231. Monroe, Charles R. *Profile of the Community College.* San Francisco: Jossey-Bass, 1973. Information about Kennedy-King College, Chicago, is given on pages 103-4, 111-19, 229-38.

2232. Norwood, Percy V. "Jubilee College, Illinois." *Historical Magazine of the Protestant Episcopal Church* 12 (1943): 44-58.

2233. *One Hundred Four Years of Excellence: National College of Education.* Evanston, Ill.: The college, 1990. In 1990 the college became National-Louis University.

2234. *One Hundred Years of Knowledge in the Service of Man: Loyola University of Chicago, 1870-1970.* Chicago, 1970.

2235. "Orchard City College and Its Founder." *Journal of the Illinois State Historical Society* 46 (1953): 309-11. Thomas Burton Greenlaw founded his business college at Flora in 1890 and operated it for thirty years.

2236. Parrott, Leslie. *The Olivet Story: An Anecdotal History of Olivet Nazarene University, 1907-1990.* Kankakee, Ill: The university, 1993.

2237. Peebles, James Clinton. *History of Armour Institute of Technology.* Chicago, 1954. Recollections by a faculty member of the early history of Armour Institute, later the Illinois Institute of Technology.

2238. Perlman, Daniel H. "Faculty Trusteeship: Concept and Experience: A History of the Governance of Roosevelt University, Chicago." Ph.D. dissertation, University of Chicago, 1971.

2239. Potts, Abbie Findlay. *House on Hill, for the Hundredth Year of Rockford College.* Rockford, Ill.: Centennial Committee of Rockford College, 1947.

2240. Prince, Aaron Erastus. *History of Ewing College.* Collinsville, Ill.: J. O. Monroe, printer, 1961.

2241. Rawlinson, Howard. *The First Fifteen Years.* Photoduplicated. N.p.: Board of Trustees, Illinois Junior College District 521, 1972. History of Rend Lake College, formerly the Mt. Vernon Community College.

2242. *Rend Lake College: 1992-93, 1993-94 College Catalog.* Ina, Ill.: Board of Trustees, Community College District 521, 1992.

2243. Rickard, Ruth. *History of the College of Lake County, 1969-1986, Reflector of and Reactor to the Needs of the Changing Times: The Story of the College under Two Administrations.* Grayslake, Ill.: College of Lake County, 1987.

2244. Roberts, Clarence N. *North Central College: A Century of Liberal Education, 1861-1961.* Naperville, Ill.: The college, 1960.

2245. Rockford College, Rockford, Ill. *Alumnae Register, 1854-1925.* Rockford: The college, 1926.

2246. Sachs, Jerome Michael. *Reminiscences about Northeastern Illinois University, or, There Must Be a Pony Here Somewhere.* Chicago: Northeastern Illinois University, 1987.

2247. *Semi-Centennial Celebration, Garrett Biblical Institute, May Fifth to Ninth, Nineteen Hundred Six.* Evanston, Ill., 1906. This Methodist seminary is affiliated with Northwestern University.

2248. *Shawnee Community College, 1993-1995 Catalog.* Ullin, Ill.: The college, 1993. Contains a brief history.

2249. Sherman, Richard G. *Prairie State College in Its First Quarter-Century, 1957-82: A Community College History.* Chicago Heights, Ill.: The college, 1992.

2250. Sherwin, Byron L. *Contexts and Content; Higher Jewish Education in the United States: Spertus College of Judaica--A Case Study.* Chicago: Spertus College of Judaica Press, 1987.

2251. Shively, Roma Louise. *Jubilee--A Pioneer College.* Elmwood, Ill.: Elmwood Gazette, 1935.

2252. Skillrud, Harold Clayton. *LSTC: Decade of Decision; A History of the Merger of the Lutheran School of Theology at Chicago with Special Emphasis on the Decade 1958-1968.* Chicago: The college, 1969.

2253. Smith, George Washington. "The Old Illinois Agricultural College." *Journal of the Illinois State Historical Society* 5 (1912-13): 475-80. Chartered in 1861 and located at Irvington, the college opened in 1866 and closed in 1877.

2254. Spielman, William Carl. *The Diamond Jubilee History of Carthage College, 1870-1945.* Carthage, Ill.: Carthage Historical Society and Carthage College, 1945.

2255. Sulkin, Howard A. "Spertus College of Judaica." In *The Sentinel's History of Chicago Jewry* (q.v.), pp. 199-201.

2256. Szymczak, Donald Ray. "Origins and Development of Southeastern Illinois College, 1960-1976." Ph.D. dissertation, Southern Illinois University, 1977. Southeastern Illinois College is located at Harrisburg.

2257. Tenney, Mary Alice. *"Still Abides the Memory."* Greenville, Ill.: Greenville College, Tower Press, 1942.

2258. Tingley, Donald Fred, ed. *The Emerging University: A History of Eastern Illinois University, 1949-74.* Charleston: Eastern Illinois University, 1974.

2259. Trares, Thomas Francis. "Ecumenical Action: A History of Springfield College in Illinois, 1929-1969." Ph.D. dissertation, St. Louis University, 1972.

2260. Troller, Bill, and Hallenstein, Ruth. "An Odyssey of Learning." *Vision* [a publication of the College of DuPage] 12, no. 3 (Spring 1992): 6-11. History of the Glen Ellyn college on the occasion of its twenty-fifth anniversary.

2261. *25* [a chronology of the 25-year history of Moraine Valley Community College]. Palos Hills, Ill.: The college, 1993.

2262. Watson, Elmo Scott. *The Illinois Wesleyan Story, 1850-1950.* Bloomington: Illinois Wesleyan University Press, 1950.

2263. Weinstein, M. M.; Mrtek, M. B.; and Mrtek, R. G. "Factors Leading to the Formation of the Chicago College of Pharmacy." *Pharmacy in History* 14, no. 1 (1972): 3-17.

2264. Wilder, William H., ed. *An Historical Sketch of the Illinois Wesleyan University, together with a Record of the Alumni, 1857-1895.* Bloomington, Ill.: University Press, 1895.

2265. William Rainey Harper College. *History.* Palatine, Ill.: The college, 1993.

2266. Wood, Susan H. *A History of Joliet Junior College, 1901-1984.* Joliet, Ill.: Joliet Junior College Foundation, 1987.

2267. Yates, Louis A. R. *A Proud Heritage: Bradley's History, 1897-1972.* Peoria, Ill.: Bradley University, Observer Press, 1974.

D. ENVIRONMENT

2268. *Bibliography and Index of Illinois Geology, Selected from Publications Indexed in GeoRef.*   Alexandria, Va.: GeoRef Information System and Champaign, Ill.: Illinois State Geological Survey. Issued annually.

2269. Bishop, David, and Campbell, Craig C. *History of the Forest Preserves of Winnebago County, Illinois.* Rockford: Winnebago County Forest Preserve Commission, 1979.

2270. Bohlen, H. David. *The Birds of Illinois.* Bloomington: Indiana University Press, 1989. Includes color plates of 87 species, painted by wildlife artist William Zimmerman. This authoritative study covers 439 species.

2271. *Bulletin of the Illinois Geographical Society.* April 1955--to date. Published twice a year for the society by the Department of Geography and Geology, Illinois State University.

2272. Burnham, J. H. "Destruction of Kaskaskia by the Mississippi River." *Transactions of the Illinois State Historical Society, 1914*, pp. 95-112. Emphasis is on the changing course of the Mississippi, but there is also substantial information about Kaskaskia and other French villages.

2273. Calhoun, John, and Loomis, Forrest D. *Prairie Whitetails.* Springfield: Illinois Division of Wildlife Resources, 1974.

2274. Caton, John Dean. *Origin of the Prairies: Paper Read before the Ottawa Academy of Natural Sciences, December 30th, 1869.* Ottawa, Ill.: Osman & Hapeman, 1869.

2275. Chandler, Josephine Craven. "The Wild Flowers of Illinois and Their Preservation." *Transactions of the Illinois State Historical Society, 1927*, pp. 132-43.

2276. Changnon, Stanley A. Jr. *Climatology of Severe Winter Storms in Illinois.* Illinois Department of Registration and Education, Bulletin 53. Urbana: Illinois State Water Survey, 1969.

2277. Colten, Craig E. "Industrial Wastes in Southeast Chicago: Production and Disposal, 1870-1970." *Environmental Review* 10 (Summer 1986): 93-105.

2278. Eifert, Virginia S. *Essays on Nature: An Anthology of Selected Writings from the Living Museum.* Edited by Herman Eifert and Orvetta M. Robinson. Springfield: Illinois State Museum, 1967.

2279. *Environmental Impact Statements: A Handbook for Writers and Reviewers.* Prepared by the Department of Landscape Architecture, University of Illinois, Urbana-Champaign. Illinois Institute of Environmental Quality, Document no. 73-8. Chicago, 1973. Bibliography, pp. 187-202.

2280. "Freaks of Nature." *Journal of the Illinois State Historical Society* 5 (1912-13): 139-41. Unusual weather and astronomical events, 1830-81.

2281. Fuller, M. L. "The Climate of Illinois: Its Permanence." *Transactions of the Illinois State Historical Society, 1912*, pp. 54-62.

2282. Garver, Jared K. "The History of the Wild Turkey in Illinois." *Selected Papers in Illinois History, 1983*. Springfield: Illinois State Historical Society, 1985. Pp. 11-16.

2283. Herkert, James R., ed. *Endangered and Threatened Species of Illinois: Status and Distribution. Volume 1: Plants*, 1991; *Volume 2: Animals*, 1992--both published by the Illinois Endangered Species Protection Board, Springfield.

2284. Hoffmeister, Donald. *Mammals of Illinois*. Urbana: University of Illinois Press, 1989. A comprehensive scientific guide to native, non-native, and prehistoric species in Illinois.

2285. Horsley, A. Doyne. *Illinois: A Geography*. Geographies of the United States. Boulder, Colo.: Westview Press, 1986. Traditional descriptions of Illinois with discussions of geographic reasons for demographic trends.

2286. Illinois Department of Energy and Natural Resources; Illinois State Geological Survey; and Illinois Hazardous Waste Research and Information Center. *Environmental Geology*. No. 1 (1965)--to date. Issued irregularly. Originally titled *Environmental Geology Notes*.

2287. Illinois Natural History Survey. *Bulletin*. Vol. 1 (1876)--1918. In those years there were three slightly different titles.

2288. Illinois State Geological Survey. *Bulletin*. No. 1 (1906)--to date.

2289. _____. *Circular*. 1906-13. Later series, nos. 1 (1931)--22 (1937) [called *Information Circular*] and 23 [*Circular*]--to date.

2290. _____. *Report of Investigations*. Irregular, 1924-67.

2291. Ivens, J. Loreena. *Annotated List of Publications, 1895-1970, Illinois State Water Survey*. Urbana: Illinois State Water Survey, 1970.

2292. Johnson, Leland R. *The Falls City Engineers: A History of the Louisville District, Corps of Engineers, United States Army, 1970-1983*. Louisville, Ky.: United States Army Engineer District, 1984. The effect of a new mandate to preserve the environment on proposed construction projects in the Louisville District, which includes Illinois.

2293. King, Frances B. *Plants, People, and Paleoecology: Biotic Communities and Aboriginal Plant Usage in Illinois.* Illinois State Museum, Scientific Papers, vol. 20. Springfield, 1984.

2294. *Living Museum.* Vol. 1 (1939)--to date. Published monthly at Springfield by the Illinois State Museum; devoted largely to articles on natural history. For the general reader.

2295. Ludlum, David M. *Early American Winters II, 1821 to 1870.* Boston: American Meteorological Society, 1968. Contains extensive descriptions of Illinois winters.

2296. McCollum, Dannel Angus, and Smith, James Oliver. *A Guide to the Big Vermilion River System.* Champaign, Ill.: Shakerag Publishing, 1982. A history and geography of the Big Vermilion and its three main tributaries, the Salt Fork, the Middle Fork, and the North Fork.

2297. McFall, Don, ed. *A Directory of Illinois Nature Preserves.* Springfield: Illinois Department of Conservation, Division of Natural Heritage, 1991.

2298. McManis, Douglas R. *The Initial Evaluation and Utilization of the Illinois Prairies, 1815-1840.* University of Chicago Department of Geography Research Paper, no. 94. Chicago, 1964.

2299. Mann, Fred L.; Ellis, Harold H.; and Krausz, N. G. P. *Water-Use Law in Illinois.* University of Illinois, Agricultural Experiment Station, Bulletin 703. Urbana, 1964.

2300. May, George W. *Down Illinois Rivers.* Ann Arbor, Mich.: Edwards Brothers, 1981. A personal narrative of float-paddle trips down eighteen rivers in Illinois.

2301. Meyer, Alfred Herman. "Circulation and Settlement Patterns of the Calumet-South Chicago Region of Northwest Indiana and Northeast Illinois: A Sequent Occupance Study in Historical Geography." *Proceedings, VIIIth General Assembly, XVIIth Congress, International Geographical Union.* Washington, 1952. Pp. 538-44. Covering the years from Potawatomi occupancy to 1952, this study emphasizes the effect of geographical features on economic development.

2302. _____. "The Kankakee 'Marsh' of Northern Indiana and Illinois." *Papers of the Michigan Academy of Science, Arts, and Letters* 21 (1935): 359-96; published 1936.

2303. Mohlenbrock, Robert H., ed. *The Illustrated Flora of Illinois.* Carbondale: Southern Illinois University Press, 1967-- . A multi-volume continuing series, by several authors, covering "every group of plants, from algae and fungi through flowering plants." Designed for the general reader.

2304. Musselman, T. E. "A History of the Birds of Illinois." *Journal of the Illinois State Historical Society* 14 (1921-22): 1-73.

2305. *Nature of Illinois.* Vol. 1, no. 1 (Summer 1986)--to date. Published by the Nature of Illinois Foundation (previously the Society for the Illinois Scientific Surveys). The foundation was created in 1984 "to promote, foster and encourage the welfare and programs of the three Illinois Scientific Surveys--The Natural History, Water, and Geological Surveys."

2306. Neely, R. Dan, and Heister, Carla G., comps. *The Natural Resources of Illinois: Introduction and Guide.* Illinois Natural History Survey, Special Publication 6. Champaign, Ill., 1987. A description of the state's natural resources, as of 1982, by some fifty specialists. The topics are as varied as agricultural production, river and lake traffic, fish and wildlife, mineral and water resources, climate, forests, etc. Tables of agricultural- and mineral-production statistics in many cases include figures from the 1930s to the 1980s. An appendix lists series publications of state and federal agencies that provide detailed, technical information about the state's environment. A separate "citation bibliography" constitutes a good basic bibliography for the environment.

2307. Page, John L. *Climate of Illinois: Summary and Analysis of Long-time Weather Records.* University of Illinois Agricultural Experiment Station, Bulletin 532. Urbana, 1949.

2308. Parmalee, Paul W. *The Fresh-Water Mussels of Illinois.* Illinois State Museum Popular Science Series, no. 8. Springfield, 1967.

2309. _____. *Reptiles of Illinois.* Illinois State Museum Popular Science Series, no. 5. Springfield, 1955.

2310. Poggi, Edith Muriel. *The Prairie Province of Illinois: A Study of Human Adjustment to the Natural Environment.* Illinois Studies in the Social Sciences, vol. 19, no. 3. Urbana: University of Illinois, 1934. Includes chapters on the state's geographic regions, glaciation, surface and ground water, climate and corn production, natural vegetation, mineral production, and settlement and development.

2311. Ridgley, Douglas C. *The Geography of Illinois.* Chicago: University of Chicago Press, 1921. Designed to be a classroom reference and an authoritative study for the general reader. With demographic information based on the 1910 census.

2312. Ridgway, Robert. *The Ornithology of Illinois . . .* 2 vols. Springfield, Ill.: H. W. Rokker, 1889, 1895. A groundbreaking scientific study.

2313. Ripley, Paula, ed. *The Great Lakes Directory of the Natural Resource Agencies and Organizations.* Produced biennially by the Freshwater Society for the Center for the Great Lakes. Chicago: Center for the Great Lakes, 1984. Illinois, pp. 81-88. Includes both private and public agencies concerned with the environment.

2314. Scarpino, Philip V. *Great River: An Environmental History of the Upper Mississippi, 1890-1950.* Columbia: University of Missouri Press, 1985. The author considers the Upper Mississippi to begin at the convergence of the Missouri and Mississippi rivers, just above St. Louis. A model of environmental history.

2315. Schlunz, Thomas P.; Sutton, Robert Mize; and White, George W. *An Annotated Bibliography of Observations on Illinois Water Resources, 1673-1850.* Water Resources Center Research Report, no. 12. Urbana, Ill: 1967.

2316. Schuberth, Christopher J. *A View of the Past: An Introduction to Illinois Geology.* Springfield: Illinois State Museum, 1986.

2317. Shockel, B. H. "Settlement and Development of the Lead and Zinc Mining Region with Special Emphasis upon Jo Daviess County, Illinois." *Mississippi Valley Historical Review* 4 (1917-18): 169-92. Effects of topography and geology on agriculture, mining, and other business.

2318. Smith, Harry R., and Parmalee, Paul W. *A Distributional Check List of the Birds of Illinois.* Illinois State Museum Popular Science Series, no. 4. Springfield, 1955.

2319. Smith, Walter M., comp. *Stream Flow Data of Illinois.* Springfield: Illinois Division of Waterways, Department of Public Works and Buildings, 1937.

2320. Thornburg, Dennis. "The Canada Goose Flock in Illinois." *Selected Papers in Illinois History, 1982.* Springfield: Illinois State Historical Society, 1984. Pp. 87-91. State and federal management, for conservation and hunting, of the Canada goose.

2321. University of Illinois Department of Geography. *Atlas of Illinois Resources,* secs. 1-6: 1. *Water Resources and Climate,* November 1958; 2. *Mineral Resources,* June 1959; 3. *Forest, Wildlife, and Recreational Resources,* January 1960; 4. *Transportation,* June 1960; 5. *Manpower,* May 1963; 6. *Agriculture in the Illinois Economy,* November 1962. Published by the Division of Industrial Planning and Development of the Department of Registration and Education.

2322. Warner, William E. *Life and Lore of Illinois Wildflowers.* Springfield: Illinois State Museum, 1988.

2323. Wegemann, Carroll H. "Some Notes on River Development in the Vicinity of Danville, Illinois," in *Studies from the Geological Department.* University Studies, vol. 3, no. 2 (January 1909). Urbana, Ill.: University Press.

2324. Westemeier, Ronald L. "The History of Prairie-Chickens and Their Management in Illinois." *Selected Papers in Illinois History, 1983.* Springfield: Illinois State Historical Society, 1985. Pp. 17-27.

2325. Willman, H. B.; Simon, Jack A.; Lynch, Betty M.; and Langenheim, Virginia A., comps. *Bibliography and Index of Illinois Geology through 1965: A Contribution to the Illinois Sesquicentennial Year.* Illinois State Geological Survey Bulletin 92. Urbana, 1968.

2326. Winsor, Roger A. "Environmental Imagery of the Wet Prairie of East Central Illinois, 1820-1920." *Journal of Historical Geography* 13 (October 1987): 375-97.

2327. Winterringer, Glen S., and Lopinot, Alvin C. *Aquatic Plants of Illinois: An Illustrated Manual Including Species Submersed, Floating, and Some of Shallow Waters and Muddy Shores.* Illinois State Museum Popular Science Series, no. 6. Springfield, 1966.

2328. Winterringer, Glen S. *Wild Orchids of Illinois.* Illinois State Museum Popular Science Series, no. 7. Springfield, 1967.

2329. Wise, Daniel L. "Tornadoes of Western Illinois Prior to 1875." *Western Illinois Regional Studies* 4 (1981): 152-62.

2330. Worthen, Amos H. *Geological Survey of Illinois.* 8 vols. in 9 (a separate vol. of vol. 8 consists of plates). Published by authority of the legislature of Illinois, 1866-90. The pioneering scientific study.

E. LIBRARIES AND PUBLISHERS

2331. *The Carnegie Library in Illinois.* Photographs by Raymond Bial. Text by Raymond Bial and Linda LaPuma Bial. Urbana: University of Illinois Press, 1991. Photographs of the eighty-three Carnegie libraries still in existence, with a history of each on a facing page. There are also histories of the twenty-two libraries no longer standing.

2332. Donnelley, Gaylord. *To Be a Good Printer: Our Four Commitments.* Chicago: Lakeside Press, R. R. Donnelley, 1977.

2333. Finkelman, Paul. "Class and Culture in Late Nineteenth-Century Chicago: The Founding of the Newberry Library." *American Studies* 16 (1975): 5-22.

2334. Frye, Lonn. *Carnegie Libraries: Restoration and Expansion.* Springfield: Illinois Historic Preservation Agency, 1993.

2335. Hallwas, John E. "The Illinois State Historical Library: Keeper of Our Cultural Tradition." *Illinois Issues,* vol. 14, no. 5 (May 1988), pp. 16-19.

2336. *Illinois Libraries.* Published monthly (except July and August) since January 1919 by the Illinois State Library and its predecessor organization. Deals primarily with school and public libraries and their concerns, although articles on manuscript, newspaper, archival, and genealogical holdings of Illinois libraries are also published occasionally. Some of general interest are listed herein.

2337. Kogan, Herman. *The Great EB: The Story of the Encyclopaedia Britannica.* Chicago: University of Chicago Press, 1958. Printed in Chicago since 1909, the *Britannica* was purchased by Sears, Roebuck in 1920 and given to the University of Chicago in 1941.

2338. Larson, Cedric A. *Who: Sixty Years of American Eminence; The Story of Who's Who in America.* New York: McDowell, Obolensky, 1958. A publishing history of the Chicago firm first headed by A. N. Marquis.

2339. McMurtrie, Douglas C. "The Contribution of the Pioneer Printers to Illinois History." *Transactions of the Illinois State Historical Society, 1938,* pp. 20-38. Reprint, Springfield: Privately printed, 1939.

2340. Regnery, Henry. *Memoirs of a Dissident Publisher.* New York: Harcourt, Brace, 1979. The native Illinoisan Henry Regnery became an ultra-right wing publisher and here expounds his political views of the problems of the World War II era.

2341. Ruff, Allen M. "Socialist Publishing in Illinois: Charles H. Kerr & Company of Chicago, 1886-1928." *Illinois Historical Journal* 79 (1986): 19-32. As the major left-wing publisher in the nation between 1899 and 1918, the firm helped shape the socialist movement of that era.

2342. Sammons, Wheeler Jr. "Sixty Years of *Who's Who*: Some Notes on the History of an Illinois Institution." *Journal of the Illinois State Historical Society* 51 (1958): 43-58. Sammons was an associate publisher of *Who's Who* and its related biographical dictionaries.

2343. Schwartz, Thomas F. "A Brief History of the Henry Horner Lincoln Collection of the Illinois State Historical Library." *Illinois Historical Journal* 82 (1989): 263-70. The collection consists of books and pamphlets related to Lincoln.

2344. Stern, Madeleine B. "Keen & Cooke: Prairie Publishers." *Journal of the Illinois State Historical Society* 42 (1949): 424-45. History of the Chicago firm founded in 1852 by David B. Cooke.

2345. Steuernagel, Bella, comp. *The Belleville Public Library, 1836-1936: An Historical Sketch.* Belleville, Ill.: The library, 1936.

2346. Taylor, Dorothy Loring. "Olive Beaupré Miller and *My Book House.*" *Illinois Historical Journal* 78 (1985): 273-88. A short history of the beloved collection of classic poetry and tales for children.

2347. _____. *Olive Beaupré Miller and the Book House for Children.* Chicago: Chicago Review Press, 1986.

2348. Waltz, George H. Jr. *The House That Quality Built: A Professional Writer Looks at R. R. Donnelley & Sons Company, Its People, and Their Work.* Chicago: Lakeside Press, R. R. Donnelley, 1957.

2349. Weber, Jessie Palmer, comp. *Alphabetic Catalog of the Books, Manuscripts, Maps, Pictures, and Curios of the Illinois State Historical Library.* Springfield, Ill., 1900. For bibliographic purposes, this publication is considered part of the series *Transactions of the Illinois State Historical Society.*

F. MEDICINE AND SCIENCE

2350. Allen, William H. "Leon Lederman: Nobel Laureate and Illinois' First Science Adviser." *Illinois Issues*, November 1990, p. 15. Former head of the Fermi National Accelerator Laboratory at Batavia, Lederman organized and became chairman of the Governor's Science Advisory Committee.

2351. Barclay, George A. "The Keeley League." *Journal of the Illinois State Historical Society* 57 (1964): 341-65. The league was organized to support recovering alcoholics who had received the Keeley treatment. This article includes the work against alcoholism of James Oughton, Jr., in the 1960s.

2352. Blankmeyer, Helen Van Cleave. "Health Measures in Early Springfield." *Journal of the Illinois State Historical Society* 44 (1951): 323-31. Medical practice, 1820-68.

2353. Bogard, Mary O. "Peoria's Pioneer Druggists, the Farrells, and Farrell's Arabian Liniment." *Pharmacy in History* 24, no. 3 (1982): 99-105.

2354. Bonner, Thomas Neville. *Medicine in Chicago, 1850-1950: A Chapter in the Social and Scientific Development of a City.* Madison, Wis.: American History Research Center, 1957.

2355. Cain, Louis P. *Sanitation Strategy for a Lakefront Metropolis: The Case of Chicago.* DeKalb: Northern Illinois University Press, 1978. A much broader study than the title indicates, this volume opens with a good discussion of the Illinois and Michigan Canal and also includes accounts of the medical problems that once resulted from inadequate water and sewage treatment.

2356. Crellin, John K. *Medical Care in Pioneer Illinois.* Medical Humanities Series. Springfield: The Pearson Museum, Southern Illinois University School of Medicine, 1982. Medical practice to the late 1800s.

2357. Custer, Milo. "Asiatic Cholera in Central Illinois, 1834-1873." *Journal of the Illinois State Historical Society* 23 (1930-31): 113-62.

2358. Davenport, F. Garvin. "Natural Scientists and the Farmers of Illinois, 1865-1900." *Journal of the Illinois State Historical Society* 51 (1958): 357-79. A study of the scientific contributions of the state's early entomologists.

2359. Grob, Gerald N. *Mental Illness and American Society, 1875-1940.* Princeton, N.J.: Princeton University Press, 1983. The author presents a discussion of work done in Illinois under the Board of Public Charities (later the Charities Commission and still later the Department of Public Welfare), especially at Kankakee State Hospital, which opened in 1880.

2360. Hendrickson, Walter B. "Nineteenth-Century Natural History Organizations in Illinois." *Journal of the Illinois State Historical Society* 54 (1961): 246-67.

2361. Himelhoch, Myra Samuels, with Arthur H. Shaffer. "Elizabeth Packard, Nineteenth-Century Crusader for the Rights of Mental Patients." *Journal of American Studies* 13 (1979): 343-75.

2362. Hyde, James Nevins. *Early Medical Chicago: An Historical Sketch of the First Practitioners of Medicine, with the Present Faculties, and Graduates since Their Organization of the Medical Colleges of Chicago.* Fergus' Historical Series, no. 11. Chicago, 1879.

2363. Illinois State Medical Society. *History of Medical Practice in Illinois. Volume I: Preceding 1850*, compiled by Lucius H. Zeuch; . . . *Volume II: 1850-1900*, edited by David J. Davis. Chicago: Illinois State Medical Society, 1927, 1955.

2364. Illinois State Museum. Scientific Papers, vol. 1 (1940)--to date, and Popular Science Series, vol. 1 (1939)--to date. Papers of general interest from these series are listed herein.

2365. Jackson, Julian, and Jackson, Eleanor. *Dentists to the World: Illinois' Influence on the Growth of the Profession.* Chicago: Quadrangle Books, 1964.

2366. Kingery, R. A.; Berg, R. D.; and Schillinger, E. H. *Men and Ideas in Engineering: Twelve Histories from Illinois.* Urbana: Published for the University of Illinois College of Engineering by the University of Illinois Press, 1967.

2367. Kogan, Herman. *A Continuing Marvel: The Story of the Museum of Science and Industry.* Garden City, N.Y.: Doubleday, 1973.

2368. _____. *The Long White Line: The Story of Abbott Laboratories.* New York: Random House, 1963. The author calls this volume "an informal narrative about one of the great pharmaceutical companies of our time."

2369. Reagan, Leslie J. " 'About to Meet Her Maker': Women, Doctors, Dying Declarations, and the State's Investigation of Abortion, Chicago, 1867-1940." *Journal of American History* 77 (1990-91): 1240-64.

2370. Richardson, B. K. *A History of the Illinois Department of Public Health, 1927-1962.* Springfield: State of Illinois, 1963.

2371. Seipp, Conrad. "Organized Medicine and the Public Health Institute of Chicago." *Bulletin of the History of Medicine* 62 (Fall 1988): 429-49.

2372. Thompson, Milton D. *The Illinois State Museum: Historical Sketch and Memoirs.* Springfield: Illinois State Museum Society, 1988. The early collections of the Illinois Natural History Society and the Illinois State Geological Survey formed the nucleus of the State Museum, created by the legislature in 1877.

G. NATIVE AMERICANS

1. Bibliography, Historiography, and Reference Works

2373. *Adventures and Sufferings: The American Indian Captivity Narrative through the Centuries; An Exhibition of Books in the Collections of the St. Louis Mercantile Library Association, A Catalogue and Checklist for an Exhibition, November 1--November 30, 1988.* St. Louis: Mercantile Library Association, 1988. Narratives of Illinoisans Sylvia and Rachel Hall and William Biggs are listed.

2374. Clifton, James A. "Old Northwest Indian Removal, 1825-1855: A Bibliography." Mimeographed. Green Bay, Wis.: The compiler, 1985-- . Periodically updated.

2375. Dockstader, Frederick J. *The American Indian in Graduate Studies: A Bibliography of Theses and Dissertations.* Contributions from the Museum of the American Indian Heye Foundation, vol. 15. New York, 1957.

2376. Driver, Harold E. *Indians of North America*. Chicago: University of Chicago Press, 1961. The author's aim was to offer "a comprehensive comparative description and interpretation of native American culture," and in this he succeeds.

2377. Fenton, William N. *American Indian and White Relations to 1830: Needs & Opportunities for Study: An Essay*. With a bibliography by L. H. Butterfield, Wilcomb E. Washburn, and William N. Fenton. Needs and Opportunities for Study Series. Chapel Hill: University of North Carolina Press, for the Institute of Early American History and Culture, 1957. A concise bibliography of the important standard sources available in 1957. Fenton's historiographical essay is subtitled "A Common Ground for History and Ethnology."

2378. Heard, J. Norman. *Handbook of the American Frontier, Four Centuries of Indian-White Relationships; Volume II: The Northeastern Woodlands*. Metuchen, N.J.: Scarecrow Press, 1990. Includes material on many of the tribes that once lived in Illinois. A useful addition to Hodge's *Handbook* (no. 2380) because of the up-to-date bibliographical citations.

2379. Hirschfelder, Arlene B.; Byler, Mary Gloyne; and Dorris, Michael A. *Guide to Research on North American Indians*. Chicago: American Library Association, 1983. A comprehensive survey of sources, with detailed annotations.

2380. Hodge, Frederick Webb, ed. *Handbook of American Indians North of Mexico*. 2 pts. Smithsonian Institution, Bureau of American Ethnology, *Bulletin 30*. Washington, 1912. Reprint, New York: Pageant Books, 1959.

2381. *Index to Literature on the American Indian* . . . San Francisco: Indian Historian Press. Published annually 1970-73. Includes both periodicals and books issued within the year.

2382. Jacobs, Wilbur R. "Native American History: How It Illuminates Our Past; A Review Article." *American Historical Review* 80 (1975) 595-609.

2383. Johnson, Steven L. *Guide to American Indian Documents in the Congressional Serial Set, 1817-1899*. The Library of American Indian Affairs series. New York: Clearwater Publishing, 1977.

2384. Kappler, Charles J., comp. and ed. *Indian Affairs: Laws and Treaties*. 2 vols. U.S. Congress. Senate. 57th Cong., 1 sess. S. Doc. 452. Washington, 1903.

2385. Litton, Gaston. "The Resources of the National Archives for the Study of the American Indian." *Ethnohistory* 2 (1955): 191-208.

2386. Murdock, George Peter. *Ethnographic Bibliography of North America.* Behavior Sciences Bibliographies. 3d ed., New Haven, Conn.: Human Relations Area Files, 1960. Midwest, pp. 175-89. Within geographic areas, entries are arranged by tribal name. Approximately seven hundred entries for the Midwest area.

2387. Nickerson, Gifford S. *Native North Americans in Doctoral Dissertations, 1971-1975: A Classified and Indexed Research Bibliography.* Council of Planning Libraries, Exchange Bibliography 1232. Monticello, Ill., 1977. There are three indexes to the bibliography: subject, geographic area, and tribes and cultures.

2388. Prucha, Francis Paul. *A Bibliographical Guide to the History of Indian-White Relations in the United States.* A Publication of the Center for the History of the American Indian of the Newberry Library. Chicago: University of Chicago Press, 1977. This guide includes publications issued through 1974--a total of 9,705 entries. Part 1 includes manuscripts in the National Archives, published federal documents, manuscript guides, reference works, etc. Part 2 entries are classified by topic. There is also a good subject index keyed to entry numbers.

2389. _____. *Indian-White Relations in the United States: A Bibliography of Works Published, 1975-1980.* Lincoln: University of Nebraska Press, 1982.

2390. Royce, Charles C., comp. "Indian Land Cessions in the United States." Smithsonian Institution, Bureau of American Ethnology. *Eighteenth Annual Report . . . 1896-97.* 2 pts. Washington, 1901-2. Pt. 2, pp. 521-964. With maps.

2391. Schoolcraft, Henry R. *Information Respecting the History, Condition, and Prospects of the Indian Tribes of the United States, Collected and Prepared under the Direction of the Bureau of Indian Affairs per Act of Congress of March 3d 1847.* 6 vols. Philadelphia: Lippincott, Grambo, 1852-57. An index, compiled by Frances S. Nichols, is *Bulletin 152* of the Bureau of American Ethnology. Washington: Government Printing Office, 1954. The index has many entries for the tribes that lived in Illinois.

2392. Smithsonian Institution, Bureau of American Ethnology. *Annual Reports.* Many studies from the *Reports* that relate to the Indians of Illinois are listed separately in this volume. The *Forty-eighth Annual Report . . . 1930-31* contains the "General Index, Annual Reports of the Bureau of American Ethnology, Vols. 1 to 48 (1879 to 1931)," compiled by Biren Bonnerjea. Pp. 25-1220.

2393. _____. *Bulletin.* Relevant titles from the series are listed separately herein. A complete list of the 199 *Bulletin* titles (together with an index to titles and authors' names) is in *Bulletin 200.* Washington, 1971. A comprehensive general index (by Biren Bonnerjea) to the *Bulletin*, nos. 1-100, is no. 178. Washington, 1963.

2394. Sturtevant, William C., ed. *Handbook of North American Indians.* 20 vols. projected. Washington: Smithsonian Institution, 1978-- . Designed as a broader replacement of Hodge, q.v. Does not have Hodge's easy-to-use dictionary arrangement of entries, nor does it have, as of volume 15, Hodge's useful list of synonymies; those for individual tribes are given at the end of the tribal history. Accounts of tribes that lived in Illinois are in volume 15 (1978). Volumes have not appeared in numerical order. Volumes 18 and 19 are a biographical dictionary in which there are biographies of many Native Americans from the northeastern region, which includes Illinois.

2395. Swanton, John R. *The Indian Tribes of North America.* Smithsonian Institution, Bureau of American Ethnology, *Bulletin 145.* Washington, 1952. A listing of tribes by state and country, with brief tribal histories and population figures.

2. Tribal Groups

a. In General

2396. Atwater, Caleb. *Remarks Made on a Tour to Prairie du Chien, Thence to Washington City, in 1829.* Columbus, Ohio: Jenkins & Grover, 1831. Describes travel up the Mississippi River, but the volume is especially valuable for its descriptions of Indians and Indian villages and the 1829 treaty councils at Prairie du Chien, Wisconsin.

2397. Barge, William D. *Early Lee County, Being Some Chapters in the History of the Early Days in Lee County, Illinois.* Chicago: Barnard & Miller, 1918. The first half of the book deals primarily with the fur traders and their relations with the Indians of north-central Illinois.

2398. Beckwith, Hiram W. *The Illinois and Indiana Indians.* Fergus' Historical Series, no. 27. Chicago, 1884.

2399. Benton, Colbee Chamberlain. *A Visitor to Chicago in Indian Days: "Journal to the 'Far-off West.' "* Edited by Paul McClelland Angle and James R. Getz. Chicago: Caxton Club, 1957. On his 1833 trip from Vermont to the Midwest, Benton visited Indian villages of northern Illinois and Indiana and southern Wisconsin.

2400. Blair, Emma Helen, ed. *The Indian Tribes of the Upper Mississippi Valley and Region of the Great Lakes . . .* 2 vols. Cleveland: Arthur H. Clark, 1911-12. Volume 2 contains an 1827 report on the Sauk and Fox by agent Thomas Forsyth and an 1820 report on the same tribes by Maj. Morrill Marston of Fort Armstrong. Appendixes contain short reports on the Potawatomi and Winnebago by twentieth-century observers.

2401. Bushnell, David I. Jr. *Villages of the Algonquian, Siouan, and Caddoan Tribes West of the Mississippi.* Smithsonian Institution, Bureau of American Ethnology, *Bulletin 77.* Washington, 1922. Discusses the Sauk and Fox, Illinois, Delaware, and Shawnee in the state of Illinois as well as west of the Mississippi. Pp. 37-43.

2402. Catlin, George. *Letters and Notes on the Manners, Customs, and Condition of the North American Indians, Written during Eight Years' Travel amongst the Wildest Tribes of Indians in North America in 1832, 33, 34, 35, 36, 37, 38, and 39 . . .* 2 vols. 2d ed., London: The author, 1841. Catlin describes the Indians he met and sketched, including many who were living, or had lived, in Illinois. A heavily edited, condensed one-volume version of *Letters and Notes* (Michael Macdonald Mooney, ed.; New York: Clarkson N. Potter, 1975) is useful for background information on Catlin and for the index.

2403. Caton, John Dean. *The Last of the Illinois, and a Sketch of the Pottawatomies: Read before the Chicago Historical Society, December 13, 1870.* Fergus' Historical Series, no. 3. Chicago: Fergus Printing, 1876.

2404. Chouteau, Auguste. "Notes of Auguste Chouteau on Boundaries of Various Indian Nations." Edited by Stella M. Drumm and Grant Foreman. Missouri Historical Society's *Glimpses of the Past* 7, nos. 9-12 (October-December 1940): 119-40. Chouteau was one of the commissioners who negotiated the 1815 treaties at Portage des Sioux, Missouri, with the various tribes living in Illinois. The original copy of this report, dated 21 February 1816, is in the National Archives, Records of the Department of the Interior, Office of

Indian Affairs, Ancient and Miscellaneous Surveys, volume 4. Chouteau discusses tribal land claims and presents brief histories of the tribes.

2405. Drake, Samuel G. *The Aboriginal Races of North America.* 15th ed., rev., New York: Hurst, 1880. Pages 637-78 are concerned with the Sauk and Fox and Winnebago, particularly the Black Hawk War of 1832 and the trip of Sauk and Fox prisoners to the East Coast in 1833.

2406. Ewers, John C. *George Catlin, Painter of Indians of the West.* Washington: Government Printing Office, 1957. Reprinted from the 1955 Annual Report of the Smithsonian Institution. Especially valuable for its catalog of the Catlin paintings in the National Museum.

2407. Fisher, Robert L. "The Treaties of Portage des Sioux." *Mississippi Valley Historical Review* 19 (1932-33): 495-508. The treaties were negotiated in 1815 to make peace with various tribes after the Treaty of Ghent. Despite stereotypical descriptions of the Indians, Fisher presents graphic accounts of calling the tribes to council and of the councils themselves. He ignores evidence available in sources cited by him that the Sauk and Fox had been threatened by British agents if they made peace in 1815.

2408. Foreman, Grant. "Illinois and Her Indians." *Transactions of the Illinois State Historical Society, 1939*, pp. 67-111. Despite a few minor errors, a good brief history.

2409. _____. *The Last Trek of the Indians.* Chicago: University of Chicago Press, 1946. A comprehensive index guides the reader to the names of tribes that once lived in Illinois and to accounts of their removal from the state.

2410. "Indian Affairs of the Iowa Region, 1827-1830." *Annals of Iowa* 3d ser. 3 (1927-28): 25-42. Letters from agents Joseph M. Street and Thomas Forsyth concern the relations between the various tribes in the Iowa-Illinois-Wisconsin area. The original letters are in the National Archives.

2411. *Indians of Illinois and Northwestern Indiana.* New York: Garland, 1974. Contains two reports presented before the Indian Claims Commission: "Anthropological Report on the Ottawa, Chippewa, and Potawatomi Indians," by Erminie Wheeler-Voegelin, and "Report on the Kickapoo, Illinois, and Potawatomi Indians," by David B. Stout.

2412. *Indians of Northeastern Illinois.* New York: Garland, 1974. This volume contains two reports presented to the United States Indian Claims Commission:

"Anthropological Report on the Chippewa, Ottawa, and Potawatomi Indians in Northeastern Illinois," by Erminie Wheeler-Voegelin and Remedios Wycoco-Moore, and "The Identity of the Mascoutens," by David A. Baerreis.

2413. Jablow, Joseph. *Indians of Illinois and Indiana: Illinois, Kickapoo, and Potawatomi Indians.* New York: Garland, 1974. This work was Petitioners' Exhibit 133, Docket 313, 315 et al. before the Indian Claims Commission.

2414. Kinietz, W. Vernon. *The Indians of the Western Great Lakes, 1615-1760.* University of Michigan Museum of Anthropology, Occasional Contributions, no. 10. Ann Arbor, 1940. Detailed descriptions of the manners and customs of the various tribes, drawn from primary sources.

2415. McKenney, Thomas L., and Hall, James. *The Indian Tribes of North America with Biographical Sketches and Anecdotes of the Principal Chiefs.* 3 vols. 1836-44. New ed., edited by Frederick Webb Hodge, Edinburgh: John Grant, 1933-34. The first edition has a slightly different title.

2416. Matson, Nehemiah. *French and Indians of Illinois River.* Princeton, Ill.: Republican Job Printing, 1874. The author also discusses the War of 1812 in Illinois and settlers of the early statehood period.

2417. _____. *Reminiscences of Bureau County [Illinois], in Two Parts.* Princeton, Ill.: Republican Book & Job Office, 1872. The book is concerned mainly with Indians, early traders, and the Black Hawk War. Anecdotal and unannotated. Despite its many factual errors, still useful.

2418. *The North American Indians: 1950 Distribution of Descendants of the Aboriginal Population of Alaska, Canada, and the United States.* Map prepared under the direction of Sol Tax. Chicago: University of Chicago Department of Anthropology, 1960.

2419. Ritzenthaler, Robert E., and Ritzenthaler, Pat. *The Woodland Indians of the Western Great Lakes.* Garden City, N.Y.: Published for the American Museum of Natural History by the Natural History Press, 1970. 2d ed., Milwaukee Public Museum, 1983.

2420. Tanner, Helen Hornbeck, ed. *Atlas of Great Lakes Indian History.* Norman: University of Oklahoma Press, for the Newberry Library, 1987. Civilization of the American Indian series, vol. 174. The thirty-three maps in this volume are based on prodigious research by Tanner and her staff into more than fifteen hundred Indian villages. Each map illustrates Indian movements in the area. A bibliography and historical narrative accompany each map.

2421. Temple, Wayne C. *Indian Villages of the Illinois Country: Historic Tribes.* Illinois State Museum, Scientific Papers, vol. 2, pt. 2. Springfield: Illinois State Museum, 1958. Companion volume to Sara Jones Tucker's portfolio of maps, this was a pioneering study.

2422. Tucker, Sara Jones. *Indian Villages of the Illinois Country: Atlas.* Illinois State Museum, Scientific Papers, vol. 2, pt. 1. Springfield: Illinois State Museum, 1942. Fifty-four maps dated from 1671 to 1830.

2423. Whitney, Ellen M. "Indian History and the Indians of Illinois." *Journal of the Illinois State Historical Society* 69 (1976): 139-46. A brief account of Illinois' principal historic tribes and their removal from the state, together with comments about some of the better histories of those tribes.

b. Illinois and Illinois Subtribes

2424. Blasingham, Emily J. "The Depopulation of the Illinois Indians." *Ethnohistory* 3 (1956): 193-224 and 361-412. Adapted from "The Illinois Indians, 1634-1800: A Study in Depopulation." Thesis, Indiana University, 1956.

2425. Brewster, Paul G. "The Piasa Bird: A Legend of the Illini." *Hoosier Folklore* 8 (1949): 83-86.

2426. Ellis, Richard N., and Steen, Charlie R., eds. "An Indian Delegation in France, 1725." Translated by Charlie R. Steen. *Journal of the Illinois State Historical Society* 67 (1974): 385-405. This report on the visit of the four chiefs of the Illinois tribe, together with representatives of the Oto, Osage, and Missouri tribes, twenty-two in all, first appeared in the December 1725 issue of *Mercure de France.*

2427. Faye, Stanley. "Illinois Indians on the Lower Mississippi, 1771-1782." *Journal of the Illinois State Historical Society* 35 (1942): 57-72. Report on the tribe of Illinois that moved first to Kaskaskia and then to Arkansas.

2428. Garraghan, Gilbert Joseph. "The Great Illinois Village: A Topographical Problem." *Mid-America* 3 n.s. (1931-32): 141-51.

2429. Good, Mary Elizabeth. *Guebert Site: An 18th Century Historic Kaskaskia Indian Village in Randolph County, Illinois.* Central States Archaeological Societies Memoir, no. 2. Wood River?, Ill., 1972. The first third of this volume deals with the historical record and the final two thirds with the archaeological record.

2430. Hauser, Raymond E. "The *Berdache* and the Illinois Indian Tribe during the Last Half of the Seventeenth Century." *Ethnohistory* 37 (1990): 45-65.

2431. _____. "The Fox Raid of 1752: Defensive Warfare and the Decline of the Illinois Indian Tribe." *Illinois Historical Journal* 86 (1993): 210-24. Shows the devastating effects of French involvement in intertribal affairs.

2432. _____. "The Illinois Indian Tribe: From Autonomy and Self-Sufficiency to Dependency and Depopulation." *Journal of the Illinois State Historical Society* 69 (1976): 127-38. A succinct but scholarly history of the Illinois tribe that lays to rest many legends. Adapted from the author's 1973 Ph.D. dissertation, Northern Illinois University.

2433. _____. "Warfare and the Illinois Indian Tribe during the Seventeenth Century: An Exercise in Ethnohistory." *Old Northwest* 10 (1984-85): 367-87.

2434. Hunt, George T. *The Wars of the Iroquois: A Study in Intertribal Trade Relations.* Madison: University of Wisconsin Press, 1940. Contains substantial information about the wars of the Illinois and Iroquois.

2435. Scott, James. *The Illinois Nation: A History of the Illinois Nation of Indians from Their Discovery to the Present Day.* 2 pts. Streator, Ill., 1973.

2436. Throop, Addison J. *The Last Village of the Kaskaskia Indians, 1700-1832* . . . East St. Louis, Ill.: Call Printing, 1953.

c. Kickapoo

2437. Custer, Milo. "Masheena." *Transactions of the Illinois State Historical Society, 1911,* pp. 115-21. Sketch of the Kickapoo chief who once lived in McLean County.

2438. Gibson, Arrell Morgan. *The Kickapoos: Lords of the Middle Border.* Norman: University of Oklahoma Press, 1963.

2439. Herring, Joseph B. *Kenekuk, the Kickapoo Prophet.* Lawrence: University Press of Kansas, 1988. Contains the history of the Vermillion River Kickapoo who lived in western Indiana and eastern Illinois in the early nineteenth century.

2440. _____. "The Vermillion Kickapoos of Illinois: The Prophet Kenekuk's Peaceful Resistance to Indian Removal, 1819-1833." *Selected Papers in Illinois History, 1983.* Springfield: Illinois State Historical Society, 1985. Pp. 28-38.

2441. Mooney, James. "The Ghost-Dance Religion and the Sioux Outbreak of 1830." Smithsonian Institution, Bureau of American Ethnology. *Fourteenth Annual Report . . . 1892-93.* 2 pts. Washington, 1896. Chapter 5 is titled "Känakûk and Minor Prophets."

2442. Nielsen, George R. *The Kickapoo People.* Phoenix, Ariz.: Indian Tribal Series, 1975.

2443. Snider, Brainerd C. *Story of the Kickapoos.* Lincoln, Ill.: Lincoln Press, 1951. An account of the Kickapoo Indians in Logan County.

> d. Ottawa, Chippewa, and Potawatomi

2444. Clifton, James A. "Chicago Was Theirs." *Chicago History* 1 n.s., no. 1 (1970): 4-17. Traces the history of the Prairie Potawatomi to 1970, noting the descendants of famous leaders who then lived in Kansas.

2445. _____. "Merchant, Soldier, Broker, Chief: A Corrected Obituary of Captain Billy Caldwell." *Journal of the Illinois State Historical Society* 71 (1978): 185-210. Caldwell became prominent among the Potawatomi of Michigan, Indiana, Illinois, and Iowa, but was in fact the son of a Mohawk woman and a British ranger captain. The author shows how Billy Caldwell came to accept the role of an "alien-sponsored manager of a tribal society."

2446. _____. "Personal and Ethnic Identity on the Great Lakes Frontier: The Case of Billy Caldwell, Anglo-Canadian." *Ethnohistory* 25 (Winter 1978): 69-94. Caldwell spent a major portion of his adult life in Chicago, where he was associated with the Potawatomi and often incorrectly identified as a member of that tribe.

2447. _____. *A Place of Refuge for All Time: Migration of the American Potawatomi into Upper Canada, 1830 to 1850.* Canadian Ethnology Service

Paper, no. 26. Ottawa: National Museums of Canada, 1975. Has information on Potawatomi removal from Illinois and some of the prominent tribal leaders.

2448. _____. "Potawatomi Leadership Roles: On *Okama* and Other Influential Personages." *Proceedings of the 1974 Algonquian Conference, Mercury Series,* 1974.

2449. _____. *The Prairie People: Continuity and Change in Potawatomi Indian Culture, 1665-1965.* Lawrence: Regents Press of Kansas, 1977. The author explains French, British, Canadian, and United States Indian policies and shows how those policies affected the Potawatomi; he also discusses the changing culture of the tribe. A broad-ranging and important study.

2450. _____. "Simon Pokagon's Sandbar: Potawatomi Claims to Chicago's Lakefront." *Michigan History* 71 (September-October 1987): 12-17.

2451. Conway, Thomas G. "Potawatomi Politics." *Journal of the Illinois State Historical Society* 65 (1972): 395-418.

2452. Davis, Charles G. "The Indian Boundary Line under the Treaty of August 24, 1816." *Journal of the Illinois State Historical Society* 28, no. 1 (April 1935): 26-48. The line (from the southern tip of Lake Michigan to the Mississippi), negotiated with the Ottawa, Potawatomi, and Chippewa, was the northern boundary of land claimed by those tribes in Illinois and was within an earlier cession of land by the Sauk and Fox.

2453. Dean, Seth. "Wabaunsee, the Indian Chief (A Fragment)." *Annals of Iowa* 3d ser. 3 (1927-28): 3-23.

2454. Densmore, Frances. *Chippewa Customs.* Smithsonian Institution, Bureau of American Ethnology, *Bulletin 86.* Washington, 1929.

2455. Dundes, Alan. "Study of Folklore in Literature and Culture: Identification and Interpretation." *Journal of American Folklore* 78 (April 1965): 136-42. The etymology of a Potawatomi folk tale.

2456. Edmunds, Russell David. "The Illinois River Potawatomi in the War of 1812." *Journal of the Illinois State Historical Society* 62 (1969): 341-62.

2457. _____. *Kinsmen through Time: An Annotated Bibliography of Potawatomi History.* Native American Bibliography Series, no. 12. Metuchen, N.J.: Scarecrow Press, 1987. A good index for the 1,092 entries.

2458. _____. *The Potawatomis, Keepers of the Fire.* Civilization of the American Indian series, vol. 145. Norman: University of Oklahoma Press, 1978.

2459. _____. "Potawatomis in the Platte Country: An Indian Removal Incomplete." *Missouri Historical Review* 68 (1973-74): 375-92. Removal of Ottawa, Chippewa, and Potawatomi from the Chicago area to Missouri, Iowa, and Kansas.

2460. _____. "The Prairie Potawatomi Removal of 1833." *Indiana Magazine of History* 68 (1972): 240-53.

2461. Gerwing, Anselm. "The Chicago Indian Treaty of 1833." *Journal of the Illinois State Historical Society* 57 (1964): 117-42. Excellent account of the treaty proceedings by which title to the last Indian-held land in Illinois was extinguished; biographical information for some of the Potawatomi leaders has been superseded by later research.

2462. Landes, Ruth. *The Prairie Potawatomi: Tradition and Ritual in the Twentieth Century.* Madison: University of Wisconsin Press, 1970. Although the tribe no longer lived in Illinois in the twentieth century, this study provides valuable insights into tribal life of an earlier era.

2463. Matson, Nehemiah. "Sketch of Shau-be-na, a Pottawattomi Chief." *Collections of the State Historical Society of Wisconsin* 7 (1876): 415-21.

2464. Meyer, Alfred Herman. "Circulation and Settlement Patterns of the Calumet Region of Northwest Indiana and Northeast Illinois: The First State of Occupance--the Pottawatomie and the Fur Trader, 1830." *Annals of the Association of American Geographers* 44 (1954): 245-74. The author shows how the environment shaped Indian trails and placement of villages.

2465. Polke, William? " 'Journal Of an Emigrating Party of Pottawattomie Indians, From Twin Lakes, in Marshall County, Ia. [Indiana], to Their Homes on the Osage River in the We[stern] Territory . . .' " *Indiana Magazine of History* 21 (1925): 315-36. Between 16 September and 10 October 1838 the emigrating Indians traveled across Illinois from Danville to Quincy. Excellent descriptions of travel conditions and towns along the route. The original journal is in the Fort Wayne, Indiana, Public Library.

2466. Quaife, Milo Milton, ed. "Documents: The Chicago Treaty of 1833." *Wisconsin Magazine of History* 1 (1917-18): 287-303. Charges about improper influence by the treaty negotiators, especially Governor George B. Porter, and Porter's response.

2467. Schmidt, Royal J. *The Potawatomi Indians of Du Page County.* Wheaton: Du Page County Historical Society, 1974.

2468. Schofield, William W. *The Trail of the Potawatomi.* Lockport, Ill.: Will County Historical Society, 1990.

2469. Skinner, Alanson. *The Mascoutens or Prairie Potawatomi Indians.* 3 pts. Bulletin of the Public Museum of the City of Milwaukee, vol. 6, nos. 1-3 (1924-27). Reprint, Westport, Conn.: Greenwood, 1970.

2470. Temple, Wayne C. *Shabbona, Friend of the Whites.* Illinois State Museum Reports of Investigations, no. 6 (Springfield, 1957).

2471. Walters, Alta P. "Shabonee." *Journal of the Illinois State Historical Society* 17 (1924-25): 381-97. Reprints sketches of Shabonee and Billy Caldwell, written by William Hickling, pages 387-96. The Hickling article appeared originally in Fergus' Historical Series, no. 10. Chicago, 1877.

2472. Winger, Otho. *The Potawatomi Indians.* Elgin, Ill.: Elgin Press, 1939.

2473. Zeman, Alice Fitch. *Wabansi: Fiend or Friend?* Henry, Ill.: M. and D. Printers, 1991. An interesting study of the Potawatomi leader.

   e. Sauk and Fox (Musquakies)

2474. Black Hawk. *Ma-Ka-Tai-Me-She-Kia-Kiak, Black Hawk: An Autobiography.* Edited by Donald Jackson. Urbana: University of Illinois Press, 1955. The tenth, and best, edition of the *Autobiography*, which first appeared in 1833. As dictated to the Rock Island Indian Agency interpreter, Antoine Le Claire, the account is an authentic historical document.

2475. Cole, Cyrenus. *I Am a Man: The Indian Black Hawk.* Iowa City: State Historical Society of Iowa, 1938.

2476. Faye, Stanley. "The Foxes' Fort--1730." *Journal of the Illinois State Historical Society* 28, no. 3 (October 1935): 123-63. Detailed account of French-Indian affairs and of the battle against the Foxes on 9 September 1730. Faye's identification of the fort site has been superseded by that of Joseph L. Peyser, q.v.

2477. Fulton, A. R. *The Red Men of Iowa: Being a History of the Various Aboriginal Tribes Whose Homes Were in Iowa; Sketches of Chiefs, Traditions, Indian Hostilities, Incidents and Reminiscences . . .* Des Moines, Iowa: Mills, 1882. A rich source of information about the Sauk and Fox.

2478. Gallaher, Ruth A. "Indian Agents in Iowa; I, Agents among the Sacs and Foxes." *Iowa Journal of History and Politics* 14 (1916): 348-94. Contains substantial information about those tribes in Illinois.

2479. Hagan, William T. *The Sac and Fox Indians.* The Civilization of the American Indian Series, vol. 48. Norman: University of Oklahoma Press, 1958. A popular history that is more useful for recent events than for the tribes' years in Illinois.

2480. Hallwas, John E. "Black Hawk: A Reassessment." *Annals of Iowa* 45 (1979-81): 599-619.

2481. Harrington, M. R. *Sacred Bundles of the Sac and Fox Indians.* University of Pennsylvania, University Museum of Anthropological Publications, vol. 4, no. 2. Philadelphia, 1914. Reprint, New York: AMS Press, 1983.

2482. Hauberg, John H. "Black Hawk's Home Country." *Transactions of the Illinois State Historical Society, 1914,* pp. 113-21. Descriptions of Saukenuk on Rock River.

2483. _____. "Black Hawk's Mississippi: From Rock River to the Bad Axe." *Journal of the Illinois State Historical Society* 22 (1929-30): 93-163. In 1928 the author cruised the Mississippi, visiting sites associated with Black Hawk and Sauk and Fox history.

2484. Hoffmann, M. M. *Antique Dubuque, 1673-1833.* Dubuque, Iowa: Telegraph-Herald Press, 1930. Information, from primary sources, about Sauk and Fox Indians on both sides of the Mississippi.

2485. Irving, Washington. *The Western Journals of Washington Irving.* Edited by John Francis McDermott. American Exploration and Travel, no. 8. Norman: University of Oklahoma Press, 1944. On 14 September 1832 Irving visited Jefferson Barracks, Missouri, just below St. Louis. He reported that the Sauk and Fox prisoners being held there were "all chained arms & ankles with cannon, but are allowed to walk about escorted by soldiers."

2486. Jackson, Donald. "Black Hawk--The Man and His Times." *Palimpsest* 43 (1962): 65-79.

2487. Jones, William. *Ethnography of the Fox Indians.* Edited by Margaret Welpley Fisher. Smithsonian Institution, Bureau of American Ethnology, *Bulletin 125.* Washington, 1939.

2488. _____. *Fox Texts.* Publications of the American Ethnology Society, vol. 1. Leyden, Netherlands: E.J. Brill, 1907. Reprint, New York: AMS Press, 1974.

2489. _____. "Notes on the Fox Indians." *Journal of American Folklore* 24 (1911): 209-37. Folklore and manners and customs.

2490. Josephy, Alvin M. Jr. *The Patriot Chiefs: A Chronicle of American Indian Leadership.* New York: Viking, 1961. Chapter 7 is titled "The Rivalry of Black Hawk and Keokuk."

2491. Metcalf, P. Richard. "Who Should Rule at Home? Native American Politics and Indian-White Relations." *Journal of American History* 61 (1974-75): 651-65. The example studied most intensively is that of the Sauk leaders Keokuk and Black Hawk. A more comprehensive presentation of Sauk and Fox political and social structure is given by Anthony Wallace; see no. 772.

2492. Michelson, Truman. Five papers by this author are published in Smithsonian Institution, Bureau of American Ethnology. *Fortieth Annual Report . . . 1918-1919.* Washington, 1925. Pp. 23-658. The papers are titled "The Mythical Origin of the White Buffalo Dance of the Fox Indians," "The Autobiography of a Fox Indian Woman," "Notes on Fox Mortuary Customs and Beliefs," "Notes on the Fox Society Known as 'Those Who Worship the Little Spotted Buffalo,' " and "The Traditional Origin of the Fox Society Known as 'The Singing Around Rite.' "

2493. _____. *Contributions to Fox Ethnology.* Smithsonian Institution, Bureau of American Ethnology, *Bulletin 85.* Washington, 1927.

2494. _____. *Contributions to Fox Ethnology--II.* Smithsonian Institution, Bureau of American Ethnology, *Bulletin 95.* Washington, 1930.

2495. _____. *Fox Miscellany.* Smithsonian Institution, Bureau of American Ethnology, *Bulletin 114.* Washington, 1937.

2496. _____. *Notes on the Fox Wâpanowiweni.* Smithsonian Institution, Bureau of American Ethnology, *Bulletin 105.* Washington, 1932.

2497. _____. *Observations on the Thunder Dance of the Bear Gens of the Fox Indians.* Smithsonian Institution, Bureau of American Ethnology, *Bulletin 89.* Washington, 1929.

2498. _____. *The Owl Sacred Pack of the Fox Indians.* Smithsonian Institution, Bureau of American Ethnology, *Bulletin 72.* Washington, 1921.

2499. _____. "What Happened to Green Bear Who Was Blessed with a Sacred Pack." Anthropological Paper no. 4 in Smithsonian Institution, Bureau of American Ethnology, *Bulletin 119.* Washington, 1938.

2500. Owen, Mary Alicia. *Folk-lore of the Musquakie Indians of North America . . .* Folk-lore Society Publications, vol. 51. London, 1904.

2501. Peyser, Joseph L. "The 1730 Fox Fort: A Recently Discovered Map Throws New Light on Its Siege and Location." *Journal of the Illinois State Historical Society* 73 (1980): 201-13. The map, discovered at the Archives Nationales in Paris, helps to pinpoint the site of one of the "major Indian battles in North America," the author asserts.

2502. _____. "The 1730 Siege of the Foxes: Two Maps by Canadian Participants Provide Additional Information on the Fort and Its Location." *Illinois Historical Journal* 80 (1987): 147-54. The maps help to limit the possible location of a month-long siege against the Foxes by a large army of Indians led by a much smaller group of Frenchmen.

2503. Rebok, Horace M. "The Last of the Mus-Qua-Kies." *Iowa Historical Record* 16-18 (1900-1902): 305-35. Traces the history of the tribe from the late seventeenth century to 1867.

2504. Schmitz, Neil. "Captive Utterance: Black Hawk and Indian Irony." *Arizona Quarterly* 48, no. 4 (Winter 1992): 1-18. A critical analysis of Black Hawk's autobiography.

2505. Skinner, Alanson. *Observations on the Ethnology of the Sauk Indians.* 3 pts. Bulletin of the Public Museum of the City of Milwaukee, vol. 5, nos. 1-3

(1923-25). Each part occupies the entire number. Reprint, Westport, Conn.: Greenwood, 1970.

2506. Snyder, John Francis. "The Burial and Resurrection of Black Hawk." *Journal of the Illinois State Historical Society* 4 (1911-12): 47-56.

2507. Steward, John F. *Lost Maramech and Earliest Chicago: A History of the Foxes and of Their Downfall near the Great Village of Maramech* . . . Chicago: Fleming H. Revell, 1903. The attack on the Fox Indians took place in 1730. For more recent discoveries on the exact sites, see Joseph L. Peyser (nos. 2501 and 2502).

f. Others

2508. Caldwell, Norman Ward. "Shawneetown: A Chapter in the Indian History of Illinois." *Journal of the Illinois State Historical Society* 32 (1939): 193-205. Shawnee removal from Pennsylvania to Illinois in 1745 and their departure four years later.

2509. Diedrich, Mark, comp. *Winnebago Oratory: Great Moments in the Recorded Speech of the Hochungra, 1742-1887.* Rochester, Minn.: Coyote Books, 1991. Historical narrative by the compiler connects the extracts of recorded oratory, some of which concerns Winnebago affairs in Illinois.

2510. Radin, Paul. "The Winnebago Tribe." Smithsonian Institution, Bureau of American Ethnology, *Thirty-seventh Annual Report*, 1915-1916. Washington, 1923. Pp. 35-550. Reprint (Bison Book), Lincoln: University of Nebraska Press, 1970.

2511. Zanger, Martin. "Conflicting Concepts of Justice: A Winnebago Murder Trial on the Illinois Frontier." *Journal of the Illinois State Historical Society* 73 (1980): 263-76. Two Winnebago who had killed two unarmed soldiers near Fort Armstrong in 1820 were surrendered by the tribe and held in jail for a year before trial in St. Clair County. They were convicted and sentenced to hang, but one died in jail before the hanging.

3. United States Indian Policy

The following titles interpret Indian policy as it related to Illinois.

2512. Abel, Annie Heloise. "The History of Events Resulting in Indian Consolidation West of the Mississippi River." *Annual Report of the American Historical Association for the Year 1906.* Vol. 1 (Washington: Government Printing Office, 1908), pp. 233-438.

2513. Anson, Bert. "Variations of the Indian Conflict: The Effects of the Emigrant Indian Removal Policy, 1830-1854." *Missouri Historical Review* 59 (1964-65): 64-89.

2514. Clifton, James A. "Escape, Evasion, and Eviction: Adaptive Responses of the Indians of the Old Northwest to the Jacksonian Removal Policy in the 1830s." Mimeographed. 1980. Draft of a paper for the Conference on the American Indian and the Jacksonian Era: The Impact of Removal, 29 February-- 1 March 1980, Middle Tennessee State University, Murfreesboro.

2515. _____. "Trial by History: A Perspective on the Indian Removal Policy in the Old Northwest." Mimeographed. 1980. Expanded version of a paper written for the Conference on the American Indian, Texas Tech University, 21 April 1980.

2516. *Federal Indian Law.* New York: Association of American Indian Affairs, 1958. An updating and revision through 1956 of Felix S. Cohen's *Handbook of Federal Indian Law*, 1940. Also contains court decisions on federal Indian laws.

2517. Gallaher, Ruth A. "The Indian Agent in the United States before 1850." *Iowa Journal of History and Politics* 14 (1916): 3-55.

2518. Grover, Frank R. "Indian Treaties Affecting Lands in the Present State of Illinois." *Journal of the Illinois State Historical Society* 8 (1915-16): 379-419.

2519. Horsman, Reginald. *Expansion and American Indian Policy, 1783-1812.* East Lansing: Michigan State University Press, 1967.

2520. Matousek, Ladislav. "Old Indian Boundary Lines in Illinois." *Illinois Libraries* 48 (1966): 454-62.

2521. Prucha, Francis Paul. *American Indian Policy in the Formative Years: The Indian Trade and Intercourse Acts, 1790-1834.* Cambridge, Mass.: Harvard University Press, 1962.

2522. _____. "Andrew Jackson's Indian Policy: A Reassessment." *Journal of American History* 56 (1969-70): 527-39.

2523. _____, ed. *Documents of United States Indian Policy.* Lincoln: University of Nebraska Press, 1975. 2d ed., expanded, 1990.

2524. _____. *The Great Father: The United States Government and the American Indians.* 2 vols. Lincoln: University of Nebraska Press, 1984. A comprehensive history with an invaluable bibliography and index.

2525. _____. *Indian Policy in the United States: Historical Essays.* Lincoln: University of Nebraska Press, 1981.

2526. Satz, Ronald N. *American Indian Policy in the Jacksonian Era.* Lincoln: University of Nebraska Press, 1975.

2527. Viola, Herman J. *Diplomats in Buckskins: A History of Indian Delegations in Washington City.* Washington: Smithsonian Institution Press, 1981.

2528. Washburn, Wilcomb E. *The American Indian and the United States: A Documentary History.* 4 vols. New York: Random House, 1973. This valuable set includes treaties, reports of Indian commissioners, and congressional debates.

4. Miscellany

2529. Belting, Natalia Maree. "The Native American as Myth and Fact." *Journal of the Illinois State Historical Society* 69 (1976): 119-26. The author discusses French, British, and American attitudes towards the Indian, especially as illustrated by examples from Illinois and the Old Northwest. The facts of Native American society and history bear little resemblance to our commonplace myths.

2530. Brinton, Daniel G. *The Myths of the New World: A Treatise on the Symbolism and Mythology of the Red Race of America.* New York: Leypoldt & Holt, 1868.

2531. Brunson, Alfred. "Memoir of Thomas Pendleton Burnett." *Second Annual Report and Collections of the State Historical Society of Wisconsin for the Year 1855.* Pp. 233-325. Burnett was Indian subagent at Prairie du Chien, Wisconsin, and the letters and papers sent and received by him (printed as part of the Memoir) are informative about the Black Hawk War and the affairs of the Sioux and Winnebago attached to the agency.

2532. Covington, James W. "The Indian Liquor Trade at Peoria, 1824." *Journal of the Illinois State Historical Society* 46 (1953): 142-50. Subagent Thomas Forsyth's letters and reports on the Peoria Subagency and private sales of liquor.

2533. Mucha, Janusz. "From Prairie to the City: Transformation of Chicago's American Indian Community." *Urban Anthropology* 12 (Fall-Winter 1983): 337-71.

2534. Neog, Prafulla; Woods, Richard G.; and Harkins, Arthur M. *Chicago Indians: The Effects of Urban Migration.* The National Study of Indian Education. Minneapolis: Training Center for Community Programs, 1970.

2535. Peithmann, Irvin M. *Indians of Southern Illinois.* Springfield, Ill.: Charles C. Thomas, 1964. An archaeologist, the author reconstructs the prehistoric life of early Indians and carries the story through their removal from the state.

2536. Quimby, George Irving. *Indian Culture and European Trade Goods: The Archaeology of the Historic Period in the Western Great Lakes Region.* Madison: University of Wisconsin Press, 1966.

2537. _____. *Indians of the Western Frontier: Paintings of George Catlin.* Chicago: Chicago Natural History Museum, 1958. Reproductions of some paintings, with an account of how they came to the Natural History Museum, now known as the Field Museum of Natural History.

2538. Viola, Herman J. *The Indian Legacy of Charles Bird King.* Smithsonian Press Publication, no. 6256. Washington: Smithsonian Institution Press, 1976. King painted portraits of more than one hundred Indian leaders who visited Washington between 1821 and 1842. The author prints forty-four reproductions in this volume; he also includes a checklist of extant portraits and historical accounts of Native American delegations to Washington.

2539. Vogel, Virgil J. "Indian-White Intermarriage on the Frontier: The Role of Mixed-Bloods in Indian-White Relations." *Transactions of the Illinois State Historical Society: Selected Papers from the Seventh Annual History Symposium and the Eighth Annual History Symposium* [1986 and 1987]. Springfield, 1989. Pp. 1-10.

2540. White, Richard. *The Middle Ground: Indians, Empires, and Republics in the Great Lakes Region, 1650-1815.* New York: Cambridge University Press, 1991.

H. NEWSPAPERS AND OTHER COMMUNICATIONS MEDIA

2541. Allaman, John Lee. "The Patterson Family of Oquawka." *Western Illinois Regional Studies* 11, no. 1 (Spring 1988): 55-70. The story of the Pattersons is the story of the *Oquawka Spectator*, a remarkable newspaper of the mid-nineteenth century.

2542. Atkins, Smith D. "Some Illinois Editors I Have Known." *Transactions of the Illinois State Historical Society, 1910*, pp. 38-41.

2543. Beasley, Norman. *Frank Knox, American: A Short Biography.* Garden City, N.Y.: Doubleday, 1936. Knox became publisher of the *Chicago Daily News* in 1931.

2544. Bliss, Thomas A. *The Goose Bone Papers: Writings of Charles W. Bliss, Country Newspaper Editor . . . A Weaver of Words.* Hillsboro, Ill.: Hillsboro and Montgomery County News, 1981. The text of the author, Charles Bliss's grandson, and the elder Bliss's own writings illuminate some of the major social issues of the twentieth century.

2545. Brophy, L. A. "Melville E. Stone: A Brief Sketch." *Journal of the Illinois State Historical Society* 26 (1933-34): 459-66. Stone was general manager of Associated Press.

2546. Butcher, Fanny. *Many Lives--One Love.* New York: Harper, 1972. *Chicago Tribune* reporter and columnist.

2547. Chicago Tribune. *WGN . . . A Pictorial History.* Chicago, 1961. Also encompasses the early years of WGN-TV.

2548. Clendenin, Henry W. *Autobiography of Henry W. Clendenin, Editor: The Story of a Long and Busy Life.* Springfield, Ill.: State Register, 1926. Editor of the *Illinois State Register*, Springfield, for forty-five years.

2549. Dante, Harris L. "The *Chicago Tribune's* 'Lost' Years, 1865-1874." *Journal of the Illinois State Historical Society* 58 (1965): 139-64. During the years covered, Horace White was editor. The article is particularly interesting for the light it sheds on Republican party schisms and other political issues of the Reconstruction era.

2550. Davis, William Osborne. "The Autobiography of William Osborne Davis." Edited by Harold Sinclair. *Journal of the Illinois State Historical Society* 39 (1946): 345-60. Davis was publisher of the *Daily Pantagraph* of Bloomington, 1868-1911.

2551. Dennis, Charles H. *Victor Lawson: His Time and His Work.* Chicago: University of Chicago Press, 1935. Detailed analysis of Lawson's work as publisher of the *Chicago Daily News.*

2552. Digby-Junger, Richard. "A New Version of the Founding of the *Chicago Daily News.*" *Illinois Historical Journal* 86 (1993): 27-40. Letters in the Henry Demarest Lloyd Papers at the State Historical Society of Wisconsin indicate that Melville Stone, the *News* founder, defrauded the financial investor whose funds made the newspaper possible.

2553. Dyche, Grace Locke Scripps. "John Locke Scripps, Lincoln's Campaign Biographer." *Journal of the Illinois State Historical Society* 17 (1924-25): 333-51.

2554. Ely, Melvin Patrick. *The Adventures of Amos 'n' Andy: A Social History of an American Phenomenon.* New York: Free Press, 1991. A scholarly study of the radio comedy "Amos 'n' Andy," which grew out of the nineteenth-century blackface tradition of minstrel shows. "Amos 'n' Andy" originated in Chicago in the 1920s.

2555. Fanning, Charles. *Finley Peter Dunne & Mr. Dooley: The Chicago Years.* Lexington: University Press of Kentucky, 1978. An analysis of Dunne's humorous pieces about Chicago, particularly its Irish-Americans, that appeared in the *Chicago Evening Post,* 1892-98.

2556. Frazer, Betty King. *Verne E. Joy, Publisher, "Egypt's Greatest Daily."* Centralia, Ill.: Evening Sentinel, 1968. The *Sentinel* masthead proclaims its status.

2557. Gardner, Gilson. *Lusty Scripps: The Life of E. W. Scripps, 1854-1926.* New York: Vanguard, 1932. Newspaperman Edward W. Scripps was born near Rushville.

2558. Gordon, J. A. "Thomas Gregg: Historian, Editor, and Publisher." *Journal of the Illinois State Historical Society* 18 (1925-26): 433-35. The writings of this Hancock County newspaper editor and publisher were widely known in his day.

2559. Hallwas, John E. *Thomas Gregg, Early Illinois Journalist and Author.* Western Illinois Monograph Series, no. 2. Macomb: Western Illinois University, 1983. Samples of the writing of this Hancock County newspaper editor portray many aspects of frontier life. They are particularly interesting for comments about Indians and Mormon affairs.

2560. Haney, David. "John Scripps, Circuit Rider and Newspaperman." *Western Illinois Regional Studies* 9, no. 2 (Fall 1986): 7-35. A longtime Methodist circuit rider, Scripps moved in 1831 to Rushville in Schuyler County and entered business. In 1849 he and his son took over the Rushville *Prairie Telegraph.*

2561. Hays, Robert G. *Country Editor: Influence of a Weekly Newspaper.* Danville, Ill.: Interstate, 1974. A discussion of the career of Noland Blair Seil, longtime editor of the *Grayville Mercury-Independent.*

2562. Hogan, Lawrence D. *A Black National News Service: The Associated Negro Press and Claude Barnett, 1919-1945.* Rutherford, N.J.: Fairleigh Dickinson University Press, 1984.

2563. Janowitz, Morris. *The Community Press in an Urban Setting: The Social Elements of Urbanism.* 2d ed. Chicago: University of Chicago Press, 1967.

2564. Jordan, Philip D. "The Prairie Hen, together with a Sketch of Its Editor, E. S. Ingalls." *Journal of the Illinois State Historical Society* 27 (1934-35): 285-96. In his lifetime Ingalls was involved with many newspapers.

2565. Joyaux, Georges J. "French Language Press in the Upper Mississippi and Great Lakes Areas." *Mid-America* 43 (1961): 242-61.

2566. Kinsley, Philip. *The Chicago Tribune: Its First Hundred Years.* 3 vols. Vol. 1, New York: Knopf, 1943. Vols. 2 and 3, Chicago: Chicago Tribune, 1945, 1946. No annotations or bibliography.

2567. Kupcinet, Irv, with Paul Neimark. *Kup, a Man, an Era, a City: Irv Kupcinet's Autobiography.* Chicago: Bonus Books, 1988. Kupcinet is a well-known Chicago newspaper columnist.

2568. Linn, James Weber. *James Keeley, Newspaperman.* Indianapolis: Bobbs-Merrill, 1937. City editor and then managing editor of the *Chicago Tribune* in the late nineteenth and early twentieth centuries.

2569. Littlewood, Thomas B. *Arch, a Promoter, Not a Poet: The Story of Arch Ward.* Ames: Iowa State University Press, 1990. Work of the *Chicago Tribune* sports editor and promoter of special events.

2570. Logsdon, Joseph. *Horace White, Nineteenth Century Liberal.* Contributions in American History, no. 10. Westport, Conn.: Greenwood, 1971. This study of the noted Chicago newsman and publisher is also a study of major political issues of the day. White was a reporter and editor for the *Chicago Tribune*, 1857-74.

2571. McCollum, William Jr., ed. *Selected Letters of Don Marquis.* Stafford, Va.: Northwoods Press, 1982. The editor presents wonderful letters by the Illinois newspaperman and author of *Archy and Mehitabel*, but the arrangement by subject, instead of date, is confusing and unsatisfactory.

2572. McCutcheon, John Tinney. *Drawn from Memory: [Autobiography] Containing Many of the Author's Famous Cartoons and Sketches.* Indianapolis: Bobbs-Merrill, 1950.

2573. McDonough, Daniel. "Chicago Press Treatment of the Gangster, 1924-1931." *Illinois Historical Journal* 82 (1989): 17-32. Newspaper stories and editorials illustrate how prohibition led to bootlegging and eventual control of the bootleggers by criminals with strong ties to political leaders.

2574. McInerny, Paul M. "Charles Wesley Bliss and the *Montgomery News.*" *Journal of the Illinois State Historical Society* 70 (1977): 201-7.

2575. McMurtrie, Douglas C. "The First Printers of Illinois." *Journal of the Illinois State Historical Society* 26 (1933-34): 202-21.

2576. Merwin, Loring C. "McLean County's Newspapers, Particularly the *Pantagraph.*" *Journal of the Illinois State Historical Society* 51 (1958): 7-27.

2577. Monaghan, Jay. *The Man Who Elected Lincoln.* Indianapolis: Bobbs-Merrill, 1956. A biography of Charles Henry Ray, a senior editor of the *Chicago Tribune* who was influential in the rise of Abraham Lincoln. Colorful and anecdotal but not always accurate about nineteenth-century political institutions.

2578. Museum of Broadcast Communications, Chicago. *This Is NBC Chicago Channel 5 WMAQ-TV: 40 Years of Distinction.* Museum of Broadcast Communications, 1989. Brochure for an exhibit at the museum, 22 October--30 December 1989.

2579. O'Connor, Len. *A Reporter in Sweet Chicago.* Chicago: Contemporary Books, 1983. The author's career as a radio and television commentator paralleled the development of television news.

2580. Pabis, George S. "The Polish Press in Chicago and American Labor Strikes, 1892 to 1912." *Polish American Studies* 48 (1991): 7-21.

2581. Schmidt, Royal J. "The *Chicago Daily News* and Traction Politics, 1876-1920." *Journal of the Illinois State Historical Society* 64 (1971): 312-26.

2582. Singer, Spiz. *"Forty Years behind the Mike": Wit, Wisdom . . . and Fascinating Facts.* Springfield, Ill.: The author, 1968. Singer worked for radio station WTAX, Springfield.

2583. Startt, James D. *Journalism's Unofficial Ambassador: A Biography of Edward Price Bell, 1869-1943.* Athens: Ohio University Press, 1979. Bell was overseas manager of the *Chicago Daily News* foreign news service for more than twenty-two years.

2584. Stevens, J. D. "Bungleton Green: Black Comic Strip Ran 43 Years." *Journalism Quarterly* 51 (Spring 1974): 122-24. The strip ran in the *Chicago Defender.*

2585. Stone, Melville E. *Fifty Years a Journalist.* Garden City, N.Y.: Doubleday, 1921.

2586. Stonecipher, Harry W., and Trager, Robert. *The Mass Media and the Law in Illinois.* Carbondale: Southern Illinois University Press, 1976.

2587. Swanson, Walter S. J. *The Thin Gold Watch: A Personal History of the Newspaper Copleys.* New York: Macmillan, 1964. 2d ed., LaJolla, Calif.: Copley Press, 1970. The Aurora *Beacon* was the first of many Illinois newspapers owned by the Copleys.

2588. Tanner, Terence A. "Newspapers and Printing Presses in Early Illinois." *American Periodicals: A Journal of History, Criticism, and Bibliography* 3 (1993): 100-113.

2589. Tebbel, John William. *An American Dynasty: The Story of the McCormicks, Medills, and Pattersons.* New York: Doubleday, 1947. Founders of the *Chicago Tribune* had publishing interests in New York and Washington as well. Robert R. McCormick and the *Chicago Tribune* are the primary focus. No annotations or bibliography.

2590. Trimble, Vance H. *The Astonishing Mr. Scripps: The Turbulent Life of America's Penny Press Lord.* Ames: Iowa State University Press, 1992. Edward W. Scripps, the newspaper tycoon, was born on a farm near Rushville.

2591. Trohan, Walter. "My Life with the Colonel." *Journal of the Illinois State Historical Society* 52 (1959): 477-502. Affectionate reminiscences about Robert R. McCormick, publisher and editor of the *Chicago Tribune*, by a friend and longtime *Tribune* correspondent.

2592. Van Meter, Andy. *Always My Friend: A History of the* State Journal-Register *and Springfield.* Springfield, Ill.: Copley Press, 1981. "Always my friend" was Abraham Lincoln's comment about the newspaper, which was fiercely partisan, as were other newspapers of the day. The author traces the changing emphasis of the press down to the present.

2593. WGN Continental Broadcasting Company. *The Wonderful World of WGN.* Chicago: Bassett Publishing, 1966.

2594. WLS (radio station) Chicago. *WLS, the Prairie Farmer Station, Chicago, April 12, 1934.* Chicago, 1934? Covers ten years of history.

2595. WMAQ (television station) Chicago. *WMAQ-TV, 1948/1968.* Chicago, 1968.

2596. Waldrop, Frank C. *McCormick of Chicago: An Unconventional Portrait of a Controversial Figure.* Englewood Cliffs, N.J.: Prentice-Hall, 1966. A detailed but incomplete portrait of the longtime publisher of the *Chicago Tribune*.

2597. Walsh, Justin E. *To Print the News and Raise Hell! A Biography of Wilbur F. Storey.* Chapel Hill: University of North Carolina Press, 1968. Storey was editor of the *Chicago Times* in the Civil War years and until 1884.

2598. Wendt, Lloyd. *Chicago Tribune: The Rise of a Great American Newspaper.* Chicago: Rand McNally, 1979. A comprehensive, annotated study.

2599. Williams, Kenny J., and Duffey, Bernard, eds. *Chicago's Public Wits: A Chapter in the American Comic Spirit.* Baton Rouge: Louisiana State University Press, 1983. An anthology of humorous Chicago newspaper columns, from Finley Peter Dunne and George Ade of the late nineteenth century to today's Mike Royko, Bill Granger, and Bob Greene. The editors provide biographical sketches of their subjects.

I. POLITICS AND GOVERNMENT

2600. Allswang, John M. *Bosses, Machines, and Urban Voters.* Port Washington, N.Y.: Kennikat Press, 1977. Rev. ed., Baltimore: Johns Hopkins University Press, 1986. Chapter 4 is on "Big Bill" Thompson and Anthony Cermak, and chapter 5, on Richard J. Daley.

2601. Black, Carl Ellsworth. "Origin of Our State Charitable Institutions." *Journal of the Illinois State Historical Society* 18 (1925-26): 175-94.

2602. Blair, George S. "The Adoption of Cumulative Voting in Illinois." *Journal of the Illinois State Historical Society* 47 (1954): 373-84. The cumulative voting system, designed by the Constitution of 1870 to insure minority-party representation in the General Assembly, was abolished by the Constitution of 1970.

2603. _____. *Cumulative Voting: An Effective Electoral Device in Illinois Politics.* Illinois Studies in the Social Sciences, vol. 45. Urbana: University of Illinois Press, 1960.

2604. Braden, George D., and Cohn, Rubin G. *The Illinois Constitution: An Annotated and Comparative Analysis.* Urbana: Institute of Government and Public Affairs, University of Illinois, 1969. Prepared for the Illinois Constitution Study Commission. Contains analyses of each section of the 1870 constitution, with a history of the development of each section through judicial decisions.

2605. Buechler, Steven M. *The Transformation of the Woman Suffrage Movement: The Case of Illinois, 1850-1910.* The Douglass Series on Women's Lives and the Meaning of Gender. New Brunswick, N.J.: Rutgers University Press, 1986.

2606. Church, Charles A. *History of the Republican Party in Illinois, 1854-1912, with a Review of the Aggressions of the Slave-Power.* Rockford, Ill.: Press of Wilson Brothers, 1912.

2607. Clark, Harry F., ed. *Illinois State Police, a Division of the Department of Law Enforcement, 1922-1972.* Springfield, Ill.: State Police Benevolent Group, 1972.

2608. Cornelius, Janet. *Constitution Making in Illinois, 1818-1970.* Studies in Illinois Constitution Making. Rev. ed. Urbana: University of Illinois Press, for the Institute of Government and Public Affairs, 1972.

2609. _____. "Popular Sovereignty and Constitutional Change in the United States and Illinois Constitutions." *Journal of the Illinois State Historical Society* 80 (1987): 228-47.

2610. Debel, Niels H. *The Veto Power of the Governor of Illinois.* University of Illinois Studies in the Social Sciences, vol. 6, nos. 1 and 2. Urbana, 1917.

2611. Due, John Fitzgerald. *State Sales Tax Administration.* Chicago: Public Administration Service, 1963.

2612. Ebel, Alice L. "The Dilemma of Local Government." *Illinois Quarterly* 33, no. 1 (September 1970): 12-29. Analysis of the problems and proliferation of local government units.

2613. Einhorn, Robin L. *Property Rules: Political Economy in Chicago, 1833-1872.* Chicago: University of Chicago Press, 1991. Reinterpretation of the relationship between political and social structures: construction of public works was achieved, the author says, despite a "low-tax consensus," by a government "clean enough to satisfy even the most fastidious of urban reformers."

2614. Erickson, Gladys A. *Warden Ragen of Joliet.* New York: Dutton, 1957. Joseph Ragen was appointed warden of the Joliet and Stateville prisons in 1935. Most of the book is devoted to the operation of the prisons.

2615. Fahrnkopf, Nancy, and Lynch, Myra C., eds. *State and Local Government in Illinois: A Bibliography, 1954-1964.* University of Illinois Bulletin, vol. 62, no. 91. Urbana: Institute of Government and Public Affairs, 1965.

2616. Fiedler, George. *The Illinois Law Courts in Three Centuries, 1673-1973: A Documentary History.* Berwyn, Ill.: Physicians' Record, 1973. This volume has considerable narrative history besides the documents reproduced.

2617. Fisher, Glenn W. *Financing Illinois State Government: A Report of the Institute of Government and Public Affairs.* Urbana: University of Illinois Press, 1960.

2618. Frum, Harold S., comp. *Fifty-Year History of the Division of the Criminologist, State of Illinois.* Springfield, 1968.

2619. Garvey, Neil F. *The Government and Administration of Illinois.* New York: Crowell, 1958.

2620. Gienapp, William E. *The Origins of the Republican Party, 1852-1856.* New York: Oxford University Press, 1987.

2621. Gould, Alan B. "Walter L. Fisher: Profile of an Urban Reformer, 1880-1910." *Mid-America* 57 (1975): 157-72.

2622. Gove, Samuel Kimball, ed. *State and Local Government in Illinois: A Bibliography.* University of Illinois Bulletin, vol. 51, no. 37. Urbana: University of Illinois Institute of Government and Public Affairs, 1953.

2623. Green, Paul M.; Everson, David H.; Colby, Peter W.; and Parker, Joan A. *Illinois Elections: Third Edition.* Springfield: *Illinois Issues,* Sangamon State University, 1986. Thirty-one essays (by the authors listed), including those introducing the five sections into which the book is divided: voting patterns in Illinois, voting patterns in Chicago, legislative and congressional elections, the decline of party, and presidential nomination politics in Illinois.

2624. Greene, William Robert. "Early Development of the Illinois State Penitentiary System." *Journal of the Illinois State Historical Society* 70 (1977): 185-95. Jails and prisons from 1780 to the early twentieth century.

2625. Grimshaw, William J. *Bitter Fruit: Black Politics and the Chicago Machine, 1931-1991.* Chicago: University of Chicago Press, 1992.

2626. Haeger, John Denis, and Weber, Michael P., eds. *The Bosses.* Rev. ed. St. Louis: Forum Press, 1979. Reprints of essays from magazines and books; no annotations, but there is a list of suggested books for further reading.

2627. Haig, Robert Murray. *A History of the General Property Tax in Illinois.* University of Illinois Studies in the Social Sciences, vol. 3, nos. 1 and 2. Urbana, 1914.

2628. Jacobs, James B. *Stateville: The Penitentiary in Mass Society.* Studies in Crime and Justice. Chicago: University of Chicago Press, 1977. A study of the administration of Stateville and relations between staff and inmates from the opening of the prison at Lockport in 1925 until 1975.

2629. James, Herman G. "The Origin and Development of the Bill of Rights in the Constitution of Illinois." *Transactions of the Illinois State Historical Society, 1910,* pp. 81-104.

2630. Kantowicz, Edward R. "The Emergence of the Polish-Democratic Vote in Chicago." *Polish American Studies* 29 (1972): 67-80. The author's studies show that the Polish-Americans were strongly Democratic as early as the late 1880s.

2631. Keane, James F., and Koch, Gary, eds. *Illinois Local Government: A Handbook.* Carbondale: Southern Illinois University Press, 1990. Articles about the various types of local governments (more than 6,500 separate units) and their operations.

2632. Keating, Ann Durkin. *Building Chicago: Suburban Developers & the Creation of a Divided Metropolis.* Urban Life and Urban Landscape series. Columbus: Ohio State University Press, 1988. The author emphasizes the importance of governmental structure in the development of suburbs. The discussion includes Chicago neighborhoods that had been separately incorporated.

2633. Kenney, David. *Basic Illinois Government: A Systematic Explanation.* Carbondale: Southern Illinois University Press, 1970. The first two chapters deal primarily with Illinois history. Later chapters on the structure of government have a sound grounding in history.

2634. Kneier, Charles Mayard. *State Regulation of Public Utilities in Illinois.* University of Illinois Studies in the Social Sciences, vol. 14, no. 1. Urbana, 1927.

2635. Kuklinski, James. "Cumulative and Plurality Voting: An Analysis of Illinois' Unique Electoral System." *Western Political Quarterly* 26 (1973): 726-46.

2636. Laudermilk, John I. "Chicago Gunboats: Ships of the Illinois Naval Militia." *Inland Seas* 41 (Fall 1985): 162-71.

2637. League of Women Voters of Illinois. *Illinois Voters' Handbook.* Chicago, 1913--to date . Issued biennially since 1929.

2638. Lindberg, Richard C. *To Serve and Collect: Chicago Politics and Police Corruption from the Lager Beer Riot to the Summerdale Scandal.* New York: Praeger, 1991. Covers the years 1831-1961. The "lager beer riot" erupted in 1855 when a group of Germans protested the increased price of liquor licenses. The Summerdale scandal of 1958 involved a thievery ring operating out of the Summerdale police station.

2639. Lusk, D. W. *Politics and Politicians of Illinois, Anecdotes and Incidents: A Succinct History of the State, 1809-1886.* 2d ed. rev. and enl. Springfield, Ill.: H. W. Rokker, 1886. The first edition was issued in 1884, and a later edition, also revised and enlarged, was issued in 1889 under the title *Eighty Years of Illinois, Politics and Politicians, Anecdotes and Incidents: A Succinct History of the State, 1809-1889.*

2640. McKay, M. K. "History of the Poll Tax in Illinois." *Journal of the Illinois State Historical Society* 12 (1919-20): 41-44.

2641. Moore, Blaine F., and Garner, J. W. *The History of Cumulative Voting and Minority Representation in Illinois, 1870-1919.* Rev. ed. University of Illinois Studies in the Social Sciences, vol. 8, no. 2. Urbana, 1920.

2642. Nardulli, Peter F., ed. *Diversity, Conflict, and State Politics: Regionalism in Illinois.* Urbana: University of Illinois Press, 1989.

2643. Nowlan, James D., comp. *Illinois Major Party Platforms, 1900-1964.* Urbana: Institute of Government and Public Affairs, University of Illinois, 1966.

2644. Oaks, Dallin H., and Lehman, Warren. *A Criminal Justice System and the Indigent: A Study of Chicago and Cook County.* Chicago: University of Chicago Press, 1968.

2645. Pegram, Thomas R. *Partisans and Progressives: Private Interest and Public Policy in Illinois, 1870-1922.* Urbana: University of Illinois Press, 1992.

2646. Petterchak, Janice A. " 'The Bounties of Nature Belong to the People': A Political Biography of the First Commissioner of Public Property in Springfield, Illinois." Paper read at the Illinois History Symposium, 1991. Typescript, Illinois State Historical Library. Willis J. Spaulding strove to establish municipally owned water and electricity systems; with the help of funds from the federal Public Works Administration, his plans came to fruition in 1935.

2647. Pisciotta, A. W. "A House Divided: Penal Reform at the Illinois State Reformatory, 1891-1915." *Crime & Delinquency* 37 (April 1991): 165-85.

2648. *Pursuit of Freedom: A History of Civil Liberty in Illinois, 1787-1942.* Chicago: Chicago Civil Liberties Committee and Illinois Civil Liberties Committee, 1942.

2649. Raum, Green B. *History of Illinois Republicanism, Embracing a History of the Republican Party in the State to the Present Time . . . with Biographies of Its Founders and Supporters . . . Also a Chronological Statement of Important Political Events since 1774.* Chicago: Rollins Publishing, 1900.

2650. Sawyer, Jack, and Macrae, Duncan Jr. "Game Theory and Cumulative Voting in Illinois, 1902-1954." *American Political Science Review* 56 (1962): 936-46.

2651. Schlesinger, Keith R. *The Power That Governs: The Evolution of Judicial Activism in a Midwestern State, 1840-1890.* New York: Garland, 1990. In the nineteenth century, Illinois courts, as a microcosm of those throughout the nation, gradually became the primary regulator of big business, especially railroads.

2652. Schwartz, Mildred. *The Party Network: The Robust Organization of the Illinois Republicans.* Madison: University of Wisconsin Press, 1990.

2653. Selcraig, James Truett. *The Red Scare in the Midwest, 1945-1955: A State and Local Study.* Studies in American History and Culture, no. 36. Ann Arbor, Mich.: UMI Research Press, 1982.

2654. Sellers, James Lee. "The Make-up of the Early Republican Party." *Transactions of the Illinois State Historical Society, 1930*, pp. 39-149. Traces the development of the party and national issues from 1840 to 1912, emphasizing the prominent roles played by Illinoisans.

2655. Snider, Clyde F., and Howards, Irving. *County Government in Illinois.* Carbondale: Southern Illinois University, 1960.

2656. Snider, Clyde F., and Andersen, Roy. *Local Taxing Units: The Illinois Experience*. Commission Papers of the Institute of Government and Public Affairs, University of Illinois. Urbana, 1968.

2657. Spiegel, Frederick C. *The Illinois Court of Claims: A Study of State Liability*. Illinois Studies in the Social Sciences, vol. 50. Urbana: University of Illinois Press, 1962.

2658. Stow, Robert N., ed. "Conflict in the American Socialist Movement, 1897-1901: A Letter from Thomas J. Morgan to Henry Demarest Lloyd, July 18, 1901." *Journal of the Illinois State Historical Society* 71 (1978): 133-42. Much of this account centers on Illinois.

2659. "Studies of Political Loyalties of Two Nationality Groups." *Journal of the Illinois State Historical Society* 57 (1964). "Isolationism and German-Americans," by Howard W. Allen, pp. 143-49. "The Rockford Swedish Community," by Dorothy Homer, pp. 149-55. Allen determined that German-Catholic communities in Hamilton County voted as a bloc and frequently changed parties in national elections, whereas the Swedish immigrant community remained staunchly Republican until the late 1920s and 1930s, later voting Democratic if economic problems were severe.

2660. Sublett, Michael D. *Paper Counties: The Illinois Experience, 1825-1867*. American University Studies. New York: Peter Lang, 1990. This study of seventeen proposed counties (never authorized by the legislature or voted down in public referenda) offers valuable insights into the economic and political history of the state.

2661. Taylor, Quintard. "The Chicago Political Machine and Black-Ethnic Conflict and Accommodation." *Polish American Studies* 29 (1972): 40-66. Machine politics and the ethnic vote from the 1890s to the present.

2662. Townsend, Walter A. *Illinois Democracy: A History of the Party and Its Representative Members, Past and Present*. 4 vols. Springfield, Ill.: Democratic Historical Association, 1935. Volumes 2-4 contain biographies.

2663. Trout, Grace Wilbur. "Side Lights on Illinois Suffrage History." *Journal of the Illinois State Historical Society* 13 (1920-21): 145-79.

2664. Van der Slik, Jack R., and Redfield, Kent D. *Lawmaking in Illinois: Legislative Politics, People, and Processes*. Springfield, Ill.: Office of Public Affairs Communication, Sangamon State University, 1986.

2665. Verlie, Emil Joseph, ed. *Illinois Constitutions.* Collections of the Illinois State Historical Library, vol. 13. Springfield, 1919. Texts of the constitutions of 1818, 1848, and 1870 and of congressional acts under which Illinois was organized as a territory and as a state. An index lists supreme court cases that construe or apply each provision of the three constitutions.

2666. Wendt, Lloyd, and Kogan, Herman. *Lords of the Levee: The Story of Bathhouse John and Hinky Dink.* Indianapolis: Bobbs-Merrill, 1943. Reprint (A Midland Book, no. 109), Bloomington: Indiana University Press, 1967. The 1967 edition has the title *Bosses in Lusty Chicago* etc., and an introduction by Paul H. Douglas. The subjects of this anecdotal political history of late nineteenth- and early twentieth-century Chicago are First Ward bosses John J. Coughlin and Michael Kenna.

J. RELIGION

2667. Arden, Gothard Everett. *Augustana Heritage: A History of the Augustana Lutheran Church.* Rock Island, Ill.: Augustana Press, 1963.

2668. Ash, James L. Jr. "American Religion and the Academy in the Early Twentieth Century: The Chicago Years of William Warren Sweet." *Church History* 50 (December 1981): 450-64. Sweet's career at the Divinity School of the University of Chicago.

2669. Avella, Steven M. *The Confident Church: Catholic Leadership and Life in Chicago, 1940-1965.* Notre Dame, Ind.: University of Notre Dame Press, 1992.

2670. Barnhart, John D. Jr. "The Rise of the Methodist Episcopal Church in Illinois from the Beginning to the Year 1832." *Journal of the Illinois State Historical Society* 12 (1919-20): 149-217.

2671. Beuckman, Frederic. "Catholic Beginnings in Southern Illinois: Shawneetown." *Mid-America* 3 n.s. (1931-32): 105-26.

2672. _____. "The Shawneetown-to-Cairo Mission Trail." *Mid-America* 3 n.s. (1931-32): 246-62. Catholic missions in southern Illinois.

2673. Brand, Edward P. *Illinois Baptists: A History.* Bloomington, Ill.: Pantagraph Printing, 1930.

2674. Browning, Clyde. *Amish in Illinois: Over One Hundred Years of the "Old Order" Sect of Central Illinois.* Decatur, Ill.: Privately printed, 1971. The day-to-day life and work of the Amish in central Illinois by a sympathetic observer who lived among them at Arthur.

2675. Buckingham, Minnie S., ed. *Church of the Brethren in Southern Illinois.* Elgin, Ill.: Brethren Publishing House, 1950.

2676. Chrisman, Richard A. "German Methodism in Illinois." *Transactions of the Illinois State Historical Society: Selected Papers from the Fifth and the Sixth Illinois History Symposiums of the Illinois State Historical Society* [1984 and 1985]. Springfield, 1988. Pp. 25-33. The author traces the history of the German Methodist church from its origins to the late twentieth century.

2677. Cole, Charles C. Jr. *The Social Ideas of the Northern Evangelists, 1826-1860.* Columbia Studies in the Social Sciences, no. 580. New York: Columbia University Press, 1954. Reprint, New York: Octagon Books, 1966.

2678. *Disciples in Illinois, 1850-1950.* Jacksonville, Ill.: Centennial Convention, Disciples of Christ in Illinois, 1950.

2679. Eller, David B. "George Wolfe and the 'Far Western' Brethren." *Illinois Historical Journal* 80 (1987): 85-100. German Baptist Brethren (Dunkards) settled in Illinois in territorial days. The author takes their story to 1908.

2680. _____. "The Pietist Origins of Sectarian Universalism in the Midwest." *Old Northwest* 12 (1986): 41-63. The author includes a brief history of German Baptist Brethren in Illinois, 1813-40. Some of these Brethren espoused the philosophy of "universal salvation."

2681. Ellis, Elizabeth. "Dutch Reformed Beginnings in Illinois." *Journal of the Illinois State Historical Society* 36 (1943): 190-207.

2682. Evers, Joseph Calvin. *The History of the Southern Illinois Conference, the Methodist Church.* Nashville, Tenn.: Parthenon Press, 1964.

2683. Field, A. D. *Memorials of Methodism in the Bounds of the Rock River Conference.* Cincinnati: Cranston & Stowe, 1886.

2684. Garraghan, Gilbert Joseph. *The Catholic Church in Chicago, 1673-1871.* Chicago: Loyola University Press, 1921. Reprint, Ann Arbor, Mich.: University

Microfilms, 1968. Contains much information about the church throughout the state as well as in Chicago.

2685. Goodykoontz, Colin Brummitt. *Home Missions on the American Frontier: With Particular Reference to the American Home Missionary Society.* Caldwell, Idaho: Caxton, 1939. Reprint, New York: Octagon Books, 1971.

2686. Haberkorn, Ruth Ewers. "The First Ordained Congregational Woman Minister in the United States." *Journal of the Illinois State Historical Society* 35 (1942): 288-94. She was Mary L. Moreland, whose first church was in Wyanet.

2687. Harlan, Rolvix. *John Alexander Dowie and the Christian Catholic Apostolic Church in Zion.* Evansville, Wis.: Press of R. M. Antes, 1906.

2688. Hastings, Robert J., comp. *We Were There: An Oral History of the Illinois Baptist State Association, 1907-1976.* Springfield: Illinois Baptist State Association, 1976. This association of Southern Baptists was organized in 1907.

2689. Haupert, Albert P. "The Moravian Settlement in Illinois." *Transactions of the Illinois State Historical Society, 1922,* pp. 79-89. History of the colony settlement at West Salem in Edwards County.

2690. Haynes, N. S. "The Disciples of Christ in Illinois and Their Attitude toward Slavery." *Transactions of the Illinois State Historical Society, 1913,* pp. 52-59.

2691. Heath, Alden R. "Apostle in Zion." *Journal of the Illinois State Historical Society* 70 (1977): 98-113. A sketch of the evangelist John Alexander Dowie and the town of Zion, Illinois, which he founded.

2692. Heckman, John, and Miller, J. E. *Brethren in Northern Illinois and Wisconsin.* Elgin, Ill.: Brethren Publishing House, 1941. History of the Church of the Brethren.

2693. *Home Missionary and American Pastor's Journal.* Published monthly, 1828-1909, with varying titles, by the American Home Missionary Society. In the early years of the periodical there were many reports from missionaries in Illinois, with valuable descriptions of the country as well as of churches and settlements.

2694. Howard, Victor B. *Conscience and Slavery: The Evangelistic Calvinist Domestic Missions, 1837-1861.* Kent, Ohio: Kent State University Press, 1990.

2695. *Illinois Mennonite Heritage.* Metamora: Illinois Mennonite Historical and Genealogical Society. Published quarterly since June 1974.

2696. Jenkins, H. D. "The History of Presbyterianism in Illinois." *Transactions of the Illinois State Historical Society, 1913,* pp. 60-66.

2697. Kantowicz, Edward R. "Cardinal Mundelein of Chicago and the Shaping of Twentieth-Century American Catholicism." *Journal of American History* 68 (1981): 52-68.

2698. _____. *Corporation Sole: Cardinal Mundelein and Chicago Catholicism.* Notre Dame, Ind.: University of Notre Dame Press, 1983. A study of the administration of the Archdiocese of Chicago, 1916-39.

2699. Koenig, Harry C., ed. *Caritas Christi Urget Nos: A History of the Offices, Agencies, and Institutions of the Archdiocese of Chicago.* 2 vols. Chicago: Archdiocese of Chicago, 1981.

2700. _____, ed. *A History of the Parishes of the Archdiocese of Chicago.* 2 vols. Chicago: Archdiocese of Chicago, 1980.

2701. Kofoid, Carrie Prudence. "Puritan Influences in the Formative Years of Illinois History." *Transactions of the Illinois State Historical Society, 1905,* pp. 261-338. Deals with Congregationalists and Presbyterians from the early 1800s to the mid-1850s.

2702. Leaton, James. *History of Methodism in Illinois from 1793 to 1832.* Cincinnati: Printed by Walden and Stowe for the author, 1883.

2703. Lentz, Eli G. "Pioneer Baptists of Illinois." *Transactions of the Illinois State Historical Society, 1927,* pp. 122-31. A discussion of pioneer Baptists from 1787 until 1831, including the most famous, John Mason Peck, the principal founder of Shurtleff College.

2704. McGovern, James J. *The Catholic Church in Chicago.* Chicago: Archdiocese of Chicago, 1891.

2705. Melton, J. Gordon. *Log Cabins to Steeples: The Complete Story of the United Methodist Way in Illinois, Including All Constituent Elements of the United Methodist Church.* Nashville, Tenn.: Parthenon Press for the Commission on Archives and History, 1974. Extensive appendixes and a comprehensive index and bibliography make this volume especially valuable.

2706. Mills, Andrew H. "A Hundred Years of Sunday School History in Illinois, 1818-1918: A Mosaic." *Transactions of the Illinois State Historical Society, 1918*, pp. 93-196.

2707. Moore, Lamire Holden. *Southern Baptists in Illinois.* Nashville, Tenn.: Benson Printing, 1957.

2708. Nystrom, Daniel. *A Ministry of Printing: History of the Publication House of Augustana Lutheran Church, 1889-1962.* Rock Island, Ill.: Augustana Press, 1962.

2709. O'Rourke, Alice A. *The Good Work Begun--Centennial History of Peoria Diocese.* Chicago: Lakeside Press, 1970.

2710. Parot, Joseph John. *Polish Catholics in Chicago, 1850-1920.* DeKalb: Northern Illinois University Press, 1981.

2711. Pennewell, Almer M. *The Methodist Movement in Northern Illinois.* Sycamore, Ill.: Sycamore Tribune, 1942.

2712. Piersel, W. G. "The Wesley Foundation in Urbana: The Origin of an Idea." *Journal of the Illinois State Historical Society* 38 (1945): 319-44. Established by Methodists for the promotion of religious education of students at the University of Illinois.

2713. Ryan, John H. "Antislavery Struggle in Illinois As It Affected the Methodist Episcopal Church." *Transactions of the Illinois State Historical Society, 1913*, pp. 67-76.

2714. _____. "Old Time Camp Meetings in Central Illinois." *Transactions of the Illinois State Historical Society, 1924*, pp. 64-69. Methodist campgrounds in central Illinois are described.

2715. Schwartzkopf, Louis J. *The Lutheran Trail: A History of the Synodical Conference Lutheran Churches in Northern Illinois.* St. Louis: Concordia Publishing, 1950.

2716. Setterdahl, Lilly. "The End of Eric Jansonism: Religious Life in Bishop Hill in the Post-Colony Period." *Western Illinois Regional Studies* 11, no. 1 (Spring 1988): 39-54. Establishment of Swedish Lutheran churches and other Swedish churches in northwestern Illinois.

2717. Shanabruch, Charles. *Chicago's Catholics: The Evolution of an American Identity.* Notre Dame, Ind.: Notre Dame University Press, 1981.

2718. Shaw, Stephen J. *The Catholic Parish as a Way-Station of Ethnicity and Americanization: Chicago's Germans and Italians, 1903-1939.* Chicago Studies in the History of American Religion, vol. 19. Brooklyn, N.Y.: Carlson, 1991.

2719. Skerrett, Ellen; Kantowicz, Edward R.; and Avella, Steven M. *Catholicism, Chicago Style.* A Campion Book. Chicago: Loyola University Press, 1993. Commemorating the 150th anniversary of the creation of the Diocese of Chicago, this volume provides a condensed history of the diocese, concentrating on ethnic and race relations and the administrations of twentieth-century cardinals.

2720. Smith, Willard H. *Mennonites in Illinois.* Studies in Anabaptist and Mennonite History, no. 24. Scottdale, Pa.: Herald Press, 1983.

2721. Stock, Harry Thomas. "Protestantism in Illinois before 1835." *Journal of the Illinois State Historical Society* 12 (1919-20): 1-31.

2722. Sweet, Leonard I. "The University of Chicago Revisited: The Modernization of Theology, 1890-1940." *Foundations* 22 (1979): 324-51.

2723. Sweet, Warren William, ed. *Religion on the American Frontier: A Collection of Source Material.* 4 vols., 1931-46. Publishers vary. Vol. 1, *The Baptists, 1783-1830*; vol. 2, *The Presbyterians, 1783-1840*; vol. 3, *The Congregationalists, 1783-1850*; vol. 4, *The Methodists, 1783-1840.*

2724. Turner, Lynn W. "The United Brethren Church in Illinois." *Transactions of the Illinois State Historical Society, 1939*, pp. 39-66.

2725. Winterbauer, Thomas Aquinas, Sister. *Lest We Forget: The First Hundred Years of the Dominican Sisters, Springfield, Illinois.* Chicago: Adams Press, 1973.

K. SOCIAL AND CULTURAL HISTORY

1. Community Development: Urbanization, Decline, and Revitalization

2726. Abbott, Carl. "Civic Pride in Chicago, 1844-1860." *Journal of the Illinois State Historical Society* 63 (1970): 399-421.

2727. _____. " 'Necessary Adjuncts to its Growth': The Railroad Suburbs of Chicago, 1854-1875." *Journal of the Illinois State Historical Society* 73 (1980): 117-31.

2728. Adams, Jane. "Creating Community in a Midwestern Village: Fifty Years of the Cobden Peach Festival." *Illinois Historical Journal* 83 (1990): 97-108.

2729. Alcorn, Richard S. "Leadership and Stability in Mid-Nineteenth-Century America: A Case Study of an Illinois Town." *Journal of American History* 61 (1974-75): 685-702. The town studied was Paris.

2730. Barth, Gunther. *City People: The Rise of Modern City Culture in Nineteenth-Century America.* New York: Oxford, 1980. The author concentrates on such distinctive features of city culture as divided space (or housing), newspapers, department stores, ball parks, and vaudeville houses. A good index points to Chicago-related entries.

2731. Broomell, Kenneth F., and Church, Harlow M. "Streeterville Saga." *Journal of the Illinois State Historical Society* 33 (1940): 153-65. History of the claim of George Wellington Streeter to the 186-acre tract of land in Chicago that comprises what is now called the Gold Coast.

2732. Conzen, Michael P., and Morales, Melissa J., eds. *Settling the Upper Illinois Valley: Patterns of Change in the I & M Canal Corridor, 1830-1900.* Studies on the Illinois & Michigan Canal Corridor, no. 3. Chicago: Committee on Geographical Studies, University of Chicago, 1989. The first study (1987) by Conzen alone, is titled *Focus on Ottawa: A Historical and Geographical Survey of Ottawa, Illinois, in the Twentieth Century*; the second (1988), also by Conzen, is *Time and Place in Joliet: Essays on the Geographical Evolution of the City.* Study no. 4 (1990), edited by Conzen and Adam R. Daniel, is *Lockport Legacy: Themes in the Historical Geography of an Illinois Canal Town.* Study no. 5 (1991), edited by Conzen and Linda S. Lim, is *Illinois Canal Country: The Early Years in Comparative Perspective.*

2733. Cronon, William. *Nature's Metropolis: Chicago and the Great West.* New York: Norton, 1991. The author sees Chicago as the creator of the agricultural frontier, not as its destroyer, and emphasizes not the men who built the city but the interaction of the developing city and the West and Northwest (thus Nature)--which were thereby environmentally damaged.

2734. Doyle, Don Harrison. *The Social Order of a Frontier Community: Jacksonville, Illinois, 1825-70.* Urbana: University of Illinois Press, 1978.

2735. _____. "Social Theory and New Communities in Nineteenth-Century America." *Western Historical Quarterly* 8 (April 1977): 151-65. Using Jacksonville, Illinois, as the primary example, Doyle shows how churches, political parties, and voluntary associations helped establish social order--"in tension with powerful forces of disorder and conflict."

2736. Ebner, Michael H. *Creating Chicago's North Shore: A Suburban History.* Chicago: University of Chicago Press, 1988.

2737. Jablonsky, Thomas J. *Pride in the Jungle: Community and Everyday Life in Back of the Yards Chicago.* Baltimore: Johns Hopkins University Press, 1993. Emphasis is on the community in its various transformations, rather than on the stockyards and packing plants.

2738. Jaher, Frederic Cople. *The Urban Establishment: Upper Strata in Boston, New York, Charleston, Chicago, and Los Angeles.* Urbana: University of Illinois Press, 1982. Chicago, pp. 453-553. An impressive scholarly, but thoroughly readable, study.

2739. Jebsen, Harry Jr. "Preserving Suburban Identity in an Expanding Metropolis: The Case of Blue Island, Illinois." *Old Northwest* 7 (1981): 127-45. A broad-based study encompassing ethnic heritage, industrialization, labor organization, race relations, prohibition, politics, and public utilities in an independent working-class suburb.

2740. Lantz, Herman R. *A Community in Search of Itself: A Case History of Cairo, Illinois.* Foreword by Oscar Handlin. Carbondale: Southern Illinois University Press, 1972. Handlin points out that this is a "systematic detailed examination of the failure of a community to grow in terms of its social structure and the character of its population."

2741. _____, with J. S. McCrary. *People of Coal Town.* New York: Columbia University Press, 1958. A study of the class structure, and decline, of a coal-mining town, believed to be Zeigler, Illinois. Especially interesting for its accounts of the assimilation of immigrants.

2742. Lossau, Carl S. "Leclaire, Illinois: A Model Industrial Village." *Gateway Heritage: Quarterly Journal of the Missouri Historical Society, St. Louis* 8 (Spring 1988): 20-31. The town was founded in the early 1890s by N. O. Nelson, plumbing manufacturer. Eventually it was annexed to Edwardsville.

2743. Mahoney, Timothy R. *River Towns in the Great West: The Structure of Provincial Urbanization in the American Midwest.* New York: Cambridge University Press, 1990. Galena, Illinois, is one of the towns studied.

2744. Mayer, Harold M., and Wade, Richard C., with the assistance of Glen E. Holt and cartography of Gerald F. Pyle. *Chicago: Growth of a Metropolis.* Chicago: University of Chicago Press, 1969. This lavishly illustrated volume offers a balanced and sound history.

2745. Pierce, Bessie Louise. "Changing Urban Patterns in the Mississippi Valley." *Journal of the Illinois State Historical Society* 43 (1950): 46-57. Chicago is used as the primary example of the urbanization process.

2746. Posadas, Barbara M. "Suburb into Neighborhood: The Transformation of Urban Identity on Chicago's Periphery--Irving Park as a Case Study, 1870-1910." *Journal of the Illinois State Historical Society* 76 (1983): 162-76.

2747. Rees, Thomas. "Nauvoo, Illinois, under Mormon and Icarian Occupations." *Journal of the Illinois State Historical Society* 21 (1928-29): 506-24.

2748. Reiff, Janice L. " 'His Statements . . . Will Be Challenged': Ethnicity, Gender, and Class in the Evolution of the Pullman/Roseland Area of Chicago, 1894-1917." *Mid-America* 74 (1992): 231-52. The author includes the nearby communities of Kensington and West Pullman in discussing settlement patterns of various immigrant groups, employment opportunities for both men and women, and socialization of ethnic groups.

2749. Slayton, Robert A. *Back of the Yards: The Making of a Local Democracy.* Chicago: University of Chicago Press, 1986. Back of the Yards was also known as Packingtown. Traditional scholarly research and hundreds of oral interviews provide a graphic account of community development, from the opening of the stockyards to the 1970s.

2750. Sutton, Robert P. "Illinois River Towns: Economic Units or Melting Pots." *Western Illinois Regional Studies* 13, no. 2 (Fall 1990): 21-31. In this study of river towns Sutton challenges the Gilmore-Wade thesis that economics determines the viability of communities.

2751. Teaford, Jon C. *Cities of the Heartland: The Rise and Fall of the Industrial Midwest.* Bloomington: Indiana University Press, 1993.

2752. _____. *The Rough Road to Renaissance: Urban Revitalization in America, 1940-1985.* Baltimore: Johns Hopkins Press, 1990. Chicago is one of twelve cities studied.

2753. Walker, Juliet E. K. "Entrepreneurial Ventures in the Origin of Nineteenth-Century Agricultural Towns: Pike County, 1823-1880." *Illinois Historical Journal* 78 (1985): 45-64. The author shows how rivers, roads, and railroads influenced early town building. Towns that have survived are those that from an early day processed agricultural produce and continued to offer services to farmers.

2754. White, William A. "Tradition and Urban Development: A Contrast of Chicago and Toronto in the Nineteenth Century." *Old Northwest* 8 (1982): 245-71.

2755. Wille, Lois. *Forever Open, Clear, and Free: The Struggle for Chicago's Lakefront.* 2d ed. Chicago: University of Chicago Press, 1991.

2756. Wolner, Edward W. "The City Builder in Chicago, 1834-1871." *Old Northwest* 13 (1987): 3-22. The city builders particularly considered are William B. Ogden and John S. Wright, whose contributions to burgeoning technological developments also led to a more prosperous hinterland.

2. Folklore, Folk Language, and Dialects

2757. Allen, John W. *Legends and Lore of Southern Illinois.* Carbondale: Southern Illinois University, 1963. Reprint, Occasional Publications of the Illinois State Historical Society, no. 53. Springfield, 1964.

2758. Allison, Lelah. "Folk Speech from Southeastern Illinois." *Hoosier Folklore* 5 (1946): 93-102.

2759. _____. "Southern Illinois Tales and Beliefs." *Hoosier Folklore* 9 (1950): 76-79.

2760. Barbour, Frances M., ed. *Proverbs and Proverbial Phrases of Illinois.* Carbondale: Southern Illinois University Press, 1965.

2761. _____. "Some Foreign Proverbs in Southern Illinois." *Midwest Folklore* 4 (1954): 161-64.

2762. _____. "Some Uncommon Sources of Proverbs." *Midwest Folklore* 13 (1963): 97-100. Based on a collection of five thousand proverbs assembled in Illinois, 1944-50.

2763. Botkin, B. A., ed. *A Treasury of Mississippi River Folklore: Stories, Ballads, Traditions, and Folkways of the Mid-American River Country.* New York: Crown, 1955. An index of "subjects, names, and places" leads the researcher to folklore related to Illinois.

2764. Briggs, Harold E. "Folklore of Southern Illinois." *Southern Folklore Quarterly* 16 (1952): 208-9.

2765. Brownell, Baker. *The Other Illinois.* New York: Duell, Sloan & Pearce, 1958. A study of southern Illinois based on folklore and archetypal backwoods characters not necessarily representative of the region.

2766. Dorson, Richard M. *Buying the Wind: Regional Folklore in the United States.* Chicago: University of Chicago Press, 1964. Folklore of southern Illinois, pp. 289-414.

2767. Flanagan, John T. "Folklore in the Stories of James Hall." *Midwest Folklore* 5 (1955): 159-68.

2768. Frazer, Timothy. "Language Variation in the Military Tract." *Western Illinois Regional Studies* 5 (1982): 54-64. The author discusses place names and folk language as indicators of regional influences on the Military Tract area of western Illinois.

2769. Hall, Elihu Nicholas. *Ballads from the Bluffs.* Elizabethtown, Ill.: Judge Hall Book Co., 1948. Folklore from the Ozarks bluff country of southern Illinois.

2770. Halpert, Herbert. " 'Egypt'--A Wandering Place-Name Legend." *Midwest Folklore* 4 (1954): 165-68. "Egypt" is a folk name for southern Illinois.

2771. Harris, Jesse W. "The Humorous Yarn in Early Illinois Local Histories." *Midwest Folklore* 2 (1952): 167-75.

2772. _____. "Illinois Folklore, Past and Present." *Midwest Folklore* 4 (1954): 134-38. This article constitutes a brief historiography of the subject.

2773. _____. "Illinois Place-Name Lore." *Midwest Folklore* 4 (1954): 217-20.

2774. _____. "Myths and Legends from Southern Illinois." *Hoosier Folklore* 5 (1946): 14-20.

2775. _____. "Pioneer Vocabulary Remains in Southern Illinois." *Journal of the Illinois State Historical Society* 38 (1945): 476-80.

2776. _____, and Neely, Julia Jonah. "Southern Illinois Phantoms and Bogies." *Midwest Folklore* 1 (1951): 171-78.

2777. Haywood, Charles. *A Bibliography of North American Folklore and Folksong*. 2d rev. ed. 2 vols. New York: Dover, 1961. Illinois, vol. 1, pp. 298-301. Volume 2 is subtitled *The American Indians North of Mexico, Including the Eskimos*. A good index in volume 2 leads the user to many more Illinois-related entries.

2778. Hoebing, Philibert, and Schleppenbach, John. "The Way It Used To Be: Folklore of the River Men." *Western Illinois Regional Studies* 7, no. 2 (Fall 1984): 18-29.

2779. Hyatt, Harry Middleton. *Folk-Lore from Adams County, Illinois*. New York: The Alma Egan Hyatt Foundation, 1935. 2d ed., rev., Hannibal, Mo.: Western Printing and Lithographing, 1965. One of the most extensive collections from a single county.

2780. *Illinois Folklore*. Vol. 1, no. 1 (October 1947)--? Published briefly at Carbondale for the Illinois Folklore Society.

2781. Jagendorf, M. A. *Sand in the Bag, and Other Folk Stories from Ohio, Indiana, and Illinois*. New York: Vanguard, 1952.

2782. McIntosh, David S. "Blacksmith and Death." *Midwest Folklore* 1 (1951): 51-54. Two folk tales from an informant in Saline County.

2783. _____. *Folk Songs and Singing Games of the Illinois Ozarks*. Carbondale: Southern Illinois University Press, 1974.

2784. _____. "Marching down to New Orleans." *Midwest Folklore* 4 (1954): 139-48. Six Illinois versions of the singing game.

2785. _____. *Sing and Swing from Southern Illinois*. Carbondale: Southern Illinois University, 1948. Folk songs, square dances, and singing games collected by the author.

2786. _____. "Southern Illinois Folk Songs." *Journal of the Illinois State Historical Society* 31 (1938): 297-322.

2787. Mulcaster, J. G. "The Quadroon Girl of Southern Illinois." *Journal of the Illinois State Historical Society* 28, no. 3 (October 1935): 214-17. The slave girl was bought by Basil Silkwood from the Cherokee on their trek west, and set free.

2788. Neely, Charles, comp. *Tales and Songs of Southern Illinois.* Menasha, Wis.: George Banta, 1938. Reprint, Herrin, Ill.: Crossfire Press, 1989.

2789. Shuy, Roger W. *The Northern-Midland Dialect Boundary in Illinois.* Publication of the American Dialect Society, no. 38 (November 1962). Tuscaloosa: University of Alabama Press for the Society, 1964.

2790. Smith, Grace Partridge. "Egyptian 'Lies.' " *Midwest Folklore* 1 (1951): 93-97. Tall tales from southern Illinois.

2791. _____. "Folklore from 'Egypt.' " *Hoosier Folklore* 5 (1946): 45-70.

2792. _____. "Four Irish Ballads from 'Egypt.' " *Hoosier Folklore* 5 (1946): 115-19.

2793. _____. "More Lincoln Lore." *Midwest Folklore* 4 (1954): 169-70.

2794. _____. "Negro Lore in Southern Illinois." *Midwest Folklore* 2 (1952): 159-62.

2795. _____. "They Call It Egypt." *Names* 2 (1954): 51-54.

2796. Vogel, Virgil J. "Some Illinois Place-Name Legends." *Midwest Folklore* 9 (1959): 155-62.

2797. Walker, Warren S. "Water-witching in Central Illinois." *Midwest Folklore* 6 (1956): 197-203.

2798. Waller, Elbert. "Kaskaskia Destroyed by a Curse: A Tradition." *Journal of the Illinois State Historical Society* 3, no. 4 (January 1911): 67-69.

2799. Wine, Martin L. "Superstitions Collected in Chicago." *Midwest Folklore* 7 (1957): 149-59.

3. Immigration and Ethnic Groups

a. In General

2800. Adelman, William J. *Pilsen and the West Side.* Chicago: Illinois Labor History Society, 1983. A study of the changing ethnic composition of two Chicago neighborhoods and the burgeoning labor movement there.

2801. Allswang, John M. *A House for All Peoples: Ethnic Politics in Chicago, 1890-1936.* Lexington: University Press of Kentucky, 1971. A pioneering study of nine ethnic groups, based on the foreign-language press, unpublished census material, and election returns.

2802. Ander, Oscar Fritiof, comp. *The Cultural Heritage of the Swedish Immigrant: Selected References.* Augustana Library Publications, no. 27. Rock Island, Ill., 1956.

2803. _____. "Some Factors in the Americanization of the Swedish Immigrant, 1850-1890." *Journal of the Illinois State Historical Society* 26 (1933-34): 136-50.

2804. Anderson, Philip J., and Blanck, Dag, eds. *Swedish-American Life in Chicago: Cultural and Urban Aspects of an Immigrant People, 1850-1930.* Ethnic History of Chicago, edited by Melvin G. Holli. Urbana: University of Illinois Press, 1992.

2805. Babcock, Kendric C. *The Scandinavian Element in the United States.* University of Illinois Studies in Social Sciences, vol. 3, no. 3. Urbana: University of Illinois, 1914. Many references to Illinois people.

2806. Barry, P. T. "The First Irish in Illinois." *Transactions of the Illinois State Historical Society, 1902,* pp. 63-70.

2807. Beijdom, Ulf. "The Role of the Ethnic Press in Chicago's Swede Town." *Swedish Pioneer Historical Quarterly* 28 (1977): 82-96.

2808. _____. *Swedes in Chicago: A Demographic and Social Study of the 1846-1880 Immigration.* Studia Historica Upsaliensia, no. 38. Translated from the Swedish by Donald Brown. Stockholm: Løaromedelsføorlagen, 1971.

2809. Bernardi, Adria. *Houses with Names: The Italian Immigrants of Highwood, Illinois.* Urbana: University of Illinois Press, 1990. Fascinating interviews with Italian-Americans in Highwood, about thirty miles north of Chicago.

2810. Birch, Brian P. "The Pleasure and the Pain: An English Miller's Impression of Life in Mid-Nineteenth-Century Illinois." *Journal of the Illinois State Historical Society* 77 (1984): 129-44. Original letters, 1851-69, about his settlement near Galena, mill work, the family's health, and frontier hardships. There is also a good, but brief, introductory account of earlier English immigrants.

2811. Blegen, Theodore C., ed. *Land of Their Choice: The Immigrants Write Home*. Minneapolis: University of Minnesota Press, 1955. Letters from Norwegian immigrants to their families in Norway. A good index locates Chicago, Springfield, and Illinois references.

2812. _____. *Norwegian Migration to America, 1825-1860*. 2 vols. Publications of the Norwegian-American Historical Association. Northfield, Minn., 1931, 1940. Volume 2 is subtitled *The American Transition*.

2813. Bodnar, John E. *Collective Memory and Ethnic Groups: The Case of Swedes, Mennonites, and Norwegians*. Swenson Swedish Immigration Research Center, Occasional Paper no. 1. Rock Island, Ill.: Swenson Swedish Immigration Research Center, Augustana College, 1991.

2814. Bukowczyk, John J. *And My Children Did Not Know Me: A History of the Polish-Americans*. Minorities in Modern America series. Bloomington: Indiana University Press, 1987. The index has many Chicago entries. Excellent bibliographical essay.

2815. Coggeshall, John M. "Legislating Ethnicity: The Temperance Brouhaha in Southwestern Illinois." *Transactions of the Illinois State Historical Society: Selected Papers from the Fifth and Sixth Illinois History Symposiums of the Illinois State Historical Society* [1984 and 1985]. Springfield, 1988. Pp. 107-17. Actions of German-Americans, especially in Belleville and nearby communities, to defeat temperance forces in the years 1855-1919.

2816. Davies, Phillips G., ed. and trans. "Early Welsh Settlements in Illinois." *Journal of the Illinois State Historical Society* 70 (1977): 292-98. This extract, from Robert D. Thomas's history of the Welsh in America, published in 1872, describes settlements made by the Welsh after the 1830s.

2817. Davis, Allen F., and McCree, Mary Lynn, eds. *Eighty Years at Hull-House*. Chicago: Quadrangle Books, 1969. Descriptions of the settlement house and its goals, primarily by people who lived or visited there.

2818. Dowie, J. Iverne, and Espelie, Ernest M., eds. *The Swedish Immigrant Community in Transition: Essays in Honor of Conrad Bergendoff*. Rock Island, Ill.: Augustana Historical Society, 1963. Of particular interest to Illinoisans are essays on Augustana College at Rock Island, one by Bergendoff on Swedish-American education, a biographical sketch of Bergendoff, and a bibliography of his writings.

2819. Ericson, C. George. "Swedish Radio Services in Chicago." *Swedish Pioneer Historical Quarterly* 24 (1973): 157-62.

2820. Fainhauz, David. *Lithuanians in Multi-Ethnic Chicago*. Chicago: Lithuanian Library Press, 1977.

2821. Fanning, Charles; Skerrett, Ellen; and Corrigan, John. *Nineteenth Century Chicago Irish: A Social and Political Portrait*. Urban Insights Series, no. 7. Chicago: Center for Urban Policy, Loyola University of Chicago, 1980.

2822. Ffrench, Charles, ed. *Biographical History of the American Irish in Chicago*. Chicago: American Biographical Publishing, 1897.

2823. Frizzell, Robert W. "Migration Chains to Illinois: The Evidence from German-American Church Records." *Journal of American Ethnic History* 7 (Fall 1987): 59-73.

2824. _____. "Reticent Germans: The East Frisians of Illinois." *Illinois Historical Journal* 85 (1992): 161-74.

2825. Galush, William J. "Purity and Power: Chicago Polonian Feminists, 1880-1914." *Polish American Studies* 47 (1990): 5-24. Study of the organized activities (rather than pro-suffrage movements) of Polish women.

2826. Gayman, Esther Palm. *Tock Sa Mecka*. Commentary and maps by David C. Schoenwetter. Galesburg, Ill.: Log City Books, 1978. The story of the life of a Swedish immigrant family in Galesburg from the late nineteenth century to the 1970s. Schoenwetter contributes a study of ethnic residential patterns in Galesburg.

2827. Hall, Thomas Randolph. "The Russian Community of Chicago." *Transactions of the Illinois State Historical Society, 1937*, pp. 102-8.

2828. Hansen, Marcus Lee. *The Problem of the Third-Generation Immigrant.* Augustana College Library, Occasional Paper no. 16. Rock Island, Ill.: Swenson Swedish Immigration Research Center and Augustana College Library, 1987. Reprint of a 1937 address.

2829. Hauberg, Marx D. *Memoirs of Marx D. Hauberg, Being a Personal Narrative of the Immigration of His Parents and Their Children from Schleswig-Holstein, 1848 . . . to 1923.* Rock Island, Ill.: Privately printed, 1923.

2830. Heimovics, Rachel Baron. *The Chicago Jewish Source Book.* Chicago: Follett, 1981.

2831. Hoerder, Dirk, ed. *American Labor and Immigration History, 1877-1920s: Recent European Research.* Urbana: University of Illinois Press, 1983. Among the twelve previously unpublished essays in this collection are an analysis of the 1877 railroad strikes, by Marianne Debouzy, and a study of Chicago's German working-class community, 1875-90, by Hartmut Keil.

2832. Hoflund, Charles J. *Getting Ahead: A Swedish Immigrant's Reminiscences, 1834-1887.* Edited by H. Arnold Barton. Carbondale: Southern Illinois University Press, 1989. The author arrived with his parents at Andover in 1850.

2833. Holli, Melvin G., and Jones, Peter d'A., eds. *Ethnic Chicago.* 1981. Rev. and enl., Grand Rapids, Mich.: Eerdmans, 1984. Essayists provide studies of group values, social structures, and political activities of various ethnic groups--arriving at differing conclusions about cultural identity. Some of the essays were published in *The Ethnic Frontier*.

2834. _____, eds. *The Ethnic Frontier: Essays in the History of Group Survival in Chicago and the Midwest.* Grand Rapids, Mich.: Eerdmans, 1977.

2835. Jaret, Charles. "Recent Patterns of Chicago Jewish Residential Mobility." *Ethnicity* 6 (1979): 235-48.

2836. Jones, Anita Edgar. *Conditions Surrounding Mexicans in Chicago.* San Francisco: R. and E. Research Associates, 1971.

2837. Kantowicz, Edward R. "A Fragment of French Canada on the Illinois Prairies." *Journal of the Illinois State Historical Society* 75 (1982): 263-76. An account of French settlers on the Kankakee River in Illinois from the early 1800s through 1920.

2838. _____. *Polish-American Politics in Chicago, 1888-1940.* Chicago: University of Chicago Press, 1975. A study of voting patterns (in the precincts and wards the author has identified as Polish) leads to discussions of Polish-American attitudes and culture.

2839. Keil, Hartmut, and Jentz, John B. "The Chicago Project: A Study in German Ethnicity." *American Studies International* 20 (Summer 1982): 22-30. The project is sponsored by several academic institutions, including the Newberry Library in Chicago, and funded since 1979 by the Volkswagen Foundation.

2840. Keil, Hartmut, ed. *German Workers' Culture in the United States, 1850 to 1920.* Washington: Smithsonian Institution Press, 1988. The book's thirteen chapters, by different authors, constitute a broad cultural history--particularly of German-American life in Chicago.

2841. _____, and Jentz, John B., eds. *German Workers in Chicago: A Documentary History of Working-Class Culture from 1850 to World War I.* Translated by Burt Weinshanker. The Working Class in American History series. Urbana: University of Illinois Press, 1988. This anthology includes 135 documents.

2842. _____, eds. *German Workers in Industrial Chicago, 1850-1910: A Comparative Perspective.* DeKalb: Northern Illinois University Press, 1983.

2843. Kim, Bok-Lim C. "Problems and Service Needs of Asian Americans in Chicago: An Empirical Study." *Amerasia Journal* 5, no. 2 (1978): 23-44.

2844. Kim, Kwang Chung, and Hurh, Won Moo. "Ethnic Resources: Utilization of Korean Immigrant Entrepreneurs in the Chicago Minority Area." *International Migration Review* 19 (Spring 1985): 82-111.

2845. Kimball, Stanley B. *East Europeans in Southwestern Illinois: The Ethnic Experience in Historical Perspective.* Research Report, no. 14, of the Coordinator of Area Development, Southern Illinois University at Edwardsville, May, 1981.

2846. Kopan, Andrew T. *Education and Greek Immigrants in Chicago, 1892-1973: A Study in Ethnic Survival.* New York: Garland, 1990.

2847. Kourvetaris, George A. *First and Second Generation Greeks in Chicago: An Inquiry into Their Stratification and Mobility Patterns.* Athens, Greece: National Center of Social Research, 1971.

2848. Lazo, Dimitri D. "Protestant Home Missions to the Immigrant: The Work of Paul Fox in Chicago's Polonia, 1924-1942." *Selected Papers in Illinois History, 1982.* Springfield: Illinois State Historical Society, 1984. Pp. 79-86.

2849. Levine, Bruce C. *The Spirit of 1848: German Immigrants, Labor Conflict, and the Coming of the Civil War.* Urbana: University of Illinois Press, 1992.

2850. Lindmark, Sture. *Swedish-America, 1914-1932: Studies in Ethnicity with Emphasis on Illinois and Minnesota.* Studia Historica Upsaliensia, 37. Stockholm: Läromedelsförlaget, 1971.

2851. Lissak, Rivka Shpak. *Pluralism & Progressives: Hull House and the New Immigrants, 1890-1919.* Chicago: University of Chicago Press, 1989. Demythologizes the Hull House philosophy and experience.

2852. Lovoll, Odd S. *A Century of Urban Life: The Norwegians in Chicago before 1900.* Northfield, Minn.: Norwegian-American Historical Association, 1988. Distributed by the University of Illinois Press.

2853. McCaffrey, Lawrence J.; Skerrett, Ellen; Funchion, Michael F.; and Fanning, Charles. *The Irish in Chicago.* Ethnic History of Chicago, edited by Melvin G. Holli. Urbana: University of Illinois Press, 1987.

2854. McGoorty, John P. "The Early Irish of Illinois." *Transactions of the Illinois State Historical Society, 1927,* pp. 54-64. Irish who arrived in Illinois before 1818.

2855. MacMillan, Thomas C. "The Scots and Their Descendants in Illinois." *Transactions of the Illinois State Historical Society, 1919,* pp. 31-85.

2856. Manfredini, Dolores M. "The Italians Come to Herrin." *Journal of the Illinois State Historical Society* 37 (1944): 317-28. Brief study of the immigration in the late nineteenth and early twentieth centuries, with accounts of their social life and customs to 1944.

2857. Mazur, Edward Herbert. *Minyans for a Prairie City: The Politics of Chicago Jewry, 1850-1940.* European Immigrants and American Society series. New York: Garland, 1990.

2858. Meites, Hyman L., ed. *History of the Jews of Chicago.* Chicago: Jewish Historical Society of Illinois, 1924. Facsimile reprint, Chicago: Chicago Jewish Historical Society and Wellington Publishing, 1990. New introduction by James R. Grossman. Biographical sketches of more than five hundred individuals are scattered throughout the book in the appropriate chapters--those of lawyers following the general chapter on "Law," etc. There is a good index.

2859. Monaghan, Jay. "The Welsh People in Chicago." *Journal of the Illinois State Historical Society* 32 (1939): 498-516.

2860. Nelli, Humbert S. *The Business of Crime: Italians and Syndicate Crime in the United States.* New York: Oxford University Press, 1976.

2861. _____. *From Immigrants to Ethnics: The Italian Americans.* New York: Oxford University Press, 1983.

2862. _____. *Italians in Chicago, 1880-1930: A Study in Ethnic Mobility.* Urban Life in America series. New York: Oxford University Press, 1970.

2863. _____. "John Powers and the Italians: Politics in a Chicago Ward, 1896-1921." *Journal of American History* 57 (1970-71): 67-84.

2864. Nelson, Helge. *The Swedes and the Swedish Settlements in North America.* 2 vols. Lund: C. W. K. Gleerup, 1943. Reprint, 2 vols. in 1, New York: Arno, 1979. Illinois, pp. 138-74, and charts and maps.

2865. Norelius, Eric. *The Pioneer Swedish Settlements and Swedish Lutheran Churches in America, 1845-1860.* Translated by Conrad Bergendoff. Augustana Historical Society Publication no. 31. Rock Island, Ill., 1984. Chapters 2-8 deal with settlements and churches in Illinois. The selections in this volume were chosen from the much-longer Swedish work published in two volumes by the Lutheran Augustana Book Concern, Rock Island, 1890-1910.

2866. Nyblom, Gösta, ed. *Americans of Swedish Descent: How They Live and Work.* Rock Island, Ill.: G. Nyblom Publishing House, 1948. The last half of this 600-page volume is devoted to biographies of approximately 1,000 Illinoisans of Swedish descent.

2867. Olson, Ernst Wilhelm, ed., in collaboration with Schön Anders and Martin J. Engberg. *History of the Swedes of Illinois.* 2 vols. Chicago: Engberg-Holmberg Publishing, 1908. Reprint, New York: Arno, 1979. Volume 2 consists of biographical sketches.

2868. _____. *The Swedish Element in Illinois: Survey of the Past Seven Decades . . . with Life Sketches of Men of To-Day.* Chicago: Swedish-American Biographical Association, 1917.

2869. Osland, Birger. *A Long Pull from Stavanger: The Reminiscences of a Norwegian Immigrant.* Publications of the Norwegian-American Historical Association. Northfield, Minn., 1945. The author not only recalls his life in Chicago but also provides general information about many other Norwegian-American immigrants.

2870. Pacyga, Dominic A. "Polish-America in Transition: Social Change and the Chicago Polonia, 1945-1980." *Polish-American Studies* 44 (Spring 1987): 38-55.

2871. Padilla, Felix M. *Puerto Rican Chicago.* Notre Dame, Ind.: University of Notre Dame Press, 1987.

2872. Parot, Joseph John. "Ethnic versus Black Metropolis: The Origins of Polish-Black Housing Tensions in Chicago." *Polish American Studies* 29 (1972): 5-33.

2873. _____. "The Racial Dilemma in Chicago's Polish Neighborhoods, 1920-1970." *Polish American Studies* 32 (1975): 27-37.

2874. Pinderhughes, Dianne M. *Race and Ethnicity in Chicago Politics: A Reexamination of Pluralist Theory.* Urbana: University of Illinois Press, 1987. This study concentrates on African-Americans, while contrasting their integration into politics and society with that of Poles and Italians. Emphasis is on the years 1910-40, but the author brings her account of developments to 1983.

2875. Polacheck, Hilda Satt. *I Came a Stranger: The Story of a Hull-House Girl.* Edited by Dena J. Polacheck Epstein. Women in American History series. Urbana: University of Illinois Press, 1989. The influence of the settlement house on an immigrant Polish-Jewish girl.

2876. Posadas, Barbara M., and Guyotte, Roland L. "Aspiration and Reality: Occupational and Educational Choice among Filipino Migrants to Chicago, 1900-1935." *Illinois Historical Journal* 85 (1992): 89-104.

2877. Prisland, Marie. *From Slovenia to America: Recollections and Collections.* Chicago: Slovenian Women's Union of America, 1978. Chapter 10 concerns Slovenian settlements in Illinois.

2878. Prpic, George J. *The Croatian Immigrants in America.* New York: Philosophical Library, 1971.

2879. Rawlings, Mrs. Isaac D. "Polish Exiles in Illinois." *Transactions of the Illinois State Historical Society, 1927,* pp. 83-104.

2880. Ropko, Gerald William. *The Evolving Residential Pattern of the Mexican, Puerto Rican, and Cuban Population in the City of Chicago.* Hispanics in the United States series. New York: Arno, 1980. The author discusses immigrant settlement patterns in Chicago as early as 1800.

2881. Schiavo, Giovanni E. *The Italians in Chicago: A Study in Americanization.* Chicago: Italian American Publishing, 1928. Reprint, New York: Arno, 1975.

2882. Schnucker, George. *The East Friesens in America: An Illustrated History of Their Colonies to the Present Time.* Translated by Kenneth De Wall. Bethalto, Ill.: Ostfriesen Ancestral Research Association, 1986. This work makes available in English information about a German immigrant group that had several settlements in Illinois.

2883. *The Sentinel's History of Chicago Jewry, 1911-1986.* Published as the 15 October 1986 issue of the *Sentinel.*

2884. Stephenson, George M. "The Stormy Years of the Swedish Colony in Chicago before the Great Fire." *Transactions of the Illinois State Historical Society, 1929,* pp. 166-84. The years were stormy in part because of theological differences in the church. These differences were reflected in Swedish-American newspapers as well. Also contributing to discontent were unscrupulous immigration agents and land companies.

2885. Strand, Algot E., comp. and ed. *A History of the Norwegians of Illinois: A Concise Record of the Struggles and Achievements of the Early Settlers together with a Narrative of What Is Now Being Done by the Norwegian-*

Americans of Illinois in the Development of Their Adopted Country. Chicago: J. Anderson, 1905. Histories of communities and organizations, with many biographical sketches, for which there is an index.

2886. Thurner, Arthur W. "Polish Americans in Chicago Politics, 1890-1937." *Polish American Studies* 28 (1971): 20-42.

2887. Unonius, Gustaf. *A Pioneer in Northwest America, 1841-1858: The Memoirs of Gustaf Unonius.* Translated by Jonas Oscar Backlund; edited by Nils William Olsson. 2 vols. Minneapolis: University of Minnesota Press, 1950, 1960, for the Swedish Pioneer Historical Society.

2888. Van Reenan, Antanas J. *Lithuanian Diaspora: Königsberg to Chicago.* Lanham, Md.: University Press of America, 1990.

2889. Vecoli, Rudolph J. "*Contadini* in Chicago: A Critique of *The Uprooted.*" *Journal of American History* 51 (1963-64): 404-17. The author disputes Oscar Handlin's interpretation of Italian peasant society and of Italian immigrants' adjustment to life in Chicago.

2890. _____. "The Formation of Chicago's 'Little Italies.' " *Journal of American Ethnic History* 2 (Spring 1983): 5-20.

2891. Wirth, Louis. *The Ghetto: A Study in Isolation.* 1928. Midway Reprint, Chicago: University of Chicago Press, 1982. Five chapters (out of fourteen) are devoted to Jews in Chicago.

2892. Wyman, Mark. *Immigrants in the Valley: Irish, Germans, and Americans in the Upper Mississippi Country, 1830-1860.* Chicago: Nelson-Hall, 1984. Immigrants in the Upper Mississippi River Valley, particularly Illinois, with consideration of their reasons for leaving their home countries and discussions of how they coped with their adopted land.

2893. _____. *Immigration History and Ethnicity in Illinois: A Guide.* Illinois Historical Leaflet, no. 3. Springfield: Illinois State Historical Society, 1990.

2894. Zenner, Walter P. "Chicago's Sephardim: A Historical Exploration." *American Jewish History* 79 (1989-90): 221-41. How the Mediterranean and Southwest Asian Jews adapted to a Jewish community that was principally from Europe (Ashkenazi).

b. African-Americans

2895. Aldrich, O. W. "Slavery or Involuntary Servitude in Illinois Prior to and after Its Admission as a State." *Journal of the Illinois State Historical Society* 9 (1916-17): 119-22.

2896. Allen, John W. "Slavery and Negro Servitude in Pope County, Illinois." *Journal of the Illinois State Historical Society* 42 (1949): 411-23.

2897. Allswang, John M. "The Chicago Negro Voter and the Democratic Consensus: A Case Study, 1918-1936." *Journal of the Illinois State Historical Society* 60 (1967): 145-75. Traces the gradual change from the Republican to the Democratic party.

2898. Anderson, Alan B., and Pickering, George W. *Confronting the Color Line: The Broken Promise of the Civil Rights Movement in Chicago.* Athens: University of Georgia Press, 1986.

2899. Andrews, Stanley Burnell. *An Ethno-Historical Survey of Negro Settlement Patterns in the Black Bottoms of Southern Illinois.* Carbondale: Southern Illinois University, 1969. The area studied includes Pope, Massac, Johnson, and Randolph counties.

2900. Blockson, Charles L., with Ron Fry. *Black Genealogy.* Englewood Cliffs, N.J.: Prentice-Hall, 1977. A general how-to book, with a directory of research sources by state (and countries) and a bibliography.

2901. Bridges, Roger Dean. "Equality Deferred: Civil Rights for Illinois Blacks, 1865-1885." *Journal of the Illinois State Historical Society* 74 (1981): 82-108.

2902. Carlson, Shirley J. "Black Migration to Pulaski County, Illinois, 1860-1900." *Illinois Historical Journal* 80 (1987): 37-46. Family sketches and census statistics illuminate this previously neglected history of deep southern Illinois.

2903. Christian, Charles. *Social Areas and Spatial Change in the Black Community of Chicago, 1950-1960.* Occasional Publications of the University of Illinois Department of Geography, no. 2. Urbana, 1972.

2904. Cooley, Verna. "Illinois and the Underground Railroad to Canada." *Transactions of the Illinois State Historical Society, 1917,* pp. 76-98.

2905. Cunningham, Eileen Smith, and Schneider, Mabel Ambrose, eds. "A Slave's Autobiography Retold." *Western Illinois Regional Studies* 2 (1979): 109-26. Reminiscences of Willis McDonald, a onetime slave who made his way north to Springfield and Jacksonville, Illinois, after the Civil War.

2906. Dilliard, Irving. "Civil Liberties of Negroes in Illinois since 1865." *Journal of the Illinois State Historical Society* 56 (1963): 592-624.

2907. Drake, St. Clair, and Cayton, Horace R. *Black Metropolis: A Study of Negro Life in a Northern City.* New York: Harcourt, Brace, 1945. Rev. and enl. ed., 1970. A classic study of African-Americans in Chicago.

2908. Durham, Joseph T. "The Negro in Illinois." *Illinois Quarterly* 33, no. 4 (April 1971): 6-27.

2909. Finkelman, Paul. "Slavery, the 'More Perfect Union,' and the Prairie State." *Illinois Historical Journal* 80 (1987): 248-69. Illinois laws and court decisions relating to slaves, fugitive slaves, and free blacks from 1787 to 1858.

2910. Fisher, Miles Mark. "Negro Churches in Illinois: A Fragmentary History with Emphasis on Chicago." *Journal of the Illinois State Historical Society* 56 (1963): 552-69.

2911. Gara, Larry. "The Underground Railroad in Illinois." *Journal of the Illinois State Historical Society* 56 (1963): 508-28. Illinois abolitionists uniformly supported giving help to runaway slaves (once they had left the slave states), but the tradition of an organized Underground Railroad, the author says, "exaggerates and oversimplifies a history which had a basis in fact."

2912. Gertz, Elmer. "The Black Laws of Illinois." *Journal of the Illinois State Historical Society* 56 (1963): 454-73. History of the laws, 1803-64, that pertained to indentured blacks.

2913. Gliozzo, Charles A. "John Jones: A Study of a Black Chicagoan." *Illinois Historical Journal* 80 (1987): 177-88. A study of the remarkable man who made his way to Chicago in 1845 and became one of the leading abolitionists in the state.

2914. Gregory, Dick, with Robert Lipstye. *Nigger: An Autobiography.* New York: Dutton, 1964. Compelling story of the prejudice Gregory faced both before and after he became a track star at Southern Illinois University. Gregory later gained fame as a comedian and a civil rights activist.

2915. _____, with James R. McGraw. *Up from Nigger.* New York: Stein & Day, 1976. Gregory's career from 1963.

2916. Harris, N. Dwight. *The History of Negro Servitude in Illinois and of the Slavery Agitation in That State, 1719-1864.* Chicago: McClurg, 1904. Reprints, Ann Arbor, Mich.: University Microfilms, 1968; New York: Negro Universities Press, 1969; and New York: Haskell House, 1969.

2917. Hirsch, Arnold R. *Making the Second Ghetto: Race and Housing in Chicago, 1940-1960.* Interdisciplinary Perspectives on Modern History. New York: Cambridge University Press, 1983.

2918. Homel, Michael W. *Down from Equality: Black Chicagoans and the Public Schools, 1920-41.* Blacks in the New World series, edited by August Meier. Urbana: University of Illinois Press, 1984.

2919. Horney, Helen, and Keller, William E., comps. "The Negro's Two Hundred Forty Years in Illinois: A Chronology." *Journal of the Illinois State Historical Society* 56 (1963): 433-38.

2920. *Illinois Generations: A Traveler's Guide to African American Heritage.* With an introduction by Charles Branham. Chicago: Performance Media, Chicago Sun-Times Features, 1994. A beautiful, useful publication (of 38 pages), funded by private businesses, the Du Sable Museum of African American History, and the Illinois Bureau of Tourism.

2921. "The Issue of Freedom in Illinois." *Journal of the Illinois State Historical Society* 57 (1964). "Under Gov. Edward Coles, 1822-1826," by John Thomas Cassidy, pp. 284-88. "Under Gov. Wm. H. Bissell, 1857-1860," by Mary Jane Hiler, pp. 288-92. "Under Gov. Richard Yates, 1861-1865," by Linda Hartman, pp. 293-97.

2922. Jones, Johnetta Y. "Black Land Tenancy in Extreme Southern Illinois, 1870-1920." *Selected Papers in Illinois History, 1980.* Springfield: Illinois State Historical Society, 1982. Pp. 41-51.

2923. Lemann, Nicholas. *The Promised Land: The Great Black Migration and How It Changed America.* New York: Knopf, 1991. The migration of blacks from the South to North between World War II and the 1970s was perhaps the greatest movement of an ethnic group "not caused by the immediate threat of execution or starvation." The author advances the account with histories of individual migrants who moved from Clarksdale, Mississippi, to Chicago; many have since returned to Mississippi.

2924. Lochard, Metz T. P. "The Negro Press in Illinois." *Journal of the Illinois State Historical Society* 56 (1963): 570-91. Focuses primarily on the *Chicago Defender.*

2925. Reed, Christopher Robert. "Black Chicago Civic Organization before 1935." *Journal of Ethnic Studies* 14 (Winter 1987): 65-77.

2926. Spear, Allan H. *Black Chicago: The Making of a Negro Ghetto, 1890-1920.* Chicago: University of Chicago Press, 1967.

2927. Stevenson, Rosemary M., comp. *Index to Afro-American Reference Resources.* Bibliographies and Indexes in Afro-American and African Studies, no. 20. New York: Greenwood Press, 1988. Entries are assigned to subject categories, which are arranged alphabetically. There are author and title indexes.

2928. Strickland, Arvarh E. *History of the Chicago Urban League.* Urbana: University of Illinois Press, 1966.

2929. Travis, Dempsey J. *An Autobiography of Black Chicago.* Chicago: Urban Research Institute, 1981. History of African-Americans in Chicago. Almost one third of the book is devoted to biographies.

2930. _____. *An Autobiography of Black Politics.* Chicago: Urban Research Press, 1987. A colorful account of African-Americans in Chicago politics and government.

2931. Walker, Juliet E. K. *Free Frank: A Black Pioneer on the Antebellum Frontier.* Lexington: University of Kentucky Press, 1983. A onetime slave who managed to buy his own freedom, Frank McWhorter settled in Pike County, where he became a successful farmer and businessman, and bought the freedom of sixteen family members.

2932. Watkins, Sylvestre C. Sr. "Some of Early Illinois' Free Negroes." *Journal of the Illinois State Historical Society* 56 (1963): 495-507. Sketches of six African-American men, including Jean Baptiste Point du Sable and John Jones.

4. Intellectual Movements and the Arts

a. In General

2933. Anderson, Paul Russell. "Hiram K. Jones and Philosophy in Jacksonville." *Journal of the Illinois State Historical Society* 33 (1940): 478-520. Jones was influential in the many literary, philosophical, and scientific societies (for both men and women) that flourished in Jacksonville throughout the nineteenth century.

2934. _____. "Quincy, an Outpost of Philosophy." *Journal of the Illinois State Historical Society* 34 (1941): 50-83. A history of the intellectual life of Quincy from 1840 to 1881.

2935. Andrews, Clarence A. *Chicago in Story: A Literary History.* Iowa City, Iowa: Midwest Heritage Publishing, 1982.

2936. Beadle, Muriel, and the Centennial History Committee. *The Fortnightly of Chicago: The City and Its Women, 1873-1973.* Edited, and with a foreword, by Fanny Butcher. Chicago: Regnery, 1973.

2937. Brent, Stuart. *The Seven Stairs.* Boston: Houghton Mifflin, 1962. Reminiscences of the Chicago bookseller.

2938. Bridges, Roger Dean. "The Origins and Early Years of the Illinois State Historical Society." *Journal of the Illinois State Historical Society* 68 (1975): 98-120. The Illinois State Historical Library was created by statute in 1889 and the Society was organized ten years later. Bridges discusses the difficult early relationships between the two entities.

2939. Cole, John Y. *The Bookseller's Art: Carl Kroch and Kroch's & Brentano's.* Washington: Library of Congress, 1988. Contains tributes and reminiscences from many authors as well as information about Kroch and the bookstore.

2940. Duffey, Bernard. *The Chicago Renaissance in American Letters: A Critical History.* East Lansing: Michigan State College Press, 1954.

2941. Duncan, Hugh Dalziel. *The Rise of Chicago as a Literary Center from 1885 to 1920: A Sociological Essay in American Culture.* Totowa, N.J.: Bedminster Press, 1964.

2942. Dunn, F. Roger. "Formative Years of the Chicago Y.M.C.A." *Journal of the Illinois State Historical Society* 37 (1944): 321-50. The founders (in 1858) had a strong religious orientation, but also provided many of the educational functions of earlier similar societies.

2943. Hendrickson, Walter B., and Langfitt, John N. "The Men's Literary Clubs of Jacksonville." *Western Illinois Regional Studies* 3 (1980): 66-83. The principal club was founded in 1861 and was still active in 1980.

2944. Hirsch, Arthur H. "Historical Values in the Mid-Century Literature of the Middle West." *Transactions of the Illinois State Historical Society, 1929*, pp. 117-25.

2945. Hoffmann, John. "The 'Upward Movement' in Illinois: Henry B. Fuller's Record of Cultural Progress, 1867-1917." *Journal of the Illinois State Historical Society* 76 (1983): 257-72. Chicagoan Henry Fuller wrote an account of "Culture in Illinois" for the state's centennial history. Hoffmann's discussion of Fuller's work is in itself a valuable essay in twentieth-century historiography.

2946. Horowitz, Helen Lefkowitz. *Culture & the City: Cultural Philanthropy in Chicago from the 1880s to 1917*. Lexington: University Press of Kentucky, 1976. Extensive discussions of Chicago's libraries, as well as of its museums, the Chicago Symphony, the University of Chicago, and artists and writers.

2947. Hughett, Barbara. *The Civil War Round Table: Fifty Years of Scholarship and Fellowship*. Chicago: Civil War Round Table, 1990. The Round Table was the idea of Ralph G. Newman of the Abraham Lincoln Bookshop who met informally with sixteen of his customers for several years before the Round Table was formally organized.

2948. "The Illinois State Historical Society." *Journal of the Illinois State Historical Society* 34 (1941): 349-65. Includes histories of earlier statewide historical societies as well as a listing of the members in 1941.

2949. Johnson, Abby Arthur. "A Free Foot in the Wilderness--Harriet Monroe and *Poetry*, 1912 to 1936." *Illinois Quarterly* 37, no. 4 (Summer 1975): 28-43.

2950. Kusmer, Kenneth L. "The Social History of Cultural Institutions: The Upper-Class Connection." *Journal of Interdisciplinary History* 10 (Summer 1979): 137-46. As illustrated by Chicago from the 1880s to 1917.

2951. Miller, Katharine Aird, and Montgomery, Raymond H. *A Chautauqua to Remember: The Story of Old Salem.* Petersburg, Ill.: Silent River Press, 1987. The Old Salem Chautauqua, one of the Midwest's largest, flourished 1898-1942, in Menard County.

2952. Raymer, John. "A Changing Sense of Chicago in the Works of Saul Bellow and Nelson Algren." *Old Northwest* 4 (December 1978): 371-83.

2953. Regnery, Henry. *Creative Chicago: From* The Chap-Book *to the University.* Evanston, Ill.: Chicago Historical Bookworks, 1993. Introduction by Joseph Epstein. This collection of essays by Regnery constitutes a cultural history of Chicago in the late nineteenth and early twentieth centuries.

2954. Reigelman, Milton M. *The Midland: A Venture in Literary Regionalism.* Iowa City: University of Iowa Press, 1975. The literary magazine *The Midland,* 1915-33, was published in Chicago in later years.

2955. Seymour, Ralph Fletcher. *Some Went This Way: A Forty Year Pilgrimage among Artists, Bookmen and Printers.* Chicago: The author, 1945. As a publisher, Seymour had many personal encounters with the leading literary and artistic figures in Chicago in the late nineteenth and early twentieth centuries.

2956. Simon, John Y., and Hughett, Barbara, eds. *The Continuing Civil War: Essays in Honor of the Civil War Round Table of Chicago.* Dayton, Ohio: Morningside House, 1992.

2957. Smith, Carl S. *Chicago and the Literary Imagination, 1880-1920.* Chicago: University of Chicago Press, 1984. A study of Chicago that successfully links history and fiction.

2958. Tingley, Donald Fred. "Ralph Waldo Emerson on the Illinois Lecture Circuit." *Journal of the Illinois State Historical Society* 64 (1971): 192-205. On Emerson's 1856 lecture tour, the author says, "the reaction of the audience to him and his impressions of the West illustrate the cultural climate of the frontier." Between 1850 and 1871, Emerson conducted eleven lecture tours in the state.

2959. Williams, Kenny J. *Prairie Voices: A Literary History of Chicago from the Frontier to 1893.* Nashville, Tenn.: Townsend Press, 1980. Emphasizes the roles played by newspapers, magazines, and Chicago publishing houses. Appendixes contain bibliographies of 1) newspapers and magazines; 2) leading publishers, with historical sketches of some; and 3) Chicago novels.

b. Architecture and Art

2960. Andrew, David S. *Louis Sullivan and the Polemics of Modern Architecture: The Present against the Past.* Urbana: University of Illinois Press, 1985. A new interpretation of the relationship between Sullivan's writings and the buildings he designed.

2961. "Auditorium Building Getting Older but Better." *Roosevelt University Magazine* 10, no. 1 (Winter/Spring 1980): 10-12. The Auditorium Building in Chicago is the home of Roosevelt University and a National Historic Landmark. Louis Sullivan was the architect.

2962. Ayers, Esther Mary. "Art in Southern Illinois, 1865-1914." *Journal of the Illinois State Historical Society* 36 (1943): 164-89.

2963. Babson, Jane F. "The Architecture of Early Illinois Forts." *Journal of the Illinois State Historical Society* 61 (1968): 9-40. More than two thirds of this article is devoted to forts built by the French, especially Fort de Chartres, Fort Massac, and Fort Kaskaskia. Also good accounts of Forts Dearborn and Armstrong.

2964. Bach, Ira J., ed., with the assistance of Roy Forrey and contributions by Carl W. Condit and Hugh Dalziel Duncan. *Chicago's Famous Buildings: A Photographic Guide to the City's Architectural Landmarks and Other Notable Buildings.* 3d ed., rev. and enl. Chicago: University of Chicago Press, 1980.

2965. Bluestone, Daniel. *Constructing Chicago.* New Haven, Conn.: Yale University Press, 1991.

2966. Bolon, Carol R.; Nelson, Robert S.; and Seidel, Linda, eds. *The Nature of Frank Lloyd Wright.* Chicago: University of Chicago Press, 1988. A collection of essays presented at a symposium celebrating the seventy-fifth anniversary of the Robie House in Chicago.

2967. Brooks, H. Allen. *The Prairie School: Frank Lloyd Wright and His Midwest Contemporaries.* Toronto, Ont.: University of Toronto Press, 1972.

2968. *Bruce Graham of SOM.* Introduction by Stanley Tigerman. New York: Rizzoli, 1989. This volume consists mainly of photographs and descriptions of buildings designed by Graham, a member of the firm of Skidmore, Owings & Merrill.

2969. Bruegmann, Robert. *Holabird & Roche; Holabird & Root: An Illustrated Catalog of Works, 1880-1940.* 3 vols. New York: Garland, in cooperation with the Chicago Historical Society, 1991. A brief history of the Chicago architectural firm precedes the 1,530 listings, many of which also have detailed descriptions and histories. Appendixes list the works by both location and type of structure.

2970. Bush-Brown, Albert. *Skidmore, Owings & Merrill: Architecture and Urbanism, 1973-1983.* New York: Van Nostrand Reinhold, 1983. Work of the Chicago firm throughout the world.

2971. Chappell, Sally A. Kitt. *Architecture and Planning of Graham, Anderson, Probst and White, 1912-1936: Transforming Tradition.* Chicago: University of Chicago Press, 1992.

2972. Coggeshall, John M., and Nast, Jo Anne; with photographs by Randy Tindall. *Vernacular Architecture in Southern Illinois: The Ethnic Heritage.* Carbondale: Southern Illinois University Press, 1988. A pioneering Illinois study of home designs by non-architects.

2973. Cohen, Stuart E. *Chicago Architects.* With an introduction by Stanley Tigerman. Chicago: Swallow Press, 1976. Catalog of an exhibit illustrating the works of outstanding Chicago architects, with biographical sketches and a bibliography.

2974. Condit, Carl W. *Chicago, 1910-29: Building, Planning, and Urban Technology.* Chicago: University of Chicago Press, 1973.

2975. _____. *Chicago, 1930-1970: Building, Planning, and Urban Technology.* Chicago: University of Chicago Press, 1974.

2976. _____. *The Chicago School of Architecture: A History of Commercial and Public Buildings in the Chicago Area, 1875-1925.* Chicago: University of Chicago Press, 1964.

2977. Connors, Joseph. *The Robie House of Frank Lloyd Wright.* Chicago: University of Chicago Press, 1984.

2978. Cunningham, Eileen Smith. *Lower Illinois Valley Limestone Houses .* Carrollton, Ill., 1976.

2979. Eastman, John. *Who Lived Where: A Biographical Guide to Homes and Museums.* New York: Bonanza Books, 1983. Illinois homes of forty-seven well-known people are located and described on pages 237-52. Includes such unexpected names as Jack Johnson, Ring Lardner, Florenz Ziegfeld, Paul Tillich, Hannah Arendt, and John Dillinger.

2980. Elbert, E. Duane, and Elbert, Rachel Kamm. *History from the Heart: Quilt Paths across Illinois.* Nashville, Tenn.: Rutledge Hill Press, 1993. Accompanying 150 exquisite color illustrations are descriptions of quilting techniques and histories of the quilt-makers and their milieus.

2981. Elder, Lucius W. "The Mississippi River as an Artistic Subject." *Transactions of the Illinois State Historical Society, 1937*, pp. 34-42. With sixteen illustrations.

2982. "Four Illinois Scenes." *Journal of the Illinois State Historical Society* 47 (1954): 442-44. Reproductions of four works, and a sketch of the life of artist William S. Schwartz of Chicago.

2983. Garner, John S., ed. *The Midwest in American Architecture.* Urbana: University of Illinois Press, 1991. Among the essays in this volume is the editor's "S. S. Beman and the Building of Pullman."

2984. Gary, Grace. "Wright at Home: Exacting Restoration of the Frank Lloyd Wright Home and Studio in Oak Park, Ill. . . . *Historic Preservation* 40 (July-August 1988): 46-51.

2985. Geraniotis, Roula Mouroudellis. "German Architectural Theory and Practice in Chicago, 1850-1900." *Winterthur Portfolio* 21 (Winter 1986): 293-306.

2986. Grube, Oswald W.; Pran, Peter C.; and Schulze, Franz. *100 Years of Architecture in Chicago: Continuity of Structure and Form; Exhibited at the Museum of Contemporary Art, Chicago.* 3d ed. Chicago: Follett, 1977.

2987. Hoffman, Donald. *Frank Lloyd Wright's Robie House: The Illustrated Story of an Architectural Masterpiece.* New York: Dover Publications, 1984. Both an architectural and historical study.

2988. Kalec, Donald. *The Home and Studio of Frank Lloyd Wright in Oak Park, Illinois, 1889-1911.* Oak Park: Frank Lloyd Wright Home and Studio Foundation, 1982.

2989. Koepfer, Frederick, ed. *Illinois Architecture: From Territorial Times to the Present--A Selective Guide.* Chicago: University of Chicago Press, 1968. A collaboration of the University of Chicago Press and the architecture committee of the Illinois Sesquicentennial Commission, this volume presents photographs and discussions of 150 examples of the state's architecture.

2990. Lane, George A. *Chicago Churches and Synagogues: An Architectural Pilgrimage.* Chicago: Loyola University Press, 1981. A study of 125 structures, selected primarily for architectural distinction.

2991. Larson, Paul Clifford, and Brown, Susan M., eds. *The Spirit of H. H. Richardson on the Midland Prairies: Regional Transformations of an Architectural Style.* Ames: Iowa State University Press, 1988.

2992. Madden, Betty I. *Arts, Crafts, and Architecture in Early Illinois.* Urbana: University of Illinois Press, 1974.

2993. Maycock, Susan E. *An Architectural History of Carbondale, Illinois.* Carbondale: Southern Illinois University Press, 1983.

2994. Monaghan, Jay. "Old Masterpieces Discovered in the Corn Belt." *Journal of the Illinois State Historical Society* 34 (1941): 366-71. Four, possibly five, portraits by the African-American artist Joshua Johnston had been discovered in Illinois by 1941.

2995. Mounce, Eva Dodge. *Checklist of Illinois Potters and Potteries.* Edited by Floyd R. Mansberger and John A. Walthall. Historic Illinois Potteries Circular Series, vol. 1, no. 3. Springfield: Foundation for Historical Research of Illinois Potteries, 1989.

2996. _____. *The Potteries of La Salle County.* Historic Illinois Potteries Circular Series, vol. 1, no. 1. Springfield: Foundation for Historical Research of Illinois Potteries, 1988.

2997. _____, with John A. Walthall and David A. McGuire. *The Potters of White Hall.* Historic Illinois Potteries Circular Series, vol. 1, no. 2. Springfield: Foundation for Historical Research of Illinois Potteries, 1988.

2998. O'Donnell, Thomas Edward "An Outline of the History of Architecture in Illinois." *Transactions of the Illinois State Historical Society, 1931,* pp. 124-43.

2999. _____. "Recording the Early Architecture of Illinois in the Historic American Buildings Survey." *Transactions of the Illinois State Historical Society, 1934*, pp. 185-213.

3000. O'Gorman, James F. *H. H. Richardson: Architectural Forms for an American Society.* Chicago: University of Chicago Press, 1987. Paperback ed., 1990.

3001. _____. *Three American Architects: Richardson, Sulllivan, and Wright, 1865-1915.* Chicago: University of Chicago Press, 1991.

3002. Pfeiffer, Bruce Brooks, ed. *Frank Lloyd Wright: The Crowning Decade 1949-1959.* Fresno: The Press at California State University, 1989.

3003. _____, and Nordland, Gerald, eds. *Frank Lloyd Wright in the Realm of Ideas.* Carbondale: Southern Illinois University Press, 1988.

3004. Pommer, Richard; Spaeth, David A.; and Harrington, Kevin. *In the Shadow of Mies: Ludwig Hilberseimer, Architect, Educator, and Urban Planner.* New York: Rizzoli, for the Art Institute of Chicago, 1988. Hilberseimer was a teacher at the Illinois Institute of Technology, as well as an architect and planner. In addition to studies by the three authors, the volume also contains the texts of four lectures by Hilberseimer.

3005. Prestiano, Robert. The Inland Architect: *Chicago's Major Architectural Journal, 1883-1908.* Architecture and Urban Design, no. 9. Ann Arbor, Mich.: UMI Research Press, 1985.

3006. Prince, Sue Ann, ed. *The Old Guard and the Avant-Garde: Modernism in Chicago, 1910-1940.* Chicago: University of Chicago Press, 1990.

3007. Reichelt, Richard. *Heartland Blacksmiths: Conversations at the Forge.* Photographs by Richard Wilbers and Richard Reichelt. Shawnee Book. Carbondale: Southern Illinois University Press, 1988. Five of the nine blacksmiths interviewed are from Illinois; four of those are artist-blacksmiths, one an agricultural blacksmith.

3008. Riedy, James L. *Chicago Sculpture.* Urbana: University of Illinois Press, 1981.

3009. Rooney, William A. *Architectural Ornamentation in Chicago.* Chicago: Chicago Review Press, 1984.

3010. Saliga, Pauline A., ed. *The Sky's the Limit: A Century of Chicago Skyscrapers.* Introduction by John Zukowsky; contributions by the editor, Zukowsky, and Jane H. Clarke. New York: Rizzoli, 1990.

3011. Siry, Joseph. *Carson Pirie Scott: Louis Sullivan and the Chicago Department Store.* Chicago: University of Chicago Press, 1988.

3012. Stamper, John W. *Chicago's North Michigan Avenue: Planning and Development, 1900-1930.* Chicago Architecture and Urbanism series. Chicago: University of Chicago Press, 1991.

3013. Stevenson, Katherine Cole, and Jandl, H. Ward. *Houses by Mail: A Guide to Houses from Sears, Roebuck and Company.* Washington: Preservation Press, 1986.

3014. Storrer, William Allin. *The Architecture of Frank Lloyd Wright.* Cambridge, Mass.: M.I.T. Press, 1974.

3015. Szuberla, Guy. "Irving Kane Pond: A Michigan Architect in Chicago." *Old Northwest* 5 (Summer 1979): 109-40.

3016. _____. "Three Chicago Settlements: Their Architectural Form and Social Meaning." *Journal of the Illinois State Historical Society* 70 (1977): 114-29.

3017. Taitt, Carolyn. With photographs by Alfred von Behren. "Mural Paintings of the Illinois Supreme Court." *Journal of the Illinois State Historical Society* 77 (1984): 11-13. Albert Henry Krehbiel was the artist.

3018. Tallmadge, Thomas E. *Architecture in Old Chicago.* Chicago: University of Chicago Press, 1941. Reprint, 1975. A study of nineteenth-century architecture to 1893, but not including buildings at the World's Columbian Exposition.

3019. Tedeschi, Martha. *Great Drawings from the Art Institute of Chicago: The Harold Joachim Years, 1958-1983.* New York: Hudson Hills Press and the Art Institute of Chicago, 1985.

3020. Tigerman, Stanley. *Versus: An American Architect's Alternatives.* New York: Rizzoli, 1982. A Chicago architect discusses how ideas as well as art and architecture have influenced his work.

3021. Walthall, John A.; Gums, Bonnie L.; and Holley, George R. *The Traditional Potter in Nineteenth-Century Illinois: Archaeological Investigations at Two Kiln Sites in Upper Alton.* Illinois State Museum Reports of Investigations, no. 46. Springfield, 1991.

3022. Williams, Paul O. *Frederick Oakes Sylvester: The Artist's Encounter with Elsah.* Elsah, Ill.: Historic Elsah Foundation, 1986.

3023. Wilson, Lizabeth. "Allegories of Justice: The Albert H. Krehbiel Murals in the Supreme Court Building of Illinois." *Journal of the Illinois State Historical Society* 77 (1984): 2-10.

3024. Wooden, Howard E. *Billy Morrow Jackson: Interpretations of Time and Light.* Urbana: University of Illinois Press, 1990. Jackson was a member of the studio art faculty at the University of Illinois for more than thirty years. Eighty-eight paintings are reproduced. The volume contains biographical information but is primarily a study of his "stylistic and technical development."

3025. *Wright Studies.* The first volume in this new series devoted to Frank Lloyd Wright was issued by Southern Illinois University Press at Carbondale in 1992. Wright was not an Illinois native, but more of his buildings are standing in Illinois than in any other state, according to Wright scholar Donald P. Hallmark.

3026. Zukowsky, John, ed. *Chicago Architecture, 1872-1922: Birth of a Metropolis.* Munich: Prestel-Verlag, in association with the Art Institute of Chicago, 1987. With essays by nineteen contributors, in addition to the editor.

3027. _____, ed. *Mies Reconsidered: His Career, Legacy, and Disciples.* New York: Art Institute of Chicago, in association with Rizzol, International, 1986. Six architects discuss the life, style, and influence of the German architect Ludwig Mies van der Rohe, who moved to Chicago in 1938.

c. Music and Theatre

3028. Armstrong, W. D. "Early Music and Musicians in Illinois." *Transactions of the Illinois State Historical Society, 1931*, pp. 60-77.

3029. Blair, Virginia K. "The Singing Societies and Philharmonic Orchestra of Belleville." *Journal of the Illinois State Historical Society* 68 (1975): 386-95.

The Belleville orchestra, founded in 1867, is "the second oldest continuing symphonic orchestra in the country (only the New York Philharmonic is older)."

3030. Brubaker, Robert L. *Making Music Chicago Style*. Chicago: Chicago Historical Society, 1985. Exhibit catalog published in place of *Chicago History*, Fall & Winter 1984.

3031. Bunn, George W. Jr. "The Old Chatterton: A Brief History of a Famous Old Opera House." *Journal of the Illinois State Historical Society* 36 (1943): 7-20. The theatre in Springfield flourished 1866-1924. *See also* "Readers' Reminiscences," ibid. 210-13. Recollections of theatre in the Midwest.

3032. Collier, James Lincoln. *Louis Armstrong, an American Genius*. New York: Oxford University Press, 1983. One chapter is devoted to Armstrong's career in Chicago.

3033. Davis, Ronald L. *Opera in Chicago*. New York: Appleton, 1966.

3034. Edlund, Lawrence L. *The Apollo Musical Club of Chicago: A Historical Sketch*. Chicago: Apollo Musical Club, 1946. The men's chorus called the Apollo Musical Club was founded in 1872. Women joined the group a few years later.

3035. Freeman, Bud, as told to Robert Wolf. *Crazeology: The Autobiography of a Chicago Jazzman*. Music in American Life series. Urbana: University of Illinois Press, 1989.

3036. Furlong, William Barry. *Season with Solti: A Year in the Life of the Chicago Symphony*. New York: Macmillan, 1974.

3037. Harris, Michael W. *The Rise of Gospel Blues: The Music of Thomas Andrew Dorsey in the Urban Church*. New York: Oxford University Press, 1992. An important portion of the book is devoted to Dorsey's work in Chicago.

3038. Hodes, Art, and Hansen, Chadwick. *Hot Man: The Life of Art Hodes*. Music in American Life series. Urbana: University of Illinois Press, 1992. The life of jazz pianist Art Hodes spans the history of jazz in Chicago.

3039. Hodge, John E. "The Chicago Civic Opera Company: Its Rise and Fall." *Journal of the Illinois State Historical Society* 55 (1962): 5-30. The company operated for ten years, 1922-32, taking over from an earlier company that had been in Chicago since 1910.

3040. Jackson, Mahalia, with Evan McLeod Wylie. *Movin' on Up.* New York: Hawthorn Books, 1966. Reminiscences of the great gospel singer are particularly interesting for her comments about African-American life in Chicago.

3041. Kennerly, Carole Reed. "The Grand Opera House of Peoria, 1882-1909." *Journal of the Illinois State Historical Society* 77 (1984): 33-44. The history of a large theatrical house that presented touring-company productions ranging from grand opera to minstrel shows to lectures.

3042. Kenney, William Howland III. "Eddie Condon in Illinois: The Roots of a 'Jazz Personality.' " *Illinois Historical Journal* 77 (1984): 255-68. Jazz string player (guitar, banjo, and ukelele), Condon grew up and learned music in Momence, Chicago Heights, and Chicago.

3043. Krummel, Donald William; Geil, Jean; Dyen, Doris J.; and Root, Deane L. *Resources of American Music History: A Directory of Source Materials from Colonial Times to World War II.* Urbana: University of Illinois Press, 1981. Illinois, pp. 92-117. Describes the music-related holdings of libraries, colleges, and historical societies, as well as of individuals and musical groups.

3044. McColley, Robert. "Classical Music in Chicago and the Founding of the Symphony, 1850-1905." *Illinois Historical Journal* 78 (1985): 289-302. The symphony was known as The Chicago Orchestra and The Theodore Thomas Orchestra in these years.

3045. Martin, Lorene. "The Unique Career of an Illinois Musician." *Journal of the Illinois State Historical Society* 35 (1942): 140-47. Albert Morris Bagby of Rushville, a piano pupil of Franz Liszt's in the late nineteenth century, became a famous impresario in New York City.

3046. Mason, Bertha K. "Sol Smith Russell, Actor from Jacksonville." *Journal of the Illinois State Historical Society* 45 (1952): 23-29. Russell appeared with stock companies throughout the United States from the time of the Civil War until his death in 1900.

3047. Mazzola, Sandy R. "Orchestras of Chicago: A Musical and Economic History." *Transactions of the Illinois State Historical Society: Selected Papers from the Fifth and Sixth Illinois History Symposiums of the Illinois State Historical Society* [1984 and 1985]. Springfield, 1988. Pp. 69-81.

3048. Mezzrow, Milton (Mezz), and Wolfe, Bernard. *Really the Blues.* New York: Random House, 1946. Many editions and reprints. The black jazz musician Mezz Mezzrow was raised in Chicago.

3049. Naeseth, Henrietta C. K. *The Swedish Theatre of Chicago, 1868-1950.* Rock Island, Ill.: Augustana Historical Society and the Augustana College Library, 1951.

3050. Neff, Robert, and Connor, Anthony. *Blues.* Boston: David R. Godine, 1975. Interviews with fifty-five American blues musicians, many of whom became prominent in Chicago.

3051. Otis, Philo Adams. *The Chicago Symphony Orchestra: Its Organization, Growth, and Development, 1891-1924.* Chicago: Clayton F. Summy, 1924.

3052. Reich, Howard. " 'Hotter near the Lake': From King Oliver to Nat 'King' Cole and Beyond, Chicago Has Been a Wellspring of Great Jazz." *Chicago Tribune Magazine*, 5 September 1993. Pp. 12-18, 24. An excellent overview of the city's jazz history.

3053. Root, George F. *The Story of a Musical Life: An Autobiography.* Cincinnati: John Church, 1891. Root was a composer and music publisher in Chicago.

3054. Rowe, Mike. *Chicago Breakdown.* Eddison Blues Books, no. 1. London: Eddison Press, 1973. Reissued as a Da Capo paperback, 1983, under the title *Chicago Blues: The City & the Music.*

3055. Schabas, Ezra. *Theodore Thomas, America's Conductor and Builder of Orchestras, 1835-1905.* Urbana: University of Illinois Press, 1989. This biography of the founder and conductor of the Chicago Symphony Orchestra is also a history of music in the nineteenth century.

3056. Selmon, Michael. "Between Prairie Wolves and Puritans: Shakespeare's Early Chicago Stages." *Old Northwest* 11 (1985-86): 127-48. Chicago theatre, 1837-65, with emphasis on Shakespearean productions.

3057. Short, Bobby. *Black and White Baby.* New York: Dodd, Mead, 1971. The noted jazz pianist writes of growing up in Danville (pages 3-131) in this autobiography.

3058. Spivey, Donald. *Union and the Black Musician: The Narrative of William Everett Samuels and Chicago Local 208.* Lanham, Md.: University Press of America, 1984. An oral history of a Chicago black jazz musician and union officer.

3059. Stallings, Roy. "The Drama in Southern Illinois, 1865-1900." *Journal of the Illinois State Historical Society* 33 (1940): 190-202.

3060. Stokes, W. Royal. *The Jazz Scene: An Informal History from New Orleans to 1990.* New York: Oxford University Press, 1991. The author says this volume is "not a formal history" but "a sort of odyssey through almost a century of jazz," with many interviews with jazz musicians. One chapter is devoted to Chicago.

3061. Travis, Dempsey J. *An Autobiography of Black Jazz.* Chicago: Urban Research Institute, 1983. A wealth of material about the Chicago jazz scene; includes white musicians as well.

3062. Woodward, Bob. *Wired: The Short Life and Fast Times of John Belushi.* New York: Simon & Schuster, 1984. Actor-comedian Belushi grew up in Wheaton and won national notice in the Second City company in Chicago.

5. Manners and Customs

a. In General

3063. Block, Jean F. *Hyde Park Houses.* Chicago: University of Chicago Press, 1978. More about the Chicago neighborhood and occupants of the houses than about architecture.

3064. Carson, Gerald. "Cracker Barrel Days in Old Illinois Stores." *Journal of the Illinois State Historical Society* 47 (1954): 7-19.

3065. Drury, John. *Old Chicago Houses.* Reprint, Chicago: University of Chicago Press, 1975. As in his *Old Illinois Houses,* Drury emphasizes the history of the houses and of the families that occupied them, rather than architecture. In 1975 only 34 of the 100 houses described were extant.

3066. _____. *Old Illinois Houses.* Occasional Publications of the Illinois State Historical Society, no. 51. Springfield, 1948. Reprinted from a series in the *Chicago Daily News,* starting in 1941. Reprint, Chicago: University of Chicago

Press, 1977. For the most part, Drury emphasizes the family and community history with which the house is associated, rather than its architectural history.

3067. Gale, Edwin O. *Reminiscences of Early Chicago and Vicinity.* Chicago: Revell, 1902. The author came as a child to Chicago in 1835, and he recalls life there throughout the century.

3068. Hawse, Mara Lou, and Throgmorton, Dianne, eds. Illustrated by Tamara Wright. *Tell Me a Story: Memoirs of Early Life around the Coal Fields of Illinois.* Carbondale: Coal Research Center, Southern Illinois University, 1992. Seventeen essays selected from entrants in a contest asking senior citizens to describe life in Illinois' coal-mining areas.

3069. Kirkland, Caroline, comp. *Chicago Yesterdays: A Sheaf of Reminiscences.* Chicago: Daughaday, 1919. Prominent Chicagoans describe life from the earliest days of the town to the World's Columbian Exposition.

3070. Loomis, Emma Morse. "Recollections of an Illinois Woman." Edited by Mark E. Nackman and Darryl K. Paton. *Western Illinois Regional Studies* 1 (1978): 27-44. This narrative offers many insights into social life and customs from the end of the Civil War to 1938. Loomis recalls life in Jacksonville and Pekin.

3071. McCarthy, Kathleen D. *Noblesse Oblige: Charity and Cultural Philanthropy in Chicago, 1849-1929.* Chicago: University of Chicago Press, 1982.

3072. Meyerowitz, Joanne. "Women and Migration: Autonomous Female Migrants to Chicago, 1880-1930." *Journal of Urban History* 13 (February 1987): 147-68.

3073. Prince, Ezra M., comp. "Prices in McLean County, Illinois, from 1832 to 1860." *Transactions of the Illinois State Historical Society, 1904,* pp. 526-42. Includes prices of farm products, farm animals, log cabins, whiskey, pins, coffee, nails, land, etc., as well as sample wages. Compiled from official county records and county histories.

3074. Rauch, Mabel Thompson. "The First Memorial Day." *Journal of the Illinois State Historical Society* 40 (1947): 213-16. The day was first observed in Carbondale, Illinois, 5 April 1867.

3075. Rissler, Howard F. "Rendleman House, Museum of the Mississippi." *Journal of the Illinois State Historical Society* 50 (1957): 295-307. The elegant Rendleman House in Cairo never became a museum of the Mississippi, but this detailed description illustrates the life of a wealthy businessman in nineteenth-century Illinois.

3076. Ross, Ishbel. *Silhouette in Diamonds: The Life of Mrs. Potter Palmer.* New York: Harper, 1960. A look at how the truly wealthy Chicagoans lived in the late nineteenth and early twentieth centuries. A rare book of this type in that it has annotations, bibliography, and index.

3077. Russell, Nelson Vance. "The French and British at Play in the Old Northwest, 1760-1796." *Journal of the Illinois State Historical Society* 31 (1938): 22-53.

3078. Schulz, Mildred Valette. "Illinois' Inaugural Balls." *Journal of the Illinois State Historical Society* 63 (1970): 180-82. Descriptions of governors' inaugural balls, 1897-1969.

3079. Schulze, Franz. *A Heritage: University Club of Chicago, 1887-1987.* Chicago: University Club of Chicago, 1987. Architectural and social history of the University Club and its building.

3080. "Summer Phenomena Historically Considered." *Journal of the Illinois State Historical Society* 34 (1941): 254-60. Extracts from newspapers, 1843-79, describe high school examinations, open to the public at Springfield; a college commencement at Jacksonville; a Fourth of July celebration at Quincy; a Jacksonville-Springfield baseball game; a Mississippi River cruise between Alton and Grafton; and a visit to a spa, the Perry Springs Hotel.

3081. Taylor, Marjorie C. "Domestic Arts and Crafts in Illinois, 1800-1860." *Journal of the Illinois State Historical Society* 33 (1940): 278-303. Frontier farming, medicine, houses and furnishings, travel, food and cooking, education, as well as arts and crafts.

3082. Turnbull, Everett R. *The Rise and Progress of Freemasonry in Illinois, 1783-1952.* Bloomington, Ill.: Pantagraph Printing, 1952.

3083. Unsicker, Joan I. "Forgotten Images: Nineteenth-Century Gravestone Motifs in Peoria County." *Western Illinois Regional Studies* 5 (1982): 172-83.

3084. Van Mell, Richard, and Van Mell, Wendy, eds. *The First Hundred Years: A History of the Chicago Yacht Club, 1875-1975.* Chicago: Carl Gorr Printing, 1975.

3085. Yeager, Lyn Allison. "Chapin's General Store." *Journal of the Illinois State Historical Society* 65 (1972): 202-43.

b. Sports and Recreation

3086. Ahrens, Art, and Gold, Eddie, comps. *Day by Day in Chicago Cubs History.* Edited by Buck Peden. West Point, N.Y.: Leisure Press, 1982.

3087. Anson, Adrian C. *A Ball Player's Career, Being the Personal Experience and Reminiscences of Adrian C. Anson, Late Manager and Captain of the Chicago Base Ball Club.* Chicago: Era Publishing, 1900.

3088. Asinof, Eliot. *Eight Men Out: The Black Sox and the 1919 World Series.* New York: Holt, 1963. Reprint, 1987.

3089. Axelson, Gustaf W. *"Commy": The Life of Charles A. Comiskey, the "Grand Old Roman" of Baseball and for Nineteen Years President and Owner of the American League Baseball Team "The White Sox."* Chicago: Reilly & Lee, 1919.

3090. Banks, Ernie, and Enright, James. *"Mr. Cub."* Chicago: Follett, 1971.

3091. Berke, Art, and Schmitt, Paul. *This Date in Chicago White Sox History.* A Scarborough book. Briarcliff Manor, N.Y.: Stein and Day, 1982.

3092. Berkow, Ira. *The Du Sable Panthers: The Greatest, Blackest, Saddest Team from the Meanest Street in Chicago.* New York: Atheneum, 1978. An account of the 1954 state basketball tournament, in which the Panthers were the first all-black team to make the finals. They were defeated by Mt. Vernon.

3093. Brickhouse, Jack, with Jack Rosenberg and Ned Colletti. *Thanks for Listening.* South Bend, Ind.: Diamond Communications, 1986. Reminiscences of the veteran broadcaster.

3094. Brown, Warren. *The Chicago Cubs.* New York: Putnam, 1946.

3095. _____. *The Chicago White Sox.* New York: Putnam, 1952.

3096. Colletti, Ned. *You Gotta Have Heart: Dallas Green's Rebuilding of the Cubs.* South Bend, Ind.: Diamond Communications, 1985.

3097. Condon, Dave. *The Go-Go Chicago White Sox.* Coward-McCann Sports Library. New York, 1960.

3098. Considine, Robert B. *The Unreconstructed Amateur: A Pictorial Biography of Amos Alonzo Stagg.* Illustrated by Ray Sullivan; edited by Ralph Cahn. San Francisco: Amos Alonzo Stagg Foundation, 1962. Stagg was football coach at the University of Chicago, 1892-1932.

3099. Ditka, Mike, with Don Pierson. *Ditka: An Autobiography.* Chicago: Bonus Books, 1986. Ditka was coach of the Chicago Bears football team.

3100. Dykes, Jimmie, with Charles O. Dexter. *You Can't Steal First Base.* Philadelphia: Lippincott, 1967. The story of White Sox manager Jimmie Dykes.

3101. Enright, James. *March Madness: The Story of High School Basketball in Illinois.* Bloomington: Illinois High School Association, 1977.

3102. _____, with Isabel S. Grossner. *Ray Meyer, America's #1 Basketball Coach.* Chicago: Follett, 1980. Meyer was the longtime coach at DePaul University.

3103. Eskenazi, Gerald. *Bill Veeck: A Baseball Legend.* New York: McGraw-Hill, 1988.

3104. Farrell, James T. *My Baseball Diary: A Famed American Author Recalls the Wonderful World of Baseball, Yesterday and Today.* New York: Barnes, 1953. Farrell's young days as a White Sox fan.

3105. Federal Writers' Project, Illinois. *Baseball in Old Chicago.* Chicago: McClurg, 1939. Covers the years 1858-1900.

3106. Gifford, Barry. *The Neighborhood of Baseball: A Personal History of the Chicago Cubs.* New York: Dutton, 1981.

3107. Gold, Eddie. *Eddie Gold's White Sox and Cubs Trivia Book.* Chicago: Follett, 1981.

3108. _____, and Ahrens, Art. *The Golden Era Cubs, 1876-1940.* Chicago: Bonus Books, 1985.

3109. _____. *The New Era Cubs, 1941-1985.* Chicago: Bonus Books, 1985.

3110. Grange, Harold Edward, as told to Ira Morton. *The Red Grange Story: The Autobiography of Red Grange.* Putnam's Sports Series. New York: Putnam, 1953.

3111. _____. *Zuppke of Illinois.* Foreword by Grantland Rice. Chicago: A. L. Glaser, 1937. Robert Zuppke was Red Grange's football coach at the University of Illinois.

3112. Guttmann, Allan. *The Games Must Go On: Avery Brundage and the Olympic Movement.* New York: Columbia University Press, 1984. Brundage was a native Illinoisan.

3113. Halas, George, with Gwen Morgan and Arthur Veysey. *Halas by Halas.* New York: McGraw-Hill, 1979. Principally concerned with Halas as owner of the Chicago Bears football team.

3114. Herzog, Dorrel Norman Elvert (Whitey), and Horrigan, Kevin. *White Rat: A Life in Baseball.* New York: Harper, 1987. Manager Herzog was a native of New Athens.

3115. Langford, Jim. *The Game Is Never Over: An Appreciative History of the Chicago Cubs, 1948-1980.* South Bend, Ind.: Icarus Press, 1980. New, updated ed., 1982.

3116. Lindberg, Richard C. *Stealing First in a Two-Team Town: The White Sox from Comiskey to Reinsdorf.* Champaign, Ill.: Sagamore Publishing, 1994.

3117. _____. *Stuck on the Sox.* Evanston, Ill.: Sassafras Press, 1978.

3118. _____. *Who's on 3rd? The Chicago White Sox Story.* South Bend, Ind.: Icarus Press, 1983.

3119. Logan, Bob. *The Bulls and Chicago: A Stormy Affair.* Chicago: Follett, 1975.

3120. _____. *So You Think You're a Die-Hard Cub Fan.* Chicago: Contemporary Books, 1985.

3121. McCarthy, Michael P. "Politics and the Parks: Chicago Businessmen and the Recreation Movement." *Journal of the Illinois State Historical Society* 65

(1972): 158-72. Development and administration of parks in Chicago and Cook County in the late nineteenth and early twentieth centuries. Contributions of social reformers and businessmen are emphasized.

3122. Meyer, Ray, with Ray Sons. *Coach.* Chicago: Contemporary Books, 1987.

3123. Minoso, Orestes, with Herb Fagen. *Just Call Me Minnie: My Six Decades in Baseball.* Introduction by Orlando Cepeda and foreword by Billy Pierce. Champaign, Ill.: Sagamore Press, 1994. A native of Cuba, Minoso was the first black to play major-league baseball in Chicago. He joined the White Sox in 1951.

3124. Paulson, Norman M., comp. and ed. *1950 Three I. League Record Book, Containing Records, Both Club and Individual, of the Three I. League, 1901-1949 Inc.* Waterloo, Iowa: Three I. League Record Book, 1950. The league included professional baseball teams in Illinois, Indiana, and Iowa.

3125. Payton, Walter, with Jerry B. Jenkins. *Sweetness.* Chicago: Contemporary Books, 1978. Autobiography of the football star nicknamed "Sweetness."

3126. Reid, Art. *Fishing Southern Illinois.* Shawnee Books. Carbondale: Southern Illinois University Press, 1986.

3127. Schoor, Gene. *The Red Schoendienst Story.* New York: Putnam, 1961. Baseball Hall of Famer Schoendienst is from Germantown.

3128. Schwab, Rick. *Stuck on the Cubs.* Evanston, Ill.: Sassafras Press, 1977.

3129. Spink, J. G. Taylor. *Judge Landis and Twenty-five Years in Baseball.* New York: Crowell, 1947. Reprint, 1953. Landis was a federal judge in Chicago before he became baseball commissioner.

3130. Stagg, Amos Alonzo, as told to Wesley Winans Stout. *Touchdown!* New York: Longmans, Green, 1927. Stagg, longtime football coach at the University of Chicago, recalls famous games, players, and coaches.

3131. Steele, James W. *The Fox Lake Country in Illinois.* Chicago: General Passenger Department, Chicago, Milwaukee & St. Paul Railway, 1900? A bit of ephemera describing recreational opportunities.

3132. Stein, Irving. *The Ginger Kid: The Buck Weaver Story.* Foreword by Jack Brickhouse. Albuquerque, N.M.: Elysian Fields Press, 1992. Weaver, a native of Chicago, was a member of the "Black Sox" team.

3133. Sterling, Chandler W. Jr. *The Icehouse Gang: My Year with the Black Hawks.* New York: Scribner's, 1972. The distinguished Episcopal bishop and writer played one season of professional hockey with the Black Hawks.

3134. Vanderberg, Bob. *Sox, from Lane and Fain to Zisk and Fisk.* Chicago: Chicago Review Press, 1982.

3135. Vass, George. *The Chicago Black Hawks Story.* Chicago: Follett, 1970.

3136. _____. *George Halas and the Chicago Bears.* Chicago: Regnery, 1971.

3137. Veeck, Bill, with Ed Linn. *Veeck--As in Wreck: The Autobiography of Bill Veeck.* 1962. A Signet book. New York: New American Library, 1986. Longtime baseball entrepreneur, Veeck bought controlling interest in the Chicago White Sox in 1959.

3138. Voigt, David Quentin. "The Chicago Black Sox and the Myth of Baseball's Single Sin." *Journal of the Illinois State Historical Society* 62 (1969): 293-306. The Chicago White Sox scandal of 1919.

3139. Whittingham, Richard. *The Chicago Bears: An Illustrated History.* Chicago: Rand McNally, 1979.

3140. Young, Linda. *Hail to the Orange and Blue! 100 Years of Illinois Football Tradition.* Champaign, Ill.: Sagamore Publishing, 1990.

6. Social Problems

3141. Addams, Jane. "Social Settlements in Illinois." *Transactions of the Illinois State Historical Society, 1906,* pp. 162-71.

3142. Allsop, Kenneth. *The Bootleggers: The Story of Chicago's Prohibition Era.* 4th impression of the 1st ed., with slightly different title. London: Hutchinson, 1968.

3143. Booth, Stephane Elise. "The American Coal Mining Novel: A Century of Development." *Illinois Historical Journal* 81 (1988): 125-40. The author shows how novels reflect manners and customs as well as public attitudes towards women and the laboring man from 1876 through 1981.

3144. Bowly, Devereux Jr. *The Poorhouse: Subsidized Housing in Chicago, 1895-1976.* Carbondale: Southern Illinois University Press, 1978.

3145. Bray, Robert. "Robert Herrick: A Chicago Trio." *Old Northwest* 1 (March 1975): 63-84. Herrick came to the University of Chicago in 1893, and the novels he wrote in the next twenty years vividly portray the social problems and manners and customs of the city.

3146. Carson, Mina. *Settlement Folk: Social Thought and the American Settlement Movement, 1885-1930.* Chicago: University of Chicago Press, 1990.

3147. Cole, Arthur Charles. "Illinois Women of the Middle Period." *Transactions of the Illinois State Historical Society, 1920,* pp. 84-116. Movements (1850 to 1919) for prohibition, dress reform, entrance into the professions, and suffrage.

3148. Duis, Perry. *The Saloon: Public Drinking in Chicago and Boston, 1880-1920.* Urbana: University of Illinois Press, 1983.

3149. Flinn, John Joseph. *History of the Chicago Police.* Reprint of the 1887 ed., with a new introduction by Mark H. Haller, and a new index. Patterson Smith Series in Criminology, Law Enforcement & Social Problems. Montclair, N.J.: Patterson Smith, 1973.

3150. Gittens, Joan. *Poor Relations: The Children of the State in Illinois, 1818-1990.* Urbana: University of Illinois Press, 1994.

3151. Haller, Mark H. "Organized Crime in Urban Society: Chicago in the Twentieth Century." *Journal of Social History* 5 (1971-72): 210-34.

3152. Halper, Albert, ed. *The Chicago Crime Book.* Cleveland: World, 1967. A collection of essays about notorious criminals and famous trials.

3153. Harring, Sidney L. *Policing a Class Society: The Experience of American Cities, 1865-1915.* New Brunswick, N.J.: Rutgers University Press, 1983. A history of the use of police to support prevailing social attitudes.

3154. Hays, Agnes D. *A Heritage of Dedication*. Evanston, Ill.: Signal Press, 1974. A history of the Woman's Christian Temperance Union, headquartered in Evanston.

3155. Hoch, Charles, and Slayton, Robert A. *New Homeless and Old: Community and the Skid Row Hotel*. Philadelphia: Temple University Press, 1989. The authors use Chicago from 1870 to the present as a case study.

3156. Holt, Marilyn Irvin. *The Orphan Trains: Placing Out in America*. Lincoln: University of Nebraska Press, 1992. Contains many examples from Illinois.

3157. Kusmer, Kenneth L. "Functions of Organized Charity in the Progressive Era: Chicago as a Case Study." *Journal of American History* 60 (1973-74): 657-78. Work of the Charity Organization Society in the late nineteenth and early twentieth centuries.

3158. McDowell, Mary E. "A Quarter of a Century in the Stockyards District." *Transactions of the Illinois State Historical Society, 1920*, pp. 74-83. The noted social worker describes the lives of the laboring man and woman in Chicago, beginning with the 1894 strike of stockyards workers.

3159. Mark, Norman. *Mayors, Madams, and Madmen*. Chicago: Chicago Review Press, 1979. A lighthearted, but sardonic, collection of stories about Chicago mores, particularly political corruption, from the beginning of the city's recorded history to the present.

3160. Mayer, John A. "Relief Systems and Social Controls: The Case of Chicago, 1890-1910." *Old Northwest* 6 (1980): 217-44. County assistance was the last resort for those needing help; churches and charitable institutions were the main sources of aid.

3161. Nelson, Otto M. "The Chicago Relief and Aid Society, 1850-1874." *Journal of the Illinois State Historical Society* 59 (1966): 48-66.

3162. Pegram, Thomas R. "The Dry Machine: The Formation of the Anti-Saloon League of Illinois." *Illinois Historical Journal* 83 (1990): 173-86. Emphasizes the lobbying efforts of the dry forces from the 1890s to 1920.

3163. Philpott, Thomas Lee. *The Slum and the Ghetto: Neighborhood Deterioration and Middle-Class Reform, Chicago, 1880-1930*. Urban Life in America Series. New York: Oxford University Press, 1978. In contrasting the experience of earlier immigrant groups with that of African-Americans and discussing the work of social reformers and social settlements, the author presents a compelling social history of Chicago.

3164. Roberts, Clarence N. "The Illinois Intercollegiate Prohibition Association, 1893-1920." *Journal of the Illinois State Historical Society* 70 (1977): 140-48. Several Illinois colleges had active chapters affiliated with the association.

3165. Smith, Alson J. *Syndicate City: The Chicago Crime Cartel and What to Do about It.* Chicago: Regnery, 1954. Law enforcement, politics, and crime from 1833 to 1953.

3166. Taub, Richard P.; Taylor, D. Garth; and Dunham, Jan D. *Paths of Neighborhood Change: Race and Crime in Urban America.* Chicago: University of Chicago Press, 1984.

3167. Taylor, Graham. *Chicago Commons through Forty Years.* Chicago: Chicago Commons Association, 1936. History of the famous Chicago settlement house by its founder.

3168. Wade, Louise Carroll. "The Heritage from Chicago's Early Settlement Houses." *Journal of the Illinois State Historical Society* 60 (1967): 411-41. The work of settlement houses led to many important social and governmental reforms. The author carries the story to 1954, concentrating on settlement houses and social workers in Chicago.

III. BIOGRAPHY

Biographies of Illinoisans of statewide or national renown are included in this section. Books or articles about those less prominent are generally placed under the chronological period (or subject classification) with which the person is associated. There are a few exceptions to this general procedure: 1) Biographies of all Native Americans are placed with the tribal histories; 2) biographies of sports figures are placed in the general Sports and Recreation category; and 3) biographies of musicians are placed in the general Music and Theatre section.

Illinoisans are considered to be those born in the state or those who have done a substantial portion of their work in the state.

Three Presidents are claimed by Illinois--Abraham Lincoln, Ulysses S. Grant, and Ronald Reagan. Lincoln moved to Illinois as a young man and soon became prominent both as an attorney and as a political figure. Reagan, on the other hand, though a native son, left the state after graduating from college. Since the publisher of this volume is also publishing a series of presidential bibliographies, only a few general biographies of either man are listed below. There are many entries, however, about Lincoln's Illinois years; and other Lincoln-related entries appear in the Politics and Government sections of both the Civil War and Early Statehood eras.

Ulysses S. Grant was living in Galena when the Civil War broke out, and entered service to help enroll the state's volunteers. Grant entries below concern only his Illinois activities and his close associations with other Illinoisans.

In recent years many agencies, particularly universities, have conducted interviews with contemporary figures that constitute a valuable source of history and biography. Transcripts of many of these oral history tapes can be found in university and research libraries. Space restrictions have made it impossible to list individual interview subjects here.

A. ARTISTS AND ARCHITECTS

3169. Burton, Shirley J. *Adelaide Johnson: To Make Immortal Their Adventurous Will.* Western Illinois Monograph Series, no. 7. Macomb: Western Illinois University, 1986. Life of the feminist/sculptor who grew up in Hancock County.

3170. Burtschi, Mary. "James William Berry, Illinois Artist." *Journal of the Illinois State Historical Society* 67 (1974): 519-29.

3171. DeMare, Marie *G. P. A. Healy, American Artist: An Intimate Chronicle of the Nineteenth Century.* New York: McKay, 1954.

3172. Farr, Finis. *Frank Lloyd Wright.* New York: Scribner's, 1963.

3173. Garvey, Timothy J. *Public Sculptor: Lorado Taft and the Beautification of Chicago.* Urbana: University of Illinois Press, 1988.

3174. Gill, Brendan. *Many Masks: A Life of Frank Lloyd Wright.* New York: Putnam, 1987.

3175. Goltra, Mabel Hall. "Peter S. Newell, Cartoonist." *Journal of the Illinois State Historical Society* 41 (1948): 134-45. A native of Bushnell, Newell's professional career began at Jacksonville. His cartoons and books later achieved national acclaim.

3176. Healy, George P. A. *Reminiscences of a Portrait Painter.* Chicago: McClurg, 1894. Born in Boston, Healy moved to Chicago in 1855, lived there until 1871, and moved back again in 1892.

3177. Hey, Kenneth R. "Ralph Clarkson: An Academic Painter in an Era of Change." *Journal of the Illinois State Historical Society* 76 (1983): 177-94. Portraitist Clarkson joined the staff of the Art Institute of Chicago in 1895. Along with many other artists he was closely associated with the writers of the literary renaissance movement of the early twentieth century.

3178. Hines, Thomas S. *Burnham of Chicago: Architect and Planner.* New York: Oxford University Press, 1974. Biography of Daniel H. Burnham.

3179. Jacobs, Herbert. *Frank Lloyd Wright: America's Greatest Architect.* New York: Harcourt, Brace, 1965.

3180. Johnson, Donald Leslie. *Frank Lloyd Wright versus America: The 1930s.* Cambridge, Mass.: The MIT Press, 1990.

3181. Krehbiel, Rebecca F. "Albert Henry Krehbiel, 1873-1945: Early American Impressionist." *Journal of the Illinois State Historical Society* 77 (1984): 14-20.

3182. Lawson, Richard A., and Mavigliano, George J. *Fred E. Myers, Wood-Carver.* Carbondale: Southern Illinois University Press, 1980. A sketch of the southern Illinois man whose powerful wood carvings came to light through the Fine Arts Program of the Work Projects Administration.

3183. Meehan, Patrick J., ed. *Frank Lloyd Wright Remembered.* Washington: Preservation Press, National Trust for Historic Preservation, 1991.

3184. Moseley, Spencer, and Reed, Gervais. *Walter F. Isaacs: An Artist in America, 1886-1964.* Seattle: University of Washington Press, 1982. The subject of this excellent biography was a native of Gillespie, and the authors' treatment of his early life in Illinois is especially well done.

3185. Paul, Sherman. *Louis Sullivan: An Architect in American Thought.* Englewood Cliffs, N.J.: Prentice-Hall, 1962.

3186. Richardson, Genevieve. "Lorado Taft and Theater." *Journal of the Illinois State Historical Society* 49 (1956): 359-74. The author discusses Taft's participation in amateur theatricals in Chicago and at the art colony he established near Oregon, Illinois.

3187. Rovelstad, Trygve A. "Impressions of Lorado Taft." *Papers in Illinois History, 1937*, pp. 18-33. Reminiscences about the famous Illinois sculptor by one of his students.

3188. Schulze, Franz. *Mies van der Rohe: A Critical Biography.* Chicago: University of Chicago Press, 1985.

3189. Secrest, Meryle. *Frank Lloyd Wright: A Biography.* New York: Knopf, 1992.

3190. Spaeth, David A. *Ludwig Mies van der Rohe: An Annotated Bibliography and Chronology.* New York: Garland, 1978. Listed in the index, among other structures designed by the famous architect, are buildings on the Illinois Institute of Technology campus.

3191. _____. *Mies van der Rohe.* New York: Rizzoli, 1985.

3192. Starr, Eliza Allen. *The Life and Letters of Eliza Allen Starr.* Edited by James J. McGovern, with an introduction by William Stetson Merrill. Chicago: Lakeside Press, 1905. Starr was an art teacher in Chicago at the turn of the century.

3193. Taft, Ada Bartlett. *Lorado Taft, Sculptor and Citizen.* Greensboro, N.C.: M. T. Smith, 1946.

3194. Taft, Lorado. *Lorado in Paris: The Letters of Lorado Taft, 1880-1885.* Edited by Allen Stuart Weller. Urbana: University of Illinois Press, 1985. The editor provides information about the sculptor's life in Illinois both before and after his Paris sojourn.

3195. Twombly, Robert. *Louis Sullivan: His Life and Work.* New York: Viking, 1986. Reprint, Chicago: University of Chicago Press, 1987.

3196. Van Zanten, David T. *Walter Burley Griffin: Selected Designs.* Palos Park, Ill.: Prairie School Press, 1970. The book contains an assessment of the Illinois architect's career as well as essays by him.

3197. White, Judson. "Patrick Henry Davenport, Pioneer Illinois Portrait Painter." *Journal of the Illinois State Historical Society* 51 (1958): 245-67. A biographical sketch of the artist with a list of his works.

3198. Wright, Frank Lloyd. *Frank Lloyd Wright Collected Writings: Volume I, 1894-1930.* Edited by Bruce Brooks Pfeiffer. New York: Rizzoli, in association with the Frank Lloyd Wright Foundation, 1992. The first of six projected volumes.

B. BUSINESSMEN AND INVENTORS

3199. Aldrich, Darragh. *The Story of John Deere: A Saga of American Industry.* Minneapolis, Minn.: McGill Lithograph, 1942. History of the farm-implement manufacturer, sponsored by his grandson. No annotations.

3200. Angle, Paul McClelland. *Philip K. Wrigley: A Memoir of a Modest Man.* Chicago: Rand McNally, 1975. Chewing-gum manufacturer Wrigley was perhaps better known as owner of the Chicago Cubs.

3201. Arnold, Isaac N. *William B. Ogden and Early Days in Chicago: A Paper Read before the Chicago Historical Society, Tuesday, December 20, 1881* . . . Fergus' Historical Series, no. 17. Chicago, 1882.

3202. Bachmann, Lawrence P. "Julius Rosenwald." *American Jewish Historical Quarterly* 66 (September 1976): 89-105. Concerned with his role at Sears, Roebuck.

3203. Becker, Stephen. *Marshall Field III: A Biography.* New York: Simon & Schuster, 1964. Best known as founder of the *Chicago Sun*.

3204. Brady, Frank. *Hefner.* New York: Macmillan, 1974. Biography of Hugh Hefner, who established Playboy clubs and *Playboy* magazine, still headquartered in Chicago. The author judges him to be an "editorial and business genius."

3205. Casey, Robert J. *Mr. Clutch: The Story of George William Borg.* Indianapolis: Bobbs-Merrill, 1948. With Marshall Beck, Borg invented the clutch "that was to be a major factor in revolutionizing the automobile business." In 1928 he joined with Warner Gear Company and several other manufacturers to create the Borg-Warner Corporation.

3206. Casson, Herbert N. *Cyrus Hall McCormick, His Life and Work.* Chicago: McClurg, 1909. A short biography of the reaper manufacturer.

3207. Clark, Neil M. *John Deere: He Gave the World the Steel Plow.* Moline, Ill.: Privately printed, 1937. A sketch for the general reader.

3208. Denison, B. W. "Captain Benjamin Godfrey, the Prairie Prophet." *Journal of the Illinois State Historical Society* 44 (1951): 332-39. Godfrey was the founder of Monticello Female Seminary and the contractor for the Chicago and Alton Railroad from Springfield to Alton.

3209. Doenecke, Justus D. "General Robert E. Wood: The Evolution of a Conservative." *Journal of the Illinois State Historical Society* 71 (1978): 162-75. Wood headed Sears, Roebuck and Company for many years.

3210. Downard, William L. "William Butler Ogden and the Growth of Chicago." *Journal of the Illinois State Historical Society* 75 (1982): 47-60. Ogden had many business interests in Chicago.

3211.   Eisenschiml, Otto.   *Without Fame: The Romance of a Profession.*
Chicago: Alliance Book Corporation, 1942.   Eisenschiml was a Chicago
businessman/chemist and Civil War author.

3212.   Farwell, John Villiers.   *Some Recollections of John V. Farwell: A Brief
Description of His Early Life and Business Reminiscences.*   Chicago: R. R.
Donnelley, 1911.   The department store owner was also an early Chicago
philanthropist.

3213.   Grubb, Anna B.   *Adventure in Enterprise: The Story of Leaton Irwin and
the Company He Founded.*   Edited by George M. Irwin.   Quincy, Ill.: Published
privately by the Irwin Paper Company, 1947.

3214.   Heath, Lawrence Seymour.   *My Footsteps on the Sands of Time: An
Autobiography.*   Robinson, Ill.: The author, 1955.   The Heath Bar evolved from
the author's confectionery and ice cream business in Robinson.

3215.   Hutchinson, William T.   *Cyrus Hall McCormick.*   2 vols.   New York:
Century, 1930-35.   Reprint, New York: Da Capo, 1968.

3216.   *In Memoriam: William Thomas Rawleigh, Born December 3, 1870, Died
January 23, 1951.*   Freeport, Ill.: W. T. Rawleigh Co., 1951?   Manufacturer of
household products, particularly vanilla extract, for door-to-door sales.

3217.   Leech, Harper, and Carroll, John Charles.   *Armour and His Times.*   New
York: Appleton, 1938.   Biography of one of the famous Chicago meatpackers,
Philip Danforth Armour.

3218.   Leyendecker, Liston Edgington.   *Palace Car Prince: A Biography of
George Mortimer Pullman.*   Niwot: University Press of Colorado, 1992.

3219.   Litvin, Martin.   *Chase the Prairie Wind: The First Biography of Robert
H. Avery, Andersonville Veteran, Noted American Inventor, and Manufacturer
of Farm Machinery.*   Galesburg, Ill.: Log City Books, 1975.

3220.   Lockwood, Frank C.   *The Life of Edward E. Ayer.*   Chicago: McClurg,
1929.   Distributor of railroad ties, Ayer became better known as the collector of
Native American artifacts and literature.   His collections were donated to the
Newberry Library and the Field Museum of Natural History.

3221. McDonald, Forrest. *Insull.* Chicago: University of Chicago Press, 1962. A sympathetic portrayal of the utilities magnate as an innovator in technology and marketing.

3222. May, George W. *Charles E. Duryea, Automaker.* Ann Arbor, Mich.: Edwards Brothers, 1973. Concentrates on Duryea's years in Peoria, one of the many places he operated factories.

3223. Mottier, C. H. "Biography of Roswell B. Mason." Mimeographed. 1938. Mason was in charge of constructing the Illinois Central Railroad and was mayor of Chicago at the time of the 1871 fire.

3224. Needham, Richard H. *Maurice H. Needham, January 19, 1889--June 11, 1966.* Chicago: The author, 1991. Maurice Needham was the founder of several Chicago advertising agencies.

3225. Nichols, Robert E. Jr., comp. *Chicago Plumber: An Account of the Trade in the Twentieth Century through the Stories Told by an American Craftsman: The Work of Robert E. Nichols, an Artisan Whose Life Touched Every Decade of the Century.* Hammond, Ind.: The compiler, 1991. A remarkable account of the work of a craftsman who eventually became chief plumbing inspector for the city of Chicago.

3226. Oursler, William Charles. *From Ox Carts to Jets: Roy Ingersoll and the Borg-Warner Story: A Biography.* Englewood Cliffs, N.J.: Prentice-Hall, 1959.

3227. *Patrick Joseph Healy, Founder of the House of Lyon & Healy: An Appreciation.* Chicago, 1907. Healy and Lyon came to Chicago in 1864 for the express purpose of opening a music store.

3228. Petrakis, Harry Mark. *The Founder's Touch: The Life of Paul Galvin of Motorola.* New York: McGraw-Hill, 1965.

3229. Petterchak, Janice A. *Mapping a Life's Journey: The Legacy of Andrew McNally III.* Skokie, Ill.: Rand McNally, 1995. Biography of the chairman of Rand McNally and Company.

3230. Schriftgiesser, Karl. *The Farmer from Merna: A Biography of George J. Mecherle and a History of the State Farm Insurance Companies of Bloomington, Illinois.* New York: Random House, 1955.

3231. Swift, Louis F. *The Yankee of the Yards: The Biography of Gustavus Franklin Swift.* Chicago: A. W. Shaw, 1927. Anecdotal account, by a son.

3232. Tarbell, Ida M. *The Life of Elbert H. Gary: The Story of Steel.* New York: Appleton, 1925. The chief executive officer of United States Steel Corporation was a native of Wheaton.

3233. Tebbel, John William. *The Marshall Fields: A Study in Wealth.* New York: Dutton, 1947. An account of the men who bore that name, from the first (born 1834) to Marshall Field III (born 1893)--and especially of the great Chicago department store founded by Marshall Field I.

3234. Thwaites, Reuben Gold. "Cyrus Hall McCormick and the Reaper." *Proceedings of the State Historical Society of Wisconsin, 1908,* pp. 233-59.

3235. Tilton, Clint Clay. "Gurdon Saltonstall Hubbard and Some of His Friends." *Transactions of the Illinois State Historical Society, 1933,* pp. 83-180. Hubbard was a fur trader and merchant in Danville and Chicago in the early 1800s.

3236. Wendt, Lloyd, and Kogan, Herman. *Bet a Million! The Story of John W. Gates.* Indianapolis: Bobbs-Merrill, 1948. Born on a farm near Chicago, Gates became a successful industrialist.

3237. Werner, M. R. *Julius Rosenwald: The Life of a Practical Humanitarian.* New York: Harper, 1939. Best known as a philanthropist, Rosenwald made his fortune in merchandising; from 1895 until his death in 1932 he was associated with Sears, Roebuck and Company--president, 1910-25, and chairman of the board, 1925-32.

3238. Worthy, James C. *Shaping an American Institution: Robert E. Wood and Sears, Roebuck.* Urbana: University of Illinois Press, 1984.

C. MILITARY MEN

3239. Alberts, Don E. *Brandy Station to Manila Bay: A Biography of General Wesley Merritt.* Austin, Texas: Presidial Press, 1980.

3240. Bakeless, John E. *Background to Glory: The Life of George Rogers Clark.* Philadelphia: Lippincott, 1957. Reprint, Lincoln: University of Nebraska Press, 1992, with an introduction by James P. Ronda. A substantial part of the book concerns Clark's operations in the Illinois country during the American Revolution.

3241. Bale, Florence Gratiot. "Galena's Memories of General Ulysses S. Grant." *Journal of the Illinois State Historical Society* 21 (1928-29): 409-18.

3242. Bodley, Temple. "George Rogers Clark and Historians." *Transactions of the Illinois State Historical Society, 1935*, pp. 73-109.

3243. Davis, George T. M. *Autobiography of the Late Col. Geo. T. M. Davis, Captain and Aid-de-camp, Scott's Army of Invasion (Mexico), from Posthumous Papers.* New York: Jenkins & McCowan, 1891. An anecdote about Abraham Lincoln and his children is reprinted in the *Journal of the Illinois State Historical Society* 38 (1945): 485-86.

3244. Dorris, Jonathan Truman. "Michael Kelly Lawler, Mexican and Civil War Officer." *Journal of the Illinois State Historical Society* 48 (1955): 366-401.

3245. Grant, Ulysses S. *The Papers of Ulysses S. Grant.* Edited by John Y. Simon et al. Carbondale: Southern Illinois University Press, 1967ff. 18 vols. to date. Volume 18 includes the dates 1 October 1867--30 June 1868. Volumes 1 and 2 contain letters from Galena and Springfield, where Grant began his Civil War service. Volumes 19 and 20 are forthcoming.

3246. Hamilton, Holman. *Zachary Taylor, Soldier of the Republic.* Indianapolis: Bobbs-Merrill, 1941. Reprint, New York: Anchor Books, Doubleday, 1966. The biography contains extensive accounts of Taylor's participation in the War of 1812 in Illinois and the Black Hawk War of 1832.

3247. Havighurst, Walter. *George Rogers Clark: Soldier in the West.* New York: McGraw-Hill, 1952.

3248. Holley, I. B. Jr. *General John M. Palmer, Citizen Soldiers, and the Army of a Democracy.* Contributions in Military History, no. 28. Westport, Conn.: Greenwood Press, 1982. The grandson of Illinois governor John M. Palmer, the younger man was an army staff officer who championed universal military training. An outstanding military history.

3249. James, James Alton. *The Life of George Rogers Clark.* Chicago: University of Chicago Press, 1928.

3250. _____. *Oliver Pollock.* New York: Appleton, 1937. Chapter 2 contains an account of village life in the last years of the French occupation. Pollock was financier and supplier for George Rogers Clark.

3251. Johnson, Barry C. *"Case of Marcus A. Reno."* English Westerners' Special Publication no. 3. London, 1969. The Civil War and western frontier military officer was a native of Carrollton and a graduate of West Point.

3252. Leckie, William H., and Leckie, Shirley A. *Unlikely Warriors: General Benjamin H. Grierson and His Family.* Norman: University of Oklahoma Press, 1984. More social history than a military analysis of the Civil War general from Jacksonville.

3253. Lewis, Lloyd Downs. *Captain Sam Grant.* Boston: Little, Brown, 1950.

3254. Longacre, Edward G. *From Union Stars to Top Hat: A Biography of the Extraordinary General James Harrison Wilson.* Harrisburg, Pa.: Stackpole Books, 1972. Born near Shawneetown, Wilson graduated from West Point and had a distinguished career in the Civil War and the Spanish-American War.

3255. Nichols, Roger L. *General Henry Atkinson: A Western Military Career.* Norman: University of Oklahoma Press, 1965. The author holds that the one time Atkinson was called upon to be a military commander (during the Black Hawk War), he was generally unsuccessful.

3256. Randall, Ruth Painter. *Colonel Elmer Ellsworth.* Boston: Little, Brown, 1960. The dashing young Zouave officer from Chicago, who was studying law in Lincoln's office at the time of his election to the presidency, became the first officer killed in the Civil War.

3257. Repp, Stephen. *Ulysses S. Grant: The Galena Years.* Galena, Ill.: The author, 1985.

3258. Salter, William. *The Life of Henry Dodge, from 1782 to 1833, with Portrait by George Catlin and Maps of the Battles of the Pecatonica and Wisconsin Heights in the Black Hawk War.* Burlington, Iowa, 1890.

3259. Schutz, Wallace J., and Trenery, Walter N. *Abandoned by Lincoln: A Military Biography of General John Pope.* Urbana: University of Illinois Press, 1990.

3260. Simon, John Y. "Ulysses S. Grant One Hundred Years Later." *Illinois Historical Journal* 79 (1986): 245-56.

3261. Stephenson, Mary Harriet. *Dr. B. F. Stephenson, Founder of the Grand Army of the Republic: A Memoir by His Daughter.* Springfield, Ill.: H. W. Rokker, 1894. The GAR was an organization of veterans of the Civil War, in which Stephenson also served. The Civil War narrative in this book was written by Stephenson himself.

3262. Wallace, Isabel. *Life & Letters of General W. H. L. Wallace.* Chicago: R. R. Donnelley, 1909. The papers of General Wallace are now in the Illinois State Historical Library.

D. POLITICAL FIGURES AND ATTORNEYS

1. In General

3263. Ackerman, Carl W. *Dawes--the Doer!* New York: Era Publications, 1924. Charles Gates Dawes had many business, political, charitable, and cultural pursuits.

3264. Affleck, James. "William Kinney: A Brief Biographical Sketch." *Transactions of the Illinois State Historical Society, 1908*, pp. 209-11.

3265. Angle, Paul McClelland. "Nathaniel Pope, 1784-1850: A Memoir." *Transactions of the Illinois State Historical Society, 1936*, pp. 111-81. Secretary of Illinois Territory until 1816 and delegate to Congress, 1816-18, Pope headed the movement in Congress for Illinois' admission to statehood in 1818.

3266. Baxter, Maurice G. "Orville H. Browning, Lincoln's Colleague and Critic." *Journal of the Illinois State Historical Society* 48 (1955): 431-55. This study of the relationship between Lincoln and Browning, 1836-65, constitutes a survey of the major state and national political and governmental issues of those years.

3267. _____. *Orville H. Browning: Lincoln's Friend and Critic.* Indiana University Publications, Social Science Series, no. 16. Bloomington: Indiana University Press, 1957.

3268. Blair, Harry C., and Tarshis, Rebecca. *The Life of Colonel Edward D. Baker, Lincoln's Constant Ally, together with Four of His Great Orations.* A Civil War memorial publication. Portland: Oregon Historical Society, 1960.

3269. Block, Marvin W. "Henry T. Rainey of Illinois." *Journal of the Illinois State Historical Society* 65 (1972): 142-57.

3270. Boxerman, Burton A. "Adolph Joachim Sabath in Congress." Pt. I, "The Early Years, 1907-1932." *Journal of the Illinois State Historical Society* 66 (1973): 327-40. Pt. II, "The Roosevelt and Truman Years," pp. 428-43.

3271. Bright, John. *Hizzoner Big Bill Thompson: An Idyll of Chicago.* New York: J. Cape & H. Smith, 1930.

3272. Browning, Orville Hickman. *The Diary of Orville Hickman Browning, Volume I, 1850-1864.* Edited by Theodore Calvin Pease and James Garfield Randall. Collections of the Illinois State Historical Library, vol. 20. Springfield, 1925. *Volume II, 1865-1881.* Edited by James Garfield Randall. Collections of the Illinois State Historical Library, vol. 22. Springfield, 1933. The index for both volumes is in volume 22.

3273. Burns, Josephine E. "Daniel P. Cook." *Journal of the Illinois State Historical Society* 6 (1913-14): 425-44.

3274. Burton, William L. "James Semple, Prairie Entrepreneur." *Illinois Historical Journal* 80 (1987): 66-84. James Semple was a land speculator, politician, and inventor. His life, the author says, "provides a virtual model of Jacksonian America."

3275. Casey, Robert J., and Douglas, W. A. S. *The Midwesterner: The Story of Dwight H. Green.* Chicago: Wilcox & Follett, 1948. Illinois governor, 1941-48, Green first won public notice in 1931 as the United States attorney who successfully prosecuted the gangster Al Capone for income tax evasion.

3276. Cavanagh, Helen M. *Carl Schurz Vrooman, Self Styled "Constructive Conservative."* Chicago: Lakeside Press, R. R. Donnelley, 1977.

3277. Chamberlin, Henry Barrett. "Elias Kent Kane, United States Senator from Illinois and Author of Its First Constitution." *Transactions of the Illinois State Historical Society, 1908*, pp. 162-70.

3278. Chetlain, Augustus L. *Recollections of Seventy Years.* Galena, Ill.: Gazette Publishing, 1899.

3279. Cleveland, Martha. *Charles Percy: A Strong New Voice from Illinois, A Biography.* Jacksonville, Ill.: Harris-Wolfe, 1968.

3280. Converse, Henry A. "The Life and Services of Shelby M. Cullom." *Transactions of the Illinois State Historical Society, 1914*, pp. 55-79. The funeral sermon and an account of the funeral services for Cullom in the Capitol accompany the article.

3281. Cook, John Williston. "Life and Labors of Hon. Adlai Ewing Stevenson." *Transactions of the Illinois State Historical Society, 1915*, pp. 23-41.

3282. Cottingham, Carl D.; Jones, Preston Michael; and Kent, Gary W. *General John A. Logan: His Life and Times.* Carbondale, Ill.: American Resources Group, 1989. A chronology of Logan's life.

3283. Cox, Isaac Joslin. "Thomas Sloo, Jr., a Typical Politician of Early Illinois." *Transactions of the Illinois State Historical Society, 1911*, pp. 26-42.

3284. Cullom, Shelby M. *Fifty Years of Public Service: Personal Recollections of Shelby M. Cullom, Senior United States Senator from Illinois.* Chicago: McClurg, 1911. Reprint, New York: Da Capo, 1969.

3285. Curran, Nathaniel B. "Levi Davis, Illinois' Third Auditor." *Journal of the Illinois State Historical Society* 71 (1978): 2-12.

3286. Donald, David Herbert. *Lincoln's Herndon: A Biography.* New York: Knopf, 1948. Several later editions, and a reprint, New York: Da Capo, 1988, with a new introduction by Donald.

3287. Douglas, Paul H. *In the Fullness of Time: The Memoirs of Paul H. Douglas.* New York: Harcourt, Brace, 1972.

3288. Edwards, Anne. *Early Reagan.* New York: Morrow, 1987. The first six chapters deal with President Reagan's life in Illinois.

3289. Edwards, Ninian W. "Some Correspondence of Ninian Edwards." Edited by Philip D. Jordan. *Journal of the Illinois State Historical Society* 24 (1931-32): 173-86. Eight letters, 1812-29, from the New York Historical Society, printed here for the first time.

3290. Egan, Gerald F. "The Eloquence of W. Willard Wirtz." *Illinois Historical Journal* 81 (1988): 283-92. Emphasizes the Illinois years of President John Kennedy's secretary of labor.

3291. Ellis, L. Ethan. "James Robert Mann, Legislator Extraordinary." *Journal of the Illinois State Historical Society* 46 (1953): 28-44.

3292. Erickson, Gary Lee. "The Last Years of William Henry Herndon." *Journal of the Illinois State Historical Society* 67 (1974): 101-19.

3293. Fehrenbacher, Don E. *Chicago Giant: A Biography of "Long John" Wentworth.* Madison, Wis.: American History Research Center, 1957.

3294. Fergus, Robert. *Biographical Sketch of John Dean Caton, ex-Chief Justice of Illinois.* Fergus' Historical Series, no. 21. Chicago, 1882.

3295. Fifer, Joseph Wilson. *"Private Joe" Fifer: Memories of War and Peace Imparted in His Ninety-Sixth Year . . .* Bloomington, Ill.: Pantagraph Printing, 1936. Based on interviews with the former governor of Illinois.

3296. Gertz, Elmer. *A Handful of Clients.* Chicago: Follett, 1965. Gertz writes about his most famous legal clients.

3297. _____, and Gilbreth, Edward S. *Quest for a Constitution: A Man Who Wouldn't Quit, A Political Biography of Samuel Witwer of Illinois.* Lanham, Md.: University Press of America, 1984. Primarily about Witwer's work as chairman of the Sixth Illinois Constitutional Convention, which drafted the Constitution of 1970.

3298. Gertz, Elmer. *To Life: The Story of a Chicago Lawyer; with a New Afterword.* Carbondale: Southern Illinois University Press, 1990. Reprint of the 1974 ed. published by McGraw-Hill. Autobiography.

3299. Gottfried, Alex. *Boss Cermak of Chicago: A Study of Political Leadership.* Seattle: University of Washington Press, 1962.

3300. Gulley, Halbert E. *Roy A. Gulley: Journey to a Larger Sphere.* N.p.: Privately printed, 1966. Businessman, teacher, and state legislator, Gulley was a resident of Sesser.

3301. Haberkorn, Ruth Ewers. "Owen Lovejoy in Princeton, Illinois." *Journal of the Illinois State Historical Society* 36 (1943): 284-315. The author adds to the sketch of Lovejoy an account of the preservation and restoration of his home in Princeton.

3302. Halbert, William U. "William Henry Bissell, Eleventh Governor of Illinois." *Journal of the Illinois State Historical Society* 36 (1943): 41-49.

3303. Harrison, Carter H. *Growing up with Chicago: Sequel to "Stormy Years."* Chicago: R. F. Seymour, 1944.

3304. _____. *Stormy Years: The Autobiography of Carter H. Harrison, Five Times Mayor of Chicago.* Indianapolis: Bobbs-Merrill, 1935.

3305. Hartley, Robert E. *Big Jim Thompson of Illinois.* Chicago: Rand McNally, 1979.

3306. _____. *Charles H. Percy: A Political Perspective.* Chicago: Rand McNally, 1975.

3307. Holt, Marilyn Irvin. "Isaac Newton Morris: A Nineteenth-Century Quincy Politician." *Western Illinois Regional Studies* 12, no. 1 (Spring 1989): 44-55.

3308. Holt, Robert D. "The Political Career of William A. Richardson." *Journal of the Illinois State Historical Society* 26 (1933-34): 222-69.

3309. Howard, Robert P. "Myths After Shadrach Bond." *Transactions of the Illinois State Historical Society: Selected Papers from the Seventh Annual History Symposium and the Eighth Annual History Symposium* [1986 and 1987]. Springfield, 1989. Pp. 21-26.

3310. _____. " 'Old Dick' Richardson, the Other Senator from Quincy." *Western Illinois Regional Studies* 7, no. 1 (Spring 1984): 16-27. The better-known senator was Orville H. Browning.

3311. Hutchinson, William T. *Lowden of Illinois: The Life of Frank O. Lowden.* Vol. 1, *City and State.* Vol. 2, *Nation and Countryside.* Chicago: University of Chicago Press, 1957.

3312. Jones, James Pickett. *John A. Logan: Stalwart Republican from Illinois.* Tallahassee: University Presses of Florida, 1982.

3313. Jones, Norman L. "John M. Palmer." *Transactions of the Illinois State Historical Society, 1923*, pp. 206-15.

3314. Kenney, David. *A Political Passage: The Career of Stratton of Illinois.* Carbondale: Southern Illinois University Press, 1990. Biography of Governor William G. Stratton.

3315. King, Willard L. *Lincoln's Manager, David Davis.* Cambridge, Mass.: Harvard University Press, 1960.

3316. Kirby, Julia Duncan. *Biographical Sketch of Joseph Duncan, Fifth Governor of Illinois; Read before the Historical Society of Jacksonville, Ill., May 7, 1885.* Fergus' Historical Series, no. 29. Chicago, 1888.

3317. Koerner, Gustav. *Memoirs of Gustav Koerner, 1809-1896.* 2 vols. Edited by T. J. McCormack. Cedar Rapids, Iowa: Torch Press, 1909.

3318. Krenkel, John H., ed. *Richard Yates, Civil War Governor.* Danville, Ill.: Interstate, 1966. The rough manuscript of this biography was written by Yates's son Richard (1860-1936) and Catharine Yates Pickering. The editor has corrected quotations and added citations as well as brief biographies of people mentioned.

3319. Krug, Mark M. *Lyman Trumbull, Conservative Radical.* New York: Barnes, 1965.

3320. Lear, Linda J. *Harold L. Ickes: The Aggressive Progressive, 1874-1933.* New York: Garland, 1981.

3321. Littlewood, Thomas B. *Horner of Illinois.* Evanston, Ill.: Northwestern University Press, 1969. Based on the Henry Horner papers in the Illinois State Historical Library and the Chicago Historical Society.

3322. Livingstone, William G. "The Thomas Reynolds Confusion." *Journal of the Illinois State Historical Society* 54 (1961): 423-30. Chief Justice Thomas Reynolds of Illinois (later governor of Missouri) and Thomas Reynolds the brother of Governor John Reynolds of Illinois are here clearly distinguished.

3323. McHarry, Jessie "John Reynolds." *Journal of the Illinois State Historical Society* 6 (1913): 5-57.

3324. McNulty, John W. "Sidney Breese: His Early Career in Law and Politics in Illinois." *Journal of the Illinois State Historical Society* 61 (1968): 164-81.

3325. _____. "Sidney Breese, the Illinois Circuit Judge, 1835-1841." *Journal of the Illinois State Historical Society* 62 (1969): 170-86.

3326. Magdol, Edward. *Owen Lovejoy, Abolitionist in Congress.* New Brunswick, N.J.: Rutgers University Press, 1967. An excellent, thorough account of the life and antislavery efforts of Elijah Lovejoy's younger brother.

3327. Masters, Edgar Lee. *Levy Mayer and the New Industrial Era: A Biography.* New Haven: Yale University Press, 1927. As a Chicago attorney, Mayer represented many industrial interests.

3328. Meese, William A. "Nathaniel Pope." *Journal of the Illinois State Historical Society* 3, no. 4 (January 1911): 7-21.

3329. Merrill, William Stetson. "Pierre Menard of Illinois." *Mid-America* 3 n.s. (1931-32): 15-38.

3330. Miller, Kristie. *Ruth Hanna McCormick: A Life in Politics, 1880-1944.* Albuquerque: University of New Mexico Press, 1992.

3331. Monroe, B. D. "Life and Services of William Wilson, Chief Justice of the Illinois Supreme Court." *Journal of the Illinois State Historical Society* 11 (1918-19): 391-99.

3332. Morton, Richard Allen. "Edward F. Dunne, Illinois' Most Progressive Governor." *Illinois Historical Journal* 83 (1990): 218-34.

3333. Murphy, Lawrence R. *Frontier Crusader: William F. M. Arny.* Tucson: University of Arizona Press, 1972. In the 1850s Arny was active in Illinois politics as well as in agricultural and educational affairs.

3334. Murray, David. *Charles Percy of Illinois.* New York: Harper, 1968.

3335. Neilson, James W. *Shelby M. Cullom, Prairie State Republican.* Illinois Studies in the Social Sciences, vol. 51. Urbana: University of Illinois Press, 1962.

3336. Norton, W. T. *Edward Coles, Second Governor of Illinois, 1822-1826.* Philadelphia: Lippincott, 1911.

3337. O'Shaughnessy, Francis. "General James Shields of Illinois." *Transactions of the Illinois State Historical Society, 1915,* pp. 113-22.

3338. Ostewig, Kinnie A. "Life of Col. Shadrach Bond, the First Governor of Illinois under Statehood." *Transactions of the Illinois State Historical Society, 1929,* pp. 187-234.

3339. Palmer, George Thomas. *A Conscientious Turncoat: The Story of John M. Palmer, 1817-1900.* New Haven, Conn.: Yale University Press, 1917. Reprint, Yale University Press and London: Oxford University Press, 1941.

3340. Palmer, John M. *Personal Recollections of John M. Palmer: The Story of an Earnest Life.* Cincinnati: Robert Clarke, 1901.

3341. Pensoneau, Taylor, and Ellis, Bob. *Dan Walker: The Glory and the Tragedy.* Evansville, Ind.: Smith Collins, 1993.

3342. Peterson, Lowell N. "Omer N. Custer: A Biography of a Downstate Political Boss." *Journal of the Illinois State Historical Society* 60 (1967): 37-63.

3343. Plummer, Mark A. "Richard J. Oglesby, Lincoln's Rail-Splitter." *Illinois Historical Journal* 80 (1987): 2-12. Sketch of the two-time governor, United States senator, and Civil War general who in 1860 created the image of Lincoln as rail-splitter.

3344. Pratt, Harry Edward. "David Davis, 1815-1886." *Transactions of the Illinois State Historical Society, 1930,* pp. 157-83.

3345. Putnam, Elizabeth Duncan. "The Life and Services of Joseph Duncan, Governor of Illinois, 1834-1838." *Transactions of the Illinois State Historical Society, 1919,* pp. 107-87. Based on primary sources. Many extracts from family letters and diaries are included in the narrative biography.

3346. Reagan, Ronald Wilson. *Ronald Reagan: An American Life.* New York: Simon & Schuster, 1990. The first six chapters (43 pages) deal with Reagan's life in Illinois, from birth until his graduation from Eureka College.

3347. Reynolds, John. *My Own Times, Embracing Also the History of My Life.* Belleville, Ill.: B. H. Perryman and H. L. Davison, 1855.

3348. Rombauer, R. E. "The Life of Hon. Gustavus Koerner." *Transactions of the Illinois State Historical Society, 1904,* pp. 286-307.

3349. Roske, Ralph J. *His Own Counsel: The Life and Times of Lyman Trumbull.* Nevada Studies in History and Political Science, no. 14. Reno: University of Nevada Press, 1979.

3350. Sager, Juliet Gilman. "Stephen A. Hurlbut, 1815-1882." *Journal of the Illinois State Historical Society* 28, no. 2 (July 1935): 53-80.

3351. Samosky, Jack A. "Congressman Noah Morgan Mason: From Wales to Washington." *Journal of the Illinois State Historical Society* 71 (1978): 252-63.

3352. _____. "Congressman Noah Morgan Mason: Illinois' Conservative Spokesman." *Journal of the Illinois State Historical Society* 76 (1983): 35-48.

3353. Schapsmeier, Edward L., and Schapsmeier, Frederick H. "Serving under Seven Presidents: Les Arends and His Forty Years in Congress." *Illinois Historical Journal* 85 (1992): 105-18.

3354. Schlup, Leonard. "Gilded Age Politician: Adlai E. Stevenson of Illinois and His Times." *Illinois Historical Journal* 82 (1989): 219-30. The first Adlai E. Stevenson was vice-president of the United States, 1893-97.

3355. _____. "Letitia Green Stevenson, Matriarch of a Political Family in Illinois." *International Review of History and Political Science* 15 (August 1978): 1-12.

3356. Scott, Franklin D. "The Political Career of William R. Morrison." *Transactions of the Illinois State Historical Society, 1926,* pp. 134-71.

3357. Snyder, John Francis. "Forgotten Statesmen of Illinois: James Harvey Ralston." *Transactions of the Illinois State Historical Society, 1908,* pp. 215-32.

3358. _____. "Forgotten Statesmen of Illinois: Richard M. Young." *Transactions of the Illinois State Historical Society, 1906,* pp. 302-27.

3359. Starr, Merritt. "General Horace Capron, 1804-1885." *Journal of the Illinois State Historical Society* 18 (1925-26): 259-349.

3360. Stevens, Frank Everett. "Alexander Pope Field." *Journal of the Illinois State Historical Society* 4 (1911-12): 7-37.

3361. Tarr, Joel Arthur. *A Study in Boss Politics: William Lorimer of Chicago.* Urbana: University of Illinois Press, 1971. As chairman of the Cook County

Republican Central Committee, elected in 1895, Lorimer exerted influence that was felt throughout Illinois.

3362. Thomis, Wayne. *Abraham Lincoln Marovitz: A Moving Profile of the Man and His City.* [Chicago, 1973?] Reprint of articles from the *Chicago Tribune*, May 21-26, 1967. Marovitz grew up in Chicago and became a state legislator and a federal district court judge.

3363. Timmons, Bascom N. *Portrait of an American: Charles G. Dawes.* New York: Holt, 1953. Before he became vice-president of the United States, Dawes practiced law and became a successful utilities magnate.

3364. Townley, Wayne C. *Two Judges of Ottawa.* Carbondale, Ill.: Egypt Book House, 1948. The judges are T. Lyle Dickey and John Dean Caton.

3365. Wallace, Joseph. *Sketch of the Life and Public Services of Edward D. Baker, United States Senator from Oregon, and formerly Representative in Congress from Illinois, Who Died in Battle near Leesburg, Va., Oct. 21, A.D. 1861.* Springfield, Ill.: Journal Co., Printers, 1870.

3366. Waller, Robert A. *Rainey of Illinois: A Political Biography, 1903-34.* Illinois Studies in the Social Sciences, vol. 60. Urbana: University of Illinois Press, 1977.

3367. Washburne, Elihu B., ed. *The Edwards Papers, Being a Portion of the Collection of the Letters, Papers, and Manuscripts of Ninian Edwards . . . Presented to the Chicago Historical Society, October 16th, 1883, by His Son, Ninian Wirt Edwards.* Chicago Historical Society's Collection, vol. 3. Chicago: Fergus Printing, 1884. The published documents are dated 1800-1832.

3368. _____. *Recollections of a Minister to France, 1869-1877.* New York: Scribner's, 1887.

3369. Watkins, T. H. *Righteous Pilgrim: The Life and Times of Harold L. Ickes, 1874-1952.* New York: Holt, 1990.

3370. Wendt, Lloyd, and Kogan, Herman. *Big Bill of Chicago.* Indianapolis: Bobbs-Merrill, 1953. "Big Bill" was the nickname of William Hale Thompson.

3371. West, Roy O., and Walton, William Clarence. "Charles S. Deneen, 1863-1940." *Journal of the Illinois State Historical Society* 34 (1941): 7-25.

3372. White, Graham J. *Harold Ickes of the New Deal: His Private Life and Public Career.* Cambridge, Mass.: Harvard University Press, 1985.

3373. White, Horace. *The Life of Lyman Trumbull.* Boston: Houghton Mifflin, 1913.

3374. Wilson, James Harrison. *The Life of John A. Rawlins, Lawyer, Assistant Adjutant-General, Chief of Staff, Major General of Volunteers and Secretary of War.* New York: Neale Publishing, 1916. Rawlins's military career was in the Civil War--under Grant--and it was President Grant who named him secretary of war.

3375. Wymbe, Norman E. *A Place to Go Back to: Ronald Reagan in Dixon, Illinois.* New York: Vantage Press, 1987.

3376. Yates, Richard. *Serving the Republic--Richard Yates, Illinois Governor and Congressman, Son of Richard Yates, Civil War Governor: An Autobiography.* Edited by John H. Krenkel. Danville, Ill.: Interstate, 1968.

3377. Zane, John M. "A Rare Judicial Service: Charles S. Zane." *Journal of the Illinois State Historical Society* 19 (1926-27): 31-48. A Springfield associate of Abraham Lincoln's, Zane became Chief Justice of the Utah Supreme Court.

2. John Peter Altgeld

3378. Altgeld, John Peter. *The Mind and Spirit of John Peter Altgeld: Selected Writings and Addresses.* Edited by Henry M. Christman. Urbana: University of Illinois Press, 1960. The selections illustrate Altgeld's greatness.

3379. Barnard, Harry. *Eagle Forgotten: The Life of John Peter Altgeld.* Indianapolis: Bobbs-Merrill, 1938. Altgeld is known today for his pardon of three of the anarchists who had been found guilty of fomenting the Haymarket riot. But in his day he was influential in both the state and national Democratic parties.

3380. Browne, Waldo R. *Altgeld of Illinois: A Record of His Life and Work.* New York: B. W. Huebsch, 1924.

3381. Ellingsworth, Huber W. "John Peter Altgeld as a Public Speaker." *Journal of the Illinois State Historical Society* 46 (1953): 171-77.

3. William Jennings Bryan

3382. Ashby, LeRoy. *William Jennings Bryan: Champion of Democracy.* Twayne's Twentieth-Century American Biography Series, no. 4. Boston, 1987. Includes an account of Bryan's Illinois years.

3383. Bryan, William Jennings, and Bryan, Mary Baird. *The Memoirs of William Jennings Bryan.* Philadelphia: John C. Winston, 1925.

3384. Cherny, Robert W. *A Righteous Cause: The Life of William Jennings Bryan.* Library of American Biography. Boston: Little, Brown, 1985.

3385. Clements, Kendrick A. *William Jennings Bryan, Missionary Idealist.* Knoxville: University of Tennessee Press, 1982. A well-documented study of Bryan and the isolationist tradition in American politics.

3386. Coletta, Paolo E. *William Jennings Bryan.* 3 vols. Lincoln: University of Nebraska Press, 1964, 1969. The definitive biography.

3387. _____. " 'Won, 1880--One, 1884': The Courtship of William Jennings Bryan and Mary Elizabeth Baird." *Journal of the Illinois State Historical Society* 50 (1957): 231-42.

3388. _____. "The Youth of William Jennings Bryan: Beginnings of a Christian Statesman." *Nebraska History* 31 (1950): 1-24.

3389. Glad, Paul W. *The Trumpet Soundeth: William Jennings Bryan and His Democracy, 1896-1912.* Lincoln: University of Nebraska Press, 1960.

3390. _____, ed. *William Jennings Bryan: A Profile.* New York: Hill & Wang, 1968. Twelve writers, in addition to the editor, consider aspects of the career of the Illinois-born politician.

3391. Koenig, Louis W. *Bryan: A Political Biography of William Jennings Bryan.* New York: Putnam, 1971. A sympathetic popular biography.

3392. Levine, Lawrence W. *Defender of the Faith, William Jennings Bryan: The Last Decade, 1915-1925.* New York: Oxford University Press, 1965.

3393. Springen, Donald K. *William Jennings Bryan: Orator of Small-Town America.* Great American Orators, no. 11. New York: Greenwood, 1991.

4. Joseph Gurney Cannon

3394. Bolles, Blair. *Tyrant from Illinois: Uncle Joe Cannon's Experiment with Personal Power.* New York: Norton, 1951.

3395. Busbey, L. White. *Uncle Joe Cannon: The Story of a Pioneer American, as Told to L. White Busbey, for 20 Years His Private Secretary.* Edited by Katherine Graves Busbey. New York: Holt, 1927.

3396. Gilbert, Dorothy Lloyd. "Joe Cannon's Carolina Background." *North Carolina Historical Review* 23 (1946): 471-82.

3397. Gwinn, William Rea. *Uncle Joe Cannon, Archfoe of Insurgency: A History of the Rise and Fall of Cannonism.* New York: Bookman, 1957. A scholarly study of the longtime Illinois congressman whose ironclad control as Speaker of the House at the turn of the century led insurgent Republicans to form the Progressive party.

5. Richard J. Daley

3398. Gleason, Bill. *Daley of Chicago: The Man, the Mayor, and the Limits of Conventional Politics.* New York: Simon & Schuster, 1970. Portrait of Daley by a newspaperman--anecdotal, somewhat affectionate, somewhat critical.

3399. Kennedy, Eugene C. *Himself! The Life and Times of Mayor Richard J. Daley.* New York: Viking, 1978.

3400. Lens, Sidney. "Mayor Daley's Last Hurrah." Reprinted from *The Progressive*, vol. 39, no. 4, in Walsh, James, comp. *The Irish: America's Political Class.* The Irish-Americans series. New York: Arno, 1976.

3401. O'Connor, Len. *Clout: Mayor Daley and His City.* Chicago: Regnery, 1975.

3402. _____. *Requiem: The Decline and Demise of Mayor Daley and His Era.* Chicago: Contemporary Books, 1977.

3403. Rakove, Milton L. *Don't Make No Waves--Don't Back No Losers: An Insider's Analysis of the Daley Machine.* Bloomington: Indiana University Press, 1975.

3404. _____. *We Don't Want Nobody Nobody Sent: An Oral History of the Daley Years.* Bloomington: Indiana University Press, 1979. The Richard J. Daley Democratic organization in Chicago.

3405. Royko, Mike. *Boss: Richard J. Daley of Chicago.* New York: Dutton, 1971. A political biography by the iconoclastic Chicago columnist.

3406. Sullivan, Frank. *Legend: The Only Inside Story about Mayor Richard J. Daley.* Chicago: Bonus Books, 1989.

6. Clarence Darrow

3407. Cowan, Geoffrey. *The People vs. Clarence Darrow: The Bribery Trial of America's Greatest Lawyer.* New York: Times Books, Random House, 1993. Darrow was charged with bribing two jurors; he was found innocent, but the author asserts convincingly that he was indeed guilty.

3408. Darrow, Clarence. *Attorney for the Damned.* Edited and with notes by Arthur Weinberg. New York: Simon & Schuster, 1957.

3409. _____. *The Story of My Life.* New York: Scribner's, 1932.

3410. Hunsberger, Willard D. *Clarence Darrow: A Bibliography.* Metuchen, N.J.: Scarecrow Press, 1981.

3411. Stone, Irving. *Clarence Darrow for the Defense: A Biography.* Garden City, N.Y.: Doubleday, 1941. Although the book is fully annotated, it has fictionalized elements.

3412. Tierney, Kevin. *Darrow: A Biography.* New York: Crowell, 1979.

3413. Weinberg, Arthur, and Weinberg, Lila. *Clarence Darrow: A Sentimental Rebel.* New York: Putnam's, 1980.

7. Everett McKinley Dirksen

3414. Dirksen, Louella, with Norma Lee Browning. *The Honorable Mr. Marigold: My Life with Everett Dirksen.* Garden City, N.Y.: Doubleday, 1972.

3415. Fonsino, Frank J. "Everett McKinley Dirksen: The Roots of an American Statesman." *Journal of the Illinois State Historical Society* 76 (1983): 17-34.

3416. MacNeil, Neil. *Dirksen: Portrait of a Public Man.* New York: World, 1970.

3417. Schapsmeier, Edward L. "Dirksen and Douglas of Illinois: The Pragmatist and the Professor as Contemporaries in the United States Senate." *Illinois Historical Journal* 83 (1990): 75-84.

3418. _____, and Schapsmeier, Frederick H. *Dirksen of Illinois: Senatorial Statesman.* Urbana: University of Illinois Press, 1985.

3419. _____. "Everett M. Dirksen of Pekin: Politician Par Excellence." *Journal of the Illinois State Historical Society* 76 (1983): 3-16. The article deals primarily with Dirksen's career after 1950.

3420. _____. "Senator Everett M. Dirksen and American Foreign Policy: From Isolationism to Cold War Interventionism." *Old Northwest* 7 (1981-82): 359-72.

8. Stephen Arnold Douglas

3421. Capers, Gerald M. *Stephen A. Douglas: Defender of the Union.* The Library of American Biography. Boston: Little, Brown, 1959.

3422. Johannsen, Robert W., ed. *The Letters of Stephen A. Douglas.* Urbana: University of Illinois Press, 1961. All the extant letters written by Douglas, and located by the editor, are published herein or calendared.

3423. _____. *Stephen A. Douglas.* New York: Oxford University Press, 1973. An objective and scholarly study.

3424. Johnson, Allen. *Stephen A. Douglas: A Study in American Politics.* New York: Macmillan, 1908. Reprint, New York: Da Capo, 1970. One of the first historians to begin rehabilitating Douglas's reputation.

3425. McConnell, George Murray. "Recollections of Stephen A. Douglas." *Transactions of the Illinois State Historical Society, 1900,* pp. 40-50.

3426. Milton, George Fort. *The Eve of Conflict: Stephen A. Douglas and the Needless War.* Boston: Houghton Mifflin, 1934.

3427. Nevins, Allan. "Stephen A. Douglas: His Weaknesses and His Great-ness." *Journal of the Illinois State Historical Society* 42 (1949): 385-410.

3428. Ostendorf, Lloyd, and Duncan, R. Bruce. "The Photographic Portraits of Stephen A. Douglas." *Journal of the Illinois State Historical Society* 67 (1974): 6-78. Twenty-nine photographic portraits, together with information about the photographers (some from Illinois).

3429. Stevens, Frank Everett. "Life of Stephen Arnold Douglas." *Journal of the Illinois State Historical Society* 16 (1923-24): 247-673. Despite inadequate annotations, this biography is still valuable for its study of Douglas's Illinois years.

3430. Stevenson, Adlai Ewing. "Stephen A. Douglas." *Transactions of the Illinois State Historical Society, 1908*, pp. 48-73.

3431. Temple, Wayne C. *Stephen A. Douglas: Freemason.* Bloomington, Ill.: Masonic Book Club and the Illinois Lodge of Research, 1982. This sketch emphasizes Douglas's affiliation with the Masonic order and the Illinois Militia and presents a history of the Douglas Monument in Chicago.

3432. Wells, Damon. *Stephen Douglas: The Last Years, 1857-1861.* Austin: University of Texas Press, 1971.

9. John Milton Hay

3433. Clymer, Kenton J. *John Hay: The Gentleman as Diplomat.* Ann Arbor: University of Michigan Press, 1975.

3434. Dennett, Tyler. *John Hay: From Poetry to Politics.* New York: Dodd, Mead, 1933. This biography won the Pulitzer Prize and is generally conceded to be the best biography of Hay, the Illinoisan who served as one of Lincoln's wartime secretaries.

3435. Gale, Robert L. *John Hay.* Twayne's United States Authors Series, no. 296. Boston, 1978.

3436. Kelly, Thurman. *John Hay as a Man of Letters.* Reseda, Calif.: Mojave Books, 1974.

3437. Kushner, Howard I., and Sherrill, Anne Hummel. *John Milton Hay: The Union of Poetry and Politics.* Twayne's World Leaders Series, no. 69. Boston, 1977.

3438. Kushner, Howard I. " 'The Strong God Circumstance': The Political Career of John Hay." *Journal of the Illinois State Historical Society* 67 (1974): 363-84. The author also discusses Hay's early life in Warsaw and Springfield, Illinois.

3439. Monteiro, George. *Henry James and John Hay: The Record of a Friendship.* Providence, R.I.: Brown University Press, 1965.

3440. _____. "Introduction: John Hay's Life and Career," in *John Hay's Pike County: Two Tales and Seven Ballads.* Edited by Monteiro. Western Illinois Monograph Series, no. 3. Macomb: Western Illinois University, 1984.

3441. Thayer, William Roscoe. *Life and Letters of John Hay.* 2 vols. Boston: Houghton Mifflin, 1915.

10. Robert Green Ingersoll

3442. Anderson, David D. *Robert Ingersoll.* Twayne's United States Authors series, no. 204. New York, 1972.

3443. Angel, Donald E. "Ingersoll's Political Transition: Patriotism or Partisanship?" *Journal of the Illinois State Historical Society* 59 (1966): 354-83. Robert Ingersoll's transition from Democrat to Republican is traced through the political issues that concerned the state from the 1850s through 1867.

3444. Cramer, Clarence H. "The Political Metamorphosis of Robert Green Ingersoll." *Journal of the Illinois State Historical Society* 36 (1943): 271-83. Focuses on the political campaigns of 1860, 1862, and 1864.

3445. _____. "Robert Green Ingersoll." *Transactions of the Illinois State Historical Society, 1940,* pp. 59-68.

3446. _____. *Royal Bob: The Life of Robert G. Ingersoll.* Indianapolis: Bobbs-Merrill, 1952. The first reliable biography.

3447. Ingersoll, Robert Green. *Ingersoll, Immortal Infidel.* Edited by Roger E. Greeley. The Skeptic's Bookshelf. Buffalo, N.Y.: Prometheus Books, 1977. Quotations from Ingersoll arranged alphabetically by subject.

3448. Larson, Orvin. *American Infidel: Robert G. Ingersoll, a Biography.* New York: Citadel, 1962. This biography concentrates on Ingersoll's career as a public speaker.

3449. Nolan, Paul T. "A Southerner's Tribute to Illinois' 'Pagan Prophet.' " *Journal of the Illinois State Historical Society* 51 (1958): 269-83. An account of Ingersoll's philosophy, together with a short morality play by Espy Williams that illustrates the symbolic life of Ingersoll. Williams was a well-known playwright at the turn of the century.

3450. Plummer, Mark A. *Robert G. Ingersoll: Peoria's Pagan Politician.* Western Illinois Monograph Series, no. 4. Macomb: Western Illinois University, 1984. Emphasizes political issues of the post-Civil War era.

3451. Reed, Scott Owen. "The Legal Philosophy of Robert G. Ingersoll." *Western Illinois Regional Studies* 6, no. 1 (Spring 1983): 42-66.

3452. Smith, Frank. *Robert G. Ingersoll: A Life.* Buffalo, N.Y.: Prometheus Books, 1990.

3453. Stein, Gordon. *Robert G. Ingersoll: A Checklist.* The Serif Series, no. 9, Bibliographies and Checklists. Kent, Ohio: Kent State University Press, 1969. Includes not only books and articles about Ingersoll but also those written by him.

3454. Wakefield, Eva Ingersoll, ed. *The Letters of Robert G. Ingersoll.* New York: Philosophical Library, 1951. Many of the letters are from the collections of the Illinois State Historical Library.

11. Abraham Lincoln and His Family

The following section includes standard general biographies and books and articles about Lincoln's life and work in Illinois, his family, and his burial in Illinois.

Sources for Lincoln's debates with Stephen A. Douglas in the 1858 campaign for a United States Senate seat are given in the section on the Civil War era. Check the Index for other Lincoln-related items.

a. Bibliography, Historiography, and Biography

3455. Abraham Lincoln Association. *Bulletin.* No. 1 (20 December 1923)--58 (December 1939). Superseded by the *Abraham Lincoln Quarterly.* Vol. 1 (March 1940)--7 (December 1952).

3456. _____. *Papers*, 1924-1939. Discontinued. The items in this series were issued annually. The *Papers* series was resumed in 1979 and the title changed in 1987 to *Journal of the Abraham Lincoln Association*, now published twice a year.

3457. Ander, Oscar Fritiof, ed. *Lincoln Images: Augustana College Centennial Essays.* Rock Island, Ill.: Augustana College Library, 1960. Three of the essays have strong Illinois connections. One, by the editor, details the story of the Swedish Galesburg newspaper *Hemlandet* and its role in Republican party politics in Illinois, 1854-60; a second, by Ralph J. Roske, is concerned with the relationship between Lincoln and Illinois Senator Lyman Trumbull; and the third, by Robert Mize Sutton, is about Lincoln and Illinois railroads.

3458. Angle, Paul McClelland. *The Lincoln Reader.* New Brunswick, N.J.: Rutgers University Press, 1947. Reprint, New York: Da Capo, 1990. Angle used selections from sixty-five of Lincoln's contemporaries to present a multi-faceted biography.

3459. _____. *The Living Lincoln.* New Brunswick, N.J.: Rutgers University Press, 1955.

3460. Barton, William E. "The Lincoln of the Biographers." *Transactions of the Illinois State Historical Society, 1929*, pp. 58-116. Includes a bibliography of biographies of Lincoln.

3461. Basler, Roy P. *A Touchstone for Greatness: Essays, Addresses, and Occasional Pieces about Abraham Lincoln.* Westport, Conn.: Greenwood, 1973. Some of Basler's essays include his interpretation of Lincoln's character, but of particular interest are those about Basler's own life, in which he discusses his work in Illinois and his relationships with others who wrote about Lincoln.

3462. Beveridge, Albert J. *Abraham Lincoln, 1809-1858.* 2 vols. Boston: Houghton Mifflin, 1928.

3463. Boritt (Borit), Gabor S., and Forness, Norman O., eds. *The Historian's Lincoln: Pseudohistory, Psychohistory, and History.* Urbana: University of Illinois Press, 1988.

3464. Boritt (Borit), Gabor S. *Lincoln and the Economics of the American Dream.* Memphis, Tenn.: Memphis State University Press, 1978. More than half the book is devoted to the pre-presidential years.

3465. Current, Richard N. *The Lincoln Nobody Knows.* New York: McGraw-Hill, 1958.

3466. _____. *Speaking of Abraham Lincoln: The Man and His Meaning for Our Times.* Champaign: University of Illinois Press, 1983. A collection of the author's lectures, several of which are concerned with Lincoln's Illinois years.

3467. Davis, G. Cullom; Strozier, Charles B.; Veach, Rebecca Monroe; and Ward, Geoffrey C., eds. *The Public and the Private Lincoln: Contemporary Perspectives.* Carbondale: Southern Illinois University Press, 1979.

3468. Fehrenbacher, Don E. *Prelude to Greatness: Lincoln in the 1850's.* Stanford, Calif.: Stanford University Press, 1962.

3469. Hanchett, William. *Out of the Wilderness: The Life of Abraham Lincoln.* Urbana: University of Illinois Press, 1994.

3470. Herndon, William H. *Herndon's Life of Lincoln: The History and Personal Recollections of Abraham Lincoln as Originally Written by William H. Herndon and Jesse W. Weik; With Introduction and Notes by Paul M. Angle.* New introduction by Henry Steele Commager. New York: Da Capo, 1983. After being discredited for many years, Herndon, a Springfield attorney and Lincoln's partner, has come to be respected as a conscientious, honorable man devoted to the truth as he saw it. In addition to his own intimate knowledge of Lincoln, Herndon had information based on scores of interviews with others who had known Lincoln.

3471. Hickey, James T. "Abraham Lincoln Chronology." *Illinois Blue Book, 1963-1964.* Pp. 35-53. Reprint, Springfield: Illinois State Historical Library, 1965, 1990. The 1990 revised and expanded edition was edited by Thomas F. Schwartz.

3472. _____. *The Collected Writings of James T. Hickey, from Publications of the Illinois State Historical Society, 1953-1984.* Springfield: Illinois State

Historical Society, 1990. Twenty-one articles, primarily about Lincoln, the Lincoln family, and Springfield, with a foreword by Mark E. Neely, Jr., who calls Hickey "the greatest Lincoln curator of his generation."

3473. Hostick, King V. "Lincoln Letters Theme Has Not Been Exhausted." *Journal of the Illinois State Historical Society* 52 (1959): 52-58.

3474. House, Albert V. Jr. "The Trials of a Ghost-Writer of Lincoln Biography: Chauncey F. Black's Authorship of Lamon's Lincoln." *Journal of the Illinois State Historical Society* 31 (1938): 262-96.

3475. Johannsen, Robert W. "In Search of the Real Lincoln, or Lincoln at the Crossroads." *Journal of the Illinois State Historical Society* 61 (1968): 229-47. An historiographical study showing how scholars have used source materials only recently made available to reinterpret crucial aspects of Lincoln's character and career, thereby distinguishing the real Lincoln from the mythical hero.

3476. _____. *Lincoln, the South, and Slavery: The Political Dimension.* Baton Rouge: Louisiana State University Press, 1991. Traces the development of Lincoln's public political stances on slavery.

3477. Lincoln, Abraham. *The Collected Works of Abraham Lincoln.* Edited by Roy P. Basler, Marion Dolores Pratt, and Lloyd A. Dunlap. 9 vols. and Index. New Brunswick, N.J.: Rutgers University Press, 1953. *First Supplement, 1832-1865*, edited by Roy P. Basler, 1974. *Second Supplement, 1848-1865*, edited by Roy P. Basler and Christian O. Basler, 1990. The supplement volumes are separately indexed. A selection of Lincoln documents, in two volumes, titled *Abraham Lincoln, Speeches and Writings . . .* , edited by Don E. Fehrenbacher, was published in New York: Library of America, 1989. The first volume contains papers, 1832-58; and the second, 1859-65.

3478. *Lincoln Herald.* Vol. 1 (1899)--to date. Published by Lincoln Memorial University, Harrogate, Tenn.; monthly, 1899-1933, and quarterly, 1937--to date; titled *Mountain Herald*, 1899-October 1937. There are gaps in the volume numbering.

3479. Lorant, Stefan. *The Life of Abraham Lincoln: A Short, Illustrated Biography.* New York: McGraw-Hill, 1954.

3480. _____. *Lincoln: A Picture Story of His Life.* 1952. Rev. and enl. ed., New York: Norton, 1969.

3481. Luthin, Reinhard. *The Real Abraham Lincoln.* Englewood Cliffs, N.J.: Prentice-Hall, 1960.

3482. Miers, Earl Schenck, ed. *Lincoln Day by Day: A Chronology, 1809-1865.* 3 vols. Washington: Lincoln Sesquicentennial Commission, 1960. Replaces earlier volumes published by the Abraham Lincoln Association. A facsimile reprint (three volumes in one) was issued by Morningside, Dayton, Ohio, in 1991.

3483. Monaghan, Jay, comp. *Lincoln Bibliography, 1839-1939.* 2 vols. Collections of the Illinois State Historical Library, vols. 31 and 32. Springfield, 1943 and 1945. Entries arranged chronologically by year of publication and alphabetically by author within the year. The last section of volume 2 lists foreign-language titles chronologically in the same manner. A separate index in volume 2 lists all publications alphabetically by author (or editor or compiler; or by title if the item is unattributed; or by publisher or sponsor if there is no author or title). Altogether, there are 3,958 entries.

3484. Nevins, Allan. *The Emergence of Lincoln.* 2 vols. New York: Scribner's, 1950.

3485. Newman, Ralph Geoffrey, ed. *Man for the Ages.* Garden City, N.Y.: Doubleday, 1960.

3486. Nicolay, John G., and Hay, John Milton. *Abraham Lincoln: A History.* 10 vols. New York: Century, 1890. Abridged ed., Chicago: University of Chicago Press, 1966.

3487. Oates, Stephen B. *Abraham Lincoln: The Man behind the Myths.* New York: Harper, 1984.

3488. _____. *With Malice toward None: The Life of Abraham Lincoln.* New York: Harper, 1977.

3489. Ostendorf, Lloyd. *Lincoln in Photographs: An Album of Every Known Pose.* Norman: University of Oklahoma Press, 1963.

3490. Peterson, Merrill D. *Lincoln in American Memory.* New York: Oxford University Press, 1994.

3491. Pratt, Harry Edward. "Albert Taylor Bledsoe, Critic of Lincoln." *Transactions of the Illinois State Historical Society, 1934,* pp. 153-80. Bledsoe was a brilliant Springfield contemporary of Lincoln's, an attorney, and editorial writer who later served the Confederacy. His assessment of Lincoln's character is perceptive, though caustic.

3492. Randall, James Garfield. *Lincoln, the Liberal Statesman.* New York: Dodd, Mead, 1947.

3493. _____. *Lincoln the President.* 4 vols. New York: Dodd, Mead, 1945-55.

3494. Sandburg, Carl. *Abraham Lincoln: The Prairie Years.* New York: Harcourt, Brace, 1926. Great literature; captures the spirit of the period and the man but has many historical errors. *The Prairie Years* and *The War Years* (4 vols., 1939) were distilled by Sandburg into one volume, issued by Harcourt, Brace in 1954.

3495. Tarbell, Ida M. *The Early Life of Abraham Lincoln.* New York: Barnes, 1974. This edition has an introduction by Paul McClelland Angle.

3496. Thomas, Benjamin Platt. *Abraham Lincoln: A Biography.* New York: Knopf, 1952. For years the standard one-volume biography of Lincoln.

3497. _____. *Portrait for Posterity: Lincoln and His Biographers.* New Brunswick, N.J.: Rutgers University Press, 1947.

3498. Wessen, Ernest James. "Campaign Lives of Abraham Lincoln, 1860: An Annotated Bibliography of the Biographies of Abraham Lincoln during the Campaign Year." *Transactions of the Illinois State Historical Society, 1937,* pp. 188-220.

b. Early Life

3499. Baber, Adin. *A. Lincoln with Compass and Chain . . .* Kansas, Ill.: The author, 1968. Hanks Family Historical Series, vol. 5. The definitive source for Lincoln's work as a surveyor.

3500. Barton, William E. "Abraham Lincoln and New Salem." *Journal of the Illinois State Historical Society* 19 (1926-27): 74-101.

3501. Coffin, Charles Carleton. "Ancestry and Early Years of Abraham Lincoln." *Harper's Weekly* 36 (1892): 153-56.

3502. Coleman, Charles H. "The 'Grocery Keeper' and His Customer." *Journal of the Illinois State Historical Society* 52 (1959): 547-51. Lincoln's work at a New Salem grocery that served liquor was mentioned by Stephen Douglas in the 1858 debates and led to banter between the two men about their early lives.

3503. Davis, Edwin David. "Lincoln and Macon County, Illinois, 1830-31." *Journal of the Illinois State Historical Society* 25 (1932-33): 63-107.

3504. Efflandt, Lloyd H. *Lincoln and the Black Hawk War.* Rock Island, Ill.: Rock Island Arsenal Historical Society, 1992.

3505. Hickey, James T. "Three R's in Lincoln's Education." *Journal of the Illinois State Historical Society* 52 (1959): 195-207. Three related frontier families made their libraries available to young Lincoln in the 1830s.

3506. Horgan, Paul. *Citizen of New Salem.* New York: Farrar, 1961. Description of the frontier Illinois village where Lincoln lived for seven years, and a study of its influences on his life.

3507. "Lincoln's Association with New Boston." *Journal of the Illinois State Historical Society* 51 (1958): 200-202. Lincoln surveyed the town site and handled several property deeds.

3508. "Lincoln Was First a Militia Captain." *Journal of the Illinois State Historical Society* 46 (1953): 188.

3509. "Model of Lincoln's River Steamboat." *Journal of the Illinois State Historical Society* 41 (1948): 145. Description of the steamboat *Talisman*, which Lincoln helped maneuver up the Sangamon River and back to the Illinois River.

3510. Myers, James E. *The Astonishing Saber Duel of Abraham Lincoln.* Springfield: Lincoln-Herndon Building Publishers, 1968. A whimsical but documented account of a duel that was arranged but never took place.

3511. Neely, Mark E. Jr. "Lincoln's Peculiar Relationship with Indiana." *Inland: The Magazine of the Middle West*, 1980, no. 1, pp. 4-7. Traces Indiana influences on Lincoln and on some of his political positions at the beginning of his career in Illinois.

3512. Sandburg, Carl. *Abe Lincoln Grows Up.* New York: Harcourt, Brace, 1928. Reprinted from the author's *Abraham Lincoln: The Prairie Years.*

3513. Spears, Zarel C., and Barton, Robert S. *Berry and Lincoln, Frontier Merchants: The Store That Winked Out.* New York: Stratford House, 1947.

3514. Strozier, Charles B. "On the Verge of Greatness: Psychological Reflections on Lincoln at the Lyceum." *Civil War History* 36 (1990): 137-48.

3515. Temple, Wayne C. "Lincoln's Arms, Dress and Military Duty before, during, and after the Black Hawk War." *Illinois Libraries* 53 (1971): 1-9.

3516. Wilson, Major L. "Lincoln and Van Buren in the Steps of the Fathers: Another Look at the Lyceum Address." *Civil War History* 29 (1983): 197-211.

c. Law Practice

3517. Bannister, Dan W. *Lincoln and the Common Law: A Collection of Lincoln's Illinois Supreme Court Cases from 1838-1861 and Their Influence on the Evolution of Illinois Common Law.* Springfield, Ill.: Human Services Press, 1992.

3518. Brown, Charles LeRoy. "Abraham Lincoln and the Illinois Central Railroad, 1857-1860." *Journal of the Illinois State Historical Society* 36 (1943): 121-63. Lincoln was an attorney for the company in those years.

3519. Davis, G. Cullom, ed. *The Lincoln Legal Papers: A Documentary History of the Law Practice of Abraham Lincoln, 1837-1861.* Working title for a documentary edition of all surviving records from Lincoln's law practice. The collection will be issued in both a complete facsimile edition on CD-ROM and a five-volume book edition of selected cases. The effort is sponsored by the Illinois Historic Preservation Agency, Abraham Lincoln Association, Sangamon State University Center for Legal Studies, and University of Illinois College of Law. Expected publication, 1997-2002.

3520. Duff, John J. *A. Lincoln, Prairie Lawyer.* New York: Rinehart, 1960. A well-written scholarly study.

3521. _____. "This Was a Lawyer." *Journal of the Illinois State Historical Society* 52 (1959): 146-63. A distillation of Duff's *A. Lincoln, Prairie Lawyer,* then in press.

3522. East, Ernest Edward. "The Melissa Goings Murder Case." *Journal of the Illinois State Historical Society* 46 (1953): 79-83. Lincoln represented the bondsmen for a Woodford County abused wife charged with murdering her husband and then fleeing the county.

3523. Frank, John P. *Lincoln as a Lawyer.* Urbana: University of Illinois Press, 1961.

3524. Gilbert, Barry. "Attorney for William Baker Gilbert." *Journal of the Illinois State Historical Society* 46 (1953): 290-93. An account of the last legal suit Lincoln was involved in before he was elected president. Lincoln's praecipe is in the Illinois State Historical Library.

3525. Gridley, J. N. "Lincoln's Defense of Duff Armstrong." *Journal of the Illinois State Historical Society* 3, no. 1 (April 1910): 24-44.

3526. Hickey, James T. "Lincoln the Real Estate Agent." *Journal of the Illinois State Historical Society* 53 (1960): 70-78. Lincoln's involvement with real property in Illinois, as both attorney and property owner.

3527. Hill, Frederick Trevor. *Lincoln, the Lawyer.* New York: Century, 1905. Reprint, 1913, as a Lincoln Centennial Association Limited Edition. Lincoln's law practice after his return from Congress in 1849.

3528. Hinchliff, Emerson. "Lincoln and the 'Reaper Case.' " *Journal of the Illinois State Historical Society* 33 (1940): 361-65.

3529. "Lincoln Tries a Suit Well." *Journal of the Illinois State Historical Society* 47 (1954): 63-66. Charles M. Chase, editor of the *DeKalb County Sentinel* and a juror in an 1859 federal case at Chicago, describes Lincoln as a defense attorney.

3530. Long, John. *Lincoln's Cases before the Illinois Supreme Court, From His Entry into the Practice of Law until His Entry into Congress.* The Law of Illinois, vol. 1. Shiloh, Ill.: Illinois Co., 1993.

3531. Matthews, Elizabeth W. *Lincoln as a Lawyer: An Annotated Bibliography.* Carbondale: Southern Illinois University Press, 1991. Contains 509 entries.

3532. Pratt, Harry Edward. "Abraham Lincoln in Bloomington, Illinois." *Journal of the Illinois State Historical Society* 29 (1936-37): 42-69. Lincoln's court cases, political speeches, and personal friends in Bloomington.

3533. _____. "Abraham Lincoln's First Murder Trial." *Journal of the Illinois State Historical Society* 37 (1944): 242-49.

3534. _____. "The Famous 'Chicken Bone' Case." *Journal of the Illinois State Historical Society* 45 (1952): 164-67. In representing two physicians who were being sued for malpractice, Lincoln used chicken bones at the trial to illustrate how a broken bone healed. The jury was unable to reach a verdict, and the suit was eventually dismissed.

3535. _____. " 'Judge' Abraham Lincoln." *Journal of the Illinois State Historical Society* 48 (1955): 28-40. Account of Lincoln's substitutions for Judge David Davis on the Eighth Illinois Judicial District in the 1850s.

3536. Schwartz, Thomas F. "The Lincoln Handbill of 1837: A Rare Document's History." *Illinois Historical Journal* 79 (1986): 267-74. The original handbill (privately owned) illustrates Lincoln's involvement in a Sangamon County land dispute.

3537. Tilton, Clint Clay. "Lincoln and Lamon: Partners and Friends." *Transactions of the Illinois State Historical Society, 1931*, pp. 175-228.

d. Early Political Career

3538. Baringer, William Eldon. *Lincoln's Vandalia: A Pioneer Portrait.* New Brunswick, N.J.: Rutgers University Press, 1949. Lincoln's work as a legislator at Vandalia and the influence of that work on his later career.

3539. Boritt (Borit), Gabor S. "Lincoln's Opposition to the Mexican War." *Journal of the Illinois State Historical Society* 67 (1974): 79-100.

3540. Bradford, M. E. "Lincoln's Republican Rhetoric: The Development of a Political Idiom." *Old Northwest* 14 (1988): 185-211. An examination of Lincoln's speeches and political positions from 1854 to the time of the 1858 debates with Stephen A. Douglas.

3541. Ewing, Thomas, ed. "Lincoln and the General Land Office, 1849." *Journal of the Illinois State Historical Society* 25 (1932-33): 139-53. Letters that illustrate the political maneuverings over appointment to head the General Land Office. Lincoln lost the position to Justin Butterfield.

3542. Fehrenbacher, Don E. "Only His Stepchildren: Lincoln and the Negro." *Civil War History* 20 (1974): 293-310.

3543. _____. "The Origins and Purpose of Lincoln's 'House-Divided' Speech." *Mississippi Valley Historical Review* 46 (1959-60): 615-43.

3544. Findley, Paul. *A. Lincoln: The Crucible of Congress.* New York: Crown, 1979. Former congressman from the Illinois district once represented by Lincoln, Findley discusses Lincoln's two-year congressional career in detail and concludes that it was not a failure, as sometimes argued.

3545. Fredrickson, George M. "A Man But Not a Brother: Abraham Lincoln and Racial Equality." *Journal of Southern History* 41 (1975): 39-58.

3546. Harris, Sheldon H. "Abraham Lincoln Stumps a Yankee Audience." *New England Quarterly* 38 (June 1965): 227-33. In 1848 Congressman Lincoln stumped Massachusetts for more than two weeks in behalf of the Whig national ticket.

3547. Lewis, Gene D., ed. "Lincoln's Cincinnati Speech of 1859." *Cincinnati Historical Society Bulletin* 23 (1965): 147-78.

3548. Lincoln, Abraham. *Abraham Lincoln's "House Divided" Address, Delivered in Springfield before the Illinois State Republican Convention, June 16, 1858.* Introduction by Clyde C. Walton. Illinois State Historical Society Pamphlet Series, no. 1. Springfield, 1958.

3549. _____. "A Newly Discovered Speech of Lincoln Delivered at Bloomington, September 26, 1854." Edited by Ernest E. East. *Journal of the Illinois State Historical Society* 28, no. 1 (April 1935): 65-77. The speech, on the Kansas-Nebraska bill, as condensed in a Peoria newspaper.

3550. "Lincoln at Galena in 1856." *Journal of the Illinois State Historical Society* 47 (1954): 410-11. Contemporary newspaper description of Lincoln as a speaker.

3551. Merwin, J. B. "Lincoln and Peter Cartwright." *Century* 93 (1917): 603-4. Joshua Speed's recollection of Lincoln's 1846 congressional campaign.

3552. Neely, Mark E. Jr. "Lincoln and the Mexican War: An Argument by Analogy." *Civil War History* 24 (1978): 5-24.

3553. _____. "War and Partisanship: What Lincoln Learned from James K. Polk." *Journal of the Illinois State Historical Society* 74 (1981): 199-216. From Polk, Lincoln learned the value of partisanship in making appointments to civilian jobs and also the value of nonpartisanship in presidential relations with military commanders. Lincoln's career in Congress and relationships with Illinois politicians during the Mexican War are discussed in detail.

3554. Olsen, Otto H. "Abraham Lincoln as Revolutionary." *Civil War History* 24 (1978): 213-24. The author concludes that Lincoln served as a "most successful promoter and leader of internal revolution in the United States."

3555. Paullin, Charles O. "Abraham Lincoln in Congress, 1847-1849." *Journal of the Illinois State Historical Society* 14 (1921-22): 85-89.

3556. Porter, Laura Smith. " 'The last, best hope of earth': Abraham Lincoln's Perception of the Mission of America, 1834-1854." *Illinois Historical Journal* 78 (1985): 207-16. The author shows how Lincoln's interpretation of the Civil War as a "fight for American mission resulted from a lifetime commitment to the doctrine of mission" that grew out of frontier attitudes and experiences.

3557. Pratt, Harry Edward. "Lincoln and the Division of Sangamon County." *Journal of the Illinois State Historical Society* 47 (1954): 398-409. Legislative operations, 1834-39, that led to the creation of three new Illinois counties.

3558. Riddle, Donald W. *Congressman Abraham Lincoln*. Urbana: University of Illinois Press, 1957. Reprint, Westport, Conn.: Greenwood, 1979.

3559. _____. *Lincoln Runs for Congress*. New Brunswick, N.J.: Rutgers University Press, 1948. Lincoln was elected to Congress in 1846.

3560. Rietveld, Ronald D. "Lincoln and the Politics of Morality." *Journal of the Illinois State Historical Society* 68 (1975): 27-44. Political positions and moral principles regarding slavery that were enunciated by Lincoln in the years 1836-58.

3561. Ruiz, Ramón Eduardo. "A Comment on Morality: Lincoln, Justin H. Smith, and the Mexican War." *Journal of the Illinois State Historical Society* 69 (1976): 26-34. As a congressman from Illinois, Lincoln opposed the Mexican War as one started by American invasion of Mexican territory. The author presents a factual and historiographical study that supports Lincoln's position.

3562. Schwartz, Thomas F. "Lincoln, Form Letters, and Fillmore Men." *Illinois Historical Journal* 78 (1985): 65-70. Lincoln's speaking and letter-writing efforts in behalf of the 1856 Republican national and state tickets, headed by John C. Frémont and William Bissell, respectively. Millard Fillmore was the candidate of the Know-Nothing party.

3563. Shaw, James. "A Neglected Episode in the Life of Abraham Lincoln." *Transactions of the Illinois State Historical Society, 1922*, pp. 51-58. The episode was Lincoln's participation in the 1847 Chicago Harbor and River Convention.

3564. Simon, Paul. *Lincoln's Preparation for Greatness: The Illinois Legislative Years.* Norman: University of Oklahoma Press, 1965. Reprint, Urbana: University of Illinois Press, 1971; paperback ed., 1989.

3565. Strickland, Arvarh E. "The Illinois Background of Lincoln's Attitude toward Slavery and the Negro." *Journal of the Illinois State Historical Society* 56 (1963): 474-94.

3566. White, Horace. "Abraham Lincoln in 1854." *Transactions of the Illinois State Historical Society, 1908*, pp. 25-47. A pivotal year in Lincoln's political career.

3567. Wiley, Earl Wellington. "Lincoln in the Campaign of 1856." *Journal of the Illinois State Historical Society* 22 (1929-30): 582-92.

e. Presidential Campaign and Election

3568. Boritt (Borit), Gabor S. "Was Lincoln a Vulnerable Candidate in 1860?" *Civil War History* 27 (1981): 32-48.

3569. Conkling, Clinton L. "How Mr. Lincoln Received the News of His First Nomination." *Transactions of the Illinois State Historical Society, 1909*, pp. 63-66.

3570. Fischer, Roger A. "The Republican Presidential Campaigns of 1856 and 1860: Analysis through Artifacts." *Civil War History* 27 (1981): 123-37. Comparison of the campaigns of John C. Frémont and Abraham Lincoln.

3571. "Lincoln Is Notified of His Nomination." *Journal of the Illinois State Historical Society* 48 (1955): 322-24. Contemporary accounts of Lincoln's notification of his nomination for the presidency.

3572. Luebke, Frederick C., ed. *Ethnic Voters and the Election of Lincoln.* Lincoln: University of Nebraska Press, 1971. Eleven articles related primarily to the 1860 election.

3573. Pratt, Harry Edward., comp. and ed. " 'The Journal Paper Was Always My Friend.' " *Journal of the Illinois State Historical Society* 46 (1953): 178-86. Stories from the Springfield newspaper, primarily in 1860, about Lincoln.

3574. Searcher, Victor. *Lincoln's Journey to Greatness: A Factual Account of the Twelve-day Inaugural Trip.* Philadelphia: Winston, 1960.

3575. Strevey, Tracy E. "Joseph Medill and the *Chicago Tribune* in the Nomination and Election of Lincoln." *Transactions of the Illinois State Historical Society, 1938,* pp. 39-63.

3576. Temple, Wayne C. "Lincoln's Fence Rails." *Journal of the Illinois State Historical Society* 47 (1954): 20-34. An account of the 1860 state Republican convention at Decatur at which the fence rails were introduced as the symbol of Lincoln the rail-splitter, champion of the workingman.

3577. "A Ticket for 1860." *Magazine of American History* 29 (1893): 282-83. In 1858 an Ohio reader of the *Cincinnati Gazette* is believed to have made the first public suggestion of Abraham Lincoln as a presidential candidate.

3578. Villard, Henry. *Lincoln on the Eve of '61.* Edited by Harold G. and Oswald Garrison Villard. New York: Knopf, 1941. A selection of Villard's discerning letters to the *New York Herald* for nearly three months after Lincoln's election to the presidency.

f. Family and Personal Life

3579. Baber, Adin. *Nancy Hanks, the Destined Mother of a President . . .* Kansas, Ill.: Privately printed (sold by the Arthur H. Clark Co.), 1963. Hanks Family Historical Series, vol. 3.

3580. _____. *Nancy Hanks of "Undistinguished Families--Second Families."* Hanks Family Historical Series, vol. 1. Bloomington, Ind.: The author, 1959.

The first of several volumes designed to set the record straight about the mother of Abraham Lincoln and her ancestors.

3581. Baker, Jean H. *Mary Todd Lincoln: A Biography.* New York: Norton, 1987. More reliable, though more provocative, than Ruth Randall's biography.

3582. Barton, William E. "The Ancestry of Abraham Lincoln." *Transactions of the Illinois State Historical Society, 1924*, pp. 123-38.

3583. Briggs, Harold E., and Briggs, Ernestine B. *Nancy Hanks Lincoln: A Frontier Portrait.* New York: Bookman, 1952.

3584. Coleman, Charles H. *Abraham Lincoln and Coles County, Illinois.* New Brunswick, N.J.: Scarecrow Press, 1955. Deals with Lincoln's family and friends as well as his law practice in the county.

3585. _____. "Lincoln's Lincoln Grandmother." *Journal of the Illinois State Historical Society* 52 (1959): 59-90. She was Bathsheba Herring Lincoln, mother of Thomas Lincoln, the president's father.

3586. _____. *Sarah Bush Lincoln, the Mother Who Survived Him.* Charleston, Ill., 1952. Reprinted from the *Lincoln Herald*, Summer 1952.

3587. Darrin, Charles V. "Robert Todd Lincoln and a Family Friendship." *Journal of the Illinois State Historical Society* 44 (1951): 210-17. The Lincolns' friendship with the Shearer family.

3588. _____. "Your Truly Attached Friend, Mary Lincoln." *Journal of the Illinois State Historical Society* 44 (1951): 7-25. The first five of the ten letters printed here deal with Mary Lincoln's friends and social life in Springfield in 1859 and early 1860.

3589. Davis, Alonzo Hilton. "Lincoln's Goose Nest Home." *Century* 44 (n.s. 22) (1892): 798-99. This was the last home of the Lincoln family in Indiana.

3590. Davis, Edwin David. "The Hanks Family in Macon County, Illinois, 1828-1939: A Biographical Directory." *Transactions of the Illinois State Historical Society, 1939*, pp. 112-52.

3591. Fehrenbacher, Don E. *The Minor Affair: An Adventure in Forgery and Detection.* Fort Wayne, Ind.: Louis A. Warren Lincoln Library and Museum, Lincoln National Life Insurance Company, 1979. Traces the story of the forged documents published in the *Atlantic Monthly* that supported a Lincoln-Ann Rutledge romance. But see nos. 3610, 3614, 3617.

3592. "Fine Lincoln Letter on Exhibit." *Journal of the Illinois State Historical Society* 45 (1952): 415-16. Letter of 4 July 1860 to Anson G. Henry, given to the Illinois State Historical Library, is one of the few in which Lincoln discusses his family and personal life.

3593. Goff, John S. *Robert Todd Lincoln: A Man in His Own Right.* Norman: University of Oklahoma Press, 1969. A scholarly, well-written biography.

3594. Hickey, James T. "The Lincoln Account at the Corneau & Diller Drug Store, 1849-1861: A Springfield Tradition." *Journal of the Illinois State Historical Society* 77 (1984): 60-66. These purchase records provide insights about daily activities of the Lincoln family.

3595. Holzer, Harold. *Abraham Lincoln [and] Mary Todd Lincoln.* Richmond, Va.: United States Historical Society, 1984. A study of the Lincoln marriage.

3596. Kincaid, Robert L. *Joshua Fry Speed, Lincoln's Most Intimate Friend.* Harrogate, Tenn.: Lincoln Memorial University, 1943.

3597. Krueger, Lillian. "Mary Todd Lincoln Summers in Wisconsin." *Journal of the Illinois State Historical Society* 34 (1941): 249-53. Mrs. Lincoln visited the spa and took the mineral waters (believed to have been high in lithium, now used as a specific for depression) at Waukesha in 1872.

3598. Neely, Mark E. Jr., and McMurtry, R. Gerald. *The Insanity File: The Case of Mary Todd Lincoln.* Carbondale: Southern Illinois University Press, 1986.

3599. Ostendorf, Lloyd. "The Story of the 'Tired Lincoln' Photograph." *Journal of the Illinois State Historical Society* 57 (1964): 400-405. Circumstances of Lincoln's family life and political obligations in August 1858, when the photograph was made.

3600. Pratt, Harry Edward. "Little Eddie Lincoln: 'We Miss Him Very Much.' " *Journal of the Illinois State Historical Society* 47 (1954): 300-305. An account of the short life and death of Abraham and Mary Lincoln's second son.

3601. _____. *The Personal Finances of Abraham Lincoln.* Springfield, Ill.: Abraham Lincoln Association, 1943.

3602. Purvis, Thomas L. "The Making of a Myth: Abraham Lincoln's Family Background in the Perspective of Jacksonian Politics." *Journal of the Illinois State Historical Society* 75 (1982): 149-60. How Lincoln contributed to the myth of himself as a self-made man.

3603. Randall, Ruth Painter. *The Courtship of Mr. Lincoln.* Boston: Little, Brown, 1957. Lincoln's courtship of Mary Todd.

3604. _____. *Lincoln's Sons.* Boston: Little, Brown, 1956. Primarily anecdotal accounts of the early lives of the four sons of Abraham Lincoln.

3605. _____. *Mary Lincoln: Biography of a Marriage.* Boston: Little, Brown, 1953.

3606. "Recollections of a Springfield Doctor." *Journal of the Illinois State Historical Society* 47 (1954): 57-63. Dr. Preston Bailhache's recollections are primarily concerned with Lincoln and his family in the years 1857-60.

3607. Ritze, C. C. "In Defense of Mrs. Lincoln." *Journal of the Illinois State Historical Society* 30 (1937-38): 5-69. Detailed study of Mary Lincoln as portrayed by Lincoln's colleagues and biographers.

3608. Ross, Rodney A. "Mary Todd Lincoln, Patient at Bellevue Place, Batavia." *Journal of the Illinois State Historical Society* 63 (1970): 5-34. Mrs. Lincoln was confined at Bellevue Place in 1875 after having been judged insane by a Cook County court. The article includes extracts from Bellevue medical records, now in the Illinois State Historical Library.

3609. Simmons, Dawn Langley. *A Rose for Mrs. Lincoln: A Biography of Mary Todd Lincoln.* Boston: Beacon Press, 1970.

3610. Simon, John Y. "Abraham Lincoln and Ann Rutledge." *Journal of the Abraham Lincoln Association* 11 (1990): 13-33. A reexamination of the historical record "overwhelmingly indicates" the reality of the Lincoln-Rutledge romance.

3611. Temple, Wayne C., ed. *Mrs. Frances Jane (Todd) Wallace Describes Lincoln's Wedding.* Harrogate, Tenn.: Lincoln Memorial University Press, 1960. This account appeared in Chicago and Springfield newspapers in 1895 and in a pamphlet published in Springfield in 1917.

3612. Temple, Wayne C. "Thomas Lincoln Buys School Land." *Illinois Libraries* 48 (1966): 450-53. The purchase of two forty-acre tracts in Coles County.

3613. Turner, Justin G. "The Mary Lincoln Letters to Mrs. Felician Slataper." *Journal of the Illinois State Historical Society* 49 (1956): 7-33. Texts of eleven letters dated from 1868 to 1874 are printed. Mrs. Lincoln's friend Eliza Slataper lived in Pittsburgh, Pennsylvania.

3614. Walsh, John Evangelist. *The Shadows Rise: Abraham Lincoln and the Ann Rutledge Legend.* Urbana: University of Illinois Press, 1993. A book-length treatment based in large part on the findings of John Y. Simon and Douglas L. Wilson.

3615. Warren, Louis A. "Lincoln Lands and Lineage." *Transactions of the Illinois State Historical Society, 1927,* pp. 144-53.

3616. _____. "Sarah Bush Lincoln, the Stepmother of Abraham Lincoln." *Transactions of the Illinois State Historical Society, 1926,* pp. 80-88.

3617. Wilson, Douglas L. "Abraham Lincoln, Ann Rutledge, and the Evidence of Herndon's Informants." *Civil War History* 36 (1990): 301-23. Largely because of the work of Paul McClelland Angle, David Donald, and James G. Randall, Lincoln scholars discredited the Ann Rutledge story for half a century. John Y. Simon, Wilson, and others have now examined the William H. Herndon papers and concluded that Herndon's informants were by and large reliable and that Lincoln and Ann Rutledge had been engaged and that Lincoln showed "excessive grief" at her death.

3618. _____. "Abraham Lincoln and 'That Fatal First of January.' " *Civil War History* 38 (1992): 101-30. A closely argued analysis and comparisons of the various primary accounts of Lincoln's broken engagement to Mary Todd and his attraction to Matilda Edwards. Wilson concludes that Lincoln's mention of the "fatal first of Jany. '41" referred most likely not to events in Lincoln's life but to those in the life of the letter's recipient, Joshua F. Speed.

3619. Woodward, Elizabeth Raymond. "Portrait of My Grandmother, Mrs. Lincoln's Kinswoman." *Journal of the Illinois State Historical Society* 41 (1948): 265-80. Biography of Helen Dodge Edwards, a sister-in-law of Mary Todd Lincoln's sister, Elizabeth Todd Edwards.

g. Miscellany

3620. Angle, Paul McClelland. *"Here I Have Lived": A History of Lincoln's Springfield, 1821-1865.* Springfield, Ill.: Abraham Lincoln Association, 1935.

3621. Boritt (Borit), Gabor S., and Borit, Adam. "Lincoln and the Marfan Syndrome: The Medical Diagnosis of a Historical Figure." *Civil War History* 29 (1983): 212-29.

3622. Chesebrough, David B. " 'His own fault': Rev. Charles H. Ellis of Bloomington Sermonizes on the Assassination of Abraham Lincoln." *Illinois Historical Journal* 86 (1993): 146-88. Ellis was an ardent abolitionist who criticized both Lincoln's character and policies--thereby precipitating public outrage, a "free speech" crisis in Bloomington, and Ellis's resignation from the Congregational church.

3623. Coleman, Charles H. "Spelling Bothered Lincoln, Too." *Journal of the Illinois State Historical Society* 49 (1956): 405-15.

3624. Croy, Homer. "Discovered: An Authentic Lincoln Fingerprint." *Journal of the Illinois State Historical Society* 49 (1956): 263-70. In providing an autograph for a friend of John Hay's assistant, Lincoln left a clear print on the sheet with his signature; and it was authenticated in a letter by the assistant, Gustave E. Matile.

3625. Dooley, Raymond N. "Lincoln and His Namesake Town." *Journal of the Illinois State Historical Society* 52 (1959): 130-45. Lincoln had many business, political, and legal associations with Logan County and its county seat, the town of Lincoln.

3626. Endy, Melvin B. Jr. "Abraham Lincoln and American Civil Religion: A Reinterpretation." *Church History* 44 (1975): 229-41.

3627. Fraysse, Olivier. *Lincoln, Land, and Labor, 1809-60.* Translated by Sylvia Neely. Urbana: University of Illinois Press, 1994. Discussions of Lincoln's ideas on disposal of public lands, on agriculture and industry, and on the place of African-Americans and Native Americans in society.

3628. George, Joseph Jr. "The Lincoln Writings of Charles P. T. Chiniquy." *Journal of the Illinois State Historical Society* 69 (1976): 17-25. Chiniquy was a onetime Catholic priest in Illinois whose anti-Catholic writings, in which he attributed similar sentiments to Lincoln, were nothing short of libelous.

3629. Heath, Caroline R., comp. and ed. *Four Days in May: Lincoln Returns to Springfield.* Springfield: Sangamon County Historical Society & Illinois State Historical Society, 1965. Funeral and burial ceremonies.

3630. Hickey, James T. "Abraham Lincoln's Lot in Lincoln, Illinois." *Journal of the Illinois State Historical Society* 46 (1953): 83-87. Lincoln acquired the property in 1858 as payment for a note.

3631. _____. "Springfield, May, 1865." *Journal of the Illinois State Historical Society* 58 (1965): 21-33.

3632. Johnson, Ludwell H. "Lincoln and Equal Rights: The Authenticity of the Wadsworth Letter." *Journal of Southern History* 32 (1966): 83-87. The argument against the authenticity of Lincoln's 1864 letter to Major General James H. Wadsworth--generally cited as one of the main sources for Lincoln's equalitarian principles.

3633. Kyle, Otto R. *Abraham Lincoln in Decatur.* New York: Vantage, 1957.

3634. Merritt, Edward L. "Recollections of the Part Springfield Bore in the Obsequies of Abraham Lincoln." *Transactions of the Illinois State Historical Society, 1909*, pp. 179-83.

3635. Monaghan, Jay. "A Critical Examination of Three Lincoln Photographs." *Journal of the Illinois State Historical Society* 52 (1959): 91-105. Consideration of the photographs involves a study of Lincoln's movements in 1856, 1857, and 1860.

3636. _____. "Lincoln's Other Boswell." *Journal of the Illinois State Historical Society* 42 (1949): 454-56. An account of Lincoln's sittings for sculptor Leonard Volk in 1860.

3637. Newman, Ralph Geoffrey. " 'In This Sad World of Ours, Sorrow Comes to All,' A Timetable for the Lincoln Funeral Train." *Journal of the Illinois State Historical Society* 58 (1965): 5-20.

3638. Nicolay, John G. "Lincoln's Literary Experiments, with a Lecture and Verses Hitherto Unpublished." *Century Magazine* 47 (n.s. 25) (1894): 823-32.

3639. _____. "Lincoln's Personal Appearance." *Century Magazine* 42 (n.s. 20) (1891): 932-38.

3640. Searcher, Victor. *The Farewell to Lincoln.* Nashville, Tenn.: Abingdon Press, 1965.

3641. Speer, Bonnie Stahl. *The Great Abraham Lincoln Hijack.* Norman, Okla.: Reliance Press, 1990. An account of the attempt in 1876 to steal Lincoln's body from his tomb in Springfield.

3642. Temple, Wayne C. *Abraham Lincoln and Others at the St. Nicholas.* Springfield, Ill.: St. Nicholas Corporation, 1968. Lincoln's many associations with the hotel, including his sittings there for the sculptor Thomas D. Jones.

3643. _____. *Lincoln's Connections with the Illinois & Michigan Canal, His Return from Congress in '48, and His Invention.* Springfield: Illinois Bell, 1986. Lincoln's invention was a ship design that used buoyant air chambers when navigating in shallow water.

3644. Tisler, C. C. *Lincoln's in Town.* Ottawa, Ill.: The author, 1941. A record of Lincoln's visits to, and associations with, the city of Ottawa; based on contemporary newspapers.

3645. Volk, Leonard Wells. "The Lincoln Life-Mask and How It Was Made." *Journal of the Illinois State Historical Society* 8 (1915-16): 238-48. Reprinted from *Century Magazine*, December 1881. See also the *Journal* article by Henry B. Rankin: "Comment and Corrections on 'The Lincoln Life-Mask and How It Was Made,' " pp. 249-59.

3646. Wadsworth, Moses Goodwin. "Some Memories of Lincoln." *Journal of the Illinois State Historical Society* 41 (1948): 281-83. The author describes Lincoln and several of his speeches.

3647. Whitney, Blair. "Lincoln's Life as Dramatic Art." *Journal of the Illinois State Historical Society* 61 (1968): 333-49.

3648. Zane, Charles S. "Lincoln As I Knew Him." *Journal of the Illinois State Historical Society* 14 (1921-22): 74-84.

12. Adlai E. Stevenson II

3649. Brown, Stuart Gerry. *Conscience in Politics: Adlai E. Stevenson in the 1950's.* Syracuse, N.Y.: Syracuse University Press, 1961. An uncritical, altogether admiring study.

3650. Busch, Noel F. *Adlai E. Stevenson of Illinois: A Portrait.* New York: Farrar, 1952. The first biography of Stevenson, rushed into print before he was nominated for president. Half of the book consists of excerpts from his speeches and writings.

3651. Cochran, Bert. *Adlai Stevenson: Patrician among the Politicians.* New York: Funk & Wagnalls, 1969.

3652. Davis, Kenneth Sydney. *The Politics of Honor: A Biography of Adlai E. Stevenson.* New York: Putnam, 1967. A revised and updated version of his *Prophet in His Own Country.*

3653. _____. *A Prophet in His Own Country: The Triumphs and Defeats of Adlai E. Stevenson.* Garden City, N.Y.: Doubleday, 1957.

3654. Doyle, Edward P., ed. *As We Knew Adlai: The Stevenson Story by Twenty-two Friends.* Foreword by Adlai E. Stevenson III. New York: Harper, 1966. These reminiscences provide source material about the good qualities of Stevenson.

3655. Harris, Patricia. *Adlai, the Springfield Years.* Nashville, Tenn.: Aurora Publishers, 1975.

3656. Hayman, LeRoy. *American Ambassador to the World: Adlai Stevenson.* London: Abelard-Schuman, 1966.

3657. Ives, Elizabeth Stevenson. *Adlai Stevenson of Illinois, by John Bartlow Martin (Doubleday, 1976): Corrections and Comments.* [Bloomington, Ill., 1977.]

3658. _____, and Dolson, Hildegard. *My Brother Adlai.* New York: William Morrow, 1956.

3659. Kneerim, Jill, ed. *Adlai Stevenson's Public Years.* With photographs by Cornell Capa, John Fell Stevenson, and Inge Morath. New York: Grossman, 1966. An uncritical pastiche of photographs and excerpts from Stevenson's writings.

3660. McKeever, Porter. *Adlai Stevenson: His Life and Legacy.* New York: William Morrow, 1989. A popular biography by a friend but by no means hagiography.

3661. Martin, John Bartlow. *Adlai Stevenson.* New York: Harper, 1952. A campaign biography.

3662. _____. *Adlai Stevenson and the World: The Life of Adlai E. Stevenson.* Garden City, N.Y.: Doubleday, 1977.

3663. _____. *Adlai Stevenson of Illinois: The Life of Adlai E. Stevenson.* Garden City, N.Y.: Doubleday, 1976. The two Martin volumes from Doubleday are halves of a single massive biography--the most important work on Stevenson.

3664. Muller, Herbert J. *Adlai Stevenson: A Study in Values.* New York: Harper, 1967. One of the earliest scholarly biographies.

3665. Roberts, John W. "Cold War Observer: Governor Adlai Stevenson on American Foreign Relations." *Journal of the Illinois State Historical Society* 76 (1983): 49-60. Because of Stevenson's background in foreign relations, foreign-policy issues figured prominently in his speeches and work in the years of his governorship, 1949-53.

3666. Ross, Lillian. *Adlai Stevenson.* Philadelphia: Lippincott, 1966. A memoir written soon after Stevenson's death.

3667. Severn, William. *Adlai Stevenson, Citizen of the World.* New York: D. McKay, 1966.

3668. Sievers, Rodney M. *The Last Puritan? Adlai Stevenson in American Politics.* Port Washington, N.Y.: Associated Faculty Press, 1983.

3669. Stevenson, Adlai E. II *Adlai E. Stevenson Speeches from the Seeley G. Mudd Manuscript Library, Princeton University, in Milner Library, Illinois State University.* Edited by Michael Maher. Normal: Illinois State University, 1980.

3670. _____. *An Illinois Legacy: Gubernatorial Addresses of Adlai E. Stevenson, 1949-1952.* Edited by Michael Maher. Bloomington, Ill: Paint Hill Press, 1985. Contains thirty-seven previously unpublished speeches.

3671. _____. *Man of Honor, Man of Peace: The Life and Words of Adlai Stevenson.* Compiled by the editors of Country Beautiful; editorial direction by Michael P. Dineen; edited by Robert L. Polley. New York: Putnam, 1965.

3672. _____. *The Papers of Adlai E. Stevenson; Volume I: Beginnings of Education, 1900-1941.* Edited by Walter Johnson; Carol Evans, assistant editor. Boston: Little, Brown, 1972.

3673. _____. *The Papers of Adlai E. Stevenson; Volume II: Washington to Springfield, 1941-1948.* Edited by Walter Johnson; Carol Evans, assistant editor. Boston: Little, Brown, 1973. The last section of this volume deals with Stevenson's successful 1948 campaign for governor of Illinois.

3674. _____. *The Papers of Adlai E. Stevenson; Volume III: Governor of Illinois, 1949-1953.* Edited by Walter Johnson; Carol Evans, assistant editor. Boston: Little, Brown, 1973.

3675. _____. *The Papers of Adlai E. Stevenson; Volume IV: "Let's Talk Sense to the American People, 1952-1955."* Edited by Walter Johnson; Carol Evans, assistant editor; C. Eric Sears, editorial assistant. Boston: Little, Brown, 1974. This volume contains both political and personal papers.

3676. _____. *The Papers of Adlai E. Stevenson; Volume V: Visit to Asia, the Middle East, and Europe, March-August, 1953.* Edited by Walter Johnson; Carol Evans, assistant editor; C. Eric Sears, editorial assistant. Boston: Little, Brown, 1974. This and the preceding volumes are well edited and have good indexes.

3677. Walton, Richard J. *The Remnants of Power: The Tragic Last Years of Adlai Stevenson.* New York: Coward-McCann, 1968.

3678. Whitman, Alden. *Portrait--Adlai E. Stevenson: Politician, Diplomat, Friend.* New York: Harper, 1965.

13. Harold Washington

3679. Grimshaw, William J. "Unraveling the Enigma: Mayor Harold Washington and the Black Political Tradition." *Urban Affairs Quarterly* 23 (December 1987): 187-206.

3680. Holli, Melvin G., and Green, Paul M. *Bashing Chicago Traditions: Harold Washington's Last Campaign, Chicago, 1987.* Grand Rapids, Mich.: Eerdmans, 1989.

3681. _____, eds. *The Making of the Mayor, 1983.* Grand Rapids, Mich.: Eerdmans, 1984. Chicago's first African-American mayor, Harold Washington.

3682. Kleppner, Paul. *Chicago Divided: The Making of a Black Mayor.* DeKalb: Northern Illinois University Press, 1985. Primarily about race and electoral politics, especially from 1955 to 1983, when Harold Washington was elected mayor.

3683. Levinsohn, Florence Hamlish. *Harold Washington: A Political Biography.* Chicago: Chicago Review Press, 1983.

3684. Miller, Alton. *Harold Washington: The Mayor, the Man.* Chicago: Bonus Books, 1989.

3685. Rivlin, Gary. *Fire on the Prairie: Chicago's Harold Washington and the Politics of Race.* New York: Holt, 1992.

3686. Travis, Dempsey J. *"Harold," the People's Mayor: An Authorized Biography of Mayor Harold Washington.* Chicago: Urban Research Press, 1989.

3687. Washington, Harold. *Climbing a Great Mountain: Selected Speeches of Mayor Harold Washington.* Commentary by Alton Miller. Foreword by Coretta Scott King. Chicago: Bonus Books, 1988. The texts of twenty-three speeches.

E. RELIGIOUS AND EDUCATIONAL LEADERS

3688. Ander, Oscar Fritiof. *T. N. Hasselquist: The Career and Influence of a Swedish-American Clergyman, Journalist, and Educator.* Augustana Library Publications, no. 14. Rock Island, Ill., 1931.

3689. *Andreen of Augustana, 1864-1940: Tributes to Gustav Albert Andreen, A Loyal Son of Augustana Synod Pioneers, Third President of Augustana College and Theological Seminary.* Rock Island, Ill.: Augustana Book Concern, 1942.

3690. Ashmore, Harry S. *Unseasonable Truths: The Life of Robert Maynard Hutchins.* Boston: Little, Brown, 1989. Hutchins was president of the University of Chicago for twenty-two years.

3691. Babcock, Rufus, ed. *Forty Years of Pioneer Life: Memoir of John Mason Peck, D.D.; Edited from His Journals and Correspondence.* Philadelphia: American Baptist Publication Society, 1864.

3692. Britt, Albert. *Ellen Browning Scripps, Journalist and Idealist.* Oxford, England: Printed for Scripps College at Oxford University Press, 1960. Ellen Scripps, founder of Scripps College in California, grew up in Illinois.

3693. Carriel, Mary Turner. *The Life of Jonathan Baldwin Turner.* 1911. Reprint, Urbana: University of Illinois Press, 1961. Turner was a professor at Illinois College at Jacksonville and a champion of agricultural education.

3694. Chamberlin, M. H. "Rev. Peter Cartwright, D.D." *Transactions of the Illinois State Historical Society, 1902,* pp. 47-56.

3695. "Charles Henry Rammelkamp, 1874-1932." *Journal of the Illinois State Historical Society* 25 (1932-33): 190-234. Sketches illustrating the life and career of the Illinois College president were written by Merrill M. Barlow, Joe Patterson Smith, Carl E. Black, Frank J. Heinl, and Clarence Edwin Carter.

3696. Donnelly, Joseph P. *Pierre Gibault, Missionary, 1737-1802.* Chicago: Loyola University Press, 1971.

3697. Dunn, J. P. "Father Gibault, the Patriot Priest of the Northwest." *Transactions of the Illinois State Historical Society, 1905,* pp. 15-34. Father Pierre Gibault arrived in the Illinois country in 1768; the author traces Catholic church history in the Kaskaskia area from 1720 to 1790.

3698. Dzuback, Mary Ann. *Robert M. Hutchins: Portrait of an Educator.* Chicago: University of Chicago Press, 1991.

3699. Findlay, James F. Jr. *Dwight L. Moody, American Evangelist, 1837-1899.* Chicago: University of Chicago Press, 1969.

3700. Fischer, Raymond P. *Four Hazardous Journeys of the Reverend Jonathan Blanchard, Founder of Wheaton College.* Wheaton, Ill.: Tyndale House Publishers, 1987. This volume, by Blanchard's last living grandson, is based on recently discovered family papers.

3701. Gettleman, Marvin E. *An Elusive Presence: The Discovery of John H. Finley and His America.* Chicago: Nelson-Hall, 1979. A native Illinoisan, Finley was president of Knox College, a political science professor at Princeton, and editor-in-chief of the *New York Times.*

3702. Girling, Katherine Peabody. *Selim Hobart Peabody: A Biography.* The author was a daughter of her subject, a nineteenth-century president of the University of Illinois.

3703. Goodspeed, Thomas Wakefield. *William Rainey Harper, First President of the University of Chicago.* Chicago: University of Chicago Press, 1928.

3704. Greeley, Andrew M. *Confessions of a Parish Priest: An Autobiography.* New York: Simon & Schuster, 1986.

3705. Gregory, Allene. *John Milton Gregory.* Chicago: Covici-McGee, 1923. A biography of the first president of the University of Illinois.

3706. Haley, Margaret A. *Battleground: The Autobiography of Margaret A. Haley.* Edited by Robert L. Reid. Urbana: University of Illinois Press, 1982. Haley was the leader of the Chicago Teachers' Federation in the early twentieth century, and her autobiography is a study of the struggle for professionalism in education.

3707. Harker, Joseph R. *Eventide Memories: Recollections of a Busy and Happy and Guided Life, by Joseph R. Harker, from 1893 to 1925 President of Illinois Woman's College, now MacMurray College.* Jacksonville, Ill.: A. B. Press, 1931.

3708. Hendrickson, Walter B. "Clarence Paul McClelland, 1883-1974." *Journal of the Illinois State Historical Society* 67 (1974): 422-28. A tribute to the historian who served as president of MacMurray College, 1925-52, and as a trustee of the Illinois State Historical Library, 1946-60.

3709. Hickey, Donald R., and Seymour, Lyle. "Louis Rodenberg: Pioneer in Braille Printing." *Journal of the Illinois State Historical Society* 75 (1982): 39-46. A native of Randolph County, Rodenberg developed a new form of braille music notation at the Illinois School for the Blind in Jacksonville.

3710. Humphrey, J. Otis. "Dr. John Mason Peck and Shurtleff College." *Transactions of the Illinois State Historical Society, 1907,* pp. 145-63.

3711. Karl, Barry D. *Charles E. Merriam and the Study of Politics.* Chicago: University of Chicago Press, 1974. Merriam's career in the political science department at the University of Chicago and his ventures into Chicago politics and government.

3712. Kelsey, Harry E. Jr. *Frontier Capitalist: The Life of John Evans.* Denver: State Historical Society of Colorado, 1969. Evans lived in Illinois for about fifteen years; he played a leading role in establishing Northwestern University.

3713. Kersey, Harry A. Jr. *John Milton Gregory and the University of Illinois.* Urbana: University of Illinois Press, 1968.

3714. Kilby, Clyde S. *Minority of One: A Biography of Jonathan Blanchard.* Grand Rapids, Mich.: Eerdmans, 1959. Onetime president of both Knox and Wheaton colleges, Blanchard crusaded for the abolition of slavery and secret societies.

3715. Kinley, David. *The Autobiography of David Kinley.* Urbana: University of Illinois Press, 1949. Kinley joined the University of Illinois in 1893 and served as president, 1921-29. Most of this book concerns his work there.

3716. Kotre, John N. *The Best of Times, The Worst of Times: Andrew Greeley and American Catholicism.* Chicago: Nelson-Hall, 1978.

3717. Lawrence, Matthew. *John Mason Peck, the Pioneer Missionary.* New York: Fortuny's, 1940.

3718. Leavitt, Edward T. "Ralph Ware of Granville: Champion of Agriculture and Education." *Journal of the Illinois State Historical Society* 70 (1977): 161-63.

3719. Leffingwell, C. W. "Bishop Chase and Jubilee College." *Transactions of the Illinois State Historical Society, 1905,* pp. 82-100.

3720. McClelland, Clarence Paul. "William Henry Milburn: Blind Man Eloquent." *Journal of the Illinois State Historical Society* 48 (1955): 137-51. The famous orator and minister grew up in Jacksonville.

3721. McInerny, Dennis Q. "John Lancaster Spalding, Poet-Bishop of Peoria." *Selected Papers in Illinois History, 1983.* Springfield: Illinois State Historical Society, 1985. Pp. 39-50. A nationally known leader of the Catholic Church, Spalding is considered the founder of Catholic University of America, though his episcopal career was spent in Peoria.

3722. McLoughlin, William Gerald. *Billy Sunday Was His Real Name.* Chicago: University of Chicago Press, 1955. Raised in Iowa, Sunday came to

Chicago to play for the White Sox. While in the city he became an evangelist and was soon known nationwide.

3723. Malak, Henry M. *Theresa of Chicago*. Translated by Ann K. Dudzik. Lemont, Ill.: League of the Servant of God Mother Mary Theresa, 1975.

3724. Marshall, Helen E. *Jesse W. Fell, Friend of Education*. Normal: Illinois State Normal University, 1957. Fell was a prominent nineteenth-century entrepreneur-attorney from Bloomington, who was perhaps best known for his educational leadership.

3725. Morehouse, Frances Milton I. *The Life of Jesse W. Fell*. University of Illinois Studies in the Social Sciences, vol. 5, no. 2. Urbana, 1916.

3726. Nef, John U. *Search for Meaning: The Autobiography of a Nonconformist*. Washington, D.C.: Public Affairs Press, 1973. A pioneer in interdisciplinary studies at the University of Chicago.

3727. Norton, John N. *The Life of Bishop Chase*. New York: General Protestant Episcopal S. School and Church Book Society, 1857. Biography of Philander Chase.

3728. Pearson, Irving F. *Three Score Ten and More: An Autobiography*. Chicago: Adams Press, 1971. Principal of a rural school at age twenty, Pearson rose in the educational world to serve for twenty-four years as executive secretary of the Illinois Education Association.

3729. Peck, John Mason. *Forty Years of Pioneer Life: Memoir of John Mason Peck*. Edited by Rufus Babcock. Philadelphia: American Baptist Publication Society, 1864. Reprint, Carbondale: Southern Illinois University Press, 1965.

3730. Rinaker, Thomas. "Gideon Blackburn, the Founder of Blackburn University, Carlinville, Illinois." *Journal of the Illinois State Historical Society* 17 (1924-25): 398-410.

3731. Scott, Walter Dill. *John Evans, 1814-1897: An Appreciation*. Evanston, Ill.: Privately printed, 1939. Evans was the founder of Evanston and one of the founders of Northwestern University.

3732. Simonds, William Edward. "Newton Bateman." *Transactions of the Illinois State Historical Society, 1935*, pp. 141-84. Bateman was an early superintendent of public instruction, and this sketch has a great deal of information about the public school system as well as about Knox College, of which Bateman was president, 1857-97.

3733. Smith, Laura Chase. *The Life of Philander Chase, First Bishop of Ohio and Illinois: Founder of Kenyon and Jubilee Colleges . . .* New York: Dutton, 1903.

3734. Smith, Thomas Vernor. *A Non-Existent Man: An Autobiography.* Austin: University of Texas Press, 1962. T. V. Smith, professor of philosophy at the University of Chicago, was well known throughout the state as congressman-at-large.

3735. Sturtevant, Julian M. *Julian M. Sturtevant: An Autobiography.* Edited by J. M. Sturtevant, Jr. New York: F. H. Revell, 1896. Clergyman, professor, and then president of Illinois College.

3736. Taylor, Albert Reynolds. *Autobiography of Albert Reynolds Taylor, President Emeritus, The James Millikin University.* Decatur, Ill.: Review Printing and Stationery, 1929.

3737. _____. *The Life Story of James Millikin, Founder of the James Millikin University.* Decatur, Ill., 1926?

3738. Taylor, Richard S. "Beyond Immediate Emancipation: Jonathan Blanchard, Abolitionism, and the Emergence of American Fundamentalism." *Civil War History* 27 (1981): 260-74. Blanchard served as president of Knox College and Wheaton College. He espoused the cause of abolition and fought secret societies. Those positions led him toward religious fundamentalism.

3739. Townsend, Lucy Forsyth. *The Best Helpers of One Another: Anna Peck Sill and the Struggle for Women's Education.* Chicago: Educational Studies Press and DeKalb: Northern Illinois University, Department of Leadership and Educational Policy Studies, 1988. Sill came to Rockford in 1848 to establish a female seminary, which became Rockford College.

3740. Weil, Rolf A. *Through These Portals: From Immigrant to University President.* Chicago: Roosevelt University, 1991. Weil was president of Roosevelt University, 1966-88.

3741. West, William Garrett. *Barton Warren Stone, Early American Advocate of Christian Unity.* Nashville, Tenn.: Disciples of Christ Historical Society,

1954. Stone, who spent the last years of his life in Illinois, was one of the founders of the Disciples of Christ denomination.

F. SCIENTISTS AND PHYSICIANS

3742. Beck, Joseph Clar. *Fifty Years in Medicine.* Chicago: McDonough, 1940. Also contains thumbnail sketches of many of the physician's associates and friends.

3743. Black, Bessie McLaughlin. "Greene Vardiman Black, 1836-1915." *Transactions of the Illinois State Historical Society, 1931*, pp. 78-123. This sketch includes a bibliography of Dr. Black's writings and speeches on dentistry.

3744. Black, Carl Ellsworth, and Black, Bessie McLaughlin. *From Pioneer to Scientist: The Life Story of Greene Vardiman Black, "Father of Modern Dentistry," and His Son, Arthur Davenport Black, Late Dean of Northwestern University Dental School.* St. Paul, Minn.: Bruce Publishing, 1940.

3745. Bonner, Thomas Neville. "A Forgotten Figure in Chicago's Medical History." *Journal of the Illinois State Historical Society* 45 (1952): 212-19. Throughout the late nineteenth and early twentieth centuries, Dr. Bayard Holmes was in the forefront of scientific medical innovation and education.

3746. Buckler, Helen. *Daniel Hale Williams.* New York: Pitman, 1968. Williams was an African-American surgeon in Chicago who performed the first open-heart surgery in 1893.

3747. Cavanagh, Helen M. *Seed, Soil and Science: The Story of Eugene D. Funk.* Chicago: Lakeside Press, R. R. Donnelley, 1959.

3748. Connaughton, Dennis. *Warren Cole, MD, and the Ascent of Scientific Surgery.* Urbana: University of Illinois Press, for the Warren and Clara Cole Foundation, 1991. Cole taught at the University of Illinois College of Medicine, 1936-66.

3749. Danforth, I. N. *The Life of Nathan Smith Davis, A.M., M.D., LLD., 1817-1904.* Chicago: Cleveland Press, 1907. Davis was a faculty member of Rush Medical College and Chicago Medical College, which became the medical department of Northwestern University. He was a proponent of professional medical organizations and a pioneer in the public health movement.

3750. Darrah, William Culp. *Powell of the Colorado*. Princeton, N.J.: Princeton University Press, 1951. Illinois teacher and scientist, John Wesley Powell led the 1869 expedition from Green River, Wyoming, through the Grand Canyon. The expedition was financed by the Illinois Natural History Society, Illinois State Normal University, and the University of Illinois.

3751. Davenport, F. Garvin. "Robert Ridgway, Illinois Naturalist." *Journal of the Illinois State Historical Society* 63 (1970): 271-89. A sketch of the Illinois man who served for many years as ornithologist at the Museum of Natural History of the Smithsonian Institution.

3752. Davis, Loyal. *A Surgeon's Odyssey*. Garden City, N.Y.: Doubleday, 1973.

3753. Ernst, Erik A. "John A. Kennicott of The Grove: Physician, Horticulturist, and Journalist in Nineteenth-Century Illinois." *Journal of the Illinois State Historical Society* 74 (1981): 109-18.

3754. Fermi, Laura. *Atoms in the Family: My Life with Enrico Fermi*. Chicago: University of Chicago Press, 1954.

3755. Fishbein, Morris. *Morris Fishbein, M.D.: An Autobiography*. Garden City, N.Y.: Doubleday, 1969.

3756. Foster, J. W. "Robert Kennicott." *Journal of the Illinois State Historical Society* 6 (1913-14): 273-87. Kennicott was already an established naturalist when he died at the age of thirty.

3757. Harris, Harry. "Robert Ridgway." *The Condor* 30 (1928): 5-118. This article contains a bibliography of the more than five hundred articles and books written by the Illinois-born naturalist.

3758. Herrick, James Bryan. *Memories of Eighty Years*. Chicago: University of Chicago Press, 1949. Herrick recalls his years as a Chicago physician and medical school teacher.

3759. Ingals, Ephraim. "Autobiography of Dr. Ephraim Ingals." With a foreword by Dr. George H. Weaver. *Journal of the Illinois State Historical Society* 28, no. 4 (January 1936): 279-308. Dr. Ingals became a prominent member of the Rush Medical College faculty in the mid-nineteenth century.

3760. James, James Alton. "Robert Kennicott, Pioneer Illinois Natural Scientist and Arctic Explorer." *Transactions of the Illinois State Historical Society, 1940*, pp. 22-39.

3761. Kinney, Janet. *Saga of a Surgeon: The Life of Daniel Brainard, M.D.* Medical Humanities Series. Springfield: Southern Illinois University School of Medicine, 1987. Brainard was the founder of Rush Medical College at Chicago.

3762. Martin, Franklin H. *Fifty Years of Medicine and Surgery: An Autobiographical Sketch.* Chicago: Surgical Publishing, 1934.

3763. Millikan, Robert A. *The Autobiography of Robert A. Millikan.* New York: Prentice-Hall, 1950. The great physicist, a native of Morrison, and a faculty member at the University of Chicago for many years, discusses not only his own life but also (for the layman) the major developments in physics up to 1950.

3764. Morris, Lindsey Gardner. "John Wesley Powell, Scientist and Educator." *Illinois State University Journal* 31, no. 3 (February 1969): 1-47.

3765. Pappas, Charles N. *The Life and Times of G. V. Black.* Chicago: Quintessence, 1983. A dentist in Winchester and Jacksonville, Illinois, Black became dean of Northwestern University Dental School and a renowned dental innovator and writer.

3766. Pearson, Emmet F. *My Sixty Years in Medicine.* Springfield: The Pearson Museum, Southern Illinois University School of Medicine, 1991.

3767. Prieto, Jorge. *Harvest of Hope: The Pilgrimage of a Mexican-American Physician.* Notre Dame, Ind.: University of Notre Dame Press, 1989. Prieto was chairman of the Department of Family Practice at Cook County Hospital, 1974-85, and president of the Chicago Board of Health, 1985-87.

3768. Shastid, Thomas Hall. *My Second Life.* Ann Arbor, Mich.: George Wahr, publisher to the University of Michigan, 1944. An 1159-page autobiography of the physician/writer/peace activist from Pittsfield.

3769. Stegner, Wallace. *Beyond the Hundredth Meridian: John Wesley Powell and the Second Opening of the West.* Boston: Houghton Mifflin, 1954.

3770. Thorek, Max. *A Surgeon's World: An Autobiography*. Philadelphia: Lippincott, 1943. An immigrant from the Austro-Hungarian Empire, Dr. Thorek worked his way through Rush Medical College and became a noted surgeon.

3771. Tucker, Edna Armstrong. "Benjamin D. Walsh, First State Entomologist of Illinois." *Transactions of the Illinois State Historical Society, 1920*, pp. 54-61.

G. SOCIAL REFORMERS AND LABOR LEADERS

1. In General

3772. Addams, Jane. *My Friend Julia Lathrop*. New York: Macmillan, 1935.

3773. Ashbaugh, Carolyn. *Lucy Parsons, American Revolutionary*. Chicago: Charles H. Kerr, for the Illinois Labor History Society, 1976. The widow of Albert R. Parsons, Lucy remained active in the radical wing of the labor movement until her death in 1942.

3774. Blumberg, Dorothy Rose. *Florence Kelley: The Making of a Social Pioneer*. New York: A. M. Kelley, 1966.

3775. Booth, Stephane Elise. *Gerry Allard, Miners' Advocate*. Chicago: Illinois Labor History Society, 1981.

3776. Bordin, Ruth. *Frances Willard: A Biography*. Chapel Hill: University of North Carolina Press, 1986. A portrait of Willard, designed to appeal to modern feminists, that downplays her piety and moralistic attitudes.

3777. Costin, Lela B. *Two Sisters for Social Justice: A Biography of Grace and Edith Abbott*. Urbana: University of Illinois Press, 1983.

3778. Earhart, Mary. *Frances Willard: From Prayers to Politics*. Chicago: University of Chicago Press, 1944.

3779. Fraser, Steven. *Labor Will Rule: Sidney Hillman and the Rise of American Labor*. New York: Free Press, 1991. Hillman rose to prominence as a labor leader in Chicago.

3780. Glück, Elsie. *John Mitchell, Miner: Labor's Bargain with the Gilded Age*. New York: John Day, 1929. A coal miner in the Illinois fields from childhood on, Mitchell became active in labor unions and, ultimately, president of the United Mine Workers.

3781. Goldmark, Josephine. *Impatient Crusader: Florence Kelley's Life Story.* Urbana: University of Illinois Press, 1953.

3782. Grant, Madeleine P. *Alice Hamilton: Pioneer Doctor in Industrial Medicine.* New York: Abelard-Schuman, 1967.

3783. Harmon, Sandra D. "Florence Kelley in Illinois." *Journal of the Illinois State Historical Society* 74 (1981): 163-78.

3784. Horwitt, Sanford D. *Let Them Call Me Rebel: Saul Alinsky, His Life and Legacy.* New York: Knopf, 1989.

3785. Kelley, Florence. *Notes of Sixty Years: The Autobiography of Florence Kelley.* Edited by Kathryn Kish Sklar. Chicago: Charles H. Kerr, 1986, for the Illinois Labor History Society. Champion of laws to protect women and children and workers' safety, Florence Kelley became Illinois' chief factory inspector in 1893.

3786. Kinneman, Marion. "John Mitchell in Illinois." *Illinois State University Journal* 32, no. 1 (September 1969): 21-35.

3787. Mayer, C. H. *The Continuing Struggle: Autobiography of a Labor Activist.* Foreword by Scott Nearing. Northampton, Mass.: Pittenbruach Press, 1989. A native of Virden, Mayer was a lifelong social activist and labor organizer.

3788. Nestor, Agnes. *Woman's Labor Leader: An Autobiography.* Rockford, Ill.: Bellevue Books, 1954.

3789. "The Other Woman." *Chicago Tribune*, 17 September 1989, sec. 6, pp. 1, 7. Sketch of Ellen Gates Starr, who, with Jane Addams, founded the social settlement Hull House in Chicago. Based on correspondence between the two women.

3790. Payne, Elizabeth Anne. *Reform, Labor, and Feminism: Margaret Dreier Robins and the Women's Trade Union League.* Urbana: University of Illinois Press, 1988. This biography of the social reformer and labor organizer concentrates on her work in Chicago.

3791. Selvin, David F. *Eugene Debs: Rebel Labor Leader, Prophet.* New York: Lathrop, Lee, and Shepard, 1966.

3792. Sicherman, Barbara. *Alice Hamilton: A Life in Letters.* A Commonwealth Fund Book. Cambridge: Harvard University Press, 1984. Dr. Hamilton came to Chicago in 1897 and lived at Hull House for twenty-two years. She taught at the Women's Medical School of Northwestern University and served on the Hull House staff and the technical staff of the Illinois Commission on Occupational Diseases.

3793. Taylor, Eleanor K. "The Edith Abbott I Knew." *Journal of the Illinois State Historical Society* 70 (1977): 178-84. Reminiscence about their social work at the University of Chicago and Hull House.

3794. Trowbridge, Lydia Jones. *Frances Willard of Evanston.* Chicago: Willett, Clark, 1938.

3795. Wade, Louise Carroll. *Graham Taylor: Pioneer for Social Justice, 1851-1938.* Chicago: University of Chicago Press, 1964. The great social activist was founder of the Chicago Commons settlement house and the Chicago School of Civics and Philanthropy.

3796. Wells, Ida B. *Crusade for Justice: The Autobiography of Ida B. Wells.* Edited by Alfreda M. Duster. Negro American Biographies and Autobiographies series, edited by John Hope Franklin. Chicago: University of Chicago Press, 1970. The daughter of a slave, Wells was noted for her militant struggles against racism.

3797. Wieck, David Thoreau. *Woman from Spillertown: A Memoir of Agnes Burns Wieck.* Carbondale: Southern Illinois University Press, 1992. Wieck was a radical labor activist and journalist long associated with Illinois' coal mines and miners.

3798. Willard, Frances E. *Glimpses of Fifty Years: The Autobiography of an American Woman.* Boston: G. M. Smith, 1889.

3799. Wilson, Howard E. *Mary McDowell, Neighbor.* Chicago: University of Chicago Press, 1928. Head resident of the University of Chicago Settlement, McDowell became known as the "Angel of the Stockyards" for her work in behalf of minorities and labor unions.

2. Jane Addams

3800. Addams, Jane. *Jane Addams: A Centennial Reader.* New York: Macmillan, 1960. Edited by Emily Cooper Johnson. Extracts from Addams's works that constitute a valuable source for her philosophy and accomplishments.

3801. _____. *The Second Twenty Years at Hull-house, September 1909 to September 1929 with a Record of Growing World Consciousness.* New York: Macmillan, 1930.

3802. _____. *The Social Thought of Jane Addams.* Indianapolis: Bobbs-Merrill, 1965. 1st Irvington ed., edited by Christopher Lasch, New York: Irvington, 1982.

3803. _____. *Twenty Years at Hull-house, with Autobiographical Notes.* New York: Macmillan, 1910. Reprint, paper, Urbana: University of Illinois Press, 1990; introduction and notes by James Hurt.

3804. Davis, Allen F. *American Heroine: The Life and Legend of Jane Addams.* New York: Oxford University Press, 1973. A brilliant study.

3805. Deegan, Mary Jo. *Jane Addams and the Men of the Chicago School, 1892-1918.* New Brunswick, N.J.: Transaction Books, 1988. Addams as a sociologist and her relationships with male sociologists at the University of Chicago.

3806. Dilliard, Irving. "The Centennial Year of Two Great Illinoisans: Jane Addams and William Jennings Bryan." *Journal of the Illinois State Historical Society* 53 (1960): 229-46. Two eminent native-born Illinoisans considered together because of their common birth year: 1860.

3807. Farrell, John C. *Beloved Lady: A History of Jane Addams' Ideas of Peace and Freedom.* Baltimore: Johns Hopkins University Press, 1967.

3808. Levine, Daniel. "Jane Addams: Romantic Rebel, 1889-1912." *Mid-America* 44 (1962): 195-210.

3809. _____. *Jane Addams and the Liberal Tradition.* Madison: State Historical Society of Wisconsin, 1971. Addams as an important force in making the nation a general welfare state.

3810. Linn, James Weber. *Jane Addams: A Biography.* New York: Appleton, 1935.

3811. Scott, Anne Firor. *Making the Invisible Woman Visible.* Urbana: University of Illinois Press, 1984. Included are an essay and a review (pages 107-48) that offer valuable insights into Addams's life and career.

3812. Tims, Margaret. *Jane Addams of Hull House, 1860-1935: A Centenary Study.* New York: Macmillan, 1961.

3. Mary Harris Jones

3813. Atkinson, Linda. *Mother Jones: The Most Dangerous Woman in America.* New York: Crown, 1978.

3814. Fetherling, Dale. *Mother Jones, the Miners' Angel: A Portrait.* Carbondale: Southern Illinois University Press, 1974. Arcturus Books ed., 1979.

3815. Jones, Mary Harris. *Autobiography of Mother Jones.* 1925. Reprint, edited by Mary Field Parton, with introduction and bibliography by Fred Thompson. Chicago: Charles H. Kerr, 1972. Mother Jones was active in the 1885 Chicago Poor People's March and the 1919 steelworkers' strike in Chicago.

3816. _____. *The Correspondence of Mother Jones.* Edited by Edward M. Steel. Pittsburgh: University of Pittsburgh Press, 1985. Letters of the remarkable labor leader include discussions of the Ku Klux Klan and strikes at Herrin, Illinois, in the 1920s.

3817. _____. *Mother Jones Speaks: Collected Writings and Speeches.* Edited by Philip S. Foner. New York: Monad Press, 1983. Although Mother Mary Harris Jones worked often in Illinois, this collection has little connection with the state; it is valuable, however, for the editor's comments about Mother Jones and her times, as well as the literature about her.

3818. _____. *The Speeches and Writings of Mother Jones.* Edited by Edward M. Steel. Pittsburgh: University of Pittsburgh Press, 1988.

3819. McDonald, Duncan. "Mother Jones, 1830-1930." *Journal of the Illinois State Historical Society* 73 (1980): 235-37. McDonald's reminiscences of Mother Jones from his manuscript autobiography in the collections of the Illinois State Historical Library.

4. John L. Lewis

3820. Alinsky, Saul David. *John L. Lewis: An Unauthorized Biography.* New York: Putnam, 1949.

3821. DeCaux, Len. *Labor Radical: From the Wobblies to CIO.* Boston: Beacon Press, 1970. In his autobiography DeCaux recalls his years in Illinois as assistant editor of the *Illinois Miner*; especially worthwhile are his reminiscences of John L. Lewis and other labor leaders.

3822. Dubofsky, Melvyn, and Van Tine, Warren. *John L. Lewis: A Biography.* 1977. Reprint, Urbana: University of Illinois Press, 1983. The definitive biography of the great labor leader.

3823. Selvin, David F. *The Thundering Voice of John L. Lewis.* New York: Lothrop, Lee & Shepard, 1969.

3824. Sulzberger, C. L. *Sit down with John L. Lewis.* New York: Random House, 1938.

3825. United Mine Workers of America. *John L. Lewis and the International Union, United Mine Workers of America: The Story from 1917 to 1952.* Washington?, 1952.

3826. Wechsler, James A. *Labor Baron: A Portrait of John L. Lewis.* New York: William Morrow, 1944.

3827. Zieger, Robert H. *John L. Lewis, Labor Leader.* Twayne's Twentieth-Century American Biography Series, no. 8. Boston, 1988.

H. WRITERS

1. In General

3828. Anderson, Margaret. *My Thirty Years' War: An Autobiography.* New York: Covici, Friede, 1930.

3829. Andrews, Clarence A. "Floyd Dell in the Western Illinois Region." *Western Illinois Regional Studies* 8, no. 2 (Fall 1985): 17-33. Dell was a native of Barry.

3830. Angle, Paul McClelland. "Benjamin Platt Thomas, 1902-1956." *Journal of the Illinois State Historical Society* 50 (1957): 7-23. A memorial tribute to the Lincoln biographer and historian.

3831. _____. "Frank Everett Stevens, January 5, 1856-October 16, 1939." *Journal of the Illinois State Historical Society* 32 (1939): 517-23.

3832. Becker, George Joseph. *John Dos Passos.* New York: Ungar, 1974.

3833. Bender, Edward J. *Mr. Dooley & Mr. Dunne: The Literary Life of a Chicago Catholic.* Charlottesville, Va.: Michie, 1981. Mr. Dooley was the creation of Finley Peter Dunne.

3834. Bowron, Bernard R. Jr. *Henry B. Fuller of Chicago: The Ordeal of a Genteel Realist in Ungenteel America.* Westport, Conn.: Greenwood, 1974. The life of this novelist, which spanned the years 1857-1929, is an important part of the intellectual history of Illinois.

3835. Branch, Edgar Marquess. *James T. Farrell.* Twayne's United States Authors Series, no. 185. New York, 1971.

3836. Bray, Robert. "The American Years of Harold Sinclair." *Illinois Historical Journal* 82 (1989): 177-94. Sketch of the historical novelist from Bloomington.

3837. Brooks, Gwendolyn. *Report from Part One.* Detroit: Broadside Press, 1972. Autobiographical.

3838. Brown, Maurice F. *Estranging Dawn: The Life and Works of William Vaughn Moody.* Carbondale: Southern Illinois University Press, 1973.

3839. Burbank, Rex J. *Sherwood Anderson.* Twayne's United States Authors Series, no. 65. New York, 1964. Born in Ohio, Anderson lived for a time in Chicago.

3840. _____. *Thornton Wilder.* Twayne's United States Authors Series, no. 5. New York, 1961. A native of Wisconsin, Wilder spent a portion of his career in Chicago.

3841. Cahill, Daniel J. *Harriet Monroe.* Twayne's United States Authors Series, no. 222. New York, 1973.

3842. Chapin, Helen Geracimos. " 'Chicagopolis'--the Double World of Harry Mark Petrakis." *Old Northwest* 2 (1976): 401-13.

3843. Cheney, Anne. *Lorraine Hansberry.* Twayne's United States Authors Series, no. 430. Boston, 1984.

3844. Conrow, Robert. *Field Days: The Life, Times & Reputation of Eugene Field.* New York: Scribner's, 1974. A native of St. Louis, the journalist/poet moved to Chicago in 1883.

3845. Dale, Edward Everett. *Grant Foreman: A Brief Biography.* Norman: University of Oklahoma Press, 1933. The Indian historian was a native of Illinois.

3846. Dell, Floyd. *Homecoming: An Autobiography.* New York: Farrar, 1933.

3847. Dennis, Charles H. *Eugene Field's Creative Years.* Garden City, N.Y.: Doubleday, 1924.

3848. Destler, Chester McArthur. *Henry Demarest Lloyd and the Empire of Reform.* Philadelphia: University of Pennsylvania Press, 1963. "As the prophet of a unique ethical, social welfare philosophy," writer Lloyd inspired "the new liberal, progressive political tradition."

3849. Dilliard, Irving. "Historian in Cowboy Boots: Jay Monaghan, 1893-1980." *Journal of the Illinois State Historical Society* 74 (1981): 261-78. With a bibliography of Monaghan's works.

3850. _____. "Paul M. Angle: Warm Recollections and Clear Impressions." *Journal of the Illinois State Historical Society* 68 (1975): 435-48. With a bibliography of Angle's works.

3851. _____. "Three to Remember: Archibald MacLeish, Stanley Kimmel, Phillips Bradley." *Journal of the Illinois State Historical Society* 77 (1984): 45-59. Personal reminiscences and biographical sketches of three writers--two native Illinoisans (MacLeish and Kimmel) and another whose professional career brought him to the University of Illinois; all died in 1982.

3852. Donaldson, Scott. *Archibald MacLeish: An American Life.* Boston: Houghton Mifflin, 1992.

3853. Drew, Bettina. *Nelson Algren: A Life on the Wild Side.* New York: Putnam, 1989.

3854. Dutton, Robert R. *Saul Bellow.* Twayne's United States Authors Series, no. 181. New York, 1971.

3855. Ellis, Elmer. *Mr. Dooley's America: A Life of Finley Peter Dunne.* Hamdon, Conn.: Archon Books, 1969.

3856. Fabre, Michel. *The Unfinished Quest of Richard Wright.* Translated from the French by Isabel Barzun. New York: Morrow, 1973. Wright was raised in Mississippi, but emerged as a writer in Chicago and reflects Chicago as the setting in *Native Son,* his masterpiece.

3857. Fitzgerald, Robert. *The Third Kind of Knowledge: Memoirs and Selected Writings.* Edited by Penelope Laurans Fitzgerald. New York: New Directions, 1994. The best-known twentieth-century translator of the Greek classics, Fitzgerald grew up in Springfield.

3858. Flanagan, John T. "John Russell of Bluffdale." *Journal of the Illinois State Historical Society* 42 (1949): 272-91.

3859. Fleming, Robert E. *Willard Motley.* Twayne's United States Authors Series, no. 302. Boston, 1978.

3860. Garrett, George P. *James Jones.* San Diego, Calif.: Harcourt, Brace, 1984.

3861. Gates, Arnold. "John J. Duff, 1902-1961." *Journal of the Illinois State Historical Society* 54 (1961): 419-22.

3862. Gayle, Addison. *Richard Wright: Ordeal of a Native Son.* Garden City, N.Y.: Anchor Press, Doubleday, 1980. Chapters 5-7 treat Wright's life in Chicago in the late 1920s and early 1930s. An excellent portrayal of African-American life in the city, race relations, and the development of the Communist party there.

3863. Goldstone, Richard Henry. *Thornton Wilder: An Intimate Portrait.* New York: Saturday Review Press, 1975.

3864. Hallwas, John E. "The Achievement of Virginia S. Eifert." *Journal of the Illinois State Historical Society* 71 (1978): 82-106. A brief biography of an author Hallwas calls "one of the great nature writers of the Midwest."

3865. _____. "Early Illinois Author John L. McConnel and 'The Ranger's Chase.' " *Journal of the Illinois State Historical Society* 73 (1980): 177-86. The author shows how McConnel's stories, from the mid-nineteenth century, illustrate frontier life. "The Ranger's Chase," for example, was set during the War of 1812.

3866. _____, ed. *Illinois Literature: The Nineteenth Century.* Macomb: Illinois Heritage Press, 1986. A rich collection of selections from Illinois authors, each preceded by a biographical sketch.

3867. _____. "The Midwestern Poetry of Eliza Snow." *Western Illinois Regional Studies* 5 (1982): 136-45. Mormon teacher and writer Eliza Snow wrote poetry that reflects the early history of the church.

3868. _____, ed. *Studies in Illinois Poetry.* Urbana, Ill.: Stormline Press, 1989. Essays that consider many lesser-known Illinois poets, with substantial biographical information about each.

3869. Halpern, Martin. *William Vaughn Moody.* Twayne's United States Authors Series, no. 64. New York, 1964.

3870. Harris, Mark. *Saul Bellow, Drumlin Woodchuck.* Athens: University of Georgia Press, 1980.

3871. Hart, John Edward. *Floyd Dell.* Twayne's United States Authors Series, no. 184. New York, 1971.

3872. Hecht, Ben. *A Child of the Century.* New York: Simon & Schuster, 1954. More than a third of the autobiography deals with Hecht's years in Chicago.

3873. Hendrickson, Walter B. "Louis William Rodenberg, an Illinois Poet." *Western Illinois Regional Studies* 4 (1981): 176-91.

3874. Henson, Clyde E. *Joseph Kirkland.* Twayne's United States Authors Series, no. 13. New York, 1962. A Chicago businessman and attorney, Kirkland became famous as a literary figure.

3875. _____. "Joseph Kirkland's Novels." *Journal of the Illinois State Historical Society* 44 (1951): 142-46. Biographical sketch of the Illinois writer whose realistic novels reflect Illinois life in the mid-nineteenth century.

3876. Howard, Jane. *A Different Woman.* New York: Dutton, 1973. Howard weaves many tales of other women's lives through this warm-hearted account of her own growing up in Illinois and her career.

3877. Howe, Irving. *Sherwood Anderson.* Stanford, Calif.: Stanford University Press, 1966.

3878. Hurt, James. "William Maxwell: The Illinoisan and the New Yorker." *Selected Papers in Illinois History, 1981.* Springfield: Illinois State Historical Society, 1982. Pp. 108-22. Maxwell, a native of Lincoln, was a longtime *New Yorker* editor and novelist.

3879. Jernigan, E. Jay. *Henry Demarest Lloyd.* Twayne's United States Authors Series, no. 277. Boston, 1976.

3880. Kent, George E. *A Life of Gwendolyn Brooks.* Lexington: University Press of Kentucky, 1990.

3881. Kimbrough, Emily. *Through Charley's Door.* New York: Harper, 1952. Writer-editor Kimbrough tells of the beginning of her career at Marshall Field's.

3882. Landsberg, Melvin. *Dos Passos' Path to U.S.A.: A Political Biography, 1912-1936.* Boulder, Colo.: Associated University Press, 1972.

3883. Litvin, Martin. *I'm Going to be Somebody: A Biography of George Fitch (Originator of the Word "Siwash").* Woodston, Kans.: Western Books, 1991. "Siwash" stories were based on Knox College, which Fitch had attended.

3884. Logan, Mary. *Mary Logan: Reminiscences of Civil War and Reconstruction.* Edited by George Worthington Adams. Carbondale: Southern Illinois University Press, 1970. An abridgment of the author's 1913 *Reminiscences of a Soldier's Wife.*

3885. MacAdams, William. *Ben Hecht: The Man behind the Legend.* New York: Scribner's, 1990.

3886. McCall, Dan. *The Example of Richard Wright.* New York: Harcourt, Brace, 1969.

3887. MacShane, Frank. *Into Eternity: The Life of James Jones, American Writer.* Boston: Houghton Mifflin, 1985.

3888. Mayer, Charles W. "J. F. Powers and the Catholic Clergyman." *Western Illinois Regional Studies* 12, no. 1 (Spring 1989): 73-85. A native Illinoisan, Powers lived in several towns in the state.

3889. Melhem, D. H. *Gwendolyn Brooks: Poetry and the Heroic Voice.* Lexington: University Press of Kentucky, 1987. The first chapter is biographical, and other biographical information is woven throughout the critical analyses of the poetry.

3890. Monaghan, Jay. "Lloyd Downs Lewis, 1891-1949." *Journal of the Illinois State Historical Society* 42 (1949): 127-46.

3891. Monroe, Harriet. *A Poet's Life: Seventy Years in a Changing World.* New York: Macmillan, 1938. Autobiography of the founder of *Poetry: A Magazine of Verse.*

3892. Nemiroff, Robert. *To Be Young, Gifted, and Black: Lorraine Hansberry in Her Own Words.* Englewood Cliffs, N.J.: Prentice-Hall, 1969. Reprint, New York: New American Library, 1970.

3893. Nevius, Blake. *Robert Herrick: The Development of a Novelist.* Berkeley: University of California Press, 1962. Herrick taught at the University of Chicago, 1893-1923.

3894. Nierman, Judith. *Floyd Dell: An Annotated Bibliography of Secondary Sources, 1910-1981.* Scarecrow Author Bibliographies, no. 69. Metuchen, N.J.: Scarecrow Press, 1984.

3895. Nolan, William F. *The Ray Bradbury Companion: A Life and Career History, Photolog, and Comprehensive Checklist of Writings, with Facsimiles from Ray Bradbury's Unpublished and Uncollected Work in All Media.* Detroit: Gale Research, 1975.

3896. Noreen, Robert G. *Saul Bellow: A Reference Guide.* Reference Publications in Literature. Boston: G. K. Hall, 1978. Writings about Bellow, arranged by year of publication.

3897. Norris, Hoke. "Illinois Writers." *What's New in Books: Book Bulletin of the Chicago Public Library* 50 (1968): 123-27. Thumbnail sketches of some of Illinois' most famous writers.

3898. Patrick, Walton R. *Ring Lardner.* Twayne's United States Authors Series, no. 32. New York, 1963.

3899. Petrakis, Harry Mark. *Reflections: A Writer's Life, A Writer's Work.* Chicago: Lake View Press, 1983. Contains an account of growing up in Chicago's Greek community and a record of his work as a writer in the 1970s.

3900. Pratt, Harry Edward. "James Garfield Randall, 1881-1953." *Journal of the Illinois State Historical Society* 46 (1953): 119-28; with a bibliography of Randall's writings by Wayne C. Temple, pp. 128-31.

3901. Price, Robert. "Mary Hartwell Catherwood: A Bibliography." *Journal of the Illinois State Historical Society* 33 (1940): 68-77. The article also contains a biographical sketch of the Illinois novelist.

3902. Randall, James Garfield. "Theodore Calvin Pease." *Journal of the Illinois State Historical Society* 41 (1948): 353-66.

3903. Randall, Ruth Painter. *I, Ruth: Autobiography of a Marriage; The Self-Told Story of the Woman Who Married the Great Lincoln Scholar James G. Randall, and through Her Interest in His Work Became a Lincoln Author Herself.* Boston: Little, Brown, 1968.

3904. Richards, John Thomas. *Luminous Sanity: Literary Criticism by John G. Neihardt.* Cape Girardeau, Mo.: Concord Publishing House, 1973. The book also contains biographical information about Neihardt.

3905. Roba, William. "Marjorie Allen Seiffert, Moline Poet." *Western Illinois Regional Studies* 8, no. 2 (Fall 1985): 5-16.

3906. _____. "Quad-Cities Writers: A Group Portrait." *Western Illinois Regional Studies* 6, no. 1 (Spring 1983): 67-81. Illinoisans considered are Floyd Dell, Harry Hansen, Marjorie Allen Seiffert, and Cornelia Lynde Meigs.

3907. Robinson, Orvetta M., comp. *The Legacy of Virginia S. Eifert: A Bibliography.* Introduction by John E. Hallwas. Macomb: Western Illinois University Library, 1981.

3908. Ruber, Peter A. *The Last Bookman: A Journey into the Life and Times of Vincent Starrett, Author, Journalist, Bibliophile* . . . New York: Candlelight Press, 1968.

3909. Scott, Clifford H. *Lester Frank Ward.* Twayne's United States Authors Series, no. 275. Boston, 1976.

3910. Shaw, Harry B. *Gwendolyn Brooks.* Twayne's United States Authors Series, no. 395. Boston, 1980.

3911. Simonson, Harold P. *Francis Grierson.* Twayne's United States Authors Series, no. 97. New York, 1966. Musician-writer-mystic, Grierson of Illinois wrote *The Valley of the Shadows*, an account of Illinois in the 1850s that remains a classic.

3912. _____. "Francis Grierson: A Biographical Sketch and Bibliography." *Journal of the Illinois State Historical Society* 54 (1961): 198-203.

3913. Starrett, Vincent. *Born in a Bookshop: Chapters from the Chicago Renascence.* Norman: University of Oklahoma Press, 1965. Autobiography of the Chicago writer who here describes the events and characters in the Chicago literary "renascence" of the 1920s.

3914. Swanberg, W. A. *Dreiser.* New York: Scribner's, 1965. Theodore Dreiser was a native of Indiana but lived for a time in Chicago, which was reflected in three of his novels.

3915. Taylor, Lloyd C. *Margaret Ayer Barnes.* Twayne's United States Authors Series, no. 231. New York, 1974. A native Chicagoan, Barnes was awarded the Pulitzer Prize in 1931 for her novel *Years of Grace.*

3916. Taylor, Welford Dunaway. *Sherwood Anderson.* New York: Ungar, 1977.

3917. Terkel, Louis (Studs). *Talking to Myself: A Memoir of My Times.* New York: Pantheon, 1977.

3918. Thompson, Slason. *Eugene Field: A Study in Heredity and Contradictions.* 2 vols. New York: Scribner's, 1901.

3919. Tingley, Donald Fred. "Allan Nevins: A Reminiscence." *Journal of the Illinois State Historical Society* 66 (1973): 177-86. An appreciative, anecdotal account of the famous historian.

3920. Travis, Dempsey J. *I Refuse to Learn to Fail*. Chicago: Urban Research Press, 1982. The author calls this book "a slice" of his life story.

3921. Van Doren, Carl. *An Illinois Boyhood*. New York: Viking, 1939. Life in Champaign County at the turn of the twentieth century.

3922. Van Doren, Mark. *The Autobiography of Mark van Doren*. New York: Harcourt, Brace, 1958. The author grew up in Champaign County and graduated from the University of Illinois.

3923. Wagenknecht, Edward Charles. *As Far as Yesterday: Memories and Reflections*. Norman: University of Oklahoma Press, 1968.

3924. Webb, Constance. *Richard Wright: A Biography*. New York: Putnam, 1968.

3925. Whitlock, Brand. *The Letters and Journal of Brand Whitlock*. Edited by Allan Nevins. Introduction by Newton D. Baker. 2 vols. New York: Appleton, 1936. Whitlock was a Chicago newspaperman early in his career. Later he became well known as a writer and diplomat.

3926. Whitney, Blair. *John G. Neihardt*. Twayne's United States Authors Series, no. 270. Boston, 1976. A native of Sharpsburg in Christian County, the novelist and newspaperman moved to Nebraska as a boy, later worked in Chicago.

3927. Williams, Kenny J. *A Storyteller and a City: Sherwood Anderson's Chicago*. DeKalb: Northern Illinois University Press, 1988.

3928. Wilson, David L. "Lloyd Lewis, Historian." *Selected Papers in Illinois History, 1983*. Springfield: Illinois State Historical Society, 1985. Pp. 51-59.

3929. Wilson, Francis. *The Eugene Field I Knew*. New York: Scribner's, 1898.

3930. Wilson, Milton L. *Biography of Mary Hartwell Catherwood*. Newark, Ohio: American Tribune Printery, 1904.

3931. Wrenn, John H. *John Dos Passos.* Twayne's United States Authors Series, no. 9. New York, 1962. Dos Passos was born in Chicago.

3932. Yardley, Jonathan. *Ring: A Biography of Ring Lardner.* New York: Random House, 1977. Lardner was a sports writer and columnist for several Chicago newspapers in the early twentieth century.

2. Ernest Hemingway

3933. Baker, Carlos. *Ernest Hemingway: A Life Story.* New York: Barnes and Noble, 1967. Reprinted many times. The standard biography of the Nobel Prize winner.

3934. *Ernest Hemingway, as Recalled by His High School Contemporaries.* Edited by Ina Mae Schleden and Marion Rawls Herzog. Historical Society of Oak Park and River Forest, monograph no. 1. Oak Park, 1973.

3935. Griffin, Peter. *Along with Youth: Hemingway, the Early Years.* New York: Oxford University Press, 1985.

3936. Hanneman, Audre, comp. *Ernest Hemingway: A Comprehensive Bibliography.* Princeton, N.J.: Princeton University Press, 1967.

3937. Hayashi, Tetsumaro, comp. and ed. *Steinbeck and Hemingway: Dissertation Abstracts and Research Opportunities.* Metuchen, N.J.: Scarecrow Press, 1980.

3938. Mellow, James R. *Hemingway: A Life without Consequences.* Boston: Houghton Mifflin, 1992 In this recent important addition to the Hemingway canon, Mellow skillfully links the author's life and his works.

3939. Meyers, Jeffrey. *Hemingway: A Biography.* New York: Harper, 1985. Chapter 1 concerns his boyhood (1899-1917) in Oak Park.

3940. Rovit, Earl H. *Ernest Hemingway.* Twayne's United States Authors Series, no. 41. New York, 1963.

3941. Sanford, Marcelline Hemingway. *At the Hemingways: A Family Portrait.* Boston: Little, Brown, 1961. The early family life of Ernest Hemingway.

3. Vachel Lindsay

3942. Camp, Dennis. "Vachel Lindsay and the Chicago *Herald.*" *Western Illinois Regional Studies* 2 (1979): 70-88. Lindsay had a poetry column in the newspaper in 1914-15.

3943. Chénetier, Marc, ed. *Letters of Vachel Lindsay.* New York: Burt Franklin, 1979.

3944. Harris, Mark. *City of Discontent: An Interpretive Biography of Vachel Lindsay, Being Also the Story of Springfield, Illinois, USA, and of the Love of the Poet for That City, That State, and That Nation.* Indianapolis: Bobbs-Merrill, 1952. Reprint, Urbana: University of Illinois Press, 1992, with a foreword by Laurence Goldstein.

3945. Hawley, Owen. "Lindsay's 1908 Walking Trip." *Western Illinois Regional Studies* 2 (1979): 156-72.

3946. Massa, Ann. *Vachel Lindsay: Fieldworker for the American Dream.* Bloomington: Indiana University Press, 1970.

3947. Masters, Edgar Lee. *Vachel Lindsay: A Poet in America.* New York: Scribner's, 1935. Reprint, New York: Biblo & Tannen, 1969.

3948. Ruggles, Eleanor. *The West-Going Heart: A Life of Vachel Lindsay.* New York: Norton, 1959.

3949. South, Eudora Lindsay. *From the Lindsay Scrapbook: Cousin Vachel.* Indianapolis, Ind.: Privately printed, 1978. Contains some good family history and interesting reminiscences but is not a sound biography.

3950. Ward, John C. "The Background of Lindsay's 'The Chinese-Nightingale.' " *Western Illinois Regional Studies* 8, no. 1 (Spring 1985): 70-80. The Lindsay family's connection with China.

4. Edgar Lee Masters

3951. Burgess, Charles E. "Edgar Lee Masters' Paternal Ancestry: A Pioneer Heritage and Influence." *Western Illinois Regional Studies* 7, no. 1 (Spring 1984): 32-60.

3952. _____. "Some Family Source Material for Spoon River Anthology." *Western Illinois Regional Studies* 13, no. 1 (Spring 1990): 80-89.

3953. Flanagan, John T. *Edgar Lee Masters: The Spoon River Poet and His Critics.* Metuchen, N.J.: Scarecrow Press, 1974.

3954. Hallwas, John E. "Masters and the Pioneers: Four Epitaphs from Spoon River Anthology." *Old Northwest* 2 (December 1976): 389-99. Parallels between the lives of pioneer members of Masters' family and the characters in *Spoon River Anthology.*

3955. Hartley, Lois. "Edgar Lee Masters, Biographer and Historian." *Journal of the Illinois State Historical Society* 54 (1961): 56-83.

3956. _____. "Edgar Lee Masters, Political Essayist." *Journal of the Illinois State Historical Society* 57 (1964): 249-60. A knowledge of Masters' political attitudes, as revealed in his essays, is essential to understanding the man and his work.

3957. Masters, Edgar Lee. *Across Spoon River: An Autobiography.* New York: Farrar, 1936. Reprint, with an introduction by Ronald Primeau, Urbana: University of Illinois Press, 1991.

3958. _____. *Spoon River Anthology: An Annotated Edition.* Edited, with an introduction, by John E. Hallwas. Urbana: University of Illinois Press, 1992. The 80-page introduction and the extensive annotations tie the famous book to the author's Illinois background.

3959. Masters, Hardin Wallace. *Edgar Lee Masters: A Biographical Sketchbook about a Famous American Author.* Cranbury, N.J.: Associated University Presses, 1978.

3960. Masters, Hilary. *Last Stands: Notes from Memory.* Boston: Godine, 1982. A memoir by Edgar Lee Masters' son, who writes of his childhood, his father, and other family members.

3961. Primeau, Ronald. *Beyond Spoon River: The Legacy of Edgar Lee Masters.* Austin: University of Texas Press, 1981.

3962. Wrenn, John H., and Wrenn, Margaret M. *Edgar Lee Masters.* Twayne's United States Authors Series, no. 456. Boston, 1983.

5. Carl Sandburg

3963. Borough, Reuben W. "The Sandburg I Remember." *Journal of the Illinois State Historical Society* 59 (1966): 229-51. The author and Sandburg worked together as newspapermen in Chicago in 1907.

3964. Callahan, North. *Carl Sandburg, Lincoln of Our Literature: A Biography.* New York: New York University Press, 1970.

3965. _____. *Carl Sandburg: His Life and Works.* Rev. ed., University Park: Pennsylvania State University Press, 1987.

3966. Detzer, Karl. *Carl Sandburg: A Study in Personality and Background.* New York: Harcourt, Brace, 1941.

3967. Flanagan, John T. "Carl Sandburg at Eighty." *Journal of the Illinois State Historical Society* 51 (1958): 191-98. A tribute to Sandburg on the occasion of his eightieth birthday in 1958.

3968. Golden, Harry L. *Carl Sandburg.* Cleveland: World Publishing, 1961. Reprint, with a foreword by Joseph Wershba and a preface by Penelope Niven, Urbana: University of Illinois Press, 1987.

3969. Heise, Kenan. *The Sandburg Shelf: An Annotated Bibliography and Price Guide for the Works of Carl Sandburg.* Evanston, Ill.: Chicago Historical Bookworks, 1993. Lists 144 items, including forewords, prefaces, and introductions by Sandburg (34 items).

3970. Jenkins, Alan. "Sandburg's Private Printings." *Journal of the Illinois State Historical Society* 46 (1953): 401-6.

3971. *Journal of the Illinois State Historical Society* 45 (Winter 1952): 295-406. The entire issue is devoted to Sandburg in honor of his seventy-fifth birthday, 6 January 1953. Articles by twenty-six authors.

3972. Mitgang, Herbert, ed. *The Letters of Carl Sandburg.* New York: Harcourt, Brace, 1968.

3973. Niven, Penelope. *Carl Sandburg: A Biography.* New York: Scribner's, 1991. Scholars consider this the best biography of the famous poet.

3974. _____. "Seeing Sandburg Plain: The Search for Carl Sandburg." *Selected Papers in Illinois History, 1981.* Springfield: Illinois State Historical Society, 1982. Pp. 113-22.

3975. Perry, Lilla S. *My Friend Carl Sandburg: The Biography of a Friend-ship.* Edited by E. Caswell Perry. Metuchen, N.J.: Scarecrow Press, 1981.

3976. Reid, Robert L. "The *Day Book* Poems of Carl Sandburg." *Old Northwest* 9 (1983): 205-18. For three years, 1914-17, Sandburg worked as a reporter for the small Chicago daily newspaper *The Day Book.* Subsidized by E. W. Scripps, the newspaper was considered radical and "decidedly pro-labor." The author discusses both the newspaper and the Sandburg poems it published.

3977. Sandburg, Carl. *Always the Young Strangers.* New York: Harcourt, Brace, 1953. Sandburg's account of the first twenty years of his life, 1878-98.

3978. _____. *Ever the Winds of Chance.* Urbana: University of Illinois Press, 1983. Sandburg's rough draft of an account of his life, 1898-1908. Scholars should be warned that Sandburg concealed as much as he revealed of this period of his life. This second volume of his autobiography was edited by Margaret Sandburg and George Hendrick.

3979. Sandburg, Helga. "Eyeing the World with All Delight: Helga Sandburg Looks Back at Her Family." *Illinois Historical Journal* 81 (1988): 82-94. Carl Sandburg's daughter recalls her childhood years.

3980. _____. *A Great and Glorious Romance: The Story of Carl Sandburg and Lilian Steichen.* New York: Harcourt, Brace, 1978.

3981. Sandburg, Margaret, ed. *The Poet and the Dream Girl: The Love Letters of Lilian Steichen & Carl Sandburg.* Urbana: University of Illinois Press, 1987.

3982. Steichen, Edward, ed. *Sandburg: Photographers View Carl Sandburg.* New York: Harcourt, Brace, 1966.

3983. Swank, George. *Carl Sandburg: Galesburg and Beyond.* Galesburg: Wagoner Printing, 1983. Notable in this remembrance are comments of the poet's friends and mentors and many snapshots of Sandburg and his friends and family.

3984. Van Doren, Mark. *Carl Sandburg, with a Bibliography of Sandburg Materials in the Library of Congress.* Washington: Published for the Library of Congress by the Gertrude Clarke Whittall Poetry and Literature Fund, 1969.

I. OTHER BIOGRAPHIES

3985. Beckford, Ruth. *Katherine Dunham: A Biography.* The Dance Program, vol. 14. New York: Marcel Dekker, 1979.

3986. Benny, Mary Livingstone, and Marks, Hilliard, with Marcia Borie. *Jack Benny.* Garden City, N.Y.: Doubleday, 1978.

3987. Blair, Harry C. *Dr. Anson G. Henry, Physician, Politician, Friend of Abraham Lincoln.* [Portland, Ore., 1950?]

3988. Block, Herbert. *Herblock: A Cartoonist's Life.* New York: Macmillan, 1993. The noted political cartoonist grew up in Chicago.

3989. *Boyce of Ottawa; "Items on Grand Account": William D. Boyce, 1858-1929.* Marseilles, Ill.: John F. Sullivan, curator, W. D. Boyce Scouting Hall of Fame, 1985. Boyce was the man who "brought scouting to America." He was a successful publisher in both Chicago and Ottawa.

3990. Brashler, William. *The Don: The Life and Death of Sam Giancana.* New York, Harper, 1977. The Chicago crime boss.

3991. Bruns, Roger. *The Damnedest Radical: The Life and World of Ben Reitman, Chicago's Celebrated Social Reformer, Hobo King, and Whorehouse Physician.* Urbana: University of Illinois Press, 1986. A scholarly biography of a well-known "character" in Chicago in the 1920s and 1930s.

3992. Brush, Daniel Harmon. *Growing Up with Southern Illinois, 1820 to 1861, from the Memoirs of Daniel Harmon Brush.* Lakeside Classics, no. 42, edited by Milo Milton Quaife. Chicago: R. R. Donnelley, 1944. Reprint, with a Civil War essay by John Y. Simon, Herrin, Ill.: Crossfire Press, 1992. The complete manuscript of Brush's memoirs is now in the Illinois State Historical Library.

3993. Burr, Barbara. "Letters from Two Wars." *Journal of the Illinois State Historical Society* 30 (1937-38): 135-58. Letters from Lindorf Ozburn during his service in the Mexican War and the Civil War. The letters are now in the Illinois State Historical Library.

3994. Cavanagh, Helen M. *Funk of Funk's Grove: Farmer, Legislator, and Cattle King of the Old Northwest, 1797-1865.* Bloomington, Ill.: Pantagraph Printing, 1952. Special ed., Springfield: Illinois State Historical Society, 1968. Biography of the Illinois pioneer Isaac Funk.

3995. Coletta, Paolo E. "Silas Bryan of Salem." *Journal of the Illinois State Historical Society* 42 (1949): 57-79. Biographical sketch of the father of William Jennings Bryan.

3996. Dickenson, Mollie. *Thumbs Up: The Life and Courageous Comeback of White House Press Secretary Jim Brady.* New York: Morrow, 1987.

3997. Dunham, Katherine. *A Touch of Innocence.* New York: Harcourt, Brace, 1959.

3998. Eaton, Leonard K. *Landscape Artist in America: The Life and Work of Jens Jensen.* Chicago: University of Chicago Press, 1964. Jensen lived and worked in Chicago, 1886-1935.

3999. Federal Writers' Project, Illinois. "Octave Chanute, Aviation Pioneer." Mimeographed. Chanute Field, Ill., 1940.

4000. Grese, Robert E. *Jens Jensen: Maker of Natural Parks and Gardens.* Baltimore: Johns Hopkins University Press, 1992.

4001. Gridley, Eleanor. "Presentation of Bronze Bust of Mrs. Myra Bradwell, First Woman Lawyer in Illinois." *Transactions of the Illinois State Historical Society, 1931,* pp. 168-71. The bust is in the Illinois State Historical Library.

4002. Harrison, Gilbert A. *A Timeless Affair: The Life of Anita McCormick Blaine.* Chicago: University of Chicago Press, 1979. The daughter of Cyrus Hall McCormick, Anita Blaine devoted her life to social and political causes and to the complicated lives of her extended family.

4003. Hendrickson, Walter B. *The Indiana Years, 1903-1941.* Indianapolis: Indiana Historical Society, 1983. An account of his early years by the MacMurray College professor.

4004. _____. "John Wickliffe Kitchell--Prairie Philanthropist, Conchologist, and Patron of the Arts." *Journal of the Illinois State Historical Society* 65 (1972): 22-42.

4005. Jarvis, Fields. " 'Incidents in the Life of an Old Pioneer': The Memoir of Fields Jarvis." Edited by John Lee Allaman. *Western Illinois Regional Studies* 9, no. 1 (Spring 1986): 5-18. Jarvis recalls early settlements on several frontiers, and relations with the Indians from 1799 to 1832.

4006. Laing, Diana Whitehill. "A Tuscolan in the War and Afterward." *Journal of the Illinois State Historical Society* 56 (1963): 372-90. John Thomas Williams of Tuscola served in the 2d Illinois Cavalry; he later became a newspaperman. His reminiscences recount his early hard life on a farm during the Civil War era.

4007. Lentz, Lula Gillespie. "The Reminiscences of Lula Gillespie Lentz." *Journal of the Illinois State Historical Society* 68 (1975): 267-88 and 353-67. The author describes life in deep southern Illinois, where she grew up in the late nineteenth century. She continues the story of her life to 1929. Excellent accounts of manners and customs.

4008. Lewis, Lloyd Downs. *John S. Wright, Prophet of the Prairies.* Chicago: Prairie Farmer Publishing Co., 1941. Founder of the *Prairie Farmer* and champion of public schools and parks as well as railroads and improved agriculture.

4009. Litvin, Martin. *The Young Mary, 1817-1861: Early Years of Mother Bickerdyke, America's Florence Nightingale and Patron Saint of Kansas.* Galesburg, Ill.: Log City Books, 1976. Mary Ann Bickerdyke was a resident of Galesburg when she went to Cairo to nurse troops in the Civil War.

4010. Mitchell, Lucy Sprague. *Two Lives: The Story of Wesley Clair Mitchell and Myself.* New York: Simon & Schuster, 1953. Mitchell, a native Illinoisan, became a world-famous economist and his wife, a noted educator.

4011. Monaghan, Jay. "North Carolinians in Illinois History." *North Carolina Historical Review* 22 (1945): 418-59. Sketches of Brigadier General Henry Atkinson, Judge Alfred Arrington, and Congressman Joseph Gurney Cannon.

4012. Morris, Ira Nelson. *Heritage from My Father: An Autobiography.* New York: Privately printed, 1947. A distinguished United States diplomat, Ira Morris was the son of Chicago meatpacker Nelson Morris.

4013. Moynihan, Ruth Barnes. *Rebel for Rights: Abigail Scott Duniway.* New Haven, Conn.: Yale University Press, 1983. Born in Tazewell County in 1834,

Abigail Scott Duniway emigrated to Oregon with her family in 1852. She became an author, newspaper editor, and suffragist.

4014. Ponting, Tom Candy. *Life of Tom Candy Ponting: An Autobiography.* Western Range Cattle Industry Study, no. 2. Evanston, Ill.: Branding Iron Press, 1952. Known as the "cattle king" of central Illinois (his home was at Moweaqua), Ponting operated throughout the United States and Canada.

4015. Roper, Laura Wood. *F.L.O.: A Biography of Frederick Law Olmsted.* Baltimore: The Johns Hopkins University Press, 1973. A study of the life and work of the landscape architect who made substantial contributions to Chicago's parks and boulevards.

4016. Sorensen, Andrew A. "Lester Frank Ward, 'The American Aristotle,' in Illinois." *Journal of the Illinois State Historical Society* 63 (1970): 158-66. The Illinois years of sociologist Ward.

4017. Sunder, John E. *Joshua Pilcher, Fur Trader and Indian Agent.* Norman: University of Oklahoma Press, 1968. Pilcher for a time was stationed as Indian agent at Rock Island.

4018. Urban, William. "Wyatt Earp Was Born Here: Monmouth and the Earps, 1845-1859." *Western Illinois Regional Studies* 3 (1980): 154-67.

4019. Walton, Clyde C., ed. *John Francis Snyder: Selected Writings.* Springfield: Illinois State Historical Society, 1962. With a biography of Snyder by Phyllis E. Connolly and a study of his archaeological work by Melvin L. Fowler. A selection of Snyder's historical and archaeological writings are reprinted.

4020. Weil, Joseph R. *"Yellow Kid" Weil: The Autobiography of America's Master Swindler, as Told to W. T. Brannon.* Chicago: Ziff-Davis Publishing, 1948. Autobiography of a Chicago mobster.

4021. Wilson, Hugh Robert. *The Education of a Diplomat.* Introduction by Claude G. Bowers. London: Longmans, Green, 1938. The autobiography of the diplomat Hugh Wilson, a native Illinoisan.

IV. GENERAL AND REGIONAL HISTORIES AND REFERENCE SOURCES

This category includes items that cover two or more chronological periods. City, county, and regional histories appear in this bibliography only if they are of statewide interest. An Illinois bibliography that did not include Chicago history would be incongruous, however, for so much of the state's history is concentrated in that city: farm markets, transportation facilities, art, labor and industry, architecture, music, and politics and government, for example. Items related to such subjects appear herein under the appropriate chronological period or subject heading, but the following sections include Chicago histories that are especially meritorious and of general interest.

A. GENERAL AND REGIONAL HISTORY

4022. Alvord, Clarence Walworth. *The Illinois Country, 1673-1818.* The Centennial History of Illinois, vol. 1. Springfield: Illinois Centennial Commission, 1920. Reprint, The Sesquicentennial History of Illinois, vol. 1, with an introduction by Robert Mize Sutton. Urbana: University of Illinois Press, 1987. Also reprinted in The American West series, with an introduction by John Francis Bannon. Chicago: Loyola University Press, 1965.

4023. Ander, Oscar Fritiof, comp. and ed. *The John H. Hauberg Historical Essays.* Augustana Library Publications, no. 26. Rock Island, Ill., 1954. Includes "The Changing Lincoln," by Paul McClelland Angle; "Abraham Lincoln in the Black Hawk War," by Harry E. Pratt; and "In the American Tradition," by Conrad Bergendoff--the last a sketch of Hauberg.

4024. Angle, Paul McClelland. "The Story of Illinois, 1673-1940: A Glorious Chapter in U.S. History." *Blue Book of the State of Illinois, 1939-1940.* Pp. 342-58.

4025. Badger, David Alan. *The County Court Houses of Illinois.* 3 vols. Havana, Ill.: Badger, 1986. Drawings and brief historical texts for each of Illinois' 102 courthouses by the artist/author. Based mainly on the "Illinois Courthouses" manuscript in the Illinois State Historical Library.

4026. Bannon, John Francis. "The Spaniards and the Illinois Country, 1762-1800." *Journal of the Illinois State Historical Society* 69 (1976): 110-18.

4027. Bogart, Ernest L. "The Movement of the Population of Illinois, 1870-1910." *Transactions of the Illinois State Historical Society, 1917,* pp. 64-75.

4028. Boggess, Arthur Clinton. *The Settlement of Illinois, 1778-1830.* Chicago Historical Society's Collection, vol. 5. Chicago, 1908. Facsimile reprint, Illinois Sesquicentennial ed., Ann Arbor, Mich.: University Microfilms, 1968. This volume constitutes a general history of the state for the years stated, with a good annotated bibliography and an index.

4029. Breese, Sidney. *The Early History of Illinois, from Its Discovery by the French, in 1673, until Its Cession to Great Britain, in 1763, Including the Narrative of Marquette's Discovery of the Mississippi . . . with a Biographical Memoir by Melville W. Fuller.* Edited by Thomas Hoyne. Chicago: E. B. Myers, 1884.

4030. Bridges, Roger Dean, and Davis, Rodney O., eds. *Illinois: Its History & Legacy.* St. Louis: River City Publishers, 1984. Eighteen essays by authorities on Illinois history, including the editors, "summarize the latest scholarship and interpretations," as the editors state was their intention. A list of suggested readings accompanies each essay.

4031. Buisseret, David. *Historic Illinois from the Air.* Illustrations and cartography by Tom Willcockson. Chicago: University of Chicago Press, 1990. This volume has historic drawings, paintings, and maps, as well as modern maps and other more recent photographs in addition to the aerial photographs. With a well-organized narrative accompanying illustrations, the volume is a comprehensive state history, with a list of sources for each chapter and an index.

4032. Buley, R. Carlyle. *The Old Northwest: Pioneer Period, 1815-1840.* 2 vols. 1950. Reprint, Bloomington: Indiana University Press, in association with the Indiana Historical Society, 1983. This work, which won the Pulitzer Prize in 1950, portrays daily life, social and economic organization, and government.

4033. Cain, Jerrilee; Hallwas, John E.; and Hicken, Victor, eds. *Tales from Two Rivers I.* Macomb: Two Rivers Arts Council and the College of Fine Arts Development, Western Illinois University, 1981. The editors selected 121 entries, from the first (1980) Tales from Two Rivers writing contest, that illustrate social history as related by residents over sixty years of age. Four additional volumes have been published. Volumes 2 and 3, with the same editors, were issued in 1982 and 1984. Volume 4, edited by John E. Hallwas and David R. Pichaske, appeared in 1987; and Volume 5, edited by Hallwas and Alfred J. Lindsey, in 1991.

4034. Calkins, Earnest Elmo. *They Broke the Prairie: Being Some Account of the Settlement of the Upper Mississippi Valley by Religious and Educational Pioneers, Told in Terms of One City, Galesburg, and of One College, Knox.* New York: Scribner's, 1937. Reprint, Westport, Conn.: Greenwood, 1971. Another reprint (1989), by the University of Illinois Press, has an introduction by Rodney O. Davis. The narrative covers a period of one hundred years.

4035. Carrière, Joseph Médard. "Life and Customs in the French Villages of the Old Illinois Country (1763-1939)." *Report of the Canadian Historical Association*, 1939, pp. 34-47.

4036. *Chicago History* 1 (1945)--8 (1969). Issued quarterly by the Chicago Historical Society as "an informal publication devoted in the main to the Society's museum, library, and activities." In 1970 the Society began a new series, with the same title (1 [1970]--to date), containing longer articles on all aspects of Chicago history.

Earlier the Society had published the *Bulletin of the Chicago Historical Society* 1 (1922)--3 (1925) and a new series 1 (1934)--2 (1939). Articles from these series have not generally been included in this bibliography.

Roberta Casey is the compiler of an index for new series volumes 8 through 16 (Spring 1979 through Fall and Winter 1987-88); it was published in *Chicago History* 18 (special index issue 1989): 1-54.

4037. Coffman, Edward M. *The Old Army: A Portrait of the American Army in Peacetime, 1784-1898.* New York: Oxford University Press, 1986. The peacetime army was important to Illinois from 1784 until 1833; this volume will therefore be useful to anyone studying those years of Illinois history.

4038. Conger, John Leonard, and Hull, William E. *History of the Illinois River Valley.* 3 vols. Chicago: S. J. Clarke, 1932. Volumes 2 and 3 consist of biographies.

4039. Currey, Joseph Seymour. *Chicago, Its History and Its Builders: A Century of Marvelous Growth.* 5 vols. Chicago: S. J. Clarke, 1912. Volumes 4-5 contain biographical sketches.

4040. Davidson, Alexander, and Stuvé, Bernard. *A Complete History of Illinois from 1673 to 1873 . . .* Springfield: Illinois Journal, 1874. Old but valuable.

4041. Dedmon, Emmett. *Fabulous Chicago.* New York: Random House, 1953.

4042. Duncan, Hugh Dalziel. *Culture and Democracy: The Struggle for Form in Society and Architecture in Chicago and the Middle West during the Life and Times of Louis H. Sullivan.* Totowa, N.J.: Bedminster Press, 1965. Despite the length of the title, it fails to indicate the vast scope of this volume, which is really a social and cultural history that includes, for example, lengthy sections on immigrant settlers, newspapers, religion, politics, oratory, humor, merchandising and money, labor, settlement houses, women, and many other artists and architects besides Sullivan.

4043. Dunne, Edward F. *Illinois, the Heart of the Nation.* 5 vols. Chicago: Lewis Publishing, 1933.

4044. Edwards, Ninian W. *History of Illinois from 1778 to 1833; and Life and Times of Ninian Edwards.* Springfield: Illinois State Journal, 1870. Reprint, New York: Arno, 1975.

4045. *Fergus' Historical Series,* nos. 1-35 (1876-1914). This series on Chicago and Illinois history was published by the Fergus Printing Company of Chicago. Some numbers include several different items; those deemed of general interest are listed separately in this volume.

4046. Flint, Margaret A., comp. "A Chronology of Illinois History, 1673-1941." *Blue Book of the State of Illinois, 1941-1942.* Pp. 469-87. Updated and published in several later volumes. Rev. ed., Springfield: Illinois State Historical Library, 1972. Chronology for the years 1969-71 prepared by Clifford H. Haka.

4047. Gilbert, Paul, and Bryson, Charles Lee. *Chicago and Its Makers: A Narrative of Events from the Day of the First White Man to the Second World's*

Fair. Chicago: Felix Mendelsohn, 1929. Also includes almost seven hundred biographies of Chicagoans.

4048. Gillespie, Joseph. *Recollections of Early Illinois and Her Noted Men. Read before the Chicago Historical Society, March 16th, 1880.* Fergus' Historical Series, no. 13. Chicago, 1880.

4049. Gray, James. *The Illinois.* The Rivers of America. New York: Farrar, 1940. Reprint, with an introduction by John E. Hallwas, Urbana: University of Illinois Press, 1989. Anecdotal history with sketches of famous Illinoisans whose connection with the river was often tenuous. Little about the river.

4050. Hallwas, John E. "The Regional Essays of Jerry Klein." *Western Illinois Regional Studies* 1 (1978): 65-85. Contains biographical information about the Peoria newspaperman as well as extracts from his essays describing western Illinois.

4051. _____. *Western Illinois Heritage.* Macomb: Illinois Heritage Press, 1983. The author's essays (arranged by subject, and chronologically within each subject division) constitute a good introduction to the history of western Illinois.

4052. Horrell, C. William; Piper, Henry Dan; and Voight, John W. *Land Between the Rivers.* Carbondale: Southern Illinois University Press, 1973. Paper, 1982. Photographs by Horrell and historical text by Piper and Voight are concerned with southern Illinois.

4053. Howard, Robert P. *Illinois: A History of the Prairie State.* Grand Rapids, Mich.: Eerdmans, 1972.

4054. Hubbs, Barbara Burr. "Rivers That Meet in Egypt." *Transactions of the Illinois State Historical Society, 1940,* pp. 1-21. Histories of early settlers and settlements on the rivers in southern Illinois.

4055. Hyman, Harold. *American Singularity: The 1787 Northwest Ordinance, the 1862 Homestead and Morrill Acts, and the 1944 G. I. Bill.* The Richard B. Russell Lectures, no. 5. Athens: University of Georgia Press, 1986.

4056. "Illinois and Illinoisans, 1876-1976: From the Collections of the Illinois State Historical Library." *Journal of the Illinois State Historical Society* 69 (1976): 242-329 and 347-48. Selections from manuscripts, newspapers, and photographs that illustrate manners and customs as well as major national historical events.

4057. *Illinois Magazine: The Magazine of the Prairie State.* Originally *Outdoor Illinois.* Vol. 1, no. 1 (March 1962)--to date. Published bimonthly at Litchfield. Eight to ten articles (two to three pages each) per issue, related to manners and customs or historic places, events, and people. No annotations; profusely illustrated.

4058. *Illinois Quarterly.* Vols. 1-44 (May 1938-Summer 1982). This journal, published by Illinois State University, was first *Teacher Education,* vols. 1-26 (May 1938-April 1964), and then *Illinois State University Journal,* vols. 27-32 (September 1964-April 1970). As the *Quarterly,* it was primarily concerned with literature but also published articles devoted to the social sciences, education, and the humanities. It was not limited to Illinois-related subject matter. Items pertaining to Illinois history are listed herein.

4059. Illinois State Historical Society. *Journal.* Volume 1 (1908-9)--to date. In Autumn 1984 (volume 77, number 3), the title was changed to *Illinois Historical Journal.* Three cumulative indexes are available, for volumes 1-25, 26-50, and 51-60; a fourth is in preparation. *Journal* volumes have been analyzed, and perhaps as many as ninety per cent of the articles are separately listed herein.

4060. _____. *Transactions.* Volumes 1-55 (1899-1989). This series of articles and society proceedings has changed titles several times over the years-- being called *Publications, Proceedings, Papers in Illinois History,* or *Occasional Publications.* The *Occasional Publications* were full-length books, volumes 50-55 (1947-89). In 1982 the titles *Selected Papers* and *Transactions* were resumed to publish papers from the annual history symposium sponsored by the Illinois State Historical Society since 1980. From the earlier *Transactions,* only those articles still deemed useful to the researcher are separately listed herein. There is a cumulative index for volumes 1-50.

4061. Jensen, Richard J. *Illinois: A Bicentennial History.* New York: Norton, 1978. A sociological approach to Illinois history, this volume is one in the American Association for State and Local History series for the states.

4062. Johannsen, Robert W. *The Frontier, the Union, and Stephen A. Douglas.* Urbana: University of Illinois Press, 1989. A collection of articles and two previously unpublished lectures, most of which are related to Douglas and Lincoln. One of the lectures, "Sandburg and Lincoln: The Prairie Years," is a study of the reception of Sandburg's work that constitutes a brief historiography of Lincoln studies.

4063. *Journal of the Illinois State Historical Society.* In the years 1938-48 and 1954-58 a chronology of the preceding year's events was published annually.

4064. Keiser, John H. *Illinois Vignettes.* Springfield, Ill.: Sangamon State University, 1977. A collection of newspaper columns about Illinois history, issued by Sangamon State University, 1974-77.

4065. Krohe, James Jr., ed. *A Springfield Reader: Historical Views of the Illinois Capital, 1818-1976.* Sangamon County Historical Society Bicentennial Studies in Sangamon History. Springfield, 1976. Many of the articles in this collection deal with events and people of statewide and national importance.

4066. Madison, James H., ed. *Heartland: Comparative Histories of the Midwestern States.* Midwestern History and Culture series. Bloomington: Indiana University Press, 1988. G. Cullom Davis's essay on Illinois, one of twelve states represented in this volume, is an impressive description and history of the state in twenty-seven pages.

4067. Mason, Edward G., ed. *Early Chicago and Illinois.* Chicago Historical Society's Collection, vol. 4. Contains biographies of several prominent Illinoisans as well as reproductions of early French and British documents from the collections of the Chicago Historical Society. The latter category includes John Todd's Record Book and John Todd Papers, Philippe de Rocheblave Papers, and lists of early citizens in what is now Illinois.

4068. _____. *Illinois in the 18th Century: Three Papers Read before the Chicago Historical Society--Kaskaskia and Its Parish Records, Old Fort Chartres, Col. John Todd's Record Book.* Fergus' Historical Series, no. 12. Chicago, 1881. Todd was the first civil governor of Illinois when it was a county of the state of Virginia.

4069. Nevins, Allan. "Not without Thy Wondrous Story, Illinois." *Journal of the Illinois State Historical Society* 46 (1953): 231-46. Nevins shows how the history of Illinois was integrated with international and national affairs.

4070. *Newberry Library Bulletin,* 1944-66; superseded by the Library's *Annual Report.* The *Bulletin* reported primarily on acquisitions and collections of the library and the related conferences Newberry sponsored. The researcher interested in American studies, genealogy, literature, rare books, maps, Native American history, and Chicago social life and reform movements, for example, will find the *Bulletin* useful.

4071. Nothstein, Ira Oliver. "Rock Island and the Rock Island Arsenal." *Journal of the Illinois State Historical Society* 33 (1940): 304-40. A brief history of the area from 1763, concentrating on the Civil War era, when the arsenal was built and the island housed a prison for Confederate soldiers.

4072. Patterson, Robert W. *Early Society in Southern Illinois: An Address Read before the Chicago Historical Society, Tuesday, October 19th, 1880.* Fergus' Historical Series, no. 14. Chicago, 1881.

4073. Pease, Theodore Calvin. *The Story of Illinois.* McClurg, 1925. 2d ed., Illinois State Historical Society, 1949. 3d ed., rev. by Marguerite Jenison Pease, Chicago and London: University of Chicago Press, 1965. Both scholarly and readable, this volume is a succinct history of the state to 1964.

4074. Perkins, James H., comp. *Annals of the West, Embracing a Concise Account of Principal Events, Which Have Occurred in the Western States and Territories, from the Discovery of the Mississippi Valley to the Year Eighteen Hundred and Fifty.* 2d ed., rev. and enl. by J. M. Peck. St. Louis: J. R. Albach, 1850.

4075. Pierce, Bessie Louise. *A History of Chicago.* 3 vols. New York: Knopf, 1937, 1940, 1947. *Volume I: The Beginning of a City, 1673-1848. Volume II: From Town to City, 1848-1871. Volume III: 1871-1893.*

4076. Pooley, William V. *The Settlement of Illinois from 1830 to 1850.* Bulletin of the University of Wisconsin, no. 220; History Series, vol. 1, no. 4. Madison, 1908. Of much broader scope than the title indicates, the book has chapters on pre-1830 settlements, roads, trails, and waterways, the Mormons, various colony and communal settlements, agriculture, pioneer life, and economic conditions.

4077. Pratt, Harry Edward. "The Illinois Story." *Illinois Blue Book, 1955-1956.* Pp. 33-73. Reprint, Illinois State Historical Society, 1957.

4078. Prucha, Francis Paul. *Broadax and Bayonet: The Role of the United States Army in the Development of the Northwest, 1815-1860.* Madison: State Historical Society of Wisconsin, 1953. Reprint, Lincoln: University of Nebraska Press, 1967.

4079. Quaife, Milo Milton. *Checagou: From Indian Wigwam to Modern City, 1673-1835.* Chicago: University of Chicago Press, 1933. A shorter and more popular version of his 1913 history.

4080. _____. *Chicago and the Old Northwest, 1673-1835: A Study of the Evolution of the Northwestern Frontier, together with a History of Fort Dearborn.* Chicago: University of Chicago Press, 1913. A comprehensive, scholarly history. Quaife's analysis of the Fort Dearborn massacre (chapters 10 and 11) is superseded by that of Mentor L. Williams, q.v.

4081. _____, comp. and ed. *The Development of Chicago, 1674-1914, Shown in a Series of Contemporary Original Narratives.* Chicago: The Caxton Club, 1916.

4082. _____. *Lake Michigan.* The American Lakes Series, edited by Milo M. Quaife. Indianapolis: Bobbs-Merrill, 1944. Popular general history of the Lakes region from the early 1600s to the 1940s. A good index indicates Illinois material.

4083. Rantoul Press and Chanute Field News. "Rantoul Salutes Chanute's Golden Anniversary, 1917-1967." Commemorative ed., published 14 June 1967.

4084. Rosenberry, Lois Kimball Mathews. *The Expansion of New England: The Spread of New England Settlement and Institutions to the Mississippi River, 1620-1865.* Boston: Houghton Mifflin, 1909. Reprint, New York: Russell & Russell, 1962. Chapter 8 deals with settlement of New Englanders in Indiana and Illinois.

4085. Schall, Robert. "The History of Fort Sheridan, Illinois . . ." Mimeographed. Fort Sheridan: The Clerical School and the Visual Training Aids Section, 1672nd Service Unit, 1944. History of the fort from its authorization by Congress in 1887 to 1943.

4086. Scheiber, Harry N., ed. *The Old Northwest: Studies in Regional History, 1787-1910.* Lincoln: University of Nebraska Press, 1969. A collection of previously published articles, primarily economic and political. Those that relate to Illinois are listed separately herein.

4087. Schlarman, Joseph H. *From Quebec to New Orleans: The Story of the French in America . . .* Belleville, Ill.: Buechler Publishing, 1929. Also covers the British period of Illinois history, as well as Native American history.

4088. Schlereth, Thomas J. "The New England Presence on the Midwest Landscape." *Old Northwest* 9 (1983): 125-42. Aspects of the influence of New England and New Englanders are considered--on education, philanthropy, architecture, business and finance, land speculation, and railroad development. Illinois figures prominently in this account.

4089. Smith, George Washington. *History of Illinois and Her People.* 6 vols. Chicago: American Historical Society, 1927. Volumes 3-6 contain biographies.

4090. _____. *A History of Southern Illinois: A Narrative Account of Its Historical Progress, Its People, and Its Principal Interests.* 3 vols. Chicago: Lewis Publishing, 1912. Volumes 2 and 3 are biographical.

4091. *Story of Illinois.* Springfield: Illinois State Museum, 1943-63. A series of thirteen pamphlets that deal with the history, archaeology, geology, ethnography, art, and flora and fauna of Illinois.

4092. Sutton, Robert P., ed. *The Prairie State: A Documentary History of Illinois.* 2 vols. Grand Rapids, Mich.: Eerdmans, 1976. These selections, from scholarly historical works as well as from little-known diaries, travelogues, and newspaper accounts, are unified by the editor's interpretive essays.

4093. Tingley, Donald Fred, ed. *Essays in Illinois History, in Honor of Glenn Huron Seymour.* Carbondale: Southern Illinois University Press, 1968. Eight scholarly essays honor the longtime history professor at Eastern Illinois University: "Anti-Intellectualism on the Illinois Frontier," by the editor; "Lincoln's Particular Friend [Ward Hill Lamon]," by Lavern M. Hamand; "John P. Altgeld, Promoter of Higher Education in Illinois," by Neil Thorburn; "Urban Immigrant Lawmakers and Progressive Reform in Illinois," by John D. Buenker; "John H. Walker, Labor Leader from Illinois," by John H. Keiser; "Harold Ickes and Hiram Johnson in the Presidential Primary of 1924," by Robert E. Hennings; and "Unemployment in Illinois during the Great Depression," by David J. Maurer.

4094. Wagenknecht, Edward Charles. *Chicago.* The Centers of Civilization Series, 13. Norman: University of Oklahoma Press, 1964. An excellent overview of the high points of Chicago history, with biographical sketches of some of the city's luminaries.

4095. Walton, Clyde C., comp. and ed. *An Illinois Reader.* An Illinois Sesquicentennial Book. DeKalb: Northern Illinois University Press, 1970. This anthology, compiled from publications of the Illinois State Historical Society, tells the story of the state from its earliest history to the present era.

4096. Way, Royal Brunson. *Rock River Valley: Its History, Traditions, Legends, and Charms . . .* 3 vols. Chicago: S. J. Clarke Publishing, 1926. The second and third volumes are biographical.

4097. Wentworth, John. *Early Chicago* (two lectures delivered before the Sunday Lecture Society and McCormick Hall on 7 May and 11 April 1876). Fergus' Historical Series, nos. 7 and 8, respectively. Chicago, 1876.

4098. Wheeler, Adade Mitchell, and Wortman, Marlene Stein. *The Roads They Made: Women in Illinois History.* Chicago: Charles H. Kerr, 1977.

4099. Wood, Walter Shea. "The 130th Infantry, Illinois National Guard: A Military History, 1778-1919." *Journal of the Illinois State Historical Society* 30 (1937-38): 193-255. The author includes militia units from those counties "included in the regimental area of the 130th Infantry." A lengthy, but cursory, unannotated account. Not dependable.

B. REFERENCE SOURCES

1. Atlases, Gazetteers, and Place Names

4100. Adams, James N., comp. *Illinois Place Names.* Edited by William E. Keller. Occasional Publications of the Illinois State Historical Society, no. 54. Springfield, 1968; reprinted from *Illinois Libraries*, vol. 50 (1968), nos. 4, 5, and 6. Reprinted, with a new addendum by Lowell M. Volkel, as Occasional Publications, no. 55. Springfield, 1989.

4101. Barge, William D., and Caldwell, Norman Ward. "Illinois Place Names." *Journal of the Illinois State Historical Society* 29 (1936-37): 189-311. Sources are given for each name listed.

4102. Barge, William D. "The Old Towns of Illinois." *Transactions of the Illinois State Historical Society, 1912,* pp. 193-97. Names that had disappeared by 1912, along with the new name if the town was still in existence.

4103. Beck, Lewis C. *A Gazetteer of the States of Illinois and Missouri Containing a General View of Each State, a General View of Their Counties, and a Particular Description of Their Towns, Villages, Rivers, &c., &c.; with a Map and Other Engravings.* Albany, N.Y.: C. R. & G. Webster, 1823. Reprint, Mid-American Frontier series. New York: Arno, 1975.

4104. Bergen, John V. "Maps and Their Makers in Early Illinois: The Burr Map and the Peck-Messinger Map." *Western Illinois Regional Studies* 10, no. 1 (Spring 1987): 5-31. Brief histories of map-making in general and the map-makers under discussion, as well as analyses of their maps.

4105. Brown, Samuel R. *The Western Gazetteer, or Emigrant's Directory . . .* Auburn, N.Y.: H. C. Southwick, 1817. Illinois Territory, pp. 17-35. Reprinted in *Transactions of the Illinois State Historical Society, 1908*, pp. 299-310.

4106. Conzen, Michael P.; Akerman, James R.; and Thackery, David T., comps. *Illinois: County Landownership Map and Atlas Bibliography and Union List.* Springfield: Illinois Cooperative Collection Management Coordinating Committee, Illinois Board of Higher Education, 1991.

4107. Curtiss, Daniel S. *Western Portraiture, and Emigrants' Guide: A Description of Wisconsin, Illinois, and Iowa; with Remarks on Minnesota and Other Territories.* New York: J. H. Colton, 1852.

4108. Federal Writers' Project, Illinois. *Cairo Guide.* American Guide Series. Cairo?, Ill.: Sponsored by Cairo Public Library, 1938.

4109. _____. *Du Page County: A Descriptive and Historical Guide, 1831-1939.* Reedited for publication in 1948 by Marion Knoblauch. Elmhurst, Ill.: I. A. Ruby, 1948.

4110. _____. *Galena Guide.* American Guide Series. Chicago: Sponsored by the city of Galena, 1937.

4111. _____. *Illinois: A Descriptive and Historical Guide.* Chicago: McClurg, 1939; rev. ed., 1947. New rev. ed., edited by Harry Hansen, New York: Hastings House 1974. Reprint of 1939 ed. (edited, with a new introduction, by Neil Harris and Michael Conzen), New York: Pantheon, 1983. The 1939 edition and a 1969 edition (the latter issued by the Illinois Sesquicentennial Commission) are generally agreed to be better than that of 1974.

4112. _____. *Nauvoo Guide.* American Guide Series. Chicago: McClurg, 1939.

4113. _____. *Princeton Guide.* American Guide Series. Princeton, Ill.: Sponsored by the city of Princeton, 1939.

4114. Flint, Timothy. *The History and Geography of the Mississippi Valley, to Which Is Appended a Condensed Physical Geography of the Atlantic United States and the Whole American Continent.* 2d ed. 2 vols. in 1. Cincinnati: E. H. Flint & L. R. Lincoln, 1832. Illinois, pp. 316-32.

4115. Hayner, Don, and McNamee, Tom. *Streetwise Chicago: A History of Chicago Street Names.* Chicago: Loyola University Press, 1988.

4116. Hoffmann, John. "Queries Regarding the Western Rivers: An Unpublished Letter from Thomas Jefferson to the Geographer of the United States." *Journal of the Illinois State Historical Society* 75 (1982): 15-28. Jefferson had questions about Thomas Hutchins's map of, and pamphlet about, the trans-Allegheny West. The author also sketches the life of Hutchins.

4117. Illinois. Secretary of State. *Counties of Illinois: Their Origin and Evolution, with . . . Maps Showing the Original and the Present Boundary Lines of Each County of the State.* Twenty-three maps and accompanying text. First published in 1906 and retained in print.

4118. Illinois Sesquicentennial Commission. *Illinois: Guide and Gazetteer.* Chicago: Rand McNally, 1969. Follows the pattern of the excellent Federal Writers' Project Guide, published in 1939, but completely rewritten.

4119. *James' River Guide, Containing Descriptions of all the Cities, Towns, and Principal Objects of Interest on the Navigable Waters of the Mississippi Valley . . . with Full Tables of Distances, and Many Interesting Historical Sketches of the Country, Statistics of Population, Products, Commerce, Manufactures, Mineral Resources, Scenery, &c., &c. Illustrated with Forty-Four Maps and a Number of Engravings.* Cincinnati: U. P. James, 1856. Town and landing entries are given under names of the various rivers, to which there is an index.

4120. Karrow, Robert W. Jr., ed. *Checklist of Printed Maps of the Middle West to 1900.* Volume 4 of this 14-volume series is for Illinois, compiled by David A. Cobb and Marsha L. Selmer. Boston: G. K. Hall, 1981. Volume 14 (Chicago: Newberry Library, 1983) is a subject, author, and title index.

4121. Landelius, Otto Robert. *Swedish Place-Names in North America.* Translated by Karin Franzén; edited by Raymond Jarvi. Carbondale: Southern Illinois University Press, for the Swedish-American Historical Society, 1985. Illinois, pp. 56-60.

4122. Lloyd, James T. *Lloyd's Steamboat Directory . . . a Complete List of Steamboats and All Other Vessels Now Afloat on the Western Rivers and Lakes . . . History of All the Rail Roads in the United States . . .* Cincinnati: J. T. Lloyd, 1856. In one section, "Distances, Towns, and Populations," Lloyd gives river landings on the Mississippi and Illinois, their distances from each other, and their populations.

4123. McDermott, John Francis. "The French Impress on Place Names in the Mississippi Valley." *Journal of the Illinois State Historical Society* 72 (1979): 225-34. A delightful etymological study.

4124. Mitchell, S. Augustus. *Illinois in 1837: A Sketch Descriptive of the Situation, Boundaries, Face of the Country, Prominent Districts, Prairies, Rivers, Minerals, Animals, Agricultural Productions, Public Lands, Plans of Internal Improvement, Manufactures, &c. of the State of Illinois; Also, Suggestions to Emigrants, Sketches of the Counties, Cities, and Principal Towns in the State* . . . Philadelphia: S. Augustus Mitchell and Grigg & Elliott, 1837.

4125. Muelder, Hermann R. "The Naming of Spoon River." *Western Illinois Regional Studies* 4 (1981): 105-14.

4126. Peck, John Mason. *A Gazetteer of Illinois, in Three Parts, Containing a General View of the State, a General View of Each County, and a Particular Description of Each Town, Settlement . . . etc. Alphabetically Arranged.* Jacksonville, Ill.: R. Goudy, 1834.

4127. _____. *A Guide for Emigrants, Containing Sketches of Illinois, Missouri, and the Adjacent Parts.* Boston: Lincoln & Edmands, 1831. Reprint, New York: Arno, 1975.

4128. Savage, James P. Jr. "Do-It-Yourself Books for Illinois Immigrants." *Journal of the Illinois State Historical Society* 57 (1964): 30-48. Discussion of the major guidebooks of the years 1840-70.

4129. Sneed, Glenn J. *Ghost Towns of Southern Illinois.* Royalton, Ill.: The author, 1977. The author includes towns in the lower seventeen counties. Town sketches are arranged by county, and then alphabetically within that grouping.

4130. Swenson, John F. "Chicagoua/Chicago: The Origin, Meaning, and Etymology of a Place Name." *Illinois Historical Journal* 84 (1991): 235-48.

4131. Thorndale, William, and Dollarhide, William. *Map Guide to the U.S. Federal Censuses, 1790-1920.* Baltimore: Genealogical Publishing, 1987. Shows county boundaries at the time of each census.

4132. Thurman, Melburn D. "Cartography of the Illinois Country: An Analysis of the Middle Mississippi Maps Drawn during the British Regime." *Journal of the Illinois State Historical Society* 75 (1982): 277-88.

4133. Vogel, Virgil J. "Indian Place Names in Illinois." *Journal of the Illinois State Historical Society* 55 (1962): 45-71, 157-89, 271-308, 385-458.   An invaluable source for both linguistics and Indian history. Reprinted as a separate pamphlet in 1963.

4134. Waller, Elbert. "Some Half-Forgotten Towns in Illinois." *Transactions of the Illinois State Historical Society, 1927,* pp. 65-82.

4135. Writers' Program, Illinois. *Hillsboro Guide.* American Guide Series. Hillsboro, Ill.: Montgomery News, 1940.

4136. _____. *Rockford.* American Guide Series. Rockford, Ill.: Sponsored by the city of Rockford, 1941. Emphasizes industrial development.

2. Bibliography, Historiography, and Indexes

Bibliographies that pertain to major subject categories or chronological periods appear throughout this volume and are reflected in the Index to Subjects under the entry Bibliographies.

4137. *America, History and Life* (originally subtitled *A Guide to Periodical Literature*). Vol. 1 (July 1964)--to date. Published by Clio Press for the American Bibliographic Center. A zero volume covers the years 1954-63. This publication includes abstracts of articles in historical publications and citations to reviews and dissertations "covering the United States and Canada," as well as an annual index to subjects, authors, and titles. Arrangement of entries has varied over the years, and annual volumes have several parts; but entries are numbered consecutively throughout the volume year. There are also five-year cumulative indexes. Difficult to use, but a comprehensive, authoritative source.

4138. *American Doctoral Dissertations 1965/66--to date.* Ann Arbor, Mich.: University Microfilms. Previously issued as the thirteenth number of *Dissertation Abstracts.*

4139. Angle, Paul McClelland, and Beyer, Richard Lawrence, comps. *A Handbook of Illinois History: A Topical Survey with References for Teachers and Students.* Reprinted from *Papers in Illinois History,* 1941. Springfield: Illinois State Historical Society, 1943. This annotated bibliography has a section on general histories and eleven chronological sections. Each section has a sound and well-written historical introduction.

4140. Angle, Paul McClelland, comp. *Supplement to Suggested Readings in Illinois History.* Springfield: Illinois State Historical Society, 1941.

4141. Boris, Eileen. "The Settlement Movement Revisited: Social Control with a Conscience." *Reviews in American History* 20 (1992): 216-21. A compelling review article that constitutes a brief historiography of social-settlement history.

4142. Bray, Robert, ed.; Pettis, Francis, assoc. ed.; with John Hallwas, James Hurt, Babette Inglehart, and John Knoepfle. *A Reader's Guide to Illinois Literature.* Springfield: Office of the Illinois Secretary of State, 1985. A bibliography of literature that "uses Illinois as setting or subject or both," arranged by type of literature and subject, each section introduced by a scholarly essay.

4143. Bridges, Roger Dean, comp. "A Bibliography of Dissertations Related to Illinois History, 1884-1976." *Journal of the Illinois State Historical Society* 70 (1977): 208-48. Dissertation titles are arranged under thirty-five subject headings.

4144. Byrd, Cecil K. *A Bibliography of Illinois Imprints, 1814-58.* Chicago: University of Chicago Press, 1966. The volume has excellent bibliographical data, as well as historical and biographical information about authors and printers.

4145. Chicago. Municipal Reference Library. *Catalogue of the Chicago Municipal Library, 1908.* Compiled and issued by Bureau of Statistics and Municipal Library, May, 1908. Chicago, 1908. By an ordinance of 31 March 1913, the Municipal Library was made the Municipal Reference Library, a branch of the Public Library. On 31 March 1918, also by ordinance, the library became a separate institution, the Municipal Reference Library.

4146. Chicago Public Library Omnibus Project. "Bibliography of Illinois Poets since 1900." Mimeographed. Chicago, 1942. Sponsored by the Federal Works Agency, Work Projects Administration (Illinois). Lists poets alphabetically, with birth and death dates, titles of collections of poems, titles of single poems and place published, and sources of biographical information.

4147. Davis, Rodney O. "Coming to Terms with County Histories." *Western Illinois Regional Studies* 2 (1979): 144-55.

4148. *Dissertation Abstracts: Abstracts of Dissertations and Monographs in Microfilm.* Ann Arbor, Mich.: University Microfilms, 1952-66; vols. 16-25 contain a thirteenth issue, which is an index. In 1967 this publication split into *Dissertation Abstracts for Humanities and Social Sciences* and *Dissertation Abstracts in Sciences and Engineering.*

4149. *Doctoral Dissertations in History.* July-December 1975--to date. Washington: American Historical Association, Institutional Services Program. Supersedes *List of Doctoral Dissertations in History.*

4150. Federal Writers' Project, Illinois. "Selected Bibliography; Illinois: Chicago and Its Environs." American Guide Series. Mimeographed. Chicago, 1937.

4151. Felt, Thomas E. "A Proposed Agenda for Illinois Historians." *Journal of the Illinois State Historical Society* 52 (1959): 503-25. This still-valuable historiographical study provides an overview of Illinois histories, emphasizing work that needed consideration in 1959.

4152. Filby, P. William, comp. *A Bibliography of American County Histories.* Baltimore: Genealogical Publishing, 1985. Histories of 99 of Illinois' 102 counties are listed on pages 71-90.

4153. Foster, Olive S. *Illinois: A Students' Guide to Localized History.* New York: Teachers College Press, 1968. In addition to suggested readings for students, this guide contains a brief history of eight chronological periods, with suggested volumes for the school library and a listing of historic sites related to each period.

4154. Gallagher, Bernice E. *Illinois Women Novelists in the Nineteenth Century: An Analysis and Annotated Bibliography.* Urbana: University of Illinois Press, 1994.

4155. Hall, Thomas Randolph. "The Illinois Historical Records Survey: A Bibliography of Its Publications." *Journal of the Illinois State Historical Society* 35 (1942): 174-79.

4156. Hallwas, John E. "The Rhetoric of Community History." *Selected Papers in Illinois History, 1983*. Springfield: Illinois State Historical Society, 1985. Pp. 1-10.

4157. Harmon, Sandra D. *A Guide to Researching and Writing Illinois Women's History*. Illinois Historical Leaflet, no. 2. Springfield: Illinois State Historical Society, 1988.

4158. Hasse, Adelaide R. *Index of Economic Material in Documents of the States of the United States; Illinois, 1809-1904*. Washington: Carnegie Institution, 1909. After a section that includes official printed legislative reports, part 2 is a topical analysis, arranged alphabetically, of reports of state agencies and officers. The content is far broader than the title would indicate, including, for example, under "Maintenance: State" entries related to the insane, delinquents, dependent children, and the blind. The material indexed was that in the New York Public Library, which must nearly have duplicated that in the Illinois State Archives for the period covered. The index is a valuable key to early Illinois documents.

4159. Hoffmann, John, ed. *A Guide to the History of Illinois*. Reference Guides to State History and Research series. Westport, Conn.: Greenwood, 1990. Fourteen historiographical essays (eight on chronological periods, six on specific subjects) by well-known scholars and twelve essays on manuscript and archival collections. The latter group includes descriptions of major holdings at the Illinois State Historical Library; the Illinois State Archives; the Chicago Historical Society; the University of Chicago; Newberry Library, Chicago; other Chicago repositories; the University of Illinois at Urbana-Champaign; Southern Illinois University; Northern Illinois University; other repositories in downstate Illinois; as well as the Library of Congress and National Archives. A superb volume.

4160. _____. "A History of The Centennial History of Illinois, 1907-1920." *Selected Papers in Illinois History, 1982*. Springfield: Illinois State Historical Society, 1984. Pp. 57-78.

4161. Jewell, Frank. *Annotated Bibliography of Chicago History*. Chicago: Chicago Historical Society, 1979.

4162. Kaige, Richard H., and Vaughan, Evelyn L., comps. "Illinois County Histories: A Checklist of Illinois County Histories in the Illinois State Library." *Illinois Libraries* 50 (1968): 694-722.

4163. Kilpatrick, Thomas L., and Hoshiko, Patsy-Rose. *Illinois! Illinois! An Annotated Bibliography of Fiction.* Metuchen, N.J.: Scarecrow Press, 1979. A selection of 1,554 books from a possible 7,000 works related in some substantial way to Illinois.

4164. Kuehl, Warren. *Dissertations in History: An Index to Dissertations Completed in History Departments of United States and Canadian Universities, 1873-1960.* Lexington: University of Kentucky Press, 1965, and . . . *1961-1970.* Lexington: University of Kentucky Press, 1972.

4165. _____. *Dissertations in History, 1970-June 1980: An Index to Dissertations Completed in History Departments of United States & Canadian Universities.* Santa Barbara, Calif.: ABC-Clio Information Services, 1985.

4166. McClellan, Larry A., comp. *Local History South of Chicago: A Guide for Research in the Southern Suburbs.* Chicago: Northeastern Illinois Planning Commission and Governors State University, 1987. In addition to the expected printed sources (given by towns), the compiler lists available newspapers and newsletters, libraries, and historical landmarks. The volume also contains a town and township index to "Where the Trails Cross," the quarterly publication of the South Suburban Genealogical and Historical Society.

4167. McMurtrie, Douglas C. *A Bibliography of Chicago Imprints, 1835-1850.* Chicago: W. Howes, 1944.

4168. _____. "A Bibliography of Peoria Imprints, 1835-1860." *Journal of the Illinois State Historical Society* 27 (1934-35): 202-27. Privately reprinted, 1934.

4169. _____. "Early Illinois Copyright Entries, 1821-1850." *Bulletin of the Chicago Historical Society* 2 (1936-37): 50-61, 92-101.

4170. _____. *The First Printers of Chicago, with a Bibliography of the Issues of the Chicago Press, 1836-1850.* Chicago: Cuneo Press, 1927. Also *Notes in Supplement to "The First Printers of Chicago."* Chicago: Privately printed, 1931. Gives the names of printers (who were for the most part newspaper publishers) and titles of the books and pamphlets they printed.

4171. _____. *The First Printing in Peoria, Illinois.* Chicago: Ludlow Typograph, 1929. Brief history of the printers, with a preliminary bibliography of Peoria imprints (excluding newspapers and periodicals), 1835-60.

4172.   *Masters Abstracts.*   [Ann Arbor, Mich.]: University Microfilms International, 1962-85.   In 1986 the title changed to *Masters Abstracts International.*   A cumulative subject index to volumes 1-15 was issued in 1978.

4173.   *Periodical Source Index, 1847-1985.*   Prepared by the Staff of the Allen County Public Library Foundation and the Allen County Public Library Genealogy Department.   8 vols.   Fort Wayne, Ind.: Allen County Public Library Foundation, 1988-90.   Annual volumes cover the years 1986 to date.   This *Index* is a continuing, comprehensive place, subject, and surname index.   When the project is completed, the editors say, more than two thousand periodicals will have been indexed.   In addition to scholarly publications of the states, newsletters of county historical and genealogical societies are also indexed.   Volume 1, for example, has entries arranged first by state general entries, then by county within the state, and then by subject within the county.   Other volumes arrange entries by family name.   Canada and other foreign countries are also covered.

4174.   Peterson, Clarence Stewart, comp.   *Consolidated Bibliography of County Histories in Fifty States in 1961; Consolidated, 1935-1961.*   Baltimore: Genealogical Publishing, 1961.   2d ed., 1963.

4175.   Petterchak, Janice A.   *Researching and Writing Local History in Illinois.*   Illinois Historical Leaflet, no. 1.   Springfield: Illinois State Historical Society, 1987.

4176.   Schlereth, Thomas J.   *The Industrial Belt: An Annotated Bibliography.*   Garland Bibliographies in American Regional Studies, vol. 1; Garland Reference Library of Social Science, vol. 272.   New York: Garland, 1987.   A general bibliography of scholarly works, published principally in the last two decades, for a region that includes northern Illinois.

4177.   Schreiner-Yantis, Netti, comp.   *Genealogical Books in Print: A Catalogue of In-Print Titles . . .*   Springfield, Va.: The author, 1975.   More than 5,000 titles are listed, arranged by subject (where appropriate), by state and geographical regions, and by family.   A second edition, published in 1976, contains approximately 6,000 additional titles; third and fourth editions (1981-90) were published by Genealogical Books in Print, Springfield, Va.   The fourth edition consists of four volumes.   Supplement 1 to volume 4 (1990) is titled *Genealogical & Local History Books in Print.*

4178.   Shipton, Dorothy.   "Illinois: A Bibliography."   *Illinois State University Journal*, vol. 31, no. 2 (December 1986), pp. 15-42.   Approximately four hundred well-chosen titles that include those for juveniles as well as adults.

4179. Smith, Bernice, ed.; Neill, Leslie Ann, comp. *Bibliography of Illinois Materials in the Member Libraries of DuPage Library System.* Wheaton: DuPage Library System, 1968.

4180. Spahn, Betty, and Spahn, Raymond J. "Wesley Raymond Brink, History Huckster." *Journal of the Illinois State Historical Society* 58 (1965): 117-38. Biography of the county-history publisher, with a bibliography.

4181. U.S. Engineer School, Library. *The Mississippi River and Valley: Bibliography, Mostly Non-Technical.* Fort Humphreys, Va.: The Engineer School, 1931. Entries 1-255 deal with discovery and exploration, history and biography, description and travel, and commerce; many of the remaining entries, 256-624, do deal with navigation, geography, and engineering. There is also a section of approximately 300 unnumbered entries that are primarily technical.

4182. Whitney, Ellen M., and Dunn, William R., comps. "Illinois Sesquicentennial Publications: A Preliminary Descriptive Checklist." *Journal of the Illinois State Historical Society* 63 (1970): 422-38. In addition to the special publications of the Illinois Sesquicentennial Commission (many of which are listed separately herein), this checklist includes forty-three county histories and fifteen city and township histories.

4183. Writers' Program, Illinois. *Chicago in Periodical Literature: A Summary of Articles; Sponsored by the State of Illinois Division of Departmental Reports and the Chicago Library Club.* Chicago, 1940. Newspapers and periodicals for the years 1812-71 were searched. Annotated entries, arranged chronologically, include many of statewide interest--on transportation, business, Indians, and agriculture.

4184. Zochert, Donald. "Research Projects in Illinois History." *Journal of the Illinois State Historical Society* 66 (1973): 404-11.

3. Biography and Genealogy (General Sources and Directories)

In addition to collections of biographical sketches, this section includes indexes to biographies and obituaries, and directories of artisans and professional people. The directories generally include little biographical information but are believed nevertheless to be of value to the researcher.

Each *Illinois Blue Book* (no. 4281) also contains biographies of state officials. See also the section Encyclopedias and Statistical Guides, which follows this.

4185. *Abridged Biography and Genealogy Master Index: A Consolidated Index to More Than 1,600,000 Biographical Sketches from over 115 Selected Current and Retrospective Biographical Dictionaries Indexed in Biography and Genealogy Master Index through 1987.* Edited by Barbara McNeil, with the assistance of Amy L. Unterburger. 3 vols. 1st ed., Detroit: Gale Research, 1988.

4186. Arnold, Isaac N. *Reminiscences of the Illinois Bar Forty Years Ago: Lincoln and Douglas as Orators and Lawyers; Read before the "Bar Association of the State of Illinois," Springfield, January 7, 1881.* Fergus' Historical Series, no. 14. Chicago, 1881. Has reminiscences about many other lawyers besides Lincoln and Douglas.

4187. Barrett, Janice Rolison, and Schuller, Jo Coolidge. *Illinois Artisans and Craftsmen: A Guide, Resource, and Reference.* Lexington, Ill.: Insearch, 1982. Sketches of the craftsmen, who discuss the nature of their work, media used, and education. The first in a projected series.

4188. Bentley, Elizabeth Petty. *Directory of Family Associations.* Baltimore: Genealogical Publishing, 1991.

4189. Bergendoff, Conrad. *The Augustana Ministerium: A Study of the Careers of 2,504 Pastors of the Augustana Evangelical Lutheran Synod/Church, 1850-1962.* Rock Island, Ill.: Augustana Historical Society, 1980.

4190. *Biographical Sketches of the Leading Men of Chicago.* Chicago: Wilson & St. Clair, 1868.

4191. Bonham, Jeriah. *Fifty Years' Recollections, with Observations and Reflections of Historical Events, Giving Sketches of Eminent Citizens--Their Lives and Public Service.* Peoria, Ill.: J. W. Franks & Sons, 1883.

4192. Chatten, Mrs. Melville C., comp. *Roll of Revolutionary Ancestors, State of Illinois.* Salt Lake City: Genealogical Society of Utah, 1972.

4193. *Chicago Bar Association Lectures.* Fergus' Historical Series, no. 22. Chicago, 1882. Recollections of the bench and bar by Isaac N. Arnold, James C. Conkling, and Thomas Hoyne.

4194. Collins, David R., and Witter, Evelyn. *Notable Illinois Women.* Rock Island, Ill.: Quest Publishing, 1982. The authors discuss the lives of twelve prominent women and twenty-eight lesser-known women of accomplishment.

4195. Crossley, Frederic B. *Courts and Lawyers of Illinois.* 3 vols. Chicago: American Historical Society, 1916.

4196. Czach, Marie. *A Directory of Early Illinois Photographers: Preliminary Investigations into Photography as Practiced in Illinois, Excluding Chicago, from circa 1846 to 1914.* Rochester, N.Y.: Light Impressions, 1977. The first section of this directory contains brief biographies.

4197. Darby, Edwin. *The Fortune Builders.* Garden City, N.Y.: Doubleday, 1986. Biographies of Chicago capitalists.

4198. Davidson, William T. "Famous Men I Have Known in the Military Tract." *Transactions of the Illinois State Historical Society, 1908,* pp. 153-61.

4199. Devanny, Mildred Smith, comp. *Soldiers of the American Revolution Buried in Illinois.* Edited by Ruth Bitting Hamm. Springfield: Illinois State Genealogical Society, 1975. This volume lists 1,053 Revolutionary War veterans and gives both military and personal information about each. There is an index by county and by name of spouse.

4200. *Directory of Illinois Political Leaders, 1991-1993.* Chicago: Social Engineering Associates, 1990. Includes winners of the 1990 primary and general elections.

4201. Droba, Daniel D. *Czech and Slovak Leaders in Metropolitan Chicago: A Biographical Study of 300 Prominent Men and Women of Czech and Slovak Descent.* Chicago: Slavonic Club of the University of Chicago, 1934.

4202. Field, A. D. *Worthies and Workers, Both Ministers and Laymen, of the Rock River Conference.* Cincinnati: Cranston & Curts, 1896. Sketches of prominent Methodists.

4203. Filby, P. William, comp. *American & British Genealogy & Heraldry: A Selected List of Books.* 2d ed., Chicago: American Library Association, 1975. Has 5,125 titles, arranged by place insofar as possible and then by subject; with an index to authors and subjects. Illinois entries, nos. 1293-1363. The entries are not family histories, but reference works of use to genealogists.

4204. *Genealogical Periodical Annual Index.* Bladensburg, Md.: Genealogical Recorders. Vol. 1 (1962)--to date.

4205. Golembiewski, Thomas E. *Index to Polish American Family Biographies, Found in Jubilee Books of St. Stanislaus Kostka and Holy Trinity Parishes.* Chicago: Polish Genealogical Society, 1982.

4206. Green, Paul M., and Holli, Melvin G., eds. *The Mayors: The Chicago Political Tradition.* Carbondale: Southern Illinois University Press, 1987. Collection of sketches of thirteen Chicago mayors, from Joseph Medill to Harold Washington.

4207. Griffith, Will, ed. *Idols of Egypt* Carbondale, Ill.: Egypt Book House, 1947. Sketches of prominent onetime residents of southern Illinois (known as Egypt): William Jennings Bryan, William E. Borah, William McAndrew, Joseph R. Harker, Robert Green Ingersoll, Elias Kent Kane, Daniel Pope Cook, Mary Logan, Morris Birkbeck, James and Sarah Lusk, Robert Ridgway, and Green Berry Raum.

4208. Harker, Oliver A. "Fifty Years with the Bench and Bar of Southern Illinois." *Transactions of the Illinois State Historical Society, 1920,* pp. 41-53.

4209. Hennessey, LeRoy; Lucas, Carter; Fox, George V.; and Callahan, J. E., comps. and eds. *Bench and Bar of Illinois, 1920.* Chicago: Bench & Bar Publishing, 1920?

4210. Hine, Darlene Clark, et al. *The Black Women in the Middle West Project: A Comprehensive Resource Guide, Illinois and Indiana.* Indianapolis: Indiana Historical Bureau, 1986. The authors compiled information from 245 women, slightly more than one third of whom were from Illinois. That information includes biographical sketches, photographs, and manuscript collections. These items are now in the Illinois State Historical Library and the Library of the Chicago Historical Society.

4211. Hollister, John H. "Biographical Sketches of Some of the Early Physicians of Illinois." *Transactions of the Illinois State Historical Society, 1907*, pp. 164-97.

4212. Hollowak, Thomas L., and Hoffman, William F., comps. *Index to the Obituaries and Death Notices Appearing in the Dziennik Chicagoski, 1890-1899.* Chicago: Polish Genealogical Society, 1984. More than 2,000 listings.

4213. _____, comps. *Index to the Obituaries and Death Notices Appearing in the Dziennik Chicagoski, 1900-1909.* Chicago: Polish Genealogical Society, 1987. More than 12,000 listings.

4214. _____, comps. *Index to the Obituaries and Death Notices Appearing in the Dziennik Chicagoski, 1910-1919.* Chicago: Polish Genealogical Society, 1988. More than 24,000 listings.

4215. _____, comps. *Index to the Obituaries and Death Notices Appearing in the Dziennik Chicagoski, 1920-1929.* 2 vols. Chicago: Polish Genealogical Society, 1991.

4216. Hollowak, Thomas L., comp. *Polish Directory for the City of Chicago, 1903.* Chicago: Polish Genealogical Society, 1981.

4217. Horsley, Jack E. *History of Craig & Craig, Attorneys, 1868-1988.* Ann Arbor, Mich.: Braun-Brumfield, Printers, 1991. History of a Mattoon law firm and its major cases, with biographies of firm members.

4218. Howard, Robert P. *Mostly Good and Competent Men: Illinois Governors, 1818-1988.* Springfield: Illinois Issues, Sangamon State University, and Illinois State Historical Society, 1988.

4219. Husband, Lori, comp. *Deaths in the Chicago Defender, 1910-1920.* Park Forest, Ill.: The compiler, 1990. Lists names alphabetically (along with age of each decedent and date of death) as they appeared in the *Defender's* "Deaths of the Week" column.

4220. Illinois. Adjutant General's Office. *Roll of Honor: Record of Burial Places of Soldiers, Sailors, Marines, and Army Nurses of All Wars of the United States Buried in the State of Illinois.* 2 vols. Springfield, Ill., 1929.

4221. *Illinois and Its Builders: A Work for Newspaper and Library Reference.* Compiled under the direction of the James O. Jones Company. Published by the Illinois Biographical Association, 1925. The biographies were of those prominent in 1925.

4222. *The Illinois Architecture Reference Directory . . .* Chicago: The Illinois Council, The American Institute of Architects and Metropolitan Press Publications. Published annually. The directory also includes a construction and allied industries directory as well as directories for preservation groups, arts organizations, engineering associations, and government organizations.

4223. *Illinois Authors: A Publication of* Read Illinois. Springfield: Illinois State Library, 1983. A 226-page listing that provides biographical information as well as a bibliography of each writer's works.

4224. *Illinois Authors on the Illinois State Library Building.* Springfield: Illinois State Library, n.d. Brief biographical sketches of the thirty-five authors whose names are etched on the fourth-floor frieze of the library building.

4225. *The Illinois Bar: A Directory of Lawyers Located throughout the State of Illinois, and the Rules of Practice.* 1st annual ed., October 1985. Northbrook, Ill.: Bar List Publishing, 1985. There is an alphabetical list, followed by a listing separated into Cook County and non-Cook County. In the latter category attorneys are listed by town. Firm-name entries include names of members of the firm, with law school and date of admission to the bar for each member. There are also lists of state and federal courts and their officers.

4226. *Illinois Marriage Listing.* Published on microfiche. Springfield: Illinois State Genealogical Society, 1994. This ongoing project now includes marriages from sixty-four counties, listed alphabetically by name of both bride and groom and including date of marriage, type of record consulted, and volume and page number (when available).

4227. *Illinois Soldiers' and Sailors' Home of Quincy: Admission of Mexican War and Civil War Veterans, 1887-1898.* Indexed by Lowell M. Volkel. Thomson, Ill.: Heritage House, 1975. A reprint of daily admission records that give information about the solder's military service, his home county, and nature of infirmity. Records for those admitted after 1895 give substantially more personal information.

4228. Johnson, Curtis L. *A Checklist of 19th Century Illinois Gunsmiths: An Introduction to Illinois Gunsmithing.* York, Pa.: Geo. Shumway, 1974. This list, compiled from census returns and city directories, includes about six hundred names.

4229. Judicial Conference of the United States Bicentennial. *Judges of the United States.* 2d ed., Washington: Government Printing Office, 1983. Judges from Illinois or those serving in Illinois are not set out in any way, but this is a valuable source of biographical information not easily available elsewhere.

4230. Kehoe, John E. "Trial Lawyers I Have Known." *Journal of the Illinois State Historical Society* 39 (1946): 179-95. Brief descriptions and characterizations of many of the state's best lawyers in the late nineteenth and early twentieth centuries.

4231. Kinneman, John A. "The School Extends Its Influence." *Journal of the Illinois State Historical Society* 50 (1957): 168-75. Brief accounts of prominent graduates of Illinois State Normal University, 1857-1957.

4232. Lincoln Academy of Illinois. *Hall of Fame of Historic Illinoisans, Established January 31, 1992.* Springfield, 1992. The Lincoln Academy of Illinois was established in 1964 to honor living Illinoisans; to date more than 150 have been so honored. In 1992 a prestigious committee selected the first 50 Illinoisans to be honored posthumously, and additional names will be added to the Hall of Fame periodically. Biographical sketches of the first 50 are presented.

4233. Linder, Usher F. *Reminiscences of the Early Bench and Bar of Illinois.* Introduction and appendix by Joseph Gillespie. Chicago: Chicago Legal News, 1879. The table of contents lists alphabetically the subjects of Linder's sketches, which are candid and idiosyncratic. They include those of several prominent men who were not attorneys.

4234. "List of Pensioners, Chicago and Cook County, Illinois, January 1, 1883." Mimeographed. Chicago: Chicago Genealogical Society, 1985. This list (extracted from volume 3 of the roll printed by the Government Printing Office, Washington), gives the pensioner's name, reason for pension, post office address, rate of payment, and date of original pension.

4235. Lunde, Mrs. O. B., comp. *Illinois State Genealogical Society Surname Index, 1981.* Decatur: Illinois State Genealogical Society, 1981.

4236. Michals, Mary Catherine, comp. "Index to Biographical Sketches in the Minutes of the Annual Meeting of the Illinois Baptist General Association, 1847-1905." Typescript, 1977. Springfield: Illinois State Historical Library.

4237. Middeke, Raphael H., and Konieczny, Stanley J., eds. *Profiles from Our Heritage: Stories of Catholics Who Helped Shape the Church of Southern Illinois.* St. Louis: Patrice Press, 1987.

4238. Moeller, Josephine S., ed. "Genealogical Collection III." *Illinois Libraries* 74 (1992): 395-479. Articles in the November issue are divided into two sections: Illinois library holdings related to ethnic history and those related to church history.

4239. Ness, George T. Jr. "Illinois at West Point: Her Graduates in the Civil War." *Journal of the Illinois State Historical Society* 35 (1942): 338-46.

4240. *Notable Men of Illinois & Their State.* Chicago: Chicago Daily Journal, 1912.

4241. Palmer, John M., ed. *The Bench and the Bar of Illinois: Historical and Reminiscent.* 2 vols. Chicago: Lewis Publishing, 1899.

4242. Parmalee, Paul W., and Loomis, Forrest D. *Decoys and Decoy Carvers of Illinois.* DeKalb: Northern Illinois University Press, 1969. After general discussions of hunting and decoy construction, biographical information about carvers and discussions of their work are presented by region. There is a good index to both the text and the many illustrations.

4243. Phillips, David Lyman. *Biographies of the State Officers and Thirty-third General Assembly of Illinois.* Springfield, Ill.: Biographical Publishing, 1883. A predecessor to the *Blue Book of the State of Illinois,* which began appearing regularly in 1903.

4244. *Prominent Democrats of Illinois: A Brief History of the Rise and Progress of the Democratic Party of Illinois; Biographical Sketches of Well Known Democratic Leaders . . .* Chicago: Democrat Publishing, 1899.

4245. Quilici, George L. *The Italian American Lawyers of Chicago.* 4th ed., Chicago: Justinian Society of Lawyers, 1968.

4246. Redmond, Mary, comp. *Mr. Speaker: Presiding Officers of the Illinois House of Representatives, 1818-1980.* An annotated collection of biographies of fifty-six Speakers.

4247. *Republicans of Illinois: A Portrait and Chronological Record of Members of the Republican Party.* Chicago: Lewis Publishing, 1905.

4248. Sawyers, June Skinner. *Chicago Portraits: Biographies of 250 Famous Chicagoans.* Chicago: Loyola University Press, 1991.

4249. Schulz, Mildred Valette, comp. "Index to Biographical Sketches in the Minutes of the Annual Meetings of the Illinois Baptist State Convention, 1906-1958." Typescript, 1978.   Springfield: Illinois State Historical Library.

4250. Scott, John M. *Supreme Court of Illinois, 1818: Its First Judges and Lawyers; Short Sketches.* Bloomington, Ill., 1896.

4251. Snively, E. A. "Newspapers and Newspaper Men of Illinois." *Transactions of the Illinois State Historical Society, 1904,* pp. 205-13. Valuable primarily for the characterizations of early newspapermen.

4252. Sobel, Robert, and Raimo, John W., eds. *Biographical Directory of the Governors of the United States, 1789-1978.* 4 vols. Westport, Conn.: Meckler, 1978. Supp. 1 for 1978-83, edited by John W. Raimo, published 1985; supp. 2 for 1983-88, edited by Marie Marmo Mullaney, published 1989. In the four-volume set, see volume 1, pages 365-92, for Illinois governors.

4253. *Soldiers' and Patriots' Biographical Album, Containing Biographies and Portraits of Soldiers and Loyal Citizens in the American Conflict, together with the Great Commanders of the Union Army, also a History of the Organizations Growing out of the War . . .* Chicago: Union Veteran Publishing, 1892.

4254. Sparks, Esther. "A Biographical Dictionary of Painters and Sculptors in Illinois, 1808-1945." Ph.D. dissertation, Northwestern University, 1971.

4255. Sperry, F. M., comp. *A Group of Distinguished Physicians and Surgeons of Chicago: A Collection of Biographical Sketches of Many of the Eminent Representatives, Past and Present, of the Medical Profession of Chicago.* Chicago: J. H. Beers, 1904.

4256. Sprague, Stuart Seely. *Kentuckians in Illinois.* Baltimore: Genealogical Publishing, 1987. The author searched biographical sketches in Illinois county histories and arranged names of native-born Kentuckians by their county of origin, together with other biographical information. There is an index.

4257. Sutton, Amy Louise. "Revolutionary War Veterans and Other Pensioners Listed in the 1840 Federal Census for Illinois." *Illinois Libraries* 48 (1966): 463-69. This supplements information given in Harriet J. Walker's *Revolutionary Soldiers Buried in Illinois,* q.v.

4258. *The United States Biographical Dictionary and Portrait Gallery of Eminent and Self-Made Men; Illinois Volume.* Chicago: American Biographical Publishing, 1876; also an 1883 ed.

4259. Volkel, Lowell M., ed. "Genealogical Collections in Illinois." *Illinois Libraries* 68 (1986): 244-84. Thirteen articles on genealogical collections and research at ten major research institutions in Illinois. This was the first issue devoted entirely to such collections.

4260. _____, ed. "Genealogical Collections II." *Illinois Libraries* 70 (1988): 479-537. The entire September issue is devoted to genealogical research. The first article, "Genealogical Research in the County Courthouse," is by Doris Roney Bowers. The remaining twenty-two articles discuss genealogical collections at twenty-two public libraries in the state.

4261. Walker, Harriet J. *Revolutionary Soldiers Buried in Illinois.* Los Angeles: Standard Printing, 1917. Reprint, Baltimore: Genealogical Publishing, 1967. Superseded by *Soldiers of the American Revolution Buried in Illinois,* compiled by Mildred Smith Devanny; edited by Ruth Bitting Hamm. Springfield: Illinois State Genealogical Society, 1976. The Walker volume contains slightly more biographical information.

4262. Walton, Clyde C., ed. *Illinois Lives: The Prairie State Biographical Record.* Hopkinsville, Ky.: Historical Record Association, 1969.

4263. Warner, Ezra G. *Generals In Blue: Lives of the Union Commanders.* Baton Rouge: Louisiana State University Press, 1964.

4264. *Who's Who in Chicago and Illinois.* Chicago: A. N. Marquis. The title changed several times after 1905 when the first edition appeared as *The Book of Chicagoans.* In 1941 the volume was enlarged to include the state.

4. Encyclopedias and Statistical Guides

4265. Allen, Howard W., and Lacey, Vincent A., eds. *Illinois Elections, 1880-1990: Candidates and County Returns for President, Governor, Senate, and House of Representatives.* Carbondale: Southern Illinois University Press, 1992.

4266. Barone, Michael; Ujifusa, Grant; and Matthews, Douglas. *The Almanac of American Politics: The Senators, the Representatives--Their Records, States and Districts, 1972.* Boston: Gambit, 1972. A continuing series, appearing every two years, from different publishers, most recently from National Journal. The political background analyses for each district are particularly valuable.

4267. Bateman, Newton, and Selby, Paul, eds. *Historical Encyclopedia of Illinois.* Chicago: Munsell, 1900. There were many later editions, and the volume was also published as part of the histories of forty-three counties. It was frequently reissued under slightly varying titles and as a two- or three-volume set (Joseph Seymour Currey, et al., eds.), beginning in 1920. For a sound criticism of these volumes, see Davis, no. 4147.

4268. *The Book of the States.* Chicago: Council of State Governments. Vol. 1 (1935)--to date. Published biennially. Statistical information about all aspects of government, from tax revenues to numbers of state employees to public school attendance to low-level radioactive waste distribution.

4269. *Catalog of State Assistance to Local Governments: Third Edition.* Springfield: Illinois Commission on Intergovernmental Cooperation, 1989. Information (arranged by state agency) describes the kind of assistance, eligibility, funds available, legislative authority, and address and phone number for the state agency involved. There is also a subject index for kinds of assistance. Published every two years.

4270. Clayton, John, comp. *The Illinois Fact Book and Historical Almanac, 1673-1968.* Carbondale: Southern Illinois University Press, 1970. A reference combining biographies, statistics, general information, and history. Indexed by subject.

4271. Clements, John. *Illinois Facts: A Comprehensive Look at Illinois Today, County by County.* Dallas: Clements Research II, 1989. The first 57 pages of this 437-page volume present an overview of Illinois--its climate and environment, economy, transportation, community resources, government, population and election statistics, etc. Similar information is given for each of Illinois' 102 counties. The volume concludes with a chronological history (given by county) and a list of place names with map locations and zip codes.

4272. Colby, Charles. *Pilot Study of Southern Illinois.* Carbondale: Southern Illinois University Press, 1956. Primarily a statistical study of the thirty-four southernmost counties of Illinois.

4273. Eldridge, Grant J., ed. *Encyclopedia of Associations: Regional, State, and Local Organizations . . . 1992-93; Volume 1: Great Lakes States . . .* 3d ed., Detroit: Gale Research, 1992. Illinois, pp. 1-149. Entries, arranged by city, include every type of organization from those of marriage counsellors to grain-elevator managers.

4274. *First Chicago Guide: A Scholl Corporate Guide, 1993-94; Major Publicly Held Corporations and Financial Institutions Headquartered in Illinois.* Deerfield, Ill.: Scholl Communications, Inc., 1993. This guide, sponsored by First Chicago Corporation since 1984, covers all of Illinois and lists banks and savings institutions as well as public corporations. The volume provides a brief description of each company, the names of directors and other officers, and a consolidated balance sheet and income statement. Companies are listed alphabetically and indexed by classification.

4275. Fremon, David K. *Chicago Politics, Ward by Ward.* Bloomington: Indiana University Press, 1988. A brief history of each of the fifty wards, with population statistics, vote in the 1983 and 1987 mayoral elections, and names of community newspapers, aldermen, and party committeemen.

4276. Gove, Samuel Kimball, ed. *Illinois Votes, 1900-1958: A Compilation of Illinois Election Statistics.* Urbana: Institute of Government and Public Affairs, University of Illinois, 1959. A supplement, titled "Illinois Votes, 1960-1962," appears in *Illinois Government* (a newsletter issued by the Institute), March 1964.

4277. *Harris Illinois Industrial Directory.* Twinsburg, Ohio: Harris Publishing. Issued annually under varying titles and by different publishers. Includes companies listed alphabetically by name, by geographical location, and by product (i.e., printing and publishing, chemicals, etc.). There are also statistical tables for the state.

4278. Heise, Kenan, and Frazel, Mark. *Hands on Chicago.* Chicago: Bonus Books, 1987. The first part of the book, the authors say, is a "mini-encyclopedia" of Chicago, and the second part describes seventy-seven Chicago neighborhoods.

4279. Historical Records Survey, Illinois. *Guide to Church Vital Statistics Records in Illinois; Preliminary Ed.* Chicago: Illinois Historical Records Survey, 1942.

4280. _____. *Guide to Public Vital Statistics Records in Illinois.* Chicago: Illinois Historical Records Survey, 1941. Reprint, Thomson, Ill.: Heritage House, 1976, with a copy of the state vital records act as amended in 1975.

4281. Illinois. Secretary of State. *Blue Book of the State of Illinois* (now called *Illinois Blue Book*). A source for Illinois local and state government. Published since 1903, it now appears every two years and contains biographies of judges and members of the General Assembly and of Congress, as well as reports on state agencies. The volume for 1931-32 lists all state legislators and officers (including judges) and Illinois members of Congress from 1818 to 1932; it also includes an index to previous issues of the *Blue Book.*

4282. Illinois Chamber of Commerce. *Illinois: Resources, Development, Possibilities.* Chicago: Illinois Chamber of Commerce, 1930. Illinois at the end of the 1920s.

4283. *Illinois Manufacturers Directory.* Chicago: Manufacturers' News. Published annually since 1912. Includes a buyers' guide, an alphabetical listing of manufacturers and processors as well as listings of those firms by location and by standard industrial classification. There are also marketing statistics by sections and counties, and a computer index that names the firms using the various computers on the market.

4284. Illinois State Historical Library/Society. "Courthouse Project Records." Manuscript in Illinois State Historical Library. Drafts of chapters for a history of Illinois' 102 county courthouses. Each chapter also contains information about early court cases and county government.

4285. Johnson, Daniel Milo, and Veach, Rebecca Monroe, eds. *The Middle-Size Cities of Illinois: Their People, Politics, and Quality of Life.* Springfield, Ill.: Sangamon State University, 1980. Studies of eight communities (Bloomington-Normal, Champaign-Urbana, Decatur, East St. Louis, Peoria, Rockford, Rock Island-Moline, and Springfield) sponsored by the Center for the Study of Middle-Size Cities at Sangamon State and written by sociologists, historians, journalists, and political scientists. Tables of statistical information conclude the volume.

4286. Layer, Robert G. *The Fundamental Bases of the Economy of Southern Illinois, 1879-1959.* Regional Studies in Business and Economics, monograph no. 2. Carbondale: Business Research Bureau, Southern Illinois University, 1965.

4287. Leighton, Morris M., comp. *Illinois Resources: An Atlas.* Chicago: Illinois Post-war Planning Commission, 1944. A report on natural resources, mining, trade, transportation, public utilities, agriculture, and industry. Insofar as possible, the statistics are presented through maps.

4288. Lohmann, Karl B. *Cities and Towns of Illinois: A Handbook of Community Facts.* Urbana: University of Illinois Press, 1951.

4289. Meyer, Douglas K., and Sublett, Michael D. *East Central Illinois: A Look into the Future.* Normal: Department of Geography-Geology, Illinois State University, 1980.

4290. Moses, John. *Illinois: Historical and Statistical.* 2 vols. Chicago: Fergus Printing, 1889. Still a useful source because of its detail and statistics.

4291. Norton, Margaret Cross, ed. *Illinois Census Returns, 1810, 1818,* and *Illinois Census Returns, 1820.* Collections of the Illinois State Historical Library, vols. 24 and 26. Springfield, 1935 and 1934. Reprints, Baltimore: Genealogical Publishing, 1969.

4292. Peyton, John Lewis. *A Statistical View of the State of Illinois, to Which Is Appended an Article upon the City of Chicago.* Chicago: Spaulding & Tobey, 1855. Reprinted from *Hunt's Merchants' Magazine* 32 (1855): 56-66, 320-32.

4293. Roberts, Robert B. *Encyclopedia of Historic Forts: The Military, Pioneer, and Trading Posts of the United States.* New York: Macmillan, 1988. Approximately 150 Illinois forts, camps, and posts are located, and some described, on pages 255-71.

4294. Southern Illinois Executive Committee. *Southern Illinois: Resources and Potentials of the Sixteen Southernmost Counties.* Urbana: University of Illinois Press, 1949.

4295. Sweet, O. P. *Sweet's Amusement Directory and Travelers' Guide from the Atlantic to the Pacific, Containing Historical Sketches and Statistical Records, with Population, Railway and Steamboat Transit, Public Buildings, Halls, Hotels, Newspapers, Printers, Bill Posters, Baggage Expresses, etc., with Maps of the Railroad and Steamboat Routes, and Distances between Places.* Rochester, N.Y.: Travelers' Publishing, 1870-71. Among other information are listings and descriptions of opera houses, together with the names of their proprietors.

4296. Trkla, Pettigrew, Allen & Payne. *Area-wide Economic and Industrial Growth Analysis of the Illinois and Michigan Canal National Heritage Corridor.* Prepared for the Upper Illinois Valley Association. Chicago: The association, 1988.

4297. Van der Slik, Jack R., ed. *Almanac of Illinois Politics, 1992.* Springfield: Illinois Issues, 1992. Contains much information not easily available elsewhere, such as key votes of legislative members, public-action committee ratings, campaign contributions to each General Assembly member, as well as demographic information for each legislative district.

5. Research Resources

a. Libraries, Historical Museums, and Research Institutions
(Directories and Guides)

4298.   American Association for State and Local History. *Directory of Historical Organizations in the United States and Canada.* 14th ed., Nashville, Tenn., 1990. Entries are arranged by state, and by town within the state sections. There is a general index by name of institution and a special interest index that arranges entries by category, e.g., genealogy, historic persons; there is also a listing of historical and archaeological areas administered by the National Park Service.

4299. *American Library Directory, 1992-93.* 2 vols. 45th ed., New York: R. R. Bowker, 1992. Illinois, vol. 1, pp. 447-558. Issued annually.

4300. Cavanaugh, Karen B. *A Genealogist's Guide to the Ft. Wayne, Indiana, Public Library.* Ft. Wayne, Ind.: The author, 1980. A useful guide to one of the nation's preeminent genealogical collections.

4301. Cerny, Johni, and Elliott, Wendy, eds. *The Library: A Guide to the LDS Family History Library.* Salt Lake City: Ancestry Publishing, 1988.

4302. *Directory of Local Historical Collections in Northern Illinois.* Compiled by a Task Force of the Genealogy and Local History Interest Group of the Illinois Regional Library Council, 1981. Chicago: Illinois Regional Library Council, 1981. The directory lists 300 institutions in 23 northern Illinois counties and indicates the types of holdings each has--photographs, manuscripts, monographs, newspapers, books, and pamphlets.

4303. Filby, P. William, comp. *Directory of American Libraries with Genealogy or Local History Collections.* Wilmington, Del.: Scholarly Resources, 1988. Illinois, pp. 52-64.

4304. *Historical and Cultural Agencies and Museums in Illinois, 1993-94.* Springfield: Association of Illinois Museums and Historical Societies, 1993. A listing by town (with address, telephone number, name of chief officer, hours of operation, and a listing of principal holdings and events), with an index by county and a general index. The listing includes college and university libraries and museums. Reissued periodically.

4305. Historical Records Survey, Illinois. *Guide to Depositories of Manuscript Collections in Illinois, Preliminary Edition.* Chicago: Illinois Historical Records Survey Project, 1940.

4306. Kaminkow, Marion J., ed. *United States Local Histories in the Library of Congress: A Bibliography.* Baltimore: Magna Carta Book Co., 1975. 5 vols. Illinois, 140 pp. of listings (approximately 15 items per page) in vol. 3.

4307. Makower, Joel, ed., and Zaleskie, Linda, assoc. ed. *The American History Sourcebook.* A Tilden Press Book. New York: Prentice-Hall, 1988. Illinois, pp. 109-24. The editors list 108 Illinois research institutions or museums and briefly describe their holdings.

4308. National Historical Publications and Records Commission. *Directory of Archives and Manuscript Repositories in the United States.* 2d ed., Phoenix: Oryx Press, 1988.

4309. Neagles, James C., assisted by Mark C. Neagles. *The Library of Congress: A Guide to Genealogical and Historical Research.* Salt Lake City: Ancestry Publishing, 1990.

4310. Reithmaier, Tina M., ed. *A Guide to the Cultural Resources in Illinois.* Springfield, Ill.: Office of the Secretary of State, 1988. Includes contributions by several authors, on archival collections as well as the Illinois State Archives, genealogical and historical societies, historic sites, libraries, the Illinois State Library, the Illinois State Historical Library, general museums and living farm museums, as well as articles on training programs, funding, and bibliographies of general reference guides and of periodicals published in the state.

4311. Sinko, Peggy Tuck. *Guide to Local and Family History at the Newberry Library.* Salt Lake City: Ancestry Publishing, 1987. A researcher working in any library in any field will find this superb guide to Newberry's holdings of inestimable value.

4312. Southern Illinois History Project. *Southern Illinois History Inventory.* Carterville, Ill.: Shawnee Library System, 1983. An inventory of southern Illinois history and genealogy materials that are available through the Shawnee Library System.

4313. *The Swenson Swedish Immigration Research Center of Rock Island: A Guide to Resources and Holdings.* Reprinted from *Swedish American*

Genealogist, March 1984. The center, at Augustana College, holds books, periodicals, newspapers, original manuscripts, photographs, and microfilms.

4314. Whittaker, Mary Jo. *Museums of Illinois*. Salem, Ill.: Weekends, Inc., 1974. Descriptions of the collections of Illinois museums.

b. Manuscript and Archival Holdings (Descriptions, Guides, and Reproductions)

(1) Of the Illinois State Historical Library

(a) Lincolniana

4315. Angle, Paul McClelland. "The Record of a Friendship: A Series of Letters from Lincoln to Henry E. Dummer." *Journal of the Illinois State Historical Society* 31 (1938): 125-37. Eleven letters, 1842-60, printed with the article, concern politics and the practice of law.

4316. " 'The Coming Rude Storms' of Lincoln's Writings: William H. Herndon and the Lincoln Legend." *Journal of the Illinois State Historical Society* 71 (1978): 66-70. Letters from Herndon and Richard J. Oglesby and extracts from Herndon's famous two-part speech in 1865 on the character of Lincoln.

4317. " 'Every body likes to shake hands with him'--Letters of Elbridge Atwood." *Journal of the Illinois State Historical Society* 72 (1979): 139-42. Letters, 1860-65, of a young Springfield man, describe Springfield, Abraham Lincoln, and the community's attitudes towards him.

4318. "From Dr. Shutes' Lincoln Collection." *Journal of the Illinois State Historical Society* 47 (1954): 312-14. Four Lincolniana items given to the Illinois State Historical Library by Dr. Milton H. Shutes.

4319. "A Generous Lincoln Collector." *Journal of the Illinois State Historical Society* 47 (1954): 68-70. Lincoln's letter of 4 November 1851 to John D. Johnston, presented to the Illinois State Historical Library by Foreman M. Lebold, is reproduced.

4320. Hickey, James T. "His Father's Son: Letters from the Robert Todd Lincoln Collection of the Illinois State Historical Library." *Journal of the Illinois State Historical Society* 73 (1980): 215-34.

4321. _____. "Lincolniana." *Journal of the Illinois State Historical Society* 65 (1972): 101-2, 206-9. Reproduced from the manuscript collections of the Illinois State Historical Library are an 1851 letter from Abraham Lincoln about the Alton and Sangamon Railroad case, an 1860 letter from Mary Lincoln, and an 1861 letter about her.

4322. _____. "Robert S. Todd Seeks a Job for His Son-in-Law Abraham Lincoln." *Journal of the Illinois State Historical Society* 72 (1979): 273-76. A letter from the Robert Todd Lincoln Collection in the Illinois State Historical Library illustrates the esteem in which Robert Todd held Lincoln, who had recently handled a law case for him.

4323. _____. "Robert Todd Lincoln and His Father's Grave Robbers; or, Left in the Lurch by the Secret Service." *Illinois Historical Journal* 77 (1984): 295-300. Letters in the Robert Todd Lincoln Collection reveal how Robert Lincoln helped financially to keep witnesses in Springfield to assist in the prosecution of the unsuccessful grave robbers.

4324. _____. "Robert Todd Lincoln and the 'Purely Private' Letters of the Lincoln Family." *Journal of the Illinois State Historical Society* 74 (1981): 59-79. History of the papers of Abraham Lincoln gathered by his son Robert Todd Lincoln and a discussion of the final disposition of those papers as well as of Robert Lincoln's own papers.

4325. _____. "A Small Receipt Reveals a Large Story." *Journal of the Illinois State Historical Society* 75 (1982): 73-80. The document illustrates Lincoln's legal practice in the 1840s.

4326. _____. "Some Robert Todd Lincoln Letters on the 'dreadful statue' by George Gray Barnard." *Journal of the Illinois State Historical Society* 73 (1980): 132-39. Robert Lincoln's dislike of the statue was buttressed by letters from people who had known Lincoln and described his appearance.

4327. "Last Pair of Gloves A. Lincoln Wore." *Journal of the Illinois State Historical Society* 49 (1956): 333-34. The gloves, along with other mementos, are part of a collection, presented by Philip R. Baker, that includes letters from Mary Todd Lincoln, David J. Baker, and Elizabeth Todd Edwards.

4328. "Lincoln and the Town of Huron." *Journal of the Illinois State Historical Society* 49 (1956): 419-21. Lincoln surveyed the site for the town, which never materialized. The original survey with Lincoln's certificate is in the Illinois State Historical Library.

4329. "Lincoln Carries Lake Fork Precinct." *Journal of the Illinois State Historical Society* 49 (1956): 329-31. An account by Hawkins Taylor of election procedures in Sangamon County in 1834, when Lincoln was first elected state representative.

4330. "Lincoln Documents from Logan County." *Journal of the Illinois State Historical Society* 45 (1952): 184-85. Eight legal documents transferred to the Illinois State Historical Library.

4331. "Lincoln Favors an Old Friend." *Journal of the Illinois State Historical Society* 46 (1953): 430-31. A letter requesting discharge for a Civil War soldier, with Lincoln's endorsement of approval.

4332. "Lincolniana." *Journal of the Illinois State Historical Society* 67 (1974): 120-23. A previously unknown letter, 6 April 1860, in which Lincoln discusses how various national politicians might be expected to fare in Illinois.

4333. "Lincolniana." *Journal of the Illinois State Historical Society* 72 (1979): 71. A brief description of the Robert Todd Lincoln Collection in the Illinois State Historical Library. Of primary interest are forty-six letter books containing copies of approximately twenty thousand pieces of outgoing mail, 1865-1912, from Robert Todd Lincoln.

4334. "Lincoln's Cane on Display." *Journal of the Illinois State Historical Society* 47 (1954): 190-91. The provenance of the cane in the collections of the Illinois State Historical Library.

4335. "Mr. Lincoln Leaves for Washington" [Entry of 11 February 1861 from diary of Henry C. Latham]. *Journal of the Illinois State Historical Society* 34 (1941): 135. Original manuscript in the Illinois State Historical Library.

4336. "The Original of a February 12, 1809 Story." *Journal of the Illinois State Historical Society* 43 (1950): 137-39. Dunham Wright's manuscript relating his grandmother's account of serving as midwife at the birth of Lincoln.

4337. "A Petition Signed by Lincoln." *Journal of the Illinois State Historical Society* 46 (1953): 190. The petition, addressed to Sangamon County commissioners, was for a bridge over Rock Creek.

4338. Pratt, Harry Edward. "Lincolniana in the Illinois State Historical Library." *Journal of the Illinois State Historical Society* 46 (1953): 373-400. General description of the books, manuscripts, and memorabilia related to Lincoln, as well as Lincoln's own letters, in the library's collections.

4339. _____. "The Lincolns Go Shopping." *Journal of the Illinois State Historical Society* 48 (1955): 65-81. The Abraham Lincoln accounts, 1842-53, at two Springfield business firms.

4340. _____. "Only Known Photograph of Lincoln in His Coffin." *Journal of the Illinois State Historical Society* 45 (1952): 252-56. The plates and all copies of the 24 April 1865 photograph were ordered destroyed. This one surviving print was discovered in the Nicolay and Hay Collection in the Illinois State Historical Library.

4341. "Presentation of Barrett Manuscripts" and "Barrett Lincoln Fund Presentation." *Journal of the Illinois State Historical Society* 45 (1952): 70-72, 181-82. Account of the purchase in 1952 by the Illinois State Historical Library of Lincolniana items in the Oliver R. Barrett Collection, and a description of the major items.

4342. "A Problem of Patronage." *Journal of the Illinois State Historical Society* 50 (1957): 65-66. An 1861 Lincoln letter is reproduced and discussed.

4343. "The Problem of the Welcoming Speech." *Journal of the Illinois State Historical Society* 44 (1951): 170-72. Manuscript of a speech by Milton Hay welcoming Lincoln back to Springfield following his Cooper Union speech. The "problem" of the speech is that there is no record of its date or place of delivery, and it may have been a letter prepared on behalf of the Republican Club of Springfield.

4344. "A Rare Autographed Photograph." *Journal of the Illinois State Historical Society* 46 (1953): 294-96. The provenance of an autographed Lincoln photograph.

4345. "Rare Lincoln Campaign Newspapers." *Journal of the Illinois State Historical Society* 46 (1953): 188-90. Description of items acquired by the

Illinois State Historical Library. These short-run newspapers were issued for the 1860 presidential campaign.

4346. "Rare Lincolniana Presented to Library." *Journal of the Illinois State Historical Society* 47 (1954): 414. Five Lincolniana items, including three volumes, in loose-leaf binders, of photographs collected by Frederick Hill Meserve.

4347. Schwartz, Thomas F. " 'About new powder': An Unpublished Lincoln Note." *Illinois Historical Journal* 84 (1991): 119-24. Lincoln's interest in gunpowder developed by a Springfield acquaintance.

4348. _____. "Grief, Souvenirs, and Enterprise Following Lincoln's Assassination." *Illinois Historical Journal* 83 (1990): 259-64. Three items related to Lincoln and his family, two of which are in the collections of the Illinois State Historical Library.

4349. Segal, Charles M. "Lincoln, Benjamin Jonas, and the Black Code." *Journal of the Illinois State Historical Society* 46 (1953): 277-82. Lincoln used the services in 1857 of Benjamin Jonas (son of Abraham Jonas of Quincy) to purchase the freedom of an Illinois free black who had been imprisoned in New Orleans for being on the street without his "free papers." The indenture of apprenticeship for the "free black," John Shelby, is in the Illinois State Historical Library; *see* "Postscript to the 'Black Code' Article," ibid., pp. 428-30.

4350. " 'Took Tea at Mrs. Lincoln's': The Diary of Mrs. William M. Black." *Journal of the Illinois State Historical Society* 48 (1955): 59-64. Diary entries illustrate the close relationship between Mary Lincoln and Elizabeth Black in Springfield.

4351. Zane, Charles S. "Impressions of Herndon and Lincoln." Edited by James T. Hickey. *Journal of the Illinois State Historical Society* 64 (1971): 206-9. Zane moved to Springfield in 1856 to study law in the Lincoln and Herndon firm. His reminiscences of those days were recorded much later.

(b) Other Collections

4352. "Andrus and Deere Contracts," "Three Letters by Robert Todd Lincoln," "Letters to Ozias Mather Hatch," "Yates Biography and Autobiography," "Letters to Isaac Funk," "Additions to the Grierson Papers,"

"Four Letters from John Russell." *Journal of the Illinois State Historical Society* 46 (1953): 213-17.

4353. Bowen, Laurel G., and Michals, Mary Catherine. "The Scott Wike Lucas Collection: Manuscripts and Audiovisual Resources." *Illinois Historical Journal* 77 (1984): 193-96. A brief guide to the papers of United States Senator Lucas, dating from 1918 through 1968. A 220-page inventory is in the Historical Library.

4354. Brubaker, Robert L. *The David Davis Family Papers, 1816-1943: A Descriptive Inventory.* Manuscripts in the Illinois State Historical Library, no. 3. Springfield: Illinois State Historical Library, 1965.

4355. _____. *The King Family Papers, 1798-1927: A Descriptive Inventory.* Manuscripts in the Illinois State Historical Library, no. 1. Springfield: Illinois State Historical Library, 1963.

4356. _____. *Manuscripts Acquired during 1963: A Descriptive Inventory.* Manuscripts in the Illinois State Historical Library, no. 2. Springfield: Illinois State Historical Library, 1964.

4357. "Dr. Samuel A. Mudd Papers." *Journal of the Illinois State Historical Society* 46 (1953): 425-28.

4358. Felt, Thomas E. "The Stephen A. Douglas Letters in the State Historical Library." *Journal of the Illinois State Historical Society* 56 (1963): 677-91.

4359. "General Benjamin H. Grierson's Papers." *Journal of the Illinois State Historical Society* 45 (1952): 280-82. Two thousand letters and some army records, 1854-91.

4360. "General John Charles Black's Papers." *Journal of the Illinois State Historical Society* 47 (1954): 330-32. Description of the large collection of papers of the Civil War general, congressman, and attorney from Danville.

4361. "General Parsons Writes of Lincoln's Death." *Journal of the Illinois State Historical Library* 44 (1951): 355-56. The letter reproduced is from the papers of Lewis Baldwin Parsons.

4362. "The Grant-McClernand Civil War Feud." *Journal of the Illinois State Historical Society* 44 (1951): 251-53. The more than two hundred Grant letters in the Illinois State Historical Library illustrate many aspects of his character and military philosophy.

4363. "Grant's Letters to Elihu B. Washburne." *Journal of the Illinois State Historical Society* 45 (1952): 257-61. Fifty-eight letters are briefly described.

4364. *Guide to the Microfilm Edition of the Pierre Menard Collection in the Illinois State Historical Library.* Paul D. Spence, project director; Kathrine Wagner Seineke, editor; and Emily W. Adler, assistant. Springfield: Illinois State Historical Society, 1972. The collection is now available in a 28-reel microfilm edition.

4365. *Illinois History: A Magazine for Young People,* vol. 42, no. 8 (May 1989). This special issue constitutes a guide to the book and manuscript resources of the Illinois State Historical Library. Valuable to adult students of history as well as the magazine's usual audience, articles concern the following subjects: the Historical Library itself, newspapers, Illinois as frontier, Native American history, the Black Hawk War Collection, Mormon history, the Lincoln Collection, the Civil War, politics and politicians, United States senators and representatives from Illinois, labor history, women's history, family history, and Illinois governors.

4366. Illinois State Historical Library. Manuscript acquisitions and guides. Four numbers in a series titled Manuscripts in the Illinois State Historical Library were published, 1963-67 (see nos. 4354-56 and 4377). A separate guide not in this series is no. 4364.

In the years 1958 through 1976 and 1979 through 1984, a listing of major manuscript acquisitions appeared in the *Journal of the Illinois State Historical Society.* In 1956, manuscript acquisitions were described in the *Journal* on pages 253-54 and 333-34. In 1979-84 the listing appeared as part of the director's annual report, also published in the *Journal.*

Now in progress is a complete listing of the library's manuscript holdings with the Online Computer Library Center, Inc.

Many major collections are listed in the *National Union Catalog of Manuscript Collections* and are being input into the Research Libraries Information Network.

Complete inventories of 113 manuscript collections have been contributed to the *National Inventory of Documentary Sources* and are available on microfiche.

4367. "Library Receives Grant and Green Letters." *Journal of the Illinois State Historical Society* 44 (1951): 83. Eight Civil War letters by Ulysses S. Grant and twenty-four Revolutionary War letters by Nathanael Green.

4368. "Lincoln before a New York Audience." *Journal of the Illinois State Historical Society* 49 (1956): 213-15. Lincoln's Springfield friend Mason Brayman describes Lincoln's presentation at Cooper Union and contrasts it with his style "at home." This is one of approximately fifteen hundred items in the Bailhache-Brayman Papers.

4369. Michals, Mary Catherine. "Photograph Acquisitions." *Journal of the Illinois State Historical Society* 74 (1981): 297-301. A history of the Prints and Photographs Section of the Illinois State Historical Library, with brief descriptions of eight major collections.

4370. "Microfilm Collections of Periodicals, Manuscripts, and Miscellany in the Illinois State Historical Library." *Illinois Libraries* 47 (1965): 276-81. Also reprinted separately.

4371. Petterchak, Janice A. "Rare Photographs of Illinois Congressmen." *Journal of the Illinois State Historical Society* 71 (1978): 57-65. A description of the Charles Lanman Collection of papers and photographs he had acquired as compiler, for five years, of the *Dictionary of the United States Congress*, 1859-63. Nine photographs and biographical sketches are reproduced.

4372. _____. "Resources for the Study of Labor History at the Illinois State Historical Library." *Labor's Heritage*, October 1991, pp. 50-55.

4373. Plummer, Mark A., ed. " 'Goodbye dear Governor. You are my best friend': The Private Letters of Robert G. Ingersoll to Richard J. Oglesby, 1867-1877." *Journal of the Illinois State Historical Society* 73 (1980): 78-116. The twenty-seven letters from the Oglesby Family Papers contain many political allusions, which the editor places in perspective.

4374. _____. "Robert G. Ingersoll and the Sensual Gods: An Unpublished Letter." *Western Illinois Regional Studies* 3 (1980): 168-72. The 1870 letter to Governor Richard Oglesby is from the Oglesby Family Papers in the Illinois State Historical Library, which also holds an extensive Ingersoll Collection.

4375. Pratt, Harry Edward. "Lewis B. Parsons: Mover of Armies and Railroad Builder." *Journal of the Illinois State Historical Society* 44 (1951): 349-57. Description of some of the five thousand items in the General Lewis Baldwin Parsons Papers in the Illinois State Historical Library. Approximately half of the papers are concerned with Parsons' career in the Civil War, in which he ultimately became chief of rail and river transportation for the Union armies. From 1853 until 1878 he was connected in one capacity or another with the Ohio and Mississippi Railroad (later the Baltimore and Ohio).

4376. Schnirring, Cheryl. "Church Collections in the Illinois State Historical Library Manuscript Section." *Illinois Libraries* 74 (1992): 456-58.

4377. Spence, Paul D. *Manuscripts Acquired during 1964-1965: A Descriptive Inventory.* Manuscripts in the Illinois State Historical Library, no. 4. Springfield: Illinois State Historical Library, 1967.

(2) Of Other Institutions and Private Collectors

4378. "Additions to Knox College Lincoln Collections." The additions were books Lincoln was known to have studied. *Journal of the Illinois State Historical Society* 52 (1959): 311.

4379. Ander, Oscar Fritiof. *Guide to the Material on Swedish History in the Augustana College Library.* Rock Island, Ill.: Augustana College Library and Augustana Historical Society, 1934.

4380. Bailey, Robert E., ed.; Evans, Elaine Shemoney, assoc. ed.; Hutchcraft, Ruth, asst. ed.; Cantrall, Daniel, and Woods, Martha, comps. *Chicago City Council Proceedings Files, 1833-1871: An Inventory.* Springfield: Illinois State Archives, 1987. The files are in the Illinois State Archives.

4381. Bailey, Robert E., and Evans, Elaine Shemoney. *Index to the Descriptive Inventory of the Archives of the State Of Illinois.* Springfield: Illinois State Archives, 1990. An invaluable research tool.

4382. _____, comps. *The Margaret Cross Norton Working Papers, 1924-1958: An Inventory and Index.* Seven microfiche. Springfield: Illinois State Archives, 1993. Norton was chief of the Archives Division of the Illinois State Library and one of the founders of the Society of American Archivists. The papers themselves fill eight rolls of microfilm.

4383.   Bailey, Robert E.; Evans, Elaine Shemoney; Heflin, Barbara; and Moore, Karl, eds. *A Summary Guide to Local Governmental Records in the Illinois Regional Archives.* Springfield: Illinois State Archives, Office of the Secretary of State, 1992. A computer-generated finding aid that is more user-friendly than Turnbaugh's 1983 volume, q.v. The guide has two parts: 1) holdings listed by county and 2) holdings listed by title. This source also brings holdings up to date.

4384.   Bailey, Robert E., ed., and Evans, Elaine Shemoney, assoc. ed. *Supplement to the Descriptive Inventory of the Archives of the State of Illinois.* Springfield: Illinois State Archives, 1985. See no. 4406.

4385.   Brichford, Maynard J., comp. *Avery Brundage Collection, 1908-1975.* Köln: Verlag Karl Hofman Schorndorf, 1977. Detailed finding aid (described by box number), with a separate index of the collection in the University of Illinois Archives. A microfilm edition is in preparation.

4386.   _____, and Maher, William J. *Guide to the University of Illinois Archives.* Microform (seven microfiche and one booklet). Urbana: The archives, 1986.

4387.   _____; Sutton, Robert Mize; and Walle, Dennis F., comps. *Manuscripts Guide to Collections at the University of Illinois at Urbana-Champaign.* Urbana: University of Illinois Press, 1976.

4388.   Bridges, Roger Dean, comp. "Illinois Manuscript and Archival Collections: A Checklist of Published Guides." *Journal of the Illinois State Historical Society* 66 (1973): 412-27.

4389.   Brubaker, Robert L. "The Development of an Urban History Research Center: The Chicago Historical Society's Library." *Chicago History* 7 n.s. (Spring 1978): 22-36. Good overview of the library's book and manuscript collections by the society's chief librarian.

4390.   Bryan, Mary Lynn McCree, ed. *The Jane Addams Papers.* Ann Arbor, Mich.: University Microfilms International, 1985. A guide to the microfilm edition of 120,000 documents (on 82 reels), from nearly 150 sources, that cover Addams's entire life.

4391.   Caldwell, John, comp. "Guide to Resources for Regional Studies." *Western Illinois Regional Studies* 6, no. 1 (Spring 1983): 86-91. Lists institutions with resources for western Illinois and eastern Iowa studies, with a brief description of the collections.

4392. Chicago. University. Library. "A Preliminary Guide to the Manuscripts and Archives in the University of Chicago Library . . ." Mimeographed. [University of Chicago Library] 1973.

4393. Crick, B. R., and Alman, Miriam, eds.; Beales, H. L., general supervisor. *A Guide to Manuscripts Relating to America in Great Britain and Ireland.* London: Published for the British Association for American Studies by Oxford University Press, 1961. Some excellent letters from Illinois are listed in the index.

4394. Downs, Robert B., ed. *Guide to Illinois Library Resources.* Chicago: American Library Association, in cooperation with the Illinois State Library, 1974. Arranged topically and/or by name of collection rather than by library.

4395. Dunlap, Leslie W. "University of Illinois Receives Fine Lincoln Collection." *Journal of the Illinois State Historical Society* 46 (1953): 296-99. A description of the gift from Dr. and Mrs. Harlan Hoyt Horner of three thousand books and pamphlets related to Abraham Lincoln and his contemporaries.

4396. George, Joseph Jr. "Lincoln Family Documents in the F. J. Dreer Collection." *Illinois Historical Journal* 79 (1986): 139-42. Description of the collection in the Historical Society of Pennsylvania and reproduction of two items.

4397. *Guide to Swedish-American Archival and Manuscript Sources in the United States.* Chicago: Swedish-American Historical Society, 1983. About one half of the 600-page volume is devoted to Swedish-American archival repositories in Illinois.

4398. *Guide to the National Archives of the United States.* Washington: National Archives and Records Service, General Services Administration, 1974. Supersedes the 1948 edition.

4399. Hale, Richard W. Jr., ed. *Guide to Photocopied Historical Materials in the United States and Canada.* Ithaca, N.Y.: Published for the American Historical Association by Cornell University Press, 1961. Photocopied records held in Illinois are listed on page 192.

4400. Hallwas, John E., ed. "Selected Letters of Virginia S. Eifert." *Western Illinois Regional Studies* 10, no. 1 (Spring 1987): 56-82. The letters are among the manuscript holdings of Western Illinois University.

4401. Ham, F. Gerald, and Hedstrom, Margaret, comps. and eds. *A Guide to Labor Papers in the State Historical Society of Wisconsin.* Madison: State Historical Society of Wisconsin, 1978. There are several index entries for Chicago and Illinois.

4402. Hamer, Philip M., ed. *A Guide to Archives and Manuscripts in the United States, Compiled for the National Historical Publications Commission.* New Haven: Yale University Press, 1961. Illinois, pp. 148-70.

4403. Harper, Josephine L. *Guide to the Draper Manuscripts.* Madison: State Historical Society of Wisconsin, 1983. These manuscripts in the State Historical Society of Wisconsin include many relating to early Illinois history, especially the British, American territorial, and early statehood periods. There is a good index that indicates entries related to Illinois, the War of 1812, the Black Hawk War, the George Rogers Clark Papers, and the Thomas Forsyth Papers, among others.

4404. Historical Records Survey, Illinois. *Inventory of the County Archives of Illinois.* Under this title, inventories for thirty-four counties were published, first under the sponsorship of the Federal Writers' Project and then of the state of Illinois. The introductory general histories of the counties and administrative histories of the offices are excellent. The series was discontinued at the opening of World War II. Inventories for Cass, Peoria, and Moultrie counties were published in addition to the thirty-one listed in Thomas Hall's bibliography, no. 4155.

4405. Illinois State Archives. *Illinois Public Domain Land Sales.* Springfield: The archives, 1985. An introduction to the microfiche records of 538,750 original land transactions.

4406. Irons, Victoria, and Brennan, Patricia C., comps., under the direction of John Daly. *Descriptive Inventory of the Archives of the State of Illinois.* Springfield: Illinois State Archives, 1978. Among other papers inventoried are those of the Illinois Historical Records Survey of the Works Progress Administration, 1936-42, now in the State Archives (Record Group 954); WPA papers for 1940-42 are at the Illinois Historical Survey, University of Illinois. Incomplete files of the Federal Writers' Project for Illinois are in the Illinois State Historical Library.

4407. Jackson, Elisabeth Coleman, and Curtis, Carolyn, comps. *Guide to the Burlington Archives in the Newberry Library, 1851-1901.* Chicago: Newberry Library, 1949.

4408. Jenkins, William Sumner, comp., and Hamrick, Lillian A., ed. *A Guide to the Microfilm Collection of Early State Records.* Washington: Library of Congress, 1950. Records listed by state under various headings, e.g., legislative journals, session laws, constitutional records, administrative records.

4409. Karrow, Robert W. Jr., and Buisseret, David. *Gardens of Delight: Maps and Travel Accounts of Illinois and the Great Lakes from the Collection of Hermon Dunlap Smith: An Exhibition at the Newberry Library, 29 October 1984--31 January 1985; Catalog.* Chicago: Newberry Library, 1984.

4410. Kimball, Stanley B., ed. *Slavic-American Imprints: A Classified Catalog of the Collection at Lovejoy Library, Southern Illinois University at Edwardsville.* Lovejoy Library Bibliographic Contributions, no. 7. Southern Illinois University at Edwardsville, 1972. There are 1,867 numbered entries in the catalog (by Rudolph Wierer and Milton Moore), each with an English translation of the title. An index gives numbers of Illinois-related entries. The catalog includes both manuscript and printed items.
  Supplement 1, Bibliographic Contributions, no. 9, 1979.

4411. Leland, Waldo G. *Guide to Materials for American History in the Libraries and Archives of Paris.* Carnegie Institution of Washington Publication, no. 392, vol. 1. Washington, 1932. A good index locates events and people connected with the Illinois country.

4412. *Library of Congress National Union Catalog of Manuscript Collections: Catalog 1990.* Washington, 1992. The 26th in the series (the first volume of which was published in 1962) includes 1,891 collections in 34 repositories. The geographic guide in the front of the volume lists repositories by state and town and the volumes in which collections from each repository are entered. Since inception, the catalog has described 62,455 collections in 1,364 repositories and has indexed them, with over 700,000 citations, to "topical subjects and personal, family, corporate, and geographical names." The index volumes are sometimes published separately; that for 1986-90 was published in 1992. This is a valuable resource, but of necessity many repositories report only their major collections.

4413. "Lincoln Letter Given to University." *Journal of the Illinois State Historical Society* 53 (1960): 78-79. Lincoln's letter of 19 August 1856 to Jesse K. Dubois is now in the University of Illinois collections.

4414. McKee, Linda, comp. *Guide to Research Collections, Lovejoy Library, Southern Illinois University, Edwardsville.* [Edwardsville, Ill.] 1971. Entries are arranged under nineteen subject categories.

4415. Meehan, Patrick J. *Frank Lloyd Wright: A Research Guide to Archival Sources.* New York: Garland, 1983.

4416. Meyer, Daniel. *Stephen A. Douglas and the American Union.* Chicago: University of Chicago Library, 1994. Exhibit catalog based on papers and artifacts from the Douglas Papers in the University of Chicago Library.

4417. Mohr, Carolyn Curtis, comp. *Guide to the Illinois Central Archives in the Newberry Library, 1851-1906.* Chicago: Newberry Library, 1951. Illinois Central records include papers of more than fifty small rail lines in all parts of the state.

4418. Mollman, Sarah C., ed. *Louis Sullivan in the Art Institute of Chicago: The Illustrated Catalogue of Collections.* New York: Garland, 1989.

4419. [Monaghan, Jay.] "Opening of the Lincoln Papers." *Journal of the Illinois State Historical Society* 40 (1947): 358-60. A brief history of the Lincoln Papers deeded to the Library of Congress in 1923 by Robert Todd Lincoln. The 26 July 1947 ceremony at the opening of the papers is also described.

4420. "Newly Discovered Lincoln Papers on Exhibit." *Journal of the Illinois State Historical Society* 55 (1962): 75-77. Items from the Elsie O. and Philip D. Sang Collection.

4421. Nollen, Sheila. "Thomas F. Railsback and His Congressional Papers." *Western Illinois Regional Studies* 9, no. 1 (Spring 1986): 59-74. Railsback's papers are in the Western Illinois University Library.

4422. Pease, Marguerite Jenison. "Guide to Manuscript Materials of American Origin in the Illinois Historical Survey." Rev. ed., Illinois Historical Survey, University of Illinois, publication no. 6. Mimeographed. Urbana, 1956.

4423. _____. "Guide to Manuscript Materials Relating to Western History in Foreign Depositories, Reproduced for the Illinois Historical Survey." Rev. ed., Illinois Historical Survey, University of Illinois, publication no. 5. Mimeographed. Urbana, 1956.

4424. Pease, Theodore Calvin, comp. and ed. *The County Archives of Illinois*. Collections of the Illinois State Historical Library, vol. 12. Springfield, 1915. In an introduction, the editor discusses the authorized county offices of Illinois and the kinds of records generated. The listing by county then describes the actual records extant in 1915. For later disposition of many of these records, see nos. 4383 and 4432.

4425. *A Preliminary Guide to the Manuscripts and Archives in the University of Chicago Library*. Chicago: Department of Special Collections, Joseph Regenstein Library, 1973.

4426. Pumroy, Eric, with Brockman, Paul. *A Guide to Manuscript Collections of the Indiana Historical Society and Indiana State Library*. Indianapolis: Indiana Historical Society, 1986. An excellent index shows many entries for Illinois.

4427. Rishel, Jane, and Shumaker, Earl, eds. "Documents to the People." *Illinois Libraries* 69 (1987): 443-530. The entire September issue is devoted to government documents (both published and unpublished) and access to those documents. One article deals with records of other countries; the remainder with United States and Illinois records.

4428. Robertson, Mary, and Preston, Jean F., comps. *Guide to American Historical Manuscripts in the Huntington Library*. San Marino, Calif.: Huntington Library, 1979. The index has several Illinois references; for a more detailed survey, see no. 4431.

4429. Smith, Alice E., ed. *Guide to the Manuscripts of the Wisconsin Historical Society*. Madison: State Historical Society of Wisconsin, 1944. *Supplement Number One*, by Josephine L. Harper and Sharon C. Smith. Madison: State Historical Society of Wisconsin, 1957. *Supplement Number Two*, by Josephine L. Harper. Madison: State Historical Society of Wisconsin, 1966. All three volumes have index entries for Illinois.

4430. Szucs, Loretto Dennis, and Luebking, Sandra Hargreaves. *The Archives: A Guide to National Archives Field Branches*. Salt Lake City:

Ancestry Publishing, 1988. Records held at the Chicago branch are described on pages 17-19.

4431. Tingley, Donald Fred. "Manuscript Materials Relating to Illinois in California's Henry E. Huntington Library." *Journal of the Illinois State Historical Society* 60 (1967): 313-19.

4432. Turnbaugh, Roy C. Jr. *A Guide to County Records in the Illinois Regional Archives.* Springfield: Illinois State Archives, 1983. Six state universities serve as regional archives depositories for local government records of permanent value. Under sixteen record group headings (one for each county office), Turnbaugh lists the counties whose records are on deposit and locates the depository. There is also a listing by county.

4433. U.S. Congress. House. Office for the Bicentennial of the United States House of Representatives. *A Guide to the Research Collections of Former Members of the United States House of Representatives, 1789-1987.* Cynthia Pease Miller, editor-in-chief. 100th Cong., 2d sess., H. Doc. 100-171. Washington, 1988. Information is given alphabetically by name of member.

4434. U.S. Congress. Senate. *Guide to Research Collections of Former United States Senators, 1789-1982.* Edited by Kathryn Allamong Jacob and Elizabeth Ann Hornyak. U.S. Senate Bicentennial Publication, no. 1. Washington: Historical Office, U.S. Senate, 1983. Supplement I issued in 1985 and Supplement II in 1987. Senators are listed alphabetically with the locations of their papers. There is a separate listing by state, giving the names of repositories and the senatorial papers held therein.

4435. Wood, Thomas J., and Keating, Meredith. *James Jones in Illinois: A Guide to the Handy Writers' Colony Collection in the Sangamon State University Library Archives.* Springfield: Sangamon State University, 1989.

c. Newspapers

(1) Bibliographies

4436. Adams, James N. "Rare Newspapers in Historical Library." *Journal of the Illinois State Historical Society* 47 (1954): 193-96.

4437. Ander, Oscar Fritiof, comp. *Swedish-American Political Newspapers: A Guide to the Collections in the Royal Library, Stockholm, and the Augustana College Library, Rock Island.* Uppsala: Almqvist & Wiksells, 1936.

4438. Belles, A. Gilbert, comp. "The Black Press in Illinois." *Journal of the Illinois State Historical Society* 68 (1975): 344-67. The compiler has identified and listed 190 black newspapers in 26 Illinois communities, together with names of editors and dates of publication.

4439. Chicago Public Library Omnibus Project of the Work Projects Administration. *Bibliography of Foreign Language Newspapers and Periodicals Published in Chicago.* Chicago: Chicago Public Library Omnibus Project, 1942.

4440. Gregory, Winifred, ed. *American Newspapers, 1821-1936. A Union List of Files Available in the United States and Canada.* New York: H. W. Wilson, 1937.

4441. *Illinois Media . . .* Chicago: Midwest Newsclip, published annually since the 1950s. The 1993-94 edition was published in December 1993. Listings in this "comprehensive directory of all print and electronic media in the state" include the names of principal editors and administrators for each medium.

4442. Illinois Newspaper Project. James A. Edstrom, senior cataloger. Underway is a program to find, catalog, and preserve Illinois newspapers from their beginning in 1814 to the present. As the project proceeds, titles and sources are being made available on the bibliographic database of the national Online Computer Library Center, Inc. The project is part of the United States Newspaper Program, which is funded by the National Endowment for the Humanities and coordinated by the Library of Congress. The catalog will eventually include holdings of libraries and universities throughout the state.

4443. "Newspapers in Libraries of Chicago: A Joint Check-List." Mimeographed. Chicago: University of Chicago Libraries, Documents Section, 1936.

4444. *Newspapers in the Illinois State Historical Library.* Published every three years, 1964 to date, by the Illinois State Library. The listings have been compiled by James N. Adams, William E. Keller, Sandra M. Stark, and Cheryl Pence.

4445. Pease, Marguerite Jenison. "Checklist of Newspapers in the Illinois Historical Survey." Illinois Historical Survey, University of Illinois, publication no. 4. Mimeographed. Urbana, 1953.

4446. Rudeen, Marlys. *The Civilian Conservation Corps Camp Newspapers: A Guide.* Chicago: Center for Research Libraries, 1991.

4447. Scott, Franklin W., comp. *Newspapers and Periodicals of Illinois, 1814-1879.* Collections of the Illinois State Historical Library, vol. 6. Springfield, 1910. In a 104-page introduction, the compiler presents political and printing histories of the state. The newspaper listings (by city) give dates of publication and names of editors. An appendix lists Illinois libraries and indicates their newspaper holdings. Another appendix lists newspapers alphabetically by title. There is also an index to names of editors and publishers.

(2) Representative Newspapers

Newspapers in this list (which were selected, in part, for geographical diversity) fit one or more of the following criteria: 1) They reflect the attitudes and emotions of their audience(s) over a sustained period of time; 2) they are in some way intrinsically important to the history of Illinois; and 3) they had or have state or national influence. Titles are not necessarily single discrete items, but more often are families of newspapers. The list is arranged chronologically.

4448. *Illinois Herald.* The first newspaper in Illinois began publication about 1814 in Kaskaskia. Matthew Duncan was the first publisher. It became the weekly *Western Intelligencer* in 1816 and achieved perhaps its greatest significance under Daniel Pope Cook, later congressman from Illinois. Upon assuming ownership in 1817, Cook used the newspaper to advocate statehood for the Illinois Territory. The title was changed to *Illinois Intelligencer* in May 1818 to celebrate the success of the statehood movement. The paper moved to Vandalia when that town became the new state capital. In 1832, the *Intelligencer* merged with the *Illinois Whig* to become the *Vandalia Whig and Illinois Intelligencer*, in which form it continued until some time in 1834.

4449. Shawneetown *Illinois Gazette.* The second newspaper in Illinois began as the *Illinois Emigrant* in 1819. (Some maintain that it was known initially as *Shawnee Chief.*) Henry Eddy and Singleton H. Kimmel, the first publishers, changed the title to *Illinois Gazette* in 1819; Kimmel sold out in 1820 to James Hall, an early literary figure in Illinois.

4450. Edwardsville *Spectator*. The *Spectator* began in 1819 under the editorial direction of Hooper Warren, an antislavery partisan. His newspaper is significant for its role in defeating the movement to call a state constitutional convention in 1824 that might well have legalized slavery. The *Spectator* ceased publication in 1826.

4451. Kaskaskia *Republican Advocate*. Begun in 1823 and probably edited by Elias Kent Kane, the *Advocate* was as important as the *Spectator* in the constitutional convention controversy of 1824, favoring slavery in Illinois and thus favoring a convention. It became the *Republican* in early 1824 and was succeeded in 1826 by the *Illinois Reporter*, which ceased publication in 1827.

4452. Galena *Miners' Journal*. The earliest newspaper in northern Illinois was begun in about 1828 by James Jones. Addison Philleo bought the *Journal* in 1832, changed the title to *The Galenian* and made it a Democratic organ. *The Galenian* was succeeded in about 1836 by the *Democrat*, which died out some time in the 1840s.

4453. Springfield *State Journal-Register*. The *Journal* branch of this title is believed to have originated in 1830 as an Edwardsville paper titled *Crisis*. If true, the *Journal-Register* has been published, in one form or another, as long as almost any other newspaper in Illinois. The *Journal* began life in Springfield in 1831 as the weekly *Sangamon* (sometimes *Sangamo*) *Journal*. It spawned a daily in 1848. An index to the *Journal*, 1831-60, is available at the Illinois State Historical Library.

The *Register* branch can be traced back to the weekly Edwardsville *Illinois Advocate*, which began in 1831 and moved in 1833 to Vandalia as the *Illinois Advocate and State Register*. When Springfield became the capital, the *Advocate and State Register* moved to that town, where it dropped the name *Advocate*. The *State Register* launched a triweekly in 1847 and a daily in 1849. It merged with the *Journal* in 1974. These two newspapers were frequently at odds during the years before their merger. The *Journal* tended to support the Whig party and then the Republicans, whereas the *Register* supported the Democrats.

4454. *Chicago Tribune*. One of the most important newspapers in the United States, the *Tribune* traces its direct history to 1847, but it actually reaches back to the first newspaper in Chicago. The *Chicago Democrat* began publication in 1833 under John Calhoun and was absorbed by the *Tribune* in

1861.   The *Tribune* family tree encompasses an array of newspapers, including the Chicago weekly, triweekly, and daily *Press*, the daily and weekly *Democrat*, the *Gem of the Prairie*, and even a branch of abolitionist newspapers beginning with the Lowell, Illinois, *Genius of Liberty* and ending with *Free West*, which was absorbed by the *Tribune*'s first weekly edition.

Under the direction of Joseph Medill, who bought an interest in the paper in 1855, and later under his grandson, Robert R. McCormick, the *Tribune* became a publication of international importance, with a strongly conservative Republican perspective.   The *Tribune* was a leading exponent of isolationism and anti-Communism into the mid-twentieth century.

4455. *Alton Observer.*   This began as the *St. Louis Observer* in 1833 and originally had a religious orientation.   Under the editorial direction of Elijah P. Lovejoy, the *Observer* became a strong exponent of the abolitionist movement.   Its removal to Alton, Illinois, did not lessen its propensity for creating controversy; mobs destroyed Lovejoy's equipment several times, and on 7 November 1836 Lovejoy was killed by a mob while attempting to defend his press.   After his death, the *Observer* was published sporadically through 1838 in Cincinnati, Ohio.

4456. *Quincy Herald-Whig.*   This dates from 1835, with the debut of the weekly *Illinois Bounty Land Register*, published by C. M. Woods & Company.   A Democratic organ and the first newspaper in Adams County, it was devoted to advertising federal public lands in Illinois between the Illinois and Mississippi rivers.   For a brief period at the end of the 1830s and the beginning of the 1840s, it was known as the *Argus*.   A daily edition commenced in the 1850s.

The *Whig* branch first appeared in 1838 as a weekly, merged with the Quincy *Republican* to become *Whig and Republican* in the 1850s, again became the *Whig* in the 1860s, merged in 1920 with the Quincy *Journal* to become the *Whig-Journal*, and in 1926 joined with the *Herald* to become the *Quincy Herald-Whig and the Quincy Journal*.   In 1943 the name was shortened to *Quincy Herald-Whig*.

4457. Alton *Telegraph*.   This began in 1836 as a weekly Whig newspaper under publishers Richard M. Treadway and Lawson A. Parks.   As one observer commented, it "promoted religion, republicanism, temperance, Unionism, United States expansion, freedom for the slaves, and community pride without screaming headlines or shock treatment reporting."   National, state, and local issues were treated with equal importance.   It published a triweekly edition for a period in the 1850s and began daily publication in

1852. The *Telegraph* is one of the oldest newspapers still in publication in Illinois. An index to the *Telegraph*, 1836-1933, is available on microfilm.

4458. Belleville *Der Freiheitsbote für Illinois*. Published and edited from May 6 through October 28, 1840, by Gustave Koerner (later lieutenant governor under Governor Joel A. Matteson, 1853-57), this was probably the first non-English newspaper in Illinois.   As a Democratic campaign newspaper, it promoted the reelection of Martin Van Buren and sharply attacked the Nativist movement.

4459. *Belleville News-Democrat*. The earliest ancestor of the *News-Democrat* was the weekly *Belleville Advocate*, which began in 1840 under the direction of James L. Boyd and John T. C. Clark.   Originally Democratic in politics, the *Advocate* supported the Free Soil party in the late 1850s and eventually became Republican. A daily edition was begun in 1898.

The other main branch of the *News-Democrat* commenced in 1858 as the *Belleville Weekly Democrat*.   The *Democrat* began a daily in 1883 and merged with the *Advocate* in 1958.

4460. *Nauvoo Expositor*. The *Expositor* was begun in 1844 by disaffected Mormons William Law and Wilson Lane, among others, to present a challenge to Mormon leader Joseph Smith's control over the city of Nauvoo. In particular, the *Expositor* criticized Smith for instituting polygamy and maintaining theocratic control of the community.   The editors urged political and religious reform.   After one issue (7 June 1844) the city council suppressed the paper.   That act led to the lynching of Joseph Smith and his brother Hyrum, which in turn precipitated the departure of the Mormons from Illinois to Utah.

4461. Bloomington *Pantagraph*. This paper probably traces its history to the short-lived weekly *McLean Register*, which began in 1845. C. P. Merriman changed the title to *Western Whig* in 1846, and to *Bloomington Intelligencer* in 1851, when Merriman became disenchanted with the Whig party. It finally became the *Pantagraph* (Greek for "to write all things") in 1854. A daily edition was begun that same year. The *Pantagraph* and its editor, Jesse W. Fell, were leaders in the movement to form the Republican party.   The *Pantagraph* continues to publish seven days a week.

4462. Peoria *Journal Star*. This began in the 1850s as the weekly and daily *Transcript* under the direction of William Rounseville and Nathaniel C. Nason.   After its sale in 1859 to Nathan C. Geer, the *Transcript* became thoroughly Republican.   Geer's successors, Enoch Emery and Edward A.

Andrews, developed it into one of the most influential newspapers in Illinois and a significant voice in the state Republican party. Increasing competition from other newspapers, however, led to a merger with the Democratic *Peoria Daily Herald* in 1898, which had commenced publication in 1889 under Henry M. Pindell. In turn, the *Herald-Transcript* merged in 1937 with the *Peoria Journal*, a generally Republican organ that was begun in 1877 by Eugene F. Baldwin and Jacob B. Barnes, and in 1955 with the *Peoria Evening Star*, which had originated in 1897 as an independent newspaper under Eugene F. Baldwin and Charles H. Powell.

4463. *Chicago Herald-American.* The *Herald-American* had one of the most colorful and complex newspaper histories in Illinois. There are at least eight distinct branches of the *Herald-American* tree: the *Times*, the *Herald*, the *News Record*, the *Post*, the *Republican*, the *Inter Ocean*, the *Examiner*, and the *American*. The *Times*, a daily, weekly, and triweekly newspaper, began in 1852 and gained notoriety by opposing the Lincoln administration (in 1863 General Ambrose Burnside ordered the *Times* shut down; the action was reversed by the President within a few days).

An important branch of the *Herald-American* was the Chicago *Post*, founded in 1860 by James W. Sheahan, André Matteson, and Francis Eastman to support Stephen A. Douglas. The *Post*, in turn, was absorbed by the Chicago *Republican*, begun in 1865 under the editorial direction of Charles A. Dana. Perhaps the most important period in the history of the *Herald-American* family began in 1900 with the appearance of William Randolph Hearst's *Chicago American*. According to its final successor, *Chicago Today* (issue of 13 September 1974), the *American* "throbbed and dazzled, charmed and chagrined. It finagled, connived, and roistered." Indeed, the *American* served as a model for the play "The Front Page" by Ben Hecht and Charles MacArthur, both of whom had reported for the newspaper. The last issue of *Chicago Today* was published in 1974.

4464. Champaign-Urbana *News-Gazette.* The first newspaper in Champaign County began as the *Urbana Union* in 1852. Published by William N. Coler, the *Union* was at the outset strongly Democratic, campaigning for the election of Franklin Pierce as president. Coler was awarded a government office for his efforts, and in 1853 J. O. Cunningham and Benjamin Roney bought the newspaper. Under Cunningham, the *Union* became solidly Republican and supported Lincoln in the senatorial election of 1858 as well as in the presidential election of 1860. The *Union* flourished with the coming of the railroad and the University of Illinois to Champaign-Urbana. The paper merged with George W. Scroggs's *Central Illinois Gazette* in the 1860s. The title fluctuated between *Gazette* and *Union and Gazette* for a number of years.

A *Daily Gazette* edition was added in 1883, and in 1919 that paper merged with the *Champaign Daily News* (founded in 1895) to form the *News-Gazette*.

4465. *Chicago Daily News.* Started by Melville E. Stone in December 1875 as an independent newspaper, the *Daily News* emphasized evenhanded reporting at a time when most newspapers were explicit in their political biases. During the Spanish-American War it initiated a highly respected foreign-news service. The *Daily News* ceased publication in 1978.

4466. Chicago *Conservator.* The first African-American newspaper in Illinois, the *Conservator* was founded by Ferdinand L. Barnett in 1878 and survived until 1914. Little information is available about the newspaper, and only scattered issues have been preserved. Activist Ida B. Wells was among those who wrote for the paper.

4467. *Chicago Defender.* One of the most influential African-American newspapers in the United States, the *Defender* was begun by Robert Abbott in 1905 as a small weekly handbill. Because of its wide circulation in the South, the *Defender* played an important role in encouraging the migration of African-Americans to the cities of the industrial North during the time of World War I, and consequently it had a significant impact upon the history and development of Chicago and the nation. The *Defender* also provided a forum for such African-American writers as Langston Hughes, Mary McLeod Bethune, and W. E. B. DuBois. A daily edition was begun in 1956.

V. HISTORIC SITES

The designation Historic Sites, as used in this section, applies not only to official state historic sites and monuments administered by the Illinois Historic Preservation Agency but also to markers of historic places, national historic sites, and places listed on the National Register of Historic Places. Histories of some state sites are presented under the appropriate chronological period.

A. IN GENERAL

4468. Bogue, Margaret Beattie. *Around the Shores of Lake Michigan: A Guide to Historic Sites.* Madison: University of Wisconsin Press, 1985. Illinois sites, pp. 97-138.

4469. *Guide to Historic Places in Southwestern Illinois.* Collinsville, Ill.: Southwestern Illinois Metropolitan and Regional Planning Commission, 1979. Locates and describes National Register sites, districts, and buildings in a seven-county area.

4470. Historic American Buildings Survey, Historic American Engineering Record. *An Inventory of Historic Structures within the Illinois and Michigan Canal National Heritage Corridor.* Washington: HAB/HAER Division, National Park Service, U.S. Department of Interior. Vol. 1 (1986)--to date.

4471. *Historic Illinois.* Published bi-monthly by the Division of Historic Sites of the Illinois Department of Conservation, June 1978--June 1985, and since then by the Division of Preservation Services, which, along with

Historic Sites, became part of the newly created Illinois Historic Preservation Agency.   Includes articles about state-owned historic sites and places in Illinois listed on the National Register of Historic Places.   An index to volumes 1-16 (June 1978--April 1994) was issued as number 6 of volume 16 (April 1994).

4472. *Historic Illinois Places* [map].   Springfield: Illinois Historic Preservation Agency and Illinois State Historical Society, 1989.   Keith A. Sculle, project coordinator; Melissa A. Records, cartographer; James A. Bier, cartographic consultant; and John A. Jakle, historical consultant.   The map shows the location of museums, state historic sites, and sites listed on the National Register of Historic Places.   The reverse side of the map lists National Register sites by county, with map location.

4473. Illinois Historic Landmarks Survey.   "Inventory of Historic Landmarks in . . . County: Interim Report."   Mimeographed, 1973.   The Survey was a division of the Illinois Historic Sites Survey, conducted under the auspices of the Illinois Department of Conservation.   Individual reports were prepared for each of Illinois' 102 counties, by several different field surveyors.   Detailed maps are a part of each report.

4474. Illinois Preservation Series.   1980 to date.   Published annually by the Division of Historic Sites of the Illinois Department of Conservation, 1980-85, and since then by the Division of Preservation Services of the newly created Illinois Historic Preservation Agency.   Technical reports, for the most part, on the preservation of historic sites.   Of more general interest, no. 6 (1985) is a listing of Illinois places on the National Register of Historic Places, and no. 4 (1983) is a brief "Prehistory of Illinois," by Alan S. Downer.

4475. Knack, Ruth Eckdish, ed.   *Preservation Illinois: A Guide to State & Local Resources.*   Springfield: Illinois Department of Conservation, with a grant from American Revolution Bicentennial Administration and Illinois Bicentennial Commission, 1977.

4476. *National Register of Historic Places, 1966-1988.*   Nashville, Tenn.: American Association for State and Local History, 1989.   Illinois, pp. 157-71.

4477. Newcomb, Rexford.   "Beginnings of Architecture in Illinois."   *Journal of the Illinois State Historical Society* 39 (1946): 303-22.   The author discusses many of the buildings that are now state historic sites.

4478. Schnedler, Marcia. *Country Roads of Illinois.* Castine, Maine: Country Roads Press, 1992. Excellent descriptions and brief histories of historic sites in thirteen regions of the state.

4479. Weil, Tom. *Hippocrene U.S.A. Guide to America's Heartland: A Travel Guide to the Back Roads of Illinois, Indiana, Iowa, and Missouri.* New York: Hippocrene Books, 1989. In 117 pages the author outlines nine trips; his narratives include an astonishing amount of history that succeeds in giving the flavor of Illinois.

B. AT CAHOKIA

4480. Babb, Margaret E. "The Mansion House of Cahokia and Its Builder, Nicholas Jarrot." *Transactions of the Illinois State Historical Society, 1924,* pp. 78-93.

4481. Donnelly, Joseph P. *The Parish of the Holy Family, Cahokia, Illinois, 1699-1949.* East St. Louis, Ill.: Cahokia Anniversary Association, 1949.

4482. Peterson, Charles E. "Notes on Old Cahokia." *Journal of the Illinois State Historical Society* 42 (1949): 7-29, 193-208, 313-43. Part 1 traces the history of the village and surrounding area from 1699 through 1773. Part 2 continues through the era of British occupation. Part 3 deals with the American colonial era, 1778-90. The author brings to date the history of such early buildings as the Cahokia Courthouse, the Church of the Holy Family, and the Nicholas Jarrot mansion.

4483. Study, Guy. "Oliver Parks Restores the Jarrot Mansion at Cahokia." *Journal of the Illinois State Historical Society* 38 (1945): 351-53.

C. CAHOKIA MOUNDS

4484. Brackenridge, Henry M. "The Cantine Mounds of Southern Illinois: The First Published Report of Their Existence and an 1811 Eyewitness Account of the Monks Who Lived There." Edited by Raymond H. Hammes. *Journal of the Illinois State Historical Society* 74 (1981): 145-56. These mounds, now part of the Cahokia Mounds State Historic Site (near Collinsville), were first reported by Brackenridge in the St. Louis *Louisiana Gazette* on 9 January 1811; the second report appeared in the same newspaper on 31 January 1811, and described the Trappist monastery, near the largest of the mounds, and the monks who lived there.

4485. *The Cahokia Mounds.* University of Illinois Bulletin, vol. 26, no. 4 (25 September 1928). Includes papers by Warren K. Moorehead, Jay L. B. Taylor, Morris M. Leighton, Frank C. Baker, and a bibliography by Thomas H. English. Some of the material was previously published in volume 19, number 35, and volume 21, number 6. Technical, but of general interest.

4486. Emerson, Thomas E., and Lewis, R. Barry, eds. *Cahokia and the Hinterlands: Middle Mississippian Cultures of the Midwest.* Urbana: University of Illinois Press, published in cooperation with the Illinois Historic Preservation Agency, 1991. Seventeen contributions by archaeologists Robert L. Hall, David Rindos, Sissel Johannessen, William I. Woods, George R. Holley, John E. Kelly, Kenneth B. Farnsworth, Rebecca Miller Glenn, Lawrence A. Conrad, Alan D. Harn, Joseph A. Tiffany, Lynne G. Goldstein, John D. Richards, Guy E. Gibbon, Charles R. Moffat, Robert J. Barth, Brian M. Butler, Jon Muller, Jeanette E. Stephens, as well as the editors.

4487. Fowler, Melvin L. *The Cahokia Atlas: A Historical Atlas of Cahokia Archaeology.* Illinois Historic Preservation Agency Studies in Illinois Archaeology, no. 6. Springfield, 1989. A study, both historical and archaeological, of the Cahokia group of mounds.

4488. Garraghan, Gilbert Joseph. "The Trappists of Monks Mound" in his *Chapters in Frontier History: Research Studies in the Making of the West.* Science and Cultural Series. Milwaukee: Bruce Publishing, 1934.

4489. Skele, Mikels. *The Great Knob: Interpretations of Monks Mound.* Illinois Historic Preservation Agency Studies in Illinois Archaeology, no. 4. Springfield, 1988. Also includes information on the historical period.

D. FORT MASSAC

4490. Caldwell, Norman Ward. "Fort Massac: Since 1805." *Journal of the Illinois State Historical Society* 44 (1951): 47-60. The fort ceased to be an active military post in 1814.

4491. _____. "Fort Massac: The American Frontier Post, 1778-1805." *Journal of the Illinois State Historical Society* 43 (1950): 265-81. In 1794 American troops constructed a fort at the site of the old French post on the

Ohio. It remained important to the defense of the frontier through the troubled territorial years.

4492. _____. "Fort Massac during the French and Indian War." *Journal of the Illinois State Historical Society* 43 (1950): 100-119.

4493. Farrar, William G., and Farrar, JoAnn S. *Historic Profiles of Fort Massac.* Edited by Brent Locke. Southern Illinois Studies, no. 5. Carbondale: University Museum, Southern Illinois University, 1970.

4494. Hogg, Victor, in association with Margaret Brown and John B. Fortier. "Historic Fort Massac: The Development of the American Fort." Mimeographed. Carbondale: Southern Illinois University, 1970.

4495. Johnson, Leland R. "The Doyle Mission to Massac, 1794." *Journal of the Illinois State Historical Society* 73 (1980): 2-16. United States Army Major Thomas Doyle's mission to Massac was authorized to quell hostilities among Indian, Spanish, and French units in the region and to reestablish United States authority there.

4496. Nelson, Paul David. *Anthony Wayne: Soldier of the Early Republic.* Bloomington: Indiana University Press, 1985. This well-documented biography will be of interest to Illinoisans for its story of General Wayne's directing the construction of Fort Massac on the Ohio in 1794.

E. AT GALENA

4497. Carroll, Virginia R. "The Galena Market House, Oldest in the Midwest." *Journal of the Illinois State Historical Society* 45 (1952): 51-54.

4498. "De Soto House: Hundred-Year-Old Galena Hotel." *Journal of the Illinois State Historical Society* 47 (1954): 315-21.

4499. "Galena Market House Restoration." *Journal of the Illinois State Historical Society* 47 (1954): 19.

4500. "Grant Home at Galena Rededicated." *Journal of the Illinois State Historical Society* 50 (1957): 221. The home of Ulysses S. Grant was rededicated after its restoration and refurbishment to look as it did when the Grants lived there.

4501. Johnson, Carl H. Jr. *The Building of Galena: An Architectural Legacy.* Galena, Ill.: The author, 1977.

4502. Laine, Christian K. "The Architecture of Galena: The Development of the Middle West's First Industrial City." *Illinois Architecture Reference Directory* 86 (1986): 33-51.

F. LINCOLN SITES AND MEMORIALS

4503. Alderfer, William K. "How Illinois Preservationists Finally Saved the Old Capitol." *Journal of the Illinois State Historical Society* 61 (1968): 431-42.

4504. Anderson, William T. "Mr. Lincoln's Springfield." *American History Illustrated* 24, no. 1 (March 1989): 26-31.

4505. "Another Lincoln Memorial for Springfield." *Journal of the Illinois State Historical Society* 53 (1960): 288. The Great Western Railroad station, where Lincoln made his famous farewell address, was purchased by businessmen, who turned the building into a Lincoln memorial. It is still a privately owned and operated Lincoln site.

4506. Brown, Virginia Stuart. *Through Lincoln's Door.* 1st ed., Springfield, Ill.: Li-Co Art & Letter Service, 1952.

4507. " 'The Chicago Lincoln' Statue Dedicated." *Journal of the Illinois State Historical Society* 49 (1956): 335-36. See also ibid. 48 (1955): 200-201, "Lincoln Statue Contest Winner."

4508. Converse, Henry A. "The House of the House Divided." *Transactions of the Illinois State Historical Society, 1924,* pp. 141-71. A detailed history of the Springfield building now known as the Old State Capitol.

4509. Davenport, Don. *In Lincoln's Footsteps: A Historical Guide to the Lincoln Sites in Illinois, Indiana, & Kentucky.* Madison, Wis.: Prairie Oak Press, 1991.

4510. Dyba, Thomas J. *Seventeen Years at Eighth and Jackson: The Story of Life in the Lincoln Home.* Lisle: Illinois Benedictine College, 1982. 2d ed., 1985, has a slightly different subtitle.

4511. Fairbanks, Avard. "Making the Lincoln Statue for New Salem." *Journal of the Illinois State Historical Society* 47 (1954): 119-32.

4512. "Fifth Custodian of Lincoln's Tomb." *Journal of the Illinois State Historical Society* 44 (1951): 187-88. Brief history of the custodianship of the tomb from 1874. It became a state monument in 1895.

4513. "Furniture from the Lincoln Home." *Journal of the Illinois State Historical Society* 44 (1951): 61-63. Authenticated pieces in private hands in 1951.

4514. Hagen, Richard S. "Back-Yard Archaeology at Lincoln's Home." *Journal of the Illinois State Historical Society* 44 (1951): 340-48.

4515. _____. " 'What a Pleasant Home Abe Lincoln Has.' " *Journal of the Illinois State Historical Society* 48 (1955): 5-27. Description of the research for, and restoration of, the Lincoln home in the 1950s.

4516. "Hearst Honored at New Salem." *Journal of the Illinois State Historical Society* 44 (1951): 271-73. Governor Adlai E. Stevenson pays tribute to William Randolph Hearst for his part in preserving the village site of Abraham Lincoln's New Salem.

4517. Hickey, James T. " 'Own the house till it ruins me': Robert Todd Lincoln and His Parents' Home in Springfield." *Journal of the Illinois State Historical Society* 74 (1981): 279-96. A history of the Lincoln home from 1861 to 1924; Robert Lincoln transferred the house title to the state in 1887 as a public memorial; it is now a National Historic Site.

4518. "Historic Lincoln Sites in Macon County." *Journal of the Illinois State Historical Society* 49 (1956): 216.

4519. Hosking, William J. "Lincoln's Tomb: Designs Submitted and Final Selection." *Journal of the Illinois State Historical Society* 50 (1957): 51-61.

4520. Irving, J. C. "The Old Court House at Metamora Presented to the State of Illinois." *Journal of the Illinois State Historical Society* 14 (1921-22): 365-67. *See also* "Dedication of Old Court House in Metamora as State Lincoln Memorial." Ibid., 368-81.

4521. Johnson, Mark; Munyer, Marianna J.; and Taylor, Richard S. "The Lincoln-Herndon Law Offices Volunteer Manual." Photoduplicated.

Springfield: Historic Sites Division, Illinois Historic Preservation Agency, 1986. A training manual for interpreters at the Lincoln-Herndon Law Offices State Historic Site. More than three fourths of this volume is devoted to a history of the building, to the leading attorneys who practiced in the federal courtroom on the second floor, and to the operation of the court itself. Fully annotated.

4522. Knotts, Mrs. Raymond. "A Living Memorial to Lincoln." *Journal of the Illinois State Historical Society* 46 (1953): 190-93. A history of the Abraham Lincoln Memorial Garden, located on Lake Springfield.

4523. "Lincoln and Douglas Plaques at Knoxville." *Journal of the Illinois State Historical Society* 53 (1960): 79. The original bronze plates, on the Old Main Building at Knox College, commemorate the 1858 debate there. Copies were mounted in the old county courthouse at Knoxville.

4524. "Lincoln Home Restoration." *Journal of the Illinois State Historical Society* 45 (1952): 283.

4525. "Lincoln Log Cabin Replica for Peoria." *Journal of the Illinois State Historical Society* 52 (1959): 311, 440.

4526. "Lincoln Statue Dedicated at Barrington." *Journal of the Illinois State Historical Society* 52 (1959): 310.

4527. "Lincoln Statue for New Salem." *Journal of the Illinois State Historical Society* 46 (1953): 103.

4528. "Marker Dedicated at Albion." *Journal of the Illinois State Historical Society* 50 (1957): 423-24. The marker commemorates an 1840 Lincoln speech.

4529. "Memorial Garden Begins Second Quarter Century." *Journal of the Illinois State Historical Society* 55 (1962): 72-75. History of the Lincoln Memorial Garden on Lake Springfield.

4530. "Mr. Lincoln at Home." *Journal of the Illinois State Historical Society* 40 (1947): 93-94. Description from the *Cincinnati Daily Gazette*, 27 August 1860.

4531. " 'A Most Beautiful Dirty Clay Color.' " *Journal of the Illinois State Historical Society* 47 (1954): 189. The quotation describes the color of the

Lincoln home in 1865; it is from the diary of Abner Foreman, in the Illinois State Historical Library.

4532. Nelson, G. E. "The Genesis of Restored New Salem." *Journal of the Illinois State Historical Society* 36 (1943): 368-77.

4533. "Newest Lincoln Marker." *Journal of the Illinois State Historical Society* 50 (1957): 422-23. The marker is located at the site of Lincoln's first home in Illinois, in what is now Lincoln Trail Homestead State Park.

4534. "New Marker in Charleston." *Journal of the Illinois State Historical Society* 47 (1954): 70. Markers commemorate the fourth Lincoln-Douglas debate.

4535. "New Memorial Garden Center Dedicated." *Journal of the Illinois State Historical Society* 58 (1965): 431-32. The center is located in the Abraham Lincoln Memorial Garden on Lake Springfield.

4536. "The Reconstruction of New Salem: Ceremonies at the Laying of the Cornerstone." *Journal of the Illinois State Historical Society* 25 (1932-33): 326-42. *See also* "The Official Name of New Salem," by Paul McClelland Angle, ibid., p. 343.

4537. "Remodeled Lincoln Home Reopened." *Journal of the Illinois State Historical Society* 46 (1953): 103-4.

4538. Rissler, Howard F. "The State Capitol, 1837-1876." *Journal of the Illinois State Historical Society* 61 (1968): 397-430. This building, later the Sangamon County Courthouse, has been reconstructed and is now the historic site known as the Old State Capitol.

4539. "Sangamon County's Remodeled Court House." *State Topics*, vol. 1, no. 10 (2 March 1901), pp. 2, 3. The courthouse is now known as the Old State Capitol.

4540. Scott, Kenneth. "Lincoln's Home in 1860." *Journal of the Illinois State Historical Society* 46 (1953): 7-12.

4541. "The Second Story of the Lincoln Home." *Journal of the Illinois State Historical Society* 49 (1956): 216-18. Remodeling of the Lincoln home in Springfield in 1856.

4542. "Springfield Lincoln Plaque Rededicated." *Journal of the Illinois State Historical Society* 52 (1959): 309. The plaque marks the Lincoln pew in the First Presbyterian Church.

4543. Swift, Lester L. "The President of the Lincoln Guard of Honor." *Journal of the Illinois State Historical Society* 33 (1940): 207-11. The guard president was Gustavus S. Dana, one of those who helped move Lincoln's remains to a safer place beneath the obelisk at the burial site.

4544. Temple, Sunderine Wilson, and Temple, Wayne C. *Illinois' Fifth Capitol: The House That Lincoln Built and Caused to Be Rebuilt (1837-1865).* Springfield, Ill.: Phillips Brothers, 1988. Now a state historic site, the reconstructed Old State Capitol houses the Illinois State Historical Library in below-ground quarters.

4545. Temple, Wayne C. *By Square and Compass: The Building of Lincoln's Home and Its Saga.* Bloomington, Ill.: Ashlar Press, 1984. Definitive information about Lincoln's home in Springfield.

4546. Thomas, Benjamin Platt. "Lincoln and New Salem: A Study in Environment." *Transactions of the Illinois State Historical Society, 1934*, pp. 61-75.

4547. _____. *Lincoln's New Salem.* 1934. Reprint of the 1973 new rev. ed., Carbondale: Southern Illinois University Press, 1987. A history of New Salem for the years Lincoln lived there, 1831-37. Thomas also discusses the restoration of the village, now a state historic site.

4548. "Tremont Courthouse Marker." *Journal of the Illinois State Historical Society* 49 (1956): 220. A marker commemorates Lincoln's associations with the building.

4549. Ward, Geoffrey C. "The House at Eighth and Jackson." *American Heritage* 40 (April 1989): 68-79. Lincoln's Springfield home.

4550. Weber, John Richard. "An Episode of Journalism in 1840." *Journal of the Illinois State Historical Society* 23 (1930-31): 503-10. An account of political journalism and violence in Springfield that followed criticism of one of the commissioners charged with building what is now known as the Old State Capitol.

4551. Whitney, Ellen M. "The Razing and Reconstruction of the Old State Capitol: A Brief Record in Pictures." Photographs by Alfred von Behren. *Journal of the Illinois State Historical Society* 61 (1968): 443-52.

G. OTHER SITES

4552. Aleshire, Ruth Cory. "Warsaw and Fort Edwards on the Mississippi." *Transactions of the Illinois State Historical Society, 1930*, pp. 200-209. Discusses United States Army posts at the site of Warsaw (Forts Johnson and Edwards) and the first settlers in the area.

4553. Angle, Paul McClelland. "Found: The State House Corner Stone." *Journal of the Illinois State Historical Society* 30 (1937-38): 260-64. The cornerstone is located in the structure, but the whereabouts of the one it replaced was not known in 1937.

4554. Appleman, Roy E. "Lost Site of Camp Wood: The Lewis and Clark Winter Camp, 1803-04." *Journal of the West* 7 (1968): 270-74.

4555. Atkinson, Mabel. "Note on the New Nauvoo." *Journal of the Illinois State Historical Society* 43 (1950): 60-61. A brief account of historic structures then standing in Nauvoo.

4556. Buder, Stanley. *Pullman: An Experiment in Industrial Order and Community Planning, 1880-1930*. New York: Oxford University Press, 1967.

4557. Burtschi, Mary. *A Guide Book of Historic Vandalia*. Vandalia, Ill.: Vandalia Historical Society, 1974.

4558. Cain, Jerrilee. *Illinois Opera Houses: A Time of Glory*. Macomb: Western Illinois University, ca. 1981. A brief history of Illinois opera houses, with a listing of seventy-one still standing in 1981. Photographs and histories of fifteen.

4559. "The Cornerstone Mystery Solved." *Journal of the Illinois State Historical Society* 37 (1944): 264-65. The missing cornerstone of the present Illinois Capitol was discovered underground in 1944.

4560. Davis, G. Cullom, research director. *Memories of a Bank: Final Report--An Oral History and Documentary Inventory at Old Shawneetown.* 3

vols. in 5. Springfield, Ill.: Sangamon State University, Oral History Office, 1979.

4561. *The 1846 Home of Poet Nicholas Vachel Lindsay.* Springfield, Ill.: Vachel Lindsay Association, 1985? Lindsay's Springfield home is now a state historic site.

4562. *Frank Lloyd Wright and Susan Lawrence Dana, from the Town and Prairie Conference, Springfield, Illinois, April 1984, April 1985.* Springfield: Sangamon State University, 1985. Contains scholarly papers by Richard S. Taylor, "Susan Lawrence Dana, Feminist," pp. 1-17, and Mark Heyman, "Wright and Dana, Architect and Client," pp. 18-37. The house Wright designed for Susan Lawrence Dana in Springfield is now a state historic site.

4563. French, Mrs. Charles L. "The Last Years of Kaskaskia." *Journal of the Illinois State Historical Society* 37 (1944): 229-41. In a description written in the 1890s, the author discusses the changing course of the Mississippi River, Riley's mill, the Church of the Immaculate Conception, the Pierre Menard home, and other Kaskaskia sites.

4564. George, Adda. "The Galesburg Birthplace." *Journal of the Illinois State Historical Society* 45 (1952): 300-305. Restoration of Carl Sandburg's birthplace.

4565. "The Governor's Mansion a Century Ago." *Journal of the Illinois State Historical Society* 48 (1955): 330-37. The 1853 legislative authorization for the Governor's Mansion, together with newspaper reports of progress on its construction.

4566. "Governor's Mansion Nearing Its Centennial." *Journal of the Illinois State Historical Society* 44 (1951): 185-86.

4567. Hallmark, Donald P. "Frank Lloyd Wright's Dana-Thomas House: Its History, Acquisition, and Preservation." *Illinois Historical Journal* 82 (1989): 113-26.

4568. Hauberg, John H. "The New Black Hawk State Park." *Journal of the Illinois State Historical Society* 20 (1927-28): 265-81. The park on Rock River was the site of the Sauk village and farmlands known as Saukenuk. The author gives a condensed history of the village and the Sauk, 1760-1832.

4569. Hay, Linda L. "Historic Preservation for Beginners." *Dispatch* [from the Illinois State Historical Society], May-June 1990, pp. 5-6. A step-by-step account of the preservation of the Pierre Martin house, a vertical-log structure built about 1790 in St. Clair County. See also "Pierre Martin House Listed on National Register of Historic Places." Ibid. pp. 6-7.

4570. *Historical Map & Guide to the Illinois & Michigan Canal National Heritage Corridor.* Chicago: University of Chicago Press, 1993, for the I & M Canal National Heritage Corridor Commission. The I & M Corridor is the nation's first national heritage corridor.

4571. *Historic Sites and Structures of Hancock County, Illinois.* Carthage, Ill.: Hancock County Historical Society Bicentennial Commission, 1979.

4572. Historic Sites Division and the Davis Mansion Staff of the Illinois Historic Preservation Agency. "The David Davis Mansion: Volunteer Manual." Mimeographed. 1985. This 422-page manual presents historical sketches of the Davis family and of Alfred H. Piquenard, the architect of their Bloomington home, and an extensive treatment of the building's architecture and artifacts.

4573. *A History of Rock Island and Rock Island Arsenal from Earliest Times to 1954.* 3 vols. and supplement. Rock Island, Ill.: U.S. Army Rock Island Arsenal, 1965.

4574. Hodges, Carl G. "The Kidnaped Cornerstone." *Journal of the Illinois State Historical Society* 53 (1960): 29-36. The story of the original cornerstone of the present Capitol in Springfield.

4575. Holt, Glen E., and Pacyga, Dominic A. *Chicago: A Historical Guide to the Neighborhoods, the Loop and South Side.* Chicago: Chicago Historical Society, 1979. Including the Loop, the authors trace the history and development of sixteen neighborhoods.

4576. Karlowicz, Titus M. "The Historic Architecture of Rock Island Arsenal." *Western Illinois Regional Studies* 10, no. 2 (Fall 1987): 9-24.

4577. Keiser, John H. "The Union Miners Cemetery at Mt. Olive, Illinois: A Spirit-Thread of Labor History." *Journal of the Illinois State Historical Society* 62 (1969): 229-66. Brief histories of some of the major Illinois strikes whose leaders and participants are buried in the Miners Cemetery.

4578. Keller, William E. "Newspaper Notes on Early Capitols." *Journal of the Illinois State Historical Society* 61 (1968): 457-62.

4579. Lankiewicz, Donald P. "The Camp on Wood River: A Winter of Preparation for the Lewis and Clark Expedition." *Journal of the Illinois State Historical Society* 75 (1982): 115-20.

4580. MacLaughlin, Ada Greenwood. "The Site of Fort Crèvecoeur." *Transactions of the Illinois State Historical Society*, 1902, pp. 179-89.

4581. Magee, M. Juliette. *Cavern of Crime.* Smithland, Ky.: Livingston Ledger, 1973. Cave-in-Rock on the Ohio River, now a state park.

4582. Martin, Lorene. "Old Jubilee College and its Founder, Bishop Chase." *Transactions of the Illinois State Historical Society, 1934*, pp. 121-52. Bishop Philander Chase was an Episcopalian who founded Jubilee College, which opened in 1840 and closed in 1868. The surviving buildings and grounds are now a state historic site.

4583. Miles, Arthur A. *Story of How the Famous and Historic Spot at Cave in Rock, Illinois, Was Made a State Park.* N.p., 1953?

4584. "Nauvoo Sun Stone a Century Later." *Journal of the Illinois State Historical Society* 50 (1957): 99. A description of the Nauvoo Temple and the history of one of the capstones that topped the thirty pilasters reinforcing exterior walls.

4585. Newberry, Lane K. "Portraits of Historic Spots in Illinois." *Journal of the Illinois State Historical Society* 28, no. 1 (April 1935): 49-64. Fourteen paintings (reproduced in black and white) and descriptions by the artist.

4586. "Old Gristmill Grinds Again." *Journal of the Illinois State Historical Society* 44 (1951): 372-73. Restoration of the Graue mill in Du Page County.

4587. Orser, Charles E. Jr., and Karamanski, Theodore J. *Preliminary Archaeological Research at Fort Kaskaskia, Randolph County, Illinois.* Southern Illinois Studies, no. 17. Carbondale: University Museum, Southern Illinois University, 1977. A military history of the Illinois country from 1703 on (by Orser) precedes histories of two forts: the one on the bluff started by the French in 1759 or 1760 (now the site of Fort Kaskaskia State Park) and Fort Gage, built by the British in the village of Kaskaskia.

4588. Osgood, Ernest Staples, ed. *The Field Notes of Captain William Clark, 1803-1805.* New Haven, Conn.: Yale University Press, 1964. Clark's notes for the period 13 December 1803--14 May 1804 were made at the Wood (Dubois) River camp in Illinois.

4589. Pacyga, Dominic A., and Skerrett, Ellen. *Chicago, City of Neighborhoods: Histories & Tours.* Chicago: Loyola University Press, 1986. The authors divided the city into fifteen districts (containing forty-odd neighborhoods), with references to historic buildings and sites on the National Register of Historic Places. The neighborhood histories consider ethnic tensions as well as urban and suburban growth.

4590. Pointner, Norbert J. III. "Pullman: A New Town Takes Shape on the Illinois Prairie." *Historic Preservation* 22, no. 2 (April--June 1970): 26-35. The "model industrial town," built in the late nineteenth century, is now a state historic site.

4591. *Pullman: Portrait of a Landmark Community; A Photographic Essay by Fred Leavitt, with a View of Historic Pullman by Nancy Miller.* Chicago: Historic Pullman Foundation, 1981.

4592. Rothert, Otto A. *The Outlaws of Cave-in-Rock: Historical Accounts of the Famous Highwaymen and River Pirates Who Operated in Pioneer Days upon the Ohio and Mississippi Rivers and over the Old Natchez Trace.* Cleveland: Arthur H. Clark, 1924. Reprint, Evansville, Ind.: Unigraphic, 1975.

4593. Smith, George Owen. *The Lovejoy Shrine: The Lovejoy Station on the Underground Railroad.* 3d ed., Princeton, Ill.: Tribune Printing, 1949. Partial reprint and rev. ed., Tiskilwa, Ill.: Bureau Valley Chief, 1987.

4594. Snyder, John Francis. "Fort Kaskaskia." *Journal of the Illinois State Historical Society* 6 (1913): 58-71. Outdated.

4595. Sorensen, Mark W., ed. *Capitol Centennial Papers: Papers Prepared for the Centennial Observation of the Completion of the Illinois State Capitol, 1988.* Springfield: Illinois State Archives, 1992. Narrative histories, profusely annotated, by the editor and Mark A. Plummer, Wayne C. Temple, and Robert W. Williams.

4596. Taylor, Richard S. "Susan Lawrence." Mimeographed. Springfield: Office of Research and Publications, Historic Sites Division, Illinois Department of Conservation, 1982. Biography of Susan Lawrence Dana, whose Springfield home was designed by Frank Lloyd Wright.

4597. Unsicker, Joan I. "Archaeological Explorations at Jubilee College Historic Site." *Western Illinois Regional Studies* 3 (1980): 36-45.

4598. Watt, Kay C. "Clayville Inn." *Journal of the Illinois State Historical Society* 66 (1973): 71-78. History of the stagestop on the line between Springfield and Beardstown.

4599. Wunderlin, Linda, comp. *"Davis Family Letters: A Selection from the David Davis Collection of the Illinois State Historical Library."* Photoduplicated. Springfield: Historic Sites Division, Illinois Historic Preservation Agency, 1986. The letters included are those that relate to the David Davis Mansion in Bloomington, a state historic site.

H. MARKERS AND MONUMENTS

4600. Angle, Paul McClelland. *"Historical Markers for Illinois Highways."* *Journal of the Illinois State Historical Society* 27 (1934-35): 109-15. Announces formation of the Illinois State Historical Society markers program, to be conducted jointly with the Division of Highways.

4601. _____. "An Old Mystery Solved: The Sculptor of the Menard Monument Identified." *Journal of the Illinois State Historical Society* 36 (1943): 316-17. The sculptor of the monument for Illinois' first lieutenant governor, Pierre Menard, was John H. Mahoney of Indiana.

4602. Baruch, Mildred C., and Beckman, Ellen J. *Civil War Union Monuments.* Washington, D.C.: Daughters of Union Veterans of the Civil War, 1978. Of the 2,600 standing monuments identified, 140 are in Illinois.

4603. Birk, Russell Charles. "The Historical Markers Program: A Brief History, 1934-1968, and an Inventory." *Journal of the Illinois State Historical Society* 61 (1968): 191-96.

4604. _____. "The Historical Markers Program: Along Illinois Highways to Historic Sites." *Journal of the Illinois State Historical Society* 62 (1969): 73-83. Includes an inventory of cast metal markers erected 1934-68.

4605. "Blockhouse Planned for Fort Edwards." *Journal of the Illinois State Historical Society* 47 (1954): 444.

4606. *Brevet's Illinois Historical Markers and Sites.* Sioux Falls, S.D.: Brevet Press, 1976. Arranged by region and county and illustrated by more than 250 photographs, this volume contains the texts of nearly 300 markers erected by the state between 1934 and 1975.

4607. "Cairo Point--Fort Defiance Park Dedicated." *Journal of the Illinois State Historical Society* 53 (1960): 315-16. A memorial at the new state park commemorates Civil War activities at the site.

4608. "Dedication of Bronze Memorial Statues of Governor Richard Yates, the Elder, and Governor John M. Palmer." *Transactions of the Illinois State Historical Society, 1923*, pp. 167-70. The statues are on the Capitol lawn in Springfield.

4609. East, Ernest Edward. "Civil War Memorials for Illinois Veterans." *Illinois Libraries* 42 (1960): 337-51.

4610. Eisendrath, Joseph L. Jr. "Illinois' Oldest Memorial--The Stephen A. Douglas Monument." *Journal of the Illinois State Historical Society* 51 (1958): 127-48. A history of the monument by Leonard Volk, built on land that was part of Douglas's estate in Chicago. Douglas is buried at the site.

4611. "Fort Edwards Monument at Warsaw, Illinois, Dedicated." *Journal of the Illinois State Historical Society* 7, no. 3 (October 1914): 298-99. Built during the War of 1812, the fort was occupied until 1824.

4612. Hochstetter, Nancy, ed. *Guide to Illinois' Historical Markers.* Verona, Wis.: Guide Press, 1986. With an index and the text for each state marker.

4613. Hurst, Richard M. "The Historical Markers Program." *Journal of the Illinois State Historical Society* 58 (1965): 301-4; 60 (1967): 181-83. The first article has a broad outline of the State Historical Society's markers policy, together with a list of existing markers. The second lists markers for 1966-67.

4614. Mayer, Robert W. "Wood River, 1803-1804." *Journal of the Illinois State Historical Society* 61 (1968): 140-49, 511-12. Geography and history of the area of the Lewis and Clark camp site. A small park and marker memorialize the site.

4615. "Monument Unveiled: Dedication of Shabbona Park, La Salle County, Illinois, Aug. 29, 1906." *Transactions of the Illinois State Historical Society, 1907*, pp. 332-41. The park contains a monument to the victims of an attack on an Indian Creek settlement during the Black Hawk War.

4616. Petterchak, Janice A. "The Historical Markers Program." *Journal of the Illinois State Historical Society* 67 (1974): 324-39. An inclusive listing of markers, by county, that also includes date of placement, title, and exact location.

4617. Russell, Don. "Illinois Monuments on Civil War Battlefields." *Transactions of the Illinois State Historical Society, 1941*, pp. 1-37.

4618. "Some Information in Regard to the Statue of Stephen A. Douglas-- Leonard Volk, Sculptor." *Journal of the Illinois State Historical Society* 7 (1914-15): 74-75.

4619. Volk, Leonard Wells. *History of the Douglas Monument at Chicago, Prefaced with a Brief Sketch of Senator Douglas' Life, Illustrations of the Monument, etc.* Chicago: Chicago Legal News, 1880. Volk was the sculptor and designer of the monument.

4620. Wentworth, John. *Early Chicago: Fort Dearborn; An Address Delivered at the Unveiling of the Memorial Tablet to Mark the Site of the Block-House, on Saturday Afternoon, May 21st, 1881 . . .* Fergus' Historical Series, no. 16. Chicago, 1881.

INDEX TO AUTHORS

101, 853, 2428, 2684, 4488
Garrett, George P., **3860**
Garrett, Romeo B., **1172**
Garrow, David J., **1665**
Garver, Jared K., **2282**
Garvey, Neil F., **2619**
Garvey, Timothy J., **1217, 1309, 3173**
Gary, Grace, **2984**
Gates, Arnold, **959, 3861**
Gates, Paul Wallace, **315-16, 669, 1100-1102, 1750-51, 1918**
Gatewood, Willard B. Jr., **1270-71**
Gayle, Addison, **3862**
Gayler, George R., **503-4**
Gayman, Esther Palm, **2826**
Gazel, Neil R., **1825**
Gazell, James Albert, **1382**
Gegenheimer, Elizabeth, **416, 874**
Geil, Jean, **3043**
George, Adda, **4564**
George, Joseph Jr., **3628, 4396**
Gephart, Ronald M., **135**
Geraniotis, Roula Mouroudellis, **2985**
Gernon, Blaine Brooks, **1173**
Gertz, Elmer, **939, 1103, 1628-29, 1691, 2912, 3296-98**
Gerwing, Anselm, **2461**
Gettleman, Marvin E., **2093, 3701**
Getz, James R., **2399**
Ghelardi, Robert, **1686**
Ghent, Jocelyn Maynard, **708**
Gibbon, Guy E., **4486**
Gibson, Arrell Morgan, **2438**
Gibson, Harold E., **2078**
Gienapp, William E., **1020-21, 2620**
Gifford, Barry, **3106**
Gilbert, Barry, **3524**
Gilbert, Dorothy Lloyd, **3396**
Gilbert, James, **1290**
Gilbert, Paul, **4047**
Gilbert, William H., **1081**
Gilbreth, Edward S., **3297**
Gill, Brendan, **3174**
Gill, John G., **819-20**
Gillespie, Joseph, **4048, 4233**
Gilman, Carolyn, **674**
Gilmore, William E., **1407**
Gilmour, J. V., **1197**
Ginger, Ray, **1138**
Giraud, Marcel, **41**
Girling, Katherine Peabody, **3702**

Gittens, Joan, **3150**
Givens, George W., **505**
Glad, Paul W., **3389-90**
Gleason, Bill, **3398**
Gleicher, David, **2195**
Glenn, John M., **1826**
Glenn, Rebecca Miller, **4486**
Glick, Frank G., **1523**
Gliozzo, Charles A., **2913**
Glück, Elsie, **3780**
Godfrey, Kenneth W., **506**
Goedeken, Edward A., **1408**
Goff, John S., **3593**
Gold, Eddie, **3086, 3107-9**
Golden, Harry L., **3968**
Goldman, Peter, **1672**
Goldmark, Josephine, **3781**
Goldstein, Laurence, **3944**
Goldstein, Lynne G., **4486**
Goldstone, Richard Henry, **3863**
Golembiewski, Thomas E., **4205**
Goltra, Mabel Hall, **3175**
Good, Mary Elizabeth, **2429**
Goode, W. T., **1272**
Goodspeed, Thomas Wakefield, **2130, 3703**
Goodykoontz, Colin Brummitt, **2685**
Gordon, Harry, **194**
Gordon, J. A., **2558**
Gordon, Joseph Hinckley, **1919**
Gordon, Rita Werner, **1524**
Gosnell, Harold F., **1525**
Gottfried, Alex, **3299**
Gottlieb, Amy Zahl, **1174, 1455**
Goudy, Frank W., **1692**
Gould, Alan B., **2621**
Gould, E. W., **2009**
Gould, M. J., **371**
Gove, Samuel Kimball, **1630-32, 1653, 2622, 4276**
Graebner, Norman A., **151**
Graebner, William, **1485**
Graff, Maurice O., **2010**
Grange, Harold Edward (Red), **3110-11**
Granger, Bill, **1633**
Granger, Lori, **1633**
Grant, A. Cameron, **581**
Grant, H. Roger, **556, 559, 1493-94, 1920-22**
Grant, Madeleine P., **3782**
Grant, Ulysses S., **940, 3245**
Gray, Francis Jerome, **2196**

Taft, Ada Bartlett, **3193**
Taft, Lorado, **3194**
Taitt, Carolyn, **3017**
Talbot, William L., **1130**
Tallmadge, Thomas E., **3018**
Tamarkin, Civia, **1610**
Tanner, Helen Hornbeck, **2420**
Tanner, Henry, **839**
Tanner, Terence A., **541, 2588**
Tanselle, G. Thomas, **1389**
Tap, Bruce, **1507**
Tarbell, Ida M., **3232, 3495**
Tarr, Joel Arthur, **1204-5, 1476, 3361**
Tarshis, Rebecca, **3268**
Taub, Richard P., **3166**
Tax, Sol, **2418**
Taylor, Albert Reynolds, **3736-37**
Taylor, Charles H., **1883**
Taylor, D. Garth, **3166**
Taylor, Dorothy Loring, **2346-47**
Taylor, Eleanor K., **3793**
Taylor, Graham, **3167**
Taylor, Jay L. B., **4485**
Taylor, Lloyd C., **3915**
Taylor, Marjorie C., **3081**
Taylor, Quintard, **2661**
Taylor, Richard S., **660, 1508, 2158, 3738,**
    4521, 4562, 4596
Taylor, Robert M. Jr., **284**
Taylor, Samuel W., **542**
Taylor, Welford Dunaway, **3916**
Teaford, Jon C., **685, 2751-52**
Tebbel, John William, **2589, 3233**
Tebbetts, William H., **976**
Tedeschi, Martha, **3019**
Temple, Sunderine Wilson, **4544**
Temple, Wayne C., **31, 917, 1131-32,**
    2421, 2470, 3431, 3515, 3576, 3611-12,
    3642-43, 3900, 4544-45, 4595
Tennery, Thomas D., **767**
Tenney, Craig D., **902**
Tenney, Mary Alice, **2257**
Terkel, Louis (Studs), **1540, 1710, 3917**
Terrell, John Upton, **32**
Thackery, David T., **4106**
Thayer, Crawford Beecher, **768**
Thayer, William Roscoe, **3441**
Thiem, George, **1655**
Thomas, Benjamin Platt, **1869, 3496-97,**
    4546-47
Thomas, Charles M., **206**

Thomas, Lewis Foulk, **414**
Thomas, R. G., **1884**
Thomas, Robert D., **2816**
Thomas, William, **769**
Thomis, Wayne, **3362**
Thompson, Charles Manfred, **127, 788,**
    801-3, 1137
Thompson, David G., **184**
Thompson, Fred, **1885, 3815**
Thompson, Milton D., **2372**
Thompson, Mitchel Andrew, **977**
Thompson, Samuel, **2111**
Thompson, Scerial, **411**
Thompson, Slason, **3918**
Thomson, Gladys Scott, **472**
Thorburn, Neil, **4093**
Thorek, Max, **3770**
Thoreson, Trygve, **1331**
Thornbrough, Gayle, **285**
Thornburg, Dennis, **2320**
Thorndale, William, **4131**
Thornton, Earle C., **1438**
Thrasher, Frederic Milton, **1681**
Throgmorton, Dianne, **3068**
Throop, Addison J., **2436**
Thurman, Melburn D., **4132**
Thurner, Arthur W., **1477, 2886**
Thurston, John Gates, **412**
Thwaites, Reuben Gold, **49, 69, 86-87,**
    185, 207, 230, 379, 452, 454-55, 459,
    474, 477, 770, 1723, 3234
Tierney, Kevin, **3412**
Tiffany, Joseph A., **4486**
Tigerman, Stanley, **2968, 2973, 3020**
Tillson, Christiana Holmes, **618**
Tilton, Clint Clay, **341, 3235, 3537**
Timmons, Bascom N., **3363**
Tims, Margaret, **3812**
Tindall, Randy, **2972**
Tingley, Donald Fred, **619, 804, 876, 903,**
    1275, 1336, 1390-91, 2258, 2958, 3919,
    4093, 4431
Tisler, C. C., **3644**
Tobias, Ruth Anne, **1640**
Tompkins, C. David, **1249**
Tonsor, Stephen J., **620**
Tonty (Tonti), Henri de, **88**
Toole, Robert C., **2027**
Townley, Wayne C., **3364**
Townsend, Lucy Forsyth, **3739**
Townsend, Walter A., **2662**

INDEX TO SUBJECTS

Only the information provided by titles and annotations has been indexed. Any given work may therefore contain substantial information not reflected in this index.

Illinois State Council of Defense, **1417-18**

Illinois State Fair, **703, 1128, 1741, 1758**

Illinois State Federation of Labor, **1879**

Illinois State Geological Survey, **2305, 2372**

Illinois State Historical Library, **3708, 4001, 4310**

  description and history, **2335, 2938, 4365, 4544**

  holdings

    catalog, **2349**

    Lincolniana, **728, 732, 789, 1020, 1111, 2343, 3524, 3592, 3594, 4315-51, 4361, 4368, 4531**

    manuscript and archival records, **241, 291, 301, 361, 415, 439, 458, 466, 535, 537, 562, 630, 648-50, 730, 743, 775, 798, 807, 869, 951, 963, 976, 991, 993, 1039, 1042, 1098, 1136, 1162, 1218, 1228, 1338, 1463, 1806, 3262, 3321, 3454, 3608, 3819, 3992-93, 4056, 4159, 4210, 4284, 4315-77, 4599**

    newspapers, **4436, 4444**

    prints and photographs, **1502, 4369, 4371**

Illinois State Historical Society, **2938, 2948, 4059-60**

  historical markers program, **4600, 4603-4, 4606, 4612-13, 4616**

Illinois State Horticultural Society, **1760**

Illinois State Journal (Springfield), **3573, 4453**

Illinois State Library, **2336, 4162, 4224, 4310, 4382**

Illinois State Lyceum, **299**

Illinois State Museum, **2294, 2372**

Illinois State Police, **2607**

Illinois State Reformatory, **2647**

Illinois State Register (Springfield), **2548, 4453**

Illinois State University (Illinois State Normal University) (Normal), **960, 1578, 2057, 2083-92, 3750, 4231**

Illinois State University (Springfield), **2187**

Illinois State University Journal, **4058**

Illinois State Water Survey, **2291, 2305**

Illinois Supreme Court, **3530, 4250**

Illinois Supreme Court Building, **3017, 3023**

Illinois Symphony Orchestra, **1521**

Illinois Terminal Railroad Company, **1916, 1934, 1961**

Illinois Territory, **231, 263, 267-68, 272, 275, 277, 279, 299, 304-6**

Illinois Traction Co. System, **1930, 1961**

Illinois-Wabash Land Company, **196, 198**

Illinois War Council, **1559, 1566**

Illinois Waterway, **1998, 2000, 2010, 2031**

Illinois Wesleyan University, **2103, 2262, 2264**

Illinois Whig (Kaskaskia), **4448**

Illinois Woman's College, **3707**

Immigrants, **381-82, 1087, 1443, 1797, 2748, 2800-2894, 3163, 3740**

  agents for, **2884**

  assimilation, **2741**

  folk language and folksongs, **2761, 2792**

  in General Assembly, **4093**

  guides for, **364, 590, 607, 4107, 4127-28**

  restrictions against, **1368**

  See also Settlers and settlements; names of nationality groups, as Italian-Americans, etc.

Immigrants' Protective League, **1368, 1370, 1374**

Independent Engineering Company, **1567**

Indiana, **232, 287, 316, 405, 456, 473, 685, 1241, 1491, 1702, 1794, 2301-2, 2398-99, 2411, 2413, 2439, 2445, 2464-65, 2781, 3124, 3511, 3589, 4084, 4509**

Indian agents and subagents, **302, 2410, 2478, 2517, 2531-32, 4017**

Indiana Historical Society, **4426**

Indiana State Library, **4426**

Indiana Territory, **219, 269-70, 272, 278, 285, 302**

Indian Claims Commission, **2411-13**

Indian Creek, **4615**

Indians. *See* Native Americans

Indian trails. *See* Highways and trails

Indigenous populations. *See* Native Americans

Industrial safety, **1485**

Industrial Workers of the World, **1885**

Industry. *See* Business and industry

Infantry, Illinois, **756, 767**. *See also* Civil War, military units

Influenza epidemic, **1511**

Ingalls, Eleazer Stillman, **2564**

Ingals, Ephraim, **3759**

Ingersoll, Robert Green, **3442-54, 4207, 4373-74**

Ingersoll, Roy, **3226**

Midland, The, **2954**
Mies van der Rohe, Ludwig, **3004, 3027, 3188, 3190-91**
Milburn, William Henry, **858, 3720**
Miles, Nelson A., **1278**
Military Tract. *See* Illinois Military Tract; Western Illinois (Two Rivers region)
Military units
    in Spanish-American War, **1268-75, 1277**
    in World War I, **1393-97, 1400-1401, 1407, 1413, 1419, 1423, 1425-26, 1429-33, 1436, 1438-40**
    in World War II, **1551, 1563-64, 1567-68, 1572, 1579-80, 1582, 1585-86**
    See also Black Hawk War, rosters; Civil War, military units; Illinois Militia; Illinois National Guard; Mexican War; Revolutionary War, rosters; War of 1812, rosters
Militia. *See* Illinois Militia; Illinois National Guard
Miller, George, **484**
Miller, Olive Beaupré, **2346-47**
Millikan, Robert A., **3763**
Millikin, James, **1796, 3737**
Millikin National Bank, **1796**
Millikin University, **2230, 3736-37**
Mills, Abel, **604**
Mills, Albert Taylor, **2230**
Mills, **306, 2810, 4563, 4586**
Milwaukee, Wis., **1927**
Mineral resources, **2306, 2310, 2321**. *See also* Coal mining; Lead mining
Mineral springs, **1214, 3080**
Miners' Journal (Galena), **4452**
Minet, ____, **89**
Mining, **4, 384, 4287**. *See also* Coal miners; Coal mining; Lead mining
Minnesota, **1425, 1429, 2850, 4107**
Minor affair, **3591**
Minoso, Orestes (Minnie), **3123**
Missions, **68, 98, 111, 116, 848, 853, 2848**
Mississippi, **219, 918, 927, 946, 964, 2923, 3856**
Mississippian people, **10, 4486**
Mississippi River, **78, 83, 89, 117, 356, 1098, 1594, 2012, 2272, 4181**
    art and artists, **389, 414, 571, 2981**
    bridges, **1971, 1978**
    discovery, **54-55, 61, 70**
    environmental history, **2314**

    ferries, **2003, 2030**
    folklore, **2763, 2778**
    geology, **2029**
    at Kaskaskia, **4563**
    logging, **1831**
    maps, **53, 56, 59**
    Native Americans on, **24, 214-15, 383, 2396, 2427, 2483-84**
    navigation, **208, 1503, 2003, 2009, 2028-29**
    pirates, **4592**
    rapids bypassed, **2029**
    source of, **217, 402-3**
    steamboats, **1503, 2020, 2022-23, 2033**
    towns, settlements, and landings on, **138, 214, 4119, 4122**
    travel on, **199, 214-15, 348, 377, 410**
    in War of 1812, **244**
Mississippi River Valley, **25, 39-40, 43, 404, 414, 682, 872, 4034, 4114, 4119, 4181**
Mississippi Territory, **219**
Mississippi Valley Review, **1700**
Missouri, **227, 232, 250, 603, 823, 1429, 1464, 1491, 2459, 4103, 4127**
Missouri (Native Americans), **2426**
Missouri Historical Society, **149, 227**
Mitchell, John, **3780, 3786**
Mitchell, Lucy Sprague, **4010**
Mitchell, Wesley Clair, **4010**
Moline, Ill., **4285**
Momence, Ill., **3042**
Monaghan, Jay, **3849**
Money-lending, **1874**. *See also* Banking and financial institutions
Monks' Mound. *See* Cahokia Mounds
Monmouth, Ill., **910, 977, 1133, 4018**
Monmouth College, **910, 2107-11**
Monopolies, **1464, 1791**
Monroe, Harriet, **1383, 1386-87, 1392, 2949, 3841, 3891**
Monroe County, **2, 287, 1990**
Montgomery, John, **149, 170**
Montgomery County, **605, 903, 1834**
Montgomery News (Hillsboro), **2574**
Montgomery Ward, **1833, 1836, 1844**
Monticello College (Monticello Female Seminary), **629, 2200, 3208**
Moody, Dwight L., **1290, 1321, 3699**
Moody, William Vaughn, **3838, 3869**
Moody Bible Institute, **2172, 2190**
Moore, George, **493**

About the Compiler and Editors

ELLEN M. WHITNEY is retired publications editor for the Illinois State Historical Library and Society. She is the editor and compiler of *The Black Hawk War, 1831–1832* (4 vols., 1970–1978).

JANICE A. PETTERCHAK is director of the Illinois State Historical Library, a division of the Illinois Historic Preservation Agency. She is former assistant executive director of the Illinois State Historical Society.

SANDRA M. STARK has been newspaper librarian and head of Reference and Technical Services at the Illinois State Historical Library and is currently senior librarian.

ISBN 0-313-28235-8

HARDCOVER BAR CODE